PSYCHOANALYTIC SCHOOLS FROM THE
BEGINNING TO THE PRESENT

PSYCHOANALYTIC SCHOOLS FROM THE BEGINNING TO THE PRESENT

by DIETER WYSS, M.D.

With an introduction by Leston L. Havens, M.D.

TRANSLATED BY
GERALD ONN

JASON ARONSON, INC.
NEW YORK

In Memory of
Victor von Weizsäcker

———◇———

*You will never find the boundaries of the soul
though you were to pace out every path—
so profound is its logos.*

HERACLITUS

*That man is a physician, who knows the
invisible element, which has no name,
which has no material form and yet has effect.*

PARACELSUS

INTRODUCTION

BY LESTON L. HAVENS, M.D.

The significance of this book transcends its presentation of the severely fragmented body of psychoanalysis. Dr. Wyss' presentation of Freud's work is detailed, accurate, and happily rests on Freud's own observations and statements; it is not so voluminous as Fenichel's but can stand beside it. If, to make another comparison, Jaspers' *General Psychopathology* carries the reader into almost every facet of psychopathology, Wyss' treatment of the schools of psychoanalysis is much more inclusive and up-to-date than Jaspers'; the latter may outweigh Wyss, but he does not outpoint him. And the non-Freudian depth psychological schools find in Wyss an expositor both sympathetic and sharp; not even Ruth Munroe exceeds him in these qualities. What gives this book its outstanding distinction, however, has less to do with presentation than with perspective.

Psychiatry and psychology today need desperately both the summary statements Wyss provides and even more his *grasp of issues.* The present confederation of psychiatric and psychological states has no common language, no reciprocal understanding, and only one commodity regularly produced: the development and secession of ever more independent states. Civil war breaks out when mutual disdain proves insufficient. And every student and critical practitioner stands baffled within the shifting boundaries.

Psychotherapeutic schools have developed widely and wildly in this century. The resulting confusion has left even the main positions in doubt; minor figures receive inordinate attention from many writers. Above all, the lines of development have been difficult to follow. Wyss sets out to clarify the relationships between schools, their relative importance, and the specific directions in which development has taken place.

Psychoanalysis springs chiefly from Freud and it is Freudianism that lies at the center of the book. A detailed presentation of psychoanalytic observations and ideas occupies the opening chapters, a refreshingly concrete and clear presentation, and Freudian concepts serve as the standard for comparison throughout. We could complain that such early workers as Charcot and Janet receive short shrift and that not so much effort is put into detailing the observational basis of Freud's later thought as is done with the earlier, but these would be small complaints. The excitement and significance of the book results from its confrontation of the major schools. Carl Jung's thought is presented with remarkable clarity, and then the philosophi-

i

cally oriented, existential school of Jaspers, Binswanger, and von Weizacker. The relationship between Freud and these provides the book's principal tension, the deepest source of disagreements about the scientific basis and practical methods of psychotherapy. In the last few pages, Wyss brings to a climax his ideas for dealing with this tension.

It was the specific aim of Freud's thought to be both scientific and humanistic, to bring concepts and order to human concerns and human concerns into the scientific community; Freud's was the most ambitious attempt ever made not only to bridge the two cultures but to see them as one. The result has been a great volume of attack on psychoanalysis from *both* sides: accusations of intellectuality, conceptual rigidity, reductionism from the humanistic side, and of vagueness, tautology, a willingness to sacrifice phenomena to theories from scientific critics. Wyss' review encompasses both these trends. He is precise in his dissection of Freudian inconsistences and thoroughgoing in his account of the ways personality and humanness do sometimes get lost in psychoanalysis.

This book could not command the interest it does, however, if it were only a *more* thorough critique of psychoanalysis, a prize so many have coveted. Nor would Wyss expect that even the *most* thorough criticism of psychoanalysis would do more than shake a body of conceptions which remains at the center of depth psychology precisely because of its variety and inclusiveness—the very qualities that expose psychoanalysis to attack from so many directions! Again, this book is not important because of its presentations *or* its criticisms but because of its grasp of the issues which have given rise to other schools, have made conflicting demands on psychotherapy, and now call out for fresh syntheses.

The reader seeking to follow these issues (or themes, as Wyss calls them) will be helped by the excellent table of contents in which many are listed in the form of catch phrases. He may also be helped by some review of the principal issues here.

Perhaps no single idea leads us more swiftly into Freud's thought and out again, much modified, to the later schools, than the idea of the *wish*. This idea, on the one hand so familiar, so much a felt phenomenon, and on the other hand so opaque, occupies a central place in Freud's *clinical* conceptions and reappears in his theoretical conceptions as instinct, energy, and object cathexes. Wish exists in Freud's thought on the level of phenomenon, intuition, clinical decision. In his speculative thought—his theories—abstract ideas replace clinical nuances. One gains logical rigor at the expense of familiarity.

The wishes he discovered in neurosis were sexual, they caused con-

Oak Park and River Forest High School

APPOINTMENT SLIP

Name _Chris Ferraro_ Room _386_

Please meet me in the deans' office, Room 308,

during _3_ period on _9/12_

Approved:

_____ _____

Study Hall Teacher Dean

Please bring this slip with you.

flict, the resulting compromises were either symptoms or culturally approved aspirations. Behind wishes were instincts with variably displaceable energies which formed now-this, now-that object cathexis. One after another these statements lay down the basis for various school developments. Some of these developments have occurred for scientific reasons, others for philosophical ones, still others because of the demands of therapy. However, none—as Wyss makes clear—has preempted the whole field because it was so broadly occupied by psychoanalysis in advance.

For example, the interpersonalists—whose data is social behavior—substituted the idea of *relationships* for wishes: everything intrapsychic and individual was to be understood socially. Instead of the "instances," as Wyss terms ego, id, and superego, these social psychiatrists studied the self in society—its adaptations, deceptions, and more recently its introjects and projections. When society and culture, in particular the family, were closely studied, it became possible to find the fantasies and conflicts psychoanalysis had discovered in the psyche occurring as acts ("behaved") in society. It then became possible to blame society, just as Freud had blamed biology, although no one knew which came first if they did not develop together. The psychoanalysts found the social psychiatrists superficial, and the social psychiatrists called analysts unrealistic.

Jung and the existential psychiatrists substituted *aspirations* for wishes. The social psychiatrists (whom Wyss calls Behaviorists) had shifted psychiatric attention to society. Existential psychiatrists now shifted it from the analyzed past into the future and from the individual understood through preformed biological concepts to the individual understood through his own point of view. Psychiatry had come to include the study of society, and now this radical subjectivity.

Jung led the movement away from Freud's biological, anatomical, sexual concepts to the religious, mythical, and value saturated ideas which existential psychiatrists would develop still more subjectively. Jung, like Freud and unlike the existentialists, threw himself into system-building; there was a structure of archetypes, opposites, psychological functions to which individuals would be found to conform; he was to that large extent reductionistic and in existential terms "unreduced"! Only with the determined application of the *phenomenological reduction* by existentialists did psychiatric system-building receive a powerful blow.

Jung, however, had clearly translated wishes into aspirations and by his method of amplification hoped to discover and develop human strivings without recourse to developmental themes. Psychoanalysis, in contrast, threw strivings back to the infantile past; it must always *suspect* them. In essence, Jung and the existential psychiatrists set about to *honor* them.

This is at first glance not so much a scientific as a temperamental, philosophical, or therapeutic dispute. If one is impressed by the infantile, destructive, selfish aspects of man's striving and the resulting havoc in the world, Jung's "idealizing" must seem sentimental hogwash; one then views religion, for example, as a compromise formation expressing and controlling the love and hate of the father. But it is perfectly consistent for a Freudian to say that religion is also a "creative solution to life's problems" or even an experience of archetypes, although his emotional tone would not be Jung's. Freudian man is a biological animal barely and occasionally civilized. Jungian man reaches for the stars.

This brings us to another issue that Wyss illuminates from the viewpoint of several schools. Again it is an issue for which Freudian psychoanalysis lays down the starting position.

Because neither the individual nor society, instinct nor culture offers a secure resting place, in short because there is no psychoanalytic *solution* to life's dilemmas, only the compromise of inevitably contending forces, *reason* is the central ideal of Freud's psychology and of his practice. The analytic technique aims to shed light on the contending forces, translate them into words, discharge their pent-up feelings, above all to *analyze* and not to act on them. Moreover, reason is to penetrate the irrational, reveal its meaning, indeed master it. The ego can guide the id. The voice of reason is soft but "persistent." In any case, there is no other guide.

This view owes much to nineteenth century neurology and biology with their hierarchical view of the nervous system and evolutionary meliorism. "Primitive" reflexes are controlled by ever more complex ones, the great neural pathways lead upward to the crown of grey matter delaying, overseeing, integrating the impulses pouring in from below. The lower neurons represent the affective, impulsive, reflexive, primitive, perhaps instinctual; above are the ego and superego organizing the impulses into reality and action, carrying the cultural heritage, compromising the demands from below. And implicit is a developmental process which every individual repeats for himself. Reason and the neopallium are both *late* developments. Freud's ego arose from the id as the tribal brothers sprang from the father. Pleasure had to be sacrificed to reality, the id to the ego.

This view, so "self-evident" for many in the contemporary climate of opinion, has been challenged from several directions. Again, Jung has been a leader. Perhaps man's highest aspirations are not the fruit of compromise and reason but the very reverse: perhaps reason illuminates man's strivings, examines them, but as often hinders as helps. Man's ideals, it is argued, are with him from the start.

Implicit is also a view of the *irrational* sharply different from Freud's. Ideas, as archetypes, are as much a part of this irrational as instincts are; and culture is not formed out of the strivings and frustrations of the irrational but also part of the irrational from the start.

In essence, reason is dethroned. At its most radical, this view doubts that reason will even illuminate the irrational. We can empathize with the basic strivings, amplify them, help them seek the light of day, but they cannot be scientifically understood, as Freud believed. This historical, human, individual world can be felt, we may discover some of its possible meanings, but it cannot be subject to scientific analysis; all such efforts scientifically to understand man fail because what cannot be experimented with is the human element itself, which is killed or escapes.

Again in contrast to Freudian psychoanalysis, this view sees the unpredictable as a basic category. The unpredictable is not what science still has to reach and clarify; it is an intrinsic feature of human life. Every effort to overcome the unpredictable either fails or, in succeeding, destroys the human. From the point of view of science, this view maintains that human life is random. The impression of determinism is an impression only. It springs from the retrospective standpoint: once things have happened they appear fixed because they are over. But from the standpoint of the present, they are unpredictable.

On the other hand, does the Universe play dice with us? Einstein could not believe it does, and threw his mind against the quantum theories which elevated indeterminacy to a principle of nature. Freud did not believe it does, either. But are these great system-builders exceeding the mind's power to understand a world perhaps to some measure random, irrational, so often absurd?

Further, can reason *lead*? Does the balanced survey and analysis of a personality ever *end*? Is there not always a moment of decision in which reason is thrown aside and a bet placed on some element of the unpredictable?

If life is unpredictable and the capacity for surprise really the capacity for neurosis, as Binswanger believed, how can therapists square their knowledge with the terrifying limitations on that knowledge?

Finally, when should reason, analysis, conversation give way to decision and action? Some of the schools are wild to act, others sick with thought. Can there be more than a personal, temperamental resolution to these differences?

Similarly, sex can be studied, even experimented with. Can love? Sex often destroys love; on other occasions it assists, even founds it. But efforts to study or conceptualize love by means of sex lose themselves in the fragile, elusive quality of love. Yet the ability to love stands as perhaps the principal sign of emotional health in modern psychopathology!

I agree with Wyss that the best efforts to understand love in psychological terms are the work of existentialists. Few of these efforts have penetrated American psychiatry, especially medical psychology, despite the work of Fromm, May, Rogers, Frankl, and others. We are more fearful to deal with love than we are with hate! Perhaps it was enough that the last hundred years should have asked psychology and medicine to deal with sex!

Closely allied is the problem of causality. The pathogenic sequences that Freud extracted from the study of hysterical cases were meant to be *causal* sequences: trauma led to affects and ideas; these were split off from the conscious mind and then found partial expression in dreams and symptoms. However, as we go from Anna O. to Dora to the Rat Man and Wolf Man the number of influences streaming in on the final common pathway becomes almost infinite. There are wishes of many kinds, past and present, memories, images, as well as the changing influences of the contemporary scene. We can *understand* some of these relationships, Jaspers wrote, but we do not approach causal clarification. That requires weighing the power of individual factors, which is beyond us. It is therefore necessary to speak of *possible meanings,* not of exact scientific laws:

Motives can be adduced *ad infinitum* for even the most trivial deed and they become more and more complex the deeper we delve into the personal life and fate of the person who performed the deed. Of course these motives, no matter whether they refer to a symptom or an act of will, do not follow the laws of logic as do the proposition of contradiction or the Aristotelian proposition of the Third Man. And so, if human activity is investigated in detail, it becomes evident that it is fed from an infinite source of conceivable conditions which lend an irrational character to even the most banal activity (p. 512).

How much more familiar to American readers is the reverse of this statement! We could say the conceivable conditions lend an understandable character to even the most *irrational* activity. *We* see the possible meanings as hypotheses, not the end of science but its start. Bowlby suggested to Harlow that he test whether oral, tactile, or some other stimulus successfully integrates the young monkey's relationship to the environment. The experiment did not come out as psychoanalysis had predicted, but without the possible meanings or hypotheses suggested by psychoanalysis there would have been no experiment and that much less understanding of development. Yes, we reply to Wyss, there are an enormous number of influences bearing on the simplest acts, but such is the case with nature in all her forms, yet scientific knowledge grows.

There are many other themes taken up and followed in this book. Each captures an element of the schools' development and leads to issues waiting for resolution. Here is a final example.

Projection is a concept the development of which Freud influenced but did not exhaust. Indeed his very method of work made any other outcome unlikely. Projection is a *social* phenomenon. It asks for social facts which the study of association and fantasy limit our securing. It is no accident that the further study of Schreber's projections waited upon learning his early life experiences. Moreover, the concepts Freud developed from the study of fantasies do not lend themselves easily to the understanding of facts (see Neiderland's efforts to relate what he believes Schreber may have experienced as a child to the psychoanalytic concepts of psychosis). One result has been the emergence of "object-relations" theories that are more intimately related to social observations than are the structural and libidinal theories. These object-relations theories, in turn, confront existential developments that challenge the subject–object split upon which theories of objects depend.

The existential theorists ask the object-relations theorists to modify their autonomy of the objects; people are never like billiard balls bouncing off one another; relationships are never merely incorporative, hostile, even adaptive. Relationships, the existentialists argue, are *creative;* they represent "achievements" which reshape each party. (Similarly, treatment is not so much an experience of discovery as of creation.) What happens between two people cannot be conceptualized as *between* them (despite Sullivan's efforts); the space between is *in* both parties who are changed to the extent that a real relationship exists; and the result is something new and unpredictable. Thus existential theory resembles systems theory and perhaps transactional analysis.

At the book's end Wyss confronts the dilemmas his own convictions have produced. Extensive as his and many schools' criticisms of psychoanalysis have been, "no other thinker has equalled the intensity, logic, and profundity" of Freud's speculations (p. 504). "There can in fact be no doubt but that psychoanalytic practice is broadly based on empirical foundations" (p. 505). To what purpose then existentialism, interpersonalism, behaviorism?

He is equally convinced that the *person* gets lost in psychoanalysis, at one time to trauma, then to instincts or the unconscious, later to archetypes or introjects. The hydraulic model of psychoanalysis has limitations; the ego must be partially independent of the drives; anxiety results not only from the thrust of forbidden drives but also from being-in-the-world; values cannot be solely derived from repression and the unconscious; reality and pleasure are not always polar opposites; transference and countertransference do not exhaust the technical understanding of psychotherapy.

Psychology and psychiatry today confront irreconcilable differences which forbid any inclusive solution. The psychotherapist must make his way by a rich mixture of conceptions and techniques unless the patient is to be imprisoned anew, now in a prison of the doctor's choosing.

The difficulty facing psychotherapy here, the need to strike a balance between perceiving and loving, the need to see through the patient whilst yet lovingly accepting him, the need to regard him not only as an object of transference but also as a human being in his own right, should not be underestimated. This point of balance, it would seem, is no sooner established than it is lost again. Indeed, if we analyze the therapist, it would appear from the thoughts, impulses and feelings to which he is subject in the course of treatment that therapy constantly oscillates between the two poles. By perceiving his patient, by seeing through him, the therapist withdraws from the patient, treats him as a thing to be thought about, reduces him to the status of a mere object. By accepting him again with understanding and love he reinstates him as a subject, as a real person (pp. 560–561).

PREFACE TO THE ENGLISH EDITION

The initial purpose of this enquiry into the history of depth psychology, which is now going into its second edition in Germany, was to enable German readers to follow the development of depth psychology from 1933 onwards. At the same time, however, it affords a general insight into analytic problems as such, and more particularly into the conceptions of Existential analysis (*Daseinsanalyse*) and allied movements which have been developing on the European continent in the course of the past 35 years (Trüb, von Weizsäcker, Ey, Binswanger, etc.). Consequently, it is felt that the book will also interest the English and American public. The synoptic discussion of the various schools and of their potentialities and limitations should also be of interest for, although excellent synoptic publications have appeared both in England and the United States (R. Munroe,[1] Cl. Thompson,[2] P. Mullahy,[3] L. Salzmann,[4] etc.), the way in which the discussion is conducted in this present book is quite new. It was this which encouraged the publisher to undertake an English version in the conviction that he would not be carrying 'coals to Newcastle'.

A warning from an analyst, not to overvalue the scientific exactitude or therapeutic potential of psychoanalysis, might well be held to be of particular interest in the country where psychoanalytic findings are already being used as slogans. Scepticism would appear to be called for when scientific sanction is claimed for enquiries which, on closer inspection, are seen to be questionable in respect both of their method and of their content. And a similar scepticism would appear to be apposite when the problems posed by psychoanalytic terminology are comparable to the (esoteric) difficulties presented by theoretical physics, which is no longer readily accessible to normal human understanding.

The author hopes to publish the enquiry into analytic anthropology included in Part III of this book in the not too distant future in a more co-ordinated and enlarged framework under the title *Mensch und Moral*[5] ('Man and Morality').

If this present work should succeed in encouraging discussion and consequently collaboration between the various analytic schools it will have achieved its purpose.

Frankfurt am Main   DIETER WYSS

PREFACE TO THE FIRST GERMAN EDITION

The fact that this enquiry into the development and problems of the various schools of depth psychology is appearing shortly after the twentieth anniversary of Siegmund Freud's death is not unintentional. It has a two-fold purpose. Firstly, to provide those interested in this field with a survey of depth psychology, which, it need hardly be added, lays no claim to comprehensiveness. The enquiries carried out by the Freudian School alone and which have been published in their books and journals run into the thousands. O. Fenichel has attempted to condense the most important of these Freudian contributions up to 1945 in his fundamental work on *The Psychoanalytic Theory of Neurosis*. It has been no part of the present author's purpose to emulate Fenichel, which in any case would only have been possible, had he shared Fenichel's views in respect of psychological doctrine. Although the selection of Freud's followers and their works has been determined by the wish to condense those findings and theses which constitute a further development of Freud's own theses, it has none the less been necessary to exclude certain of Freud's followers, whose contributions would surely have merited consideration, simply for reasons of space. In other words, although the selection was based on objective considerations, it remains both subjective and restricted. The second purpose of this enquiry is in part occasioned by the twentieth anniversary of Freud's death and is concerned with the question: what is the position of depth psychology to-day, twenty years after the death of its founder and seventy years after the publication of his first psychoanalytic paper (1892)? The systematic clarification of this question, its solution within the limits imposed by our present knowledge, is the further objective of this book, particularly of the Third Part, which—be it noted—does not claim to anticipate a new conception of neuroses but merely to indicate *possible ways* in which the various problems might be solved. This question is intimately connected with the further question as to whether we are at all justified in regarding depth psychology as a scientific discipline. For to-day, especially in the United States, it is assumed—and the assumption is given concrete expression in the form of Institutes, Technical Journals and Congresses—that depth psychology is as much a scientific discipline as the exact natural sciences.

The objective description of the various doctrines of depth psychology is the criterion which I have endeavoured to observe in the First and Second Parts of my book. It is for this reason that the most important representatives of the various theories have been allowed to speak for themselves in quotations from their own works, a method of procedure which also enables the reader to gain an immediate impression of the various authors. Then, in the Third Part of the book, in which the fundamental problems attendant on the various theories are formulated and the theories themselves criticized and compared, I have expressed my own view, which has been deeply influenced in the course of its development by the personality and work of Viktor von Weizsäcker. One factor that emerges from this book, and particularly from the Third Part, is the difficulty involved in siding with any one of the schools of depth psychology, which, although related to one another in general, cannot unite because of the many issues on which they are divided.

The material with which the book deals is arranged both formally (see Table of Contents) and thematically (e.g. symbol). The various themes, which recur throughout the whole length of the book, are also listed in the Table of Contents in the form of catch-phrases.

I would like to take this opportunity of thanking the *Notgemeinschaft deutscher Wissenschaft* (German Research Body) for having made it possible for me to devote a total of four of my ten years of clinical training and study to a practical and theoretical enquiry into the problems of depth psychology, and consequently for having indirectly contributed to the composition of this present enquiry.

Frankfurt am Main,   DIETER WYSS

CONTENTS

15

Contents

22

CONTENTS

CONTENTS

CONTENTS

PART TWO

PHILOSOPHICALLY ORIENTED SCHOOLS OF DEPTH PSYCHOLOGY

CONTENTS

33

34

G. HENRI EY   437

PART THREE

FUNDAMENTAL PROBLEMS OF THE VARIOUS THEORIES OF DEPTH PSY-CHOLOGY WITH SUGGESTIONS AS TO HOW THESE MIGHT BE RESOLVED

39

PART ONE

THEORIES OF DEPTH PSYCHOLOGY BASED ON THE NATURAL SCIENCES

I

SIEGMUND FREUD'S PSYCHOANALYSIS

A

FROM THE SYMPTOM TO THE PERSONALITY

(1880–1905)

I. BIOGRAPHICAL SKETCH[1]

Siegmund Freud was born on May 6, 1856, in Freiburg, a small town in Moravia, where his father was a business man. For financial reasons the family moved to Vienna when Freud was four years old. From 1860 to 1938, when Austria was occupied by Hitler, Freud lived and worked in Vienna. Externally his life followed the pattern laid down for the nineteenth-century Liberal scholar, unfolding itself in sober and settled circumstances. Freud's day was divided between the laboratory (later his clinic and practice), the care of his relatively large family and his research, to which he devoted his evenings and part of his nights.

His personality, however, was subject to powerful contrasts, stamped as it was on the one hand by passionate intensity and on the other by the scientific objectivity to which he had disciplined himself. The hard struggle for existence which he was required to wage in his practice, a struggle which he was obliged to continue at a later date against the world at large because it rejected psychoanalysis, endowed his person with certain authoritarian and fanaticizing tendencies. Only in old age did these recede into the background, due partly to the resignation, partly to the pessimism and scepticism, of his later outlook.

Freud left the 'Gymnasium' in Vienna, where he had been 'top boy' for seven years, and passed his University Entrance in 1873. Although his father's financial circumstances were by no means favourable, he had none the less urged his son to follow his own bent in his choice of a

---

[1] A biographical sketch of Freud's early life has been given because it casts light on the origins of psychoanalysis. No such biographical sketch has been given in respect of Freud's followers.

faculty. This was no easy matter for Freud, since—with his unusual combination of talents—practical research and theoretical subjects were both equally attractive to him. He decided to study medicine but found no satisfaction in this field until *Ernst Brücke* took him on as a 'Volontärassistent' [1] in the Physiological Laboratory, where Freud was engaged on physiological problems. He worked in this Institute from 1876 to 1882 but was obliged to give up the idea of a career in physiological research because his financial situation would not permit it. At the Brücke Institute he was principally concerned with investigations into the nervous system of the lower species of fish; the results of his investigations were published at the time. After leaving the Institute and with a view to preparing himself for the practice of medicine he became a Sekundärarzt[2] in the General Hospital, whilst still continuing with his physiological and histological investigations into the central nervous system in human beings. His activities at the Physiological Institute were now replaced by his work at the Institute of Brain Anatomy and whilst he was there he published a large number of neuro-pathological works on the course of the fibrous tissue in the medulla oblongata and the spinal cord.

The then Professor for Psychiatry, *Meynert*, whose influence on Freud will be dealt with, together with Brücke's, on a later page, invited Freud to accept the post of Director of the Laboratory for Brain Anatomy and to take over his own series of lectures, an offer which Freud declined. As a result of his research work Freud was now considered one of the leading neurologists and neuro-pathologists in Vienna.—In 1885 he was appointed lecturer in Neuropathology and in the autumn of the same year he went to Paris to enter the Salpêtrière as an Elève of *Charcot*.

At the time Charcot was one of the leading neurologists and neuro-pathologists of Europe and it is understandable that Freud should have hoped to learn from him. But over and above this there were practical reasons for his visit to Charcot. In view of the fact that Freud intended to engage in the treatment of nervous disorders he was obliged to concern himself with *hypnosis*, since at that time this constituted one of the few weapons in the therapeutic arsenal at the disposal of the physician working in this field. Many of the Professors of Psychiatry of the day declared hypnosis to be a swindle—a declaration which they were subsequently to make in respect of psychoanalysis as well. But Freud had been able to assess the validity of hypnotic symptoms and hypnotic conditions whilst still a student. With Charcot hypnosis was employed as a valid therapeutic instrument. In his famous *leçons du mardi*, at which the Parisians would appear *haute volée*, he used hypnosis to

---

[1] Volontärassistent: assistant on part salary. (Tr.)
[2] Sekundärarzt: assistant on full salary. (Tr.)

produce symptoms and also—but usually for a short time only—to cure them.

But the patients who were the subjects of these demonstrations did in fact suffer from hysteria and Freud acquired a thorough knowledge both of the range of this illness and of its detailed ramifications. When he returned to Vienna he reported his observations to his colleagues of the Viennese medical fraternity, but they simply held him up to ridicule and refused to take him seriously. Meynert was offended by Freud's interest in hysterical symptoms; as a representative of a psychiatric school based exclusively on brain anatomy he was, for example, unable to accept that hysterical paralysis could be induced by hypnosis. The break between Meynert and Freud came about in connection with their discussions of this question. Freud then largely withdrew into general practice, where, in the course of the following five years, he prepared the series of investigations which were to lead to the discovery and development of psychoanalysis.

II. HYSTERIA AND HYPNOSIS

Hysteria had caught the imagination of neurologists at the turn of the century—especially in France—because it produced neurological symptoms, which appeared to be of an organic nature, such as insensitivity or hyper-sensitivity (anaesthesia, hyperaesthesia) of the limbs and parts of the body, paralysis, spasms and convulsions that were reminiscent of epilepsy.

Charcot had made a noteworthy contribution to the analysis and systematization of the various hysterical symptoms, but their psychological ramifications were only of incidental interest to him, since his main concern was with the neurological investigations as such. Apart from the neurological symptoms of hysteria, which at that time were still considered by a large number of researchers to be of an organic nature, hysteria could also be distinguished by the particular *state of consciousness* which accompanied it. Hysterical patients entered into states of consciousness, especially during the so-called *grande attaque*, which brought about a distinct change in their personality, resulting in a limitation of consciousness and an impaired sense of temporal and spatial orientation. They were, moreover, confused and after waking from this condition had no recollection of what they had experienced or expressed during the fit (amnesia). Furthermore, it was possible, by means of hypnosis, to cause (apparently) healthy persons to enter into a state of consciousness resembling hysteria and to instruct them under hypnosis to form symptoms such as the above-mentioned hysterical fit or, for example, paralysis of a leg. On the other hand it was also possible under hypnosis to heal a person suffering from hysteria by telling him that when he awoke he would, for example, be able to flex his arm again.

Freud discovered these last two techniques in 1889 when he visited the *School of Nancy*, where *Liébault* and *Bernheim* were working. The School of Nancy, which Freud visited in connection with his own enquiries into hysteria, was famous for the methodological development of suggestion and autosuggestion. Freud translated works of both Charcot and Bernheim.

The use of hypnosis was still known to the medical men of the nineteenth century as a relic of romantic medicine under the name of 'animal magnetism'. The hypnotic condition was induced either by stroking certain parts of the body—especially the arms, neck and chest—in a rhythmical manner or by requiring the person who was to submit to the hypnosis to fix his gaze on a certain object. The two methods were also used in combination. Anton *Mesmer* may be regarded as the father of our modern theory of hypnosis, although the art was never entirely lost to the medical fraternity since the days of antiquity.

III. FREUD'S FIRST PUBLICATION ON A CASE OF SUCCESSFUL TREATMENT BY HYPNOTISM (1892)

In this publication Freud tells of a young woman who was prevented by lack of appetite, sleeplessness, the drying up of her milk and a mild condition of excitation from suckling her child following her first confinement. Freud succeeded in placing the patient under hypnosis and in suggesting to her that not only would she have no more ailments but that she would also be able to suckle her child. The patient was cured after two sessions of hypnosis. A similar success was achieved following a third confinement.

Freud explained that the cure was brought about by means of the following 'mechanism'. When a human being carries out a given action (in the case of the patient that of giving suck), the action releases certain expectant ideas and certain affects which are linked with those ideas. The success of an action (in this case that of giving suck) depends on the importance of the action to the person concerned and the degree of inner security or, alternatively, insecurity possessed by that person. People of a nervous disposition incline more to insecurity than do healthy people, this insecurity being caused by a 'sum of ideas', which Freud calls 'painful, antithetic ideas' (in the case of this particular patient: 'I cannot give suck'). Whilst a healthy person *suppresses* and *inhibits* the antithetic ideas which precede the execution of a given action, 'excludes them from association',[1,2] the neurasthenic or nervous person is unable to do so. He is a victim of the antithetic ideas, which, however, are capable of being inhibited under hypnosis by means of a counter-suggestion to the extent that they no longer influence the patient in his waking state. The patient is often *unconscious*[3] of the antithetic ideas, a factor which is related to the tendency, which is implicit in hysteria, towards disassociation (*split*) of consciousness (see above—Change in state of consciousness in hysterics). The antithetic idea continues to exist as a disconnected idea and at the time of the action (in the above case that of giving suck) it is capable of physical expression in the same way as, in normal circumstances, is an idea determined by the will. The antithetic idea appears as a 'counter-will', i.e. the patient notes to her consternation that, although she wishes to give suck, she is unable to do so. Freud draws the further inference that the hysterical condition is characterized by the exhaustion and weakness of '. . . those elements of the nervous system which form the material foundation of the ideas associated with the primary consciousness—that is, from the normal ego—the inhibited and suppressed ideas are not exhausted, and they consequently predominate at the moment when the disposition to hysteria emerges'.[4] These elements of the nervous system—the material basis of the ideas or, subsequently, the ideas themselves—are, Freud maintains, 'excluded from the chain of associations of the normal ego'. The inhibited and repressed ideas, on the other hand, are not exhausted and it is these that will prevail once the hysterical condition sets in. This explains why people who were perfectly decent when in their normal state of health tended to produce the most extraordinary and incredible reactions when they became hysterical: because the antithetic idea, the counter-will, is given a free rein.

This first attempt of Freud's to interpret hysterical symptoms is of particular importance, because it contains *in nuce* the elements of his subsequent psychoanalysis. These elements are as follows:

1. Affect and idea are differentiated. They can be separated from one another or linked with one another. This conception is to prove of prime importance for the subsequent explanation of the various forms of neurosis.

2. Idea and painful antithetic idea: Freud's later unconscious is present here in the limited form of the antithetic idea and the counter-will. The importance of ambivalence, of discord, which was to have great influence in the later development of psychoanalysis, is here anticipated.

---

[1] In a comparative study of organic and hysterical paralysis (*Arch. d. Neurologie*, 77, 1893) Freud demonstrates the fundamental difference between the two types of paralysis.   [2] S. Freud, *Coll. Paps.*, Vol. V, p. 39.
[3] *Ibid.*, p. 40.   [4] *Ibid.*, p. 43.

3. 'Subjective insecurity' is linked with a neurasthenic condition, with a nervous disposition; this facilitates the emergence of the antithetic idea.

4. The healthy person 'suppresses' or 'inhibits' the antithetic idea. (Subsequently repression and defence.)

5. The inhibition or repression consists in the fact that the painful ideas are excluded from the chain of associations of the normal ego.

Freud *observed* in his patient the *symptoms* of sleeplessness, loss of appetite and inability to give suck (*a*) Other hysterical patients displayed that changed state of consciousness, in which they did things which they would never have dreamt of doing in their normal lives. (*b*) The fact that hysterics tended to do the opposite of what they wanted Freud connected with the following observation taken from normal psychology. (*c*) That in anticipating or carrying out an intended course of action a healthy person will also consider the possibility that he might come to grief. Freud extends this observation from the sphere of normal psychology:

1. to the concept of the painful antithetic idea;
2. which is repressed by the healthy person;
3. which is often unconsciously present in the hysteric, in whom it exists as a 'disassociated idea';
4. which then asserts itself as the counter-will.

Observation (*a*) was linked with observation (*b*) and both were explained by (*c*), resulting in the introduction of three hypotheses:

1. the hypothesis of the antithetic idea;
2. the hypothesis of the repression and inhibition of the antithetic idea in healthy persons;
3. the hypothesis of the (pathogenic) unconscious and disassociated idea in hysterics.

The fact that the antithetic idea is not pathogenic (does not produce illness) in a healthy person, although it logically follows that in the healthy person it is also unconscious and also excluded from the interchange of associations made by the normal ego, Freud explains by the introduction of two further hypotheses:

1. The antithetic ideas in hysterics are not 'exhausted', whereas in healthy persons they are, in which respect Freud understands under 'exhaustion' a reduction of the sum of excitation contained in the ideas, which excitation has been determined by the affect;
2. What has been exhausted in the hysteric, however, are 'those

elements of the nervous system which form the material foundation of the ideas associated with the primary consciousness'.

Freud considered on the one hand that these elements were constitutionally determined changes within the cellular elements of the brain and on the other hand that they formed the basis of the later 'ego'.

These statements of Freud's constitute the first attempt to deal with a question which psychoanalysis has yet to answer, namely why repressed (i.e. unconscious) ideas should prove pathogenic in one case and not in another. The separation of affect—which Freud here provisionally defines as the sum of excitation—and idea (association) enables him (a) to increase or decrease the sum of excitation and (b) to move it up and down the chains of associations. This hypothesis is based on the observation taken from the sphere of normal psychology that ideas with strong or weak affects or with no affects at all can in fact be linked with one another.

IV. FURTHER INVESTIGATIONS INTO HYSTERICAL SYMPTOMS

Whilst he was still an 'Assistent' with Brücke (1880) Freud made the acquaintance of Josef *Breuer*, a man fifteen years his senior, who had a large practice in Vienna as a specialist for internal diseases and who was also engaged on scientific research. Breuer was a highly respected, highly respectable person, who promoted Freud's interests over a period of ten years, afforded him financial help, and kept him regularly informed between 1880 and 1882 about one of his patients, Anna O., who was undergoing treatment with him at that time. This patient was suffering from an abundance of the most varied hysterical symptoms, which included paralysis, contractions and states of confusion with reduced conscious orientation. Breuer placed the patient under hypnosis and then induced her to talk about the things that oppressed and frightened her. It soon became apparent that the discussions conducted under hypnosis, which the patient was unable to recall after being wakened, were causing the symptoms to yield. Over and above this, however, it also became apparent that these symptoms were closely linked to a period in the patient's life when she had nursed her sick father for a considerable length of time. The symptoms were meaningful if they were understood in terms of the patient's affects and her situation during the period of nursing. They were recollections of particular situations at her father's sick-bed in the sense that the patient had suppressed certain thoughts and ideas at that time. *The symptom had subsequently appeared in place of the repressed impulse or inhibited idea. The recollection—under hypnosis —of the situation in which a certain idea had been suppressed caused the symptom to yield.*

This therapy, in which the patients were permitted to unburden themselves (abreact) under hypnosis was called the 'cathartic method'. Stimulated by both Breuer and Charcot and also by the activities of the school of Nancy Freud used the same method of treatment with some of his own patients and achieved similar results. In 1893 he published the results of his investigations in *On the Psychical Mechanism of Hysterical Phenomena: Preliminary Communication*, a work of which Breuer was joint author. This was followed in 1894 by the publication of *The Neuro-psychoses of Defence*, in which Freud extended the results which Breuer and he had drawn from hysteria to other disturbances of psychic behaviour, namely the so-called anxiety and obsessional neuroses. Then in 1895, again jointly with Breuer, the *Studies on Hysteria* were published. What were the most important conclusions established in these works?

V. THE THEORETICAL AND FOUNDATION DEVELOPMENT OF PSYCHOANALYSIS IN THE SCIENTIFIC PUBLICATIONS OF FREUD AND BREUER (BETWEEN 1892 AND 1899)

(a) Trauma, Symptom and Catharsis

Charcot differentiated between 'traumatic' and 'idiopathic' hysteria. In the case of the former the link between the accident—a shock or a shattering experience—and the illness was an obvious one, even if the reason *why* the accident should have caused an hysterical condition to develop was not clarified. 'Idiopathic hysteria' on the other hand was considered to be a form of degeneration. The discovery that the trauma, here understood in the sense of a shattering experience, was also an important factor in this type of hysteria was destined to be made by Freud and Breuer (1880–1882), although *Delbouef, Binet* and *Janet* had already expressed *similar* views in France before the publication of the Preliminary Communication.

The trauma as understood by Freud and Breuer is not, however, to be equated with Charcot's accident trauma. On the contrary, it is characterized as any experience that is linked with anxiety, fright or shame. Instead of one big trauma—comparable to an accident or a fright—a succession of 'partial traumas' are often to be discovered in the life history of hysterics, whose influence is increased by summation. It is also possible for apparently trivial causes to combine on the one hand with the event which actually exercises the influence and on the other hand with a particular sensitivity or irritability in the person concerned. The recollection of the trauma, in its extended sense of an unpleasant experience, is then activated under hypnosis. If it is linked with a corresponding affect, then it can be 'abreacted'. Only those recollections which are linked with affects are of therapeutic value. However, the relationship between the symptom and the recollection is not always apparent. Often the connection is merely *symbolic and not so direct*. Let us take as an example the case of the doctor who, when assisting at an operation in which his brother's anchylosed (ossified) hip joint was being stretched under narcosis, felt a violent pain in his own hip at the precise moment when his brother's hip gave way to the accompaniment of a loud crack. In this case the relationship between the cracking noise in the brother's hip and the pain in his own—which lasted for more than a year—was a direct one. In other cases of hysterical hemianaesthesia (insensitivity of one side of the body) or in cases of hysterical fits the connection between the trauma (experience) and the symptom cannot be so readily detected. *The importance of traumas in the development of hysteria was to become one of the cornerstones of psychoanalytic theory.* As has already been stated, it is essential that the patient should *not* remember the traumas but should only gain access to them in a state of modified consciousness (hypnosis). Breuer and Freud have summed up the importance of the trauma for the hysteric in the following sentence: 'The hysteric suffers from reminiscences'.[1]

The fact that in one person recollections have a pathogenic effect whilst in another they have not Freud and Breuer explained—in accordance with Freud's initial research into the 'counter-will'—by stating that different people reacted to a given experience with a greater or lesser degree of affect. If the 'sum of excitation' contained in the idea is discharged, then the memory fades and no longer produces a pathogenic effect. This pathogenic effect can also be rendered harmless if, through the influence of other ideas, the memory can be altered, corrected, or incorporated into the sequence of associations. These two methods, namely, (*a*) that of affective reaction to an experience and (*b*) that of conscious transformation of the experience, can prevent any such experience from triggering off hysterical symptoms. In later psychoanalytic therapy these two methods were to become pillars of therapeutic technique.

Their importance is summarized by Freud and Breuer as follows:[2]

'It brings to an end the operative force of the idea which was not abreacted in the first instance, by allowing its strangulated effect to find a way out through speech; and it subjects it to associative correction by introducing it into normal consciousness (under light hypnosis) or by removing it through the physician's suggestion, as is done in somnambulism by amnesia.'

[1] Sigmund Freud, *Complete Works*, Standard Edition; London, Hogarth Press; New York, Macmillan; Vol. II, pp. 6 ff. [2] *Ibid.*, p. 17

(b) Hypnoid States

It is characteristic for the development of Freud's concept of the unconscious that in his early psychopathological publications, including the *Studies*, it played only a subordinate role (see above p. 52 ff.). The dominant theme at that time was the analysis of the problem of split consciousness or diasssociation as revealed in hysterics, which Charcot's disciple, Janet, took as the starting-point for his theory of hysteria, which theory Freud then augmented with his conception of 'acquired hysteria'. (This is the leading concept in traumatic and idiopathic hysteria.) The dimming of consciousness and the restriction which hysterics develop in an hysterical fit Freud and Breuer call 'hypnoid states' by analogy with the state produced by means of hypnosis. 'Hypnosis is artificial hysteria'.[1] In contrast to this hypnoid hysteria, however, Freud's acquired hysteria, which is illustrated by the detailed case histories reported in the *Studies*, deserves special attention.[2]

'We have found, however, that a severe trauma (such as occurs in a traumatic neurosis) or a laborious suppression (as of a sexual affect, for instance), can bring about a splitting off of groups of ideas even in people who are in other respects unaffected; and this would be the mechanism of psychically acquired hysteria.'

In Freud's view the essential characteristic of the hypnoid states is the exclusion of the emerging idea from the 'interchange of associations' with the other contents of consciousness (above all in the waking state). Hysterical symptoms were similarly explained. When Freud and Breuer separated at the end of the 'nineties, they did so largely because they were unable to agree on the evaluation of these 'hypnoid states'. Breuer considered them to be the decisive pathogenic factor in the development of hysteria, whilst Freud, who had meanwhile become interested in other parapsychological phenomena, tended to place hysteria within the larger context of a general psychopathology and structure of the personality, rather than to accord it a special position. The difference between the 'Preliminary Communication' (*Studies on Hysteria*) and the work on the 'counter-will' lies in the following points:

(a) In the *Studies* the emphasis is placed on the (discovery of the) importance of the traumatic experience for the patient. The memory of the suppressed thoughts and impulses associated with specific situations will exercise a pathogenic affect to the extent to which it has not been effectively or consciously transmuted. The memories form a pathogenic

---

[1] S. Freud, *St. Edn.*, Vol. II, p. 12.   [2] *Ibid.*, p. 12.

group in the unconscious, which is split off from the (conscious) ego and 'revenges itself' (see below p. 59 ff.) for its isolation from consciousness by forming symptoms. The dominant theme of the *Studies* is that of therapy: the discovery of the 'cathartic method'.

(*b*) The exclusive theme of the work of the 'counter-will' is that of the *dynamic* aspect of the suppressed antithetic idea, which is unconsciously active and is excluded from the 'interchange of associations' with the normal ego. The importance of the pathogenic ideas, however, had not yet been discovered, from which it follows that the therapeutic method was limited in scope. The concepts of the antithetic idea and of the counter-will tip the balance in favour of the unconscious.

(*c*) Defence and Conversion

Freud's work on the *Neuro-psychoses of Defence*, published in 1894, mentions the concept of 'defence' for the first time. This was subsequently replaced by the concept of 'repression'. To some extent these two expressions are used synonymously. Referring back to the 'Preliminary Communication' of 1893 Freud now distinguishes between 'defence hysteria' and hypnoid hysteria. He found with several of his patients that the characteristic condition of the former was the denial of incompatible, painful ideas. A painful, incompatible idea, which, in the case of female patients, is often connected with their '*sexual experiences*',[1] is rejected by the ego and produces physical symptoms. How is this possible ? Here Freud applies his above-mentioned hypothesis of the separation of affect and idea (sum of excitation and association), to explain that the repressing ego wrests the sum of excitation (the affect) from what had once been an intense idea and discharges this sum of excitation into the physical sphere. There, by *conversion* of the affect into physical terms, the hysterical symptom is formed, which subsequently yields to the recalled affect in the course of cathartic treatment. (The sum of excitation is freed from the physical symptom.) In the case of persons who are not given to conversion—and here Freud is saying that the basis of conversion is constitutionally determined—the affect that has been split off from the idea will remain within the psychic sphere. The consequence of this is the appearance of obsessional neuroses and phobias (specific types of anxiety).

(*d*) Other Forms of Defence

The affect hooks on to other ideas, which need not necessarily be incompatible, and these may then turn into—for example—obsessional ideas. Although as a result of the conversion of the affect into the physical sphere—in the case of hysteria—the ego achieves freedom from contra-

---

[1] S. Freud, *St. Edn.*, Vol. III, p. 47.

diction, on the other hand it burdens itself with a 'memory symbol', which, in the form of an 'insoluble motor innervation' ... 'lives like a parasite in the unconscious mind and continues to exist until such time as a conversion in the opposite direction has taken place'. (The memory symbol is eradicated by the cathartic recollection.)

In obsessional neurosis and phobias, however, the ego is not able to free itself from contradiction to the same extent, since the affect remains unchanged and *only the incompatible idea is excluded from the memory.* The affect hooks on to the modified ideas. In all cases of obsessional neurosis and phobias, to which Freud applied the cathartic method, the repressed idea was related to experiences in the patient's sex life. The disassociated affect can in fact tack on to any ideas, but often there is an inner connection between the 'dislocated' affects and the ideas. These latter are usually taken from the sphere of sexuality. The following case may be quoted as an example, one of several described by Freud in this work, in which the fear of incontinence *replaces* the fear of sexual excitation.[1]

'Another girl suffered from the dread of being overcome by the desire to urinate, and of being unable to avoid wetting herself, ever since a need of this kind had in fact once obliged her to leave a concert hall during the performance. By degrees this phobia had made her completely incapable of enjoying herself or of going into society. She only felt well if she knew there was a WC near at hand which she could reach unobtrusively. There was no question of any organic complaint which might justify this mistrust in her power to control her bladder; when she was at home, in quiet conditions, or at night, the need to urinate did not arise. A detailed examination showed that the need had occurred first in the following circumstances. In the concert hall a gentleman to whom she was not indifferent had taken a seat not far from her. She began to think about him and to imagine herself sitting beside him as his wife. During this erotic reverie she had the bodily sensation which is to be compared with an erection in a man, and which in her case—I do not know if this is always so—ended with a slight need to urinate. She now became greatly frightened by the sexual sensation (to which she was normally accustomed) because she had resolved within herself to combat this particular liking, as well as any other she might feel; and the next moment the affect had become transferred on to the accompanying need to urinate and compelled her after an agonizing struggle to leave the hall. In her ordinary life she was so prudish that she had an intense horror of everything to do with sex and could not contemplate the thought of ever marrying. On the other hand,

[1] S. Freud, *St. Edn.,* Vol. III, p. 56.

she was so hyperaesthetic sexually that during every erotic reverie, in which she readily indulged, the same voluptuous sensation appeared. The erection was each time accompanied by the need to urinate, though without its making any impression on her until the scene in the concert hall. The treatment led to an almost complete control over the phobia.'

Now psychosis as we know it to-day in the various forms of schizophrenia can be said to obtain when the ego has completely repudiated the idea and the affect and in consequence suffers a complete loss of reality. In support of his view Freud reports the following case:[1]

'A girl had given her first impulsive affection to a man, and firmly believed that he returned her love. In fact she was wrong; the young man had a different motive for visiting the house. Disappointments were not wanting. At first she defended herself against them by effecting an hysterical conversion of the experience in question and thus preserved her belief that one day he would come and ask for her hand. But at the same time she felt unhappy and ill, because the conversion was incomplete and because she was continually being met by fresh painful impressions. Finally, in a state of great tension, she awaited his arrival on a particular day, the day of a family celebration. But the day wore on and he did not appear. When all the trains by which he could arrive had come and gone, she passed into a state of hallucinatory confusion; he had arrived, she heard his voice in the garden, she hurried down in her nightdress to receive him. From that time on she lived for two months in a happy dream, whose content was that he was there, always at her side, and that everything was as it had been before (before the time of the disappointments which she had so laboriously fended off). Her hysteria and her depression of spirits were overcome. During her illness she was silent about the whole latter period of doubt and suffering; she was happy so long as she was left undisturbed, and she broke out in fury only when some rule of conduct insisted on by those around her hindered her in something which seemed to her to follow quite logically from her blissful dream. This psychosis, which had been unintelligible at the time, was explained ten years later with the help of a hypnotic analyst.'

In his work on the *Neuro-psychoses of Defence* Freud enlarges on the points of view put forward in his work on the 'Counter-will' and establishes the following extended premises, which are of importance for the further development of psychoanalysis.

1.   The symptom arises out of the interplay of forces between the ego,

[1] S. Freud, *St. Edn.*, Vol. III, p. 58.

which represses an unpleasant idea, and the repressed idea and the affect. The affect can either be discharged into the physical sphere, resulting in 'conversion', or it is split off from its own idea and linked up with another idea, resulting in an obsessional neurosis or a phobia.

2. The painful ideas, which are repressed, derive for the most part from sexuality.

3. It was primarily as a result of his use of the 'cathartic method' that Freud began to collect the observations and experiences which prompted him to put forward the following hypotheses:

(*a*) (conversion) the physical symptom disappears as a result of the affect-laden recollection of the repressed ideas and situations,

(*b*) the recollection of the repressed idea (see the case of the girl whose phobia was designed to banish all thought of sexuality) is able to contribute to the dissolution of the phobia. In the case of this patient fear of incontinence had replaced the fear of sexual excitation. The anxiety *affect* was then linked with the fear of incontinence.

4. The conditions found to exist in respect of hysteria also applied to other disturbances of psychic life. With this realization Freud advanced from a psychotherapy of hysteria to a psychotherapy of neurosis and a general psychopathology. Moreover, the psychology which was now developing was not restricted to psycho*pathology* but was extended to embrace a psychology of the normal person. The interplay of forces between the successful and unsuccessful repression of unpleasant ideas and affects was subsequently to be considered an integral part of the p ychological attitude of the normal person. In addition to this there w the discovery of the extraordinary importance of sexuality for the aet ology of neurosis, which was to develop more and more into a nucleus of psychoanalytic theory.

(*e*) The Trauma of Early Childhood

Two years after the appearance of the *Neuropsychoses of Defence* a further publication appeared, in which the ideas first set down in that work were developed along the following lines: The 'reminiscences of hysterics' (see above p. 53) can be traced back to specific sexual traumas of puberty and childhood. The special condition for hysteria lies in the *passivity* with which the traumas are experienced by the patient. It is not the actual experiences which have a traumatic effect but the 'recollection' of those experiences at the time of sexual maturity. What are the implications of this formulation as compared with its predecessor, in which the stress was placed on the importance of the trauma for the aetiology of hysteria? In the further pursuit of his psychoanalytic investigations (the term *psychoanalytic* is here used for the first time in its later meaning of 'rendering previously unconscious material conscious') Freud had noticed that[1] the farther he went in his examinations of his patients, the farther back in time their traumatic experiences in the sexual sphere were found to lie. The more the therapist enquired into the symptoms, the more they revealed a temporal organization and stratification. As soon as the individual reached sexual maturity, then, as a result of the increase in sexual excitability, the memories of those traumas were—inexplicably—aroused, resulting in the development of hysterical symptoms. Subsequently a parallel was to be drawn on the basis of this last hypothesis between the frequency of sexual traumas observed in childhood and the further observation of the importance of traumas as such for the emergence of hysteria or neuroses.

(f) The Symptom as Compromise

In respect of obsessional neurosis Freud put forward in this same publication the hypothesis of active sexual participation during early childhood, to which patients responded with self-reproach.[2]

'*Obsessional ideas* are invariably transformed *self-reproaches* which have re-emerged from *repression* and which always relate to some *sexual* act that was performed with pleasure in childhood.'

Freud describes the development of obsessional neurosis in connection with the development of human sexuality, thus anticipating his later *Essays on the Theory of Sexuality*. He describes an early period of childish immorality, in which children engage in aggressive sexual actions towards other children. In the period of growing sexual maturity (puberty) these actions of early childhood are first remembered with pleasure but are then subjected to defence or *repressed*. By way of a reaction to the successful repression conscientiousness, shame and lack of self-confidence are developed in the so-called healthy period. The illness appears when the defence can no longer be successfully maintained and the repressed memories of the sexual activity of early childhood emerge and meet with reproaches (obsessional ideas). The repression continues to be exercised by the ego. But it is also possible for the reproach *affect* to be repressed and *transformed* into any other type of affect.[3]

'Thus self-reproach (for having carried out the sexual act in childhood) can easily turn into *shame* (in case someone else should find out about

[1] S. Freud, *St. Edn.*, Vol. III, p. 164.   [2] *Ibid.*, p. 169.
[3] *Ibid.*, p. 171.

THEORIES OF DEPTH PSYCHOLOGY

it), into *hypochondriacal anxiety* (fear of being punished by society for the misdeed), into *religious anxiety*, into *delusions of being noticed* (fear of betraying the act to other people), or into *fear of temptation* (a justified mistrust of one's own moral powers of resistance), and so on. In addition, the mnemic content of the act involving self-reproach may be represented in consciousness as well, or it may remain completely in the background —which makes diagnosis much more difficult.'

Whilst obsessional symptoms represent the *return of the repressed material* in the form of a compromise and whilst obsessional *ideas* constitute the most important aspect of those symptoms, obsessional *actions*, i.e. the ceremonial rituals observed by an obsessional neurotic, also have a further meaning. Freud interprets them as the ego's 'secondary defence', with which it seeks to defend itself against the 'descendants of the memories that were repressed in the first place'. And so repression—or defence—reveals three phases in obsessional neurosis

(*a*) primary repression during puberty of the sexual activity of early childhood;
(*b*) secondary repression which is effected by means of a compromise reached between the repressed and the repressing idea;
(*c*) tertiary defence effected by means of protective actions designed to counter the emergence of the ideas mentioned under (*b*) (so-called obsessional actions).

If we compare the two works which Freud published on the *Neuropsychoses of Defence*, the importance of the latter one, that of 1896, which closes with the analysis of a condition of chronic paranoia, is seen to lie in the following considerations:

1. Freud's realisation of the importance of sexuality for the aetiology of hysteria and of neuroses is extended, with the result that not only current sexual traumas are considered to exercise a pathogenic effect but also those experienced in early childhood. These are recalled at the time of sexual maturity; and it is the recollection and *not* the trauma which triggers off the illness.
2. The symptoms of obsessional neurosis are compromise formations, e.g. between the repressed reproach and the repressing ego. The *compromise character* of these symptoms is spontaneously extended to all psychoneurotic symptoms, including the trauma.
3. Repression is also seen to be a process which is organized both *temporally* and *dynamically* and which, in the case of obsessional neurosis, can be sub-divided into three phases.
4. The affects and the ideas linked with them are capable of *transforma-*

tion. This thesis is of particular importance for the understanding of numerous psychoneurotic symptoms which, according to this thesis, can all be traced back to a primary or original affect, an affect, however, which is capable of transformation (e.g. sexuality into reproach). This assumption is based on the further assumption that affect and idea can be separated and it demonstrates the direct influence exercised on Freud by the physico-energic ideas contained in the theory of the constancy of energy (see below p. 79 ff.). The affect is defined as the sum of excitation, a definition which proclaims its purely quantitative character and allows transformation into any other 'form of energy' to take place without hindrance.

5. Character traits such as conscientiousness, lack of confidence, shame are conceived for the first time as *reaction formations* in the sense of reactions formed in response to the repression of painful ideas.

6. The concept of 'projection' is introduced for the first time. A case of chronic paranoia, which Freud himself analysed, induced him to advance the hypothesis that the paranoic *projects* the reproach, which emerges together with the suppressed sexual experiences of childhood, on to the environment. He sums up as follows:[1,2]

'It only remains for me now to employ what has been learned from this case of paranoia for making a comparison between paranoia and obsessional neurosis. In each of them repression has been shown to be the nucleus of the psychical mechanism, and in each what has been repressed is a sexual experience in childhood. In this case of paranoia, too, every obsession sprang from repression; the symptoms of paranoia allow of a classification similar to the one which has proved justified for obsessional neurosis. Part of the symptoms, once again, arise from primary defence— namely, all the delusional ideas which are characterized by distrust and suspicion and which are concerned with ideas of being persecuted by others. In obsessional neurosis the initial self-reproach has been repressed by the formation of the primary symptom of defence: *self-distrust*. With this, the self-reproach is acknowledged as justified; and, to weigh against this, the conscientiousness which the subject has acquired during his healthy interval now protects him from giving credence to the self-reproaches which return in the form of obsessional ideas. In paranoia, the self-reproach is repressed in a manner which may be described as *projection*. It is repressed by erecting the defensive system of *distrust of other people*. In this way the subject withdraws his acknowledgement of the self-reproach; and, as if to make up for this, he is deprived of a protection against the self-reproaches which return in his delusional ideas.'

[1] S. Freud, *St. Edn.*, Vol. III, p. 183.   [2] *Ibid.*

(g) From Catharsis to Psychoanalysis
Initial Topography of the Unconscious

Freud's far-reaching *quantitative-dynamic* formulations were preceded by his initial *topical* formulation in his work on 'The Psycho-therapy of Hysteria' (which formed part of the *Studies*). The so-called dynamic, economic and topical aspect was to prove decisive for the whole of the subsequent description of the psychic apparatus. Moreover, this work represents the transition from Breuer's 'cathartic' method to the actual psychoanalytic method. Why did Freud decide to develop an alternative therapeutic process ? He was prompted to do so for three reasons:

1.   The cathartic process did not appear to be effective in respect of causes but merely effected symptomatic cures. In other words, if the physician succeeded in bringing about the desired discharge of affect in the patient, although the symptom disappeared, the possibility remained that it might reappear in another part of the body. The structure of the illness and of the personality remained *unaltered*. Over and above this not all patients were able to achieve the desired abreaction.
2.   Not all patients could be placed under hypnosis—how were such patients to be treated ?
3.   Freud discovered the importance of resistance and of transference, i.e. of the relationship between the therapist and the patient, which develops in the course of treatment.

From the outset hypnosis created an unequal relationship between doctor and patient, for by placing the patient completely in the doctor's power it encouraged the so-called transference infatuation, expecially in the case of women. Freud tell how[1] one of his women patients, on waking from hypnosis, threw her arms around his neck, and that the embarrassing situation was only brought to an end by the timely entrance of a servant. He and his patient then reached a tacit agreement to discontinue treatment by hypnosis. He also describes the difficulties attendant on the analytic method and in the following passage he gives his first observations on the nature of transference:[2]

The procedure is laborious and time-consuming for the physician. It presupposes great interest in psychological happenings, but personal concern for the patient as well. I cannot imagine bringing myself to delve into the psychical mechanisms of an hysteria in anyone who struck me as low-minded and repellent, and who, on closer acquaintance, would not be capable of arousing human sympathy; whereas I can keep the treatment of a tabetic or rheumatic patient apart from personal

---

[1] S. Freud, *St. Edn.*, Vol. XX, pp. 26 ff.
[2] *Ibid.*, Vol. II, pp. 265–6.

approval of this kind. The demands made on the patient are not less. The procedure is not applicable at all below a certain level of intelligence, and it is made very much more difficult by any trace of feebleness of mind. The complete consent and complete attention of the patients are needed, but above all their confidence, since the analysis invariably leads to the disclosure of the most intimate and secret psychical events. A good number of the patients who would be suitable for this form of treatment abandon the doctor as soon as the suspicion begins to dawn on them of the direction in which the investigation is leading. For patients such as these the doctor has remained a stranger. With others, who have decided to put themselves in his hands and place their confidence in him—a step which in other such situations is only taken voluntarily and never at the doctor's request—with these patients, I say, it is almost inevitable that their personal relationship to him will force itself, for a time at least, unduly into the foreground. It seems, indeed, as though an influence of this kind on the part of the doctor is a *sine qua non* to a solution of the problem.'

The next step in the progression from cathartic to analytic treatment was the method of so-called 'free association', which Freud now developed and which to this day has remained one of the central therapeutic methods employed by the Freudian schools of psychoanalysis. Freud's patients were still required to lie down on the couch—as in the hypnotic sessions—but right at the beginning of the session he gave them a theme, one taken from their own life, on which they were expected to comment *without exercising any control* over their thoughts. Usually he took as his starting-point the events which had preceded the appearance of a symptom. If the flow of thoughts began to dry up Freud would lay his hand on the patient's brow and exert gentle pressure. At the same time he would encourage the patient by suggesting that he could surely remember this or that event. He considered that the resistance which the patient occasionally developed and which took the form of his not wanting to remember a specific event, one perhaps of a sexual nature, was identical with the *force of the defence* or repression which prevented the memory from emerging. Moreover, the resistance appeared to him to be the consequence of a censorship exercised by the ego, whose object was to prevent certain ideas from becoming conscious.[1]

'It has indeed been generally admitted by psychologists that the acceptance of a new idea (acceptance in the sense of believing or of recognizing as real) is dependent on the nature and trend of the ideas already united in the ego, and they have invented special names for this process of

[1] S. Freud, *St. Edn.*, Vol. II, p. 269.

censorship to which the new arrival must submit. The patient's ego had been approached by an idea which proved to be incompatible, which provoked on the part of the ego a compelling force of which the purpose was defence against this incompatible idea. This defence was in fact successful. The idea in question was forced out of consciousness and out of memory. The psychical trace of it was apparently lost to view. Nevertheless that trace must be there. If I endeavoured to direct the patient's attention to it, I became aware, in the form of *resistance*, of the same force as had shown itself in the form of *repulsion* when the symptom was generated. If now I could make it appear probable that the idea had become pathogenic precisely as a result of its expulsion and repression the chain would seem complete.'

In the further development of psychoanalysis the concept of the censor was also destined to play a central part.

Freud subsequently discontinued the method involving encouragement and the application of pressure for purposes of suggestion, retaining only the method of 'free association'. This process, moreover, aroused in Freud

'. . . a deceptive impression of there being a superior intelligence outside the patient's consciousness which keeps a large amount of psychical material arranged for particular purposes and has fixed a planned order for its return to consciousness. I suspect, however, that this unconscious second intelligence is no more than an appearance.'[1]

When this process was employed the unconscious appeared to operate as a 'second intelligence', a phenomenon which at that time Freud still viewed with scepticism and reserve. None the less, he states in this same work his intention of *ordering* this unconscious pathogenic material, which he *assumes* is present, but which is not at the disposal of the patient's ego. And with this Freud has laid the cornerstone for the topography of the psychic apparatus that was to follow:[2]

'The psychical material in such cases of hysteria presents itself as a structure in several dimensions which is stratified in at least three different ways. (I hope I shall presently be able to justify this pictorial mode of expression.) To begin with there is a nucleus consisting in memories of events or trains of thought in which the traumatic factor has culminated or the pathogenic idea has found its purest manifestation. Round this nucleus we find what is often an incredibly profuse amount of other mnemic material which has to be worked through in the analysis and which is, as we have said, arranged in a threefold order.

[1] S. Freud, *St. Edn.*, Vol. II, p. 272.   [2] *Ibid.*, pp. 288-9.

'In the first place there is an unmistakable linear chronological order which obtains within each separate theme. As an example of this I will merely quote the arrangement of the material in Breuer's analysis of Anna O. Let us take the theme of becoming deaf, of not hearing. This was differentiated according to seven sets of determinants, and under each of these seven headings ten to over a hundred individual memories were collected in chronological series. It was as though we were examining a dossier that had been kept in good order. The analysis of my patient Emmy von N. contained similar files of memories though they were not so fully enumerated and described. These files form a quite general feature of every analysis and their contents always emerge in a chronological order which is as infallibly trustworthy as the succession of days of the week or names of the month in a mentally normal person. They make the work of analysis more difficult by the peculiarity that, in reproducing the memories, they reverse the order in which these originated. The freshest and newest experience in the file appears first, as an outer cover, and last of all comes the experience with which the series in fact began.

'I have described such groupings of similar memories into collections arranged in linear sequences (like a file of documents, a packet, etc.) as constituting themes! These themes exhibit a second kind of arrangement. Each of them is—I cannot express it in any other way—stratified concentrically round the pathogenic nucleus. It is not hard to say what produces this stratification, what diminishing or increasing magnitude is the basis of this arrangement. The contents of each particular stratum are characterized by an equal degree of resistance, and that degree increases in proportion as the strata are nearer to the nucleus. Thus there are zones within which there is an equal degree of modification of consciousness, and the different themes extend across these zones. The most peripheral strata contain the memories (or files), which, belonging to different themes, are easily remembered and have always been clearly conscious. The deeper we go the more difficult it becomes for the emerging memories to be recognized, till near the nucleus we come upon memories which the patient disavows even in reproducing them.

'It is this peculiarity of the concentric stratification of the pathogenic psychical material which, as we shall hear, lends to the course of these analyses their characteristic features. A third kind of arrangement has still to be mentioned—the most important but the one about which it is least easy to make any general statement. What I have in mind is an arrangement according to thought content, the linkage made by a logical thread which reaches as far as the nucleus and tends to take an irregular and twisting path, different in every case. This arrangement has a dynamic character, in contrast to the morphological one of the two stratifications mentioned previously. While these two would be represented in a spatial diagram by a continuous line, curved or straight, the course of the logical train would have to be indicated by a broken line which would pass along the most roundabout paths from the surface to the deepest layers and back, and yet would in general advance from the periphery to the central nucleus, touching at every intermediate halting-place—a line resembling the zigzag line in the solution of a Knight's move problem, which cuts across the squares in the diagram of the chess-board.'

In this stratification of pathogenic material, which Freud deduces from his observations, the most important characteristic of the symptom apart from compromise formation appears to be its over-determination.[1] The new factors which emerge from the last part of the *Studies* may be summarized as follows:

1. The transition from the (hypnotic) cathartic method to that of 'encouragement' and free association;
2. the first steps towards a psychology of transference are taken as a result of the application of the method of 'encouragement';
3. the resistance exercised by the patient in the course of the treatment is analogous to the force of repression;
4. the concept of censorship is introduced;
5. the unconscious is topically organized into periphery and nucleus. It appears as a 'superior intelligence' and also as an isolated, pathogenic group that has been split off from the ego;
6. the symptom is over-determined.

(h) Early Versions of the Libido Theory

In the works published between 1892 and 1896 it was not only the cornerstones of psychoanalytic theory and therapy that Freud laid but also those of the *Libido theory*, which was to occupy a central position in the further development of psychoanalysis. Freud took the concept of the Libido from *Moll*, a contemporary physician and sexologist, who used it in the sense of a sexual drive. At first Freud defined the libido in terms of a 'sexual affect',[2] 'sexual drive'[3] 'psychic desire',[4] his object being to fix a quantitative value on this concept in order to express energic ideas. This purely quantitative conception of the libido, which is analogous to the concept of the affect as a sum of excitation, is already implicit in the concepts of 'sexual affect' and 'psychic desire'. But these attempts to establish a purely quantitative definition were faced from

[1] See below p. 96 ff.
[2] S. Freud: *Origins of Psychoanalysis*; London, Imago; New York, Basic Books; p. 93.   [3] *Ibid.*, p. 97.   [4] *St. Edn.*, Vol. III, p. 107.

the outset with the difficulty, which arose out of the fact that, as compared with other drives, the sexual drive possessed a *specific quality*, a quality which Freud was obliged to make use of, if his idea of the nature of the libido was to be rendered at all intelligible. And so from the very beginning the libido has been a problematical and hybrid concept. On the one hand it is intended as a purely quantitative term, whilst on the other hand it is required to demonstrate the specific quality of the sexual drive.

In his attempts to arrive at the aetiology of so-called neurasthenia and of anxiety neurosis (1895) Freud considered that he had established the fact that neurasthenia—the 'vegetative dystonia' of the turn of the century—can be traced back to sexual abuse: excessive masturbation and self-pollution. Anxiety neurosis, on the other hand, he assumed to be linked with frustrated and pointless sexual excitation, such as may be caused by *coitus interruptus*, for example. The discontinuance of the particular sexual abuse often had a beneficial effect on the neurasthenic or anxiety condition, causing it to disappear. In respect of those patients who complained of a decrease in libido coupled with anxiety conditions Freud developed the following theory: the sexual drive has a somatic source in the seminal vesicles, in which the sexual substances are produced. When a certain quantity of these substances has been amassed the stimulus is passed via sensory nerve endings to the cerebral cortex, where it is registered as a sexual drive—i.e. the psychic component of the libido. In a person suffering from anxiety conditions the somatophysical production of sexual substances remains unimpaired, from which it follows that the somatic conditioning of the drive is also unimpaired. The only thing that is disturbed is the process whereby somatic libido is converted into psychic libido, a disturbance which is felt by the patient in the form of a deficiency in his sexual drive, but which also promotes anxiety. And so anxiety is produced because somatic sexual excitation—i.e. sexual substances—are put to an abnormal use; and after failing to achieve their proper purpose, namely, the conversion of somatic libido into psychic libido, they are transformed into anxiety.[1] This complicated hypothesis is based on the observation that anxiety neuroses are often combined with an abuse of sexuality (in the sense of frustrated excitation); at the same time, however, it is also based on the further observation that such neuroses are often accompanied by a libido deficiency. If the first of these situations—i.e. frustrated excitation leading to anxiety—had obtained in isolation, then the hypothesis might have been put forward that *pent-up libido, that has not been abreacted, results in anxiety*. (This thesis did in fact play a certain part in Freud's thinking. See *Origins of Psycho-analysis*, pp. 77-8.)

[1] *St. Edn.*, Vol. III, p. 108.

But with the occurrence of the second category of anxiety neuroses Freud was obliged to distinguish between the *somatic* and the *psychic* sections of the libido and to develop his toxological theory of anxiety, according to which anxiety is produced as a result of an abnormal application and transformation of the sexual substances. Freud explains that what prompted him to put forward these theses in the first instance —he was subsequently obliged to withdraw them to a large extent— was the total lack of frightening experiences or traumas in the lives of many patients suffering from anxiety neuroses. These would have supplied an immediate explanation—by analogy with hysteria—of the states of anxiety occurring in such patients. The apparent lack of traumas on the one hand and the frequency of the disturbances of sexual behaviour on the other strengthened him in his assumption of the abnormal transformation of sexual substances in patients suffering from anxiety. Over and above this, however, the traumas and experiences of fright and shock which he had observed failed to satisfy Freud as a specific cause that might adequately explain the development of states of anxiety; his growing interest in sexuality was leading him along another trail, that of 'toxicology'.

(i) The Symptom (Summary)

The following summary indicates the development of Freud's views, as revealed in his scientific works between 1892 and 1896, on (1) the hysterical symptom and subsequently (2) the neurotic symptom.

1892: The symptom is the realization by the counter-will of the antithetic idea within the physical sphere. The antithetic idea exists in the unconscious as an idea that has been isolated from the interchange of associations with the ego. Only if the patient is subjectively insecure will the antithetic idea be thus realized.

1893: ('Prel. Communication') The symptom emerges in place of a trauma which has not been remembered and has consequently become pathogenic. 'Hysterics suffer from reminiscences.'

1894: (*Neuropsychoses of Defence*) The symptom emerges because an unpleasant idea or an unpleasant affect has been repressed. The latter is usually connected with sexuality. The sum of excitation contained in the affect is split off and is (a) discharged into the physical sphere (conversion), (b) linked with another idea (obsessional neurosis/phobia).

1895: (On the Psychotherapy of Hysteria [*Studies*]) and

1896: 'Further Remarks on the Neuropsychoses of Defence.'

1.   The symptom emerges as a compromise between the repressing ego and the repressed idea (affect).

2.   The symptom emerges as a consequence of the recollection of a trauma at the time of sexual maturity (and not as a direct consequence of the trauma at the time of its occurrence).

3.   The symptom is *over-determined*: various causal sequences are seen to be involved in the process of its causation.

4.   The symptom emerges as a projection on to the environment (paranoia).

1899: The symptom is represented, in summarized form, in Freud's work on 'Screen Memories' as follows:[1]

'I have elsewhere had occasion to describe a very similar instance of substitution which occurred in the analysis of a patient suffering from paranoia. The woman in question hallucinated voices, which used to repeat long passages from Otto Ludwig's novel "Die Heiterethei" to her. But the passages they chose were the most trifling and irrelevant in the book. The analysis showed, however, that there were other passages in the same work which had stirred up the most distressing thoughts in the patient. The distressing affect was a motive for putting up a defence against them, but the motives in favour of pursuing them further were not to be suppressed. The result was a compromise by which the innocent passages emerged in the patient's memory with pathological strength and clarity. The process which we here see at work—conflict, repression, substitution involving a compromise—returns in all psychoneurotic symptoms and gives us the key to understanding their formation. Thus it is not without importance if we are able to show the same processes operating in the mental life of normal individuals.'

(*k*) *The Ego* (*Summary*)

The part played by the ego in the theories which Freud was formulating during this period is as follows:

1.   It is the ego which represses those ideas which the patient is intent on supressing (which 'excludes them from the interchange of associations') (1892).

2.   The ego splits the idea off from the affect (of the sum of excitation) and either discharges this affect into the physical sphere or links it with other ideas (1894) or projects it in the form of a reproach affect on to the environment (1896) (Defence).

3.   The ego represses both the idea and the affect, the result of which is psychosis (1894).

[1] *St. Edn.*, Vol. III, p. 308.

4. The ego is enriched by the previously pathogenic memories (1895).[1]

5. The ego exercises a censorship; unpleasant ideas are not admitted into consciousness.

6. The ego guards the entrances to perception and motor activity.

1. The Unconscious (Summary)

The importance attached to the unconscious during this period is as follows:

1892: The unconscious appears as a 'realm of shades', in which the 'inhibited intentions are stored' and where they 'enjoy an unsuspected existence till they emerge like bad spirits and take control of the body, which is as a rule under the orders of the predominant ego consciousness.'[2]

1894: (Neuropsychoses of Defence)[3]

'The separation of the sexual idea from its affect and the attachment of the latter to another, suitable but not incompatible idea—these are processes which occur without consciousness. Their existence can only be presumed, but cannot be proved by any clinico-psychological analysis. Perhaps it would be more correct to say that these processes are not of a psychical nature at all, that they are physical processes whose psychical consequences present themselves as if what is expressed by the terms "separation of the idea from its affect" and "false connection" had really taken place.'

1895: (Studies) The unconscious appears as a 'superior intelligence', etc.[4]

'It remains I think a fact deserving serious consideration that in our analysis we can follow a train of thought from the conscious into the unconscious (i.e. into something that is absolutely not recognized as a memory), that we can trace it from there for some distance through consciousness once more and that we can see it terminate in the unconscious again, without this alteration of "psychical illumination" making any change in the train of thought itself, in its logical consistency and in the interconnection between its various parts. Once this train of thought was before me as a whole I should not be able to guess which part of it was recognized by the patient as a memory and which was not. I only, as it were, see the peaks of the train of thought dipping down into the unconscious—the reverse of what has been asserted of our normal processes.'

[1] St. Edn., Vol. II, p. 299.   [2] S. Freud: Coll. Paps., Vol. V, pp. 44–45.
[3] S. Freud: St. Edn., Vol. III, p. 53.   [4] Ibid., Vol. II, p. 300.

Here the unconscious is not a 'superior intelligence', but that which is 'absolutely not recognized as a memory'. In these same *Studies* the unconscious is also described as a 'disassociated psychic group'.[1]

'The actual traumatic moment then is the one at which the incompatibility forces itself upon the ego and at which the latter decides on the repudiation of the incompatible idea. That idea is not annihilated by a repudiation of this kind, but merely repressed into the unconscious. When this process occurs for the first time there comes into being a nucleus and centre of crystallization for the formation of a psychical group directed from the ego—a group around which everything which would imply an acceptance of the incompatible idea subsequently collects. The splitting of consciousness in these cases of acquired hysteria is accordingly a deliberate and intentional one. At least it is often introduced by an act of volition; for the actual outcome is something different from what the subject intended. What he wanted was to do away with an idea, as though it had never appeared, but all he succeeds in doing is to isolate it psychically.'

In the works published in French in this period the expressions *sub*conscious and *un*conscious (subconscient, inconscient) are used synonymously. The concept of the libido in this period is used synonymously with that of 'sexual affect', 'psychic desire' and also, on the basis of Moll's usage, in the sense of a sexual drive.

VI THE THEORETICAL FOUNDATION AND DEVELOPMENT OF PSYCHOANALYSIS 1892–1900.

(a) *From the Correspondence with Wilhelm Fliess*

Freud's correspondence with the Berlin nose, ear and throat specialist and founder of the so-called 'law of periods', Wilhelm Fliess, which was published in 1950, enables us to study in detail the genesis of psychoanalysis. The correspondence took place during the period in which Freud's earliest scientific works of a psychoanalytic nature were published and it constitutes the link between these and the *Interpretation of Dreams* (1900). From the correspondence we see above all just how closely Freud's explanations of psychopathological phenomena were related to contemporary electrophysiological and energic ideas. By contrast with the restraint exercised in respect of theory and speculation in the published works of these years, in the letters, drafts and notes which he sent to Fliess, Freud freely indulges in psychological and

[1] S. Freud: *St. Edn.*, Vol. II, p. 123.

electrophysical speculations, which he subsequently condensed into the first *Project for a Scientific Psychology*.

Between 1892 and 1894 Freud repeatedly turned his attention to the problem of the conservation of the constancy of psychic energy. What is meant by this process is that the 'psychic apparatus' is at pains to maintain its store of energy, whose composition is subject to increases and decreases of excitation, in a state of balance. The 'neuroses are disturbances of equilibrium due to increased difficulty in discharge'.[1] The organism makes 'attempts at compensation of limited efficiency'.[2] The ultimate cause in the process leading up to a neurosis Freud sees as a *quantitative* factor. In his reply to Loewenfeld's criticism of anxiety neurosis he writes:[3]

'1. Whether a neurotic illness *occurs at all* depends upon a quantitative factor—upon the total load on the nervous system as compared with the latter's capacity for resistance. Everything which can keep this quantitative factor below a certain threshold value, or can bring it back to that level, has a therapeutic effect, since by so doing it keeps the aetiological equation unsatisfied.

'What is to be understood by the "total load" and by the "capacity for resistance" of the nervous system, could no doubt be more clearly explained on the basis of certain hypotheses regarding the function of the nerves.

'2. What *dimensions* the neurosis attains depends in the first instance on the amount of the hereditary taint. Heredity acts like a multiplier introduced into an electric circuit, which increases the deviation of the needle many times over.'

It was this apparently quantitative character of the affects (see above) —on which the principle of constancy is based—which, in 1894, induced Freud to describe three mechanisms of transformation of affects:[4]

'I know three mechanisms (1) conversion of affect (conversion hysteria); (2) displacement of affect (obsessions) and (3) transformation of affect (anxiety neurosis and melancholia). In all these cases what seems to undergo the change is sexual excitation; but what precipitates the change is not always something sexual. That is to say, wherever neuroses are acquired, they are acquired owing to disturbances of sexual life; but there are people in whom the behaviour of their sexual affects is

[1] S. Freud: *Origins of Psychoanalysis* pp. 87–8.   [2] *Ibid.*, p. 88.
[3] S. Freud: *St. Edn.*, Vol. III, pp. 138–9.
[4] S. Freud: *Origins of Psychoanalysis*, p. 84.

disturbed hereditarily, and they develop the corresponding forms of hereditary neurosis.'

If the affects are considered to be quantitative, so too are the *drives*. In his scientific works of this period Freud's analysis of the drives had as yet played no part—save that they were mentioned in connection with sexuality. In 1894 they are quantitatively defined for the first time as a 'tension', the source of which lies in the body. Tensions arise somatically and are not felt (perceived) intra-psychically until they have exceeded a certain threshold value.[1] It is on this conception that the theory of anxiety neurosis described above is based. By analogy with this theory of anxiety affects Freud also developed a theory of melancholia (depression) based on libido loss resulting from psychic inhibition. —The sorrow of melancholics, however, is sorrow over *loss* of libido. Fifteen years are to pass before this theory of melancholia is again taken up by Freud, but then it is substantially expanded.

Apart from (*a*) his interest in the quantitative problems of the constancy of psychic energy, which was to lead Freud to set up pleasure and displeasure as the regulators of the psychic apparatus, (*b*) his definition of the drives as conditions of tension, which are somatic in origin, (*c*) the above-mentioned explanation of melancholia, the correspondence with Fliess also contains the following viewpoints and perceptions which constitute aspects of psychoanalysis:

1.   The thesis, put forward in the second publication on the neuropsychoses of defence (see above), that it was not the actual trauma but the recollection of pre-sexual traumas that formed the symptom, was specified as follows:[2]

(*a*)   The 'pre-sexual' traumas (i.e. those occurring before sexual maturity, before puberty) are attributed to specific age groups.

(*b*)   These age groups are classified as:

(i) up to 4 years of age (pre-conscious)
(ii) from 4 to 8 years of age (infantile)
(iii) from 8 to 14 years of age (pre-pubescent)
(iv) maturity.

(*c*)   Repression is fitted into these age groups in phases, namely, in the 'transitional periods' (subsequent latency periods) between 8 and 10 and 10 and 13 years of age. This conception anticipates the inferences which Freud draws in respect of the sexuality of early childhood in his 'Three Essays on the Theory of Sexuality'. The importance of the

[1] S. Freud: *Origins of Psychoanalysis*, p. 101.   [2] *Ibid.*, p. 84.

erotogonic zones, which is dealt with at length in this work, is likewise anticipated in his discussion of *perversions* in the year 1896.[1] At that time he spoke of the erotogenic zones as the numerous parts of the body in which sexuality may be felt.

2. Then in 1897 the erotogenic zones were divided into oral and anal zones and were linked for the first time with the concept of *repression*.[2]

'In so far as a memory refers to an experience connected with the genitals, what it produces by deferred action will be libido. But in so far as it refers to the anus, mouth, etc., it will produce *internal* disgust. And the final result of this will be that a certain amount of libido will be unable to make its way through, as it normally would, to action or to translation into psychical terms, but will be obliged to proceed in a *regressive* direction (as happens in dreams). Libido and disgust would here seem to be associatively linked. We owe it to the former that the memory cannot lead to general unpleasure, etc., but can be employed psychically; while the latter results in this psychical employment producing nothing but symptoms instead of purposive ideas.'

3. Repression is brought about by 'intellectual processes of development such as morals, shame, etc.'[3]
'The whole of this, then, arises at the cost of extinguished (virtual) sexuality. From this we can see how, with the progressive steps of a child's development, he becomes invested with piety, shame, etc., and how, in the absence of any such extinction of the sexual zones, 'moral insanity' may result as a developmental inhibition'.[4]

4. In the correspondence we witness the inception and the (temporal) course of Freud's self-analysis. Stimulated both by his patients and by the progress of his self-analysis Freud became more and more interested in dreams. In 1895 he discovered that *wish-fulfilment* was the real motivation underlying the dream of Irma's injection (see below). It is true that several contemporary authors had already expressed similar ideas. Freud, however, in his attempt to advance from a pathological psychology to a psychology of the normal personality, immediately linked the wish-fulfilment character of the dream with that of the *symptom*. He saw in the composition of the dream the key to the understanding of hysteria.[5] At the same time he recognized the self-punitive character of the symptom (and subsequently of certain dreams).[6]

[1] S. Freud: *Origins of Psychoanalysis*, pp. 179 ff.   [2] *Ibid.*, pp. 233–4.
[3] *Ibid.*, p. 232.   [4] *Ibid.*, pp. 232–3.
[5] *Ibid.*, pp. 270 ff.   [6] *Ibid.*, pp. 208–9.

'Remembering is never a motive, but only a method—a mode. The first motive force, chronologically, for the formation of symptoms is libido. Thus symptoms are *fulfilments of wishes*, just as dreams are. (At later stages the defence against libido has made a space for itself in the unconscious as well.) Wish-fulfilment has to meet the requirements of this unconscious defence. And this takes place if a symptom is able to operate as a punishment (for an evil impulse) or as a self-hindrance due to self-distrust. The motive forces of *libido* and of *wish-fulfilment* as a punishment can then act together by way of summation. In this the general tendency towards abreaction and to the irruption of the repressed is unmistakable—a tendency to which the two other motive forces are added.'

The importance of Freud's self-analysis for the development of psychoanalysis lies in the following points:

(*a*) Apart from dreams and hysterical symptoms the different levels of unconscious motivation underlying the so-called faulty actions (slip of the tongue, mislaying of objects, forgetfulness) are also elucidated. In 1898, in his publication on the *Psychic Mechanisms of Forgetfulness*, Freud describes for the first time the complex resolution of an incident, in which he himself had (unconsciously) 'intentionally' forgotten something. He summarizes his observations in his book *On the Psychopathology of Everyday Life*.

(*b*) Freud discovered the so-called Oedipus Complex as a result of his self-analysis. The scenes of seduction from early childhood, about which his hysterical patients were constantly informing him, obliged Freud to consider very seriously, whether these seductions were in fact real-life experiences or the product of wish-fulfilment phantasies. This decision he found so difficult that for a time he doubted the validity of his whole undertaking. Not until he had analysed and interpreted his own dreams with reference to particular memories did he arrive at the hypothesis that sexual desires, which the little boy feels for his mother, the little girl for her father, can give rise to phantasies such as the seduction scenes to which his patients laid claim. (The discovery of the *positive* Oedipus complex in the man preceded that of the *negative* Oedipus complex in the woman.) In this connection Freud writes:[1]

'Only one idea of general value has occurred to me. I have found love of the mother and jealousy of the father in my own case too, and now believe it to be a general phenomenon of early childhood, even if it does

---

[1] S. Freud: *Origins of Psychoanalysis*, pp. 223-4.

not always occur so early as in children who have been made hysterics. (Similarly with the "romanticization of origins" in the case of paranoics —heroes, founders of religion.) If that is the case, the gripping power of Oedipus Rex, in spite of all the rational objections to the inexorable fate that the story presupposes, becomes intelligible, and one can understand why later dramas were such failures. Our feelings rise against any arbitrary, individual fate such as shown in the Ahnfrau, etc., but the Greek myth seizes on a compulsion which everyone recognizes because he has felt traces of it in himself. Every member of the audience was once a budding Oedipus in phantasy, and this dream-fulfilment played out in reality causes everyone to recoil in horror, with the full measure of repression which separates his infantile from his present state.'

And in an earlier letter he mentions for the first time the importance of aggression.[1]

'Hostile impulses against parents (a wish that they should die) are also an integral part of the neuroses. They come to light consciously in the form of obsessional ideas. In paranoia the worst delusions of persecution (pathological distrust of rulers and monarchs) correspond to these impulses. They are repressed in periods in which pity for one's parents is active—at times of their illness or death. One of the manifestations of grief is then to reproach oneself for their death (cf. what are described as "melancholias") or to punish oneself in an hysterical way by putting oneself into their position with an idea of retribution. The identification which takes place here is, as we can see, merely a mode of thinking and does not relieve us of the necessity for looking for the motive. It seems as though in sons this death wish is directed against their father and in daughters against their mother.'

Freud tells us that when he was two years old he spent the night with his mother in a sleeping car compartment on board a train and saw her without any clothes on. He assumed that this experience had a lasting effect on him in terms of the Oedipus complex.

(c) Freud also recognized within the context of his self-analysis the importance of phantasy—the part it plays in poetry and art. He writes of phantasies:[2]

'Phantasies arise from an unconscious combination of things experienced and heard, constructed for particular purposes. These purposes aim at making inaccessible the memory from which symptoms have been

[1] S. Freud: *Origins of Psychoanalysis*, p. 207.　　　　[2] *Ibid.*, p. 204.

generated or might be generated. Phantasies are constructed by a process of fusion and distortion analogous to the decomposition of a chemical body which is combined with another one. For the first kind of distortion consists in a falsification of memory by a process of fragmentation, which involves a disregard of chronological considerations (Chronological corrections seem to depend precisely on the activity of the system of consciousness). A fragment of a visual scene is then joined up to a fragment of an auditory one and made into a phantasy, while the fragment left over is linked up with something else. This makes it impossible to trace their original connection. As a result of the construction of phantasies of this kind (in periods of excitation) the mnemic symptoms cease. But instead there are now unconscious fictions which have not succumbed to defence. If the intensity of such a phantasy increases to a point at which it would have to force its way into consciousness, it is repressed and a symptom is generated by a backward drive from the phantasy to its constituent memories.'

At another point he writes of the relationship of phantasies to poetry[1]:

'The mechanism of creative writing is the same as that of hysterical phantasies. Goethe combined in Werther something that he had experienced (his love for Lotte Kästner) and something he had heard of (the fate of young Jerusalem, who killed himself). He probably toyed with the idea of killing himself and found a point of contact in this for identifying himself with Jerusalem, whom he provided with a motive from his own love story. By means of this phantasy he protected himself against the consequences of his experience.'

The above-mentioned topical organization (see p. 62 ff.) of the unconscious into periphery and nucleus, which derived from the temporal course of the analysis in as far as the peripheral sections of the unconscious became conscious at an earlier and the deeper sections at a later juncture, is extended during the correspondence to embrace the distinction between the *pre-conscious* and the *unconscious*. This more precise distinction, however, is linked with theoretical investigations (cf. *Project*) which are outlined below. The assumption of a pre-conscious within the unconscious is accompanied by the submersion in the unconscious of certain sections of the repressing ego.[2]

'It appears as though at later stages on the one hand complicated structures (impulses, phantasies, motives) are produced by transference from memories, while on the other hand defence, arising from the pre-

[1] S. Freud: *Origins of Psychoanalysis*, p. 208.   [2] *Ibid.*, p. 209.

conscious (the ego), seems to force its way into the unconscious—so that defence as well becomes multilocular.'

6. For the first time identification is considered as a mode of ego-repression.[1]

'The formation of symptoms by means of identification is linked to phantasies, that is to say, to their repression in the Ucs., and is analogous to the modification of the ego in paranoia.

7. Reality—the reality principle of later years—is recognized more and more as a factor opposing the wish and of importance in the formation of symptoms.[2]

'It is not only dreams that are fulfilments of wishes, but hysterical attacks as well. This is true of hysterical symptoms, but it probably applies to every product of neurosis—for I recognized it long ago in acute delusional insanity. Reality—wish fulfilment, it is from this contrasting pair that our mental life springs. I believe I now know the determining condition which distinguishes dreams from symptoms that force their way into waking life. It is enough for a dream to be the the wish-fulfilment of the repressed thought; for a dream is kept apart from reality. But a symptom, which has its place in actual life, must be something else as well—the wish-fulfilment of the repressing thought. A symptom arises where the repressed and the repressing thoughts can come together in the fulfilment of a wish.'

8. The importance of the anal sphere as opposed to the genital sphere is observed:[3]

'I read one day that the gold which the devil gave his victims regularly turned into excrement; and next day Herr E., who reports that his nurse had money deliria, suddenly told me (by way of Cagliostro—alchemist—Dukatenscheisser).[4] that Louise's money was also excrement. Thus in the witch stories it is only transferred back into the substance of which it originally consisted.'

9. The perversions, which Freud was prompted to study not least by the kindly encouragement of *Krafft-Ebing*, Professor of Psychiatry in

---

[1] S. Freud: *Origins of Psychoanalysis*, p. 209.   [2] *Ibid.*, p. 227.
[3] *Ibid.*, pp. 188–9.
[4] *Dukatenscheisser*, lit. one who excretes ducats. Fig. one who throws his money around.

Vienna, were declared to be a 'negative of hysteria'. Freud was to hold this view for the rest of his life.

10. Femininity and masculinity are contrasted and their importance for the psychology of neuroses anticipated.[1]

'It is to be suspected that the essential repressed element is always femininity. This is confirmed by the fact that women no less than men admit more easily to experiences with women than with men. What men essentially repress is their paederastic element.'

The theses and theories anticipated in this correspondence received their final clarification when they were published, first in 1900 in the *Interpretation of Dreams*, and a few years later (in 1904) in *Three Essays on the Theory of Sexuality*. The theoretical ideas, which formed the basis of his thought in the decennium 1890–1900, Freud summarized in his *Project for a Scientific Psychology*, which has already been mentioned above.

(b) The 'Project for a Scientific Psychology'

The purpose of this project, as envisaged by Freud, was to establish a psychology according to the principles of the natural sciences:[2] i.e. 'psychical processes as quantitatively determined states of specifiable material particles'. This project attempts to represent psychic processes as quantitative processes within the nervous system. This consists of neurones, i.e. nerve cells and their dendrites (the motor or sensory nerve endings). The psychic processes are described by analogy with electro-physiological processes of a quantitative nature. Although Freud may be said to have withdrawn from this (extremely mechanistic) conception, for it would appear that he sent the Project to W. Fliess without asking for it to be returned, the Project none the less presents ideas which were to accompany him throughout his life. Freud merely withdrew at a later date from the direct equation within the nervous system of electro-physiological processes and processes susceptible to quantitative measurement with psychic processes. But he always remained faithful to the mechanistic character of his conceptions.

He differentiates between a primary system of neurones, a secondary and a tertiary. The primary system is phylogenetically the oldest and corresponds to the (hypothetical!) cell, whose only reaction (reflex) is concerned with the intake of external stimuli and their discharge outwards. This cell is subject to the principle of constancy or inertia: i.e. it endeavours to keep itself entirely free from stimuli. (The primary function of the cell is the discharge of stimuli, cf. cathartic method!)

[1] S. Freud: *Origins of Psychoanalysis*, pp. 203–4.   [2] *Ibid.*, p. 355.

If an excess of stimuli presses in on the cell from the outside world, the cell will withdraw from them by 'taking flight from the stimuli': *secondary function*. The 'necessities of life' impose on the cell the need for further development and differentiation. It cannot withdraw from the internal needs (hunger, thirst, sexuality) by taking flight. And from this it follows that the original system can no longer pursue the principle of lethargy, but is obliged to accumulate 'quantity'—instead of keeping it to a bare minimum—in order to satisfy the necessities of life.[1]

'All the performances of the neuronic system are to be comprised under the heading either of the primary function or of the secondary function imposed by the exigencies of life.'

The neurones are capable of being cathected with energy or of discharging energy. In doing so they are obliged to overcome resistances in the paths of conduction: the so-called contact barriers. The assumption of contact barriers makes it possible to differentiate between consciousness (perception) and memory. For a second system of neurones also exists, one which is permeable in all directions and which contains no contact barriers. In this it differs from the first system, in which the contact barriers transform conscious perceptions into memories by the introduction of resistances (dams). The memory comes into being as a result of the facilitations between those neurones which are equipped with contact barriers. These facilitations serve the primary function (discharge of stimuli) in as far as they make it possible for displacement and discharge to take place between the different neurones.

And so we have these two systems of neurones, the primary, which is permeable to stimuli (perception), and the secondary, which is impermeable to stimuli (memory). The primary system corresponds to the primary brain. Consequently the primary function (the discharge of stimuli) coincides with the permeability of the system to stimuli. This primary system with its primary function has no direct connection with the outside world but only via the secondary system of neurones. *It corresponds to the later 'id'*.

The structure of the neuronic system, considered as an entity, serves to restrict quantity (irruptions of stimuli, e.g. in pain), whilst its function serves to discharge stimuli. In other words, pleasure and displeasure are the basic principles underlying the structure and function of the nervous system. Displeasure produces an increase in quantity, pleasure a discharge of quantity. In the final analysis pleasure and displeasure serve the principle of inertia or constancy. The theory of the importance of the death wish, which was to be developed twenty-five years later, is

[1] S. Freud: *Origins of Psychoanalysis*, p. 358.

here anticipated, the death wish corresponding to the principle of inertia.

In order that qualitative perception might take place within these otherwise purely quantitative processes Freud postulated a third system of neurones.[1]

'a third system of neurones—"perceptual neurones" they might be called—which are excited along with the others during perception but not during reproduction, and whose states of excitation give rise to the different qualities—are, that is to say, conscious sensations.'

Psychologically this system corresponds to the ego. Not only is it capable of qualitative feeling, but of conscious qualitative feeling.[2]

'. . . a word upon the relation of this theory of consciousness to others. According to a modern mechanistic theory, consciousness is no more than an appendage added to physiologico-psychical processes, an appendage whose absence would make no difference to the course of psychical events. According to another theory consciousness is the subjective side of all psychical events and is thus inseparable from physiologico-mental processes. The theory which I have here propounded lies between these two. According to it consciousness is the subjective side of a part of the physical processes in the neuronic system —namely, of the perceptual processes (w-processes); and its absence would not leave psychical events unchanged but would imply the absence of any contribution from the W (w)-system.'

The primary neuronic system is entirely at the mercy of the endogenous—somatic—driving force (cf. below the later definition of the id). This driving force (sums of excitation) can gradually increase (summation), thus producing a wish, or be released, thus producing an affect. A small child, at the mercy of its somatic needs, will express those needs in the form of motor statements (kicking) and other types of statement (crying). It has as yet no facility for channelling its urge (facilitations!) and is dependent on outside help if its discharge of affect is to reach a satisfactory conclusion (breast).[3]

'This path of discharge thus acquires an extremely important secondary function—viz. of bringing about an understanding with other people; and the original helplessness of human beings is thus the primal source of all moral motives.'

[1] S. Freud: *Origins of Psychoanalysis*, p. 370.   [2] *Ibid.*, pp. 372–3.
[3] *Ibid.*, p. 379.

At a later stage it learns to procure the 'experience of satisfaction' for itself, namely by the association of wish and wish-fulfilment in its memory as simultaneous happenings. For example, it will form an association between being thirsty and being given its bottle. Consequently an image is formed in the second neuronic system on the basis of this association, i.e. the image: bottle/thirst. The next time the child feels thirsty this memory image is resuscitated, namely, by the facilitation or cathexis of the secondary neurone by the primary neurones. What Freud understands under cathexis in this respect is that quantities of energy transfer from the primary to the secondary neurone.

The recollection of sexual traumas and the symptoms which these may conceivably produce is a process of a similar order. The cathexis and counter-cathexis between the unconscious and the ego (which he formulated at a later date) Freud also conceived as conforming to these electro-physiological processes. With the formulation of subsequent hypotheses the ego, which was postulated on the basis of this triple neuronic system, came to be equipped with *constant* amounts of energy, whereby it acquired a correspondingly permanent and autonomous character (cf. later the ego-function in *The Ego and the Id*, 1923).

Reality is introduced as follows: the ego becomes nervous when, in a 'wishful' state, it re-cathects the memory of an object and, instead of finding satisfaction in reality, finds it only in phantasy (in the recathected memory of the object). If phantasy is to be distinguished from reality —a task which presents difficulties to the small child—a special 'indication of reality' is required, which is supplied by the triple neuronic system (the reality test is an ego function in *The Ego and the Id*, 1923). This indication of reality is of a *qualitative* nature and is accompanied by a specific excitation, which makes it possible for reality to be recognised as reality. Re-stated in quantitative terms this means:[1]

'. . . indications of quality derived from outside make their appearance whatever the intensity of the cathexis, those derived from ψ only do so if the intensities are large. Accordingly, it is the inhibition brought about by the ego that makes possible a criterion for distinguishing between a perception and a memory.'

Freud also endeavours to trace the thought processes—i.e. judging, cognitive and reproductive thought—back to similar quantitative changes, but these were hypotheses to which he reverted only occasionally. To reproduce these complicated trains of thought here would be to exceed the limits set for this book. It should, however, be mentioned that within the various schools of depth psychology nobody has under-

[1] S. Freud: *Origins of Psychoanalysis*, p. 388.

taken research into this problem that could even remotely compare with Freud's profound, if mechanistically determined, enquiries. He summarizes his views on the different forms of thinking as follows:[1]

'Thus the aim and end of all processes of thought are the establishment of a state of identity, the transportation of a cathectic quantity ($o\acute{\eta}$) emanating from outside into a neurone cathected by the ego. Cognitive or judging thought seeks for an identity with a somatic cathexis; reproductive thought seeks for an identity with a psychical cathexis (an experience of the subject's own). Judging thought operates in advance of reproductive thought, since the former furnishes the latter with ready-made facilitations to assist further associative travelling. If at the conclusion of the act of thought the indication of reality also reaches perception, then a judgement of reality, a belief, is achieved and the aim of the whole activity is attained.'

The primary processes (= primary brain, see above) are suppressed in the course of development (cf. *The Ego and the Id*, 1923). In sleep, however, when the secondary system ceases its activity, they again adopt a dominant role. It was this above all else that moved Freud to equate the symptoms of the psychoneuroses with dreams. In sleep the ego withdraws its 'cathexes',[2] whilst at the same time the 'endogenous charge' in the primary system is lowered. In consequence primary processes, which appear in the symptoms of the various forms of psychoneurosis, can also appear in dreams.

The hypotheses put forward in the *Project* represent the ideational background, against which Freud's views on psychopathology were built up. The concepts of the displacement of energy and of the cathexis of different systems—especially of the memory images, which were subsequently to be of primary importance for psychoanalytic theory—derive exclusively from the realm of electro-physiological ideas described above. But it would be unjust if we were to assume that Freud first put forward these hypotheses and then used them to explain the psychopathological phenomena. From the very beginning observation and hypothesis went hand in hand. The more precise the clinical observations became, the more detailed and complicated were the energic theses. The two processes are inseparable. Not until the *Interpretation of Dreams* did Freud venture on a statement of psychic activity in *exclusively* energic terms.

(c) The Interpretation of Dreams

Dream analysis, dream interpretation, is, in Freud's own words, 'the royal road to the unconscious'. It has remained so to this day for the

[1] S. Freud: *Origins of Psychoanalysis*, pp. 394-5.　　[2] *Ibid.*, p. 398.

majority of psychoanalytic schools. *The Interpretation of Dreams* was the most extensive psychoanalytic work which Freud produced. Those who know how short is the life-span of scientific works will also know just what it means for a book such as *The Interpretation of Dreams* to have retained its authority over a period of sixty years. It stood head and shoulders above the scientific dream literature of its day, although Freud was undoubtedly stimulated by the research that had already been carried out on the dream in respect of its wish-fulfilment character (*Scherner, Robert*), its symbolism (*Schubert*), its relationship to internal (endogenous) and external stimuli, its archaic-infantile character (*Havelock-Ellis*), its relationship to the memory (*Delbouef, Binz*), etc. Many peculiar features of the dream had been described and explained both by earlier and by contemporary authors. But in respect of these authors Freud's achievement is none the less firmly established in that (1) he recognized the importance of the dream in quite general terms for both normal and pathological conditions of psychic life, (2) he was able to integrate the dream as a *meaningful* component of psychic life, (3) he established a direct connection between dreams and psycho-neurotic symptoms.[1]

(i) *The Dream of Irma's Injection*

'A large hall—numerous guests, whom we were receiving—Amongst them was Irma. I at once take her on one side, as though to answer her letter and to reproach her for not having accepted my 'solution' yet. I said to her: "If you still get pains it's really your own fault." She replied: "If you only knew what pains I've got now in my throat and stomach and abdomen—it's choking me."—I was alarmed and looked at her. She looked pale and puffy. I thought to myself that after all I must be missing some organic trouble. I took her to the window and looked down her throat, and she showed signs of recalcitrance, like women with artificial dentures. I thought to myself that there was really no need for her to do that.—She then opened her mouth properly and on the right I found a big white patch; at another place I saw extensive whitish grey scabs upon some remarkable early structures which were evidently modelled on the turbinal bones of the nose.—I at once called in Dr. M, and he repeated the examination and confirmed it . . . Dr. M. looked quite different from usual; he was very pale, he walked with a limp and his chin was clean-shaven. My friend Otto was now standing beside her as well, and my friend Leopold was percussing her through her bodice saying: "She has a dull area low down on the left." He also indicated that a portion of the skin on the left shoulder was infiltrated. (I noticed this, just as he did, in spite of her dress.) . . . M. said:

[1] S. Freud: *St. Edn.*, Vol. IV, p. 107.

"There's no doubt, it's an infection, but no matter; dysentry will supervene and the toxin will be eliminated"...We were directly aware, too, of the origin of the infection. Not long before, when she was feeling unwell, my friend Otto had given her an injection of a preparation of propyl, propyls...propionic acid...trimethylamine (and I saw before me the formula for this printed in heavy type)... Injections of that sort ought not to be made so thoughtlessly [Tr: "casually"]...And probably the syringe had not been clean.'

The dream of Irma's injection was one of the first dreams to impress on Freud not only the wish-fulfilment character but other peculiarities of dreams as well. The detailed reproduction of the analysis of this dream also reveals the *method*, whereby Freud elucidates dream activity. He reports his associations in respect of each individual part of the dream, thus relating the dream to current or past events. He subsequently implemented this same method of free association with his patients, having until then, i.e. until the end of the 'nineties, simply given them his own interpretations and left them to decide whether to accept or reject them. Meanwhile, however, he had himself experienced how important, indeed decisive, for the success of the treatment it was that the patient should himself gain access through his own associations to the corresponding sections of his dream.

The situation obtaining immediately prior to Freud's dream was that Irma's condition—Irma had been treated by Freud for various hysterical symptoms—was not entirely satisfactory, although the cure had been completed. Freud had been given this news by a colleague, with whom he was personally acquainted, the Otto who appears in the dream. This colleague, in whose report of Irma's condition he had sensed a veiled reproach, had angered Freud. In the dream he blames him for Irma's bad condition, whereby the character of wish-fulfilment is clearly demonstrated.

Wishes in dreams can derive from various sources: (1) from endogenous stimuli (hunger, thirst); (2) from the events of the day, during which the wishes were suppressed; (3) from strata which 'emerge from their suppressed state and come to life in us' only at night; and finally (4) from situations of early childhood.

(ii) *Manifest and Latent Dream Content*
The idea that Otto is to blame for Irma's condition is not expressed directly in the dream but only 'covertly'. Freud's presumably semi-conscious or unconscious idea that his colleague was to blame for Irma's condition undergoes complicated processes, making a detour via the injection, before achieving expression. This prompted Freud to differentiate between the *manifest* and *latent* dream contents. The

manifest content is related to the course of events in the dream, the latent content to the actual dream ideas underlying those events or to wish motivation.

How does the manifest dream come about? Why is the latent idea not expressed directly?

(iii) *Dream Censorship and Distortion—The Dream as the Guardian of Sleep*

Freud concedes that there are dreams which, for example, give direct expression to erotic or aggressive wish impulses. The overwhelming majority of such wish impulses, however, are expressed indirectly by means of *distortion*. The *distortion* is the consequence of a dream censorship which stands guard in sleep to ensure that inadmissible, painful and offensive ideas will not come directly to the surface of dream consciousness. In the analysis of a dream the distortion makes its presence felt in the form of a *resistance*. Wishes might be coupled with powerful excitations, which would result in the sleeper waking up, whereby the dream would lose its function as the guardian of sleep. The 'subjective insecurity' of nervous persons was one of the contributory factors which prompted Freud to develop the concept of the 'counter-will' in his publication of 1892. The sleeper finds himself in a similar state of 'subjective insecurity', for the centres of control to which ego activity is connected during waking hours are to all intents and purposes eliminated. (Compare the primary process of the 'Project'.) Wishes and affects might be stimulated in sleep for the simple reason that they are not suppressed to the same extent as in waking life. If this were to happen the sleeper would wake up in order to satisfy his wishes in real life. It is at this point that the dream takes over, providing 'hallucinatory' satisfaction of the wish by linking it with memory images and thus ensuring the continuance of sleep. And so dream censorship serves sleep (or the wish for sleep) to the extent that it contributes to the satisfaction of the wish by distorting the latent dream ideas. Freud mentions the concept of censorship for the first time within the framework of the repression of painful ideas and affects in hysteria (see p. 60 ff.). In the correspondence with Fliess he expanded this concept by analogy with 'the censorship of the press carried out in Russia': whole sentences are struck through, with the result that—just as in the interpretation of dreams—the reader can only *reconstruct* the context.

(iv) *Displacement and Condensation. Identification. Ambivalence*

In his analysis of Irma's dream Freud makes an association—in connection with the examination of her throat—between Irma and her friend, who is also a young widow. This friend, whose mouth readily opens in the dream, would have told more. As a more intelligent and more tractable patient she would perhaps have been preferable to Irma (wish). And so *displacement* took place in the dream from one person to another, the essential point here being that the 'amount of affect' (love or hate) felt for a person in reality is often transferred in dreams either to strangers or to persons who mean nothing to the dreamer. This view is based on the separation of affect and idea. In the dream of Irma's injection it is probable that Freud's interest in Irma was transferred to Irma's friend, which means that it was subject to censorship and consequently to distortion—because Freud was not prepared to admit to himself that he entertained such feelings for a patient. (That he will have recognized them in his analysis of the dream is hardly to be doubted.)

The analysis of the dream of Irma's injection covers several pages in the *Interpretation of Dreams*, i.e. the presentation of the latent dream ideas with their manifold references is out of all proportion to the brevity of the dream. This process, whereby a short dream is formed from a plenitude of possible wishes and ideas, Freud defines as *condensation*. Distortion and condensation he considers to be the chief factors in the 'dream work', and he cites numerous examples in support of his view. In point of fact, the dreamer's identification with other persons also serves to shorten the dream, for example when other persons in the dream do things which the dreamer does not permit himself to do but would in fact like to do. Freud rejects Otto's behaviour in the dream; he even blames him for Irma's 'bad condition'—but the clearly sexual nature of the injection of trimethylamine (according to Freud's associations a sexual substance) would indicate that Freud had perhaps identified with Otto. He would also like to do what Otto had so 'casually' done, namely, have intercourse with Irma, even if as a result she did get into a 'bad condition' (according to Freud's associations the pregnancy of a married woman). Thus the dream realizes the ambivalence, the discord, implicit in the dreamer's actions by permitting other persons —often of lower moral standing—to rush in where the dreamer, even in a dream (censorship), fears to tread. Moral judgement is passed on the activity—intercourse with the patient—by allowing this activity to be implemented by a 'casual' figure (Otto), and in these circumstances it is passed by the censor. In other words the censor acts as a second intelligence, whilst the displacement and condensation which take place in the dream point to the unconscious as a 'superior intelligence'.

(v) *The Symbol*

It is not the object of this enquiry to provide a complete commentary to Freud's *Interpretation of Dreams*, a work of some 700 pages. Instead dreams will be considered from the more limited point of view of their importance within the development of psychoanalytic theory and of the analogy between dreams and the explanation of psychoneurotic symptoms. In respect of these symptoms Freud noticed (see above p. 52 ff.) that they were not so much directly as symbolically connected to the patient's traumatic experiences. As a result of his research into dreams he put forward whole series of symbols, which he related for the most part either to the male or female genitals or to the act of sexual union. In respect of these symbols he held the same view, namely a simple mechanistic-materialist view, as he held in respect of all processes which were not susceptible to direct explanation. He agrees with Sperber,[1] who considers[2]

'that all primal words referred to sexual things but afterwards lost their sexual meaning through being applied to other things and activities which were compared with the sexual ones'.

Freud himself writes:[3]

'Things that are symbolically connected to-day were probably united in prehistoric times by conceptual and linguistic identity.'

The break between C. G. Jung and Freud came about as a result of their discussion of symbols. And indeed it is scarcely possible to defend Freudian symbolism against the accusation of an extreme formalism, for it is capable of logical reduction to a point where all open or closed hollow objects, from a shoe to a room, symbolize the female genital and all upright or pointed objects the male genital. Almost all activities, from flying or running to gliding or leaping, are attributed to sexual functions.

(vi) *Anxiety Dreams and Over-Determination. Conversion into the opposite*

The attempt to interpret the numerous dreams in which anxiety or other feelings of displeasure appeared as wish-fulfilment dreams met with difficulties. The realization that symptoms have a certain punitive value (see above p. 59 ff.) provided the link whereby dreams of anxiety and displeasure might be considered as punitive dreams. This link implies the presence of an instance within the psyche, through which the dreamer punishes himself. In Irma's dream the dreamer makes use of Irma's worsening condition in order to punish himself for the failure

---

[1] See H. Sperber: 'Über den Einfluss sexueller Momente auf Entstehung und Entwicklung der Sprache', *Imago*, Vol. I, 1912.
[2] S. Freud: *St. Edn.*, Vol. V, p. 352.   [3] *Ibid.*, p. 352.

of his therapeutic measures. The multiple stratification of the dream—judged merely from the single incident of Irma's 'bad condition'—is at once revealed (The 'bad condition' implied (1) wish-fulfilment: the wish that Irma should get worse because she did not accept the dreamer's interpretations; (2) wish-fulfilment: she gets worse through Otto's fault; (3) wish-fulfilment: the dreamer's wish to get the patient into a 'bad condition' himself instead of Otto, i.e. to make her pregnant; (4) Self-chastisement: the patient is worse because the dreamer did not cure her.)

Every dream and every part of every dream is always multiply determined. It consists of numerous strata.

The nature of dreams involving anxiety and displeasure is not exhausted, however, by such tendencies towards self-chastisement; and in fact such dreams are interpreted by analogy with actual situations in which anxiety is released. In other words, the dream repeats a situation in which anxiety originally arose. Whether in view of this the character of wish-fulfilment can still be upheld becomes questionable. The repetitive nature of anxiety dreams following traumas was one of the contributory factors leading to the development of the death wish theory. Over and above this, however, anxiety dreams often have a latent sexual content, a typical example of this being the case of the woman who dreams that she is being pursued by a man. The woman's desire to be pursued by the man is not allowed by the censor, the situation is *converted into its opposite*, desire for the man is replaced by fear of the man in conformity with social taboos and with censorship. For the censor will allow sexual desires for the man to be expressed only under 'negative auspices', under cover of anxiety.

The study of anxiety dreams in the *Interpretation of Dreams* led to the discovery of the 'fear of castration', which was to prove of critical importance for Freud's new conception of his anxiety theory, which he formulated in his later works (see below p. 160).

(vii) *Revaluation of All Values. The 'Infantile'. Aggression*

The thesis of the 'conversion of a given situation into its opposite' is not far removed from the further thesis that dreams undertake a revaluation of all values (cf. Nietzsche). According to this thesis—which is anticipated in the distinction made between the latent and the manifest contents of dreams—the dream thought can express the opposite of the manifest dream and vice versa. From this it follows that no limits are set to dream interpretation, which may be applied on a purely dialectical basis. Such a state of affairs, in which all situations may be converted into their opposite and all values revalued, corresponds to the wishful thinking, by means of which children, for example, change the living into the dead and the dead into the living. From this it follows that the dream character is infantile and belongs to an earlier stage of man's development. Aggression is closely allied to infantile wishful thinking and often finds expression in dreams in the form of disguised death wishes against parents and brothers and sisters (Oedipus complex).

(viii) *Dream Work and the Unconscious*

Distortion, displacement, condensation, symbolization, wish-fulfilment and aggression, the revaluation of all values, the separation of the latent and the manifest dream contents—all these processes are part of the 'dreamwork'. The dream work transforms latent dream thoughts into manifest dream thoughts by means of endogenous and exogenous stimuli during sleep and of reminiscences of the day's events (remnants of the day) or of events going back over the years. The dream work takes place at an unconscious level. Indeed, in the interpretation of dreams the unconscious comes into its own as that self-same 'superior intelligence' which Freud had introduced in his *Studies*.[1] with sceptical reserve in the form of a question.

'All the attributes which we value highly in our train of thought, and which characterize them as complex achievements of a high order, are to be found once more in dream-thoughts. There is no need to assume, however, that this activity of thought is performed during sleep—a possibility which would gravely confuse what has hitherto been our settled picture of the psychical state of sleep. On the contrary, these thoughts may very well have originated from the previous day, they may have proceeded unobserved by our consciousness from their start, and may already have been completed at the onset of sleep. The most that we can conclude from this is that it proves that the most complicated achievements of thought are possible without the assistance of consciousness—a fact which we could not fail to learn in any case from every psychoanalysis of a patient suffering from hysteria or from obsessional ideas. These dream thoughts are certainly not in themselves inadmissible to consciousness; there may have been a number of reasons for their not having become conscious to us during the day. Becoming conscious is connected with the application of a particular psychical function, that of attention—a function, which, as it seems, is only available in a specific quantity, and this may have been diverted from the train of thought in question on to some other purpose.'

Dream Censorship (see above p. 86 ff.) is also an essential part of the dream work. It corresponds to the defending, repressing ego of the psychoneurotic symptoms, which now emerge as a compromise between

---

[1] S. Freud: *St. Edn.*, Vol. V, pp. 592–3.

the repressed idea and the repressing ego. By analogy with this the dream is also seen as a compromise between the censorship and the wish, with the one difference that in respect of the dream the work of the *censorship* also takes place at an unconscious level.[1] 'We have seen that we were only able to explain the formation of dreams by venturing upon the hypothesis of their being two psychical agencies, one of which submitted the activity of the other to a criticism which involved its exclusion from consciousness.'

(ix) *Inferences drawn from Dream Interpretation for the Psychic Apparatus*

By direct analogy with the *Project for a Scientific Psychology* Freud also made a project for the psychic apparatus which was based on the reflex processes but was not directly connected with the anatomy.[2]

'This, however, does no more than fulfil a requirement with which we have long been familiar, namely that the psychical apparatus must be constructed like a reflex apparatus. Reflex processes remain the model of every psychical function.'

The primary apparatus (see *Project*, p. 30 ff.) is permeable to endogenous stimuli and subject to the law of inertia (constancy), whilst the secondary apparatus forms the basis for the memory. The 'critical (criticizing) instance' (the censorship, the ego, the third neuronic system of the *Project*) is located between the two systems 'like a screen', but nearer to the activating motor part of the primary system than to the perceptive part. The *pre-conscious* is situated between the unconscious and the above-mentioned conscious 'criticizing instance'. It is distinguished by the fact that it has direct access to the conscious mind, an access denied to the unconscious. As has already been stated (see above p. 71 ff.), Freud's decision to postulate a pre-conscious was not made solely for speculative reasons—such as the desire to establish a functionally flawless system. His work on the dream, which he declared to be a compromise between the censorship (ego) and the wish (unconscious), indicated to him that the unconscious does not have direct access to the conscious mind but is 'censored' in the pre-conscious.[3]

The excitation in the psychic apparatus moves in the direction of the two large arrows on the left and the right of the diagram from the perceptive end to the motor end. This is the normal progressive direction. In the dream, however, a movement must also be assumed in the opposite direction, if the excitation is to produce an hallucinatory stimulation of

[1] S. Freud: *St. Edn.*, Vol. V, p. 540. [2] *Ibid.*, p. 538.
[3] Diagram taken from S. Freud, *St. Edn.*, Vol. V, p. 541.

the memory images. Freud calls this the *regressive* direction and from it he develops the concept of *regression,* which was first mentioned in the correspondence with Fliess (see p. 73 ff.). But regression is not only an attribute of dreams. Memory images are regressively cathected with

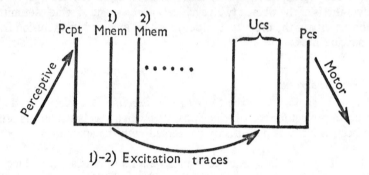

1)-2) Excitation traces

amounts of excitation both in the memory of a normal person and in the formation of psychoneurotic symptoms. In terms of the dream work repression means that a thought is transformed into an image by virtue of the fact that excitation recedes from the thinking process and attaches itself to the archaic process of the images within the excitation traces.[1]

'(*a*) *topographical* regression, in the sense of the schematic picture of the ψ-systems which we have explained above; (*b*) *temporal* regression, in so far as what is in question is a harking back to older psychical structures; and (*c*) *formal* regression, where primitive methods of expression and representation take the place of the usual ones. All these three kinds of regression are, however, one at bottom and occur together as a rule; for what is older in time is more primitive in form and in psychical topography lies nearer to the perceptual end.'

(ψ-system $=$ Pcs and Ucs)

But regression is also important for wish-fulfilment, since the majority of wishes represented in dreams originate in the pre-conscious, whereas their intensity is cathected by amounts of excitation deriving from 'wish structures' of early childhood. (Freud drew this conclusion when he found that a wish arising in a dream, e.g. a wish of an everyday nature, could be traced back to a childhood wish.) In this connection Freud attributes to the activity of 'wishing' a prominent position within the unconscious (primary activity of the unconscious).[2]

[1] S. Freud, *St. Edn.,* Vol. V, p. 548.
[2] *Ibid.,* pp. 566–7.

'In order to arrive at a more efficient expenditure of psychical force, it is necessary to bring the regression to a halt before it becomes complete, so that it does not proceed beyond the mnemic image, and is able to seek out other paths which lead eventually to the desired perceptual identity being established from the direction of the external world. This inhibition of the regression and the subsequent diversion of the excitation become the business of a second system, which is in control of voluntary movement—which for the first time, that is, makes use of movement for purposes remembered in advance. But all the complicated thought-activity which is spun out from the mnemic image to the moment at which the perceptual identity is established by the external world—all this activity of thought merely constitutes a *roundabout path to wish-fulfilment* which has been made necessary by experience. Thought is after all nothing but a substitute for a hallucinatory wish; and it is self-evident that dreams must be wish-fulfilments, since nothing but a wish can set our mental apparatus at work. Dreams, which fulfil their wishes along the short path of regression, have merely preserved for us in that respect a sample of the primary apparatus's *primary* method of working, a method which was abandoned as being inefficient. What once dominated waking life, while the mind was still young and incompetent, seems now to have been banished into night—just as the primitive weapons, the bows and arrows, that have been abandoned by adult men, turn up once more in the nursery. Dreaming is a piece of infantile mental life that has been superseded. These methods of working on the part of the psychical apparatus, which are normally suppressed in waking hours, become current once more in psychosis and then reveal their incapacity for satisfying our needs in relation to the external world.'

The relationship between the wish and the psychoneurotic symptom is immediately apparent:[2]

'A symptom is not merely the expression of a realized unconscious wish; a wish from the preconscious which is fulfilled by the same symptom must also be present. So that the symptom will have *at least* two determinants, one arising from each of the systems involved in the conflict. As in the case of dreams, there are no limits to the further determinants that may be present—to the "over-determination" of the symptoms. The determinant which does not arise from the Ucs is invariably, so far as I know, a train of thought reacting against the unconscious wish—a self-punishment, for instance. I can therefore make the quite general assertion that an hysterical symptom develops only where the fulfilments

[1] S. Freud: *St. Edn.*, Vol. V, p. 569.

of two opposing wishes, arising each from a different psychical system, are able to converge in a single expression.'

By the same token an analogy is made between the dream work (see above p. 90 ff.) and psychoneurosis; the neurotic symptom arises in the same way as the dream:[1]

'In hysteria, too, we come across a series of perfectly rational thoughts, equal in validity to our conscious thoughts; but to begin with we know nothing of their existence in this form and we can only reconstruct them subsequently. If they force themselves upon our notice at any point, we discover by analysing the symptom which has been produced that these normal thoughts have been submitted to abnormal treatment: they have been *transformed into the symptom by means of condensation and the formation of compromises, by way of superficial associations and in disregard of contradictions, and also, it may be, along the path of regression.* In view of the complete identity between the characteristic features of the dream-work and those of the psychical activity which issues in psychoneurotic symptoms, we feel justified in carrying over to dreams the conclusions we have been led to by hysteria.

We accordingly borrow the following thesis from the theory of hysteria: *a normal train of thought is only submitted to abnormal psychical treatment of the sort we have been describing if an unconscious wish, derived from infancy and in a state of repression, has been transferred on to it.*'

Freud's derivation of repression conforms to his conception of the primary function of the psychic apparatus, i.e. in response to the 'necessities of life' the secondary system (remnants of memories) is developed and with it repression. If the fictive organism, consisting of the primary system alone, was able to withdraw from an overwhelming external stimulus (Pain) by taking flight, the secondary system makes it possible, through the memory of pain previously experienced, firstly, for such experiences to be avoided in future ('learning') and, secondly, for the painful memory to be regarded, or disregarded, at will. This process constitutes the model for repression. The primary system is not in a position to incorporate an experience of 'displeasure' into the thinking process. It can only 'wish'; or—in the formulation of later years—the id is controlled by the pleasure principle. But if the second system is to function, the unrestricted wish activity of the first system must be inhibited (see Contact Barriers and Facilitation in the *Project*). This inhibition is applied in Freud's later work by the adaptation of the

[1] S. Freud: *St. Edn.*, Vol. V, pp. 597-8.

secondary system to reality, with the resultant partial sacrifice of the 'pleasure principle'. In the dream work a predominantly displeasing memory (e.g. of previously experienced pain, e.g. 'learning') is cathected, whilst the displeasure to which it might conceivably give rise is inhibited. This (hypothetical) activity Freud calls the secondary process in contrast to the primary process of pleasure and displeasure in the primary system.[1]

'The primary process endeavours to bring about a discharge of excitation in order that, with the help of the amount of excitation thus accumulated, it may establish a *"perceptual identity"* (with the experience of satisfaction). The secondary process, however, has abandoned this intention and taken on another in its place—the establishment of a *"thought identity"* (with that experience). All thinking is no more than a circuitous path from the memory of a satisfaction (a memory which has been adopted as a purposive idea) to an identical cathexis of the same memory which it is hoped to attain once more through an intermediate stage of motor experiences.'

Freud looks upon thinking—as is indicated by the quotation—as purposive. It serves the purposes of the secondary system and of adaptation to reality.[2]

'Accordingly, thinking must aim at freeing itself more and more from exclusive regulation by the unpleasure principle and at restricting the development of affect in thought-activity to the minimum required for acting as a signal.'

As has already been mentioned, the primary system contains those wishes deriving from childhood (e.g. incest wishes), which, if realized in life, would produce displeasure. For this reason they are repressed and can only achieve expression in the pre-conscious after undergoing a change of form. One essential aspect of repression is that of the transformation of affects, i.e. pleasure turns into loathing (e.g. the pleasure taken by the child in playing with its own excrement turns into a loathing of excrement at a later age).

The function of consciousness *vis à vis* the unconscious is that of a sense organ engaged in the perception of psychic qualities.[3]

'The unconscious is the true psychical reality; *in its innermost nature it is as much unknown to us as the reality of the external world, and it is as*

[1] S. Freud: *St. Edn.*, Vol. V, p. 602.   [2] *Ibid.*, p. 602.
[3] *Ibid.*, p. 613.

incompletely presented by the data of consciousness as is the external world by the communications of our sense organs.'

(x) Dream and Symptom

Repeated references have already been made (see above p. 90 ff.) to the analogy between the explanation of the dream and that of the hysterical symptom. Eight years after the appearance of the *Interpretation of Dreams* Freud summarized the determinants of the psychoneurotic symptom. But in this new formulation the ego was replaced by the drive, a change of concept that was to prove as contradictory and as grave as any in the history of psychoanalytic theory. If for 'hysterical symptom' we read 'dream' or 'faulty action', then, with the exception of Clause 2 the two formulations are interchangeable. Implicit in Clause 2. is the question of the specificity of symptom formation, which psychoanalysis was unable to clarify, although it did indicate two directions in which the answer might lie: (1) in hereditary and constitutional moments, (2) in attempts to attribute, for example, hysteria more to disturbances in the genital phase and anxiety neurosis to disturbances in the anal phase (see below).

Freud's formulation is as follows:[1]

'1. Hysterical symptoms are mnemic symbols of certain operative (traumatic) impressions and experiences.

2. Hysterical symptoms are substitutes, produced by 'conversion', for the associative return of these traumatic experiences.

3. Hysterical symptoms are—like other psychical structures—an expression of the fulfilment of a wish.

4. Hysterical symptoms are the realization of an unconscious phantasy which serves the fulfilment of a wish.

5. Hysterical symptoms serve the purpose of sexual satisfaction and represent a portion of the subject's sexual life (a portion which corresponds to one of the constituents of his sexual instinct).

6. Hysterical symptoms correspond to a return of a mode of sexual satisfaction which was a real one in infantile life and has since been repressed.

7. Hysterical symptoms arise as a compromise between two opposite affective and instinctual impulses, of which one is attempting to bring to expression a component instinct or a constituent of the sexual constitution, and the other is attempting to suppress it.

8. Hysterical symptoms may take over the representation of various unconscious impulses which are not sexual, but they can never be without a sexual significance. . . .

[1] S. Freud: *St. Edn.*, Vol. IX, pp. 163–4 and 5.

9. Hysterical symptoms are the expression on the one hand of a masculine unconscious sexual phantasy, and on the other hand of a feminine one.'

VII. HISTORICAL INFLUENCES

Psychoanalysis is not an 'autochthonous' creation. It did not come into being independently of related or similar movements of its time, neither was it uninfluenced by them. Indeed, autochthonous creations are not to be found in the history of culture. From the heterogeneous influences of his day Freud erected the relatively homogeneous structure of psychoanalysis. Clinical observations drawn from his daily practice together with self-observations constituted the materials which he endeavoured to combine into a meaningful whole. He was a genius both of observation and of speculative combination. Others had described the hysterical symptom and the dream both before him and at the same time as him, but nobody had thought of combining them. This was only possible within the framework of an *explanatory* psychology, which attempted to combine both normal and pathological phenomena in a causal and therefore (scientifically) meaningful relationship. Freud's achievement was the creation of just such an explanatory psychology, an undertaking on which his contemporaries had also embarked and with which, indeed, they had succeeded to the extent of establishing a system, but not to the extent of establishing a *method*.[1]

The direct and indirect influence on Freud of *Herbart's*, *Fechner's* and *Wundt's* psychology and of the theoretical ideas propounded by *Meynert* has been demonstrated by *H. Hartmann, M. Dorer* and in the detailed studies carried out by the *Bernfelds*.

(a) Herbart

Herbart, who was a Kantian, ressembled Freud in that he sought to establish a psychology based on scientific and as far as possible on mathematical considerations. In psychology it is not possible to apprehend the 'soul' itself—here defined as a simple substance—but only the 'contrasts' and 'inhibitions' contained in the ideas (association).

---

[1] (In 1874 *Herbart's 'Psychologie vom empirischen Standpunkt* was published. *Brentano* was the founder of phenomenology and taught in Vienna in Freud's day. *Dilthey's* main works also appeared at the end of the 'seventies. At the end of the 'eighties the works of Lotze, Kuelpe and Jodl were also published. *M. Dorer* justifiably expresses her astonishment at the fact that in his medical publications Freud reveals a detailed knowledge of contemporary literature but fails to make any mention of these scholars. Further bibliography: S. Bernfeld, 'Freud's Earliest Theories and the School of Helmholtz'; *Psa. Quart.* Vol. XIII, p. 3, 1944. H. Hartmann, *Die Grundlagen der Psychoanalyse*, Leipzig, 1927.)

Herbart's psychology is concerned with the *dynamic* interplay of forces to which such ideas are subject. These ideas, however, are susceptible only to quantitative description. Qualitative considerations are not suitable for scientific enquiry. The movement of the ideas is determined by 'a drive contained within them', this drive being a property of all ideas, which gravitate towards a state of *equilibrium*. This basic gravitation on the part of the ideas towards a state of equilibrium (Freud's principle of constancy or inertia) is opposed by disturbances of the equilibrium, which originate either in the outside world or in the deeper layers of the personality (Freud's endogenous and exogenous sources of stimuli in the primary system of the *Project* and *The Interpretation of Dreams*). If, within the mass of an idea that is gravitating towards a balance of tension, a new idea should appear—from one of the two sources of stimuli—then this new idea can *inhibit* the old one by forcing it below its 'static point'. The 'static point' or the 'static threshold' corresponds to Freud's pre-conscious, for an idea that has sunk below its static threshold can quickly rise again and be taken up by other ideas. But an idea can also sink below its 'mechanical threshold'—Freud's unconscious—when, although it acts in opposition to a conscious idea, it is no longer accessible to consciousness (Freud's efficacy of unconscious ideas). In order to describe the dynamics of these mutually antagonistic ideas Herbart employs not only the concept of inhibition but also that of *repression*.

If no further proof is needed for the conformity of Herbart's and Freud's views in respect of the dynamics and also of the topography of associations, they none the less differ in the importance which they attribute to the affect. Whereas Freud defines the affect as the sum of excitation of the ideas which can be separated from those ideas and also develops a dynamics of the affect in the course of his psychoanalytic theory, with Herbart the affects are the result of the quantitative summation of the ideas. (If, for example, a person concentrates his thoughts on a rival, an affect of hatred develops as a result of the summation of ideas.) With Herbart the principle of inertia refers only to the ideas, whilst with Freud it is also transferred to the affects. Freud's dynamics of affects is subsequently developed (1923) into his metaphysics of drives. In spite of this difference Herbart was none the less aware of the concept of *conversion*, which he referred to as the 'hardening of the affect in the nervous system', thus anticipating by one hundred years the psychosomatic theories of F. Alexander. Like Freud he defines the drive as a tension and the ego as a drive! In conformity with *Fichte*, however, he derives both drive and ego from the will and—in contrast to Freud—attributes to consciousness a greater function than that of a mere epiphenomenon of the unconscious. With Herbart the

98

function of consciousness is still determined in terms of Idealistic philosophy.

(b) Fechner

Fechner, who—in contrast to Herbart—is frequently mentioned by Freud, endeavoured to furnish proof of Herbart's psychological principles by means of the psychophysical investigations in which he was engaged. One result of these investigations was the Weber–Fechner law of the function of the 'threshold'. It is not merely that Freud uses the concept of the threshold in order to lend credibility to the transformation of quantity into quality (as in the theory of anxiety, where somatic substances are psychically perceived after they have crossed the threshold). Rather the threshold anticipates the censor, and Freud uses the two terms synonymously when he describes in topical terms the transition of an idea from the unconscious to the pre-conscious and from the pre-conscious to consciousness. To this end the idea requires a certain amount of energy, which it takes from the sums of energy attached to the repressed ideas in the unconscious and which enables it to cross the threshold. Thus the concept of the threshold represents the psychophysical part of the censor.

Quite apart from the concept of the threshold, Freud's fundamental conceptions on the course of psychic activity in terms of the principle of the constancy of energy or of pleasure and displeasure are also based on corresponding theories of Fechner's. Analogous statements by Fechner on the unconscious, the dream and sleep reveal the essential conformity of Freud's and Fechner's views, as has been pointed out by *M. Dorer*.

Herbart's and Fechner's theories, together with the electrophysical theses of Helmholtz, formed the focal point of intellectual interest amongst the scientists of Vienna at the time when Freud was engaged on his own Studies and was about to embark on his scientific activities.

The only psychologist in Vienna at that time to put forward an anti-mechanistic viewpoint was Franz *Brentano*. It is possible, but it cannot be proved, that Brentano's conception of the ego as an act may have influenced Freud's early ideas on the ego. The importance attributed to the ego in the defence process (see above pp. 57 ff.) is only feasible if the ego is defined in terms of an autonomous function (in other words, as an act), i.e. as will, consciousness (mind) and aim. The function of the ego in Freud's works prior to the *Three Essays* would indicate the assumption on his part of such a definition, even if he never openly stated it (although he may perhaps have considered it to be axiomatic). In the *Project for a Scientific Psychology* he endeavoured to strengthen the autonomy of the ego by means of a specific third neuronic system (see above p. 79 ff.). In his later definition of the ego as a self-preservation drive, and following the introduction of 'narcissism', complicated hypotheses are needed if the ego is to retain even a relative degree of autonomy (see below p. 114 ff.).

(c) Breuer

Freud never failed to acknowledge the decisive influence exercised by Breuer on psychoanalytic theory. Freud writes:[1]

'If the account I have so far given has led the reader to expect that the *Studies on Hysteria* must, in all essentials of their material content, be the product of Breuer's mind, that is precisely what I myself have always maintained and what it has been my aim to repeat here. As regards the theory put forward in the book, I was partly responsible, but to an extent to which it is to-day no longer possible to determine. That theory was in any case unpretentious and hardly went beyond the direct description of the observations. It did not seek to establish the nature of hysteria but merely to throw light upon the origin of its symptoms. Thus it laid stress upon the significance of the life of the emotions and upon the importance of distinguishing between mental acts which are unconscious and those which are conscious (or rather capable of being conscious); it introduced a dynamic factor, by supposing that a symptom arises through a damming-up of an affect, and an economic factor, by regarding that same symptom as the product of the transformation of an amount of energy which would otherwise have been employed in some other way. (This latter process was described as *conversion*.) Breuer spoke of our method as *cathartic*; its therapeutic aim was explained as being to provide that the quota of affect used for maintaining the symptom, which had got on to the wrong lines and had, as it were, become strangulated there, should be directed on to the normal path along which it could obtain discharge (or *abreaction*).'

Breuer—together with Freud—advocated a combination of the German localization theory and the French excitation theory of the nervous system, which were then in the ascendancy. According to this conception nervous (psychic) energy is conducted like a fluid in communicating tubes along the neural pathways. The 'neural fluid' in the tubes of the nervous system gravitates towards a balance of tension whenever external or internal stimuli produce an actual increase or decrease of tension. In catharsis tension is 'discharged'.

Breuer quotes the neuro-physiologist *Cabanis*.[2]

[1] S. Freud, *St. Edn.*, Vol. XX, pp. 21–22.
[2] Quoted from Dorer, *Historische Grundlagen der Psychoanalyse*, Leipzig, 1932, p. 123.

'Excitation would appear to function like a fluid whose total quantity is fixed, so that whenever the quantity of excitation is increased in one of the tubes it is proportionately reduced in the others.'

Breuer's conception of the nature of affects leans heavily on *Meynert*, who considered that affects were produced by chemical processes in the brain. Freud maintained his belief in the chemical conditioning of the affects throughout his life, but the time came when he rejected the assumption that they were locally dependent on the brain. The fact that Breuer assumed, in addition to the two psychic conditions of sleeping and waking, a third 'hypnoid' condition was one of the factors leading to his estrangement from Freud (see above).

(d) Meynert

In his time Theodor Meynert was considered one of the most steadfast advocates of the localization theory. Together with *Wernicke* he argued that human behaviour, human actions and emotions, the whole of man's emotional and mental life, was dependent on the brain. Meynert advocated an atomistic-mechanistic philosophy, which was inspired by Herbart and Fechner. In psychology he also stood for a psychology of associations. His influence on Freud, both as a teacher and a superior, was considerable, as Freud himself concedes. For Meynert consciousness is 'cerebral life'. The outside world and the ego are states of cerebral life which, because they have not yet been clarified in terms of mechanistic causation, give man the illusion of freedom. In actual fact, however, there is no freedom. On the contrary, every process is strictly determined. Consciousness is awakened in the nerve cell only through external stimuli. If these dry up, then consciousness is extinguished. And consciousness—as with Freud—is an epiphenomenon. The fibres attached to the nerve cells *project* the stimuli from the outside world (noise, colour, smell, etc.) into the conscious mind in the form of qualities. 'The fibres project ... as it were man's image of the world into the hollow sphere of the cortex as though into a camera.'[1] The Freudian conception of *projection* as a mechanism of defence can be traced back to this description of Meynert's.

Meynert—like Freud—defines the affect as a sum of excitation, when he writes:[2]

'We may say that everything that is linked with the ego by virtue of the strong excitations which we call affects or affection, whose quantity is

---

[1] *Über den Wahn*, p. 85, quoted from Dorer.
[2] Dorer, *Historische Grundlagen der Psychoanalyse*, p. 136.

always determined by the number of elements subject to the excitation, is a component part of the ego.'

But Meynert was not aware of the susceptibility of affect and idea to disassociation. The development of this hypothesis was to remain Freud's prerogative.

Freud's characteristic theory of development (see above p. 79 ff.), much of which is based on Darwin, can be clearly traced back to Meynert. For Meynert—as also for Freud—the *primary* process is the reflex process, out of which the secondary process of consciousness is developed in response to the 'necessities of life'. This interpretation of the genesis of human consciousness caused Meynert to postulate a topography of the brain, which anticipated the topography of Freud's psychic apparatus. (See p. 149 ff.) The cerebral cortex becomes the secondary organ, the carrier of consciousness and of moral responsibility. It *inhibits* the activity of the primary organ (brain stem), which Meynert elevates to the status of the seat of the drives and instincts, of 'evil', but which he also defines as the 'childlike'. This primary brain Meynert further defines as the 'unconscious ego', which is opposed by the inhibiting and regulating conscious ego of the secondary brain. From this it follows that the primary organ is (*a*) unconscious, (*b*) the seat of the drives, (*c*) childlike—statements which anticipate the essential attributes of the unconscious in Freud's definitions. Freud's subsequent division of the psychic apparatus into id, ego and super-ego constitutes a translation of Meynert's brain topography into psychic processes.

We are indebted to Maria Dorer for having revealed how closely Freud followed Meynert in the formulation of his psychoanalytic theory. Her conclusions, which even Freud's most faithful disciples were unable to disregard, she summarizes as follows:[1]

'Both (Freud and Meynert) accord a position of central importance to associations, i.e. to ideas and the further ideas to which they give rise; psychic life is an inter-play of associations, which is dominated by 'ideational goals'. These associations of ideas and memory images are linked with an affect. With Meynert and with Freud the affect has both a physical (cf. Freud "secretory!") and a psychic aspect. Affects are quantitative factors and as such are capable of subsumption; they are also known as sums of excitation and as energy; with Meynert the physiological aspect predominates, with Freud the psychological aspect; but both aspects are present in both.—The qualities of the affects are pleasure and displeasure. The pleasure principle is primary; adaptation to the external world and its requirements is only a secondary process. 'Consciousness is a secondary phenomenon; it only comes into being

[1] M. Dorer, *Historische Grundlagen der Psychoanalyse*, pp. 149 ff.

in response to stimuli from the outside world. Consciousness is preceded by reflex processes, which take place unconsciously; thus unconscious motor activity is primary in contrast to conscious, intellectual activity, which is secondary. Only when the necessities of life intervene is consciousness aroused in the reflex organism.

'Consciousness—or in Freud's case the pre-conscious—exercises an inhibition *vis-à-vis* motor activity. With Meynert consciousness embraces all those activities which with Freud are divided between consciousness and the pre-conscious: the registration of sensations and stimuli and the storing of remnants of memories for purposes of the free interplay of associations.

'The various psychic "localities", the top and the bottom (the "depth" of the "motor" unconscious) are pre-formed in the cortical centres as distinct from the sub-cortical centres, which are the source of the unconscious reflexes. Whereas with Freud the pre-conscious, by inhibiting the unconscious, establishes all that is clear, civilized and premeditated in man's nature, whilst the unconscious is tantamount to all that is savage and untamed and is entirely subservient to the pleasure principle, with Meynert the cortical centres are quite simply the source of all that is good, whilst the sub-cortical centres are the source of all that is bad; in the cortical centres the secondary ego is formed, which is socially oriented and maintains contact with what we would call the objective mind (according to Freud = the products of sublimation); Meynert's sub-cortical centres create and maintain the primary ego, which is egoistic, thinks only of itself, of its own well-being, and is a "parasite".

'The primary ego is infantile; the unconscious is infantile. The difference between madness and normal psychic life is purely quantitative; both are grounded in the same psychic organization. Madness and myth are conceived as related phenomena; both constitute a projection of man's inner life on to the external world.

'Quantitative factors are dominant in both theories; both theories are mechanistic.'

Freud's recourse to Meynert is most marked in his later writings, above all in *Beyond the Pleasure Principle*. The theses put forward there on the genesis of consciousness and the regulation of the life processes by pleasure and displeasure (see below p. 149 ff.) can be traced back, in detail, to Meynert's statements.

(e) Summary

We may sum up the historical background of psychoanalysis with the following observations: Psychoanalysis is not an original structure and could not have come into being independently of the teachings and opinions prevailing at the turn of the century. Its basic elements (the dynamics of psychic processes, the classification of these processes into the primary and secondary process, into the unconscious and conscious [topography]) and their economy (pleasure/displeasure) were pre-figured in Herbart, Fechner, Helmholtz and Meynert. In attempting to establish a causal, purposive and above all *ontogenetic* explanation of hysteria, anxiety, obsessional neurosis, paranoia, and subsequently of faulty actions and of dreams Freud drew on their work. By analogy with faulty actions and dreams the symptom was traced back to the dynamics of various forces, which are localized (topically) in the psychic apparatus and are governed by the economy of pleasure and displeasure; in this formative phase of psychoanalytic theory symptom and personality tended necessarily to become largely *identical*. The question posed by the above-mentioned determination of the symptom (see p. 94 ff.) as to the cause of that determination is answered by reference to the dynamics, topography and economy of the personality. The classification of the personality under unconscious, pre-conscious and conscious is based on the separation of the primary (reflex) process from the secondary (conscious) process. Anatomically this classification is based on the difference between the cerebral cortex (consciousness), the brain stem (pre-conscious) and the spinal cord (reflex). The 'way in which the personality functions' is established by analogy with the way in which a machine functions, this latter being determined by its topography, the positioning of its parts in relationship to one another. For Freud anatomy —conceived as an idea—is the basis of function. Nor is this invalidated by the fact that he is less than specific in respect of the connection be-tween function (psyche) and anatomy (brain localization): for purposes of comprehending the 'psyche' the anatomy of the nervous system serves as a *model*. In nature stillness and activity are both expressions of the life process, the only difference being one of degree. Absolute stillness or a complete lack of movement is achieved only in death. The machine on the other hand is either set in motion or it is stationary. And this applies to every model that is won from abstraction and then transferred to living processes. The way in which the 'psychic apparatus' (a favourite expression of Freud's) functions, corresponds to the activity of a mach-ine: the individual parts are driven by energy (libido = sums of excita-tion of the affects). As a result of work done there are constant displacements in the relationship of forces between the component parts (cs, pcs, ucs). The machine, however, is regulated; it is an auto-matic manometer: pleasure/displeasure ensures that the relationship of forces between the components will remain constant. This relationship of forces is maintained even in neurosis and psychosis: the symptom brings a pleasure yield. Each movement or piece of work carried out by the machine arises out of the total relationship of the forces to one another. In other words, the symptom, the dream, the faulty action —and every other activity besides—*are to be understood as the resultants of the various parts of the personality* or, alternatively, of the machine. This is what makes it so difficult, indeed impossible, for psychoanalysis to differentiate between genetically healthy and pathological material. Since the personality is conceived as a model machine, *every* activity undertaken by the personality is determined by analogy with the hysterical symptom (see above). The separation of pathological material from healthy material requires special hypotheses involving constitutional factors and the search for the 'ultimate cause', which, with the infinite regression of causality, is never-ending. This ultimate cause has been shifted back from the Oedipus complex to anality, to orality, and finally to the birth trauma (see below p. 362 ff.).

The dependence of Freud's thought on the physiology and physics of the last century obliged him to work with concepts of models which originated in these sciences but which were both unbiological and unphysiological to a degree (see below). He retained these concepts throughout his life and chose virtually to ignore the development of biology and physiology from 1910 to 1938. An investigation of the genesis of Freud's hypotheses in the light of the great industrial and capitalist expansion of the nineteenth century would constitute a task which can only be touched on here. The analogy between libido and capital is striking, the former the main driving force of the personality, the latter that of the economy. Both are accumulative, both can be discharged or converted. The displacement of the 'sum of excitation' from one point to another in the sequence of ideas corresponds to the possibilities of capital investment. It would not be true to say that the Stock Exchange stood godfather to the nineteenth-century concept of energy on which Freud's libido concept was based. Such a judgement would be both one-sided and materialistic. What is true, however, is that both were children of the one 'spirit', a spirit which sought technical dominion over the individual, the earth and nature. None the less, Freud's dissatisfaction with these concepts comes through time and again in his works, even if it sometimes amounts to no more than a self-effacing sceptism. On such occasions his dissatisfaction was simply 'repressed'. And out of this repression there grew in Freud's last phase that irrational mythology of drives, which established the work of the strictly scientific founder of psychoanalysis as being closely akin to the related, modern (irrational) enquiries of a *Bergson* and a *Klages*, to the inroads made by the irrational in Surrealism and Existentialism, and even to the writings of *C. G. Jung, but which failed to grasp the true nature of the irrational* (see below p. 499 ff.). However, this last phase was preceded by Freud's middle phase, in which he struggled to establish a meaningful definition of 'personality'.

B

THE PERSONALITY

I. THE PERSONALITY AND PERSONALITY DEVELOPMENT

The historical nature of the personality, its living development, constitutes the greatest stumbling-block to a mechanistic conception of the personality. *Driesch* has long since demonstrated in his analysis of *Roux's* development mechanism that the concept of a mechanism, no matter how formed, is incompatible with living development, with its capacity for reproduction, reparation, assimilation, etc. Driesch made his observations on the now famous (dismembered) sea urchins. We need not agree with all of the conclusions which Driesch felt obliged to draw to find it remarkable that Freud should have taken note of Roux and *Weismann* but not of Driesch and not of the biologists, especially *Spemanns* and his school, who to this day have been unable to furnish a complete explanation of the extraordinarily complicated process involved in living development. Freud too drew on contemporary literature only when it supported his views. And so it was that in his most important work (apart from *The Interpretation of Dreams*), his *Three Essays on Sexuality*, he created that strange, hybrid conception of a 'mechanistic history of the development of the individual', the theory of which derives largely from Darwin. The importance of this work, if we disregard the above-mentioned dubious premises on which it is founded, lies in the connection, here established for the first time, between 'neuroses and perversions' on the one hand and the development of the personality on the other in what would appear to be (at least in part) a flawless demonstration of the relationship of neuroses and perversions to specific stages in the sexual development of the individual. Over and above this the work introduces several of Freud's fundamental definitions which constantly recur in the subsequent development of psychoanalysis.

Thus the libido is equated with the sexual drive (see above p. 66 ff.) and is defined as follows:[1]

'We have defined the concept of libido as a quantitatively variable force which could serve as a measure of processes and transformations occurring in the field of sexual excitation. We distinguish this libido in respect

[1] S. Freud, *St. Edn.*, Vol. VII, p. 217.

of its special origin from the energy which must be supposed to underlie mental processes in general, and we thus also attribute a qualitative character to it. In thus distinguishing between libidinal and other forms of psychical energy we are giving expression to the presumption that the sexual processes occurring in the organism are distinguished from the nutritive processes by a special chemistry.'

The drive is defined as follows:[1]

'By an instinct (drive) is provisionally to be understood the psychical representative of an endosomatic, continuously flowing source of stimulation, as contrasted with a 'stimulus', which is set up by single excitations coming from without. The concept of instinct is thus one of those lying on the frontier between the mental and the physical. The simplest and likeliest assumption as to the nature of instincts would seem to be that in itself an instinct is without quality, and, so far as mental life is concerned, is only to be regarded as a measure of the demand made upon the mind for work. What distinguishes the instincts from one another and endows them with specific qualities is their relation to their somatic sources and to their aims. The source of an instinct is a process of excitation occurring in an organ and the immediate aim of the instinct lies in the removal of this organic stimulus.'

The *sexual object* is the person who exercises sexual attraction, whilst the action on which the drive is intent is the *sexual aim*.[2]

(a) The Perversions

Freud differentiates between deviations (divergences) in respect of the sexual object, which include homosexuality and sodomy, and deviations in respect of the sexual aim. These latter fall into two categories: anatomical transgressions of the normal sexual aim, which Freud sees in genital union, and the fixation of 'preliminary sexual aims'.

At this stage in the development of psychoanalytic theory Freud sees the source of homosexuality in the young boy's identification with his mother; it is this which produces the subsequent attraction to young men who are prepared to love persons with homo-erotic tendencies 'just as their mothers had loved them'. Deviations in respect of the sexual aim (e.g. cunnilingus, fellatio, fetishism) Freud derives from the normal psychology of love life. A person in love 'overvalues' the sexual object and the result of this is 'intellectual infatuation' (i.e. his powers of judgement are weakened).[3] This overvaluation is transferred to the whole body of the loved one, resulting, amongst other things, in the elevation

---

[1] S. Freud, *St. Edn.*, Vol. VII, p. 168.   [2] *Ibid.*, pp. 136–7.
[3] *Ibid.*, p. 150.

of other parts of the body to the status of sexual aims. The 'libidinal overvaluation of the sexual object' is opposed only by the person's sense of loathing, which may conceivably prevent fixation to a sexual goal, i.e. perversion, from taking place. Under 'fixation to preliminary sexual goals' Freud includes exhibitionism, scopophilia, sadism and masochism. He notes the 'two-fold development of the sexual goal', the passive development (scopophilia, masochism), and the active development (exhibitionism, sadism), and this he also derives from the development of normal sexuality. He considers scopophilia and exhibitionism to be connected with the civilizing influence of clothes and sadism to be pre-figured in the aggressiveness of the sexual act. At all events perversion, considered as a pathological symptom, can only be said to obtain *when it constitutes the sole content of the sexual act.* Shame, loathing and morality are the forces which the drive (libido) has to overcome if it is to achieve satisfaction. The overcoming of these forces is the hallmark of perversion. Perversion is to be understood more as a release from inhibition, as the victory of the drive over certain barriers by which it was being suppressed, kept down, in neurosis. There are certain perversions which require a multiple motivation. Sadism, for example, derives from a combination of scopophilia, aggression and libido. This observation led Freud to assume the presence of partial drives in the libido. He speaks of a scopophilic drive or an aggressive component of the sexual drive. In accordance with his definition of the drive as a somatically conditioned stimulus Freud established a connection between the partial drives and certain 'erotogenic zones' of the body in which the partial drives originate. These zones include the mucous membrane of the mouth and of the anus, the nipples and the buttocks.

(b) Infantile Sexuality

Freud's observation that neurosis involves the presence of a symptom and his diagnosis, made in the *Studies* (see p. 52 ff.), of a history of the symptom that is linked to the periods, during which specific indications of illness appear, receive a more definitive formulation when he combines neuroses and perversions with infantile sexuality. By the end of the 'nineties (see above p. 71 ff.) conjectures as to the relationship of neurotic symptoms to specific periods of infantile sexuality were already presenting themselves to his mind. The Oedipus complex and the Castration complex had already been formulated and both pointed to the special importance of infantile sexuality. But was there such a thing as 'infantile sexuality'? In contemporary research into the origins of perversions (Krafft-Ebing, Havelock-Ellis, Bloch, etc.) no importance had been attached to infantile sexuality. It was Freud's achievement, one which was much disputed at the time but which to-day enjoys general recognition, to have destroyed the taboo concerning the innocence of childhood as far as sexuality is concerned. Although he concedes that children do not reveal a sexual drive such as is present in adults, he claims that they carry out a large number of actions and manipulations which are clearly connected with experiences of pleasure and satisfaction. In order to master the difficulty arising out of the difference between infantile and adult sexuality—a difference which Freud is often prone to overlook—he employs the concept of the 'libido', which embraces both infantile and adult sexuality. The problematical nature of this concept is thus instantly revealed, but so too is its strength, which consists in its ability to subsume all tendencies which are similar to sexual behaviour. Infantile sexuality is characterized by the following considerations:

1. It arises in connection with one of the essential physical functions, e.g. taking suck, which can develop at a later stage into sensual sucking.
2. It is not directed towards a sexual object but restricted to the infant's own body; it is in fact auto-erotic.
3. Its sexual aim is tied to a specific erotogenic zone (see above).

The close connection which exists between the erotogenic zone and pleasure on the one hand and the neurotic symptom on the other Freud describes as follows:[1]

'The character of erotogenicity can be attached to some parts of the body in a particularly marked way. There are predestined erotogenic zones, as is shown by the example of sucking. The same example, however, also shows us that any other part of the skin or mucuous membrane can take over the functions of an erotogenic zone, and must therefore have some aptitude in that direction. Thus the quality of the stimulus has more to do with producing the pleasureable feeling than has the nature of the part of the body concerned. A child who is indulging in sensual sucking searches about his body and chooses some part of it to suck—a part which is afterwards preferred by him from force of habit; if he happens to hit upon one of the predestined regions (such as the nipples or genitals) no doubt it retains the preference. A precisely analogous tendency to displacement is also found in the symptomotology of hysteria. In that neurosis repression affects most of all the actual genital zones and these transmit their susceptibility to stimulation to other erotogenic zones (normally neglected in adult life), which then behave exactly like genitals. But besides this, precisely as in the case of sucking, any other part of the body can acquire the same susceptibility

[1] S. Freud, *St. Edn.*, Vol. VII, pp. 183–4.

to stimulation as is possessed by the genitals and can become an erotogenic zone. Erotogenic and hysterogenic zones show the same characteristics.

'The sexual aim of the infantile instinct consists in obtaining satisfaction by means of an appropriate stimulation of the erotogenic zone which has been selected in one way or another. This satisfaction must have been previously experienced in order to have left behind a need for its repetition; and we may expect that nature will have made safe provisions so that this experience of satisfaction shall not be left to chance. We have already learnt what the contrivance is that fulfils this purpose in the case of the labial zone: it is the simultaneous connection which links this part of the body with the taking in of food. We shall come across other, similar contrivances as sources of sexuality. The state of being in need of a repetition of the satisfaction reveals itself in two ways: by a peculiar feeling of tension, possessing, rather, the character of unpleasure, and by a sensation of itching or stimulation which is centrally conditioned and projected on to the peripheral erotogenic zone. We can therefore formulate a sexual aim in another way: it consists in replacing the projected sensation of stimulation in the erotogenic zone by an external stimulus which removes that sensation by producing a feeling of satisfaction. This external stimulus will usually consist in some kind of manipulation that is analogous to the sucking.'

Infantile sexuality reaches its peak between three and five years of age. The *latency* period which then sets in continues right through to *puberty*, when the primacy of the genital zone over the other erotogenic zones is established (Oedipus complex). In the case of the little boy the latency period is also determined by the Oedipus complex, the fear of the father (castration complex) putting an end to infantile sexual activity and curiosity. To Freud it was obvious that masturbatory tendencies on the part of the child were connected with sucking or bowel movement. It is well known that special importance is paid to bowel movement in the child's upbringing, a fact which the child is not slow to appreciate. The child establishes a connection between the pleasurable stimulation of the mucous membrane of the anus, which is produced by the emission of the faeces, and the demands made by adults for regularity and punctuality of bowel movement. Thus the child can defiantly 'withhold' its faeces or 'make a present of them'. Psychoanalysis attached special importance to this process and Freud linked specific human characteristics with the 'anal' phase (see below). Masturbatory activity may be said to correlate with the anal phase if, for example, the child withholds its faeces—out of defiance—and derives pleasure from the ensuing stimulation of the mucous membrane.

The relationship of homosexuality to this phase of sexual development is obvious.

The peak of sexuality in the child is characterized by the simultaneity or the close proximity of the various auto-erotic activities. Sucking, retention of faeces, playful stimulation of the genitals may all take place at the same age. In addition there are the child's cruel impulses, its sadism, its scopophilic drive, the exhibitionism of little girls: the child is 'polymorphously perverse'. But the simultaneity of the most diverse sexual activities does not preclude the existence of periods or phases. There is the oral or cannibalistic phase, which is characterized by the fact that sexual activity is coupled with the intake of food (sucking). This is then followed by the phase in which bowel movement forms the focal point of the child's development:[1]

'A second pregenital phase is that of the sadistic-anal organization. Here the opposition between two currents, which runs through all sexual life, is already developed: they cannot yet, however, be described as 'masculine' and 'feminine', but only as 'active' and 'passive'. The activity is put into operation by the instinct for mastery through the agency of the somatic musculature; the organ, which, more than any other, represents the passive sexual aim is the erotogenic mucous membrane of the anus. Both of these currents have objects, which, however, are not identical. Alongside these other component instincts operate in an auto-erotic manner. In this phase, therefore sexual polarity and an extraneous object are already observable. But organization and subordination to the reproductive function are still absent.

'This form of sexual organization can persist throughout life and can permanently attract a large portion of sexual activity to itself. The predominance in it of sadism and the cloacal part played by the anal zone give it a quite peculiarly archaic colouring. It is further characterized by the fact that in it the opposing pairs of instincts are developed to an approximately equal extent, a state of affairs described by Bleuler's happily chosen term "ambivalence".'

A third phase, the phallic, which is characterized by the Oedipus complex and the concentration of the libido on the genitals, Freud does not describe in detail until 1923, when he adds it to the two other phases.

But what are the sources of infantile sexuality? We have already indicated their connection with the erotogenic zones and their organic origin. Freud answers this question in the following summary:[2]

[1] S. Freud, *St. Edn.*, Vol. VII, pp. 198–9.
[2] *Ibid.*, pp. 200–1.

'. . . sexual excitation arises (*a*) as a reproduction of a satisfaction experienced in connection with other organic processes, (*b*) through appropriate peripheral stimulation of erotogenic zones and (*c*) as an expression of certain "instincts" (such as the scopophilic instinct and the instinct of cruelty) of which the origin is not yet completely intelligible'.

To these sources there must be added, amongst other things, the body vibration set up by movements to which the child is passively subjected, as on a swing or in a motor car, the active flexing of the muscles involved in wrestling or romping and all intense affect processes, such as those produced by fear or joy, which can easily trigger off sexuality in a child. Thus, by tracing sexuality back to its origin and its essence, we see that it is capable of assuming an extraordinarily rich variety of forms.

(c) The Further Development of Sexuality (Libido)

In the investigation of infantile sexuality, to which perversions are related, perversions appear as *fixations* to stages in early childhood which every person must pass through. Such fixations, however, are only made manifest in puberty when, as a result of the relevant biological changes, the 'primacy of the genital zones' is asserted. Previously the sexual drive had been largely autoerotic, but now (in puberty) it finds its 'sexual object'.[1] The choice of a sexual object is determined by a 'mutual choice of objects'. In this respect Freud differentiates between a 'sensual' and an 'affectionate current' in sexual life. In the first thrust of sexual development the sensual current is dominant but is then repressed in the latency period. The sexual object, towards which this sexuality of early childhood is directed, is nearly always the mother or the person charged with the care of the child. The sexual object is not taken directly over into puberty and in the latency period a great deal of affection may be bestowed on it. Affection may be considered as a substitute for successfully repressed sensuality. In puberty the old sexual objects are brought to life again, the sensual current becomes stronger, but is then repressed once more by the affectionate current, thus paving the way for 'calf love'. But this increase in affection is not the only response to the resuscitation of the old sexual objects in puberty. Memories of the 'incest barrier', the Oedipus complex, lead to a rejection of parental authority, which takes the form of a protest against the parents, particularly the father, the source of which is to be found in the rivalry of the Oedipus complex.[2]

[1] S. Freud, *St. Edn.*, Vol. VII, p. 208.
[2] *Ibid.*, p. 227.

"At every stage in the course of development through which all human beings ought by rights to pass, a certain number are held back;[1] so there are some who have never got over their parents' authority and have withdrawn their affection from them either very incompletely or not at all. They are mostly girls, who, to the delight of their parents, have persisted in all their childish love far beyond puberty. It is most instructive to find that it is precisely these girls who in their later marriage lack the capacity to give their husbands what is due to them; they make cold wives and remain sexually anaesthetic. We learn from this that sexual love and what appears to be non-sexual love for parents are fed from the same sources; the latter, that is to say, merely corresponds to an infantile fixation of the libido.'

We may sum up the *Three Essays* as follows:

The various sexual perversions had already been investigated and described in detail by Freud's contemporaries. Concepts such as the latency period and autoerotism were already in existence (*Fliess, Havelock-Ellis,* etc.). But contemporary psychiatry had been unable either to explain perversions or to establish a meaningful correlation between perversions and the lives of psychiatric patients. Homosexuality, for example, was considered by authors of repute (*Magnus Hirschfeld*) to be the product of an unalterable predisposition or a form of degeneration. Freud was the first to recognize in homosexuality a neurotic symptom that is caused by disturbances in the development of the individual. It was he who attempted to understand perversions in terms of normal human development and to explain them as fixations to phases of the sexuality of early childhood. Over and above this, the questions which his recognition of the importance of dreams for neurosis had failed to answer were now resolved as a result of his investigation and elucidation of infantile sexuality—the questions as to when and in which phase of infantile development the damage is done.

In the subsequent development of psychoanalysis and of its various schools the three phases of sexuality were to be taken as the starting-point for numerous hypotheses on the specificity of particular neuroses and even psychoses. Damage done in the earliest, oral phase was considered to be of prime importance for the emergence of, for example, schizophrenia, whilst disturbances caused by external factors in the anal stage were said to promote anxiety neurosis. The same held true of disturbances in the phallic stage for hysteria. Furthermore, the neurotic symptoms were linked with the perversions; neurosis and perversion complemented each other; the symptoms of neurotic patients were to be understood in part as perverse fixations to early stages of infantile

[1] This refers to 'incestuous phantasies' (cf. *St. Edn.*, Vol. VII, p. 227.)

sexuality. As a consequence of the distinction made between the affectionate and the sensual current the so-called mature sexuality of adults was often assessed as an underdeveloped sexuality (sensuality). The dependence of the love relations of puberty and maturity on the impressions received in early childhood and infancy now appeared to be firmly established.

The mechanistic model on which Freud's ideas were based was characterized by the concepts of fixation and libido. Under 'normal development' he understood a comparatively constant increase in libido analogous to fluid in communicating tubes:[1]

'The various channels along which the libido passes are related to each other from the very first like inter-communicating pipes, and we must take the phenomenon of collateral flow into account.'

When the libido is *fixated* as a result of the trauma it has presumably stuck or adhered to the inside of the tubes, either because the tubes themselves have been twisted or because, for other reasons, a change in the 'viscosity' of the libido has taken place. (The comparison which springs to mind is with the mercury in a barometer, the height of which is determined by air pressure.) The Darwinian moment that joins with these mechanistic conceptions is less concerned with the principle of selection than with the marked degree of the individual's adaptation to his environment and his other-directedness.

II.   THE INTRODUCTION OF NARCISSISM (EGO PSYCHOLOGY)

The most critical modification and extension of psychoanalytic theory between 1900 and 1290, however, was brought about as a result of the 'Introduction of Narcissism'. In the 'Three Essays' Freud mentions, almost in passing, that the earliest pleasure-toned emotions in infants occur in connection with the intake of food. The intake of food is primary; it is based on the 'self-preservation drive' which, in this initial stage of human development, coincides with the pleasures derived from sucking, with the libido. But at later stages pleasure can sever its connection with the intake of food and become its own goal as, for example, in masturbation and sucking. The self-preservation drive was allotted to the ego as an ego drive, the ego and the self-preservation drive being treated as identical concepts on repeated occasions. In this connection, however, it should be noted that Freud's conception of the functions performed by the ego was by no means constant (see below). But whereas

[1] S. Freud, *St. Edn.*, Vol. VII, p. 151 n.

in the previous development of psychoanalysis the libido—the sexual drive—had been regarded as the sole source of energy in the individual, Freud now introduced a second source: the self-preservation drive. The ego, no matter how formed, had previously been postulated as an instance which repressed the drive, whereas now it was conceived as a drive. It was not only as a result of his observations of infantile sucking that Freud felt induced to make this assumption, for biological and psychiatric hypotheses also tended to confirm his view that the sexual drive and the self-preservation drive should be separated. From the biological point of view he considered it important to establish that sexuality is subordinated to procreation and thus to the species. The species makes use of sexuality in order to ensure its continuity. But procreation can come into conflict with self-preservation when, for example, an animal that is in season risks its life to win its mate. The same is true of neuroses which, Freud now considers, originate in the conflict between the sexual drive and the self-preservation drive. The development of hysteria is due to the repression of a sexual desire. This desire was repressed, because its fulfilment would have placed the person in jeopardy; i.e. self-preservation has proved stronger than sexual desire. This process is elucidated by the Oedipus complex: if the little boy were to give in to his urge to have intercourse with his mother, then he would be punished in one way or another (e.g. by the threat of castration), as a result of which his self-preservation would be endangered. The self-preservation drive suppresses the sexual drive and *neurosis arises out of a conflict of drives, i.e. a conflict between the sexual drive and the self-preservation drive*. The psychiatric hypothesis to which Freud also has recourse is based on *Abraham's* observations of schizophrenia. The loss of reality suffered by schizophrenics (see above) was due to the fact that the libido, which the ego normally transfers to objects (in the environment), had been withdrawn into the ego.[1]

'But the question then arose of what happened to the libido of dementia praecox patients which was turned away from objects. Abraham did not hesitate to give the answer: it is turned back on to the ego and this reflexive turning-back is the source of the megalomania in dementia praecox. Megalomania is in every way comparable to the familiar sexual overvaluation of the object in (normal) erotic life.'

Thus the ego is not only equated with the self-preservation drive but also serves as a 'reservoir' both for the libido and for the sexual drives, which are withdrawn into the ego as a result of the reality loss incurred in psychosis. The combination is confusing.

[1] S. Freud, *St. Edn.*, Vol. XVI, p. 415.

(a) Narcissism

The cathexis of the ego with object libido (sexual energy directed towards the outside world) Freud calls 'narcissism'.[1]

'To put the matter shortly, we pictured the relation of ego-libido to object-libido in a way which I can make plain to you by an analogy from zoology. Think of those simplest of living organisms (the amoebas) which consist of a little-differentiated globule of protoplasmic substance. They put out protusions, known as pseudopodia, into which they cause the substance of their body to flow over. They are able, however, to withdraw the protusions once more and form themselves again into a globule. We compare the putting-out of these protusions, then, to the emission of libido on to objects, while the main mass of libido can remain in the ego; and we suppose that in normal circumstances ego-libido can be transformed unhindered into object-libido and that this can once more be taken back into the ego.'

The fact that the ego is identical with the self-preservation drive on the one hand and is a 'reservoir' for the libido on the other Freud explains by reference to the undifferentiated condition of the ego in early childhood, when breast-feeding served the dual purpose of self-preservation and the satisfaction of 'sexual' desire. An infant is 'primarily narcissistic' since, apart from its feeding times and the short periods during which it is otherwise awake, its libido is exclusively and *auto-erotically* directed towards its own body. *Secondary* narcissim then appears in connection with the development of neurotic tendencies. The narcissistic neuroses include the various forms of schizophrenia, which are caused not only by the patient's 'loss of reality' but above all by his *lacking the ability to effect a transference*. *Abraham's* observations to the effect that schizophrenics, unlike neurotics, do not transfer their parent images on to the physician seemed to Freud indication enough of their inability to effect a transference and consequently of their 'narcissism'.[2] Yet another of the narcissistic neuroses is hypochondria, in which object libido is pathologically withdrawn and directed on to the patient's own body—in the case of psychoses on to the ego—after the pattern of infantile autoerotism (see above p. 108 ff.). Sleep is also a narcissistic process, one in which object libido is withdrawn from the environment and which consequently differs only in degree from psychosis. Narcissistic object selection lies at the root of homosexuality, as also of other forms of unconscious self-love, in which the ego (or the

[1] S. Freud, *St. Edn.*, Vol. XVI, p. 416.
[2] This observation has since been largely refuted (see works by *Sechehaye, Benedetti, F. Fromm-Reichmann, D. Wyss* inter alia).

sex, i.e. male or female) becomes the object of its own attentions. Narcissistic object selection—the self-infatuation of the ego—also derives from early childhood and is in direct contrast to the object selection of the attachment type (or anaclitic type), whose subsequent attachments bear the stamp of the nurse (or the mother).[1]

'A person may love
 1. According to the narcissistic type:
    (a) what he himself is (i.e. himself),
    (b) what he himself was,
    (c) what he himself would like to be,
    (d) someone who was once part of himself.
 2. According to the anaclitic (attachment) type:
    (a) the woman who feeds him,
    (b) the man who protects him.'

(b) The Ideal Ego ('Super Ego')

The (hypothetical) elucidation of psychoses led beyond narcissism to a further sub-division of the 'ego'. When his patients suspiciously complained that they were being watched, criticized and blamed by other people, Freud assumed the existence within the ego of a further instance which enables human beings to exercise self-observation and self-criticism. In paranoia this self-observation, of which everyone is capable, is transferred to the outside world in a pathological manner, a conception which Freud had already advanced in 1895. At that time (see above p. 71 ff. in his correspondence with Fliess) he differentiated between the 'forces of conscience', establishing their dependence on cultural and civilizatory influences, and the suppression of drive life, which resulted from such dependence. The 'forces of conscience', which appear in tangible form in critical self-observation, are the offspring of education. Children take note of parental reproofs and criticisms and by a process of identification with the parents establish within their ego an instance which Freud (in 1917) called the 'Ideal Ego'. This was the decisive step. Conscience had now been psychologized, transformed, for the purposes of psychoanalytic theory, into an environmentally conditioned instance of the 'psychic apparatus'.

(c) The Development of Ego-psychology, 1895–1917

In the initial period of psychoanalytical research (see Summary, p. 69 ff.) the ego had for the most part still been interpreted in terms of *Herbart's* psychology either as a group of ideas or as will and goal (will = drive). It effected the division of affect and idea, was the agent

---

[1] S. Freud, *St. Edn.*, Vol. XIV, p. 90.

of defence where ideas were to be suppressed, was capable of rejecting both idea and affect, and it administered the censorship. A connection was established between the ego and the other defence processes—projection and identification—and the control which it exercised over perception and motor activity was also recognized. The censorship was subsequently taken over by the ideal ego, whilst the other processes were written into the libido economy. But the ego, when it becomes a drive (self-preservation drive), is still the reservoir for the libido,[1] and as such it cathects and de-cathects the objects in its environment—like an amoeba. Whereas previously it had split ideas from affects, or rejected them both (psychosis), now it withdraws libido from one idea in order to transfer it to another. Or, alternatively, it withdraws its libido entirely from ideas, affects and reality and stores it up within itself, with psychosis—e.g. megalomania—as the result ('libido economy').

(d) Conflicts of Drives and Symptoms

In the *Psychoanalytic View of Psychogenic Disturbance of Vision* (1910) Freud describes for the first time the consequences of a conflict of drives for the emergence of symptoms. The symptom (see above, p. 68 ff.) had previously been looked upon as a compromise formation between the suppressed drive and the repressing instance. Now it was to be considered as the outcome of a conflict of drives, a conflict between the self-preservation drive and the sexual drive. The ego drive and the sexual drive depend for their fulfilment on the same physical organs. For example, in eating the mouth serves the self-preservation drive, whilst in kissing it serves sexuality. In the case of the psychogenic disturbance of vision, i.e. so-called hysterical blindness, excessive claims are made on the ego by a partial sexual drive, the scopophilic drive. The scopophilic drive is in a position to threaten the self-preservation drive and a conflict thus arises between the two drives. As a result of this conflict the ego loses its control over the eye—or, by analogy, over any other organ—whereupon it withdraws its libido from the eye, thus relinquishing it to the sexual drive. The ego does not want to see anything at all (blindness) 'now that the sexual interest in seeing has made itself so prominent.[2] The repressed drive takes its revenge, as it were, for having been prevented over an inordinately long period of time from making its demands on the organ concerned by assuming absolute control over that organ. The essential point about this concep-

---

[1] The closest possible fusion of self-preservation drives and sexual drives in early childhood is an essential prerequisite of narcissism. Since libido is not the only feature of the self-preservation drives, Freud was obliged to define the ego as a reservoir of libido.

[2] S. Freud, *St. Edn.*, Vol. XIV, p. 216.

tion—in contrast to the first phase of psychoanalytic theory—is that the conflict of drives is described as a conflict *within* the libido. Previously it had been the ego, conceived in terms of consciousness and will, which had suppressed the unpleasant idea. Now it is one drive fighting against the other:[1]

'It had been said that repression was set in action by the instincts of self-preservation operating in the ego (the "ego-instincts") and that it was thought to bear upon the libidinal instincts. But since the instincts of self-preservation were now recognized as also being of a libidinal nature, as being narcissistic libido, the process of repression was seen to be a process occurring within the libido itself; narcissistic libido was opposed to object libido, the interest of self-preservation was defending itself against the demands of object-love, and therefore against the demands of sexuality in the narrower sense as well.'

(e) Conflict of Drives and the Causation of Neuroses

Between 1895 and 1905 Freud had considered the causation of neuroses to lie:

(1) in the activation of an infantile trauma,
(2) in the conflict, resulting from such activation, between the suppressed drive and the repressing instance,
(3) in the compromise formation arising out of the conflict between these two forces, namely, the symptom. But with the differentiation between sexual drives and self-preservation drives the importance of the ego was to increase both as a factor in normal personality and in neurosis. It is clear from the description of the phases of infantile sexuality given above that the ego is subject to pathological deformation in the course of its development. The development of the self-preservation drive is considered to follow a more or less parallel course to that of the sexual drive. And so if, as a result of the repercussions of a trauma, the libido should be fixated, for example, in the anal stage, then this fixation will also be a matter of some consequence to the ego. If the ego accepts the fixation, then it will become perverted or infantile, whereas if it rejects it, it will incur a repression at the precise point in its development at which the libido was fixated. From this it follows that the development of the ego will have some influence on the conflict, which is an important factor in the emergence of the neurotic symptom. An infantile or perverted ego can, for example, hinder the emergence of the neurotic symptom, since the sexual drives, although fixated to infantile phases, can be lived out within these phases relatively freely. Not until it is

---

[1] S. Freud, *St. Edn.*, Vol. XX, p. 56.

confronted with reality—in the case of homosexuals, for example, with society—is the infantile ego once more subjected to influences which are likely to activate its repressive function and thus conceivably lead to conflict and the formation of a neurotic symptom. The slow process whereby the ego turns from the pursuit of pleasure towards reality Freud has called the transformation of the pleasure ego into the reality ego. He describes this process in his work *On The Two Principles of Mental Functioning*, where he also links it with the primary and secondary processes of the Interpretation of Dreams (see above, p. 91 ff.). Now that external reality has been set up as a *reality principle* it follows that the pursuit of pleasure is no longer an exclusive aim but that adaptation to reality also takes place. The repression of one drive by another (self-preservation drive by sexual drive) is replaced by an objective assessment, the pleasure ego yields to the reality ego, adapts to it, and pursues the same goals in a different guise. In Freud's early version (1910) the secondary process was developed from the primary process due to the 'necessities of life'. Now it is the reality ego (secondary process) which emerges from the pleasure ego (primary process) due to the reality principle.

(*f*) *Provisional Assessment of the Problems attendant on the Ego Concept*
  (*see below p. 489 ff.*)

The equation of the ego with the self-preservation drive has made it extraordinarily difficult to follow the processes involved in repression and in the emergence of neuroses. In as far as the earlier ego concept involved both the will and a goal and thus the conscious mind the process of repression could be observed and formulated from the point of view of consciousness: a painful idea enters into consciousness and is there subjected to defence, it becomes unconscious (or pre-conscious), whereupon it may well exercise a pathogenic effect. This concept of the ego was coherent both in terms of *substance* and of structure, corresponding by rough analogy to the piston in the mechanical model which, when introduced at one end of the communicating tubes, keeps water under pressure. It is of course true that the ego, considered as a drive, is able to suppress another drive within the field of tension set up by the parallelogram of forces, but Freud has omitted to explain how it is that a drive is able to maintain the necessary (repressive) pressure over a period of years until such time as the symptom emerges. Over and above this, however, the ego is a basic constituent of the character, even if the character is said to be infantile or perverse. The ego can be 'twisted' (see above) or repressed, its development can be retarded or promoted—abilities which are scarcely compatible with the concept of a drive (see p. 106 ff. for the definition of a drive). The fact that the sexual drives have been listed under the pleasure principle and the self-preservation drives under the reality principle makes the problem even more complicated. During the child's development the self-preservation drive conforms to 'reality', which Freud understands in a general sense as the influences and requirements of the world at large ('the necessities of life'). Adaptation to reality takes place at the expense of the pleasure principle, i.e. of the sexual drives. *How* a drive is able to submit to the exigencies of life whilst at the same time continuing to develop and to provide the foundation for character formation is not explained. The difficulty is due to the fact that the ego concept is used *simultaneously* in terms of a substance (capable of development, plastic, subject to change) and in terms of a drive. In the last phase of Freudian theory, of course, the problem is to become even more complicated (see below, p. 156 ff.).

(g) An Example of Character Development: Anal Erotism

In 1908 Freud published a work on the relationship between *The Character and Anal Erotism*. Persons with a reputation for orderliness, thrift and obstinacy revealed that in their childhood the act of defecation had occupied a special position and consequently the anal zone had been given priority. Cleanliness and orderliness are thus interpreted as *reaction formations* on the part of the person concerned, i.e. as reactions to an excessive preoccupation with faeces during infancy. Obstinacy constitutes a continuation of the child's defiance, when it refuses to 'give up' its faeces, a quality which also finds expression in thrift. Reaction formations on the part of the ego in response to pleasurable but forbidden experiences of the anal phase develop into character traits.

(h) The Ego (Summary, 1895–1917)

Briefly, the ego performs the following functions:

(*a*) it is part of consciousness and controls perception and motility;

(*b*) it is a drive (self-preservation drive);

(*c*) it is a reservoir of libido;

(*d*) it is the cause of repression ('Self respect', see below III The Dynamics of the Personality);

(*e*) it conforms to reality, is to some extent identical with the reality principle (reality ego/pleasure ego);

(*f*) as a reaction to the drives it constitutes the basis of character formation;

(*g*) it carries out reality testing (see below, p. 125 ff.).

Thus seven widely differing functions are seen to combine in the ego, not to mention its other instance, the 'Ideal Ego'.

III. THE DYNAMICS OF THE PERSONALITY

(a) Ideal Ego and Sublimation

The difficulties ensuing from the equation of the ego with the self-preservation drive for the process of repression have been described above. Time and again Freud is obliged to have recourse to his early conception of the ego as a substance in order to render the process of repression intelligible. For example, in his fundamental work *On Narcissism: an Introduction*:[1]

'We have learnt that libidinal instinctual impulses undergo the vicissitude of pathogenic repression if they come into conflict with the subject's cultural and ethical ideas. By this we never mean that the individual in question has a merely intellectual knowledge of the existence of such ideas; we always mean that he recognizes them as a standard for himself and submits to the claims they make on him. Repression, we have said, proceeds from the ego; we might say with greater precision that it proceeds from the self-respect of the ego. The same impressions, experiences, impulses and desires that one man indulges or at least works over consciously will be rejected with the utmost indignation by another, or even stifled before they enter consciousness. The difference between the two, which contains the conditioning factor of repression, can easily be expressed in terms which enable it to be explained by the libido theory. We can say that the one man has set up an ideal in himself by which he measures his actual ego, while the other has formed no such ideal. For the ego the formation of an ideal would be the conditioning factor of repression.'

Here Freud sees the immediate cause of repression in self-respect, an extraordinarily complicated concept. The Ideal Ego has already been mentioned (see p. 117 ff.) as a preliminary stage of the super ego in its relationship to paranoia, to conscience, to the censor. When the narcissistic self-love of a child, reinforced by the love of those caring for it, is forced to yield to reality, it attaches itself to the ideal ego. The self-love which the ego enjoyed in childhood is retained in this ideal ego, which serves as a store room for personal memories of the happy childhood years. Thus the realization of an ideal always means the fulfilment of the wish to be restored to the long lost condition of childhood. Every object—and with Freud an object may also be a person—can be idealized, which means that it is 'overvalued', as in the case of falling in love (cf. ideal ego).

[1] S. Freud, *St. Edn.*, Vol. XIV, p. 93.

Sublimation, on the other hand, is not concerned with the object but with the drive. A drive is sublimated when it is directed away from its original goal—e.g. one of a sexual nature—towards another, culturally more elevated goal. Sublimation can be said to have taken place, for example, when a child who was inclined to smear faeces subsequently becomes a painter. In his study, *A Childhood Memory of Leonardo da Vinci*, Freud has attempted to present, on the basis of his own reconstruction of Leonardo's childhood experiences, both the artist's predominantly artistic phase and his subsequent scientific phase as a sublimation of the sexual experiences and inquisitiveness of childhood.

(b) Drive, Affect and Idea

If it is possible to sublimate the drive, then the question arises as to whether it cannot also be repressed. In his comprehensive work on *The Unconscious* (1913)—which was written after his theory of dreams—Freud says that it cannot. 'An instinct can never become an object of consciousness—only the idea that represents the instinct can',[1] to quote Freud's own words, with which he inaugurated a transcendentalism of drives. But apart from the sublimation of drives or, alternatively, the sublimation of the ideas and affects representing the drives, drives can also be transformed into their opposite: e.g. love into hate, scopophilia into exhibitionism. There are two processes involved in this reversal of a drive into its opposite: the transformation from active to passive (scopophilia into exhibitionism) and the reversal of the content. But apart from its ability to undergo such a transformation into its opposite the drive is also capable of turning against its own person; e.g. in masochism, which is introverted sadism. This process is illustrated by the following:[2]

'(a) Sadism consists in the exercise of violence or power upon some other person as object.

'(b) This object is given up and replaced by the subject's self. With the turning round upon the self the change from an active to a passive instinctual aim is also effected.

'(c) An extraneous person is once more sought as object; this person, in consequence of the alteration which has taken place in the instinctual aim, has to take over the role of the subject.

'Case (c) is what is commonly termed masochism. Here, too, satisfaction follows along the path of the original sadism, the passive ego placing itself back in phantasy in its first role, which has now in fact been taken over by the extraneous subject. Whether there is, besides this, a more direct masochistic satisfaction is highly doubtful. A primary masochism,

---

[1] S. Freud, *St. Edn.*, Vol. XIV, p. 177. [2] *Ibid.*, p. 127.

not derived from sadism in the manner I have described, seems not to be met with. That it is not superfluous to assume the existence of stage (b) is to be seen from the behaviour of the sadistic instinct in obsessional neurosis. There there is a turning round upon the subject's self without an attitude of passivity towards another person: the change has only got as far as stage (b). The desire to torture has turned into self-torture and self-punishment, not into masochism. The active voice is changed, not into the passive, but into the reflexive, middle voice.'

Freud explains the process whereby the drive turns against its own person by reference to the preliminary narcissistic stage of drive life, i.e. as a regression on the part of the drive concerned to an infantile, narcissistic stage. For purposes of the reversal of love into hate Freud postulates *three polarities* which govern psychic life: that of subject (ego) and object (environment), that of pleasure and displeasure and that of active and passive. In narcissistic autoerotism the separation of subject and object has not yet taken place and the child finds satisfaction in itself. Hatred arises only when by means of the most varied stimuli the environment imposes itself on the subject and the child protests against the displeasure which this involves.[1]

'Hate, as a reaction to objects, is older than love. It derives from the narcissistic ego's primordial repudiation of the external world with its outpouring of stimuli. As an expression of the reaction of unpleasure evoked by objects, it always remains in an intimate relation with the self-preservation instincts; so that sexual and ego instincts can readily develop an antithesis which repeats that of love and hate.'

Love is secondary. It comes into existence as a result of the pleasure and satisfaction which the child derives from its own body, whence it is transferred to other environmental objects. Thus for Freud 'evil' would seem to be the primary condition of man, which would be in accordance with *Meynert's* conception of the primary brain (see above, p. 101 ff.). The transformation of love into hate, therefore, is always accompanied by a return to the stage which in all probability precedes auto-erotic satisfaction, the stage of 'original rejection of environmental stimuli'. Freud summarizes as follows:[2]

'... the essential feature in the vicissitudes undergone by instincts lies in *the subjection of the instinctual impulses to the influence of the three great polarities that dominate mental life.* Of these three polarities we might describe that of activity-passivity as the *biological*, that of ego-

---

[1] S. Freud, *St. Edn.*, Vol. XIV, p. 139.   [2] *Ibid.*, p. 140.

external world as the *real*, and finally that of pleasure-unpleasure as the *economic* polarity.'

Even in the unconscious the drive exists merely as an idea, although it is capable of manifestation in the form of affect. *The affect, however, is not identical with the drive*, although it does[1] 'correspond to the instinct in so far as the latter has become detached from the idea and finds expression, proportionate to its quality, in processes which are sensed as affects'. In Freud's early phase (up to 1905) both drive and affect had been described as purely quantitative processes. To this day the drives have *not acquired a qualitative value*. The affects, however, have been endowed—over and above their quantitative sum of excitation—with quality (in the form of feelings). The separability of affect and idea remains a factor of fundamental importance for psychoanalytic theory. Both affect and idea may be subjected to repression. But the affect is always a discharge process, which differs from the idea in respect of its unconscious condition. The speed with which it can emerge, the ease with which it can be transformed (e.g. into fear), the possibility which exists of repeated repression, would all seem to indicate that its fate in the unconscious differs from that of the idea. For the idea, even when it has become conscious, continues to lead an unconscious existence as well. The impression of the father which the child receives, the father image, the imago, stays with the child, even after it has been brought into consciousness in the course of dream analysis. Years later it may reappear in the child's mind. But what becomes of the unconscious idea? Its energy charge—the sum of its affect in quantitative terms—'sharpens' the idea, so to speak, thus enabling it to impose itself upon the conscious mind.

(c) *Repression*

It is repression which removes the sum of excitation from the idea, which splits off the quantity of affect. This process takes place either in the conscious mind or—more frequently—in the *pre-conscious* (see pp. 90-1 ff.). When this happens the idea either remains deprived of its energy charge or it receives a supply of energy from the unconscious. But how can the idea, which has been repressed and which is perhaps receiving new energy from the unconscious, be prevented from thrusting itself back into consciousness? Clearly the process of repression must take place in two phases: a first phase, in which the energy is split off from the idea, is followed by a second phase, in which the repression is maintained. This is made possible by a *counter charge* (*counter cathexis*) of the repressed idea either from the conscious mind or from the pre-

[1] S. Freud, *St. Edn.*, Vol. XIV, p. 152.

conscious. If this process is reproduced on a mechanical model,[1] it is seen to observe the following pattern: the idea I_1 loses its energy to the unconscious due to repression but receives further sums of excitation from the unconscious and forces its way back towards consciousness. Consciousness then counter-cathects the idea (I_2) by 'superimposing' on it another idea with another energy charge.

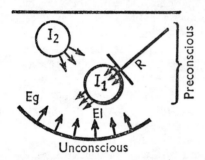

I_1 Idea
I_2 Substitute Idea
R   Repression
EL   Energy Loss
EG   Energy Gain

This other idea is a so-called '*substitute idea*', such as may be observed in animal phobias. Fear of horses is substituted for the actual fear of the father—in the analysis of the phobia of the five-year-old boy, Hans, —and the image of the horse replaces the image of the father. In this way the child is able to remain in his father's presence without fear, which he feels only when he sees a horse.[2]

'Further, we may lay stress on the interesting consideration that by means of the whole defensive mechanism thus set in action a projection outward of the instinctual danger has been achieved. The ego behaves as if the danger of a development of anxiety threatened it, not from the direction of an instinctual impulse, but from the direction of a perception, and it is thus enabled to react against this external danger with the attempts at flight represented by phobic avoidances. In this process repression is successful in one particular: the release of anxiety can to some extent be dammed up, but only at a heavy sacrifice of personal freedom. Attempts at flight from the demands of instincts are, however, in general useless, and, in spite of everything, the result of phobic flight remains unsatisfactory.'

These complicated processes of the cathexis and counter-cathexis of energy are necessitated by the dualism obtaining between idea and energy (libido). Freud would have liked to have expressed the psychic processes in the purely dynamic concepts of the libido theory. It would

[1] Author's model.   [2] S. Freud, *St. Edn.*, Vol. XIV, p. 184.

be reasonable to assume that in this particular phase of theory formation the quantum theory will have appealed to him as an ideal model. But any such wishes were opposed by the *real existence* of *ideas*, which cannot be interpreted in purely energic terms without losing the character of ideas. Over and above this, of course, the ideas 'represent' the drives, which, but for such representation, would transcend consciousness. And so compromise solutions are called for which are capable of presenting a dynamics of ideas in the language of a dynamics of drives (libido, energy, quantity). The only way in which this can be done is by displacing the ideas in accordance with both quantum and electromagnetic models: cathexis of a given idea with 'libido quanta'. The contrast between substance (idea) and function (drive) is particularly noticeable here, likewise the attempt—one that was doomed to failure—to convert substance into function, a further example of which is provided by the ego theory.

In this connection Freud was obliged to introduce a further hypothesis, which differentiated between an object presentation and a word presentation, in order that, for example, schizophrenic new word formations might be considered as substitute formations. In the conscious idea object and word coincide, whereas in the unconscious not only are they disparate but the unconscious retains only the object presentations. A child's first attempts to comprehend an object—e.g. a ball or a doll—, which it makes before it is able to speak, leave impressions in the unconscious mind which precede the word presentation. These are the so-called object cathexes or object presentations. Patients suffering from schizophrenia often make statements which, although apparently meaningless, become meaningful once it is realized that they are governed by the word idea alone without reference to any considerations of similarity between objects or things. Symptom formation amongst neurotics functions in a similar way, as, for example, in the case of the hypochondriac, whose obsession for bursting blackheads is a substitute for the guilty masturbation of earlier years.[1]

'If we ask ourselves what it is that gives the character of strangeness to the substitutive formation and the symptom in schizophrenia, we eventually come to realize that it is the predominance of what has to do with words over what has to do with things. As far as the thing goes, there is only a very slight similarity between squeezing out a blackhead and an emission from the penis, and still less similarity between the innumerable shallow pores of the skin and the vagina; but in the former case there is, in both instances, a "spurting out", while in the latter the cynical saying "a hole is a hole", is true verbally. What has dictated

[1] S. Freud, *St. Edn.*, Vol. XIV, p. 200.

the substitution is not the resemblance between the things denoted but the sameness of the words used to denote them.'

Apart from (1) psychiatric observations of schizophrenic word formation, (2) the probability that in early childhood the object cathexis precedes the word cathexis (or presentation), it was his assumption (3) that thinking is brought about as a result of speech and perception which persuaded Freud of the validity of this attitude, the logical outcome of which—*universalia sunt post realia*—he has formulated in his own words:[1]

'When we think in abstractions there is a danger that we may neglect the relations of words to unconscious thing-presentations, and it must be confessed that the expression and content of our philosophizing then begins to acquire an unwelcome resemblance to the mode of operation of schizophrenics. We may, on the other hand, attempt a characterization of the schizophrenic's mode of thought by saying that he treats concrete things as though they were abstract.'

The concepts of counter-cathexis and of substitute formation (substitute presentation) already constitute a considerable advance in the theory of repression. The next step in its development is the differentiation made between primal repression and repression proper, which Freud had already anticipated in the 'Interpretation of Dreams'. Primal repression takes place in infancy, at a time when the sexual and self-preservation drives are still undifferentiated but when the reality principle of the self-preservation drives has already begun to suppress the pleasure principle. The actual mechanism of primal repression is the counter-cathexis of the sexual drives, which are striving to achieve autonomy in the face of the reality principle. The result of this counter-cathexis is that the drives themselves are rendered incapable of conscious realization and have to be represented in the conscious mind by ideas and affects. Repression proper (i.e. all subsequent repressions) are simply displacements of energy from one conscious idea to another.

The withdrawal or splitting off of energy cathexis in respect of ideas which are to be repressed is something which repression and substitute formation have in common. In both processes the repressed idea is replaced by a new idea (the father is replaced by the horse in the phobia). But changes in the ego such as take place in obsessional neurosis are also a substitute formation: e.g. conscientiousness and defiance may emerge as a reaction to sadistic impulses. Chronologically, however, substitute formation *follows* repression.

[1] S. Freud, *St. Edn.*, Vol. XIV, p. 204.

(d) The Unconscious

How is the unconscious presented in this period of psychoanalytic development? Freud supplies the following summary:[1]

'The nucleus of the Ucs consists of instinctual representatives which seek to discharge their cathexis; that is to say, it consists of wishful impulses. These instinctual impulses are coordinate with one another, exist side by side without being influenced by one another, and are exempt from mutual contradiction. When two wishful impulses whose aims must appear to us incompatible become simultaneously active, the two impulses do not diminish each other or cancel each other out, but combine to form an indeterminate aim, a compromise.

'There are in this system no negation, no doubt, no degrees of certainty: all this is only introduced by the work of the censorship between the Ucs and the Pcs. Negation is a substitute, at a higher level, for repression. In the Ucs there are only contents, cathected with greater or lesser strength.

'The cathectic intensities (in the Ucs) are much more mobile. By the process of *displacement* one idea may surrender to another its whole quota of cathexis; by the process of *condensation* it may appropriate the whole cathexis of several other ideas. I have proposed to regard these two processes as distinguishing marks of the so-called *primary psychical process*. In the system Pcs the *secondary process* is dominant. When a primary process is allowed to take its course in connection with elements belonging to the system *Pcs*, it appears "comic" and excites laughter.

'The processes of the system *Ucs* are *timeless*; i.e. they are not ordered temporally, are not altered by the passage of time; they have no reference to time at all. Reference to time is bound up, once again, with the work of the system *Cs*.

'The Ucs processes pay just as little regard to *reality*. They are subject to the pleasure principle; their fate depends only on how strong they are and on whether they fulfil the demands of the pleasure-unpleasure regulation.

'To sum up: *exemption from mutual contradiction, primary process* (mobility of cathexes), *timelessness*, and *replacement of external by psychical reality*—these are the characteristics which we may expect to find in processes belonging to the system Ucs.'

In the pre-conscious, on the other hand, the contents of the ideas are arranged in terms of time sequence, reality, censorship and memory. The pre-conscious already approximates to a thought process, albeit a

[1] S. Freud, *St. Edn.*, Vol. XIV, p. 186.

pre-conscious thought process. The great difficulty about the unconscious—including the pre-conscious—lies in the fact that on the one hand it is purposive and on the other hand a-logical (see above for definition of the unconscious). Freud's proof of the existence of the unconscious is a purposive one:[1]

'All these conscious acts remain disconnected and unintelligible if we insist upon claiming that every mental act that occurs in us must also necessarily be experienced by us through consciousness; on the other hand they fall into a demonstrable connection if we interpolate between them the unconscious acts, which we have inferred. A gain in meaning is a perfectly justifiable ground for going beyond the limits of direct experience. When, in addition, it turns out that the assumption of there being an unconscious enables us to construct a successful procedure by which we can exert an effective influence upon the course of conscious processes, this success will have given us an incontrovertible proof of the existence of what we have assumed.'

The psycho-analytic interpretation of neurotic symptoms, of faulty actions, of dreams, is largely purposive and the economic character of psychic processes derives from the application to the psyche of Darwinian teleology. Psychoanalytic interpretation is diametrically and irresolvably opposed to the a-logicality of the processes, which, it is assumed, take place in the unconscious. And so, apart from the censorship between the pre-conscious and the unconscious (see above, pp. 90-1 ff.), a second censorship, that between the pre-conscious and consciousness, was introduced into the (topical) organization of the unconscious. This instance also resembles a purposively directed intelligence, whose task is to separate those ideas capable of being rendered conscious from the repressed ideas, and to do so in accordance with the principles of the psychic economy. It is this instance which makes itself felt in the course of psychoanalytic treatment as a conscious resistance to the emergence of particular contents. As compared to the unconscious and pre-conscious systems, consciousness becomes a mere *symptom*. From this it follows that conscious observation and perception are rendered impotent *vis-à-vis* the complicated hypotheses on the composition and interrelatedness of the unconscious and the pre-conscious, which hypotheses have all been *inferred*.[2]

'The reason for all these difficulties is to be found in the circumstance that the attribute of being conscious, which is the only characteristic of psychical processes that is directly presented to us, is in no way

---

[1] S. Freud, *St. Edn.*, Vol. XIV, p. 167.　　　　[2] *Ibid.*, p. 192.

suited to serve as a criterion for the differentiation of systems. Apart from the fact that the conscious is not always conscious but also at times latent, observation has shown that much that shares the characteristics of the system *Pcs* does not become conscious; and we learn in addition that the act of becoming conscious is attendant on the attention of the *Pcs* being turned in certain directions. Hence consciousness stands in no simple relation either to the different systems or to repression. The truth is that it is not only the psychically repressed that remains alien to consciousness, but also some of the impulses which dominate our ego—something, therefore, that forms the strongest functional antithesis to the repressed. The more we seek to win our way to a metapsychological view of mental life, the more we must learn to emancipate ourselves from the importance of the symptom of "being conscious".'

(e) Logic and A-logic of the Unconscious[1]

The difficulties which arise from this psychoanalytic conception of the unconscious may be summarized as follows: (1) The unconscious is inferred from psychic actions (symptom, dream, faulty action); (2) these actions appear to be a-logical but in fact are seen to be determined within the framework of the unconscious by purposive, rational and economic considerations; (3) from this it follows that the unconscious functions logically and purposively (the 'second intelligence' of the *Studies* 1895). At the same time the unconscious is a-logical (free from contradiction and timeless).

This essential contradiction stems from the dialectics of logic and a-logic. Each of these concepts involves the other. But logic cannot be derived from a-logic, neither can a-logic be derived from logic. All human activity—all psychic actions—are determined by the dialectics of the contrast between logic and a-logic. The whole of Freud's work may be looked upon as an attempt to explain the a-logical in logical terms. His whole system of instances, which mediate between the unconscious and the pre-conscious, was built up as a part of this attempt to present a logical account of what is unconscious and a-logical by means of a gradual process of rationalization. But the true purpose of psychoanalytic therapy, that of rendering unconscious material conscious, is also pursued by logical methods (reason). By his assertion that consciousness is only a symptom (see above) and that the seat of philosophy is to be sought in the vicinity of schizophrenia Freud is questioning his own purpose—even his therapeutic purpose—because by these assertions he in fact capitulates in the final instance to the inexplicability of the a-logical. It is dialectically impossible to deduce

---

[1] See Part Three, p. 504 ff. (The problem of the drives and the will.)

that which is a-logical by logical argument. All such explanations must remain hypothetical. This does not mean to say that the a-logical is not *effective*, as Freud himself has observed. Merely, the question as to *how* it is effective is probably largely unanswerable or, alternatively, necessitates complicated hypotheses, as may be seen from the example of counter-cathexis as applied to repression and substitute formation. Psychoanalytic treatment is the proof of the efficacy of the a-logical, an efficacy which is surely demonstrated by the fact that the patient enters into an inner, dialectical process between a-logical and logical factors, a process which, however, is not of a rational but a 'libidinal' nature. Any attempt to explain it by rational means must necessarily fail.

The *Dynamics of the Personality* may now be summarized as follows: In the early version of psychoanalytic theory (see above, p. 95 ff.) the symptom and the personality had been almost identical concepts. Meanwhile, however, the image of the personality has been complicated by the fact that the symptom is now chiefly considered to constitute a disturbance in the 'equilibrium' of the various forces at work within the personality. Freud tries to describe the historical nature of the personality, its living development, in terms of the libido concepts; this development appears as a sort of rise and fall under pressure, which is liable to be mechanically blocked, twisted or disturbed and which is comparable to the mechanically controlled rise and fall of a column of mercury. But he is constantly obliged to exceed the limits imposed by this concept of a model, since the complex processes of the psyche refuse to be tied down to a rational assessment. This model of human development, conceived as a process taking place within collateral tubular systems, breaks down at the very outset, due to the expansion of the unconscious, the a-logical, (which is to be the dominant theme of the second period of Freud's thought). Thus consciousness is increasingly undermined by the concept of the unconscious, whose expansion takes place to the accompaniment of an incipient mythologization of the drives, which are already being declared transcendent (see above, p. 105). The dynamics of the forces at work within the personality is conceived on the one hand as a dynamics of different drives (i.e. functionally), on the other hand, however, in terms of substance, e.g. (in the case of the ego) in terms of the repression resulting from the act of judgement or self-esteem. The ideal ego is an offshoot of the individual's upbringing that has taken root within the personality. The concept of introjection, of the incorporation into the ego of parental images, gains substance from the presentation of this inner-psychic process. The ideal ego raises the tension between the warring forces by the highly repressive tendencies which it quickly acquires. The unconscious is described for the first time as the 'seat' both of the repressed wishes, thoughts and affects (primal repression, see above p. 125 ff.) and of those forces which are free from contradiction and timeless. The unconscious is a-logical in the fullest sense of the word. It is faced by the pre-conscious, which is screened off from the unconscious and from consciousness by a censor, a 'doorkeeper'. Repression, described both in terms of primal repression and of repression proper, is categorized in detail in the processes of cathexis and counter-cathexis. And so the *Dynamics of the Personality* passes through the three 'stages' of its existence—consciousness, pre-conscious and unconscious—beyond which are the drives, which Freud will shortly be defining as 'mythological powers'.

IV. CULTURE AND REPRESSION

(a) Cultural Morality and Sexuality

In 1908 Freud published his essay on *'Civilized' Sexual Morality and Modern Nervous Illness*, in which he castigated the civilization of his day. He followed *von Ehrenfels* in contrasting the suppression of the instincts and the falseness and hypocrisy, which accompanied it and which were undoubtedly one cause of neurosis, to the 'natural' morals of primitive peoples. He pointed out that monogamy was in fact a dangerous institution because it hindered natural selection and he developed ideas which he had acquired from Darwin and Nietzsche and which were later to be appropriated by National Socialism (!). Although this 'model' conception of Freud's—like all his other theoretical attempts —is restricted to a simplified version of biology and although his primitive people with its 'natural' morals can no more be said to have existed than his primal horde, this investigation of his none the less leads to the heart of Freudian 'philosophy'. It is a conception to which he will return in his later work, *Civilization and its Discontents*. Although he considers that morals have a dangerous and pathogenic influence on drive life, he also holds that the suppression of the drives and the resultant latency periods, which the child passes through prior to puberty, are a prerequisite of culture. Culture itself has a dual nature: it suppresses the drives and exercises a pathogenic effect, but it is this same suppression which promotes its growth. (1) The suppression of the drives and (2) the latency periods (as a biological factor) are followed by (3) the sublimation of the drives as an additional agent in the propagation of culture:[1]

'The development of the sexual instinct then proceeds from auto-erotism to object-love and from the autonomy of the erotogenic zones to their subordination under the primacy of the genitals, which are put at the service of reproduction. During this development a part of the sexual

[1] S. Freud, *St. Edn.*, Vol. IX, pp. 188-9.

excitation which is provided by the subject's own body is inhibited as being unserviceable for the reproductive function and in favourable cases is brought to sublimation. The forces that can be employed for cultural activities are thus to a great extent obtained through the suppression of what are known as the perverse elements of sexual excitation.

'If this evolution of the sexual instinct is borne in mind, three stages of civilization can be distinguished; a first one, in which the sexual instinct may be freely exercised without regard to the aims of reproduction; a second, in which all of the sexual instinct is suppressed except what serves the aims of reproduction; and a third, in which only legitimate reproduction is allowed as a sexual aim. The third stage is reflected in our present-day "civilized" sexual morality.'

Thus, according to Freud, the sexual repression on which culture insists affects a man's whole character: the man who bows to culture, who does not dare to assert his claims on the sexual object—woman—, will be a weak and frightened man in every other department of life as well. The healthy, strong man is identified with 'natural' sexual morality. —The proximity to *Nietzsche* and to *Darwinian* natural selection is pronounced. And this proximity will become even more pronounced in Freud's book, *Totem and Taboo*.

(b) Totem and Taboo

Totem and Taboo represents the phylogenetic parallel to the ontogenetic account of sexuality given in the *Three Essays*. Although the theses which Freud develops here have not been confirmed by the investigations of social psychologists, they are none the less important for our understanding of psychoanalysis. The primal horde—a sort of clan of brothers—is ruled over by the strongest man, who is the father and owner of the women (mothers and daughters). The brothers kill and devour him, in order that they may share the women amongst themselves. Because they feel guilty about the death of the father they arrange a sacrifice in order to atone. The victim then atones for the deed on their behalf and the murdered father is consecrated as a god. He becomes a totem. The women of the clan are pronounced taboo and only women from other tribes may be taken in marriage. The genesis of religion, especially of the Christian and Jewish religions, is to be found in this kind of totemism (Christ's sacrifice on the cross on behalf of mankind; the last supper as a totem meal). The primal horde is superseded by the clan of brothers, the clan of brothers by a matriarchy, the matriarchy by a second patriarchy. The cultural cycle proceeds from revolt against the reality principle (father) to suppression of the pleasure principle (or, alternatively, subjection to the reality principle). With the increasing de-sexualization of the drives within a culture destructive (aggressive) tendencies are released, which may then possibly drive that culture to its own destruction. If a given culture permits a more potent expression of sexuality, then a regression will set in, the effects of which will be inimical to that culture and anarchic. Culture can only assert itself within the field of force set up by the endless conflict between the suppression of the drives and the revolt against the drives, between the Scylla of sexuality and the Charybdis of aggression. In his analysis and criticism of Freud's theory of culture *Marcuse* summarizes Freud's conception of the process involved in the creation of a culture as follows:[1]

'The revolt against the father is a revolt against the biological authority' his murder destroys the order by which the life of the group is vouchsafed· The rebels have committed a crime both against the community and against themselves. They are guilty towards the others and towards themselves and they must atone. Patricide is the greatest crime, for it is the father who has established the order of procreative sexuality, and so the father *is*, in his own person, the type and the genus that creates each living individual and ensures his survival. The composite figure of patriarch, father and tyrant unites sex and order, pleasure and reality, arouses love and hatred and guarantees the biological and sociological foundation on which the history of mankind is built. The elimination of his person threatens to eliminate the life of the group and to re-establish the pleasure principle with its prehistoric and supra-historic powers of destruction. But the sons want to have what the father has; they want lasting satisfaction of their needs. And they can only achieve this goal by the re-institution, in a different form, of the law and order which had controlled and supervised pleasure and thus ensured the survival of the group. The father lives on as a God. In their adoration of the God the sinners repent, in order that they may continue to sin, whilst the new fathers undertake the suppression of pleasure necessary for the continuance of their rule and the organization of their group. The progression from absolute rule to party rule is accompanied by a 'social diffusion' of pleasure and the voluntary acceptance of repression (suppression of pleasure) on the part of the ruling group, the members of which are obliged to conform to the taboos if they wish to retain their power. Suppression now penetrates the life of the suppressors and a proportion of their drive energy is made available for sublimation in the form of "work".'

(c) Freud's Concept of Culture

We have already seen that Freud's concept of culture is on the one

---

[1] Marcuse, *Eros und Kultur*, Stuttgart, 1957, p. 68 f.

hand extremely complex and on the other hand extremely simplified. It is complex in that biological considerations—selection, struggle for existence—are combined with problems of authority, of order imposed by 'strength', work and achievement. It is simplified in that these concepts are then subsumed under the further concept of the 'necessities of life' or the reality principle. But the chief factor in the creation of culture is phantasy, and phantasy—with all that it implies—entirely escaped Freud, as has been pointed out by *Marcuse*. The purely negative assessment of work as a 'necessary evil' in the sense of suppression of the pleasure principle by reality is characteristic of an epoch of growing industrialization, in which only working capital was able to satisfy the requirements of pleasure. Freud underestimated the cultural importance of the satisfaction derived from achievement and from the skill which this involves. But quite apart from this, questions of 'strength', of authority, of the institution of a social order, of the establishment of power and supremacy, involve a multitude of problems, which have yet to be settled and of which all that can be said with certainty is that at different times they have been solved in different ways by different cultures and peoples. This has been revealed above all by the investigations carried out during the past twenty to thirty years by the psychoanalytically trained ethnologists—*Malinovski, Kardiner, Linton, Mead, Levi-Strauss, inter alia.*

For example, as far as the thesis of patricide in the primal horde is concerned, Levi-Strauss has described in his reports the harmonious and orderly communal life led by the (last) Indian tribes in Brazil, and this despite the fact that the women were in a minority and were, moreover, the exclusive property of the chief of the tribe. The derivation of feelings of guilt from aggression or, alternatively, from the patricide arising out of the aggression, would appear to be particularly problematical. It is difficult to see how and why a specific feeling, such as a feeling of guilt, a *consciousness* of guilt, should arise in consequence of aggression, since the consciousness of guilt and the fear of punishment, although related, are by no means one and the same. The guilt is a separate thing from the fear of punishment, which might well have been introjected into the hypothetical brothers in the course of their upbringing. And a feeling of guilt, in the sense of a specific consciousness of guilt, would appear to be a human attribute, the psychological source of which is not readily discernible. Whether the conditions appertaining to certain species of wild animal and the fighting in which their rivalry involves them may be transferred to man, even to prehistoric man, is questionable. In this field hypotheses may be bold, for they have a free rein. Certainly there is no proof as yet that animals are capable of feelings of guilt. Freud's prehistoric man combines traits of animal rivalry with the model ideas of the primary process and the pleasure principle. If, like Freud, we consider the drives to be a blind force, then the question as to whether order and guilt can grow from drive activity must surely be answered in the negative. This does not preclude the possibility that in the animal world instinct and order will be very closely related. What it does mean, however, is that the animal instinct would appear to be differently constituted, or that now, after the waning of the Darwinian era, it is seen against a different background (see Part Three). Freud's pessimistic and negativist interpretation of culture—mid-way between sexuality and destruction—may reasonably be looked upon as illuminating *one* aspect of culture, but in no sense can it be said to afford an adequate 'explanation' of its multifarious and contrasting institutions or of its spiritual and artistic achievements. Quite apart from this, however, Freud fails to contrast culture with civilization, and civilization would have been more suited to the task of representing repressive and suppressive tendencies. For all of these reasons the arguments which Freud advanced in his dispute with Adler are *not* very convincing:[1]

'... in a discussion at the Vienna Society, he[2] said: "If you ask where repression comes from, you are told, 'from civilization'; but if you go on to ask, where civilization comes from, you are told, 'from repression'. So you see it is all simply playing with words." A tithe of the acuteness and ingenuity with which Adler has unmasked the defensive devices of the "nervous character" would have been enough to show him the way out of this pettifogging argument. What is meant is simply that civilization is based on the repressions effected by former generations, and that each fresh generation is required to maintain this civilization by effecting the same repressions. I once heard of a child who thought people were laughing at him, and began to cry, because when he asked where eggs come from he was told "from hens", and when he went on to ask where hens come from he was told "from eggs". But they were not playing with words; on the contrary, they were telling him the truth.'

In point of fact, the truth of the matter is that the act of repression and thus culture are specifically human attributes, which cannot be derived either from hypothetical stages in man's evolution from the animal world[3] or from the antithesis between the 'necessities' of life and the primary process. Man and his culture have always *co-existed*,

[1] S. Freud, *St. Edn.*, Vol. XIV, p. 56.
[2] The reference is to Adler (cf. *St. Edn.*, Vol. XIV, p. 56).
[3] Freud's conception is basically Darwinian: certain apes abandoned their life in the trees, then established culture by discovering fire.

as have culture and 'repression'—they are simultaneous phenomena and not derivatives of one another. Although this is not what Adler was getting at, his 'pettifogging' argument none the less went to the heart of the matter and was by no means invalidated by Freud's reference to the chicken and the egg. The child rightly felt that it had been fobbed off, because it had not been told about the simultaneity of the chicken and the egg, which are interdependent, just as repression and culture are interdependent.

V. PHANTASY AND DREAM

(a) Phantasy

Freud was quick to recognize (in his correspondence with W. Fliess, see p. 71 ff.) the importance of phantasy as a compensation for repressed wishes. Only an unsatisfied person will indulge in phantasies, seeking in his day-dreams and his castles in the air the satisfaction denied him by reality or by the structure of his personality—e.g. by an over-developed ideal ego. Phantasy enables the pleasure principle, which had reigned supreme in the autoerotic stage of infancy, to continue its reign. Dreams too are highly organized and stratified events, in which repressed wishes are very seldom expressed as wishes. Freud describes the relationship of phantasy to *time* as follows:[1]

'The relation of a phantasy to time is in general very important. We may say that it hovers, as it were, between three times—the three moments of time which our ideation involves. Mental work is linked to some current impression, some provoking occasion in the present which has been able to arouse one of the subject's major wishes. From there it harks back to a memory of an earlier experience (usually an infantile one) in which this wish was fulfilled; and it now creates a situation relating to the future which represents a fulfilment of the wish. What it thus creates is a day-dream of phantasy, which carries about it traces of its origin from the occasions which provoked it and from the memory. Thus past, present and future are strung together, as it were, on the thread of the wish that runs through them.'

Within the psychoanalytic system phantasy enjoys an exceptional position, since it is able to give direct expression to repressed material. Why this 'outlet' in the libido economy of the personality should not in itself prove adequate to the task of raising repressed material into consciousness, thus rendering further suppression and the dynamics between the conscious and the unconscious mind largely superfluous, is

[1] S. Freud, *St. Edn.*, Vol. IX, pp. 147-8.

a question which Freud has failed to pose. For him phantasy remains a marginal phenomenon, a psychopathological symptom; he failed to see the creative force of phantasy as a cultural factor. And so, in his investigations into art and artists such as Leonardo, Michelangelo and Dostoievsky, he endeavoured to trace important works by these artists back to the activation of infantile phantasies by actual experiences (see especially *Creative Writers and Day-Dreaming*).

(b) Dreams

The *Interpretation of Dreams*, Freud's most comprehensive and complete work, remained virtually unchanged—apart from a few minor additions to the text—in the course of the twenty years of psychoanalytic development which followed its publication. Not until 1916—16 years after *The Interpretation of Dreams* was written—did Freud attempt a more precise formulation of dream processes in terms of the libido economy. In this respect his short essay 'A Metapsychological Supplement to the Theory of Dreams' is one of his most profound statements on the interpretation of dreams. Taking the narcissism of sleep (see above, p. 116 ff.) as his point of departure, the characteristic of which is the withdrawal by the ego of its (energy) cathexes, he asked himself how this withdrawal of cathexes could be reconciled with the formation of dreams, with the dream work. Part of the function of dreams is that they serve the desire for sleep. External and internal stimuli, which might possibly disturb sleep, are transformed by dreams in an hallucinatory manner and thus make it possible for sleep to continue undisturbed (e.g. a falling object is incorporated into the action of the dream and thus prevented from waking the sleeper). But where does the dream get its energy from, if in sleep this energy is completely withdrawn into the ego (narcissism)?

The situation is only rendered plausible if both the drives and the repressed ideas, the so-called remnants of the day, around which the dream crystallizes, retain a part of their energy instead of surrendering it all to the ego. Thus the narcissism of sleep is not absolute but is penetrated by the dream.[1]

'The wish to sleep endeavours to draw in all the cathexes sent out by the ego and to establish an absolute narcissism. This can only partly succeed, for what is repressed in the system *Ucs* does not obey the wish to sleep. A part of the anticathexes has therefore to be maintained, and the censorship between the *Ucs* and the *Pcs* must remain, even if not at its full length. So far as the dominance of the ego extends, all the

[1] S. Freud, *St. Edn.*, Vol. XIV, p. 225.

systems are emptied of cathexes. The stronger the *Ucs* instinctual cathexes are, the more unstable is sleep.'

The dream wish arises in connection with the remnants of the day stored in the pre-conscious, but it receives its energy from the unconscious. This energy, which is invested in the dream, is awaiting discharge. Normally it would obtrude into consciousness, but that would mean waking the sleeper, and consequently this path is denied to it, as also is discharge through motor activity. On the contrary, the energy flows in the opposite direction, away from consciousness and towards the unconscious, i.e. it *regresses*. Freud calls this regression *topical regression*, because energy flows from one system (the pre-conscious) to another (the unconscious). He differentiates between topical regression and temporal regression, i.e. regression arising out of living development, in which, for example, sexual energy flows back from the genital phase to the anal phase. In the *Interpretation of Dreams* Freud had already described regression as a process, in which thoughts are converted into images or word presentations into object presentations (see above, p. 91 ff.). He considers the difference between dreams and schizophrenia to be as follows:[1]

'Let us, furthermore, bear in mind the great practical importance of distinguishing perceptions from ideas, however intensely recalled. Our whole relation to the external world, to reality, depends on our ability to do so. We have put forward the fiction that we did not always possess this ability and that at the beginning of our mental life we did in fact hallucinate the satisfying object when we felt the need for it. But in such a situation satisfaction did not occur, and this failure must very soon have moved us to create some contrivance with the help of which it was possible to distinguish such wishful perceptions from a real fulfilment and to avoid them for the future. In other words, we gave up hallucinatory satisfaction of our wishes at a very early period and set up a kind of "reality-testing".'

Reality differs from hallucination in that, whereas the latter consists of an energy cathexis of consciousness by internal stimuli, the former can only be perceived through an action (motor activity) or disposed of through the elimination of perception (e.g. by closing one's eyes), as when an infant kicks off its blankets in order to be free or counters the oppressive stimulus of the light by closing its eyes. On the one hand this reality test is tied to consciousness, on the other hand it constitutes one of the most important functions of the ego (see above, p. 118 ff.). Now, in the dream, which serves the desire for sleep (see above), the reality

[1] S. Freud, *St. Edn.*, Vol. XIV, p. 231.

test that is linked with consciousness is eliminated or, in other words, sleep withdraws the cathexis from the 'Cs system'.

But the state of hallucinatory confusion which obtains in psychosis is such that the ego is too shattered to carry out the reality test—and here we may note a further connection between dreams and psychosis. The simple thesis of energy withdrawal from the 'Cs system' and the elimination of the reality test which this involves appears upon reflection to be an over-simplification of what are in all probability highly complex processes. The central question—see above—as to *how* the dream becomes conscious, despite the fact that it moves in the opposite direction to regression, has only been apparently solved. For although all the attributes of reality—colours, noises, tactile stimuli, heat and cold— are present in dreams and are *felt to be real*, the consciousness of a dreaming person is none the less different from that of a waking person. But for Freud there is no difference between the consciousness of dreams and the consciousness of waking life. Both are identical with the 'Cs system'. Although the dreamer is lying in bed and asleep, in his dream he experiences himself as active: walking, swimming or climbing. Now if reality is held to consist of a profusion of the most diverse qualitative perceptions and of the individual person's reactions to those perceptions (motor activity), then such attributes of reality are all contained in dreams. The criterion of the 'reality test', the ability to eliminate real-life phenomena or to cause them to disappear, is also fulfilled in dreams, when, for example, the dreamer has the experience of turning away from something or of causing something which is actively unpleasant to disappear.[1] From this it follows that the Freudian definition of reality testing is incapable of clarifying the difference between reality as experienced in dreams and reality as experienced in waking life. It neither takes into consideration the considerable difference between dream consciousness and waking consciousness nor does it adequately illumine the nature of dream reality for the dreamer or the nature of reality testing itself. But these fundamental objections do not reduce the importance of the 'Metapsychological Supplement to the Theory of Dreams' as a contribution within the framework of psychoanalytic theory. In it Freud has attempted to expand the reality principle in terms of the libido economy and to shed light on the relationship between dreams and psychosis from new angles—those of the libido economy.

VI. THE PROBLEM OF ANXIETY

The nomination of the ego as the 'seat of anxiety' constituted the chief further contribution to the problem of anxiety between 1900 and 1920.

---

[1] Cf. below *P. Federn's* investigations (p. 235 ff.).

Anxiety may be compared to the signal which warns the ego of impending danger. By comparison with real anxiety, i.e. anxiety felt in the face of danger in real life, neurotic anxiety takes the form of a reaction to inner libido. A child, who realizes with a sudden shock that it has mistaken a strange woman for its mother, feels the onrush of surplus libido which should have signified its filial longing in the form of anxiety. The ego is threatened from within both by surplus libido, i.e. libido which has not been discharged, and by aggressions, in much the same way as it might be threatened from without by the dangers of real life. To both of these threats it reacts with anxiety, the anxiety appearing as a transformed and undischarged affect. The transformation of affects was a central concept in Freud's early theory of anxiety, especially in his toxological theory, according to which anxiety arose from pent-up sexual substances. Freud based his thesis of the transformation of affects on the observation of conditions of hysterical anxiety, in which anxiety replaced other reactions, such as anger, shame or embarrassment. The obsessional neuroses function in a similar manner: the numerous symptoms associated with these neuroses develop in place of anxiety, but anxiety immediately takes over if the symptom—e.g. a compulsive action—fails to assert itself. Thus, both in respect of obsessional neurosis and hysterical anxiety conditions, it may be inferred that anxiety either replaces another affect or that it can be 'restricted' to symptoms. The phobias, in which by definition anxiety appears only in specific situations, are related to obsessional neurosis in as far as they attempt to restrict anxiety:[1]

'In phobias, for instance, two phases of the neurotic process can be clearly distinguished. The first is concerned with repression and the changing of libido into anxiety, which is then bound to an external danger. The second consists in the erection of all the precautions and guarantees by means of which any contact can be avoided with this danger, treated as it is like an external thing. Repression corresponds to an attempt at flight by the ego from libido which is felt as a danger. A phobia may be compared to an entrenchment against an external danger which now represents the dreaded libido. The weakness of the defensive system in phobias lies, of course, in the fact that the fortress which has been so greatly strengthened towards the outside remains assailable from within. A projection outwards of the danger of libido can never succeed thoroughly. For that reason, in other neuroses other systems of defence are in use against the possible generation of anxiety.'

Despite these clear-cut theses Freud conceded the following weakness in his theory of anxiety:[2]

[1] S. Freud, St. Edn., Vol. XVI, p. 410.   [2] Ibid., p. 405.

'The anxiety which signifies a flight of the ego from its libido is after all supposed to be derived from that libido itself. This is obscure and it reminds us not to forget that after all a person's libido is fundamentally something of his and cannot be contrasted with him as something external. It is the topographical dynamics of the generation of anxiety which are still obscure to us—the question of what mental energies are produced in that process and from what mental systems they derive.'

VII. FEMININE SEXUALITY

In Freud's psychoanalysis woman is man deprived. In the last decade of the nineteenth century and the early years of the twentieth century Freud's chief concern was to furnish an explanation of male sexuality and of the psychopathology of men, but in *The Interpretation of Dreams*, as also in the *Three Essays*, he began to sketch out the framework of a psychology of women. Then, in the case history of an hysteric ('Dora, Fragments from the Analysis of a Case of Hysteria'), the observation of female sexuality became the focal point of Freud's investigations over a limited period of time. In the phase of infantile sexuality little girls do not differ from little boys. Their autoerotic and masturbatory behaviour is largely analogous. Freud writes:[1]

'So far as the autoerotic and masturbatory manifestations of sexuality are concerned, we might lay it down that the sexuality of little girls is of a wholly masculine character. Indeed, if we were able to give a more definite connotation to the concepts of "masculine" and "feminine", it would even be possible to maintain that libido is invariably and necessarily of a masculine nature, whether it occurs in men or in women and irrespectively of whether its object is a man or a woman.'

In the phallic phase, however, whereas the little boy discovers the erotogenic zone of the penis and above all of the glans, the little girl's first experience of sexual excitation comes from the clitoris. In this phase the boy passes through the 'positive' Oedipus complex, the girl through its 'negative' counterpart. She desires her father and tries to displace her mother ('Electra Complex'). In the case of the little boy this phase is often terminated by the 'castration complex', whilst in the case of the little girl the comparison which she makes between herself and the little boy leads to the development of so-called penis envy, a complex of central importance to the understanding of the female psyche and one whose existence can scarcely be denied. It is true that for purposes of masturbation the clitoris is as effective as the penis, but it is the size of

[1] S. Freud, *St. Edn.*, Vol. VII, p. 219.

the penis which produces envy and jealousy in the girl. These may develop into driving forces in the character of the grown woman—ego reactions—e.g. in the woman, whose adult life is stamped by activities of a particularly ambitious and often intellectual order. According to Freud the struggle for emancipation, the growing independence of women and their desire to get on equal terms with men all ultimately derive from penis envy. On the other hand, however, penis envy can be translated—with the aid of dolls—into a love of children, which achieves full fruition in motherhood. First the doll, then the child serves to compensate the woman for the anatomical deficiency which may otherwise develop into a character defect. But basically a woman is a castrated man, to whom in the final analysis a child is only a partial compensation for her lack of a penis.

Freud summarizes the development of female sexuality in puberty as follows:[1]

'If we are to understand how a little girl turns into a woman, we must follow the further vicissitudes of this excitability of the clitoris. Puberty, which brings about so great an accession of libido in boys, is marked in girls by a fresh wave of *repression*, in which it is precisely clitoridal sexuality that is affected. What is thus overtaken by repression is a piece of masculine sexuality. The intensification of the brake upon sexuality brought about by pubertal repression in women serves as a stimulus to the libido in men and causes an increase of its activity. Along with this heightening of libido there is also an increase of sexual over-valuation which only emerges in full force in relation to a woman who holds herself back and who denies her sexuality. When at last the sexual act is permitted and the clitoris itself becomes excited, it still retains a function: the task, namely, of transmitting the excitation to the adjacent female sexual parts, just as—to use a simile—pine shavings can be kindled in order to set a log of harder wood on fire. Before this transference can be effected, a certain interval of time must often elapse, during which the young woman is anaesthetic. This anaesthesia may become permanent if the clitoridal zone refuses to abandon its excitability, an event for which the way is prepared precisely by an extensive activity of that zone in childhood.'

VIII. SUMMARY

The chief characteristic of the first phase of Freudian theory (see p. 71 ff.) was its close dependence on the mechanical model of the 'psychic apparatus', on which the topography, economy and dynamics of the

[1] S. Freud, *St. Edn.*, Vol. VII, p. 220.

psyche were based. The symptom and the personality were derived from similar topical, economic and dynamic points of view, from which it followed that they were almost identical. The characteristic of the second phase is the rejection to a considerable extent of the mechanical model, this being replaced by the concept of the libido economy, whilst at the same time an attempt is made to describe psychic activity largely in terms of the libido economy. The static, anatomical conception of the first phase is superseded by an energic conception. The dynamics of the drives—the libido economy—is the dominant factor in psychic processes. The personality is assessed from a historical perspective, even though the assessment is made in the terms of the mechanistic sciences. The second phase of psychoanalytic theory constitutes an advance over the first phase in that it continues the development of certain viewpoints already present in latent form (especially in the correspondence with W. Fliess) and introduces other entirely new viewpoints. These we may summarize as follows:

1. Topography:
   The topography of the personality is still organized under the three categories: unconscious, pre-conscious and conscious. But now two censors are introduced: between the unconscious and the pre-conscious and between the pre-conscious and conscious (see p. 129 ff.).
2. Dynamics:
   The dynamics of the processes taking place between consciousness and the unconscious are re-stated in terms of cathexis and counter-cathexis (see p. 125 ff.).
3. The dynamics of the personality (pleasure displeasure) undergoes a considerable transformation due to the introduction of the reality principle, as a result of which the pleasure principle can no longer be represented as the sole determinant of psychic activity (see p. 117 ff.).
4. Repression is conceived as a process within the libido, as the resultant of two interacting drives (see p. 114 ff.).
5. The ego is defined (functionalized) as a drive (self-preservation drive), although this definition is subject to constant modification (see p. 125 ff.). The evaluating, criticizing instance within the ego, the conscience, is called the ideal ego (see p. 122 ff.).
6. The drives, like the unconscious, are transcendent, even though Freud continues to postulate a somatic origin for them.
7. The decisive influence of infantile sexuality—the historical nature of the personality—on the subsequent development of the individual and of his psychic disturbances is now recognized.
8. Observations on the psychopathology of the individual person are transferred (phylogenetically) to the history of mankind. Culture is

conceived as the resultant of the pleasure and reality principles, but is interpreted primarily in a negative sense as the suppression of drives (see p. 133 ff.).

C

FROM PERSONALITY TO MYTHOLOGY

I. THE DEATH DRIVE (AGGRESSION)

(a) The Derivation of the Death Drive

If the sexual drive is the chief characteristic of the first phase of psychoanalytic theory, the self-preservation drive that of the second, then the death drive is the hallmark of the third phase (1923–1939). Freud gives three reasons for introducing the death drive:

1. The compulsive repetition which he had observed in neurotics suggested to him that psychic activity involved factors, which—even after the introduction of the reality principle—could not be regulated by the pleasure/displeasure principle. What did he understand under compulsive repetition? He employed this concept to describe, for example, the regular recurrence in the dreams of accident or pension neurotics of traumas, in which their lives were threatened. If, for example, a man had been knocked down by a motor car, the accident might well reappear in great detail in his dreams years after the event. Factors such as this were not easily reconciled with the concept of the regulation of psychic processes by pleasure and displeasure and of the repression of predominantly displeasurable experiences. Furthermore, the urge to repeat unpleasant childhood situations could be observed in the patient's transference to his physician and these could not be explained simply by positing the existence of an unconscious desire for punishment.

2. The shattering experiences of the First World War had again impressed on Freud the importance of aggression, whose function he had already more or less established in his correspondence with W. Fliess. But at that time the importance of aggression had not yet been appreciated or investigated; in sadism and masochism it was held to be a subsidiary component of the sexual drive. But the fearful destruction wrought by the Great War impressed on Freud the need to consider aggression as a drive in its own right, i.e. as a destructive drive. But how were destruction and compulsive repetition to be reconciled with man's apparently over-riding desire for pleasure, with his 'libido economy'?

3. At this point Freud had recourse to the biological-physical ideas

which he had already sketched out twenty-five years before in his 'Project'. He considered that life originated in a simple vesicle, which was helplessly exposed to environmental stimuli until eventually it was so 'burnt up'[1] by those stimuli that it formed a protective layer. This protective layer was inorganic, it was living substance which had 'died off' in the struggle with the environmental stimuli and thus offered protection from those stimuli. The ability of the living substance to assert itself *vis-à-vis* its environment, to preserve itself, was ultimately determined by the property of the protoplasm, of the living substance, which enabled it to form an inorganic protective layer by 'dying off', as a result of which life might be preserved. From this it follows that the self-preservation drives (the ego drives) are of a *conservative nature*; in the process in which the protective layer was formed they represent the original condition which prevailed before life ever existed—the condition of *death*. The speculative derivation of the self-preservation drives from stimulus protection is expanded by Freud into the thesis that all living phenomena are subject to the desire to return to an earlier inorganic condition which existed before the development of organic life. All drives—apart from the sexual drive—are endowed with a conservative character, or, in Freud's own words:[2]

'*It seems then that an instinct is an urge inherent in organic life to restore an earlier state of things* which the living entity has been obliged to abandon under the pressure of external disturbing forces; that is, it is a kind of organic elasticity, or, to put it another way, the expression of the inertia inherent in organic life.'

This drive, which he calls the death drive, Freud considers to be operative both in the compulsive repetition of the neurotic and also in aggression. Aggression (which transforms living substance into dead substance by means of destruction), sadism and masochism are all subject to the death drive. Seen in this light life appears as an ultimately absurd detour leading to death. 'The goal of all life is death.'[3] Freud, who was himself perhaps not entirely convinced by the hypothesis of stimulus protection and ego development, tried to strengthen his argument regarding the conservative nature of the drives by reference to ontogenesis, the repetition of phylogenesis in embryo development, as also by reference to specific, apparently conservative migratory drives amongst certain classes of fish and birds. The fact of phylogenesis, the multiplicity of classes and species that has been perpetuated throughout the millennia, is traced back 'to external disturbing and diverting

---

[1] S. Freud, *St. Edn.*, Vol. XVIII, p. 27.   [2] *Ibid.*, p. 36.
[3] *Ibid.*, p. 38.

influences'.[1] The sexual drives are now contrasted to the death drives. The former are supposed to organize the living (hypothetical) elementary organisms, which are still helplessly exposed to external stimuli, into larger units, which can then offer a concerted defence against the onslaught of the outside world. But these sexual drives are also conservative (!),[2] 'in that they bring back earlier states of living substance; but they are conservative to a higher degree in that they are peculiarly resistant to external influences; and they are conservative in another sense also, in that they preserve life itself for a comparatively long period'. What is not clear, however, is just how these drives, which are also conservative, counteract the death drives and assume responsibility for the development of life. Freud sought support for his thesis in the work of *Weismann*, who divided the germ-cell plasma into a mortal and an immortal substance. And so, in formulating his hypothesis of the death drive, Freud had recourse to biological theories which were already thirty years old. Apart from Weismann, he also drew on the Cosmos literature, which had been popular at the turn of the century, and on the theories of *Lipschütz*, *Bölsche*, *Doflein* inter alia. After investigating these biological theories of the turn of the century Freud came to the conclusion that they were certainly not opposed to his assumption of a death drive and that to some extent they even supported it, since individuals were either destroyed by the products of their own metabolism or were rejuvenated by copulation. But in order to establish the derivation of the sexual drives, which on the one hand are conservative but on the other hand preserve life, he is obliged to turn to Plato:[3]

'Shall we follow the hint given us by the poet-philosopher, and venture upon the hypothesis that living substance at the time of its coming to life was torn apart into small particles, which have ever since endeavoured to reunite through the sexual instincts? that these instincts, in which the chemical affinity of inanimate matter persisted, gradually succeeded, as they developed through the kingdom of the protista, in overcoming the difficulties put in the way of that endeavour by an environment charged with dangerous stimuli—stimuli which compelled them to form a protective cortical layer? that these splintered fragments of living substance in this way attained a multicellular condition and finally transferred the instinct for reuniting, in the most highly concentrated form, to the germ-cells?—But here, I think, the moment has come for breaking off.'

[1] S. Freud, *St. Edn.*, Vol. XVIII, p. 38.   [2] *Ibid.*, p. 40.
[3] *Ibid.*, p. 58.

The conclusion which Freud finally drew was that the libidinal sexual and death drives originally existed in a state of fusion and must in some way or other have been present in this state in the first elementary being. For psychology this involves the assumption of an original and thus ultimate union of aggression and libido—of Eros and Thanatos.

(b) *Viewpoints Common to Both the Last and the First Phase of Psychoanalytic Theory*

The common ground in Freudian theory between Freud's last period and the theses formulated in the 'nineties, especially those set out in the *Project*, may be summarized as follows:

1. In the *Project* the biological and psychic processes are subject to the 'principle of inertia' (see p. 79 ff.), which is identical with the assumption of a death drive and with the 'Nirvana principle'.

2. Pleasure and displeasure are reactions to external and internal stimuli, they are subject to the principle of inertia, in as far as displeasure is superseded by pleasure, which in its turn is superseded by repose ('relaxation'). In other words: life is a detour leading to death.

3. The derivation of the secondary process from the primary process (see p. 79 ff.) and the need for a third neuronic system corresponds to the idea of a helpless vesicle exposed to stimuli (primary process), which then forms a protective layer (secondary process), which in its turn forms the basis of the ego (third neuronic system).

II. THE DEATH DRIVE AND THE TOPOGRAPHY OF THE PERSONALITY

(a) *Ego-Ideal, Identification and Aggression*

The ego ideal had already been described in the metapsychological investigations undertaken before the First World War as a criticizing and observing instance within the ego which is subject to educational influences. In his investigation into *Group Psychology and the Analysis of the Ego* Freud considers the importance of this process chiefly in terms of group formations. Just as a person under hypnosis will blindly follow the hypnotist and a person in love the loved one, so the group will blindly follow its leader. What is common to all three processes is that the object (the hypnotist, the loved one, the leader) has taken the place of the ego ideal. Both the group and the person in love have identified with the love object. The Oedipus complex is based on just such a process of identification, for the little boy identifies with his father, admires him and emulates him. But there are two different forms of this process: (1) *the objective choice of the father* and (2) *the (subjective) identification with the father*. In the first case the father

149

is chosen as an object, the child would like to possess him or, in the language of the oral phase, to eat him. In the second case the little boy would like to *be* like his father. In both cases the ego ideal is superimposed on to the process of identification, in the first case as an object to be introjected or incorporated, in the second as a model worthy of emulation. *But even in its original form identification or introjection is ambivalent:* the desire to eat someone may be prompted by tender feelings or by hostile feelings. In other words, death drive and libido (tenderness = libido: to eat someone up = destruction) were indissolubly united from the outset and the original structure of man was *ambivalent* or dualistic. The most basic form of objective identification (the desire to possess somebody) or of subjective identification (the desire to be like somebody) is repeated in the formation of every community, when the leader of the community is set up as an ego ideal or *super ego*. As a component part of the ego the ego ideal (super ego) is now able to enter into many different types of relationship with the ego. The investigation of these different forms of relationship is the task of ego analysis. If, for example, 'something in the ego'[1] coincides with the ego ideal, the result is a feeling of triumph; but if the relationship between these two is one of tension, then a feeling of guilt or even inferiority may develop. The process of identification apart, Freud has attempted a more detailed account of the development of the super ego from the ego in *The Ego and the Id*. It has been pointed out (p. 120 ff.) that the relationship between the ego and character formation is of the order of a reaction to repressed material. The super ego develops out of the ego in a similar manner, namely, as a reaction to the father:[2] 'You may not be like this (like your father)—that is, you may not do all that he does.' Thus the super ego is also dualistically structured, as Freud himself states:[3]

'This double aspect of the ego ideal derives from the fact that the ego ideal had the task of repressing the Oedipus complex; indeed, it is to that revolutionary event that it owes its existence. Clearly the repression of the Oedipus complex was no easy task. The child's parents, and especially his father, were perceived as the obstacle to a realization of his Oedipus wishes; so his infantile ego fortified itself for the carrying out of the repression by erecting this same obstacle within itself. It borrowed strength to do this, so to speak, from the father, and this loan was an extraordinarily momentous act. The super-ego retains the character of the father, while the more powerful the Oedipus complex was and the more rapidly it succumbed to repression (under the influence of

[1] S. Freud, *St. Edn.*, Vol. XVIII, p. 131.   [2] *Ibid.*, Vol. XIX, p. 34 f.
[3] *Ibid.*, p. 34 f.

authority, religious teaching, schooling and reading), the stricter will be the domination of the super-ego over the ego later on—in the form of conscience or perhaps of an unconscious sense of guilt.'

The severity of the super ego, its despotic and destructive power, which, in the case of obsessional neurosis for example, it unleashes on to the ego, derives from aggression, from the death drive. The introduction of the death drive was the last critical step in the topical organization of the personality; henceforth the structure of the personality was to be determined by the interaction of both destructive and libidinal components.

(b) Extension of the Oedipus Complex

Besides the introduction of aggression as a component part of the structure of the personality ego analysis made another important discovery, that of the double Oedipus complex. On the one hand the little boy would like to appear in his mother's eyes like his father, on the other hand he is quite capable of expressing tender and devoted feelings for his father, just as if he were a little girl; in the second of these two conditions he identifies with his mother. The same holds true for the little girl, who is not only able to identify with her father, thus revealing the normal Oedipus complex of the little boy, but would also dearly like to play her mother's part *vis-à-vis* her father. Freud bases the double Oedipus complex not only on his observations of neuroses but also—and predominantly—on the assumption, founded on biological evidence, of human bisexuality. In the final analysis it is human bisexuality which enables the Oedipus complex to fulfil its dual function. This thesis is one which first arose at Fliess' instigation but, although Freud had constant recourse to it, it was not until twenty-five years later that he gave it definitive expression in the formulation of the double Oedipus complex. The importance of the double Oedipus complex for the ego is to be found in the ego's identifications with the parents; the history of these identifications is crystallized in the attitude of the ego. A gentle, submissive father, elevated for purposes of identification, will also cause his son to appear in a passive and submissive light. And if the son should identify with his masculine and active mother, then his ego will be stamped by this process in a similar manner.

(c) The Dependence of the Ego. The 'Id'

The introduction of the death drive and of aggression, the differentiation between ego and super ego and the formulation of the double Oedipus complex could scarcely fail to influence the position of the ego. In the last phase of Freudian theory the ego does, it is true, display rather more of an autonomous character, one that recalls the first phase of psycho-analytic theory, but at the same time its dependence on other instances is very much more marked. The degree of autonomy which Freud permits the ego largely appertains to the exercise of repression, which is now once again interpreted in terms analogous to those of the early definitions (see p. 55 ff.):[1]

'We have formed the idea that in each individual there is a coherent organization of mental processes; and we call this his *ego*. It is to this ego that consciousness is attached; the ego controls the approaches to motility—that is, to the discharge of excitations into the external world; it is the mental agency which supervises all its own constituent processes, and which goes to sleep at night, though even then it exercises the censorship on dreams. From this ego proceed the repressions, too, by means of which it is sought to exclude certain trends in the mind not merely from consciousness but also from other forms of effectiveness and activity.'

However, the autonomy thus accorded to the ego is cancelled out again for all practical purposes by the recognition that *large sections of the ego may also be unconscious*. The existence of unconscious guilt feelings and the observation of processes in the unconscious analogous to repression prompted Freud to extend the concept of the ego into the unconscious sphere. But important parts of the super ego were also said to be unconscious, a statement likewise based on the observation of instances exercising unconscious criticism and producing guilt feelings. *With these theses Freud radically exceeds the limits of the earlier topography of Ucs, Pcs and Cs.* Consciousness remains an epiphenomenon, having been designated by Freud as such in his earlier investigation of the 'Unconscious', and its functions are restricted to perception and motility (movement). The unconscious, as always the seat of the drives and of all repressed material, is established, as in earlier formulations (see p. 70 ff.), as the domain of the pleasure principle; in genetic terms it is identical with the primary process. What is new in this phase is Freud's designation of the unconscious as the *id*, a concept which he now adopts—via *Groddeck*—from *Nietzsche*. The equation of the unconscious with the id constitutes an attempt on the one hand to objectivize the unconscious and on the other to invest it with the physical necessity, the driving, forceful character with which Groddeck (and before him Nietzsche) had stamped this new expression. Both the ego and the super ego are rooted in the id, or rather they are superimposed on to it in much the same way as Freud imagines the development of

[1] S. Freud, *St. Edn.*, Vol. XIX, p. 17.

the single-celled, helpless, original vesicle into a vesicle provided with a cortical layer, with a 'stimulus screen'. His perception of the unconscious sections of the ego and the super ego was the cause of his radically new topography of id, ego and super ego. He represents the topography of the personality in this phase of his theory by the following graph;[1]

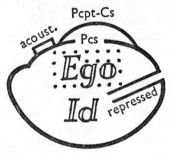

Freud describes the role of the ego in this connection as follows:[2]

'It is easy to see that the ego is that part of the id which has been modified by the direct influence of the external world through the medium of the Pcpt. Cs.; in a sense it is an extension of the surface differentiation. Moreover, the ego seeks to bring the influence of the external world to bear upon the id and its tendencies, and endeavours to substitute the reality principle for the pleasure principle which reigns unrestrictedly in the id. For the ego, perception plays the part which in the id falls to instinct. The ego represents what may be called reason and common sense, in contrast to the id, which contains the passions. All this falls into line with popular distinctions which we are all familiar with; at the same time, however, it is only to be regarded as holding good on the average or "ideally".

'The functional importance of the ego is manifested in the fact that normally control over the approaches to motility devolves upon it. Thus in its relation to the id it is like a man on horseback, who has to hold in check the superior strength of the horse; with this difference, that the rider tries to do so with his own strength while the ego uses borrowed forces. The analogy may be carried a little further. Often a rider, if he is not to be parted from the horse, is obliged to guide it where it wants to go; so in the same way the ego is in the habit of transforming the id's will into action as if it were its own.'

Freud assumes that the development of the ego from the id, which is graphically represented in his vesicle images, takes place in the same

---

[1] S. Freud, *St. Edn.*, Vol. XIX, p. 24. [2] *Ibid.*, p. 25.

way as the differentiation between object and word presentation (see above, p. 125 ff.). Conscious thought and thus the ego derive from bits of memory of things heard, from word presentations, which are without question of the order of perception. Nothing can become conscious, nothing can be *thought*, unless it has previously been perceived or heard in some form or other—this corresponds in the above diagram to the ('acoustic') ear on the surface of the ego. *Nihil est in intellectu, quod non fuerit in sensu* is a central concept of sensualism which Freud surely confirms. Compared with the Platonic horseman the ego appears to be largely autonomous; in actual fact, however, it is a shuttlecock for the opposing forces by which it is flanked, i.e. the id and the super ego. Both are essentially unconscious, but the super ego, which derives from the Oedipus complex, and thus from the initial object cathexis of the id, is much closer to the id than is the ego. In obsessional neurosis, in melancholia and in other afflictions of psychic life the super ego sub-jugates the ego quite mercilessly, tormenting it with reproaches to its conscience, demonstrating to it—in melancholia—the utter senselessness of its existence. In these illnesses the super ego represents for the ego the aggressive, sadistic impulses of the id, of the death drive; *it is the representative of the death drive.*[1]

'What is now holding sway in the super-ego is, as it were, a pure culture of the death instinct, and in fact it often enough succeeds in driving the ego into death, if the latter does not fend off its tyrant in time by the change round into mania.'

The helplessness of the ego, faced on the one hand with the punitive impulses of the super ego, which are supposed to derive in direct line from the id, and on the other hand with the drive impulses of the id, is described by Freud as follows:

'Helpless in both directions, the ego defends itself vainly, alike against the instigations of the murderous id and against the reproaches of the punishing conscience. It succeeds in holding in check at least the most brutal actions of both sides; the first outcome is interminable self-torment, and eventually there follows a systematic torturing of the object, in so far as it is within reach.'[2]

'From the other point of view, however, we see this same ego as a poor creature owing service to three masters and consequently menaced by three dangers: from the external world, from the libido of the id, and from the severity of the super-ego. Three kinds of anxiety correspond

[1] S. Freud, *St. Edn.*, Vol. XIX, p. 53. [2] *Ibid.*, p. 53.

to these three dangers, since anxiety is the expression of a retreat from danger. As a frontier-creature, the ego tries to mediate between the world and the id, to make the id pliable to the world and, by means of its muscular activity, to make the world fall in love with the wishes of the id. In point of fact it behaves like the physician during an analytic treatment: it offers itself, with the attention it pays to the real world, as a libidinal object to the id, and aims at attaching the id's libido to itself. It is not only a helper to the id; it is also a submissive slave who courts his master's love. Whenever possible, it tries to remain on good terms with the id; it clothes the id's *Ucs* commands with its *Pcs* rationalizations; it pretends that the id is showing obedience to the admonitions of reality, even when in fact it is remaining obstinate and unyielding; it disguises the id's conflicts with reality and, if possible, its conflicts with the super-ego too. In its position mid-way between the id and reality, it only too often yields to the temptation to become sycophantic, opportunist and lying, like a politician who sees the truth but wants to keep his place in popular favour.

'Towards the two classes of instincts the ego's attitude is not impartial. Through its work of identification and sublimation it gives the death instincts in the id assistance in gaining control over the libido, but in so doing it runs the risk of becoming the object of the death instincts and of itself perishing. In order to be able to help in this way it has had itself to become filled with libido; it thus itself becomes the representative of Eros and thenceforward desires to live and to be loved.

'But since the ego's work of sublimation results in a defusion of the instincts and a liberation of the aggressive instincts in the super-ego, its struggle against the libido exposes it to the danger of maltreatment and death. In suffering under the attacks of the super-ego or perhaps even succumbing to them, the ego is meeting with a fate like that of the protista which are destroyed by the products of decomposition that they themselves have created. From the economic point of view the morality that functions in the super-ego seems to be a similar product of decomposition.'[1]

Freud casts light on the sadistic nature of morality and of moralists (e.g. Calvin, Robespierre) with his observation that a man's ability to control his external aggression is often in direct proportion to the reinforcement of his inner aggressiveness (the aggressiveness of his super ego towards his ego).

The fundamental difference between the conception of id, ego and super ego and all previous attempts to develop a topography of the personality may be summarized as follows:

[1] S. Freud, *St. Edn.*, Vol. XIX, p. 56.

1. The previous organization of the personality in terms of unconscious, pre-conscious and consciousness is now replaced by an organization in terms of id, ego and super ego; in this new organization, however, *all* parts of the personality are predominantly unconscious and constantly interact within the unconscious.

2. With the introduction of the death drive (aggression) into intra-psychic conflicts it was possible to establish the extraordinary importance of self-aggression on the one hand and the relationship between aggression and guilt feelings on the other.

3. The personality—like nature and life—is conceived as a battlefield for the two types of drive, libido (eros) and death drive (thanatos).

III. FURTHER CONSEQUENCES OF THE INTRODUCTION OF THE DEATH DRIVE

If we disregard the hypothetical derivation of the death drive, the recognition of aggression as such remains a factor of the greatest importance for psychology and psychopathology. We have already indicated above in the passages dealing with the scope of the ego the connection which exists between aggression and religious and moral problems on the one hand and between aggression and illness on the other. The thesis of the fusion of drives sheds light both on the destructive nature of certain moral ideas and on the masochism of those who submit to them. Both self-inflicted aggression and aggression against others are accompanied by an erotic desire, one which is demonstrably present in masochism, where the aggressive, sadistic super ego turns on the passive ego, which seeks satisfaction in suffering. The masochism which Freud in his second phase had conceived as a secondary, reactive phenomenon arising out of an unconscious desire for punishment he now identifies with the death drive within the organism.[1]

'If one is prepared to overlook a little inexactitude, it may be said that the death instinct which is operative in the organism—primal sadism—is identical with masochism. After the main portion of it has been transposed outwards on to objects, there remains inside, as a residuum of it, the erotogenic masochism proper, which on the one hand has become a component of the libido and, on the other, still has the self as its object. This masochism would thus be evidence of, and a reminder from, the phase of development in which the coalescence, which is so important for life, between the death instinct and Eros took place. We shall not be surprised to hear that in certain circumstances the sadism, or instinct of destruction, which has been directed outwards, projected, can be once more introjected, turned inwards, and in this way regress to its

[1] S. Freud, *St. Edn.*, Vol. XIX, p. 164.

earlier situation. If this happens, a secondary masochism is produced, which is added to the original masochism.'

But even Freud's philosophy of culture reveals—in his last three psychological investigations of culture: *The Future of an Illusion, Civilization and its Discontents* and his book on *Moses*—the marked influence of the death drive (or aggression).

If sexual repression was the dominant theme of Freud's psychological contributions to culture in his earlier phases, then the need to suppress aggression was surely the dominant theme of the last. Man's longing for happiness, which, according to Freud, can only be satisfied by the fulfilment of a childhood wish, is opposed by his urge to destroy: the discrepancy between these two tendencies forms the basis of *Civilization and its Discontents*. If culture is to be maintained, not only sexuality but also aggression must be repressed. The failure to suppress aggression is illustrated both by wars and by the sadistic, aggressive impulses which are unleashed in times of social change or social decadence. The fact that aggression was indissolubly linked with guilt feelings did not, in Freud's view, constitute the sole importance of aggression for the development of the individual. Statements, which in the second phase of psychoanalytic theory would have been quite unjustifiable, were now justified by the dynamics of aggression, guilt feeling and super ego: for example, the statement that the son of a gentle and passive father was just as likely to develop an aggressive super ego as was the son of a tyrannical father. For the child who is the object of love finds no outlet for its aggression and is obliged to turn it inwards upon itself.[1] This discovery was a momentous one, involving, as it did, a departure from the environment and trauma theories which until then had dominated psychoanalysis. Assuming approximately equivalent behaviour on the part of children from two different home environments, the children from both environments might well develop the same rigid and aggressive super ego, despite the fact that in the one environment the children were pampered, whilst in the other they were subjected to suppression and denial. Whereas previously it had been considered axiomatic that there was a direct parallel between a child's development and the number of denials which it had experienced, now the whole concept of parallelism was being questioned. This made it extremely difficult, indeed wellnigh impossible, to foresee the future course of any development, since the child's reaction, which is composed of an as yet indeterminable number of determinants, had now become an imponderable. But, as might have been expected, in his philosophical investigations into culture Freud did not depart

[1] S. Freud, *St. Edn.*, Vol. XXI, pp. 130 ff.

from the formulae of his *Totem and Taboo* and was still adhering to the hypotheses, which he had advanced in this work, in his last book on Moses. Chief amongst them is the hypothesis of the derivation of guilt feelings from the fear of both external and (subsequently) internal authority. His rejection of any form of *Weltanschauung*, which he often stressed (particularly in his critical analysis of Marxism), did not prevent him from propagating his own *Weltanschauung*. He used the arguments which he had formulated in the *Future of an Illusion* as psychological data (e.g. atheism) with which to destroy each and every *Weltanschauung*. And the vacuum thus created was filled, not so much by nihilism, as by that strange, positivistic mythology of drives which was the hallmark of Freud's last phase.

IV. REPRESSION, ANXIETY AND SYMPTOM IN THE LAST PHASE
OF FREUDIAN THEORY

(a) *The Development of the Concept of Repression, 1892–1932*

1. In the phase of psychoanalytic theory extending from 1892 to 1900 repression is conceived as follows:

(i) The process of repression is both exclusively pathogenic and *conscious*; unpleasant ideas are excluded from the 'interchange of associations' (1892).

(ii) Repression can also take place *unconsciously* (1896).

(iii) Repressed material consists of unpleasant memories (ideas) which are linked to sexual experiences (1894–1895).

(iv) In a more mature person repression only takes place when the memory of a childhood trauma is triggered off by a related experience.

(v) Repressed material exercises a pathogenic effect (1894–1895).

(vi) The repressed idea does *not* have to be a painful idea. An idea which originally afforded pleasure may afterwards afford displeasure due to subsequent environmental influences and may then be repressed (see also p. 68 ff.) (1896).

(vii) Repression and defence are identical.

(viii) The repressed material appears in the symptom. The symptom is the outcome of the repression. It is also a compromise between the forces of repression (ego) and the repressed material.

(ix) The affect is split off from the idea by repression.

2. The phase between 1900 and 1920.

(i) Repression is not necessarily a pathogenic process. It is also the basis for the development of normal psychic life.

(ii) The difference between primal repression and repression proper is established. Both are processes of repression, the former from the pre-conscious to the unconscious, the latter from consciousness to the pre-conscious.

(iii)   It is not only ideas which are repressed but also *affects*.

(iv)   Repression is a conflict of drives, i.e. a conflict between the self-preservation drives and sexuality (reality principle and pleasure principle). It is a process within the libido.

(v)   Repression is described in terms of the Quantum theory and of cathexis and counter-cathexis. If the cathexis is withdrawn from an object, repression takes place.

(vi)   Repression and defence are no longer identical. The former can take place only after the separation of conscious and unconscious material. Defence processes, however, can take place before this differentiation is made. Repression is now one of the possible forms of defence against the drives or against unpleasant ideas.

(vii)   In more mature persons repression is replaced by the conscious rejection of a given idea.

3.   The phase between 1920 and 1932.

(i)   Whereas in the two preceding phases anxiety was considered to be the result of repression (cf. p. 141 ff.), now *repression is considered to be the result of anxiety*. Anxiety is the sign of displeasure given by the ego in the face of external danger (actual fear) or internal danger (onrush of drives), as a result of which repression is instituted (1926: *Inhibition, Symptom, Anxiety*).

(ii)   Repression and defence are again used synonymously. Repression is one of the ego's defence mechanisms, which it establishes after the initial differentiation between feelings of pleasure and displeasure has taken place. Another defence mechanism is that of undoing or of isolation, as found in obsessional neurosis. Yet another is reaction formation (1926).

(iii)   The final changes in the concept of repression were made in 1932. The ego perceives a drive, indulges in phantasies relating to the satisfaction of that drive, recalls the danger associated with such satisfaction, and then proceeds to repress both drive and associated idea. The reappearance of early theses (1892) concerning the function of the ego and of repression is quite evident (see p. 52 ff.).

(iv)   1939 (*Moses*) Freud sums up:[1]

'In the case of the individual we believe we can see clearly. The memory-trace of his early experience has been preserved in him, but in a special psychological condition. The individual may be said to have known it always, just as one knows about the repressed. Here we have found ideas,

[1] S. Freud, *St. Edn.*, Vol. XXIII, pp. 94–5.

which can be confirmed without difficulty through analysis, of how something can be forgotten and how it can then reappear after a while. What is forgotten is not extinguished but only "repressed"; its memory-traces are present in all their freshness, but isolated by "anti-cathexes". They cannot enter into communication with other intellectual processes; they are unconscious—inaccessible to consciousness. It may also be that certain portions of the repressed, having evaded the process (of repression), remain accessible to memory and occasionally emerge into consciousness; but even so they are isolated, like foreign bodies out of connection with the rest. It may be so, but it need not be so; repression may also be complete, and it is with that alternative that we shall deal in what follows.

'The repressed retains its upward urge, its effort to force its way to consciousness. It achieves its aim under three conditions: (1) if the strength of the anti-cathexis is diminished by pathological processes which overtake the other part (of the mind), what we call the ego, or by a different distribution of the cathectic energies in that ego, as happens regularly in the state of sleep; (2) if the instinctual elements attaching to the repressed receive a special reinforcement (of which the best example is the processes during puberty); (3) and if at any time in recent experience impressions or experiences occur which resemble the repressed so closely that they are able to awaken it. In the last case the recent experience is reinforced by the latent energy of the repressed, and the repressed comes into operation behind the recent experience and with its help. In none of these three alternatives does what has hitherto been repressed enter consciousness smoothly and unaltered; it must always put up with distortions which testify to the influence of the resistance (not entirely overcome) arising from the anti-cathexis, or to the modifying influence of the recent experience or to both.'

(b) The Transformation of the Concept of Anxiety

The decisive changes which Freud made in his concept of anxiety during his last phase (in 1926 and 1932) in fact constituted a complete reversal of his previous ideas. Although previously anxiety had been described as an 'ego signal' (1917) (see p. 141 ff.), it had none the less occurred as a *consequence of repression*: the ego had reacted in terms of anxiety to an onrush of libido or of external danger. Now, however, repression followed anxiety, was a consequence of anxiety. The phobia of the small boy, a case history to which Freud constantly refers, was interpreted in the earlier phase in terms of a reaction to libidinal tenderness *or* aggression towards the father. This libido had been suppressed and had thus produced anxiety. The horse phobia, in which the horse was a substitute for the father, enabled the little boy to live with his father *without* fearing him. Thus the symptom—the horse phobia—served a double purpose in that (1) it restricted anxiety to an actual confrontation with the horse, (2) it repressed anxiety *vis-à-vis* the father. Over and above this the symptom effected a compromise between the self-preservation drive and the libido or, alternatively, between the ego and the id, since it limited anxiety to specific and rare situations, thus ensuring a high degree of ego autonomy. Now in the last phase (see above) the little boy's phobia is considered exclusively from the point of view of the Castration complex. It is the fear of castration—the fear of the father—which leads to the repression of libidinal and aggressive impulses. This fear is then aroused in the little boy at the sight of a horse, which serves as a substitute for the father.

(c) The Relationship between Symptom and Inhibition

In the development of the phobia the ego has, as it were, left one sphere open, a sphere in which it is powerless. This sphere is in fact the symptom, which Freud now also describes as an inhibition: the ego is now restricted or inhibited at a given point in its function of regulating the libido economy. The concept of the symptom is based on the compromise between the ego and the unconscious, whereas the concept of inhibition is centred around the ego and the limitations imposed on the ego by the neurosis. The ego may subject itself to inhibitions, in order to avoid conflict with the unconscious: e.g. in hysterical paralysis, which is caused by the repression of an affect directed against a parent and in which the ego suffers the paralysis as a means of evading a further conflict of drives. The ego may also avoid a conflict with the super ego by subjecting itself to inhibitions—e.g. an unsuccessful career—in the cause of self-chastisement. Whereas in the earlier phases of Freudian theory the transformation of affects had been both an extremely important and a highly problematical concept, it now disappeared entirely from this new version of the anxiety problem. Whereas previously Freud had been obliged to consider the fate of those impulses, which were activated in the unconscious and subsequently repressed and which in their turn had posed the further problem as to how the objective of a drive impulse, namely pleasure, could be transformed into anxiety, now the whole problem was dropped following the assumption of an unconscious sector in the ego. The ego was now in a position to suppress a drive impulse (to which it had previously reacted in terms of anxiety) whilst that impulse was still in the unconscious, i.e. in *statu nascendi*, and thus to prevent it from taking shape at all. This assumption constituted the second new and important thesis concerning the emergence of anxiety, the first being the reversal of the previous relationship between anxiety and repression.

V. THE DISSOLUTION OF THE OEDIPUS COMPLEX

Apart from the important discovery of the double Oedipus complex in men and women Freud's last phase also produced several no less important theses on the 'dissolution' of the Oedipus complex.

The Oedipus complex in the boy is brought to an end by the threat of castration, no matter what the source of this threat may be. In the normal Oedipus complex—the little boy's identification with his father—the penis is directly involved. In the inverted Oedipus complex—identification with the mother—the mother's lack of a penis implies the assumption of castration. The fear of castration initiates the formation of the super ego, the introjection of parental figures into the child's ego. This is the second stage of the dissolution of the Oedipus complex. After the threat of castration has been initiated the super ego is established in the ego as the 'heir of the Oedipus complex'. This development is only partially shared by the little girl. In her capacity as a 'little boy who has received short measure' she is also exposed to the threat of castration, which she relates to the clitoris. But then she would appear to accept castration, to make her peace with it, as a result of which, and in contrast to the little boy, if often happens that the little girl's super ego is not established. This means that the little girl, unlike the little boy, fails to resolve the Oedipus complex and remains in the Oedipal phase—with its concomitant father fixation—for a much longer period of time.

VI. PSYCHOANALYTIC THERAPY FROM 1895 TO 1938 (WITH PARTICULAR REFERENCE TO TRANSFERENCE)

It is noteworthy that the therapeutic method employed in psychoanalysis has not changed significantly since it was first developed from hypnosis (see p. 62 ff.). It is restricted to the development of free association, to dream analysis and the analysis of transferences and resistances. Freud had already fully acknowledged the importance of transference in his *Studies*, whilst in his *Recollecting, Repeating, Working Through* he defines it as the real 'battlefield' of analytic treatment. In his work on *The Dynamics of Transference* (1912) Freud differentiates for the first time between positive transference, in which the patient's affection and need for love are projected on to the physician, and negative transference, which is the expression of belligerent tendencies originating in the patient's attitude towards his parents. Both forms of transference may be exploited by resistances in order to hinder the progress of the analysis; in a positive transference the patient's infatuation may have the effect of diverting his attention from the therapy and directing it exclusively on to the physician, whilst in a negative transference aggressive and belligerent impulses may inhibit the development of associations and quite conceivably wreck the analysis. Both in the negative and the positive transference the patient *acts out* childhood experiences and re-enacts them by projecting them on to the physician. Thus, since the transference gives direct expression to the neurotic symptoms, the way in which it is handled by the physician is a factor of paramount importance for the success of the analysis. *Recollecting, Repeating, Working Through* are the key words for the effective resolution of a transference, for although the patient may remember his childhood experiences, he may also act them out *without remembering them*, thus living out his neurotic tendencies, which then have to be consciously worked through by therapist and patient. The difficult problem which is posed when, in the course of transference, the patient falls in love with the physician, as may easily happen in the case of a female patient, is dealt with by Freud in his work, *Observations on Transference Love* (1915). He comes to the conclusion that falling in love in the course of transference is not so very different from falling in love in the normal way. He writes:[1]

'Transference love has perhaps a degree less of freedom than the love which appears in ordinary life and is called normal; it displays its dependence on the infantile pattern more clearly and is less adaptable and capable of modification; but that is all and not what is essential.

'By what other signs can the genuineness of a love be recognized? By its efficacy, its serviceability in achieving the aim of love? In this respect transference love seems to be second to none; one has the impression that one could obtain anything from it.

'Let us sum up, therefore. We have no right to dispute that the state of being in love which makes its appearance in the course of analytic treatment has the character of a "genuine" love. If it seems so lacking in normality, this is sufficiently explained by the fact that being in love in ordinary life, outside analysis, is also more similar to abnormal than to normal mental phenomena. Nevertheless, transference-love is characterized by certain features, which ensure it a special position. In the first place, it is provoked by the analytic situation: secondly, it is greatly intensified by the resistance, which dominates the situation; and thirdly, it is lacking to a high degree in a regard for reality, is less sensible, less concerned about consequences and more blind in its valuation of the loved person than we are prepared to admit in the case of normal love. We should not forget, however, that these departures from the norm constitute precisely what is essential about being in love.'

He describes the task with which the analyst is here faced as follows:[2]

[1] S. Freud, *St. Edn.*, Vol. XII, pp. 168-9.   [2] *Ibid.*, p. 170.

'And yet it is quite out of the question for the analyst to give way. However highly he may prize love he must prize even more highly the opportunity for helping his patient over a decisive stage in her life. She has to learn from him to overcome the pleasure principle, to give up a satisfaction which lies to hand but is socially not acceptable, in favour of a more distant one, which is perhaps altogether uncertain, but which is both psychologically and socially unimpeachable. To achieve this overcoming, she has to be led through the primal period of her mental development and on that path she has to acquire the extra piece of mental freedom which distinguishes conscious mental activity—in the systematic sense—from unconscious.

'The analytic psychotherapist thus has a threefold battle to wage—in his own mind against the forces which seek to drag him down from the analytic level; outside the analysis, against opponents who dispute the importance he attaches to the sexual instinctual forces and hinder him from making use of them in his scientific technique; and inside the analysis, against his patients, who at first behave like opponents but later on reveal the overvaluation of sexual life which dominates them, and who try to make him captive to their socially untamed passion.'

In his last work on the technique of therapy, *Analysis, Terminable or Interminable* (1937), he asks whether a neurosis can in fact be said to be curable. In the same work he also carries out a detailed investigation into the importance of the counter-transference, i.e. the physician's transference to the patient (on which *Ferenczi* had laid great stress), assessing it in terms of the influence it might have on the patient's chances of cure. But the discrepancy between the pleasure-seeking and ultimately insatiable drives on the one hand and the largely dependent and feeble ego on the other makes a cure in the sense of a single, definitive event appear dubious. The 'constitutional strength of the drives' and the 'unfavourable alteration of the ego acquired in its defensive struggle in the sense of its being dislocated and restricted'[1] are limiting factors opposing a permanent cure. By contrast the prognosis for neuroses which arise in connection with a trauma or a chance incident is far more favourable. Freud considers that in such cases analysis should be entirely successful. This particular work of Freud's contains several noteworthy formulations which shed new light on the part played by the ego in analytic therapy. He considers the analytic cure to lie—almost in the sense of Greek (Platonic) philosophy—in 'the taming of the drives', in their integration into the 'harmony of the ego'.[2] He defines the achievement of analytic therapy as follows:[3]

[1] S. Freud, *St. Edn.*, Vol. XXIII, p. 221.   [2] *Ibid.*, p. 225.
[3] *Ibid.*, p. 227.

'Analysis, however, enables the ego, which has attained greater maturity and strength, to undertake a revision of these old repressions; a few are demolished, while others are recognized but constructed afresh out of more solid material. These new dams are of quite a different degree of firmness from the earlier ones; we may be confident that they will not give way so easily before a rising flood of instinctual strength. Thus the real achievement of analytic therapy would be the subsequent correction of the original process of repression, a correction which puts an end to the dominance of the quantitative factor.'

The changes, which take place in the ego and which, if they are profound, cast doubt on the therapeutic prognosis, assume tangible shape in the defence processes instituted by the ego. These include—and by now Freud is able to refer to the book by *Anna Freud, The Ego and the Mechanisms of Defence*—not only repression but also identification, regression, projection and resistance. These 'defence mechanisms' are developed by the ego in its struggle against displeasure and anxiety and assume tangible shape in the actual therapy, in the transference. The outcome of the analysis depends principally on 'the strength and on the depth of root of these resistances that bring about an alteration of the ego.'[1] But a factor of extraordinary importance for psychoanalytic ego therapy is Freud's statement that the ego is furnished *from the outset* 'with individual dispositions and trends'.[2]

What he is in fact postulating here—and this despite the fact that the ego is developed from the id—is the primary autonomy of the ego; and logically this must lead to a relativization of the *topical* differentiation between the ego and the id.[3] But this idea, in which Freud questions the validity of his own findings on the ego and the id, is one which he does not pursue further (see below, p. 217 ff.; H. Hartmann).

In Freud's view the final obstacle in the path of analytic treatment is the death drive or destructive drive, to whose intractable activities he was obliged on more than one occasion to attribute the breakdown of an analysis. He associates himself with Empedocles, whose world consisted of love and discord (hate), and thus with the (ultimately irrational) mythology of drives,[4] which was the delta into which his work flowed from its distant source in the mechanistic conceptions of the turn of the century:[4]

'The theory of the instincts is, so to say, our mythology. Instincts are mythical entities, magnificent in their indefiniteness. In our work we cannot for a moment disregard them, yet we are never sure that we are seeing them clearly.'

[1] S. Freud, *St. Edn.*, Vol. XXIII, p. 240. [2] *Ibid.*, p. 240.
[3] See especially Part Three, p. 511 ff.
[4] S. Freud, *St. Edn.*, Vol. XXII, p. 95.

2

THE FREUDIAN SCHOOL

The Freudians dealt with in this chapter should not be regarded as a homogeneous group for they differ from one another in many respects in their interpretation of psychic activity. The issues over which Melanie Klein, Franz Alexander, Wilhelm Reich, Paul Federn and Theodor Reik departed from orthodox Freudian theory were not only minor ones, including, as they did, questions of fundamental importance (see below). The reasons why these authors have none the less been listed as disciples of Freud are (1) none of them made a complete break with Freudian theory, as (to a large extent) did the Neo-Freudians and C. G. Jung; (2) the great majority of these authors continued to adhere to the following Freudian theses: (a) to the libido theory; (b) to the development, structure (theory of instances) and dynamics of the personality as formulated by Freud (see especially *The Ego and the Id*); (c) to the topography and dynamics of the conscious and the unconscious mind, to the concepts of cathexis and counter-cathexis and to Freud's theory of drives and affects.

A

KARL ABRAHAM

Abraham's most important contributions to depth psychology may be categorized as follows:

(a) Contributions to libido development.
(b) Contributions to character formation and character development.
(c) Contributions to the psychopathology of manic-depressives and of psychotics.
(d) Psychopathological and clinical contributions on various subjects, for example, on the Castration complex in Females, Hysterical Dream Phantasies and Ejaculatio Praecox.

His studies of myths and dreams, his historical and literary investigations of Segantini and Amenhotep IV should also be mentioned, although we shall not be enquiring into them here.

(a) Contributions to Libido Development

In the light of his interpretation of (a) the attitude, (b) the dreams and (c) the associations of manic-depressive patients Abraham broke down the three stages of libido development (see Freud, p. 106 ff.) into more precise sub-divisions, which he condensed into the following schema:[1]

Stages of libidinal Organization	Stages of Object-love	
VI. Final Genital Stage	Object-love	(Post-ambivalent)
V. Earlier Genital Stage (phallic)	Object-love with exclusion of genitals	
IV. Later Anal-Sadistic Stage	Partial love	
III. Earlier Anal-Sadistic Stage	Partial love with incorporation	Ambivalent
II. Later Oral Stage (cannibalistic)	Narcissism (total incorporation of object)	
I. Earlier Oral Stage (sucking)	Auto-erotism (without object)	(Pre-ambivalent)

In this schema sexual development is considered from two points of view, that of the sexual aim (action) and that of the sexual object. The earliest stage, in which the infant sucks at its mother's breast, is characterized by pure autoerotism and by the absence of any form of object orientation. The baby is quite unable to differentiate between itself and the outside world—i.e. the breast. Not until it enters the narcissistic phase, which is characterized by total or partial incorporation of the object (the mother's breast), are the drives subjected to their first inhibitions, which may already assume the proportions of a pathogenic anxiety. This stage presupposes an initial separation between the child and its environment. The child's attitude is no longer exclusively auto-erotic and the child is able to differentiate between itself and the mother's breast. The *cannibalistic* stage may be observed in those babies who bite their mother's breast and do not want to let go of it. They are then punished by their mother and develop guilt feelings. Through these guilt feelings they overcome their desire to bite (the cannibalistic phase) and enter the *anal-sadistic* stage. This is characterized by the partial incorporation of the object. What Abraham understands under partial incorporation of the object is that the child has an ambivalent attitude towards the love object, irrespective of whether this object is part of its own body (autoerotic: penis or excrement) or part of its environment (e.g. its mother's breast). This ambivalent attitude, which

[1] Karl Abraham, *Selected Papers on Psychoanalysis* (Ed. by Ernest Jones) Hogarth Press, London, 1949, p. 496.

167

requires that the love object be incorporated and rejected at one and the same time, remains with the child until it reaches the fourth stage. Only with the gradual development of guilt feelings in the second stage (cannibalism, see above), of loathing and compassion in the third stage and, finally, of shame in the fourth stage of its sexual development does the child reach the point where, in the fifth and six stages, it is able to overcome the ambivalence which had marked the earlier stages. In the third stage the child displays for the first time its loathing and repugnance for—*inter alia*—its own excrement, which it now begins to detest, whilst at the same time it develops compassion both for itself and its environment. The third stage is also characterized by the desire to *retain* possession of the excrement, in contrast to the second stage, which was dominated by hostile tendencies directed towards the total destruction of the excretia. Abraham attempts to demonstrate the sequence of these stages chiefly by reference to depressive patients. Linking his observations with *Freud's* interpretation of depression (melancholia)—to which Abraham had made a significant contribution— he describes the regression of the patient's libido into progressively earlier stages of development. The loss of the love object which in a normal person results in grief—e.g. when a loved one dies or goes away —will prompt a melancholic to draw the lost object into his own ego, to incorporate it into himself. The libido intended for the environment is withdrawn in a narcissistic manner and the object, which was first lost and then incorporated, is cathected with it. At the same time there is a total regression of libido to the pre-ambivalent stage, in which the child sucked at its mother's breast. In the manic condition the love object is expelled—in accordance with the above-mentioned stages and by analogy with the child's expulsion of excrement—, whereby libido is freed and consequently able to cathect environmental objects, a process in which it invariably overshoots the mark. In the final analysis Abraham considers the rhythmical alternation between the depressive and the manic conditions to derive from the reciprocating rhythm of intake (incorporation) and expulsion. Whilst it is in the nature of melancholics to devour the love object—in this they may be compared to primitive peoples partaking of totem meals (Roheim[1]: *Nach dem Tode des Vaters*)—, the obsessional neurotic constantly opposes his desire for total incorporation of the object. This difference in attitude towards incorporation is one of the factors contributing towards the marked division that exists between depressive and obsessional patients, although it should be born in mind that the harmful experiences to which the obsessional neurotic is subjected are to be found above all in the third and fourth stages of libido development.

[1] G. Roheim, 'Nach dem Tode des Vaters' in *Imago*, Vol. XIII, 1927.

(b) Contributions to Character Development

Like *Freud*, who attempted to present scientific character traits as reactions to drives, Abraham illustrated the 'oral', 'anal' and 'genital' character by reference to clinical material drawn from a wide field of characterological research.

He describes a female patient, the middle child in a family of three, who, having been brought up in difficult conditions, had been taught that cleanliness was obligatory. She developed into a perfect model of cleanliness, punctuality and propriety. She was also humble and obedient. But later, as an adult, she was engaged in a constant battle with her own desire to revolt, and so she found herself poised between a conscious desire to sacrifice herself for others and an unconscious desire for revenge and rebellion. Her mother had impressed the need for cleanliness on her by engendering in her a fear of dirt, instead of letting her come to appreciate and accept cleanliness for its own sake. In this way it is of course possible to postulate many more such anal character traits (over and above the three put forward by Freud—love of order, meanness and defiance), which traits would then constitute patterns of reaction to environmental influences exercised in the anal phase. In the case of this particular patient the reaction consisted of a *need for cleanliness coupled with ambivalence between rebellion and submission*. Apart from the positive aspects of its dealings with its excrement—the pleasure of achievement, the pleasure derived from the actual process of excreting the faeces—the child also learns to obey and by its obedience ('giving up its faeces') to gain parental favour. Neurotic problems, in which the fear of loss of love plays a central part, are rooted in the anal phase with its central theme of obedience or rebellion (defiance). But persons who lack initiative, who tend to take the path of least resistance or to make up for a lack of sexual fertility or sexual activity with gifts of money (patronage) are also suffering from an anal fixation. Those with a passion for collecting, an inordinate desire to possess people or objects, would seem to indicate that as children they are loath to part from their faeces. But there are also people whose characters are such that they display a marked preference for doing the opposite of what is required of them. Idiosyncrasies of this order may also be explained in terms of possible disturbances in the anal phase.

The oral phase of libido development, although it is even less differentiated than the anal phase, also has a far-reaching effect on character formation. The oral elements of sexuality are of course less inhibited by environmental pressures than are the anal-sadistic or genital sections of the libido. The oral pleasures—eating and drinking—are encouraged and cultivated in a large number of different cultures. Character formation can only be influenced by really serious disturbances of the oral phase, such as might be caused by extreme hunger or extreme fastidiousness. Hunger might cause the child to start biting prematurely, a development which would favour the sadistic elements in character formation. Oral fastidiousness would encourage tendencies which would make it difficult for the child at a later stage of its life to suffer demands and deprivations. Disturbances of the oral phase often appear during the weaning period. The self-denial which the child must learn to accept, especially if it sees that a younger brother or sister is still being suckled, forms the basis of later jealousy. Fastidiousness in the oral phase is one of the underlying causes of the characteristics displayed by a certain type of neurotic, who is full of unbounded optimism and firmly convinced that he will always be successful and that everything 'will be all right'. This optimism can assume such proportions that the individual concerned labours under the delusion that, no matter where he goes, he will always find somebody—a mother substitute—who will look after him. By contrast it is hunger, together with other oral denials, which sets its stamp on the future pessimist, a person who is imbued with a profound scepticism with regard to his own achievements or one who 'grasps' hungrily at all that life has to offer. The generous 'givers' of this world identify with the all-providing mother, they enjoy being generous and make frequent donations to charity. The tensions which exist between giving and taking and which appear to assume importance only in the anal phase in fact derive from the oral phase.

In the genital phase the individual is at pains to overcome all trace of the earlier stages. Over and above this, however, a considerable structural influence is exercised by the Oedipus and Castration complexes. The final form taken by the individual's character will depend on the way in which he assimilates the Oedipus complex. His ability to transfer, in an appropriate form, the feelings of affection or hostility which he entertains towards his parents on to his environment will determine his subsequent adaptation to society. This conception raises the question as to what constitutes a normal character, a question to which Abraham fails to provide a clear answer. The essence of Abraham's argument is contained in the thesis in which he graphically describes the way in which particular character traits develop and interact throughout the sequence of stages. In this connection character traits and symptoms cannot be differentiated from one another, since both arise as a compromise between wish and reality, i.e. between the pleasure principle and the reality principle. And so—by summation—a person's 'character' might be defined as the sum-total of his symptoms.

(c) Contributions to the Psychopathology of Manic-depressives (and of Psychotics)

In the foreword to the English edition of Abraham's writings Ernest Jones states that these contributions were obscured by Freud's investigations into *Mourning and Melancholia*, even though these two works were written at very nearly the same time and quite independently of one another. At a later date Abraham adapted and elaborated the nucleus of these contributions in his work on the development of the libido (see above, p. 166 ff.) and so we need not deal with them here. But an earlier work of Abraham's on the clinical aspects of hysteria and schizophrenia (dementia praecox), which he composed within the framework of his activities at the Bleuler Institute, contained those important references which were to stimulate Freud to advance his theory of narcissism, namely, the references to the inability of schizophrenics to effect a transference or to sublimate. He listed numerous features that were common to both schizophrenic and hysterical patients, features which related not only to their symptoms but also to their life history. Abraham attributes particular importance to the regression to autoerotic stages which the schizophrenic (and also the melancholic) undergoes. In order to formulate the difference between hysteria and schizophrenia in analytically precise terms he is obliged to emphasize the (allegedly) much deeper origins of the autoerotic tendencies in schizophrenics.

(d) Psychopathological and Clinical Contributions

Abraham made a detailed investigation of the problem of ejaculatio praecox. The cause of this disturbance is to be found in the maldevelopment of urethral (pre-phallic) sexuality. As an expression of his narcissism this type of patient tends to over-value the penis as an excretory organ (urination) and, for purposes of exhibitionism, he would (unconsciously) dearly like to urinate in the presence of a woman. But since he knows that the woman would probably despise him if he were to indulge in such activities, he develops feelings of aggression and sadism towards the woman. Because of these aggressive impulses he then fears that he might really harm the woman; and this leads to ejaculatio praecox: due to a premature but unconsciously intentional pollution the penis has to be quickly withdrawn or, alternatively, cannot even be inserted. Denials of love encountered by the child in its relationship to its mother and the hostility which these produce are the chief factors involved in fixation to the urethral stage. Ejaculatio praecox observed the following sequence:

1. Fixation to the urethral phase: urination.
2. Exhibitionist desire to urinate in the presence of the woman.

3. Suppression of this desire and reaction formation.
4. Development of sadistic impulses *vis à vis* the woman, because the exhibitionism had to be suppressed.
5. Sadistic impulses produce the fear that coitus might be harmful to the woman.
6. These impulses are again repressed and lead to
7. Ejaculatio Praecox.

In another important work Abraham deals with the female castration complex. In this work he defines two types of women who, although strictly speaking inseparable, none the less represent the two reaction patterns of women to the discovery of castration made in childhood, as opposed to the reaction patterns of men. One type *identifies* with the man and would like to adopt the positive masculine features, e.g. masculine activity and leadership. The other type would like to *revenge herself* on the man for the castration that has been inflicted on her. With the latter type of woman, phantasies in which she cuts or bites off the penis, predominate. The frigidity, which occurs with both types, is interpreted as a desire to disappoint the man, in order to be able to despise him. Abraham illustrates these tendencies by reference to numerous neurotic symptoms such as vaginismus, frigidity, emesis and even conjunctivitis.

The influence exercised by Abraham's arguments on the libido theory has been reflected above all in *Melanie Klein's* conceptions. Klein's theory of infantile depression—as a hurt inflicted in the oral stage—derives directly from Abraham. But even H. Schultz-Hencke has recourse to Abraham in his descriptions of various aims (captative, retentive), so that Abraham's influence has also made itelf felt in the Neo-Freudian schools.

B

SANDOR FERENCZI[1]

Like *Abraham, Sachs, Rank* and *Jones* Ferenczi was one of the first of Freud's disciples. He was also one of the most prolific. There are very few spheres of psychoanalysis to which he did not contribute. His investigations will be dealt with here under four main headings:

(*a*) Contributions to the structure and dynamics of the personality.
(*b*) Contributions to the psychopathology of neuroses.
(*c*) Contributions to therapy.
(*d*) Theoretical conceptions.

[1] S. Ferenczi, *Contributions to Psychoanalysis*, Vol. I, p. 11, London, 1952 and *Thalassa, Versuch einer Genitaltheories*, Vienna, 1922.

(a) Contributions to the structure and dynamics of the personality

In his work on introjection and transference Ferenczi comes to the conclusion—one which Freud had in fact already drawn—that transference
is not a specific type of behaviour peculiar to the doctor-patient relationship but, on the contrary, is generally applicable to social intercourse.
Special attention should be paid to the *identification* which constitutes
one aspect of every transference, for the patient will imitate and identify
with his physician in exactly the same way as he imitates and identifies
with other members of the community. For Ferenczi transference is
simply a displacement—cf. Freud's *Interpretation of Dreams* (see above
p. 84 ff.)—or, as Freud himself put it, 'a wrong connection'. But whereas
transference is quite harmless in a healthy person the neurotic's 'passion
for transference'[1], which prevents him from recognizing objective connections, actually makes him sick. On the other hand Ferenczi does not
investigate the question as to whether human relationships are always
transference relationships or whether they are also capable of being
'genuine'. Having established on the one hand that transference is always
a form of displacement and on the other hand that it is frequently
accompanied by identification Ferenczi proceeds to establish an
analogous relationship between transference and *introjection*. The
neurotic, according to Ferenczi's definition, incorporates into his ego
parts of external reality, irrespective of whether they are *pleasant* or
unpleasant—in contrast to the paranoic, who projects parts of himself on
to external reality. Easily inflamed and 'large-hearted',[2] the neurotic
rushes from object to object, incorporating, 'introjecting' them, in
accordance with the pleasure principle. Consequently introjection, as a
preliminary oral stage of identification, is also held to be a form of
transference. Over and above this it constitutes an attempt on the part of
the neurotic to heal himself.

Although for all practical purposes Ferenczi equates displacement,
identification, introjection and transference, although every identification, every introjection, every transference is a displacement, he does not
draw the conclusions which logically follow from this conception nor
does he appreciate the problems which it involves. It would be perfectly
feasible to describe all of these patterns of behaviour as displacements—
but in that case why mention identification and introjection? Freud
considers that the specific quality of introjection is linked to the oral
phase—although at a later date the concept is expanded to include all
forms of *in*corporation. Introjection is held to be the basis of identification, which latter Freud derives from imitation. But imitation presupposes incorporation.

[1] Ferenczi, *Contributions*, Vol. I, p. 45.
[2] Ferenczi, *ibid.*, Vol. I, p. 48.

The problematical nature of these concepts, their high degree of interchangeability, is exposed by Ferenczi. The task of isolating these patterns of behaviour is rendered even more complex when they become defence mechanisms, when introjection, identification, transference and displacement become forms of ego defence against the outside world or against the drives. The difficulty attendant on the use of these concepts derives (1) from *Freud's* attempt to reduce the spheres of human communication to a few neurotic mechanisms, without being able to define what constitutes healthy or normal behaviour in human intercourse, (2) from their high degree of synonymity. The problematical nature of these concepts will be dealt with in detail in the final part of this book.

One of Ferenczi's most important contributions is his work on the *Stages in the Development of the Sense of Reality*. It provides a fundamental complement to Abraham's investigations into the pre-genital stages of the libido, even though it is concerned with different spheres. The blissful condition of the embryo in the womb, a condition in which it knows nothing of the outside world, changes[1] decisively and profoundly as a result of its birth. The sense of omnipotence, which dominates the early years of a young child's development and persuades it that the moon and the stars themselves are well within its grasp, Ferenczi considers to derive from the blissful, intra-uterine condition in which the embryo lacked for nothing. Accordingly he describes the first period in the development of the sense of reality as 'the period of unconditional omnipotence'. This period, which begins immediately after birth, is succeeded by 'the period of magical-hallucinatory omnipotence', in which the child satisfies its desires by means of phantasies. During this same period the child begins to make uncoordinated movements, which express any discontent it might feel. 'The period of omnipotence by the help of magic gestures' is only reached when, by means of purposive movements, the child is able to attract the attention of other people and to grasp at things *for itself*. The pathological counterpart to this period is represented by hysteria, since the hysteric also expresses repressed desires by the use of his limbs (gestures) once conversion has taken place. The phase of incipient differentiation between external and internal reality is characterized by introjection and projection. This phase gives way in its turn to the animistic period. In this period both the objects and the persons in the child's environment are magically brought to life or transformed by means of introjection and projection. This stage corresponds to the symbolic phase of childhood, for the child now learns to interpret and control the outside world in terms of its own body. The criticism which has been levelled at

---

[1] Rank's thesis of the birth trauma is relevant here. Rank tried to trace all psychopathology back to the day of birth. (See p. 362 ff.)

psychoanalysis to the effect that it restricts symbolism to the phallus and the vagina is born out by Ferenczi when he refers to the child's comprehension of the outside world in terms of images which the child has of its own body, since the phallus and the vagina (anus) are by far the most powerful images which the child then possesses. By acquiring the power of speech, which Ferenczi also considers to precede thought, the child is better able to communicate with the outside world, and it then enters into the period of 'magic thoughts and magic words'. Only when the child has passed through this period, which, like all the other periods, is resuscitated in neuroses and psychoses, does it engage in objectively valid thoughts and actions. Ferenczi assumes that the regression of libido to pregenital stages of development, which occurs in psychic illnesses, will be accompanied by an analogous regression of the sense of reality. Hysteria and obsessional neurosis would be characterized by a regression to the period of omnipotence, in the case of hysteria of omnipotence through gestures, in the case of obsessional neurosis of omnipotence through thoughts. This work of Ferenczi's, which was to play a leading part in the subsequent development of psychoanalytic child psychiatry, suffers from one regrettable deficiency in that it fails to furnish an adequate explanation or definition of the concept of the 'sense of reality'. Ferenczi does not define the sense of reality at the beginning of his essay, but in as far as he goes on to develop from the pleasure principle a human activity based on man's ability to form judgements (in the sense that thought can save man from displeasure), it is probable that what he understands under the sense of reality is thoughts and actions which are 'objectively valid' (see above).

In his work on symbolism Ferenczi deals with *Silberer's* thesis, that it is not only the contents of the phantasies and wishes which appear in dream symbolism, but that the psychic functions also represent themselves in symbolic form.[1] In the Greek myth Oedipus represents the reality principle, since he is seeking enlightenment and insight. By contrast Jocaste is the embodiment of the pleasure principle. For she begs Oedipus to desist from further enquiry, because she wishes to spare him pain and suffering (displeasure). Consequently the Oedipus myth not only represents the incestuous desires of humanity but over and above this also demonstrates the possibility of avoiding tragedy, e.g. by accepting the pleasure principle, i.e. by not asking Jocaste. In this way myths and dreams also symbolize the principles of the psychic functions, i.e. the principles of pleasure and reality. Ferenczi accepts this thesis of Silberer's to a large extent but considers the emergence of symbolism in exclusively empirical terms. The child's first attempts to speak develop out of condensed word forms, which often represent

[1] See the section on Ernest Jones, p. 199 ff.

many different things in one. These initial word formations are the equivalent of symbols. Moreover, from the psychoanalytic point of view the only genuine symbols are those resulting from the cathexis of an object by an affect, which the conscious mind is unable to explain and which is the property of another object or another idea, which is unconscious. In the condensed word forms which it first makes the child will tend, for example, to employ a synonym for penis in order to denote all pointed objects, since it quite naturally derives pleasure from the autoerotic handling of its penis and so subsequently transfers that pleasure on to the outside world. By analogy it will equate all holes with the anus, all liquids with urine. When the child has been taught to repress sexuality the condensed word forms, each cathected with its specific affect, are also repressed, only to be raised to the status of symbols and hallucinated as such in dreams.

The most important works of Ferenczi's later years (from the early 'twenties onwards) concerning the dynamics and structure of the psyche include a short essay on the psyche as an inhibiting organ and also 'The Problem of the Acceptance of Unpleasant Ideas' (1926), in which he endeavours to establish a more precise definition of the nature and development of the sense of reality. But this latter work would scarcely be conceivable without Freud's study of 'negation'. Freud considered the importance of negation to lie in its function as mediator between the denial and the acceptance of reality. The outside world, which is a source of displeasure, is admitted to consciousness via negation and in a negative form. A child's reality is not composed of those objects provided to satisfy its craving for pleasure. Probably it does not even notice them. The acceptance of reality can only be effected via pain (e.g. hunger) and the expedients which the child devises to render that pain more tolerable. Particular importance is attached to those objects— e.g. the mother's breast—which on some occasions are capable of satisfying the child but which on other occasions cause displeasure and consequently ambivalence. The memory traces cling to these objects, they are *re*-discovered as sources of pleasure or of suffering and are again recognized as such at a later date. For both Freud and Ferenczi *re*-discovery is the basis of the discovery of reality and negation an attempt to accept hateful objects as well as lovable ones—for they too are re-discovered. If ambivalence leads to the discovery of reality, the recognition of objective reality is achieved only after the neutralization of hatred and love. These two must first reunite, re-amalgamate, after which, in their neutralized form, they can endow the individual with the capacity for objective recognition, with a fully-fledged 'sense of reality'.

Ferenczi considers the act of consciousness—a prerequisite for the discovery of reality—to consist of the inhibition of all psychic activities, a process which he describes in terms of concentration on a given task achieved by an *act of will*. Concentration of this kind, whether it be applied to a mathematical problem or a physical action, precludes all other psychic processes within the conscious mind. Thus concentration involves the inhibition and blocking of all psychic processes. It is this specific, consciously controlled inhibition of the psychic processes, which transforms the reflex action by which the original life of the psyche (primary process) is determined into the 'specific quality' of psychic life. In the intentional act of will psychic energy flows in one direction only, since all the others are blocked—and this blockage, or inhibition, is part of the essence of consciousness. It is the will that *constitutes* consciousness and it is the will that raises the psyche from the level of a reflex action to the level of those complicated processes which are the distinctive feature of psychic life in human beings.

(b) Contributions to the Psychopathology of Neuroses

Ferenczi's contributions to the psychpathology of neuroses, many of them written in a condensed form, are indeed numerous. From his 'Psychoanalytical Observations on Tic' to the so-called 'Sunday Neuroses', from his observations on 'Rubbing the Eyes as a Substitute for Onanism' to 'The Dread of Cigar and Cigarette Smoking' there is scarcely a single subject on which Ferenczi has not made stimulating observations. Within the framework of this present enquiry it will not be possible to deal with more than a few of them. In his book on the psychoanalytic theory of neuroses *Fenichel* has condensed and appraised a considerable number of them.

Ferenczi was the first to conduct a thorough investigation into impotence in males, a psycho-neurotic disorder which is by no means rare. Without entering into a detailed analysis of this disturbance it may be said that impotence, like all neurotic symptoms, is over-determined and, in Ferenczi's experience, may be sub-divided into the following strata:

1. An unconscious prohibition inhibits sexual activity.
2. Severe traumatic experiences (threats of castration) or less severe but none the less harmful environmental influences, coupled with a corresponding neurotic disposition, further inhibit sexual activity.
3. Incestuous mother fixations, feelings of extreme shame in early childhood, masturbatory and incestuous phantasies opposed by fear of castration are critical factors in the development of a potency disturbance.

In another of his condensed works Ferenczi deals with the genesis of homosexuality. *Freud*, together with *Fliess*, had considered that homosexuality was rooted in the bi-sexual nature of human beings and was capable of being activated in the appropriate environmental conditions.

Sadger had attempted to furnish a more detailed genesis of homosexuality by demonstrating the homosexual's extreme mother fixation and by advancing the thesis that homosexuals identify with their mother because, when the time comes, they would like to be loved by men in the capacity of a mother. According to Sadger the homosexual tries (1) to re-establish the original mother-son relationship; (2) by loving his own sex to love himself; (3) to love his own sex; (4) to love himself as his mother had loved him. In his enquiry Ferenczi endeavours to elucidate the difference between the 'active' (male) and the 'passive' (female) homosexual. Only the second of these two could be said to have identified with the mother; the first, the active type, must have 'genuine' male feelings. What had happened in his case was that the love object had undergone a transformation. If the second type could be explained in terms of the inverted Oedipus complex (in which the child assumes the mother's role as a woman), then the active homosexual must surely be an obsessional neurotic. In his case, due to the effects of a strict upbringing, woman had already been declared taboo in the anal-sadistic phase, and it was really his fear of castration which made him prefer his own sex. Ferenczi disagrees with Freud's view, that perversion is the negative of neurosis, on the grounds that neurotics also regress to pre-genital stages of sexuality and so display symptoms which are both neurotic and perverse.

In his investigation into hysterical materialization Ferenczi enquires into the problem of *conversion*. Hysteria constitutes a regression to stages of development which precede the separation of objectively valid thought from the pleasure principle. Consequently powerful sexual impulses verge directly on the intellectual sphere. The libido, which is seen to be dangerous, is again repressed and returns as an hallucination within the sphere of the senses or as a *materialization* of impulses in motor activity. In the course of its progress from repression to materialization the libido is enriched with symbols—the precipitate of its earliest intellectual activities—which determine the specific symbolism of the hysterical gestures. In other works on hysteria Ferenczi attempts to demonstrate the close connection between hysterical symptom formation and the erotogenic zones both in respect of hysterical stigmas and hysterical hypochondria.

(c) Contributions to Therapy

The methods which Ferenzi employed in an attempt to reduce the length of time required for psychoanalytic treatment (involving increased activity on the part of the analyst) led to his growing estrangement from Freud. This estrangement was made manifest when, in 1927, Ferenczi radically altered his therapeutic method by acting on the assumption that the patient must receive genuine love if the disturbances which had been caused by a lack of love were to be cured. On the basis of Freud's requirement that, for example, a patient suffering from a phobia should constantly expose himself to situations which promoted the phobia he set his patients tasks, whereby they were required actively to confront the problems with which they were burdened. He tells of a patient in whom trivial actions which she herself performed and conditions which she induced in the course of the sessions—such as rubbing her hand, crossing her legs and, occasionally, the desire to pass water—triggered off latent masturbatory tendencies. For as long as the analyst failed to notice these tendencies, more and more unconscious libido was able to impinge on them and build up into a resistance. It was not until Ferenczi had forbidden the patient to perform these actions that the analysis, which had been stagnating until then, came to life. This case prompted him to require of certain of his patients that they should renounce specific pleasurable activities during their sessions—and sometimes between sessions as well—and that they should learn to endure disagreeable conditions. The increased resistance which this produced was calculated to transform a chronic or merely stagnant case into a condition of acute exacerbation. This was achieved above all by Ferenczi's insistence that the patients should do things which they found disagreeable. For example, a female patient refused to go to the swimming pool because she was convinced that her breasts were too big. Only when Ferenczi ordered her to go swimming were the exhibitionist phantasies revealed which her conviction had served to conceal. These experimental therapeutic methods of Ferenczi's were subsequently adopted above all by the so-called Neo-Freudian schools, chiefly by Sullivan in the USA and by H. Schultz-Hencke in Germany. Ferenczi's most important theoretical discovery was the fact that in the course of the analysis the patient undergoes new experiences which are of the greatest possible therapeutic importance: when the patient expresses sexual desires or aggression the therapist does not respond with prohibitions or punishments but with positive understanding. In this way the patient's attitude, ingrained since childhood, may be profitably disrupted and the patient may learn to accept and to have tolerance for himself and his desires.

(d) Theoretical Conceptions

The highly characteristic combination of observation and speculation which was the distinctive feature of Freud's work was also typical of Ferenczi's, save that Ferenczi did not possess the critical reserve and objectivity *vis-à-vis* his theses which distinguished Freud's attitude. Of all the psychoanalytic authors only Sandor Rado and Melanie Klein can equal Ferenczi for boldness of speculation and for simplifications of psychological, physiological and biological problems. His theoretical work, *Thalassa, Versuch einer Genitaltheorie,* now appears to the critical reader as a curious by-product of psychoanalytic theory. It is one of the works which have exposed psychoanalysis—not without some justification—to the charge of having indulged in uncritical speculation and 'pan-sexuality'. In *Thalassa* Ferenczi expands the symbols of phallus and vagina into cosmic symbols, not by reference to myths, however, but by his interpretations—which are based on crude analogies—of embryonic, physiological and psychological facts. As a complement to *Freud's* death drive Ferenczi develops the view that the whole of life is determined by a tendency to return to the womb. What he understands under the womb is not the mother's *physical* womb but the mysterious sea in which all life originated. The phylogenetic transition of animal life from water to land is equated with the process of birth, in which the infant is obliged to exchange the placenta for the cradle. Coitus constitutes a frustrated attempt to return to the womb, in which the man uses his penis to drill into the mother's body, just as the child uses its teeth 'as tools with which it tries to drill into its mother's body'. The tooth is the primeval penis—but the penis is the symbol of the 'original drill, the tooth'. Apart from re-enacting the transition of animal life from water to land birth is also an act of 'oral-erotic aggression' on the part of the mother. The child makes itself independent of the mother by producing excrement and thus combining 'in its own person both the mother's body and the child (excrement)'. The act of giving suck is equated with coitus, the nipple is equated with the penis—and this also symbolizes the return to the mother's womb. Ejaculations, of course, are a further symbol of this return, and Ferenczi does not hesitate to assert that the 'permanent invagination of the glans in a fold of mucous membrane (the foreskin) is quite simply a womb existence in miniature.'

Ferenczi considers that the preliminary stage of repression, i.e. of the 'withdrawal of psychic cathexis from anything unpleasant', is demonstrated in the biological sphere by the reaction of the lizard, which finds no difficulty in 'leaving its tail behind in the hand of a pursuer and promptly growing another'. He also considers that the sexual act begins 'as a tendency to eject the genital entirely', but which 'then contents itself with the ejection of the secretion'. The secondary sexual characteristics appear to him to be 'weapons in the battle' 'to decide which of the two belligerents will succeed in enforcing sexual penetration of the partner's body in its capacity as a substitute for the mother's body'. Coitus is not only a return to the mother's womb but also the 'simultaneous repetition and subjugation in the form of play of all the dangers attendant on the struggle for birth and the adaptation to life'. In the act of copulation the penis not only enacts 'the natal and ante-natal Existenzangst of man' but also the battles of that 'primeval animal, which was his progenitor and as such took part in the great catastrophe whereby animal life was transferred to dry land. Coitus is based on the 'idea of thalassal regression', 'the longing for the sea-life from which man emerged in primeval times'.

C

OTTO FENICHEL[1]

Freudian psychoanalysis is indebted to Otto Fenichel not only for his numerous contributions to the psychopathology of neuroses and the structure of the personality but also for the most thorough and detailed presentation of psychoanalytic theory to date: *The Psychoanalytic Theory of Neurosis*. In this work Fenichel condensed both Freud's views and the most important contributions made by his disciples (up to 1944), presenting them in an arrangement which illustrated the clinical and dynamic aspects of neurosis with which they were concerned.

Fenichel's own contributions to psychoanalytic theory may be considered from the following points of view:

(*a*) Contributions to the psychopathology of neuroses.
(*b*) Contributions to the structure of the personality.
(*c*) Contributions to metapsychology.

(*a*) *Contributions to the Psychopathology of Neuroses*

As far as the psychopathology of neuroses is concerned the most important of Fenichel's works (most of which were written between 1925 and 1935) are those in which he stresses the importance of the castration complex for the emergence and development of neuroses. From the mid-'twenties to the early 'thirties there was a tendency amongst Freud's disciples to attribute to the castration complex a key position in the psychopathology of neuroses (to wit *Alexander, Ferenczi, Sachs, Reich*, etc.). In his investigations into the psychology of transvestitism Fenichel emphasizes the important part played by the castration complex in this perversion. He describes a patient who identified with his dead mother and who, as his 'mother', desired sexual intercourse with his father (so-called negative Oedipus complex). But this desire was repressed by

---

[1] *Collected Papers of Otto Fenichel*, Vols. I & II, London, 1954. *The Psychoanalytic Theory of Neurosis*, London, 1955.

the fear that his father would make him pregnant and consequently formed the basis of a castration complex. Transvestitism can be reduced to the formula: 'I would like to be a woman and be able to bear children, whilst still retaining my penis.' Like the neurotic symptom perversion constitutes a compromise between repressed wishes and the repressing instance. In his view, which emphasizes the combination of phallic and feminine tendencies, Fenichel is opposed to *Sadger*,[1] who, in his interpretation of the transvestite, lays stress on the negative Oedipus complex (in which the transvestite desires to be loved by his father either as a woman or as his own mother). Fenichel also attaches importance to the transvestite's belief that both his mother and the world at large will love him more as a woman, a belief which is strengthened when the presence of sisters introduces an element of rivalry. *Boehm*[2] also considers the combination of phallic and feminine components in the figure of a mother equipped with a penis and the transvestite's identification with that figure to constitute an important factor.

When *Freud* embarked on his investigations into perversions (1906) he described them as the negative of neurosis (see above, p. 107 ff.), but subsequently (1917) he enlarged on this distinction by stating that perverts reacted to sexual frustrations by regressing to early sexual stages (polymorphous perversion), whereas neurotics employed other defence mechanisms. In opposing this view Fenichel insisted that perverts, unlike children, were not given to 'polymorphous perversion'. On the contrary, they were usually dominated by the *one* drive, the satisfaction of which was accompanied by a full genital orgasm. Neurotic symptoms on the other hand were desexualized, their discharge was accompanied by displeasure—as in an hysterical fit—, whereas the active pursuit of perversions was accompanied by pleasure. Over and above this perverts were also capable of repression and the structure of their personalities was similar to that of neurotics. Fear of castration and feelings of guilt would undermine the primacy of genitality in perverts no less than in neurotics. In advancing these views in his theory on the genesis of perversions Fenichel opposes Freud. But he resembles Freud in his inability to supply a satisfactory explanation of the genesis of perversions. For Fenichel the constitutional factor and fixation to experiences of early childhood (which Freud had already recognized as important elements in the genesis of perversions), together with the strength of the partial sexual drive in any given case and the theory of *imperfect repression*, constituted the decisive factors. Whereas neurotics, having repressed a given thing, proceeded to repress everything associated with it, repression

---

[1] J. Sadger, *Die Lehre von den Geschlechtsverirrungen auf psychoanalytischer Grundlage*, Vienna, 1921.

[2] F. Boehm, 'Bemerkungen über den Transvestitismus', *Int. Z. Psa.* 9, 1923.

in perverts was incomplete, leaving gaps through which specific areas of infantile sexuality could enter consciousness. These specific areas of infantile sexuality which penetrated consciousness were the determining factors for perversions.

Fenichel conducts a detailed investigation into the castration complex in his work on *Introjection and the Castration Complex*. He tells of a female patient who consulted him and who was suffering from a large number of neurotic symptoms, chief among them her extreme insecurity and shyness. The patient had several older (step-)sisters and brothers. Her own mother had died two weeks after her birth. The patient was reared by an aunt and was bottle-fed. Fenichel established, *inter alia*, the following factors:

1. The loss of the mother's breast,
2. jealousy *vis-à-vis* breast-fed children,
3. the replacement at a later date of the friendly aunt by a strict governess,
4. the observation of the father's penis, which was felt to constitute a threat.

He then interpreted these factors in a logical sequence and proceeded to draw far-reaching conclusions from his interpretation. Fenichel argues, by analogy with Abraham's investigation into melancholia and on a basis of part fact part inference, that this patient's oral aggression had produced in her the desire to bite off first her step-mother's (aunt's) breast nipple and subsequently her father's penis—i.e. to castrate him. This castration was simultaneously accompanied by the incorporation, or introjection, of the father's penis and of his personality. In the patient's wish phantasy the father's penis was bitten off *pars pro toto*— i.e. it stood for the whole person. Following its introjection, however, it continued to lead an independent existence within the patient as her super-ego. (The patient's super ego was the father or, alternatively, the father's penis.) The incorporation of the lost love object, which was characteristic of Freud's and Abraham's concepts of depression (see p. 171 ff.), Fenichel now extended to include the desire to castrate and incorporate the father. In order to explain why the patient suffered from hysteria instead of depression—which would have been more logical in terms of Abraham—Fenichel was obliged to put forward further hypotheses: in the case of this particular patient genital and oral libido had predominated and the difference could be accounted for purely in terms of the *libido economy*.

Fenichel published a further investigation on the importance of the castration complex under the title *The Pre-oedipal Libido Phases in Girls*. When the little girl discovers that, unlike the little boy, she has been castrated, her narcissistic sensitivity is dealt a heavy blow. Without exception the mother is blamed. She it was who took the little girl's penis away. Perhaps the father will give it back again! Fenichel—in contrast to other authors, above all Melanie Klein (see below)—supports Freud's thesis that girls in the pre-oedipal phase have not yet discovered the existence of the vagina and that their sexual development is centred around the clitoris. For this reason Fenichel considers vaginal masturba-ion in little girls to be no more important than similar occasional stimulation of the skin or other tissues.

In his investigation into anxiety defence Fenichel opposes those analysts who consider that the primary purpose of the libido is to neutralize anxiety. In this regard *Bergler* and *Eidelberg*[1] advance the view that the oral-libidinal cathexis of the penis stems from the need to neutralize oral-sadistic fears. When Ernest Jones maintains that the phallic phase is the *consequence* of the fear of castration, then Freud's libido theory ceases to be a biological cum psychological development and becomes instead a reaction to the fears produced by conflicts of drives. *Edward Glover* sees perversions as the (libidinal) sexualization and neutralization of the fears and dangers which the perversions conceal. From this it would follow that a person who had seen a female genital as a child and had experienced the fear of castration as a con-sequence and who had then developed a fetish about legs or feet would have done so because, 'by cathecting his feet or his legs with libido', he hoped to save himself from ever catching sight of a female genital again. In point of fact (according to Fenichel) the opposite is the case: it was the sight of the female genital which aroused in him the fear of castration and it was in order that he might overcome this fear that his legs or feet were pressed into service as a substitute for the penis which the female genital lacked. For *Glover* the man's own penis is 'libidinized' for purposes of *protection* and replaced by his leg or his foot. For Fenichel (as also for Freud) the leg or the foot replaces the penis, which the woman lacks: 'When I see this I am able to forget that girls have no penis.' In perversions, Fenichel considers, it is necessary to differentiate between two different factors: the first is the movement away from adult sexuality, the second is the movement towards infantile sexuality. In the second case 'libidinization' for the purposes of overcoming fear (see above) might be applicable. But 'libidinization' is not generally applic-able, for, if it is applied to the first factor, that of 'movement away from' adult sexuality, it is quite incapable of explaining it. This factor can only be satisfactorily explained in terms of the fear of castration—an explanation which *Glover* found too one-sided.

[1] E. Bergler and L. Eidelberg, 'Der Mammakomplex des Mannes', *Int. Z* *Psa.* Vol. 19, 1933.

The discussion of anxiety defence broaches one of the fundamental problems of psychoanalytic theory. What is primary and what is a reaction and thus secondary? In the second phase of his development Freud considered anxiety to be a signal of external or internal (libidinal) danger. Anxiety defence could take place by repression of the anxiety, seeking the protection of parental figures or overcoming the anxiety by replacing it with pleasure. The last of these methods applied particularly to perversions, which transformed situations that had previously been charged with anxiety (e.g. the fear of castration aroused at the sight of the female genital) into pleasurable situations, i.e. libidinized them. But this view, which was espoused by *Glover* and *Jones*, does not solve the dilemma. For if (1) the individual is to develop anxiety as a result of a drive or a conflict of drives and (2) the same drive, which appears to the individual in the form of a threat, is to be expressed as anxiety, (3) this self-same drive or conflict of drives is then to libidinize itself (it is always a question of libido) and (4) become a source of pleasure—then it would appear that we are faced with a self-contradictory proposition. Glover's and Jones' attempt to place libido in opposition to anxiety and to interpret the phases of libido development as reactions to anxiety, strikes a blow at the root of sexual development, but leaves the dilemma intact, whereby one and the same drive can be registered as a threat, then libidinize and neutralize itself and finally become a source of pleasure.

A further work of Fenichel's on the psychopathology of neuroses is given over to the Pseudologia phantastica. In contrast to liars, who repress truth by negation, the pseudolog enlarges the world to suit his own wishes and attempts to convice the person to whom he is speaking that his ideas are perfectly sound. For, if a lie may be true, then, conversely, a truth may also be a lie. By such means the pseudolog unconsciously tries to win over the person to whom he is lying as a witness to the fact that a real-life experience (a truth) can be untrue. One such real-life experience would doubtless be the observation of parental intercourse, which the pseudolog would rather were untrue. By now Fenichel's explanation of the pseudologia phantastica has found its way back to the Oedipus complex and proceeds to demonstrate, with considerable intellectual dexterity, how this complex may be made responsible for a number of totally different clinical phenomena.

The Oedipus complex, however, is by no means restricted to the phallic phase, as *Freud* had supposed. In his *Precursors of the Oedipus Conflict* Fenichel tries to demonstrate, on the basis of case histories, that ties between infant and mother also exist in the pre-phallic 'oral' or 'anal' stages, which Fenichel already designates as oedipal stages. He considers the loss of the breast through weaning and the loss of faeces through bowel opening to be precursors of the castration complex and its attendant anxieties. During these stages the nipple, faeces or penis are introjected (or, more precisely, 'partially introjected'), and in the case of girls this process of introjection is followed by phantasies concerning the mouth, the anus and finally the vagina. Active, phallic libido—the urge to penetrate with the penis—is pre-figured in the excretion of faeces. For ejection and retention alternate with one another in every stage of libido development.

(b) Contributions to the Structure of the Personality

A detailed investigation which Fenichel undertook into the complex problem of identification led him to formulate its various forms as follows:[1]

A: Primary Identification (of the child with its parents).
B: Regressive Identification (occurring in conflicts of drives, neuroses and psychoses).

I. Total Identification.
(a) In melancholia (schizofrenia).
(b) In the formation of the super ego in the normal person.

II. Partial Identification.
(a) In cases revealing a common aetiological origin and in cases where guilt feelings have been taken over (hysterical identification).
(b) In normal persons after loss (grief) or in love (i.e. 'falling in love').
(c) In homosexuals.
(d) On the basis of common factors of recent occurrence.
(e) In the formation of the super ego in neurotics.

The process whereby the object is first cathected observes the following sequence: (1) Perception of the object, (2) formation of an inner representation of that which has been perceived, (3) cathexis of this inner representation by the id, (4) emergence of drive needs, (5) actions determined by the drives and directed towards the object. The process whereby the child first 'meets' its environment (object cathexis) is subject to two types of disturbance: (1) the environment denies itself or (2) the ego defends itself against the drives which are bent on gratification (anxiety situation). In the second case the denied drive is subject to transformations and one such transformation is the process of *identification*. For example, the child fears the mother and identifies with her because of its fear. From this it follows that this identification is a transformation of the drive and, as such, changes both its *object* and its

[1] Fenichel, *Precursors of the Oedipus Conflict*, Vol. 1, pp. 108 ff.

aim. The object, which was denied to the drive by the ego, is now taken over by the *ego*. (See the example of identification with the mother: for fear of the mother the ego forbids the drive, the libido, to adopt a (real) attitude towards the mother, e.g. to give her affection. Instead the ego identifies with the mother, in order that the libido may then re-discover the mother within the ego.) This process, in which the ego identifies with the object, transforms the ego in its turn by concentrating its libido, which it withdraws from the environment, exclusively on the ego. Identification thus appears as a defence mechanism, which is operated by the ego *vis-à-vis* the id, which is related to *repression* and accompanied by a regression to narcissistic stages (by virtue of the fact that libido is turned away from the environment back on to the ego). Fenichel assumes that this defence mechanism may well be more primitive and more fundamental than repression. These partial identifications which take place in the ego become the precursors of the super ego within the ego, since—and this we already have from Ferenczi—obedience and identification with the person in command are one and the same process. In this connection Ferenczi coined the phrase 'Sphincter morality' to illustrate the child's obedience in matters relating to cleanliness training. These partial identifications within the ego are to be contrasted with the *total* identifications which characterize the super-ego following the disintegration of the Oedipus complex: due to the fear of castration the father is introjected into the super-ego in his entirety. Total identification within the ego is also characteristic of psychotics and in the case of schizophrenics it is already established within the oral phase. The child ego, which is still weak in this stage, incorporates (introjects) the person in whose care it is at the precise moment when this person either withdraws from it or rejects it, as a result of which the full weight of its ambivalent feelings (affection and hostility) is thrown on to the introjected individual within its own ego. Whereas in psychosis orality and narcissistic introversion of libido on to the ego are the determining factors, in the formation of the super ego the process involved, although analogous to the psychotic process in other respects, does not include orality or narcissistic regression. If total identification may be equated with narcissism, then partial identification may be considered synonymous with *hysterical* identification. This latter is likely to recur, even in adults, at any time—in falling in love, in hypnosis or in group formations (see p. 149 ff., *Freud*). In the case of a partial identification within a group, however, the super ego is projected on to the outside world, whereupon an object cathexis begins to take place in the sense that *the object assumes ego functions.* This is particularly evident in persecution mania: the greater the estrangement between super ego and ego the nearer the super ego is to the outside world; it can then quite easily be projected on to the outside world in the form of a punishment or of persecution. But partial identification may also be observed in jealousy, both in masculine women and feminine men. And character is likewise stamped by identification.[1]

Fenichel devotes a further comprehensive work to the problem of the defence mechanisms and their relationship to character traits (see p. 121 ff, *Freud*). Fenichel goes farther than Freud in attempting to draw a clear line of demarcation between the drives and defence against the drives in the composition of the character. But this attempt ran into difficulties and Fenichel was obliged to concede that the drives and defence were in fact relative to one another.

Whereas F. Alexander, for example, maintained that it was necessary to distinguish between two types of conflict in neurosis—the conflict between the (defending) ego and the id on the one hand and the conflict between different drives within the id on the other (e.g. between an actively incestuous desire and a readiness passively to accept castration) —Fenichel attempted to demonstrate that there is no such thing as a *conflict* of drives within the id. The concept of contradiction was meaningless in terms of the id, so the concept of conflict was also meaningless. Such conflicts of drives as may occur must always occur within the structure of the personality, since one set of drives was always nearer to the ego and thus to defence. Consequently a drive, which was nearer to the ego than it was to the id (for example, the so-called self-preservation drive), might also serve for purposes of defence. Neurosis consisted of the multiplicity of the following processes: drive—defence against the drive—renewed breakthrough of the drive—defence against the drive—repression of the defence.

Character, Fenichel argues in his investigation into the psychoanalysis of character, is an habitual attitude. It is necessary to distinguish between two different types of character traits within the character, those which appear only in specific situations and those which are constant. But the character as such (unlike the symptom) should not be thought of as the expression of a conflict between the id and the ego—since defence and drive are relative to one another. The 'fundamental' character, which, despite the relativity of defence and drive, Fenichel again proceeds to postulate, finds its chief application in the discharge of affects. It is opposed to the *reactive* character, whose habitual attitudes may be considered above all in the light of defence mechanisms. These reactionary character traits achieve their primary purpose, which is to control anxiety, by the adoption of specific attitudes, which *Freud* had

[1] P. Schilder assumes the existence of several ego ideals and a corresponding number of identifications. ("Zur Pathologie des Ich-Ideals", *Int. Z. Psa.* Vol. 8, 1922 and *Introduction to a Psychoanalytic Psychiatry*, New York, 1928.)

already delineated in his work on the anal character (see p. 121 ff.). They may be distinguished from *transitory* neurotic symptoms and from dreams—which also represent a compromise between the ego and the id—by virtue of their rigidity and durability. They are the neurotic mask of the personality and are subjected to character *analysis* (see below under Reich), when they make their presence felt in the form of a resistance either in the analysis (e.g. as defiance) or in the transference.

But the direct relationship which exists between 'reactive' character traits and neurotic symptoms also exists between affects and neurosis. In his investigations into the relationship of the ego to the affects Fenichel equates the discharge of affects (rage or fear) with the weakening of ego-control in neurosis, because a discharge of affects is also accompanied by weakness on the part of the ego. If the ego was overcome in childhood by an affect—e.g. anxiety—then the ego will subsequently tighten its grip on the anxiety affect with further submission—e.g. to a discharge of anxiety such as occurs in hysteria—as the possible result. The ego defends itself against the affect by blocking it, by postponing and dragging out its discharge, by transforming it, 'displacing' it into a different situation, in short, by denial, isolation and projection. The fact that Fenichel does not speak of the repression of affects is a matter of no little importance from the point of view of psychoanalytic theory. He deals with the difficult concepts of ego-weakness and ego-strength in a work of the same name (*Ego Weakness and Ego Strength*). The hallmark of the strong, healthy ego is its ability to assert itself in the face of demands made by the id no less than in the face of those made by the super ego. The strong ego differs from the neurotic ego by dint of its ability to anticipate—by heeding the signals of anxiety, loathing or shame—the threat of subjugation which the affects offer and by its consequent ability to produce and to exploit the affects in accordance with the dictates of reason. (None the less, in contrast to the authors discussed below, such as Hartmann and Kris, the ego remains for the most part a product of the id, whose nature is conditioned by environmental influences.)

(c) Contributions to Metapsychology

Apart from an early investigation into the relationship of psychoanalysis to philosophy Fenichel's contribution to metapsychology is virtually restricted to his criticism of *Freud's* assumption of a death drive. Without wishing to deny that a tendency towards death may well be inherent in life, he considered that the chief factor emerging from the death drive hypothesis was the facility which it afforded for oversimplification. Fenichel cites as an example of such oversimplification the enquiries by

Bergler and *Jekels* into *Triebdualismus im Traum*,[1] in which the authors claim that the death drive is active in the sphere of dreams. But Fenichel is also aware of the dangers attendant on an unadulterated biologism of drives (*Rado* in his early phase) which would attribute every neurosis to the conflict between death drive and eros. A large number of divergent phenomena, such as masochism, sadism, super ego formation and introjection, need not be explained *solely* in terms of the death drive, as had been assumed by many analysts in the twenties and thirties. In Fenichel's opinion it is more than questionable whether the somatic origin of drives—to which he subscribes—is applicable to the death drive. He also doubts the validity of the process whereby the death drive and the 'life drive' (Eros) are fused and unfused. He argues that in precisely those stages in which the fusion of these two drives is assumed to take place the life drive is in the ascendancy, whilst the death drive is prominent during the period of unfusing and differentiation, although it would be logical to expect that the fusion of the drives would have led to some form of neutralization. The dubious nature of the psychoanalytic conception of the drives (which is doubtless based, at least in part, on accurate observations) becomes manifest, when Fenichel, following Freud, tries to explain drive displacement (i.e. energy displacement) by means of drive quantities (so-called desexualized libido). It seemed to Freud that the transformation of love into hate was impossible without the assumption of this 'desexualized libido' and, indeed, in the years leading up to the development of the death drive hypothesis he endeavoured to think of love and hate, not as opposing factors, but as factors arising out of a specific development. Fenichel advocates a similar genesis from an *undifferentiated* substance for eros and thanatos, in contrast to *Freud*, who considers that these two types of drive have existed in their separated conditions from the outset.

In summing up it may be said of Fenichel that he was one of the most serious and most important of Freud's disciples and one who recognized the dangers of oversimplified generalizations (to which, for example, Ferenczi fell victim) and endeavoured to avoid them. He occupies a conciliatory position mid-way between the extremes of *Melanie Klein's* biologism (see below) and the milieu theory of the Neo-Freudians (Horney). He strove to preserve the inheritance of Freud's thought against the deviations of both *Glover* and *Alexander* and he did not associate himself with *Hartmann's* ego psychology. He nonetheless constantly demanded that psychoanalysis should adapt itself to the changed conditions obtaining in the world forty years after its inception (1940).

[1] *Imago*, 20, 1934 ('The Dualism of Drives in Dreams').

D

THE BRITISH GROUP AND ITS MOST IMPORTANT REPRESENTATIVES

I. EDWARD GLOVER

The investigations carried out by Glover, who may be regarded as the most important and certainly the most critical representative of Freudian psychoanalysis within the British group, will be considered from the following two viewpoints:

(a) Contributions to the structure and dynamics of the personality.
(b) Contributions to the psychopathology of neuroses.

(a) Contributions to the structure and dynamics of the personality.

In these contributions Glover attempts a critical analysis and reformulation of certain fundamental concepts of Freudian psychoanalysis. As early as 1924, in his publication[1] on the importance of the mouth in psychoanalytic theory and on anal character formation, he subjected Abraham's generalizations regarding oral character to specific criticisms. He insisted that psychoanalytic characterology should not be based on the primacy of libido development alone but that the effect of the functions of perception and consciousness on the early ego structure should also be taken into consideration. He also indicated the dangers of projecting back into very early childhood specific character traits which only arise in later phases of development. This would apply, for example, to character traits such as envy, impatience, ambition, generosity, etc., which were attributes of the urethral phase. It seemed to him that Abraham's use of the concept of 'getting' for the oral phase, 'keeping' for the anal phase and 'giving up' for the phallic phsse (see p. 169 ff.), although basically correct, did not provide a satisfactory explanation of the character traits derived from these phases. Glover criticized the characterization of pre-oedipal character traits, because these preceded the clear-cut separation of ego and object, which only took place after the resolution of the oedipal phase by the castration complex. 'Oral character' was often no more than an amalgam of qualities which had to do with the mouth and with feeding and which were over-zealously applied or transferred to this so-called 'oral character'. In spite of his critical attitude towards psychoanalytic

[1] E. Glover, 'On the Early Development of Mind', *Collected Essays*, London, 1956.

191

characterology and in spite of his realization that oral tendencies are less suppressed than is sexuality, since far greater opportunities for the satisfaction of orality are vouchsafed by the eating customs of the various cultures, Glover himself also treads the path of simplification. For example, when he describes the infant's identification with the nipple,[1] when he considers weaning to be a preliminary stage of the castration complex or when he derives passive and active homosexuality from passive or active types of suckling! (The mammae of course are phallic symbols.) The ambivalence of Glover's attitude, which made it possible for him to recognize and criticize crucial weaknesses in psycho-analytic theory and then promptly to have recourse to the same clichées (omnibus concepts) which a moment before he had been attacking, was also to be one of the characteristics of his later works. He criticizes those analysts who, following the example set by Freud in his publication on the Ego and the Id, anthropomorphize these concepts to a marked degree (especially *Alexander*, see above under *Fenichel*, p. 181 ff.) and play them off, one against the other, as virtually independent instances. Influenced as he was during this phase of his investigation by *Melanie Klein* (see below p. 213 ff.), he himself came dangerously near to anthropomorphizing, when he argued that the differentiation of the ego in the pregenital stages proceeded, due to a synthetic function of the psyche, from numerous ego nuclei, which are relatively *independent*. These primitive ego nuclei are characterized by the basic functions of the primary or primitive ego, namely, the expression of drive demands and the perception of tensions within the ego. This primitive ego identifies with its environment—irrespective of whether it consists of animate or inanimate objects—in accordance with the principle of pleasure and dis-pleasure, which is also the criterion by which it distinguishes between 'good' and 'bad' objects (see also *Melanie Klein*, p. 213 ff.). The number of ego-nuclei corresponds to the number of sources of pleasure, i.e. to the number of possible identifications and erotogenic zones. At a later point they join together to form the ego. The ego-nuclei possess both somatic and psychic character, they are both unconscious and pre-conscious; and Glover defines the early ego as consisting of two drives, the self-preservation drive and the libido. The disintegration of the personality in psychoses and addictions, its partial regressions to very early oral or anal-sadistic stages, led Glover to assume—*inter alia*—that the ego was a polymorphous structure. In these illnesses the synthetic function of the psyche dries up and the old 'mechanisms' of the ego-nuclei, their relationship to denial and gratification on the one hand and their synthesis into an organic whole on the other, will determine the ego-weakness of a later date. The greater the number of ego-nuclei that

[1] See also *Fenichel*, p. 186 ff.

remain autonomous and receive cathexis from the libido, the weaker the future ego will be—and the greater will be its danger. What is quite unclear in this conception is what Glover understands under the 'synthetic power' of the psyche, which joins the ego-nuclei into an organized whole and which, judging from its importance, must surely be quite extraordinary.

Glover's criticism of sublimation[1] reveals crucial weaknesses in the *Freud*ian concept of sublimation but without providing a preferable alternative. In Freud's view sublimation takes place (see p. 122 ff.) when the external aim, towards which the libido is directed, undergoes a change due to internal or external frustration. The one essential difference between sublimation and other defence mechanisms lies in the fact that in sublimation the libido is not repressed; instead the aim, towards which it was directed, is simply displaced. However, apart from this displacement of the aim, it is further claimed that the libido becomes a-sexual. The new aim usually has nothing in common with the old sexual aim, even though in certain cases modified libidinal aspirations are satisfied when the new aim is achieved. As has been demonstrated by *Bernfeld*,[2] *Freud* first uses the concept of sublimation as a special case of reaction formation and then proceeds to use the reaction formation as a special case of sublimation (which in both cases presupposes *repression*). The relationship of sublimation to guilt feelings (which are presumably its origin) and its very dubious relationship to culture would seem to indicate that this concept is intended to embrace highly contradictory processes. The relationship of sublimation to cultural values is rendered difficult by virtue of the fact that, for example, greed as a sublimation of anal-erotic tendencies is not necessarily of cultural value. Over and above this *Bernfeld* advances the view that there is only a difference of degree between the cultural activities of children and those of adults—whether these are of an artistic or a scientific nature—and this difference is as easily explained in terms of repressive processes as it is in terms of 'ego aims' (Bernfeld) *without* represssion. When anal-erotic components are sublimated, as in the case of a collector of *objets d'art*, then the new activity is in part determined by the objects, i.e. by the *objets d'art*, and not simply by the fact that a libidinal impulse has become a-libidinal.

The problem becomes even more difficult when the relationship between sublimation and replacement (substitution) is investigated. For *Freud* substitution—which is akin to phantasy—applied only to the ideational representation of a drive in the conscious mind. This ideational

[1] "Sublimation, Substitution, and Social Authority," *Int. J. Psa.*, Vol. XII/3, 1931.
[2] Bernfeld. See "Bemerkungen über Sublimierung," *Imago*, 8, 333, 1922.

representation included in the conscious idea the return of the repressed material and was identical with symptom formation. What is the difference between the substitution of a drive representation (idea) and sublimation? In either case the aim of the libido is involved. Moreover, how are we to view the relationship between sublimation and reaction formation? The latter is considered to be a counter-cathexis (see p. 125 ff.) (e.g. character), but the energy employed in counter-cathexis is drawn from repressed material. At a later date a distinction is made between reaction formation and repression and reaction formation becomes a special defence mechanism (*Freud* after 1925). If reaction formation and substitute formation are counter-cathected by drives as a result of the representation of other ideational elements, then it will no longer be possible to distinguish between them and sublimation or between sublimation and the symptom, and the thesis that sublimation is independent of repression will no longer be tenable.[1] The dilemma becomes tractable only if sublimation is considered as *one* of a group of psychic activities, co-existent with, for example, repression or reaction formation. But this conception would necessitate the renunciation of a genetic interpretation and the recognition of the interrelatedness of psychic activities. *Jones* seeks a compromise solution by considering sublimation as the only direct continuation of unconscious impulses and reaction formation as a further ego activity. But inhibition is also defined by *Freud* as an ego activity and on the basis of this definition *Melanie Klein* puts forward the thesis that certain ego activities are cathected with libido as the result of a displacement of sexual symbols in early childhood. (Melanie Klein expresses the view that sublimation cannot take place without repression and fixation—in which case why use this concept, when symptom or reaction formation would serve?) But this interpretation also conflicts with *Jones'* thesis (see below), who, however, is prepared to concede that sublimated ideas may also temporarily sink back into the unconscious, regress and become symbols of complexes. This raises the question as to whether dream symbols may not also be considered as sublimations.

The only way in which Glover is able to extricate himself from this confusion is by using the concept of sublimation in a purely descriptive manner, whereby he lays his main emphasis on its energic origin *and* ascribes to it a certain protective and defensive function. He considers its relationship to social and cultural values to be so questionable—on account of the repression on which these values are based,—that he virtually dispenses with it. It is because Glover's investigations clearly

---

[1] R. Sterba, "Zur Problematik der Sublimierungslehre" (*Int. Z. Psa.* XVI, 3, 4, 1930) advances the view that sublimation (as desexualization) must precede reaction formation.

reveal the problematical aspects of fundamental psychoanalytic concepts (see also Part III of this book) and illustrate the difficulties attendant on the introduction of new concepts that they have been dealt with here at such length.

Glover subjects the relationship between the sense of reality and perversions to a critical enquiry which has far-reaching consequences for psychoanalytic theory (see Fenichel p. 181 ff.). He defines the concepts of the sense of reality and reality testing as follows:[1]

'1.   Reality-sense is a faculty, the existence of which we infer by examining the processes of reality testing.
'2.   Efficient reality testing, for any subject who has passed the age of puberty, is the capacity to retain psychic contact with the objects that promote gratification of instinct, including here both modified and residual infantile impulse.
'3.   Objectivity is the capacity to assess correctly the relation of instinctual impulse to instinctual object, whether or not the aims of the impulse are, can be or will be gratified.'

Apart from Freud both *Ferenczi* and *Abraham* have subjected the relationship between the sense of reality and libido development to a close investigation (see p. 172 ff.). And these authors were followed by *Federn* (see below p. 235 ff.) and *Melanie Klein* (see below p. 212 ff.). On the basis of these investigations Glover postulates that the development of the sense of reality should not be described merely in terms of object and drive but also in terms of the control which the individual gradually gains over his anxiety. With this he is suggesting a method based on a combination of behaviourism and analytic introspection.

In his investigations into addictions (see below) Glover expresses his belief that the addict is able to maintain his relationship to reality because he has concentrated his infantile mechanisms of projection and introjection on the drug to which he happens to be addicted (morphium, alcohol, etc.). For Glover addiction occupies a position mid-way between psychosis and neurosis, because the addict overcomes his fears and maintains his relationship to reality by projecting his fears on to the object of his addiction (by 'libidinizing' it). He further asserts that the pervert's relationship to reality is maintained by an analogous process, one in which the pervert protects himself from infantile fears of introjection and projection by excessive libidinization of those parts of his body which he feels to be threatened. The fetishist will libidinize his leg, for example (because, as a penis substitute, it will then protect him from castration. See p. 181 ff., *Fenichel*). It is by means of this process that he

[1] Glover, 'On the Early Development of Mind,' *Collected Essays*, p. 217.

is able to maintain his relationship to reality. And for Glover the fear of castration, which for *Freud* and *Fenichel* supplied the motive power of perversions, becomes a defence against pre-oedipal anxieties which, if succumbed to, would produce psychosis. The influence of *Melanie Klein's* theories, according to which the pre-oedipal phase is decisive for the development of the personality, is particularly noticeable in this aspect of Glover's work. The pervert positively seeks out the fear of castration, in order that he may protect himself thereby from earlier anxieties which would expose him to psychosis. *Libido development* becomes a process of protection and defence directed against those primitive anxieties of early childhood which, due to the interpenetration of projection and introjection, Glover considers to be virtually tantamount to psychosis. Glover does not see libido development as a sequence of biological-somatic processes but rather as a sequence of anxieties over which the individual slowly gains ascendancy and control by the 'libidinization' of those parts of the body that have been threatened (castration, see above, fetishist) or by a specific type of drive satisfaction (sensual sucking, masturbation). The sense of reality of perverts and addicts is *not* disturbed because—as has already been stated—the individual concerned has learned to control his anxieties by 'libidinizing' the drug or the particular part of the body that is threatened. This type of anxiety defence is less successful in neurotics and consequently their sense of reality *is* disturbed. Psychotics achieve libido gratification in a relatively free and uninhibited manner but at the cost of a considerable restriction of their sense of reality.

But Glover is obliged to advance new and far-reaching hypotheses to explain the libidinization of primitive anxieties between the ages of six and eighteen months, a period in which it is scarcely possible to speak of a structure within the personality. It is 'neutralized sadism', i.e. sadism that has been freed from its destructive tendencies and transformed into a sort of self-preservation drive which forms the basis for the libidinization of anxiety and for subsequent repression. The problem of 'neutralized sadism' is typical of the problems attendant on psychoanalytic theories of affect. Glover is prepared to concede, however, that our understanding of the different forms of infantile affects and the mutations which these undergo, is clouded in obscurity.[1] He looks upon affects as the primary derivatives and responses to the *stress* to which the drives may be exposed. Of the various methods by which the grouping of affects may be accomplished, i.e. according to the principle of pleasure and displeasure, according to the relationship of affects to their attendant drives, according to their drive content or according to their 'mixture', Glover preferred the method, which *Freud* had already

[1] Glover, *ibid.*, p. 298.

followed, of grouping them on the basis of tension and discharge.[1] (As far as the problem of 'mixed' affects is concerned it should be noted that Glover, following the line pursued by Joan Rivières,[2] included jealousy in their number. He concluded that the development of 'mixed' affects was not a *simple* process but one which resulted from a variety of psychic experiences. This he also considered to apply to depression.) In the method of grouping based on tension and discharge the rise and fall in the tension of the affect is conceived in terms of a qualitative change in a specific quantity (energy). Taking anxiety as an example, Glover attempts to isolate the specific tension content of the anxiety, i.e. to reduce anxiety to a condition of pure tension. It seemed to him—and here he refers to *Melitta Schmideberg's*[3] investigations—that this was demonstrated by the sensation of 'disruption'. M. Schmideberg (one of Melanie Klein's collaborators) stresses the fact that the infant projects love and hate on to those parts of the body which cause it pain or pleasure. It fears a possible conflict between those parts of the body and develops the sensation of 'disruption' as a tension affect which, in Glover's view, is the precursor of a more complex anxiety condition. In a later phase Glover partially rejected his earlier conceptions, especially his theory of ego nuclei, and moved away from Melanie Klein. The theory of ego nuclei, from which he had derived a classification of psychoses, addictions and neuroses in terms of their relationship to the sense of reality and to regression, no longer seemed to him to offer an adequate answer to (1) the problem of psychosomatic illnesses and (2) the question as to when an unconscious childhood conflict triggered off a neurosis or a psychosis (i.e. the question as to the specificity (*a*) of the emergence of mental disturbances as such, (*b*) of the form which those disturbances assumed: whether hysteria, obsessional neurosis, addiction or psychosis, etc.). In order that he might master these difficulties Glover again had extensive recourse to *Freud's* views on the 'metapsychological phase'. He developed the idea of a 'primary functional phase', which the child enters shortly after birth and which is governed by the following considerations: (1) since the ego does not yet exist, neither do conflicts exist; (2) the pleasure principle is dominant. Displeasure, once felt, is avoided or arrested by counter-cathexis; (3) displeasure is equated with the trauma—in which Glover sees the precursor of conflict; (4) the counter-cathexis is the precursor of an ego organization; it serves to separate the pre-conscious from the un-conscious. The concept of conflict is only admissible after the development of a primitive ego organization, the emergence of which is then

---

[1] Note: and which Freud had taken from Wundt.
[2] 'Jealousy as a Mechanism of Defence', *Int. J. Psa.* Vol. XIII, 1932.
[3] Quoted from Glover, *op. cit.*, p. 304.

promoted above all by the incest phase and the development of the super ego.

The 'primary functional phase' may be equated with the Freudian concept of the' primary function'. Glover clarifies this idea by defining the limits which separate it from the conflict and the trauma, which latter he now designates, by a process of summation, as 'stress'.

(b) Contributions to the Psychopathology of Neuroses

Glover's considerable contributions to the psychopathology of neuroses are primarily concerned with addiction and alcoholism. He considers the following factors (drive modifications) to be responsible for alcoholism: the alcoholic's oral demands were subjected to extreme frustration. Consequently he has a partial fixation to the oral phase, to which he regresses when new burdens are imposed on him. *Oral* sadism, which is brought about as a result of frustrations, plays an important part in alcoholism. Apart from the oral fixation there is also an anal fixation with corresponding regressive and anal-sadistic tendencies. These fixations stunt the alcoholic's genital, phallic development and set the stage for a regression—which is triggered off by the fear of castration—to the anal and oral phases during his oedipal phase. And this regression is accompanied by a strong homosexual element. But above all it is the fear of castration which, in a particularly intense form, turns a man into an alcoholic. By analogy the same holds true for addictions as for alcoholism, merely, in respect of addictions Glover goes beyond the orthodox psychoanalytic interpretation by ascribing to the addict the above-mentioned position mid-way between perversions and psychoses.

It is characteristic of the problems facing psychoanalysis (see Part Three of this book) that its clinical descriptions reveal a high degree of similarity irrespective of the nature of the case in question. Whether it relates to an addiction, a potency disturbance or an obsessional neurosis the so-called pathological material frequently contains not only the stereotype castration complex but, over and above this, a regression to the anal stage, or to earlier stages, which arises out of the castration complex and corresponds to a partial fixation of a similar order, etc. But this problem, which is critical for psychoanalytic theory, will be investigated in detail in Part III (see below, sub-section g, p. 556 ff.).

Glover's development to date may be considered as falling into four phases which, although partly overlapping, reveal the following pattern:

1. Glover follows Freud closely.
2. He is influenced by Melanie Klein and moves away from Freud.
3. He turns back to Freud, criticizes and moves away from Melanie Klein.
4. He again moves away from Freud, develops a strongly pragmatic,

behaviouristic psychology and subjects psychoanalytic method in its present form to fundamental criticism.

In this last phase Glover insists that psychoanalysis should draw on other scientific disciplines and enter into close collaboration with them. These include biology, bio-chemistry, endocrinology and sociology. The main emphasis should be placed on the direct, empirical observation of patients, and especially of infants. He considers the method whereby far-reaching conclusions are drawn on the basis of material taken almost exclusively from case histories to be inadequate.

II. ERNEST JONES

The numerous contributions made by Freud's late disciple (1957†) to psychoanalysis include—over and above his work on nightmares,[1] his three volume biography of Freud and writings in which he presents and comments on Freud's works—

(a) his metapsychological studies and

(b) his studies on the psychopathology of neuroses.

Of the above-mentioned enquiries only the last two fall within the scope of this book.

(a) Metapsychological Studies

Amongst the most important of Ernest Jones's metapsychological studies are those in which he deals with the theory of symbols, with the phallic phase and with female sexuality.

The work on the theory of symbols is of particular importance because in it Jones analyses both *Silberer's* views and those advanced by C. G. Jung in his Complex psychology. He contrasts the Freudian conception of the nature of symbols, as developed above all by Rank and Sachs in their work on 'The Importance of Psychoanalysis for the Mental Sciences', with the interpretations put forward by Complex psychology. What is Jones's view of the function and purpose of the symbol?

1. The symbol replaces another concept or an idea in the sense that the idea contained in the concept is weakened by the symbol. For example, a semaphore signal can reproduce in a simplified form various complicated concepts by means of a single sign.

2. The symbol can represent a (simple) 'primary' element by analogy with the knot in a handkerchief, because it has something in common with that primary element.

[1] Jones's work on Nightmares is a comprehensive survey which sets out to demonstrate on the basis of material drawn both from antiquity and from the Middle Ages that the various superstitious forms of so-called nightmare are always linked with the inhibition of sexual drives (Freud's toxicological theory of anxiety).

3. The symbol is not expressed by means of the abstract communication characteristic of concepts but rather by means of a concrete optical or acoustic sign.

4. The use of the symbol corresponds to the early primitive stages of human development (both phylogenetically and ontogenetically).

5. The symbol can express a hidden or veiled concept.

6. The production of symbols is normally spontaneous and unconscious.

According to Jones only those symbols which can be categorized under the above six headings constitute 'genuine symbolism' and he differentiates between these and other types of indirect statement such as allegory and metaphor. In contrast above all to the metaphor, however, Jones ascribes to the symbol four additional properties, which he describes as follows: (1) Symbols represent *repressed* unconscious material. (2) Their meaning is constant and largely independent of spatial, temporal, hereditary and environmental factors. 3. This constancy derives from the largely analogous development of the psychic apparatus. (4) Symbols often reveal a relationship to linguistic expression. And then comes what is perhaps the most important point, namely that all symbols represent concepts of the self, of one's immediate blood relations, of death, birth and love. Jones tries to deal with the indisputable fact that, if his thesis is correct, it means that there are literally thousands of symbols representing these few basic facts of life, by referring to the arguments advanced by *Rank and Sachs*, which, however, are quite incapable of solving this problem.

Jones—in conformity with the assumptions already advanced by Freud—held that the symbol derives from three factors:

1. From identification: because their capacity for conceptual thought is under-developed, children and savages fuse and simplify the objects of their perception. This is exemplified by the child who calls all four-legged animals 'bow-wows'.

2. From the principle of pleasure and displeasure: if a child is required to understand a new object its first inclination is to *shy away* from the effort involved in forming a new concept that would adequately describe the object. Instead it will attempt to fit the object to the concepts which it already has at its disposal (e.g. bow-wow for all quadrupeds).

3. Jones quotes *Rank and Sachs*:[1]

'Psychologically considered, symbol-formation remains a regressive phenomenon, a reversion to a certain stage of pictorial thinking, which in fully civilized man is most plainly seen in those exceptional conditions in which conscious adaptation to reality is either restricted, as in

[1] Ernest Jones, *Papers on Psychoanalysis*, London, 1950, p. 108.

religious and artistic ecstasy, or seems to be completely abrogated, as in dreams and mental disorders. In correspondence with this psychological conception is the original function, demonstrable in the history of civilization, of the identification underlying symbolism as a means to adaptation to reality, which becomes superfluous and sinks to the mere significance of a symbol as soon as this task of adaptation has been accomplished. Symbolism thus appears as the unconscious precipitate of primitive means of adaptation to reality that have become superfluous and useless, a sort of lumber-room of civilization to which the adult readily flees in states of reduced or deficient capacity for adaptation to reality, in order to regain his old, long-forgotten playthings of childhood. What later generations know and regard only as a symbol had in earlier stages of mental life full and real meaning and value. In the course of development the original significance fades more and more or even changes, though speech, folk-lore, wit, etc., have often preserved more or less plain traces of the original association.'

But the fact that it is always the church tower which symbolizes the phallus and never the phallus which symbolizes the church tower is due less to the similarity between the two objects as such than to the intervention of specific affects, which repress the one in favour of the other. Symbols arise by analogy with symptoms as a compromise between repressed material and a repressing instance. Jones contrasts this psycho-analytic conception of the symbol with the conceptions of *Silberer* and *C. G. Jung*, to both of which he applies the title of 'functional symbolism'. Since for Jung libido simply means psychic energy as such, it follows that all indirect representations are symbols, i.e. if one psychic process replaces another it is then a symbol. Accordingly a castration complex that was associated with hysterical blindness *is for Jung the symbol of the symptom of blindness*. In *Freud's* view, however, the opposite is true: the symptom is a consequence and, in certain circumstances, a symbol of the castration complex, whereas the castration complex could never be a symbol of the blindness.

Silberer[1] noticed that, if he thought of certain things when he was tired, his thought concepts were transformed into images (symbols), which bore a direct relationship to the concepts. This process, which he called an 'auto-symbolic phenomenon', may be sub-divided into three component processes: (1) 'functional phenomena', which show how the psyche works, e.g. quickly or slowly; (2) 'material phenomena', which present the contents of the concepts; (3) 'somatic phenomena', under which Silberer understands the symbolic representation of physical processes. The first of these three processes is initiated when, due perhaps to tiredness, the psyche is unable to grasp a concept or when, for

[1] See Ernest Jones, *Papers on Psychoanalysis*, London, 1950, pp. 110 ff.

hereditary or other biological reasons, the mental faculties have been impaired. In either case a regression to more primitive stages takes place, involving the interplay of two mutually antagonistic factors, one of which (the positive one) tries to raise the concept into consciousness, whilst the other (the negative one) tries to prevent it from doing so. The first draws its energy from the affect which has been invested in the concept, whilst the second arises either from the apperceptive weakness of the psyche's powers of comprehension or from affects which prevent the concept from being raised into consciousness (repression). For *Silberer* Freud's dream censorship is the other side of apperceptive weakness—although he does concede that this weakness is not to be considered as the cause of symbolism. However, he is chiefly interested in the factors which *make it possible* for symbolism to take place and less interested in those which actually produce it. The actual point at which Silberer deviates from Freud's conception is when he lists repression and all the affective processes under the general concept of functional symbolism. These processes—e.g. repression—are now *themselves* symbols and as such they characterize the course of the psychic processes (see under Ferenczi, p. 175 ff.). From this it follows that the symbol of the snake, when equated with the phallus in Freudian psychoanalysis, does not pay sufficient attention to the loathing and fear of the snake which are also expressed in this symbol and which in fact constitute the forces of repression. These forces are no less present in the symbol of the snake than is the indication of the phallus: in other words the process of repression represents itself in the symbol of the snake, it is itself the symbol of the concept of loathing or fear. For Silberer, therefore, the symbol consists of the concept which is portrayed and the subjective (affective) attitude of the individual to this concept. According to Jones[1] Silberer attaches no importance to the decisive cause of the symbol, namely, the suppression of certain affects and the concepts with which they are linked. Consequently the difference between the *Jungian* and *Freudian* interpretations of the symbol consists in the fact that, whereas the Jungians consider the symbol to be a combination of an objective (abstract) concept and a (secondary) affect, for the Freudians the symbol remains a compromise between the repressing instances and the repressed content. Thus for *Jungians* the snake is a symbol of sexuality as such and—with the aid of Oriental myths—also comes to represent such qualities as wisdom, whilst for *Freudians* it is restricted to its phallic character. For *Jung* the symbol already contains the abstract idea *in nuce* and is therefore related to the future, whilst for *Freud* the symbol serves the purpose of concealing the conceivable concept that is contained within it. Jones considers that *Jung's* and *Silberer's* view would seem to indicate the possible *sublimation* of the symbol to the status of an idea and he distinguishes between three groups of psychic material: (1) the unconscious complexes, (2) the repressing instances (censorship), (3) the sublimating tendencies deriving from the unconscious complexes. Symbols are the products of inner-psychic conflicts between the first and second groups. The content (the conceptual definition) of the symbols was derived from the third group, the sublimations, and constituted no more than a secondary process. In Jones's opinion Silberer had confused the process of symbolic equation or definition with the process whereby the symbol actually came into being. For the definition of the symbol in terms of meaning was a secondary process, deriving from the process of sublimation, which, according to Silberer, represents itself in the process of symbol formation. Whether this argument succeeds in clarifying the relationship between symbol and concept will be dealt with in Part Three of this book.

Jones's work on the phallic phase reveals strong affinities to *Melanie Klein's* theories on the pre-oedipal phases (see below). The Oedipus complex is re-formulated with special regard to the *oral* phase and the little boy's oral-sadistic impulses *vis-à-vis* his mother's breasts. The little boy transfers these sadistic impulses of the oral phase (biting) to his own penis, which penetrates the mother's body, there to meet and destroy the father's penis. This bold conception—which Melanie Klein and Jones believe they can substantiate on the basis of clinical material— is developed in the following way: oral-sadistic impulses are aroused in the little boy as a result of weaning and the denial which this involves. The little boy equates the nipple with the penis and consequently believes that the mother cannot lose her penis (=nipple) and is moreover able to incorporate and retain every penis that approaches her. This applies above all to the father's penis, which she keeps inside her stomach. And so, apart from the nipple, the mother also possesses a penis—just like the father—, but it remains inside her stomach and is therefore invisible. In dreams it is symbolized by dragons living in caves.

The little boy's feelings of hatred and destructiveness arise as a result of the denial which weaning constitutes for him. These feelings are first directed towards the nipple, which he proceeds to bite, but are subsequently transferred to the father's penis, which he assumes to be inside his mother's body. His desire to penetrate his mother's body with his own penis is prompted by the possibility of discovering his father's penis and of destroying it with his own. This of course would mean that his penis would suffer the same fate as that which had befallen his father"s, namely, castration at the hands of his mother. For his penis would then also remain in the mother's body. On the other hand, in the phallic phase the little boy needs this conception of his mother with the father's penis inside her, because it protects him from his fear of castration: for the mother also has a penis, one which, it is true, is invisible, but none the less there has been *no* castration. This conception involves the process of 'libidinization' of fear, which was criticized by *Fenichel* (see above). The phallic phase, in which the conception of the mother with the penis is developed as a protection against castration, appears to Jones to be 'more a neurotic compromise than a natural consequence of sexual development'. Jones considers that the only way in which the boy may regain a positive attitude to the female sex and thus banish the fear of castration, which would otherwise be released during intercourse upon his penetrating the vagina, would be for him first to regress to the 'proto-phallic' stage, in which the child is unaware of sexual differences. This stage precedes the 'deutero-phallic' stage, in which the child becomes aware of the differences between the two sexes, which are destined to have such grave repercussions. Just how the little boy who regresses to the proto-phallic stage following his Oedipus complex then develops a 'normal sexuality', whether indeed this 'normal sexuality' can even be said to exist or whether in fact the neurotic compromise of the phallic phase does not continue for the rest of his life—these are questions which remain shrouded in darkness.

Jones considers the little girl's development to be analogous. In his investigations into the early stages of female sexuality he uses the concept of 'aphinisis' to denote the process whereby the fear of castration, which applies only to the penis, is expanded into a fear of total destruction of sexuality, such as may be occasioned by the denials met with in the pre-oedipal stages. From the oral stage the little girl passes to the stage in which her sexual satisfaction is chiefly derived from her discovery of the clitoris and from phantasies in which she sucks her father's penis (fellatio). This stage is then succeeded by the anal stage and ultimately by the discovery of the vagina. The discovery of the mouth, the anus and the vagina is characterized by a corresponding identification with the mother. In this phase the Oedipus complex reaches its peak and the little girl desires to replace her mother *vis-à-vis* her father. Her attitude towards the penis in this period is one of typical penis envy, in which connection Jones, following the example set by *Karen Horney*[1] in her investigations, speaks of primary and secondary penis envy. Karen Horney links the primary stage of penis envy with the numerous actions which the little boy is able to perform with his penis, such as urination, exhibitionism, masturbation, etc. The little girl envies the little boy these activities. The secondary stage of penis envy is characterized by the desire to share in the possession of the penis by coitus-like undertakings. The constant frustration which the little girl feels—never to have a

[1] See Ernest Jones, *Papers on Psychoanalysis*, London, 1950, p. 444.

204

penis like her father, never to have a child from him—constitutes the primary cause of penis envy in this secondary stage (see especially Helene *Deutsch*[1]). How is the little girl to find a way out of this insoluble conflict, in which she must either renounce her father or her own vagina? If she renounces the father and transfers her affections to another object, she will be in a position to develop normal erotic desires and a normal erotic attitude. But if she renounces her own vagina and clings to the notion that she possesses a penis of her own, then the relationship to the father may be maintained on the basis of her identification with him. (In the case of both boys and girls such an attitude leads to homosexuality.) In both cases incest is overcome by the appropriate defence mechanisms. *Freud's* 'phallic' stage in girls is that in which the girls maintain their belief that they possess a penis. Jones considers that a defence mechanism is at work in this stage analogous to that operative in the deutero-phallic stage in little boys (i.e. neurotic compromise).

(b) Studies on the Psychopathology of Neuroses

Of the investigations undertaken by Jones into the psychopathology of neuroses only one—that on *Fear, Guilt and Hate*—will be mentioned here. It should be pointed out that Jones had not yet come under the influence of Melanie Klein when he made this investigation, in which he argues that fear, guilt and hatred arise above all as reactions to the Oedipus complex. Fear, guilt and hatred are to be considered as attempts on the part of the individual to cope with his incestuous desires without losing control of the situation, despite the presence of strong libidinal tension. Affects, such as fear and hatred of the father, together with the guilt feelings to which these give rise, Jones interprets as a defence against incestuous desires. On the one hand, due to extreme aphinisis,[1] i.e. the inhibition of all libidinal desires, the child runs the risk of losing all control of the libido—such as would be the case if, due to total repression, the libido were to withdraw—or else it develops feelings of fear, guilt and hatred which, whilst affording temporary relief from the libidinal tensions, lay the foundations for a future neurosis. Within the general context of this investigation Jones points out that, for purposes of therapy, it is important that the patient should learn to accept guilt feelings and to suffer hatred.

III. ANNA FREUD

Psychoanalysis is indebted to Anna Freud, not only for her numerous investigations and observations within the field of child psychiatry, but

[1] See Ernest Jones, *Papers on Psychoanalysis*, London, 1950, p. 441.
[2] See above.

also for having been the first to have attempted a comprehensive account of the ego's defence mechanisms *vis-à-vis* the id and the outside world.[1] Her investigations will be considered here under two separate headings:

(a) The Ego and the Mechanisms of Defence.

(b) Contributions to Child Psychiatry.

(a) *The Ego and the Mechanisms of Defence*

Symptoms, faulty actions, symbols, specific character patterns may be regarded as compromise actions in the struggle between the (defending) ego and the id. Since psychoanalysis has engaged primarily in the study of the id and psychoanalytic techniques and therapy have been devoted to the analysis and reconstruction of the primary drive impulses, ego activity has necessarily been neglected. Anna Freud tries to fill this gap in psychoanalytic theory and technique by investigating the ego processes as revealed by the defence mechanisms which the ego employs against drive impulses. In terms of the actual analysis the ego occupies three main positions: it helps the analysis in as far as it places at its disposal its capacity for self-observation; it hinders the analysis when it opposes the dissolution of resistances and compromise formations; and, finally, it becomes the object of the analysis when its defensive actions come under scrutiny. Siegmund Freud had himself investigated the defence processes and given individual descriptions of each of them, although it was not until 1926 that he revived the actual term 'defence', which he had first introduced in 1894. It was on the basis of these investigations that Anna Freud put forward the following defence mechanisms:

(a)	Regression	(f)	Projection
(b)	Repression	(g)	Introjection
(c)	Reaction-formation	(h)	Turning against the self
(d)	Isolation	(i)	Reversal
(e)	Undoing		

Repression is still considered to be the chief factor at work in the genesis of neuroses. The other forms of defence, 'even when they assume an acute form, remain more within the limits of the normal. They manifest themselves in innumerable transformations, distortions and deformities of the ego, which are in part the accompaniment of and in part substitutes for neurosis'.[2]

Anna Freud quotes the following case as an example of a process of repression and displacement [3]

[1] In her book, *The Ego and the Mechanisms of Defence*, London, Hogarth Press; New York, International Universities Press.

[2] Anna Freud, *ibid.*, p. 54.　　　　[3] Anna Freud, *ibid.*, p. 52.

'I will take as an illustration the case of a patient, who also suffered in very early childhood from acute penis-envy, in her case in relation to her father. The sexual phantasies of this phase reached their climax in the wish to bite off her father's penis. At this point the ego set up its defence. The shocking idea was repressed. It was replaced by its opposite—a general disinclination to bite, which soon developed into a difficulty in eating, accompanied by hysterical feelings of disgust. And part of the prohibited impulse—that represented by the oral phantasy—had now been mastered. But the aggressive content, i.e. the wish to rob her father or a father-substitute, remained in consciousness for a time, until, as the super-ego developed, the ego's moral sense repudiated this impulse. By means of a mechanism of displacement, which I shall discuss more fully later, the urge to rob was transformed into a peculiar kind of contentedness and unassumingness. We see that the two successive methods of defence produced a substratum of hysteria and, superimposed on this, a specific ego-modification, not in itself of a pathological character.'

Whether it is that repression opposes drive impulses of a purely sexual nature, whilst the other defence processes are concerned with aggressiveness or other such wishes remains an open question. *J. Lampl de Groot* advances the view that the other defence mechanisms deal with any material that repression was unable to cope with,[1] whilst *Helene Deutsch* assumes that 'each defence mechanism is first evolved in order to master some specific instinctual urge and so is associated with a particular phase of infantile development'.[2] Siegmund Freud considers it possible 'that before its sharp cleavage into an ego and an id, and before the formation of a super ego, the mental apparatus makes use of different methods of defence from those which it employs after it has attained these levels of organization'.[3] *Melanie Klein's* view (see below) that introjection and projection are the first defence processes to take place in infancy is not shared by Anna Freud. She considers that the earliest neurotic disturbances observable in infancy are of a hysterial nature and thus presuppose repression. But she does concede that the chronology of the defence processes is still quite uncertain, a fact born out above all by the differences of opinion which obtain regarding the genesis of the super ego. Anna Freud considers the defence processes from three different points of view: (1) Defence prompted by fear of the super ego (which applies chiefly to adult neurosis); (2) Defence prompted by fear of reality, which characterizes infantile neuroses. 'The infantile ego fears the instincts because it fears the outside world. Its

[1] Reported by Anna Freud, *The Ego and the Mechanisms of Defence*, p. 55.
[2] *Ibid.*, p. 55.
[3] *Ibid.*, p. 55. (From S. Freud *Inhibition, Symptom and Anxiety*.)

defence against them is motivated by dread of the outside world, i.e. by objective anxiety.'[1] This applies to all prohibitions and punishments to which the child might expose itself by gratifying a drive; (3) Defence prompted by fear of drive strength. (This applies when the ego fears it will be overpowered or overwhelmed by the drives. Anna Freud assumes a primary hostility to the drives on the part of the ego in respect of sexuality, which, she maintains, is phylogenetically determined and constitutes the basis of the ego's irresolvable ambivalence.) In addition to these types of defence against the drives, which are largely structurally determined, i.e. in terms of the differentiation between ego, id and super ego, there are also other modes of defence against the drives, which stem from opposing tendencies within the drives themselves.[2] Homosexuality and heterosexuality, passivity and activity, can come into conflict and thus trigger off ego defence.

Anna Freud quotes numerous clinical examples from both child and adult analysis in support of her thesis of the defence processes. The avoidance of objective displeasure and objective danger by the application of various defence processes are two of the most important conditions illustrated by these examples: objective danger is denied in phantasy, as in the case of the phobia of the five-year-old boy, Hans,[3] whose fear of castration was denied in the phantasy of the plumber who unscrewed his buttocks and penis with a spanner, in order to replace them with bigger and better ones. Objective displeasure may also be denied in phantasy by means of reversal, e.g. a threatenening person is transformed into a protective person. The denial in phantasy of objective reality may be complemented by words and actions, e.g. the 'little man' who with hat and cane plays the part of his father's 'father'. The 'restriction of the ego', which is prompted by objective fear or displeasure, also constitutes one of the defence processes in that it enables the child (and less frequently the adult) to avoid situations which would engender objective fear. Common examples of this particular defence process are those in which the individual shuns physical effort (e.g. gymnastics) in favour of intellectual pursuits or restricts his human relationships to inferior persons. The difference between ego restriction and inhibition (which Freud called a restriction of the ego functions) lies in the fact that in the case of ego restriction the defence process is due solely to displeasurable *environmental* impressions, whereas inhibitions are directed against the danger from within, from the id. In ego

---

[1] Reported by Anna Freud, *The Ego and the Mechanisms of Defence*, p. 61.
[2] See especially F. Alexander 'Verhältnis von Struktur zu Triebkonflikten', *Int. Z. Psa.* Vol. XX, 1934, p. 33. (Relationship between Structural and Drive Conflicts) and Fenichel's criticism of this view.
[3] S. Freud, *Analysis of the Phobia of a Five Year Old Boy*.

restriction those situations are avoided which 'would resuscitate displeasurable objective impressions from the past'.[1] The inhibited person, on the other hand, will avoid situations calculated to endanger his inner equilibrium by arousing forbidden and fear-laden drives (e.g. phobia). Anna Freud summarizes her findings as follows:

'In the foregoing chapters I have tried to classify the various defence mechanisms according to the specific anxiety situations which call them into action and I have illustrated my remarks by a number of clinical examples. As our knowledge of the unconscious activity of the ego advances, a much more precise clarification will probably become possible. There is still considerable obscurity about the historical connection between typical experiences in individual development and the production of particular modes of defence. My examples suggest that the typical situations in which the ego has recourse to the mechanism of denial are those associated with ideas of castration and with the loss of love objects. On the other hand, the altruistic surrender of instinctual impulses seems, under certain conditions, to be a specific means of overcoming narcissistic mortification.

'In the present state of our knowledge we can already speak with greater certainty about the parallels between the ego's defensive measures against external and against internal danger. *Repression* gets rid of instinctual derivatives, just as external stimuli are abolished by *denial*. *Reaction-formation* secures the ego against the return of repressed impulses from within, while by *phantasies in which the real situation is reversed* denial is sustained against overthrow from without. *Inhibition* of instinctual impulses corresponds to the *restrictions* imposed on the ego to avoid "pain" from external sources. *Intellectualization* of the instinctual processes as a precaution against danger from within is analogous to the constant *alertness* of the ego for dangers from without. All the other defensive measures which, like reversal and turning against the subject, entail an alteration in the instinctual processes themselves have their counterpart in the ego's attempts to deal with the external danger by actively intervening to change the conditions of the world around it. Upon this last side of the ego's activities I cannot enlarge here.

'This comparison of parallel processes suggests the question: whence does the ego derive the form of its defence mechanisms? Is the struggle with the outside forces modelled on the conflict with the instincts? Or is the converse the case: are the measures adopted in the external struggle the prototype of the various defence mechanisms? The decision between these two alternatives can hardly be a straightforward one. The infantile ego experiences the onslaught of instinctual and external

[1] Anna Freud, *The Ego and the Mechanisms of Defence*, pp. 108 ff.

stimuli at the same time; if it wishes to preserve its existence it must defend itself on both sides stimultaneously. In the struggle with the different kinds of stimuli which it has to master it probably adapts its weapons to the particular need, arming itself now against danger from within and now against danger from without.

'How far does the ego follow its own laws in its defence against the instincts and how far is it influenced by the character of the instincts themselves? Perhaps some light may be thrown on this problem by a comparison with an analogous process, that of *dream-distortion*. The translation of latent dream thoughts into the manifest dream content is carried out at the behest of the censor, i.e. the representative of the ego in sleep. But the dream work itself is not performed by the ego. Condensation, displacement and the many strange modes of representation which occur in dreams are processes peculiar to the id and are merely utilized for purposes of distortion. In the same way the various measures of defence are not entirely the work of the ego. In so far as the instinctual processes themselves are modified, use is made of the peculiar properties of instinct. For instance, the readiness with which such processes can be *displaced* assists the mechanism of *sublimation,* by which the ego achieves its purpose of diverting the instinctual impulses from their purely sexual goals to aims which society holds to be higher. Again, in securing repressions by means of *reaction-formation* the ego avails itself of the instinct's capacity for *reversal*. We may conjecture that a defence is proof against attack, only if it is built up on this two-fold basis—on the one hand the ego and, on the other, the essential nature of instinctual processes.

'But even when we admit that the ego has not an entirely free hand in devising the defence mechanisms which it employs, our study of these mechanisms impresses us with the magnitude of its achievement. The existence of neurotic symptoms in itself indicates that the ego has been overpowered, and every return of repressed impulses, with its sequel in compromise-formation, shows that some plan for defence has miscarried and the ego has suffered a defeat. But the ego is victorious when its defensive measures effect their purpose, i.e. when they enable it to restrict the development of anxiety and "pain" and so to transform the instincts that, even in difficult circumstances, some measure of gratification is secured, thereby establishing the most harmonious relations possible within the id, the super ego and the forces of the outside world.'[1]

(b) Contributions to Child Psychiatry

During the Second World War Anna Freud and her colleagues had the

[1] Anna Freud, *The Ego and the Mechanisms of Defence*, pp. 190–3.

opportunity of observing evacuated children living apart from their parents in communal centres. These observations[1] constitute one of the earliest attempts to study child development on a broad clinical basis with the object of collating the results thus obtained with psychoanalytic theory. Not until after 1945 was the method combining Behaviourist observation with psychoanalytic techniques systematically pursued on a large scale, chiefly by *R. Spitz* and *A. Gsell*. The reconstruction of early libido development, which was made by Siegmund Freud on the basis of information furnished by neurotic adults, must surely be one of the most remarkable achievements in the whole of psychoanalytic theory. Anna Freud's observations regarding libido development, however, persuaded her that the oral and anal phases overlapped to a considerable degree, a view which was to some extent contrary to S. Freud's view. She warns against treating the various stages of libido development as separate entities. Even children who had been breast-fed over a long period continued to reveal both oral wishes and anal tendencies for an astonishing length of time. These children persevered with sensual sucking and occasional sensual biting far into the anal stage. It was easier to separate the phases, however, in terms of the child's attitude towards its mother or foster-mother: the extreme dependence (of the oral phase) was succeeded by the tormenting possessiveness (of the anal phase) or the mania for self-assertion (of the phallic phase).

Another of the remarkable observations, which Anna Freud and *D. T. Burlingham* illustrated by reference to numerous case histories, indicates that parts of the so-called primary process continue far on into the second year of life.[1] The behaviour of the two-year-old child fluctuates strongly between surrender to the pleasure principle (primary process) and acceptance of the reality principle. On the other hand the influence of the ego—its defence against the drives and its intellectual achievements—is demonstrably present. Another striking observation reveals that children, who are subjected to traumas, immediately *regress* to oral or anal stages without giving any hint of conflict. This observation contradicts the psychoanalytic view of regression, which, although it considers aggression to be a defence mechanism, none the less envisages a conflict between the desire for drive satisfaction, which is the object of the regression, and the ego or super ego. But there was no sign of conflict in the regressive behaviour patterns of these children, a fact which Anna Freud tries to explain by the assumption of a concomitant regression on the part of the ego and the super ego.

Further observations, which are not easily reconciled with psychoanalytic theory, include the following:

[1] Anna Freud and D. T. Burlingham, *War and Children*, London, 1942; also *Infants without Families*, London, 1944.

1.   The appearance of penis envy in girls between 18 and 24 years of age.

2.   Violent reactions in the form of shame and loathing *before* cleanliness training.

3.   The frequent 'telescoping', in the recollection of adults, of numerous traumatic and auto-erotic experiences (masturbation) into a single incident or a small number of incidents.

4.   Little children playing at sexual intercourse, although they had had *no* previous opportunity of observing sexual intercourse between adults.

5.   The adoption by little boys between the anal and phallic phases of a male, paternal pattern of behaviour (e.g. protective, solicitous), although there had been no father on whom they might have modelled themselves or whom they might have imitated.

6.   The development on the part of the children, within a matter of days, of typical 'family patterns of behaviour', when they had the opportunity of staying with a family for a short period (e.g. for purposes of adoption. Three days after his adoption by a married couple a four and-a-half-year-old boy had a specifically oedipal fit of jealousy at the breakfast table, although there had been no previous opportunity for this complex to develop).

IV.   MELANIE KLEIN[1]

Melanie Klein is undoubtedly one of the most interesting but also one of the most controversial personalities within the British Group. Her influence on the other members of this group is undeniable—even though a split has meanwhile taken place between the 'Kleinians' and the orthodox Freudians. *Glover*, who was strongly influenced by her until the mid-'forties, has since undertaken a critical assessment[2] of her work, in which he retreats from his former position. Melanie Klein's theses are based on the analyses of children between three and a half and twelve years of age, which she 'interpolates' with the statements of schizophrenics and neurotic adults.

(a)   The Development of Child Analysis

Melanie Klein's earliest works on child analysis, which, like Freud's analysis of the phobia of a five-year-old boy, are based primarily on observations of neurotic children, go back to 1920, to writers such as Hug-Helmuth, Pfister and v. Tausk (the last of whom, v. Tausk, wrote chiefly on masturbation). Before 1920 there was no such thing as independent child analysis or child therapy. And to this day every

---

[1] Melanie Klein, *Contributions to Psychoanalysis*, London, 1950; see also Bibliography in this work.

[2] *The Psychoanalytic Study of the Child*, 1945, p. 75 ff.

attempt to establish an analytic therapy for children has in fact amounted to little more than a confirmation of psychoanalytic theory (see also Glover *op. cit.*, p. 77 ff.). If we disregard *Ferenczi's* and *Abraham's* attempts to describe the pre-oedipal phases in terms of the child's sense of reality or of its libido, then the contribution in terms of new clinical material made by child analysis to psychoanalytic theory is a minor one. It was Melanie Klein's achievement to have provided, by means of her system of play therapy and her own doubtless considerable powers of intuitive perception, new theses with which to fill the gaps, which then existed, above all in the interpretation of the pre-oedipal stages. Her observations may be divided into two periods. The first of these ended in 1932 with the publication of her *Psychoanalysis of Children*, whilst the second (beginning in 1934) was chiefly concerned with her investigations into manic-depressive illness. Prior to 1932 she was content to extend the boundaries of knowledge regarding the per-oedipal phases in children, but in her second period she proceeded to draw far-reaching conclusions from the data which she had established in the first period, conclusions which deviated from Freudian theory to no small degree.

(b) The First Phase

The development of both boy and girl is stamped in equal measure by the trenchant experience to which they are subjected in weaning, but they have different ways of dealing with this severe oral denial. The nipple of the mother's breast is replaced by the father's penis, which both boy and girl would like to incorporate during the phase of oral sadism. This desire for incorporation is identical with the introjection of the penis. But the child imagines that the mother is preventing it from realizing its desire, for has not the mother herself already incorporated the father's penis? Consequently the child's sadism does not stop short of the mother's body. On the contrary it wishes to destroy it. But these sadistic impulses then engender in the child a *fear* of themselves—for Melanie Klein fear is the consequence of aggression—, against which the child protects itself by the phantasy of incorporatng its father's penis. The child establishes the father's penis within itself as an introjected object, which then forms the basis of the super ego. The super ego serves a dual purpose. It enables the child to project its impulses of hate on to the outside world, whilst at the same time inhibiting the child's sadistic desires by virtue of its severity. The destructive impulses projected on to the world at large provide the child with 'bad' objects, which, by a process of oral aggression, it again incorporates and introjects—and thus strengthens the foundation of the super ego. The process may be summarized as follows:

1. Sadism towards the mother's breast	I
2. is transferred to the father's penis;	The phase
3. the father's penis is in the mother's body;	of
4. the sadism is directed towards the mother in general.	Oral Aggression.
1. The penis is introjected;	II
2. it forms the basis of the super ego,	The phase
3. (which enables aggression to be projected on to the outside world)	of Defence.
4. and is able to stem the tide of aggression by virtue of its severity.	
1. The projection of sadistic impulses on to the outside world creates 'bad objects';	III The phase of alternating
2. these are re-incorporated and re-introjected by oral aggression;	projection and
3. they strengthen the foundations of the super ego.	introjection.

In Melanie Klein's view oral aggression is also responsible for the children's unconscious knowledge of their parents' sexual activities. They develop aggressive impulses to 'stick' something into their mother's body long before they know what a penis is. The little boy is more frightened by this mother with the incorporated penis, since he believes her to be an antagonistic combination of both parents. The consequence of such beliefs is: (1) the development of the super ego in the oral phase, (2) a correspondingly early development of the Oedipus complex before the actual oedipal phase.

The phase of alternating projection and introjection (III) is not restricted to the projection of aggressive objects and the introjection of bad objects. It also applies to 'good' objects—e.g. the breast that gives suck—in as far as these do not oppose the child's desires with denials. But this conception of 'good' and 'bad' objects, which is doubtless based on the child's tendency—demonstrably present in all children's statements—to paint everything either black or white, is one of the least clear of Melanie Klein's theses. Nor is this the only complication attendant on the child's development in the pre-oedipal phase. A further characteristic of this phase is the fact that each stage of libido development constitutes a successful defence effected by the libido against the aggressive impulses (see also 'libidinization' of anxiety, p. 191 ff.). The possibility of introjecting 'good' objects is only given when the corresponding phase of libido development has been reached, one which is accompanied by an increase in the child's adaptation to reality—which means that the child is able to control its fears and aggressions. In the anal stage fear is linked with guilt feelings. It is in this phase that obsessional neuroses are rooted (see also *Freud*), whilst the schizophrenic and manic-depressive psychoses with their intensified projections and introjections (depressions) derive exclusively from disturbances of the oral phase and constitute a repetition of that phase. The difference between the little boy and the little girl lies in the following points:

1. The little girl identifies with the mother, who has incorporated a penis. Consequently she believes that she too has a penis. These phantasies are one of the reasons why the little girl develops a stronger super ego than the little boy and why she remains prone to illusions of omnipotence over a far longer period.

2. The little boy discovers the existence of his penis at an early age and his main endeavours are given over to destroying his father's penis within his mother's body (see also Jones, p. 199 ff.). He only develops the fear of castration, which is typical of his sex, when he conceives the desire to destroy his father's penis.

(c) The Second Phase

When Melanie Klein enlarged on her theses she adopted the view that the position occupied by 'infantile depression' in the child's development was one of critical importance for its whole future life. What is this infantile depression, which Melanie Klein postulates for the first six months of human existence? It is an (unconscious) phantasy, in which the 'good' object is totally destroyed or dismembered and can never again be reconstituted. Depending on the particular circumstances the 'good' object might be the mother's breast, or it might be the mother and father image, i.e. the image of the parents compounded from projection and introjection. The ego, having introjected the good objects, realizes that it is unable to defend them against its own destructive impulses. All neuroses and psychoses are to be considered as attempts on the part of the ego to overcome this very early anxiety, which derives from the ego's inability to defend the 'good' objects against its own sadistic impulses, which in turn derive from both the id and the introjected 'bad' objects.[1] This process applies above all to *mania*, which Melanie Klein interprets as an attempt on the part of the ego to fuse in a feeling of omnipotence the inwardly 'dismembered' objects, which, because of their disintegration, are no longer able to satisfy the total demand for love.

(d) Problems and Criticisms of Melanie Klein's Theories

E. Glover, W. Foulkes and Melitta Schmideberg[2] have subjected

---

[1] See also Joan Rivière, quoted from *Psa. St. of the Child*, Vol. I, pp. 45, 90 ff.
[2] *Psychoanalytic Study of the Child*, ibid., Vol. I, p. 45.

Melanie Klein's system to detailed criticism from the point of view of Freudian psychoanalytic theory. They consider that Melanie Klein failed adequately to distinguish the concept of introjection from phantasy, from the object presentation, from the feelings arising out of the physical sphere and from the desires of the id. In point of fact Melanie Klein's phantasy concept was indistinguishable from Freud's id, in spite of which she attributed to the id no more than a substitute function. Melanie Klein considers that phantasy becomes operative within a few weeks of birth and that the relationship between phantasy and the unconscious corresponds to the relationship between the preconscious and the unconscious. Susan Isaacs,[1] a student of Melanie Klein's, asserts that phantasy is the primary content of all the conscious and unconscious activities of the psychic apparatus. The distinctions which Freud draws between memory trace, object presentation, object imago, phantasy, introjection and identification are lost in Melanie Klein's phantasy concept. The separation of affect and idea—basic to the Freudian conception—is likewise suspended. And the contrast between the denial and the fulfilment of wishes becomes pointless when, as in Melanie Klein's view, the child's development depends only in a very limited sense on environmental influences. By virtue of its phantasy the child is largely independent of the denial experiences of real life, which can lead to neurosis or psychosis. A conception such as this must necessarily end in biologism and Klein, like *Rank*, did in fact adopt a completely fatalistic view of the development of neuroses or psychoses. In place of Rank's birth trauma Melanie Klein put forward the traumatic withdrawal of love in the third month of the infant's life as the chief source of infantile depression. Due to the interlacing of projection and introjection the incipient testing and acceptance of reality is not taken into consideration. For Melanie Klein phantasy is both the psychic representation of the drive and also an agent of defence against the drive. According to Freud the ability to distinguish between external and internal reality and the ability to establish a relationship between the subject, the aim of his drives and the object of his drives are all part of the function of phantasy, which, in his view, is a relatively late product of development. Its introduction—according to Freud—depends on three factors: (1) the failure of hallucination as a source of substitute satisfaction, (2) the development of a relationship to reality and (3) the function of repression. These differentiating factors with their important metapsychological implications do not apply in Melanie Klein's system. Since she traces introjection and projection back to very early bodily functions—'taking in' and 'giving out'—it is impossible to distinguish them from bodily functions as such. Activities, which for

[1] See footnote Glover, *ibid.*

Freud (and also for *Abraham* and *Ferenczi*) are analogous, are identical for Klein: eating (taking in) is identical with thinking in early infancy.

For Melanie Klein aggression also occupies a central position. She attributes to it qualities which resemble those attributed to the libido by Freud. Anxiety arises primarily as a result of aggression, as fear *of* aggression, but not as a result of 'frustrated' libido (in his first phase Freud postulated pent-up libido as the source of aggression). According to Klein libido can only neutralize anxiety.

Glover concludes his criticism of Melanie Klein by accusing her of a tendency towards *Weltanschauung* and 'biological mysticism' and compares the supposedly critical trauma of the third month of life with original sin.

E

THE NEW YORK GROUP

I. H. HARTMANN, E. KRIS, R. LOEWENSTEIN[1]

Over the past twenty-five years the majority of members of the New York Group of Freudian analysts have published their work in the *International Journal of Psycho-analysis* and also, since 1945, in *The Psycho-analytic Study of the Child*. By now these contributions, which include both casuistic and metapsychological studies, run into the thousands. For purposes of this enquiry, however, only those authors will be considered, whose writings represent a specific advance on the basic tenets of Freudian psychoanalysis. Chief amongst these is *Heinz Hartmann*, who, both as a critic of and a contributor to psychoanalytic theory, has gained a key position within this group similar to that occupied by E. Glover within the British group. Together with *E. Kris* and *R. Loewenstein* Hartmann has made important contributions to the psychology of the structure and the dynamics of the personality.[2]

(a) Contributions to Ego Psychology

Structures—psychic systems—are defined in terms of their functions. How to accord the ego a greater degree of autonomy than *Freud* had

[1] W. E. Hoffer may also be considered as belonging to this same group centred around Hartmann. See esp. 'Mutual Influences in the Development of Ego and Id, Earliest Stages' (*Ps. St. of the Child*, Vol. VII, p. 31), also 'Development of the Body Ego' (*Ps. St. of the Child*, Vol. V, pp. 18 ff.), where Hoffer postulates, on the basis of his observations of the interaction of hand and mouth in infants. the autonomy of the ago in infancy.

[2] See also H. Hartmann, 'Mutual Influences in the Development of Ego and Id' (*Ps. St. of the Child*, Vol. VII, pp. 9 ff.). 'Comments on the Formation of Psychic Structure' (*P.St. of the Child*, Vol. II, p. 11 ff.). 'Comments on the Psychoanalytic Theory of the Ego' (*Ps. St. of the Child*, Vol. V, pp. 74 ff.).

allowed was the problem on which Hartmann and his collaborators focused their attention. Although Freud's conception of the structure and function of the ego had undergone repeated transformations and although in his later writings[1] he attributed to the ego a larger degree of independence *vis-à-vis* the id and the super ego, from the *metapsychological* point of view the ego was none the less a derivative of the id. Hartmann tries to deal with the problem of ego weakness *vis-à-vis* the id, which is a necessary concomitant of Freud's view, by assuming the embryonic existence within the id of an original ego autonomy. According to Hartmann perception, movement and memory are not created by the drives but emerge autonomously under the influence of the drives.[2] Hartmann considered that the relationship between that part of the personality which presses for immediate gratification of its wishes (the id) and that part which is prepared to accept delay had not yet been satisfactorily explained. A logical explanation is only possible if the ego participates from the outset in the process of the individual's development as an *independent variable*. This process is compounded of growing *differentiation*, i.e. the emergence of distinct structures, and *integration*, i.e. the synthesis of those structures. Freud had assumed that the child's ability to distinguish between itself and its environment stemmed from the painful process of being weaned from its mother's breast. Hartmann goes one step further. In his view, the weaning process is preceded by the condition of growing differentiation, whereby the child is able to distinguish between itself and its environment by means of the *cognitive* function of the ego. But this cognitive function cannot be derived from the id. And so Hartmann postulates a 'primary' ego, which is independent of the id (primary autonomy); he then attributes to this primary ego a considerable number of rational and cognitive functions, which constitute the 'secondary autonomy of the ego' and as such determine both the way in which the ego comes to terms with reality and the ego's resultant relationship to reality.[3] He considers *intentionality* to be one of the most important functions of the ego. In order to encompass the ego's relationship to its environment Hartmann is obliged to assume the existence of a 'sphere within the ego that is free from conflict'.

[1] 'Analysis Terminable and Interminable', *Complcte Works of S. Freud*, St. Edn., Vol. XXIII.

[2] With regard to the autonomy of the ego and its synthetic functions *H.* Nunberg may be said to have foreshadowed Hartmann's view in his *Allgemeine Neurosenlehre* (General Theory of Neurosis'), Bern, 1923. (See also Nunberg 'Ich-Staerke und Ich-Schwaeche' ('Ego Strength and Ego Weakness') *Int. Z. Psa.* Vol. XXIV, 1939).

[3] In his 'Two Principles of Mental Activity', Freud also attributes to the ego a considerable number of cognitive functions such as thinking, attentiveness, judgement, consciousness, etc.

The attitude of Hartmann and his collaborators to various individual problems of psychoanalytic theory is as follows:

(b) The Problem of Ambivalence

In his last phase *Freud* considered that ambivalence was based on the duality of the drives, eros and thanatos; at the same time, however, he suspected that it was also a defence mechanism which, by means of projection and introjection, afforded defence against destructive impulses (cf. *Melanie Klein*). *Ferenczi* on the other hand considered that ambivalence derived exclusively from the child's attitude towards an environment by which it was neglected or even denied. Neither of these assumptions appeared to Hartmann to be sufficiently well founded, especially in view of the fact that it was quite impossible to demonstrate a correlation between the denials of childhood and the subsequent aggression of the adult. Hartmann does not solve the problem concerning the origin of ambivalence, but he inclines towards a compromise between Freud's and Ferenczi's viewpoints. For Hartmann all the basic drives are compounded from libidinal and aggressive components, which are susceptible to extensive modification due to environmental attitudes on the one hand and the control exercised by the ego in the learning process on the other.

(c) The Mechanisms of Defence

These are not only of a pathological nature, but rather—as has been demonstrated by Jeanne Lampl de Groot[1] in a detailed investigation— they are in the first instance perfectly normal stages in the process whereby the individual comes to terms with his environment. Defence mechanisms become character traits (attitudes or distorted attitudes) when the ego reveals a special preference for one particular defence mechanism, e.g. denial. Repression and identification are two of the defence mechanisms whose application results in a marked change of personality.

(d) The Development of the Super Ego

In contrast to ego development the development of the super ego is largely independent of biological processes. No special biological structure is required for the formation of the super ego. The super ego comes into being in connection with the phallic phase and its structure is determined by the dissolution of the Oedipus complex (see Freud p. 162 ff.). When the Oedipus complex recedes the child identifies not so much with its real parents as with its *idealized* parents or, as Freud argues, with the parents' super ego. Consequently a distinction must be

[1] On Defence and Development, *Ps. St. of the Child*, Vol. XII, p. 114.

made between the primary identification of early childhood, which accompanies incorporation, and the process of secondary identification, which takes place in the phallic phase. In secondary identification the libido that has been concentrated on the mother is desexualized and part of it is adapted for purposes of idealization.

(e) Aggression

The simple formula, whereby aggression is virtually proportional to denial, cannot be upheld since the child's reaction to denial is always multiply[1] over-determined. The similarity between the functioning of libido and of aggression led Hartmann to advance the following points:

1. Libido can be temporarily inhibited or it can replace an action which is inhibited. In the first case discharge is hindered and displeasure may be felt, in the second case substitute formations or sublimations occur.
2. The situation with regard to aggression is analogous, merely, in the second case substitute formation is more intense due to the particular danger to which the object is exposed.
3. Libido and aggression are related one to the other in terms of antagonism. Thus libido protects the object—or the ego—from aggression.
4. Conflicts between libido and aggression may be sub-divided into (a) conflicts of drives, e.g. between hate and love, (b) conflicts between reality and aggression, in which, for example, the object of the hatred reacts in a way which endangers the individual, (c) structural conflicts, in which the ego or the super ego opposes the urge to give aggression its head.

(f) Thesis of the Parallelism of Desexualized Libido and Neutralized Aggression

Hartmann's most important thesis concerns the parallelism of desexualized libido and neutralized aggression. (He replaces the concept of sublimation—cf. *Glover* p. 191 ff. for the problematical nature of sublimation—by that of *neutralization* or desexualization.) *Freud* postulated a 'desexualized libido', for without it sublimation and lasting object relationships would have been meaningless. *Menninger*,[2] *Kardiner*, *Lampl de Groot, etc.*[3] had already pointed to the gap in Freud's theory

---

[1] J. Dollard and others, 1939, *Frustration and Aggression* (quoted from *P. St. of the Child*, Vols. III, IV, p. 34).

[2] Apart from his numerous works in the field of psychosomatic medicine Menninger is also well known for his casuistic work on the self-destructive tendencies in man, *Man against Himself* (London & New York, 1938).

[3] See summary in Hartmann and others, *Ps. St. of the Child*, Vols. III, IV, pp. 25 ff.

created by his inability to accept the possibility of the neutralization of aggression. Hartmann and his collaborators demonstrated that a constant object-relationship is only made possible by the toleration of denials. But this presupposes the sublimation of aggression. Sublimated aggression is to be equated with *neutralized* aggression, which would also appear to be a prerequisite for the formation of the ego and of the super ego.

(g) Contributions to the Problem of the Reality Principle

Freud is inclined to look upon the reality principle as consisting exclusively of the influences exercised on the subject by his environment. He contrasts it with the individual's desire for pleasure. On the other hand, however, (in 'Beyond the Pleasure Principle') the subject choses the reality principle in preference to the pleasure principle on the grounds of self-preservation and, as an indirect consequence, the reality principle becomes a part of the psychic structure. Hartmann proceeds further along these lines and postulates that the ego places the reality principle above the pleasure or Nirvana principle. Hartmann further argues that the contrast between the reality and pleasure principles is misleading, since there are a large number of activities which are performed in accordance with the reality principle but which are none the less pleasurable.[1] The acceptance of the reality principle means that the individual postpones the gratification of his desires and in certain circumstances even learns to forestall them: such, according to *Nunberg* and *Anna Freud*, is the basic function of the ego. Consequently control of the pleasure principle is dependent to a considerable extent on the development of the ego. The assumption of an autonomous section of the ego, which already existed in the id before birth, determines and in a sense predetermines the relationship between the reality principle and the pleasure principle. This conception is of far-reaching importance for the future development of psychoanalytic theory. For what it in fact says is that the formation of the individual is not exclusively determined by his reaction to denials, by the conflict between the reality and pleasure principles, but that pre-formed ego structures *regulate* the struggle between the individual's striving for reality and his striving for pleasure.

Hartmann's analysis of the concept of 'reality' is extremely thorough. (Analogous attempts to define the limits of 'reality' in children have been made by *Charlotte Buehler*,[2] *Piaget*[2] and *Rapaport*.[2]) For Hartmann this concept embraces both environmental (objective) reality and

[1] Loewald and Szekely have demostrated that Freud's conception of reality is determined chiefly by the fear of castration and by the father, whilst the mother is relatively unimportant (*Ps. St. of the Child*, Vol. XI, p. 53.

[2] See H. Hartmann, 'Notes on the Reality Principle', *Ps. St. of the Child*, Vol. XI, p. 31 ff.

'inner reality'. The child's relationship to its own body and to external objects teaches it what reality is. Thus the child's reality is stamped by multifarious influences, by its relationship to its parents no less than by its own maturing super ego. *Adaptation* means to behave and act in conformity with one's knowledge of reality. But this definition, although biologically correct, appears to Hartmann to be too narrow and he points to the French *savoir vivre, savoir faire* and *savoir tout court* as modes of behaviour which illustrate the extreme elasticity of 'adaptation'. The child's understanding of reality will depend firstly on its ability to distinguish between its own body and its environment and subsequently both on its ability to speak and its ability to form judgements. Thus the child's relationship to reality is largely a relationship between the ego and the environment. Hartmann proffers a twofold definition of reality: on the one hand it is scientifically *objective* and is determined by the application of specific methods, whilst on the other hand it is the totality of social and conventional ideas including the subjectivity of the person. He then attempts to overcome the misgivings to which this definition gives rise by positing the historical development of man and of his psyche as a further factor determining the nature of reality. What part is played by projection and introjection in the child's understanding of reality ?[1] It seems that no solution to this difficult question is to be found as yet and Hartmann refers to *Buytendijk*, who considers that the subject's world is composed of opinions, i.e. of values.

(h) Relationships between the Id and the Ego

In enlarging on Freud's postulate 'Id must become Ego' (cf. von Weizsäcker: 'Ego must become Id') Hartmann describes the development of (1) vitally important ego functions, the effects of which are (2) felt to be pleasurable and which (3) differ from the id function by virtue of their adaptation to reality. He emphasizes the fact that the reversibility of the ego functions, which is demonstrated in dreams and in psychosis, constitutes a yardstick by which ego strength (or ego weakness) may be measured. The less reversible the ego is and the more able it is to assert its independence *vis-à-vis* the id (secondary autonomy), the stronger it is.

II. RENÉ SPITZ[2]

Psychoanalysis is indebted to René Spitz for the practical application on a scale large enough to permit of statistical findings of the method

[1] Cf. Zilboorg, 'The Sense of Reality' (*Psa. Quart.*, Vol. X, 1941).

[2] R. Spitz, 'Hospitalism' (*Ps. St. of the Child*, Vols. I and II)—'Environment *v.* Race' (*Arch. d. Neurol. und Psychiat.* Vol. 57, p. 1, 1947.)—'Auto-erotism' (*Ps. St. of the Child*, Vol. III, IV, pp. 85 ff.)

combining (Behaviourist) observation of infants with psychoanalytic theory. His writings on the harmful effects of hospitalization on young children (in which he establishes a causal link between the infant's depression and the mother's absence) are no longer entirely unknown in Germany. R. Spitz considers the causes of neurotic behaviour or the appearance of psychosomatic disturbances almost exclusively from the point of view of the mother-child relationship. His work on psychogenic illnesses in babies and young children is divided up into (a) his observations of the mother-child relationship and (b) his observations of the child's reactions to its mother.

An investigation into autoerotism which he carried out on 170 children is of particular importance for psychoanalytic theory, since it contradicts Freud's thesis that autoerotism is virtually automatic and largely independent of environmental influences (cf. primary narcissism). Spitz was able to demonstrate that autoerotic activities (rocking, playing with the genitals or with the faeces) only take place after a relationship to an external object, usually to the mother, has been established. These activities do not take place at all unless the child has an emotional relationship to its environment, usually to its mother. If its relationship to its mother or its foster-mother is a good one, then the child will quite naturally indulge in autoerotic play with its genitals. But if the mother, by imposing a rigorous upbringing, prevents the child from establishing contact with its environment, then it will prefer to rock. If the mother's attitude towards the child is ambivalent, then the child will prefer to play with its faeces.

In his two publications, *Die Entstehung der ersten Objectbeziehungen*[1] and *Nein und Ja, Ursprünge der menschlichen Kommunikation*,[2] Spitz has presented further important material concerning the infant's world and its reactions. The infant's future relationships will follow the pattern established by its very first object relationship, namely, its relationship to its mother's breast. In this relationship the mother's attitude to her child—cf. above—is decisive. Spitz has compiled a scale of maternal attitudes towards the child which correspond to somatic or psychic disturbances in the infant. 'Psychotoxic' disturbances are for the most part psychosomatic disturbances in infants ranging from diarrhoea with vomiting to asthma or allergies, in which psychic changes go hand in hand with functional disturbances of a physical nature and which are held to be the outcome of an ambivalent attitude on the part of the mother towards her child.

Spitz lists the following maternal attitudes together with the effects they produce in infants:

[1] Stuttgart, 1957. ('The Emergence of the First Object Relationships').
[2] Stuttgart 1959 ('No and Yes, Origins of Communication').

1. Primary, undisguised but passive rejection of the child produces coma.
2. Active rejection: vomiting.
3. Primary anxiety: three months colic.
4. Disguised animosity in the form of anxiety: atopical dermatitis.
5. Ambivalence on the part of the mother ranging from pampering to animosity: hypermotility (hypersensitivity).
6. Cyclical aternations of mood on the part of the mother: coprophagy.
7. Animosity with conscious compensation: hyperthymia.
8. Partial withdrawal of love: anaclitic depression.
9. Complete withdrawal of love: marasmus.

The absence of mother love leads to a disturbance in the child's object relationship, which it establishes by means of transference and identification, and thus to a disturbance of its inter-personal relationships in general. The child then turns its aggression in upon itself and succumbs to mental retardment or to neglect.

In spite of the copious material which Spitz has presented, analysts who are aware of the sheer impossibility of an unambivalent attitude on the part of any mother towards her child will feel bound to treat the conclusion which Spitz has drawn with sceptical reserve; if they did not they would have to ask themselves how it is that man has managed to go on living at all. The conclusion which may legitimately be drawn from these investigations is that 'mother love' has yet again turned out to be the alpha and omega of healthy human behaviour and that, over and above this, infant children are evidently in possession of means with which to compensate for the first eight of the disturbances listed above. It is of course hardly surprising that as yet little or nothing is known about these means save by those who accept the theories advanced by *Melanie Klein*.

In his investigation into 'Yes and No' Spitz tries to demonstrate that the gesture which the child employs in order to deny a thing (i.e. shaking its head) stems from the movements made by a newly born infant in seeking its mother's breast. This searching movement undergoes a functional change, in as far as, once the child has been satisfied, it then also serves to express the child's first 'no' statements; subsequently, from the age of 15 months onwards, when the child has already begun to identify with adults, it will also use this 'no' gesture for matters quite unconnected with feeding. In the same way the child's 'yes' gestures have an antecedent in the motor sphere in the form of a nodding movement directed towards the mother's breast, which is prompted by hunger and which is a characteristic of autophagi. (Spitz overlooks the fact that man is not autophagous.) As a result of its 'no' gestures the child reaches a new stage of integration between the ages of 15 and 18 months, which, since it enables the child to say 'no' to itself (from 2 years of age onwards), is a precursor of its capacity for abstract thought and for its subsequent super ego formation.

III. PHYLLIS GREENACRE

Both in her main work, *Trauma, Growth and Personality*,[1] and in numerous other publications the authoress sets out her theory of specific phases. She takes as her starting-point the fact that the *Freudian* phases of libido development both before and after the phallic phase overlap to a considerable extent, which makes strict classification impossible. Greenacre speaks of specific peaks of maturation, which, however, defy strict classification. She differentiates between children's ability to provide a specific response to specific stimuli and the peaks of their biological maturity, which render them capable of providing the actual, specific and commensurate response. If, for example, a younger child is seduced by an older child into participating in sexual play, the older one may achieve a gratification commensurate with its stage of maturity. The younger child, however, will not yet be in a position to give an adequate response to the specific stimulus to which it is exposed as a result of the seduction. The claims made on it are excessive for the stage of maturation which it has reached and it reacts either by rushing into maturity or by regressing out of fear. The seduction then turns into a trauma and distorted actions of neurotic origin may well occur. But the seduction does not turn into a trauma if an adequate response to the stimulus is forthcoming, for example, if both children gratify their desires in accordance with the stage of biological maturity which they have reached.

IV. ERIK HOMBURGER ERIKSON

The observation of infants by psychoanalytically trained investigators, a practice which has grown considerably since its inception in the early 'forties, has been supplemented of late by the investigation and description of the parent-child relationship in so-called primitive societies.[2] *Without* departing from the fundamental concepts of Freudian psychoanalysis Erik H. Erikson has combined the two viewpoints, which arise from the observations of infants and the investigation of primitive societies, with Freud's theses. In his main work *Childhood and Society*[3]

---

[1] New York, 1952.
[2] Cf. esp. Kardiner, Mead, Kluckhohn, Linton *inter alia*, see below, pp. 311 ff.
[3] London, 1956.

Erikson derives from the combination of these viewpoints new conceptions of infantile development. He too differs from Freud in his assessment of the trauma. He does not consider that a neurotic disorder is caused by a trauma alone, but rather by three different factors: (1) the relationships between the various members of a group (group means a social or family community or a combination of both), (2) the constitution or physis (in which connection it should be noted that the endeavours of the organism are directed towards maintaining homoestasis, i.e. a state of internal organic equilibrium, (3) the ego and its attitude towards drives and wishes. As far as the concept of the group is concerned, this embraces all historical conditions; it forms and determines the parents' behaviour within its conventions—which behaviour then determines the fate of the children. With this concept of the group Erikson acknowledges the relativity of environmental conditions, which need not necessarily be determined by the course of the oedipal schema. Erikson unfolds his own conceptions regarding the course of the child's pre-genital and genital development in terms of the ego concept—which, unfortunately, he does not define. To his mind Freud's libido theory runs the risk of trying to explain animate beings in terms of marionettes driven by the 'mythical Eros'.[1] He opposes Freud's theory with his own conception of the multiple potency of *possible* patterns of behaviour in animate beings, which patterns of behaviour influence and regulate one another. Libido development does not take place in accordance with the concept of phases which are anatomically produced and subsequently disappear. Animate beings possess a multiple structure and multiple reactions to environmental stimuli. The question as to which patterns of behaviour will be formed and developed is not decided by the simplified process of stimulus and reaction to stimulus (reflex) but rather by the concerted effect of the multiple determinants which the above-mentioned factors constitute. For the oral stage of child development Erikson assumes the following patterns of behaviour, which he describes as the merging of different zones: (1) Incorporation, (2) Retention, (3) Elimination, (4) Oral Intrusion (e.g. when powerful babies press their head and neck firmly against the mother's breast). The variability of these patterns of behaviour depends to a considerable extent on the cultural conditions within the group. Basic trust is established in the oral stage but so too is the child's sensitivity to badness.[2] Badness arises in connection with teething, which is the cause of the child's first conflicts and of three types of anger, namely, anger with its mother, who withdraws her breast when the tooth hurts her, anger with the tooth, which may con-

---

[1] Erik H. Erikson, *Childhood and Society*, pp. 60 ff.

[2] Author's note: It is probable that Erikson was influenced by Melanie Klein's conception of 'good' and 'bad' objects.

ceivably be felt to be a foreign body, and finally, due to a general feeling of impotence, anger with itself. Although on the one hand Erikson tries to change the traditional three-phase libido theory by demonstrating its considerable variability, he still adheres to Freud's conception of the union of libido and self-preservation drive.[1] He is then obliged to have further recourse to special hypotheses in order to reconcile the phenomena appearing in the anal stage with the concept of self-preservation. The new social patterns of behaviour which are developed in the anal stage are: letting go or holding on (defiance). What Erickson considers to be important—again in contrast to *Freud* and also to *Abraham*—is the extension of patterns of behaviour which were originally oral, such as incorporation or retention, both to the anal and urethral spheres as also to the whole of the muscular system. For the oral ego the original conflict is between basic trust and fear of badness (cf. teething); for the anal ego it is between independent self-assertion (in pathological cases: defiance) and shame and doubt. Erikson considers the genital (phallic) stage chiefly from the point of view of the control exercised by the child over its muscular system. The characteristics acquired in the oral and anal stages, including such conflicts as may occur, are extended to the phallic phase. The capacity for penetration which was aroused in the oral stage (see above) reaches its optimum in the phallic stage. Aggressive and early sexual phantasies join with these characteristics to prepare the ground for the mature genitality that is to follow. The new characteristics acquired in the phallic phase include that of 'doing', i.e. the child enjoys creating, competing, overcoming. This applies chiefly to the little boy, whilst the little girl tends to take delight in her own powers of attraction and provocation. Erikson also considers that the incest wishes which can never be realized constitute the chief problem in this phase.

With these concepts of 'basic trust', of 'letting go' and 'holding on', of 'doing', Erikson goes beyond Freud's and Abraham's conceptions, for he treats as central characteristics and abilities in the child which they had scarcely mentioned. The fundamental overlapping of, for example, oral patterns of behaviour into the anal or genital phases is also a new departure, but not one that is confined to Erikson alone. Numerous other authors have drawn attention to the merging of one phase with anothers Nor did Abraham consider that the boundaries of the individual phase. were rigidly fixed. What is not clear is what Erikson understood under the 'ego', although he accords to the ego a position of central importance in the genesis of neuroses. Erikson occupies a position somewhere

[1] Cf. H. Hartmann, *Ps. St. of the Child*, Vol. XI, p. 31 ff., who demonstrates that the so-called self-preservation drive is anything but homogeneous. Erikson does go along with Hartmann and his collaborators, however, in recognizing that human drives are more plastic and variable than animal instincts.

between the neo-Freudians and Freudian orthodoxy, but he has not adequately defined that position in theoretical terms. He tries to overcome the theory of phases whilst adhering to its formulae; he considers the transition from pre-genital libido to be fluid, yet he also considers the actual conflict of the phallic phase to be invested in the incest wishes. He pays heed to the cultural variability of the patterns of behaviour whilst holding that omly a few uniform characteristics are capable of cultural variation without giving rise to *new* abilities.

F

THEODOR REIK

Theodor Reik is the only disciple of Freud's to have presented his psychoanalytic experiences and his psychological testimony in autobiographical form. Of recent years he has turned towards Neo-Freudianism. Reik's intuitive method, which involves a detailed self-analysis on the part of the analyst, who records the inner experiences which he himself undergoes in the course of the treatment, is far removed from systematic analysis. Because of this systematic analysts are not altogether favourably disposed towards him. Reik analyses human behaviour from the fullness of his own wide experience both of analysis and of life itself. He gives a very candid account of his own life in *The Confessions of an Analyst*. In his earlier investigations, which met with the general approval of both Freud and his followers, Reik dealt chiefly with the application of psychoanalytic theories to the faculty of the mental sciences and especially to religion. He describes how his own experience of obsessional states helped him to discover the close connection between religious ceremonies and the obsessional acts of neurotics. In both conditions what people seek is confirmation of their belief and of themselves, in both conditions they carry out obsessional acts as a defence against fear and doubt. Reik was also prompted by personal experience when he wrote his *Geständniszwang und Strafbedürfnis*,[1] one of the most important works to date on the interconnections between psychology and jurisprudence. In this work Reik makes extensive use of case material to describe the way in which unconscious guilt feelings and a concomitant unconscious desire for punishment drive the delinquent to confess his crime.

Whilst Freud's followers are still concerned with tracing the specific psychic impulses of the moment back to the corresponding impulses of childhood (Phyllis Greenacre[2] traces awe back to the corresponding emotions felt by the child at the sight of its father's penis), Reik moved

---

[1] Vienna, 1925.   [2] *Ps. St. of the Child*, Vol. XI, pp. 9 ff.

away from this genetic attitude in the course of his further development. Without actually breaking with Freud his method became more 'phenomenological' in its orientation. Not in terms of Husserl's phenomenology, however, but rather in terms of an empirically descriptive psychology, which sets out to consider specific phenomena, e.g. jealousy, from many different points of view. Where psychoanalysis describes jealousy in terms of a reaction formation of the Oedipus complex (Joan Rivière, E. Jones),[1] Reik attempts to demonstrate the difference between the jealousy of a man and the jealousy of a woman. When a man is jealous his chief feeling is one of weakness and of being at the mercy of a rival, a condition which he opposes with every means at his disposal, but when a woman is jealous her jealousy acts as a driving force, which moves her to purposive action. In psychoanalytic literature the psychology of women[2] is chiefly considered from the limited viewpoint of penis envy and the castration complex. In contrast to such enquiries Reik is concerned with describing the woman in terms of the multiple relationships in which she partakes, such as her relationships to clothes, to money, to love, etc. He tries to distinguish between what is 'feminine' and what is 'womanly' in the sense of Goethe's 'Ewigweibliche' (lit. 'Eternal-womanly'). In doing so of course he oversteps the boundaries of empirical psychology and opens the door to philosophical speculation —but then, didn't Freud do the same?

Having made this distinction between what is 'womanly' and what is 'feminine' Reik goes on to distinguish between love and sexuality. He was satisfied from the testimony of numerous detailed case histories, that Freud's libido theory does justice only to sexuality and not to love. Sexuality may derive from somatic sources but there is no evidence to suggest that this is also true of love.

'The fact that love and sexuality are so often united and fused together does not prove that they are essentially the same. Affinity is not identity. You can be friendly with a man without resembling him. You can associate with a man who is not a member of your family.

'The differences between love and sexuality are so decisive that the claim made by the psychoanalysts to the effect that both have the same origin and the same character is very improbable. These differences are most readily apparent when the two phenomena are placed in contradistinction to one another in their purest form. To quote a few examples: sexuality is a biological urge, a product of chemical processes within the organism; love is a strong emotional wish, a creation of personal

---

[1] See above, pp. 000 ff.   [2] See especially H. Deutsch, *Psychologie der Frau* ('Psychology of Women') Vols. I and II, Berne 1953.

phantasy. Implicit in sexuality is the urge to dispose of an organic tension; implicit in love is the need to free oneself from one's own insufficiency. In the former man seeks physical satisfaction, in the latter he seeks happiness. In the former it is a question of choosing a body, in the latter a personality. Sexuality has a general meaning, love has a personal meaning. The first is a call of nature, the second a call of culture. Sexuality is common to man and beast; love or romantic love was unknown to man for thousands of years and to this day it is still unknown to millions of people. Sexuality does not differentiate between persons; love is directed towards a particular person. The one relaxes the muscles, the other opens the sluice gates of the personality. And a man who is sexually satisfied can be hungry for love. The sexual drive is extinguished in an act, which consists of tension, cramp and release. Afterwards it is impossible to remember the final moment of pleasure just as it is impossible to remember the exact taste of a particular dish. But where the phenomenon of love is concerned there is no such ultimate indifference towards the object of one's feelings. Every word, every movement of the loved one is an enchanting memory. Sexuality is dramatic; love is lyrical. The sexual object is only desired during the short period of excitation and does not otherwise appear to be desirable; the loved one is the object of constant tenderness.

'When I speak of the powers of attraction possessed by a particular object I differentiate between sexual charms and the charms of the personality. But it is not simply that these two factors appear to be distinct in my description; they actually are distinct. Sexual charms disappear after the sexual act. Once the deed has been done it has been temporarily done with. But the other charms endure. Many men and not a few women confuse these two types of demand despite the fact that in the light of self-observation they assume quite different appearances. When sexuality and love are united and directed towards the same goal it is sometimes difficult to know which of these two needs is receiving the lion's share, but for the most part we are able to keep them clearly apart.'[1]

With Reik the complicated problems of the pre-oedipal phase, the boundaries between the drive and defence against the drives, the stereotype emphasis of the castration and Oedipus complexes have receded into the background in favour of broadly based psychological experience. The ambivalent position which Reik occupies in respect of method must be born in mind, however, for although it enables him to do greater justice to the psychological *phenomenon*, it also means that he

[1] Th. Reik. *Geschlecht und Liebe* ('Of Love and Lust'), Stuttgart 1905. pp. 24 ff.

fluctuates between Neo-Freudianism with its over-emphasis of cultural factors and the more biologically oriented school of psychoanalysis. This does not apply, however, to Reik's major work, *Masochism in Modern Man*,[1] which, although it also makes extensive use of case material in order to demonstrate moral masochism in a great variety of attitudes and actions, is none the less more strictly psychoanalytic in its approach. In Reik's view the business man who never succeeds and the man or woman filled with jealousy are examples of moral masochism and he gives a clear exposition of their masochistic character. (People who expose themselves to situations to which they react with jealousy are subject to unconscious masochism.) Reik points out the masochistic tendency involved in anticipating experiences which are expected to be disagreeable. A child who has to go under the cold shower following a hot bath will anticipate the cold shower, which it expects to find disagreeable, by splashing itself with cold water before taking the hot bath. The various practices of sexual masochism are similar in character to the processes involved in anticipation: the punishment attendant on the erotic experiences of infancy is anticipated in masochistic practices. But not even this thesis of Reik's with its emphasis on anticipation and the possibility which is thereby given for pleasure and punishment to merge within the processes of anticipation is capable of explaining the abnormal phenomenon whereby displeasure is felt to be pleasurable.

G

WILHELM REICH

Although Wilhelm Reich's relationship to Freud is more ambiguous than that of the Freudians so far dealt with, he none the less followed Freud in all essentials up to the point where he developed his 'Orgone' theory. If we disregard his attempts in the late 'twenties to combine Marxism with psychoanalysis,[2] his contributions to psychoanalytic theory can be divided into three main categories:

(*a*) The function of the orgasm and the function of anxiety.
(*b*) Characterology.
(*c*) The Orgone.

(*a*) The Function of the Orgasm and the Function of Anxiety

Psychoanalysis is indebted to Reich for the most detailed phenomenological description of the sexual act to date. Reich accords to the

---

[1] *Masochism in Modern Man*, New York, 1941.   [2] Bernfeld writes in this respect, 'Reich is a philosopher, who might well be described as an anarchical sexual moralist.' *Int. Z. Psa.*, Vol. XVIII, p. 384, 1932.

orgasm, to which Freud paid but scant attention, a position of central importance in the abreaction of every conceivable form of tension. He tries to prove that every neurotic suffers from difficulties in the sexual sphere, usually in the form of incomplete orgasms. In his book, *The Function of the Orgasm*,[1] Reich tries to resuscitate the old concept of symptomatic neurosis, which Freud had developed towards the end of the 'nineties but which he subsequently dropped. A symptomatic neurosis expresses conscious conflicts and it becomes a neurosis proper when these conflicts are joined by a somatic blockage of libido. The blockage is the consequence of an unsatisfactory orgasm. The limitation and inhibition of the orgasm is determined by the sexual morality of the day. Reich considers that the 'organic' blockage of libido is the decisive factor in the development of neuroses, a view which clearly casts doubt on their psychogenesis and questions the whole concept of psychic conflicts. This extreme somatic-naturalistic attitude is by no means the only one of its kind within the sphere of psychoanalysis. The members of the present-day French school, especially *S. Nacht*,[2] are moving along similar lines with their application of Selye's principles of stress and strain, including those theories which postulate the origin of psychic disturbances in diencephalic and hormone action. It should be added, however, that Nacht did not use the concept of libido blockage in the sense in which it was employed by Reich and before him by Freud. Reich does not explain the anxiety resulting from the disturbance in the orgasm—as Freud had once explained it—by assuming the presence of particular toxic materials but rather by postulating the presence of blocked neural impulses which reach the heart via the vegetative nervous system, where they then trigger off anxiety. 'Anxiety is a phenomenon of the process of excitation in the vasovegetative system which in the sensitive system would make itself felt as pleasure.'[3]

(b) Characterology

Reich's writings within the sphere of characterology constitute his most valuable contributions to psychoanalytic theory. These contributions have been compiled and presented in his work on 'Character Analysis'.[4] In his criticism of previous attempts by psychoanalytic theorists to explain neuroses Reich writes:

'To try to explain a particular case to-day by demonstrating that it

[1] Vienna, 1927.
[2] S. Nacht, *La Psychanalyse d'aujourdhui*, Vol. I, p. 11, Paris, 1956. ('Modern Psychoanalysis').
[3] Reich, *Funktion des Orgasmus* ('The Function of the Orgasm').
[4] Berlin, 1933.

embodies the same mechanisms and experiences as other types of illness is no longer good enough. We must admit that our analytic literature suffers a great deal from this shortcoming.'[1]

In an attempt to make up for this shortcoming Reich applies himself to the task of interpreting the *specificity* of a given character, taking character traits as reaction formations and stressing the difference between these and symptoms. One of the purposes for which he uses this interpretation is the analysis of the compulsive character.[2] The symptoms emerge because the basis of reaction—the character—is neurotic and therefore produces a libido blockage (see above in connection with 'orgasm'). Since the character is the basis of the neurotic reaction a cure can only be achieved if a character change is effected, which means that the symptom is not to be treated as the focal point of analytic work. For Reich the compulsive character occupies a position midway between symptomatic neurosis and psychosis. It is characterized by uninhibited activity. Reich establishes the specificity of this type of disturbance as follows:

'In respect of drive-inhibited neuroses what happens is that the nucleus of the super ego effects a successful and systematic repression, the dynamic repression being limited to the process whereby unconscious material is made conscious. Although the ego is not allowed to know anything about the nucleus of the super ego and only knows its rationalizations, it none the less subjects itself to its demands that the id-strivings be repressed. We know that it is the breakdown of this process of repression which creates symptoms. In respect of drive-inhibited symptomatic neuroses the psychic conflict is acted out between the ego plus the super ego on the one hand and the repressed section of the id (the disdained object relationships) on the other. In respect of the compulsive character the super ego has been "dynamically" and "unsuccessfully" repressed and the systematic repression is incomplete. It is easy to see that the incompleteness of the systematic repression (like that of the partial drives and of sadism) is a consequence of the dynamic repression of the super ego by the (pleasure-) ego. In this case the psychic conflict is acted out between three instances; on the one hand the ego defends itself in the service of the super ego against the id (like the drive-inhibited neurotic) whilst on the other hand it defends itself in the service of the id against the super ego. It is this double

[1] Reich, 'Der Masochistische Charakter' (The Masochistic Character) *Int. Z. Psa.* Vol. XVII, 3, p. 325, 1932.
[2] Reich. 'Der Triebhafte Charakter' ('The Compulsive Character'); *Neue Arb. z. aerztl. Psa.*, Vol. IV, Vienna, 1925.

H*　　　　　233

battle (double counter-cathexis) which makes the compulsive type so disrupted.'[1]

Reich describes the masochistic character, in contrast to the compulsive character, as follows:

'For these reasons, the masochistic character cannot be a leader, although he usually develops grandiose phantasies of heroism. His anal fixation makes him passive, and in addition, the inhibition of exhibitionism leads to self-depreciation.'[2]

By contrast the masochist's ego ideal is 'phallic and active', but it is unrealizable, since the structure of the ego is contrary to that of the ego ideal. Reich attempts to explain the specificity of character formation in terms of these manifestly hypothetical structural conflicts. Character analysis simply means that the neurotic basis of reaction operative in the analysis, i.e. the patient's individual character traits, must be treated as the focal point of the therapy. Passivity on the part of the patient, masochistic tendencies or 'phallic' desires for activity, demands for love, which are hidden behind a front of defiance and a desire for self-chastisement but which none the less stamp the patient's character, are constantly analysed and worked through by the analyst in a stereotype manner.

Reich interprets the ambivalence of loving and hating almost exclusively in terms of environmental influences and sub-divides the process into three stages:

1. 'I love you but I am afraid of being punished for it.'
2. 'I hate you because I am not allowed to love you, but I am afraid of expressing my hatred.'
3. 'I do not know whether I love you or hate you.'

The first stage goes back to the time when the libido tried to cathect the outside world 'like an amoeba', was forced to withdraw in the face of denials, took fright and subsequently developed the second and third stages (ambivalence).

Only character analysis is in a position to resolve the wellnigh insuperable resistances which arise out of this situation and which may be regarded either as character traits (e.g. defiance/passivity) or as resistances to the transference. In his description of character analysis, which has made a significant contribution to psychoanalytic therapy, Reich cites numerous case histories.

[1] W. Reich, *Der Triebhafte Charakter.*
[2] W. Reich, *Der Masochistische Charakter, Int. Z. Psa.*, Vol. XVIII, p. 3.

(c) The Orgone

The development of Reich's last phase was determined by his discovery of the 'Orgone'. Under this concept Reich understands a bio-physical fluid that is present both in the organism and in the cosmos, that is in fact concentrated in fields both around and within the organism. All the psychic processes involved in character analysis, the resolution of resistances, the interpretation of the transference, ambivalence, etc., are no more than psychic descriptions of the bio-physical processes of the Orgone. These may be observed in the muscular tensions, in the movements of the diaphragm and in the vegetative phenomena and emotions which occur in the course of the analysis. Whereas for Freud these were merely by-products of the analysis, for Reich they constitute the *fundamental bio-physical processes* of the analysis, for which he created his own special terminology and which he considered to be the decisive factors involved in therapy. What actually takes place in the projections of a schizophrenic, for example, is that the schizophrenic perceives his own Orgone field. Orgone energy can be measured with oscillographs; it kills bacteria and cancer cells. Reich's Orgone theory is no longer taken seriously by the majority of analysts and scientists, which is not surprising in view of the fact that what he actually measured was without any doubt simply the electric potential found in all animate bodies. But the abstruse mysticism of his ideas did not prevent him from founding an Orgone Institute in New York, effecting successful(?) cures and acquring both a staff of collaborators and an independent journal.

H

PAUL FEDERN[1]

Although Paul Federn's contributions to ego psychology go beyond Freudian psychoanalysis, they constitute an important complement to the structure of the personality and may on no account be overlooked. (For reasons of space Federn's fundamental writings on schizophrenia will not be dealt with here.) Federn, who was influenced both by *Scheler's* (and *Brentano's*) *Act Psychology* and by P. *Schilder's* investigations into the body scheme, considered the ego to be a *homogenous* structure, which is characterized by a specific ego feeling and an ego (self-)experience (*Erlebnis*). Federn conceives ego feeling as the individual's ability to experience space, time and causality as an entity. Whereas in waking life this feeling permeates the whole of a person's being, in states of fatigue, in sleep, in illness and psychosis it is subjected to severe limitations.

[1] He was joint editor with Meng of the Psychoanalytisches Volksbuch (Stuttgart 1926) and was one of the pioneers in the treatment of psychotics. See P. Federn, *Ich-Psychologie und Psychosen* ('Ego Psychology and the Psychoses'), Bern, 1956.

Federn attempts to define the extent to which the ego feeling undergoes structural modification due to such changes and to the normal fluctuations of daily life by reference to 'inner' and 'outer' ego boundaries. He develops this idea in his discussion of reality testing by the ego. In Federn's view reality testing as described by, *inter alia*, *Freud*, *Glover* and *Hartmann* does not provide an adequate explanation of the nature of the reality of dreams or hallucinations. The comprehension of data appertaining to the ego or the non-ego is effected by means of the sense of reality, a specific sensation which, however, is also present in the dream state. Federn explains the nature of the reality of dream images as being due to a weakening of the 'inner ego boundaries'. (The 'outer ego boundary' is the line of demarcation between the ego and external reality, the 'inner ego boundary' that between the ego and the inner reality of the id.) These boundaries are dynamic and represent a combination of structure and function. As a result of the weakening of the inner ego boundaries stimuli from the ego enter consciousness and are felt by the sense of reality to be real, because, although the sense of reality differentiates between 'outer' and 'inner' in respect of the ego, it does not do so in respect of the total psyche. If the inner ego boundary is weakened, then the relationship of the sense of reality to the ego is disturbed and the sense of reality is no longer able to distinguish the outer stimulus from the inner stimulus. For Federn delusions and hallucinations are harmful to the ego. They are not, as they are for Freud, attempts at restitution. Although these ego boundaries are extraordinarily flexible, the ego still maintains its continuity throughout the whole of life, which, however, does not preclude the possibility of earlier ego states, which had been repressed and forgotten, being resuscitated under hypnosis.

How do Federn's concepts of ego structure compare with Freud's ego theory? Federn accepts in principle the division of the psyche into id, ego and super ego, which Freud made in the last phase of his research. He differs from Freud, however, in that he extends the sphere of the ego's influence to the pre-conscious. Although the contents of the pre-conscious do not constantly reveal themselves to the ego feeling by becoming conscious, it is none the less due to the ego feeling that people feel confident of fitting in with their environment in an integrated fashion, because the ego feeling—due to the interconnections which exist between it and the unconscious—necessarily has access to the relevent pre-conscious data. Fitting in with the environment in an integrated fashion means, amongst other things, having access to all the memories, attributes and skills which pre-consciously facilitate this process of fitting in. For example, it is only possible to recognize a street crossing or to find a house which one has seen before if the ego has access to the relevant pre-conscious data which enable such a process of re-discovery to take place. It is the ego feeling—and not consciousness—which makes it possible for the unity between ourselves and the discovery of the house, i.e. between ourselves and an activity, to be established. Federn also refers to this unity between other-directed activity and the ego feeling as an ego state. Ego states occur in dreams in which people are constantly taking positive action *vis-à-vis* their environment or are subjected to its influence. Consequently Federn distinguishes between those dream images which are predominantly cathected by the id, i.e. the unconscious, and those which reflect ego states. Whereas in waking life the ego feeling rests both on a physical basis, which is manifest in all human actions (motor activity), and a psychic basis (psychic ego and body ego), these two aspects of the ego are quite disparate in dreams, in psychosis and under narcosis. The images occurring in dreams under narcosis, in which the dreamer has no sensation of his own body, are particularly representative of states of the psychic ego. Actions performed by the dreamer in his dream such as running, swimming and flying always take place without the dreamer's being aware of the specific body feeling which accompanies these activities in reality. Whereas in reality activity is characterized, amongst other things, by volition and by the materialization of the will in activity, in dreams volition, real activity and the body feeling which accompanies it are not present, volition having been replaced by a wish, which is its opposite. Accordingly reality is dominated by volition, whilst dreams are dominated by wishes. On those rare occasions when volition is represented in a dream this is due to the effect of a correspondingly active body ego feeling and in such a case the wish, e.g. the wish to fly, reinforced by volition in the form of ability, is experienced as the wish 'to be able to fly', the experience on this occasion being rendered correspondingly realistic by the accession of the body ego feeling.

This short excursion into the world of Federn's thought reveals him as a profound, determined and powerful thinker amongst Freud's followers. It is a matter of deep regret that he was not to be allowed to give a systematic account within a larger framework of his stimulating ideas, which have greatly enriched psychoanalysis. Above all else Federn was a therapist who always gave priority over his scientific research to the claims of the sick individual.

I

FRANZ ALEXANDER AND PSYCHOSOMATIC MEDICINE

The systematic development of psychosomatic medicine is linked with

F. Alexander's investigations in all essential respects. It should be pointed out, however, that long before Alexander various specialists for internal diseases, above all *Ludolf von Krehl* and *von Bergmann*, had indicated the existence of psychosomatic connections, i.e. the existence of relationships between psychic experiences and distorted attitudes of neurotic origin on the one hand and the disease of internal organs on the other. Within the psychoanalytic field *Felix Deutsch* and *Edoardo Weiss* had pioneered the psychoanalytic examination and treatment of patients with functional or organic disturbances which did not come under the heading of conversion hysteria or other types of neurosis (1922). The reserve with which Freud viewed these first attempts prevented any systematic expansion at that time. He expressed his scepticism with regard to psychosomatic medicine in a letter to Viktor von Weizsäcker:

'The explanation of the functional disturbance, in this case micturition, as the outcome of the eroticization imposed on the urinary organs is in complete accord with analytic theory, which I once tried to elucidate by a banal equation to the effect that it was as if the master of the house had started up a love affair with the cook, a course of action scarcely calculated to improve the cooking. And you reveal to us the more precise workings of this disturbance by indicating the antithetical innervations, which must suspend or confuse one another. *I was obliged to restrain the analysts from such investigation for pedagogic reasons, for innervations, vascular dilations and neural pathways would have been too much of a temptation for them; they had to learn to restrict themselves to psychological modes of thought.*[2] We are indebted to the specialist for internal diseases for this extension of our knowledge.'

German endeavours (after 1945) to explain internal diseases from psychoanalytic points of view are closely linked with the research carried out by von Weizsäcker[3] and the 'Heidelberg School'. This school is composed on the one hand of those who worked their way through the problems of the Gestaltkreis and of anthropology under von Weizsäcker, e.g. *P. Christian* and *W. Kütemeyer*, and on the other hand of *Mitscherlichs* and his collaborators, whose psychosomatic investigations, like those of F. Alexander, are more closely attuned to the theoretical premises of Freudian psychoanalysis. Within the Neo-

---

[1] V. von Weizsäcker, *Körpergeschehen und Neurose*, Stuttgart, 1947.

[2] Author's Italics.

[3] See V. von Weizsäcker and D. Wyss, *Zwischen Medizin und Philosophie* ('Between Medicine and Philosophy'), Göttingen, 1957, where von Weizsäcker's attitude to Freud and to psychoanalysis is formulated.

Freudian schools *H. Schultz-Hencke* has been the leading protagonist of psychosomatic research.

Apart from F. Alexander and his numerous collaborators[1] *F. Dunbar*[2] has also devoted a comprehensive work to psychosomatic illnesses, which is in part independent of Alexander and in which the authoress (like *Glatzel*) tries to describe the 'Accident' or 'Asthma' or 'Ulcer' personality less in terms of depth psychology than in terms of descriptive personality profiles. But although Dunbar pays greater heed to psychoanalytic aspects than does Glatzel, it is not the intention of this present enquiry to deal with this kind of descriptive personality interpretation.

F. Alexander's development, which proceeded from his earliest investigations (1922) to the phase in which he held the influence of the castration complex to be decisive for character formation, thence to the 'Psychoanalysis of the Total Personality' and finally to his psychosomatic studies, moves progressively away from the structure of the personality as the source of conflicts (id/ego/super ego) in favour of an interpretation of psychic activity based on *conflicts of drives*.

(a) Structural Conflicts (Instances)

The 'Psychoanalysis of the Total Personality', especially the first part, is particularly concerned with the *tendency towards self-chastisement* as a component of neurotic symptoms. These symptoms—as well as numerous dreams—are interpreted by Alexander in such a way as to reveal the ambiguity which makes it possible for them to constitute both wish-fulfilment and self-chastisement. He describes the 'corruptibility' of the neurotic conscience:

'The neurotic gratification of repressed wishes is only possible if the super ego is bribed with suffering, as a result of which the motive underlying the repression—the ego's fear of the super ego—disappears.'[3] Alexander describes, *inter alia*, how the neurotic's super ego, as the representative of the parents or guardians, proceeds with undue severity against the ego in order to give the id, i.e. the drive, permission to 'sin'. This permission is paid for with suffering (self-chastisement).

Alexander understands under 'The Psychoanalysis of the Total Personality' 'the total economic balance of the two fundamental tendencies'—i.e. the demands of the drives and the counter-demands of reality, which latter assume the form of fear and morality. These forces and counter-forces endeavour to achieve a balanced economy. He describes three different types of endeavour:

[1] See especially F. Alexander and T. French, *Studies in Psychosomatic Medicine*, New York, 1948.　　[2] F. Dunbar, *Emotions and Bodily Changes*, New York, 1943.
[3] F. Alexander, *Psychoanalysis of the Total Personality*, New York, 1949.

1. The mechanism of conversion hysteria: the demands of the con-science and the demands of the drives are both satisfied in a single act by virtue of the ambiguity of the symptom.

2. The mechanism of obsessional neurosis: the demands of the con-science and the demands of the drives are simultaneously satisfied but by different psychic processes.

3. The mechanism of manic-depression: the demands of the conscience and the demands of the drives are satisfied one after the other at different times.

Alexander has been accused in many quarters (*Glover, Fenichel inter alia*) of anthropomorphism because of the way in which he describes the interactions between the instances (super ego, ego, id). And it is quite true that in Alexander's writings the instances interact in the same way as do individual human beings. But his critics tend to overlook the fact that in 'The Ego and the Id' Freud also anthropomorphized the instances (see p. 151 ff.) and that Alexander was in fact merely continuing a practice initiated by Freud.

(b) Conflicts of Drives[1] ('emotional tensions')

Although Alexander—like Freud and various other authors—explains the neurotic symptoms of conversion hysteria as structural conflicts between the various instances of the personality he makes the following distinction between conversion hysteria and vegetative neurosis:[2]

'We can now define the difference between a conversion symptom and vegetative neurosis. A conversion symptom is a symbolic expression of an emotionally charged psychological content: it is an attempt to dis-charge the emotional tension. It takes place in the voluntary neuro-muscular or sensory-perceptive systems whose original function is to express and relieve emotional tensions. A vegetative neurosis is not an attempt to express an emotion but is the physiological response of the vegetative organs to constant or to periodically returning emotional states. Elevation of blood pressure, for example, under the influence of rage does not relieve the rage but is a physiological component of the total phenomenon of rage. As will be shown later, it is an adaptation of the body to the state of the organism when it prepares to meet an emergency.'

Vegetative neurosis forms the link between conversion hysteria and the group of psychogenic organic illnesses which in Alexander's view are

[1] F. Alexander, 'Relation of Structural and Instinctual Conflicts'. *Psa. Quart.*, Vol. II, p. 181, 1933.

[2] F. Alexander, *Psychosomatic Medicine*, London, Allen & Unwin, 1952, p. 42.

brought about as the result of lasting conscious or *unconscious* emotional tensions. Both in psychosomatic illness and in vegetative neurosis *conflicts of drives* produce corresponding psychosomatic reactions. Alexander has reproduced these correspondences in the following schemata:[1]

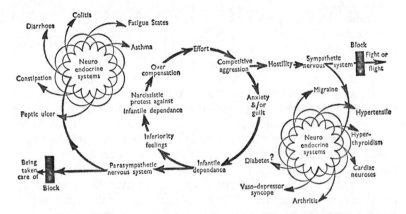

The difference between this schema of conflicts of drives, which Alexander substantiates in his psychosomatic investigations with numerous case histories, and structural conflicts is twofold:

1. Whereas the id is represented by the single concept of 'infantile dependence' the ego is represented by three concepts, namely, 'narcissistic protest', 'over-compensation' and 'efforts of will'. The aggressive aspirations of the id appear in a secondary and reactive form as 'aggression accompanied by feelings of rivalry'.

2. The decisive concept of the *blockage* either of infantile dependence or of aggressive tendencies is not adequately substantiated by Alexander. He often equates it with inhibition. In respect of hypertonia, for example, he speaks of a 'chronically inhibited state of hostility'. Does this blockage stem from the super ego and inhibit the id (aggression/regression) or is the inhibition to be understood in the Freudian sense as an inhibition of ego activity? We are not told.

In dispensing with the various instances of the personality as the spheres within which the conflicts take place Alexander runs the risk of reducing psychology to a purely dialectical process between action and reaction, which involves him in a vicious circle of causality. (The physiological problems attendant on the division of illnesses into the vagus and sympathetic groups will not be dealt with here.) Infantile dependence (action) is followed by feelings of inferiority (reaction);

[1] F. Alexander, *Ibid* p. 67.

these are then followed by a narcissistic process (action), which is followed by over-compensation (reaction), etc. Whereas Freud and his followers (see especially *Abraham, Ferenczi, Fenichel, Glover, Anna Freud, H. Hartmann,* etc.) were still concerned with questions of structure (instances) and the qualitative and quantitative differences between id, ego and super ego, Alexander, having represented conflicts as emotional tensions, was no longer interested in these problems. They were replaced by a psychology of action and reaction, which was more akin to a psychology of consciousness and which to some extent used Freud's findings in a purely dialectical sense.

In fact the representation of conflicts as emotional tensions need not by any means involve a renunciation of the theory of instances or of the assumption of structures, provided the question as to *what* is in conflict with *what* is kept firmly in mind. The psychology which Alexander sought to establish has its antecedent in Freud's second phase, in which Freud defined the ego as a drive (self-preservation drive) and thereby ran the risk of defining the personality as consisting of no more than the interplay of dynamic and diametrically opposed drives. But—quite apart from the errors attendant on such an interpretation of the personality— Freud was quick to recognize the dialectical psychology of consciousness which must necessarily grow from it and so concerned himself once more with questions regarding the structure (instances) of the personality. Not that Freud succeeded in solving the problem of the structure and function of the psyche! On the one hand his super ego is determined by the drives and is therefore dynamic, whereas in respect of the ego it is structured.

(c) Special Psychosomatic Problems

If a psychosomatic disturbance differs from conversion hysteria by virtue of the lack of symbolism of its symptoms, then the following two questions arise:

1. Why should one person suffer from hysteria whilst another suffers from a psychosomatic disturbance?
2. What determines the particular specificity of the psychosomatic symptom, i.e. why does one patient suffer from a stomach ailment and another from high blood pressure?

Alexander considers the aetiology of each illness to be contained in the following factors:[1]

'D (disease) = f(function of) (a.b.c.d.e.g.h.i.j. ... n)
(*a*)   hereditary constitution

---

[1] F. Alexander, *Psychosomatic Medicine,* p. 52.

(b)   birth injuries
(c)   organic diseases of infancy which increase the vulnerability of certain organs
(d)   nature of infant care (weaning habits, toilet training, sleeping arrangements, etc.)
(e)   accidental physical traumatic experiences of infancy and childhood
(h)   emotional climate of family and specific personality traits of parents and siblings
(i)   later physical injuries
(j)   later emotional experiences in initimate personal and occupational relations'

Although *Freud* considered the first question to be unanswerable and although the first question must be answered before the second can be answered, Alexander considered that his own solution of the second question was probably correct. Indeed, in his late publications he even considered the question as to the specificity of psychosomatic illnesses to have been solved. He sees the specificity of various diseases as follows:

1.   Diarrhoea in conjunction with colitis:
'Frustration of oral dependent longings—oral-aggressive responses—guilt—anxiety—overcompensation for oral aggression by the urge to give (restitution) and to accomplish—inhibition and failure of the effort to give and accomplish—diarrhoea'[1]
2.   A stomach ulcer caused by 'over-functioning' of the stomach:
(a)   'Frustration of oral-receptive longings—oral-aggressive response—guilt—anxiety—overcompensation for oral aggression and dependence by actual successful accomplishments in responsible activities—increased unconscious oral-dependent cravings as reaction to excessive effort and concentration—gastric hypersecretion.
(b)   Prolonged frustration of oral-receptive longings—repression of these wishes—gastric hypersecretion.'[2]
3.   High blood pressure:
'Hostile competitive tendencies—intimidation due to retaliation and failure—increase of dependent longings—inferiority feelings—reactivation of hostile competitiveness—anxiety and resultant inhibition of aggressive hostile impulses—arterial hypertension.'[3]
Although Alexander emphatically rejects any symbolic meaning for psychosomatic disturbances, this does not prevent him from having recourse to symbols—provided the symbolism fits his hypothesis. For how, if not symbolically, are we to interpret the relationship between

[1] F. Alexander, *Ibid*, 1952, p. 128.
[2] *Ibid*., p. 115.   [3] *Ibid*., p. 153.

diarrhoea and the (unsuccessful) attempt to give, or between hypertonia and the chronic 'internal' pressure to which the patient is subjected? (See Part Three, p. 459 ff.)

(d) F. Alexander's Positivism

Although in his desparture from Freud's theory of instances (to which, however, Alexander still continued to subscribe, thus complicating the task of assessing his position within psychoanalysis) we may detect a deviation from the master's teaching on the part of the disciple, Alexander none the less consistently pursued Freud's positivism. Although for Freud the drives are mythical beings (see p. 146 ff.), they still remain subjective representations of physiological (chemical) processes. By enlisting the services of endocrinology and of physiological knowledge of the vegetative nervous system Alexander is able to treat the psychogony of organic or functional disturbances as a purely provisional concept: all psychic activity and the dualism of body and psyche, which appears to be a problem, can only be said to exist in as far as we have not yet succeeded in working out better methods of expressing psychic activity in physiological formulae.

'Whereas physiology approaches the functions of the central nervous system in terms of space and time psychology approaches them in terms of various subjective phenomena which are the *subjective reflections of physiological processes.*'[1]

Where monism is so consistent the personality must ultimately appear as the sum-total of its physiological processes and the body as a 'complicated machine',[2] which illustrates with particular clarity the dependence of Freudian-type psychoanalysis on the rationalism of the French and English Enlightenment.

The imprint which Alexander's influence left on psychoanalysis in the USA may be summed up in the following points:

1. Depth psychology and structural psychology are replaced by a dialectical psychology of emotional forces and drives.
2. The problem of the connection between physical and psychic disturbances is solved in terms of *parallelism* (as practised by *Wundt*), i.e. the simultaneous investigation of physiological and psychological processes, on the basis of a materialistic monism. The connection between body and psyche is an unreal problem.
3. Freud's revolutionary findings—revolutionary because of what they revealed—are sacrificed to a rational optimistic cultural philosophy. (See F. Alexander: *Irrationale Kräfte unserer Zeit.*)

[1] F. Alexander, *Psychosomatic Medicine*, pp. 36–7.
[2] *Ibid.*, p. 38.

K

SUMMARY

The most important extensions of psychoanalytic theory within the Freudian school may be summarized from the following points of view:

(a) The Development of S. Freud's Concept of the Drive

Psychoanalytic drive theories have not been expanded or modified to any significant extent since the death of Siegmund Freud. In 1936 E. Bibring[1] presented a comprehensive survey of the drives and this work is still valid to-day. But since in Freudian psychoanalysis all the psychic functions possess a drive character, including the ego and the super ego, any survey of the psychoanalytic theory of drives must be devoted exclusively to the 'drive'. This Freud defines as follows:

'By an "instinct" is provisionally to be understood the psychical representative of an endosomatic, continuously flowing source of stimulation, as contrasted with a "stimulus", which is set up by *single* excitations coming from *without*. The concept of instinct is thus one of those lying on the frontier between the mental and the physical. The simplest and likeliest assumption as to the nature of instincts would seem to be that in itself an instinct is without quality, and, so far as mental life is concerned, is only to be regarded as a measure of the demand made upon the mind for work. What distinguishes the instincts from one another and endows them with specific qualities is their relation to their somatic sources and to their aims. The source of an instinct is a process of excitation occurring in an organ and the immediate aim of the instinct lies in the removal of this organic stimulus.[1]

Bibring summarizes the development of the drives in Freud's work as follows:[2]

'The psychoanalytic study of the instincts is made up of two main parts, a general theory of the instincts and a specialized one. The general theory includes, besides the concept of instinct, the theory of the instincts in the narrower sense, that is, the question of the number and nature of the instincts, the question of the criteria of their classification, and the question of their causation and function; the general theory further includes the theory of instinctual transformation, i.e. the question

---

[1] S. Freud, *St. Edn.*, Vol. 7, p. 168.
[2] E. Bibring, *Int. J. Psa*, Vol. 22, pp. 102 ff., 1941.

of the variability of instincts and the laws which such variations (which are in part the same as what are called instinctual vicissitudes) obey; and it includes, finally, the concepts and problems connected with the energic aspects of the instincts. The specialized theory is concerned with the development of the instincts in the individual, together with the working hypotheses which that development entails and the problems to which it gives rise.

'In the following pages I shall confine myself to the general theory and in particular to that part of it which is devoted to the theory of the instincts in the narrower sense. This field too has been the main subject of psychoanalytic discussions upon the instincts during the last few years. . . .

'Freud's theory was a dualistic one from the beginning, and it remained so, in spite of all the changes that it underwent. What was changed was never the number but only the nature of the instincts, or rather the groups of instincts, that were to be distinguished.

'The theory of the instincts reached its present position in four steps.

'1. The first step was the setting up of two groups of instincts—the sexual and the ego instincts. The sexual instincts were closely studied, whereas the ego instincts remained to begin with a relatively unknown quantity.

'2. The next step was an addition to the theory. The introduction of the concept of narcissism into the libido theory led to the postulation of a libidinal component of the ego instincts. Nevertheless, Freud held firmly to the view that besides this libidinal component there must exist a primary, non-libidinal component; this he called "interest" in a non-committal way, rather in the sense of non-libidinal egoism.

'3. The third step—a step which has for the most part been overlooked in psychoanalytical writings—was that the aggressive trends were ascribed to the ego instincts as being among their essential constituents. This view was set out by Freud in the last sections of his paper on "Instincts and their Vicissitudes" and was based upon a discussion of the relation between love and hate, in which he came to the conclusion that hate was to be regarded as a non-libidinal reaction of the ego.

'4. The fourth step was due to a growing knowledge of the structure of the mental apparatus as a whole and its division into a "vital" stratum (the id) and an organized part (the ego), and, more especially, to a study of the unconscious region of the ego, the super ego. The gist of this view was that the aggressive trends were no longer regarded as primary attributes of the ego instincts but as independently existent instincts of aggression and destruction existing side by side with the sexual instincts in the vital strata of the mind. The ego instincts ceased to be independent entities and were derived partly from the libidinal and partly from the aggressive instincts.

'To this fourth step in the development of instinctual theory there was now added a further theory. It postulated the existence of the primal instincts—what are known as the instincts of life and of death. This postulate served to extend the theoretic basis that underlay the fourth step, to solve certain unexplained problems and to bring together and to simplify the various theoretical hypotheses that had so far been set up.'[1]

In the first phase of the theory of drives, which was largely concerned with sexuality, the following sections are important:[1]

'(1) The thesis of the component instincts, which is linked to the concept of erotogenic zones; (2) the thesis of an ontogenetic development of the sexual instincts taking place in successive stages and following a fixed order prescribed by biological laws; and (3) the libido theory (which amplifies and underpins the first two theses) and also, perhaps, the theory of the transformations of the sexual instincts in general.'

The essential nature of the drives in this phase is characterized as:[2]

'Instinct, then, is an energy which arises from the vital stratum of the mind, which has a direction that is determined inherently, which presses forward towards a particular aim and is directed somewhat loosely towards things and persons as its object. It is linked to an organ of origin as its source and to a terminal organ as the site of its satisfaction. Its satisfaction consists in the removal of those changes in the zones of excitation which accompany the instinctual tension. Or, to put it more shortly, an instinct is something that "comes from outside", produces energy and is the cause of particular mental processes.'

In the second phase of Freud's theory of drives the following changes take place:

1. The ego drives, which Freud—without defining them (hunger and thirst, self-preservation drive)—had originally placed in opposition to sexuality, are now said to be libidinal. Further psychiatric observations (see p. 114 ff.) and the introduction of primary and secondary narcissism had prompted this assumption.

2. The dualism between the ego drives and sexuality is removed; both develop from 'primal' libido.

3. On the other hand Freud tries to maintain the dualism of his drive theory by introducing the concept of 'interest', which constitutes an analogue to the libido theory for the ego concept.[3]

[1] E. Bibring, *Int. J. Psa.*, Vol. 22, pp. 104–5, 1941.
[2] *Ibid.*, pp. 106–ü7, 1941.   [3] *Ibid.*, p. 109, 1941.

'Freud therefore introduced the notion of ego interest in the sense of a non-libidinal egoism; or, to put it more correctly, he asserted that what was known as egoism had two components, a libidinal-narcissistic component and a non-libidinal component. Narcissism, as he wrote, is only the "libidinal complement to the egoism of the instinct of self-preservation, a measure of which may be justifiably attributed to every living creature." Originally these two components were undifferentiated.'

Aggression is the focal point of the third phase of Freud's theory of drives. Sadism, which was originally conceived as a libidinal partial drive, was not easily reconciled with the aims of the libido. Related phenomena which made their presence felt in human relationships in the form of power or a power drive, prompted Freud (he was also prompted by Adler) to speak of the sadism of the 'ego drives'. And so sadism was again withdrawn from sexuality and attributed to the ego drives, whilst at the same time it was assumed that sexuality and aggressive ego drives intermixed. As a result interest in the source of the drive (erotogenic zones) was displaced by interest in the drive aims. No source could be found for the ego drives comparable to the erotogenic zones, but these could still be fitted in to the proposed schema as the 'demands for work' made on the psychic apparatus.

In the fourth phase of Freud's theory of drives the aggressive drive is also removed from the ego drives and made independent.[1]

'In this way the new theory asserted that there are two groups of instincts in the vital layer—the libidinal and the aggressive (or destructive) group. Each instinctual group moves forward towards satisfaction on its own account; and, partly through a free struggle to obtain it, partly through the influence of an ego which is subjected to the pressure of the external world and of the super ego, each enters into a great variety of relationships with the other, whether of an associative or an antagonistic kind. Both can easily come into opposition with those trends of the system which operate in a self-preservative sense and which are represented in the ego (ego instincts). In contradistinction to the instincts of sex and of aggression, which work in the vital layer and are directed to objects, are the ego instincts, whose field of operation is the ego.'

His observations of masochism and of severe (so-called endogenic) depression were the decisive factors leading to Freud's assumption of an independent aggressive drive, for these clinical observations were incompatible with the self-preservation character of the ego drives. In this phase of his theory the ego has to assert itself *vis-à-vis* both aggression and sexuality.

[1] E. Bibring, *Int. J. Psa.*, Vol. 22, p. 114, 1941.

In the last phase of his theory of drives Freud assumed a life drive and a death drive, which he tried to substantiate on speculative grounds (see p. 146 ff.).

(b) Extensions of Freud's Theory of Drives

A considerable number of Freud's followers have rejected his death drive hypothesis (for summary see *Bruns*)[1] but we shall not be dealing with their opinions here. *J. Lampl de Groot*[2] seeks to establish a compromise between these divergent views by restricting the concept of the drive to psychological phenomena and that of force (energy) to somatic phenomena. She argues that the death and life drives are the 'ultimate' forces underlying the psychologically tangible drives, which ultimate forces are no less mystical than the concept of a physical force. *Fenichel*, who very much doubted the existence of a death drive (see p. 189 ff.), assumed a primary congruence between ego drives and aggressive drives in the earliest oral phase (monism). For *Melanie Klein* the aggressive drive is the focal point of interest: fear is always fear of aggression (see also *K. Horney*) and the primary purpose of the libido is that of defence against fear (see p. 215 ff.). For *Hartmann* and his collaborators, who assume the presence in the id of a largely autonomous ego sphere (see p. 217 ff.), the energy within this sphere and thus the energy of the ego drives consists for the most part of 'neutralized aggression'. (The way in which the ego neutralizes aggression, however, and uses it for purposes of cathexis and counter-cathexis is largely hypothetical.) *S. Novey*,[3] on the other hand, assumes that ego energy is supplied by the life drive in the fullest sense of the word (Eros), which, he contends, should be considered independently of the sexological view of the libido. *E. Weiss*[4] postulates (a) a reservoir of energy which feeds id, ego and super ego and which should not be confused with (b) the specific reservoir of the drives. Drives, wishes and cathexes all originate in the reservoir of energy.

II. EXTENSIONS OF THE LIBIDO THEORY

These include:

(a) *Abraham's* division of libido development into six stages;
(b) *Ferenczi's* development of the sense of reality as a counterpart to the Libido theory;

[1] *Psyche*, Vol. VII, 1953.
[2] J. Lampl de Groot: 'The Theory of Instinctual Drives', *Int. J. Psa.*, Vol. XXXVIII, pp. 137 ff., 1956.
[3] S. Novey, 'The Theory of Instinctual Drives', *Int. J. Psa.* Vol. XXXVIII, pp. 137 ff., 1957.
[4] E. Weiss, 'A Comparative Study of Psychoanalytic Ego Concepts', *Int. J. Psa.*, Vol. XXXVIII, p. 209, 1957.

(c) *E. Homburger Erikson's* investigations into the correlation between social behaviour and libido development;

(d) the British school and the psychologization of libido development: libido as a defence against anxiety and aggression (*M. Klein, E. Jones, E. Glover*);

(e) the controversy between *Fenichel* (libido development as a biological process) and the British school;

(f) contributions by Anna Freud and members of the New York group regarding the extensive *overlapping* of the phases of libido development.

III. EXTENSIONS OF FREUD'S CONCEPTION OF INSTANCES (EGO AND SUPER EGO)

(a) The ego as an autonomous and synthetic sphere (investigations by *Nunberg, Anna Freud, H. Hartmann* and his collaborators and P. Federn);

(b) Glover's theory of the 'ego-nuclei' as precursors of the ego, which are subsequently joined together, due to the synthetic power of the psyche, to form an ego;

(c) a large number of cognitive activities which regulate motor activity are attributed to the ego (*Hartmann* and his collaborators, *P. Federn*);

(d) the genesis of the super ego is located in the pre-oedipal phases by *M. Klein, O. Fenichel, E. Jones*: (they are opposed by *Anna Freud, H. Hartmann* and his collaborators *inter alia*);

(e) a 'pre-Oedipal' Oedipus complex is assumed by *M. Klein, E. Jones* and in part by *O. Fenichel*: (they are opposed by *Anna Freud, H. Hartmann* and his collaborators *inter alia*).

IV. CHARACTER AND DEFENCE

Works on this subject include those by *W. Reich, O. Fenichel* and *Anna Freud*. Reich and Fenichel demonstrate the close connection between character traits and defence against the drives and against anxiety. Anna Freud, continuing the investigations of Siegmund Freud, describes in all nine patterns of behaviour which serve as a defence against anxiety. But by no means all of the defence mechanisms are pathological from the outset; rather they form a part of normal development.

V. THE IMPORTANCE OF ANXIETY

All the authors of the Freudian school are agreed on the fact that anxiety plays a specific and decisive part in the emergence of neuroses (as also of psychoses and of psychosomatic illnesses). The fact that writers like Melanie Klein place anxiety and the depression to which it gives rise in the first six months of infantile development, whilst other writers consider the rise of anxiety to be more closely correlated with the various stages of libido development, does not in any way detract from their general unanimity in this respect.

VI. DIRECT OBSERVATIONS OF SMALL CHILDREN

It is probable that observations of this kind will play a decisive part in the further development of psychoanalysis. *Anna Freud* and *D. Burlingham* have demonstrated that *both complexes and character traits are largely independent of the environment.* They are, so to speak, pre-formed and the environment serves merely as a 'release' mechanism. The controversy between the 'biological' and the 'cultural' (Neo-Freudian) nature of neurosis will be dealt with in greater detail in Part Three (see p. 556 ff.).

VII. PSYCHOTHERAPY IN THE FREUDIAN SCHOOL

Siegmund Freud's psychotherapy, which was the product of a development extending over many decades (see p. 162 ff.), restricted the physician's activity almost entirely to interpretation and the patient's activity to the production of material for interpretation, namely, dreams, free associations, resistances, transference, faulty actions and character patterns. No radical alterations have ever been made to this method of treatment by members of the Freudian school. On the contrary, a positive welter of publications has appeared, all of which deal in great detail with the same crucial question as to when and how the physician is to give his interpretation. As far as the instrument of analysis is concerned, i.e. the interpretation (in which the physician makes conscious the unconscious motivations revealed in resistances, dreams, associations or specific character patterns), there has been a considerable amount of agreement. Differences of opinion did occur, however, as to the how and the when of the proposed interpretation. These differences of opinion, which are of a technical nature, are revealing in that they document not so much the problems attendant on Freudian therapeutic method as the care with which Freudians enquire into those problems. The difference between Freudian therapy and the therapy of the Neo-Freudians or of C. G. Jung and his adherents is clearly demonstrated by the sheer quantity of such investigations, which may be justly considered to substantiate the claim that the practice of psychoanalysis in accordance with Freud's principles is the most thoroughly tested, the best proved and the most widely investigated of all the therapeutic methods. The findings reached by the Freudian school in the province of practical therapy have been taken over to a considerable extent by the other schools, which—with the exception of C. G. Jung—have contributed little of their own to psychotherapy (see below, p. 317 ff.).

Anna Freud[1] opened up a new path to therapy (theoretically) when she differentiated between the work on the ego and the defence mechanisms on the one hand and the raising into consciousness of repressed materials (the id) on the other. In both cases the physician intervenes verbally by repeatedly pointing out to the patient his faulty actions and by encouraging—i.e. in his interpretation of dreams or of free associations—the process whereby the unconscious material is freed and revealed. Anna Freud's work on child psychotherapy should be a sufficient indication of the importance of a *more active* form of psychotherapy. Children could not be treated in the same way as adults, in respect of whom the analyst was required to remain largely passive and to exercise considerable self-restraint in respect of interpretation. Child therapists did not concentrate exclusively on play therapy but also used other methods whereby the contents of the child's unconscious could be raised either directly or indirectly into consciousness, methods which presupposed greater activity on the part of the therapist.

These methods of treatment, which were: established for purposes of child therapy, were to open up new paths in the treatment of psychotics, especially of schizophrenics, most of whom had remained inaccessible to analysis conducted along traditional Freudian lines. Although differences of opinion regarding the choice of psychotherapeutic method of treating psychoses are even greater than in respect of neuroses,[2] it is none the less true to say that in the treatment of psychosis—as distinct from neurosis—there is a growing movement towards greater participation on the part of the therapist, who, it is considered, should actively encourage the formation of a transference and the establishment of a doctor-patient relationship. This movement is associated with names such as *Frieda Fromm-Reichmann, M. A. Sechehaye, A. Rosen, G. Benedetti inter alia.* In the psychotherapy of schizophrenics, as in the psychotherapy of children, the therapist tries to induce the patient to give direct expression to unconscious contents or conflicts by means of play therapy, psychodrama (i.e. the expression of psychic conflicts in dramatic form) or other symbolic media. But whereas *Rosen*, for

---

[1] *The Ego and the Mechanisms of Defence*, London, 1952.
[2] For summary see *P. Matussek* in *Handbuch der Psychotherapie* ('Handbook of Psychotherapy'), Ed. v. Gebsattel and others, Munich, 1957.

example, will give an interpretation—often of a simple sexual nature—to his schizophrenic patients of the actions which they have performed, other therapists are opposed to this method of direct interpretation.

The activity involved in the psychotherapeutic treatment of children and psychotics was to exercise a certain influence on the treatment of neurotics. It was chiefly *F. Deutsch*[1] and *F. Alexander*[2] who, with their concepts of 'sector therapy' (Deutsch) and 'vector therapy' (Alexander) urged greater activity on the part of the analyst *vis-à-vis* his patient. What Deutsch understood under 'sector therapy' was that the analyst should select from the associations made by the patient those which appeared to him to be important and should then proceed to relate them to the patient's symptoms. In Alexander's 'vector therapy' the analyst also plays a leading part. The patient is recommended to set himself specific therapeutic goals with fixed time limits (cf. especially similar endeavours by *Ferenczi*), whilst a simultaneous attempt is made to advance the therapy, to speed it up, by the 'expressive' cultivation of the contact between physician and patient. It should be added, however, that to some extent F. Alexander subsequently withdrew his support from this type of treatment, which had met with considerable opposition amongst Freud's followers. However, the conception of the analyst as an almost entirely passive figure who simply gives his patient an occasional interpretation has been revealed as a fiction. In their investigations both into the course taken by analytic treatment and above all into the problem of transference and counter-transference *R. Loewenstein*,[3] *S. Nacht*,[3] *M. Bouvet*[3] *and W. R. Eissler*[3] have recognized the need for the analyst to abandon on occasions his attitude of extreme passivity. It is of course difficult to make rules which would stipulate when and in what way the physician should break the fundamental rule of strict reserve. This will depend on the individual case. Lagache's analysis[4] of the transference situation, which cannot by any means be said to embrace the concept of ideal neutrality on the part of the analyst, is particularly revealing in this respect. Lagache[4] demonstrates |that, if an analysis is to be successful, the patient must submit to the fundamental rule of saying everything that comes into his head and, if necessary, of lying down on the analyst's couch. This submission, which is demanded on objective grounds ('dynamic causes of transference'), normally arouses resistance in the patient and can grow into a serious obstacle. No matter how much the

[1] F. Deutsch, *Applied Psychoanalysis*, New York, 1949.
[2] F. Alexander, *Fundamentals of Psychoanalysis*, London, 1949.
[3] See *Int. J. Psa.*, Vol. XXXIX, Symposium (Conclusions of the Paris Congress, 1957, with special reference to analytical therapy).
[4] D. Lagache, 'Some aspects of Transference' *Int. J. Psa.*, Vol. XXXIV, 1953, p. 1.

physician may keep himself in the background his activity must also be a matter of some moment, since it influences the 'shadow-boxing' (F. Alexander) which goes on between the physician and the patient. *R. A. Waelder*[1] (cf. also *H. Nunberg*[2]) summarizes the patient's situation in transference as follows:

'Transference develops in consequence of the conditions of the analytic experiment, viz. of the analytic situation and the analytic technique. Among these one may mention:

1. The fact that the patient suffers and comes to the analyst in expectation of help—a fact that puts him in the position of a child turning to an adult;

2. the unilateral exposure, by the patient, of the most intimate aspects of his life—putting him in the position of the child that is nude in the presence of adults;

3. the analytic rule of free associations, requiring the patient to give up, as far as possible, goal-directed behaviour and defences against the rise of impulses—a rule which changes the balance between id and ego and thereby favours (temporary) regressions;

4. the reassurance, explicit or implied, offered by the analyst, against the anxiety provoked by the rise of unconscious material, thus putting the patient in the position of a protected child; and

5. the passivity of the analyst; i.e. the fact that the analyst does not respond to the patient's attitudes on the level of reality and does not play out his own personality, so that the patient's phantasies are not stopped prematurely by counter-actions from the outside world.'[2]

The problems attendant on the transference situation are made manifest when Waelder contrasts three different aspects of this process: (1) by virtue of the processes described above transference represents a regression to infantile stages and as such may contribute towards the formation of a resistance against the insight and maturity which the analysis is expected to produce. (2) It becomes a vehicle for infantile conflicts which can be abreacted on to the analyst. (3) It can cause the patient to identify with the analyst and thus create a new super ego structure in the patient, which would provide the analyst with numerous possibilities of influencing the patient. Although this last aspect is not strictly analytical—*Aichhorn* made use of it in order to influence juvenile criminals—on the other hand there is no doubt but that Freud himself had occasional recourse to it in order to overcome resistances. There are differences of opinion with regard to transference, for

[1] R. A. Waelder, See *Int. J. Psa.*, Vol. XXXVII, 1956, pp. 367 ff.
[2] H. Nunberg, 'Transference and Reality', *Int. J. Psa.*, Vol. XXXII, 1951.

example, between *Melanie Klein* and *Anna Freud*. The former assumes that it is primarily the patient's super ego that is transferred on to the analyst, whilst the latter—like *Sterba*[1] and *Bibring*[2]—postulates that it is chiefly aspects of the ego that are transferred. These differences of opinion, which may well appear to an outsider as just so much hair-splitting, are in fact all part of the intensive enquiries into the nature of the complicated therapeutic processes which take place between the physician and his patient and should be regarded in this light.

In summing up we may say of psychotherapy within the Freudian school:

1. It does not differ in its essentials from Freud's postulates and has undergone no decisive changes in respect of the treatment of neurotics. On the other hand the 'how' and the 'when' of interpretation, the details of the technique of treatment, have been subjected to a thorough investigation both from a practical and a theoretical point of view.

2. Attempts to speed up or to force psychoanalytic treatment by means of a more active attitude on the part of the analyst have resulted in fundamental changes primarily in the sphere of child therapy and of therapy for psychotics. In the treatment of neurotics, however, these attempts have proved abortive.

[1] R. Sterba, 'The Fate of the Ego in Analytic Therapy', *Int. J. Psa.*, 1934, pp. 117–26.
[2] E. Bibring, 'Therapeutic Results of Psychoanalysis', *Int. J. Psa.*, 1937, pp. 170–89.

3
THE NEO-FREUDIANS

Several of the authors in this section were disciples of Freud's over a period of years before making what was in most cases a radical break with their preceptor. Despite the differences of opinion which undoubtedly exist between these various authors, they none the less constitute a group (i.e. the Neo-Freudian group) by virtue of their divergence from Freud in respect of the following factors:

1. They reject the libido theory.
2. As a consequence the majority of these authors—H. S. Sullivan and H. Schultz-Hencke are exceptions—have only a limited interest in genetic conceptions of personality development (i.e. of psychological development).
3. Instead, they attach major importance to environmental influences.
4. The structural concepts of the Freudian theory of instances are for the most part abandoned, as also is the theory of the mechanisms of defence.
5. Instead the so-called distorted attitudes which the individual develops are subjected to detailed examination (Behaviour research).
6. The unconscious, as Freud understood it, loses much of its meaning; it is considered as a mere marginal phenomenon.
7. The role played by sexuality is reduced to minor proportions.
8. No particular importance is attached to the investigation of symbols (dreams, faulty actions) or to the analysis of symptoms. (E. Fromm, Thomas French and H. Schultz-Hencke are exceptions.)
9. The great majority of these authors do not write for the specialist but rather for the educated layman.

A

ALFRED ADLER (INDIVIDUAL PSYCHOLOGY)

Theorie und Praxis der Individual psychologie, Vienna 1923.
The Neurotic Constitution, New York, 1917
A Study of Organ Inferiority and its Psychical Compensation,
New York, 1917
The Education of Children, London, 1930

Adler, the founder of Individual Psychology, was the first of Freud's disciples to break away (1911) and follow his own line of research.

The deficiencies of Individual Psychology, judged as a total system, are far too great for it to be capable of presenting a comprehensive explanation of human activity such as had been furnished by Freudian psychoanalysis. It none the less gained rapid popularity due to the ease with which its concepts could be understood and it found special favour with both educationalists and interested laymen. Unencumbered as it was by the tricky problem of sexuality—which for Adler is virtually non-existent—its wide diffusion was due in no small measure to this very fact. There was, moreover, the additional factor of Adler's *missionary zeal and fervour*, for he felt himself to be the herald of a new doctrine and won his disciples largely from socialist circles. To-day Individual psychology is practically extinct as a school, but this does not mean to say that its requirements and findings may be disregarded, for these were the precursors of paths subsequently pursued by the Neo-Freudians, on whom—and especially on K. ´Horney—they had a marked influence.

Individual Psychology considers human behaviour to be based on two main principles:

(*a*) feelings of inferiority, which are determined by a man's social situation;

(*b*) the attempt to 'compensate' for these feelings of inferiority by a commensurate striving for power.

(*a*) *Feelings of Inferiority*

Adler considers that feelings of inferiority, which are of crucial importance for his explanatory psychology, are determined by genetic, organic and situational factors. The genetic source of feelings of inferiority lies in the fact that in its relationship to adults *every* child is helpless and this helplessness must in *every* case give rise to a sense of inferiority on the part of the child. Quite irrespective of whether it is loved by its parents or rejected by them this sense of inferiority will impress itself on the child to such an extent that its later development must always be considered as an attempt to overcome its primary experience of inferiority. Adler defines the *life style* as the biography of the individual with particular regard to the forces involved in overcoming this primary sense of inferiority. The object of individual psychology, especially its therapeutic object, is to investigate the individual's *behaviour* from the point of view of the conflict between his feelings of inferiority and his striving for power and superiority (compensation). The organic source of feelings of inferiority lies both in the above-mentioned situation, which is common to all men, and also in physical disabilities, so-called organic inferiority. These disabilities are not necessarily anatomical but can also be functional, e.g. stuttering. Adler likes to quote Demosthenes as an example of a man who, plagued by feelings of inferiority because of his stutter, overcame both the stutter and the inferiority by systematically practising speech therapy and became an outstanding orator.

Feelings of inferiority can be said to derive from a situational source if the primarily helpless child is maltreated or rejected by its parents, i.e. if its feelings of inferiority are strengthened by its parents' attitude towards it. For Adler the Oedipus complex is relevant only in as far as parents who *spoil* their children tend to bestow undue affection on a child of the opposite sex and may thereby arouse sexual feelings and phantasies in the child. In their turn these sexual feelings may strengthen the child's primary feelings of inferiority, for, in as far as they contravene the social mores, they may produce secondary guilt in the child and consequently further feelings of inferiority. In order to overcome its feelings of inferiority the child will then try to dominate its father or mother, i.e. to exercise its power over the parent of the opposite sex. Incestuous phantasies which the child develops in this connection would simply be an expression of its domination over and subjugation of the parent and should be evaluated as such. For Adler—as also for *Horney*—the Oedipus complex is the consequence of a parental attitude of spoiling the child and not an event arising 'automatically' out of libido development. As a consequence of its being spoiled the child's sexual desires are placed in the service of its striving for power and thus in the final analysis they too serve to overcome the feelings of inferiority deriving from the situational source (see above).

(b) Overcoming Feelings of Inferiority

It is surprising that Freud should have considered that the part played by the phenomenon of power and of the individual's striving for power was only a minor one, even where rivalry between brothers and sisters was involved.[1] Due to his over-riding preoccupation with questions of sexuality and of the libido economy he continued, even in his second and third phases, to interpret the phenomena which he observed in the sphere of group sociology, in which he was then interested, in the light of his theory of instances and his theory of transference. However, his rejection of Adler and of Adler's Individual Psychology may also have contributed to the fact that Freud avoided enquiring into the phenomenon of power. Adler—and here he resembles Nietzsche—was to come to regard the individual's striving for power as one of the driving forces of human activity. It should be added, however, that for Adler

---

[1] It was only due to the influence exercised by Adler after his secession that Freud and his disciples began to take an interest in a 'power striving' within the ego.

power usually presupposed neurosis, i.e. its sole purpose was to compensate in an abnormal manner for feelings of inferiority. Adler—in contrast to Nietzsche—also had recourse to ethical and moral postulates which enabled man to adapt to society, for Adler totally rejected Nietzsche's amorality and his attempt to construct an ethical system on the basis of intensities of power. All that he actually has in common with Nietzsche is the fact that he too considers 'striving for power' to be a crucial source of human activity. The more acutely a child suffers from feelings of inferiority the more intent it will be on assuming the role of the superior, powerful, aggressive and domineering adult, whereby it lays the foundations for subsequent neurotic behaviour. In this connection the child's identification with parents, nurses or teachers is important. The 'life style', i.e. the way in which the individual lives his life under the necessity of constant reappraisal and readjustment of his feelings of inferiority, is determined in early childhood, usually at about four years of age. It is then that the decision is taken as to whether the individual's future development will be neurotic or healthy. The neurotic child will identify itself completely with the *powerful* figures which appear in its dreams and phantasies. Unrealistic in itself, it will arrange its life according to principles that are both rigid and wrong and if in the course of its upbringing it was rejected by its environment it will also constantly project its own animosity on to its environment. In contrast to the neurotic child the healthy child, whose development towards its life's goal has not been disturbed—i.e. the child that overcame its feelings of inferiority with a minimum of compensation—will develop at an early age a sense of *inner security*. It will be able to adapt itself to the demands of life without seeing in every situation with which it is faced a struggle between inferiority and the neurotic patterns of aggressive behaviour whose purpose is to overcome inferiority by a display of force. For Adler the individual's striving for power, understood in the primary sense of an attempt to come to terms with feelings of inferiority, is identical with the 'masculine protest'. He understands under this concept an attitude which is particularly prevalent in European and American culture and which is identical with authority, privilege, masculinity and power. Where this attitude prevails women and children appear as weak and inferior beings, who are not taken seriously and are consequently exploited and subjugated. To Adler it is only too obvious that in order to overcome their feelings of inferiority both women and children ardently wish to play, and in fact do play, the part of a man, i.e. they identify with the 'masculine protest'. Adler rejects the view advanced by Freud on the grounds of the anatomical and biological differences between the two sexes that there is a fundamental difference between men and women. He considers that such differences as do exist are determined purely by social and cultural considerations. In support of his argument Adler refers to periods of matriarchal rule when man was dominated by woman. The role of the father in the European—western—family has been predominantly authoritarian ever since Christianity gained power in Europe. Because of his behaviour, his 'secret' comings and goings, his decisions and resolutions the child sees a power in the father which it hopes will free it from its feelings of inferiority. The identification with the father which then ensues, particularly the identification with his power and authority, leads to the development of the 'masculine protest', which in turn leads to the formation—especially in the case of women—of grotesque images indicative of a severe neurotic disorder. Since it was in the rivalry between brothers and sisters that the striving for power within a family manifested itself most clearly, Adler examined this rivalry in detail. Where there are several brothers and sisters the oldest son will run the risk of becoming a 'dethroned crown prince', whilst the youngest child will be given to duplicity, since it is constantly obliged to compensate for its keenly felt inferiority *vis-à-vis* its brothers and sisters.

Apart from the 'striving for power' and the 'masculine protest' a further pattern of behaviour pursued for purposes of overcoming feelings of inferiority is that of 'the need for recognition' (*Geltungsbeduerfnis*), to which Adler also paid close attention. If the need for recognition is disproportionately strong, then it constitutes a further indication of neurosis both in children and adults and Adler argues that the desire to secure recognition from other people is an attempt to overcome feelings of inferiority. In Adler's view a considerable number of neurotic symptoms are simply a desire to attract the attention of other people, e.g. bed-wetting.

(c) Life Style and Social Feeling

Although confirmation of the diagnosis[1] as to whether a person is neurotic or healthy is afforded by an investigation of his life style (see above)—one expression of which, be it noted, is to be found in dreams and phantasies—Adler also considers 'social feeling' to be a criterion of health. But the reader will seek in vain for a clear definition of this concept (and of many others too) in Adler's writings. Amongst other things the three central problems of life are manifested in the 'social feeling', namely, one's relations to one's fellows, to one's profession and to love. Repeated failure in these essential spheres of life reveals a lack of social

---

[1] Adler was the first to concern himself with the question of the individual's *earliest* childhood memory, which he considered to be symbolic for the whole of his future life style. This question was subsequently taken over by nearly all the other schools of psychoanalysis.

feeling and indicates the presence of neurosis. The growing estrangement which marks human relations and which is caused by the civilization in which we live finds expression in the lack of social feeling such as is demonstrated above all by criminal and a-social elements.[1] Despite his optimism for the future of mankind Adler considers this to be one of the greatest dangers threatening our present civilization.

The personality revealed in the life style and the social feeling Adler considers to be entirely *one-dimensional*. He rejects all forms of pluralism of psychic motivations and drives in favour of a simple and *purposive* (teleological) 'life tendency'. This life tendency is the logical consequence of man's (compensatory) striving for power. The need for adaptation and security recedes in the face of this primary striving. For Adler the personality is an indissoluble, purposive entity. Regarded from this point of view a healthy personality differs from a sick personality only in so far as it does not come into conflict with its environment, i.e. with the cultural standards of a given civilization. From this it is clear that for Adler the question as to how conflicts arise is easily answered: conflicts arise only when the individual, in striving for power, clashes with society. Intrapsychic conflicts—e.g. the conflict between feelings of inferiority and striving for power—Adler rejects. He does not consider that the struggle between the individual's feelings of inferiority and his striving for power is a conflict but rather what might be called a natural condition, which always and 'automatically' gives rise to the process of striving for power. In itself this process is *not* of a pathogenic nature. It only becomes neurotic when unfavourable environmental conditions combine to reinforce feelings of inferiority, whereby the individual is obliged to exert himself to an exceptional degree in order to overcome them. In consequence of these exertions, which are rendered necessary by environmental pressures, the social feeling and the life style are subjected to changes which are of a pathogenic nature.

(d) The Importance of Anxiety

Although anxiety and the coupling of anxiety with conflicts are pathological factors whose importance is inescapable, Adler none the less paid but scant attention to them. Anxiety, which several Neo-Freudians (e.g. Horney and Rado) regard as the chief factor underlying the formation of neuroses, was only af minor interest to Adler. He did ascribe a certain importance to it but only in as far as it could be said to constitute fear of inferiority. For him the fear of castration is no more than a symbolic expression of inferiority. Freud and his followers consider the

---

[1] In Adler's view aggression, sadism and masochism are merely by-products of the process whereby the individual comes to terms with his feelings of inferiority.

relationship between inferiority and anxiety from a diametrically opposed point of view.

(e) The Unconscious

Adler at all times assumes the existence of the unconscious, for otherwise it would not be possible for the individual to remain unaware of the motive—for Adler there is only the one motive—underlying his actions. But he describes the unconscious as a phenomenon of purely marginal interest in the sense of people 'knowing more than they think they know'. He considers the division between the conscious and unconscious minds to be largely artificial and a consequence of 'psycho-analytic fanaticism'. In contrast to the structure of the personality, its various instances and the sub-divisions of id, ego and super ego he advances his own conception of a simple, purposive personality. Due to the workings of the life style, however, a *selection* of infantile wishes and tendencies is made, from which it follows that certain other infantile wishes and tendencies are not recognized, namely, those whose recognition would give rise to feelings of guilt and therefore of inferiority. But this indirect confirmation of *repression* is not followed by its direct confirmation and Adler fails to give any further explanation of this process, which is the key to any understanding of psychic activity. Adler regards *resistance* as no more than a kind of natural defence against any interventions threatening the life of the individual, interventions which might well include the conceivably shattering insights gained in the course of therapeutic treatment. The protest against such insights is identical with the individual's striving for power, for superiority, and with the masculine protest. Although Adler was aware of resistance and repression, when he came to explain them he invariably did so in terms of his holistic outlook. This rather stereotype kind of explanation was extended to dreams and phantasies as well: for example, dreams in which the dreamer finds himself falling are interpreted in terms of a loss of rank suffered or desired by the dreamer, dreams in which the dreamer finds himself climbing on the other hand are frequently interpreted in terms of (professional) advancement. Adler considers that dreams are motivated by wish-fulfilment only to a limited extent and that their chief purpose is to provide a commentary on the real-life situation of the dreamer.

(f) The Neurotic Symptom

Adler sees the neurotic symptom primarily in terms of an attempt to attract the attention of other persons (Freud's so-called secondary illness gain). A dynamics of symptoms, the possible over-determination of symptoms, the differentiation between individual forms or complexes of symptoms are only of incidental interest to Adler. In this respect medicine was obliged to yield to his social and pedagogic bent. The choice of symptoms is facilitated above all by organic inferiority, which had already been described by Freud in terms of the constitutional component of neurosis. After dealing with the problem of illness as a refuge Adler made no attempt to enlarge on the differences between neurosis and psychosis. As a result there is a positive dearth of clinical material in Adler's writings. In his analysis of a case of obsessional neurosis, for example, he is chiefly concerned with the patient's self-assertion *vis-à-vis* his environment, which takes the form of obsessions.

(g) Freud and Adler

Freud, who undertook a critical analysis of his ex-disciple's theories, stated some of his views on Individual Psychology in the following passage:[1]

'The third part of the Adlerian theory, the twisted interpretations and distortions of the disagreeable facts of analysis, are what definitely separate "Individual Psychology", as it is now to be called, from psychoanalysis. As we know, the principle of Adler's system is that the individual's aim of self-assertion, his "will to power", is what, in the form of a "masculine protest", plays a dominating part in the conduct of life, in character-formation and in neurosis. This "masculine protest", the Adlerian motive force, is nothing else, however, but repression detached from its psychological mechanism and, moreover, sexualized in addition —which ill accords with the vaunted ejection of sexuality from its place in mental life. The "masculine protest" undoubtedly exists, but if it is made into the (sole) motive force of mental life the observed facts are being treated like a springboard that is left behind after it has been used to jump off from. Let us consider one of the fundamental situations in which desire is felt in infancy: that of a child observing the sexual act between adults. Analysis shows, in the case of people with whose life story the physician will later be concerned, that at such moments two impulses take possession of the immature spectator. In boys, one is the impulse to put himself in the place of the active man, and the other, the opposing current, is the impulse to identify himself with the passive woman. Between them these two impulses exhaust the pleasurable possibilities of the situation. The first alone can come under the head of the masculine protest, if that concept is to retain any meaning at all The second, however the further course of which *Adler* disregards or which he knows nothing about, is the one that will become the more important in the subsequent neurosis. Adler has so merged himself in the jealous narrowness of the ego that he takes account only of those

[1] S. Freud, *Complete Works*, Standard Edition, Vol. XIV, p. 54.

instinctual impulses which are agreeable to the ego and are encouraged by it; the situation in neurosis, in which the impulses are opposed to the ego, is precisely the one that lies beyond this horizon.'

B

KAREN HORNEY

Karen Horney was a faithful disciple of Freud's for more than fifteen years but after emigrating to the United States (New York) she made a radical break with him. Within the framework of her extensive and successful clinical activities she founded, together with others who shared her views, the Society for the Advancement of Psychoanalysis, of which she remained the director throughout her lifetime. Her four books, *The Neurotic Personality of our Time*, *New Ways in Psychoanalysis*, *Our Inner Conflicts* and *Neurosis and Human Growth*[1] were written not so much for the specialist as for the educated layman, for doctors and educators interested in this field. In these works she states her views on the nature and origins of neuroses in considerable detail and with the aid of colourful clinical material.

(a) Healthy Behaviour and Sick Behaviour

Horney acts on the assumption that there is no such thing as the so-called psychology of the normal personality or a universally applicable psychology of human behaviour. In her view libido development as conceived by Freud, i.e. on a biological basis, is not an adequate criterion by which to distinguish the sick from the healthy or the neurotic from the normal. Freud's libido theory was only applicable, and that only to a limited extent, to the civilization of central Europe at the turn of the century. It was not applicable to a Latin civilization let alone to non-European cultures. It was therefore impermissible to look upon libido development as a norm and deviations from that development as pathogenic. For it is only the so-called 'cultural patterns', i.e. the patterns of behaviour created by a given civilization, which determine whether a person is sick or healthy. By the standards of European civilization a person who is able to talk with his deceased grandfather is sick, indeed psychotic. And yet there are Indian tribes who consider such behaviour to be healthy and normal. In view of the investigations carried out above all by ethnologists such as *Kardiner, Linton, Mead*[2] *inter alia*, who demonstrated the extraordinary variability and relativity of human behaviour within different cultures, Horney concludes that it is not

[1] London, 1937: New York, 1940, 1945, 1950.
[2] See below, p. 311 ff.

possible to distinguish between sickness and health on the basis of biological schemata (libido theory), but that any such distinction can only be made by reference to the principles laid down by a given culture as a guide to normal behaviour within that culture. What then constitutes health and illness in Western civilization (America and Europe)? K. Horney first attempts to differentiate between health and illness in descriptive, clinical terms. She establishes a provisional common denominator and describes neurotic behaviour as behaviour which is characterized by 'a certain rigidity in reaction and a discrepancy between potentialities and accomplishments'.[1] In contrast to the healthy person a neurotic would usually react to particular situations with preconceived opinions and a predetermined attitude, since he lacks flexibility and thus the possibility of adapting to different situations in different ways. His attitude is uncreative, 'unproductive'—he keeps getting in his own way. But Horney refrains from a more precise analysis of this concept of the 'uncreative' attitude.

(b) Neurosis as Defence against Anxiety

Since clinical viewpoints based on the observation of symptoms (behaviour) were in themselves inadequate as a means of distinguishing between healthy and neurotic behaviour, the problem of defence against anxiety very soon became the focal point of Horney's observations. Whereas for Adler the individual's striving for power is the main driving force underlying human actions, for Horney it is defence against anxiety or the overcoming of anxiety. Anxiety lies at the heart of every neurosis and is largely responsible for determining neurotic behaviour and for the fact that in the neurotic personality *neurotic* conflicts are in conflict with one another. Thus for Horney all neuroses are character neuroses and are typified by behaviour disturbances to which the defence against anxiety gives rise. This conception dispenses with any enquiry into individual neurotic *symptoms*, irrespective of whether the case in question is one of hysteria, obsessional neurosis or phobia, for Horney is interested neither in individual symptoms nor in the genetic source of behaviour disturbances (= deformations of character). And so, whilst symptoms are to be regarded as no more than the formal expression of deformations of character, genetic considerations are displaced by enquiries into behaviour disturbances, whose source lies in environmental situations. *How* a character neurosis comes about (i.e. its genetic origin) is only of relative importance, whereas absolute importance attaches to the *situations* in which the character disturbance is made manifest. On the other hand these situations are closely connected with the patterns of behaviour favoured by a given culture, which

[1] Horney, *The Neurotic Personality of our Time*, London, 1937.

would explain the submissive behaviour of innumerable people in professional life towards aggressive and domineering personality types. In Horney's view it is wrong to trace such behaviour back to the father who ruled over his family and the patient's childhood with a rod of iron, or, in other words, to the Oedipus complex. In the case of many of those patients who were always submissive in their dealings with their superiors no authoritative father and no unresolved Oedipus complex could be discovered. Behaviour such as this could not be explained in terms of biological processes—*viz.* Freud's libido theory—but only in terms of real-life processes, i.e. 'submissiveness' in terms of defence against anxiety. The key to an understanding of the patient's neurosis could only be provided by an *accurate analysis of the situations* in which the patient behaved submissively and not by a genetic analysis of his behaviour reaching back into infancy.

(c) Anxiety and Aggression

Horney—like Freud—differentiates between anxiety and fear. Whereas fear is related to objective situations anxiety is largely concerned with an internal and subjective source of danger, of which the patient is unaware. For Horney this internal source of danger includes the repressed hostility which gives rise to the patient's anxiety. 'Hostile impulses of various kinds form the main source from which neurotic anxiety springs.'[1] Consequently the submissive behaviour described above is in fact an expression of the patient's anxiety and his anxiety is above all else a reaction to the repressed aggression of which he is unaware but which he unconsciously directs towards his superior. And so the reason why the key to an understanding of the patient's neurosis is to be found in his *situation* is that the patient's repressed aggressions, his reaction (in the form of anxiety) to those aggressions and finally his submissive behaviour are all contained in his situation.

(d) Forms of Defence against Anxiety

Horney considers (unconscious) anxiety to be the driving force behind neurosis and neurotic behaviour. She puts forward four forms of defence against anxiety: (1) the rationalization of anxiety, (2) the denial of anxiety, (3) the dulling of anxiety and (4) the avoidance of all situations which might give rise to anxiety. An example of rationalization is provided by the over-anxious mother who 'rationalizes' her own anxiety by transferring it to her children. For all practical purposes the denial of anxiety is equivalent to repression, whilst the dulling of anxiety is the most common cause of alcoholism and of other forms of addiction. The avoidance of situations which might give rise to anxiety is such a

[1] Horney, *The Neurotic Personality of our Time*, p. 63.

common occurrence in life that there is no need to quote examples. Apart from these four forms of defence against anxiety Horney speaks of specific neurotic 'trends', traits or characteristics which may also be interpreted as a reaction to and a defence against anxiety. These include 'neurotic striving for love' (affection), and in this connection Horney describes patients whose striving for unconditional recognition assumes the proportions of a character change. Sexuality, to which Horney, like Adler, attributes only a partial influence within the total sphere of possible neurotic change, is also used by such patients for the sole purpose of obtaining love and recognition. These people are ungifted when it comes to chosing friends, placing quantity above quality and yet remaining affectively dependent on a few individuals. They try to please everybody, agree with their acquaintances' every word, not daring to contradict for fear of losing the favour of their social group. As a further instance of neurotic defence against anxiety Horney describes people whose behaviour is determined by their striving for power and who include in their number most of the so-called 'manager' class and others in positions of authority. But she tries in vain to establish a clear-cut distinction between a neurotic and a healthy desire for power, for, as she herself concedes, not all persons engaged in the intellectual and economic life of the community are neurotics. It may very well be that a man who possesses power will also possess special qualities, a special aptitude for the exercise of power. Perhaps the man with a neurotic desire for power can be distinguished from his normal counterpart by the particular style which he affects: he is more pompous, he looks on his subordinates as mere lackeys and robots, as 'flunkeys', and he often betrays his own sense of inner insecurity, etc., etc. The neurotic manager sees a potential rival in everyone and fights against everyone, for, since he is quite incapable of recognizing merit in anyone else, he must needs stand alone and unrivalled. Horney contrasts such people with others in positions of power who exercise their power without indulging in the same ostentatious display of neurotic weakness and who might therefore be considered to possess a healthy desire for power.

In her later works (*Neurosis and Human Growth*)[1] she reduces the four types of neurotic defence against anxiety to three: the compliant type, the aggressive type and the detached type, i.e. the type that tends to withdraw from contact with people, to avoid people.

(e) Causes of Anxiety
An enquiry into the cause of anxiety leads to an enquiry into the cause of neurosis itself. Horney does not agree with Freud that neurosis

[1] New York, 1950; London 1951.

derives from specific disturbances in libido development brought about as a result of the conflict between the drives and the environment. She considers that neurosis derives exclusively from a lack of warmth, security and love in the patient's childhood. If a child is deprived of acceptance, warmth and love it develops feelings of hostility which then effect a neurotic character change, and this in its turn produces anxiety and the various forms of defence against anxiety. If a child is exposed to such an unfavourable environment it will develop[1] 'an insidiously increasing, all-pervading feeling of being lonely and helpless in a hostile world. The acute individual reactions to individual provocations crystallize into a character attitude. This attitude as such does not constitute a neurosis but it is the nutritive soil out of which a definite neurosis may develop at any time. Because of the fundamental role this attitude plays in neuroses I have given it a special designation: the basic anxiety; it is inseparably interwoven with a basic hostility.'

Basic anxiety and basic hostility give rise to basic conflict, which consists of the incompatible tendencies to which the child is prone, namely, 'to go towards people', 'to withdraw from people' and 'to oppose people'. The outcome of these conflicting tendencies are the neurotic basic attitudes of submissiveness ('towards people'), withdrawal and aggressiveness. But to assume that children or adults adopt only one of these attitudes would be to think too formalistically. Especially in the case of children all three tendencies often obtain simultaneously and often in conflict with one another, whilst neurotic adults also fluctuate on occasions between these different attitudes, until eventually one or another of them finally succeeds in asserting and maintaining its supremacy.

(f) The Oedipus Complex and Narcissism

Since Horney considers that anxiety and thus neurosis is determined by the general environmental conditions obtaining in childhood it is not surprising that she attaches only minor importance to the Oedipus complex. In her opinion the Oedipus complex arises only if the parents spoil or fondle their child to such an extent as to arouse in the child sexual impulses with which it is unable to cope, or if one parent rejects the child and thus drives it to seek warmth and love from the other parent alone (cf. Adler). But even in this latter case what the child seeks from the parent of its preference is not so much sexual gratification as warmth and protection.

In contrast to Freud Horney does not consider that narcissism constitutes a deformation of libido development but simply a sort of 'ego-inflation'. This can be said to obtain when an individual admires

[1] Horney, *The Neurotic Personality of our Time*, p. 89.

qualities and abilities in himself, the existence of which cannot be veri-fied by objective means.

(g) 'Self-realization' and the 'Idealized Image'. Basic Conflict (Final version)

Horney devotes her last work, *Neurosis and Human Growth*, to the prob-lem of self-realization. She assumes that rooted in every person there is an original and irreducible striving towards self-realization, i.e. the realization of latent possibilities and potentials. This striving towards self-realization appears to her to be the source of all human development and she speaks of an 'autonomous striving towards self-realization'.[1] Neurosis gets in between the individual and his natural bent towards self-realization. This happens because the neurotic's 'idealized image', like some Frankenstein monster,[2] devours his natural energies and potentials. This ideal image of himself, an image of almost God-like perfection, which the neurotic develops is of course a mere phantasy, a perfectionist illusion, which, however, causes him to hate himself, i.e. his real self. Horney defines the basic conflict of neurosis as a conflict between the ideal image (the 'system of neurotic pride') and the real self, whose realization is hindered by the idealized image. The idealized image, i.e. the neurotic's phantasy image of himself, and the 'system of neurotic price' are one and the same. This system is maintained by the individual's neurotic tendencies: his 'search for glory' and his 'neurotic claims', i.e. the desire for preferential treatment, the desire to be singled out by destiny. Futher attributes of this system are arro-gance and pride and the tyranny of 'thou shalt', which Horney considers to be the epitome of all moral, conventional and social demands and expectations. These tendencies all support the idealized image, and the neurotic strives to realize this idealized image either by his boundless ambition, by the demands—often gigantic demands—which he makes or by his scrupulous observance of rules and regulations. Caught up in a maze of neurotic mal-development he comes to hate and despise himself, since, due to the development of his idealized image, he is naturally made aware of the discrepancy between that idealized image and his actual existence. Horney calls this discrepancy 'self-estrange-ment', by which she means that the true self is completely hidden behind the neurotic conflict between the ideal image and the forces which realize the true self. The neurotic solutions of this conflict, Horney suggests, are analogous to those which she describes in her earlier works: the 'expansive solution' (gaining power over other people), the 'self-effacing solution' (e.g. charitable activity as an appeal for love) or resig-nation (apparent freedom from neurotic conflicts as expressed, for

[1] K. Horney, *Neurosis and Human Growth*.   [2] K. Horney, *ibid.*

example, in the attitude of *laisser faire—laisser aller* of the man about town, which of course is simply resignation).

How does Horney differentiate between, for example, the 'tyranny of thou shalt' and Freud's super ego? She states that whereas for Freud the super ego normally represents conscience and morality and becomes sadistic only in neurosis, for her the precepts of 'thou shalt' and 'thou must' together with taboos and laws are all part of a neurotic force which merely imitates genuine morality and genuine (irreducible) conscience. Whereas for Freud the super ego is the derivative partly of drive tendencies and partly of moral tendencies (Oedipus complex), her own concept expresses the neurotic's unconscious striving to transform himself into something other than he is (ideal image), which is also the reason why he hates himself when this transformation goes wrong.

(h) Psychology of Women

In her criticism of *Helene Deutsch*,[1] who, in her *Psychology of Women*, attributes an even more radical anatomically based penis envy to women than Freud himself, Horney—like Adler—comes to the conclusion that there is no fundamental psychological difference between men and women. She argues that such differences as do exist are cultural and thus *relative* and that only a patriarchal, male-oriented society would attribute to the penis that exaggerated degree of importance which produces the various neurotic forms of penis envy. Penis envy is not biologically determined but culturally determined. In a culture which has come to place a high value on masculine attributes such as independence, professional success, courage, strength, etc., it is only to be expected that the penis, as a special symbol of such masculine attributes, should be treated with a like reverence (phallus cult of antiquity). Often what women envy is not so much the penis as the masculine attributes and the opportunities which the culture in which they live offers to men but not to women.

(i) The Unconscious

In her criticism of Freud (*New Ways in Psychoanalysis*) Horney denies the existence of an unconscious which is beyond time and which, as a reservoir, so to speak, of infantile wishes, conserves those infantile

---

[1] In H. Deutsch's view the psychology of women is primarily determined by their various attempts to overcome their anatomical deficiency, i.e. their lack of a penis (compensations). Underlying these substitute solutions, however, is their original *masochistic* need, namely, to be raped by a man. Until such time as a woman has had the sexual experience of being raped, she will remain frigid.

wishes throughout the individual's lifetime. Consequently the concepts of fixation, of regression and of the obsessional recollection of repressed material are of no interest to Horney. Violence rather than sustained argument is the keynote of the polemic which she conducted against Freud and in which she studiously disregarded the great wealth of empirical material which Freud after all was able to submit in support of his theories. She rejects Freud's views in general as being purely hypothetical and considers that the only valid factors are environmental influences and the extremes of helplessness and hostility between which the child fluctuates together with the consequences to which these give rise (see above). She does not entirely dispense with the concept of the unconscious, however, for the environmental influences mentioned above give rise to *unconscious* patterns of behaviour and also to unconscious *affects*, *ideas* and *wishes* which have their due effect on the neurotic's life. Neurotic character traits constitute the sum-total of the patient's childhood experiences. The details of these experiences have receded into the patient's unconscious. They may become conscious in the course of the therapy, but it is by no means essential that they should do so. Just as Adler's 'life style' embraces a large number of unconscious life experiences, so too do Horney's 'pattern' and 'neurotic trend'. Horney's definition of repression and its relationship to anxiety, on the other hand, is analogous to Freud's late definition, in which Freud stated that anxiety was the chief cause of repression. The question concerning the *specificity* of certain neuroses was of no more interest to Horney than it was to Adler. She quotes the case of a schoolmistress, who, after being censured by a superior, fell into a depression which, in Horney's submission, was a reaction to the *anxiety* which the schoolmistress felt on account of her unconscious aggression towards her superior. The fact that she reacted by falling into a *depression* rather than by developing bouts of neurotic vomiting or some other such symptom is only of minor interest to Horney. In her attitude to dreams and dream symbolism Horney has no new viewpoints to offer, nor does she attribute particular importance to these phenomena.

C

ERICH FROMM

Erich Fromm, who came to analysis from sociology, set out in his two principal works, *Escape from Freedom*[1] and *Man for Himself*,[2] the main

[1] *Escape from Freedom*, New York, 1941.
[2] *Man for Himself*, New York and London 1947 and 1949.

points of a philosophically and anthropologically oriented system of psychoanalysis, whose chief purpose was to *interpret* human development. His influence on the various schools of psychological thought has been considerable.

(a) The Theory of Drives

There is reason to suppose that *Karen Horney's* conceptions were influenced not only by Adler but also by Fromm. Fromm's criticism of the *Freudian* theory of drives is more soundly based than Horney's. Within the various psychoanalytic movements he is almost the only thinker to have raised the critical question as to the validity of Freud's definitions of the drive. By contrast Horney contents herself for the most part with opposing her own thesis of the social and cultural determination of drives to Freud's biological thesis and does not proceed to a more trenchant criticism of the Freudian conception. Fromm's theory of drives takes as its starting-point the difference between animal instincts and human drives. Animal instincts are organically determined forms of behaviour which pursue a stereotype course and which are far less supple and flexible than human drives. The susceptibility of the human drives to modification and control was bought at the price of man's comparative biological and anatomical immaturity (by comparison with mammals). But man's lack of set patterns of instinctual behaviour is the prerequisite for his powers of reason and understanding. Caught up in the Darwinian concepts of his epoch Freud failed to see the decisive difference—a difference in principle—between animal behaviour, in which the animal is obliged to follow its instincts, and human behaviour, in which man is relatively free to choose whether to follow his drives or not. Although it is true that sexuality, hunger and thirst are drives which man and beast alike must satisfy, the real crux of the matter lies in the fact that from the very beginning man—unlike animals—has left his own cultural and specifically human mark on the processes involved in the satisfaction of such drives, a mark which cannot be accounted for simply in terms of the antithesis between drives and society. This conception of Fromm's involves (1) a difference of man's own making between the processes of the drive life of human beings and the instinctual life of animals and (2) the socially determined form of human drives, which also existed from the very beginning—i.e. from the first appearance of the human type in the process of evolution— and which is part of the essential nature of *homo sapiens*. Any attempt to interpret man on the sole basis of sexual suppression must in Fromm's view be over-simplified and inadequate. The diverse, multifarious and colourful forms of human society and culture should only be made the object of scientific investigation and research for purposes of enquiring into the individual's specific relationship to his environment, to his society and to himself.

(b) Historical and Individual Development

In contrast to Freud, Fromm considers that there is a definite purpose in the historical and individual development of man, namely, individuation (cf. also *Jung* and *Rank*!). He reveals his affinity with *Hegel* when he defines individuation as a process of growing maturation on the part of the individual, i.e. a process of self-realization, as a result of which the individual is obliged to renounce his atavistic allegiance to nature. Primitive man and infant children, in whom self-awareness and reason are virtually non-existent, live their lives in the *natural* conditions of primitive societies on the one hand and in the security and seclusion of maternal care on the other. Even to-day every individual person is obliged to undergo in a concentrated form the same evolutionary process whereby the individual gradually separated out over a period of many centuries from the mythical conditions of prehistoric times, i.e. from the psychic conditions which Levy Brühl has called 'participation mystique'. Severance of the old bonds, which join the individual to myth, clan or family is accompanied by the *risks of freedom*. Fromm defines freedom as a creative task, namely, that of establishing ordered systems commensurate with a mature and conscious outlook. The ability to endure freedom involves amongst other things exchanging the security of the old bonds for insecurity, of exchanging certainty for doubt, communal living for isolation. Fromm describes the process of individuation chiefly in terms of the historical development of the Western World since the Reformation and the concomitant separation of the individual from institutional (religious) bonds. The expansion of the bourgeoisie, the breaking up of feudal systems based on kinship, the growth of individual self-awareness in the period of the Enlightenment are in his view symptoms of a logical development which is a prerequisite for the self-realization of man. But this development merely offers the necessary conditions for the establishment of freedom, which Fromm defines in its historical aspect as 'freedom from' (coercive bonds) and in terms of the future as 'freedom to' (act spontaneously). Only a very few are capable of making use of these conditions and the great majority of people seek refuge in new bonds, since they are quite incapable of enduring 'freedom from'. In the twentieth century these new bonds have been embodied above all in the totalitarian and authoritarian regimes which pledge themselves to provide substitutive pseudo-bonds in place of the old bonds. And the majority of individuals, terrified of freedom, swallow the bait. By means of these pseudo-bonds man is then shamelessly exploited in the interests of power politics and kindred undertakings.

(c) The Individual and Neurosis

It follows from the previous section that the development of the individual is determined by three factors:

1. man's biological weakness and instinctual deficiency compared with animals,
2. the possibility of human freedom which is thereby given,
3. the history of the western world and of the individual considered as an attempt to sever the bonds which, in the form of specifically human institutions and attributes, have superseded the compulsive instinctual behaviour of animals (e.g. myth, clan, family, traditions; but also non-secular authoritarian bonds such as those imposed by the church.) Neurosis only occurs when the 'freedom from' and the 'freedom to' which have been granted to the individual prove more than he can endure and he either (a) regresses into old bonds or pseudo-bonds or (b) misuses his freedom in a neurotic manner by developing particular distorted attitudes. Apart from this source of neurosis, to which man is exposed by virtue of his historical development and the special position which he occupies in the animal world, there are also existential and historical dichotomies which may give rise to pathogenic developments. One of the 'existential dichotomies' is caused by the duality of human existence, for, although as a part of nature man is bound to perish, yet he transcends nature, although he is able to foresee his death, he will still think himself immortal, although he is homeless, still he is chained to the home. These dichotomies have come into being as a result of man's special position in nature. His 'break with the universe', which disrupted his 'harmony with nature', his biological weakness in comparison to animals, were the basis for—to quote but one example—the existential dichotomy of his knowledge of death. For it was his 'break with nature' which led him to develop his rational powers and all that these involved namely, his recognition of himself as a being separate from nature, capable of imagining the future, of recalling the past and of designating objects and events by means of symbols.

The 'historical dichotomies' include all those processes which bind man to a particular culture or ideology but which also involve him in contradictions within his particular culture. Thus in our present civilization, although there is an abundance of technical and material opportunities, man is unable to make adequate use of them. Both the 'existential' and 'historical' dichotomies become cardinal points of neurosis when man is unable to accept the actual facts which they involve and instead devises ways—neurotic ways—of deluding himself as to their true nature.

(d) Flight Mechanisms

Fromm describes over and above the process of regression to atavistic or pseudo-bonds four mechanisms, by means of which man is able to withdraw from freedom. These mechanisms of escape are (1) (moral) masochism, (2) sadism, (3) destructiveness and (4) automaton conformity. In the first category Fromm places those neurotics whose loyal or affectionate behaviour conceals a powerful desire to submit and to subjugate themselves to external authority. *Horney* would have described such types as 'submissive'. The sadistic types of Fromm's second category and the destructive types of his third category strive to make others dependent on themselves, to inhibit and block the productive capacity of others and to exploit other people by abusing their own authority (*Horney's* manager). The fourth category, the conformists, are people with no opinion of their own and with no real identity, who are carried aimlessly along on the tide of public opinion like so much 'driftwood', a ready prey for any dictator. These are persons whose behaviour conforms to that of 'other people'—'other people' do this, 'other people' do that—and whose judgement is largely determined by the judgements of 'other people'.

(e) Ways of Accepting Freedom

But how can a man avoid the neurotic solution, gain strength and prove himself worthy of the 'risk of freedom'? 'Assimilation' and 'Socialization' are in Fromm's opinion the two fundamental tendencies which determine in a positive sense man's relationship to his environment, to himself and to his freedom (see above). Assimilation means taking in the environment in the fullest sense of the word. It applies not only to the satisfaction of the drives but also to learning and to every form of psychic participation. 'Socialization' (Adler's social feeling, cf. p. 260 ff.) means the primary directedness of man towards a 'Thou', towards social contact. This applies in every sphere—in play, in love, in rivalry, in the dissemination of knowledge and experience and in the acquisition of property and knowledge. In the four neurotic mal-developments described above (masochism, sadism, destructiveness and automaton conformity) the process of socialization was disturbed. Disturbances in the process of assimilation occur in five further types, i.e. in five further distorted attitudes: (1) the (exclusively) receptive character, (2) the character who exploits, (3) the character who saves (acquires), (4) the character who is exclusively concerned with economic or material ends and (5) the creative character. Only the creative character, who is the counterpart of the loving character of the social types, can do justice to the demands of freedom. But in order to understand this creative character we shall first have to investigate the distorted images of false

275

assimilation. The characteristic of the first type, the type who is exclusively receptive, lies in the fact that he assumes that every single thing he does should be determined by some external authority, i.e. his whole life is given over to consumption. This type passively permits some outside source to determine his needs and desires, his interests, his knowledge and his pleasures and as a result he is obliged to attach himself to others and stands in constant need of an external authority that will take his decisions for him. People with this sort of character are normally frank, friendly and optimistic. But the moment their external, environmentally determined sources of self-esteem dry up they react with a display of panic. By contrast the second type, the exploiter, takes whatever he can, is aggressive and self-assured in his actions, but is quite as uncreative and quite as bereft of independent thoughts and ideas as the receptive, passive type.

The third group, the acquisitive type, includes both obsessional neurotics and those people whose inner security is based on possessions of every kind, be they material or intellectual. For such people love is largely a matter of taking possession of another person, whilst they feel the external world to be a predominantly hostile and threatening place. This type will shut himself off from his fellow men and has no faith in the productive forces of life.

The fourth character type, whose attentions are directed exclusively towards economic aims, is the counterpart to the automaton conformist (Type 1). Whilst the latter unreservedly submits to the social conventions, the former sees life simply as a process of buying and selling. Both spiritual and material goods are valued for their utility. Success is the sole criterion. And success is measured by materialistic standards.

Fromm contrasts these distorted images of human development with the productive character (No. 5). In this character Fromm draws the ideal image of the un-neurotic type, the man who is able to love others because he genuinely loves himself—in accordance with the words of Jesus Christ, 'Thou shalt love thy neighbour as thyself'. Although present-day Western and European civilization preaches the doctrine of brotherly love in the traditional sense, its preaching is contradicted by its practice, in which egoism is the only force that is taken seriously, especially where economic matters are concerned. The postulate of brotherly love and the grossly dominant position accorded to egoism are both rooted in the failure to appreciate the fact that genuine love for oneself based on the inner acceptance and tolerance of one's own person is the prerequisite for overcoming one's own egoism and for extending understanding and recognition to others. Fromm describes 'productive characters' as persons who, in the process of assimilation, were able to avoid the temptations of exclusive receptivity and exclusive exploitation and who, in the process of socialization, were equally well able to avoid the temptation of masochism or sadistic distortions. Productivity need not necessarily be of an artistic nature and no spiritual or material products (works of art) need be involved. A man is productive when he participates with genuine care in the life of another, when he extends his interests from the narrow confines of his own person and begins to recognize his partner; for every act of recognition is itself an act of loving participation. Fromm supports his thesis by reference to the ethical postulates of the great philosophers from Plato to Spinoza and Kant. In his view conscience is the keynote of the creative type and he considers that Freud's super-ego affords only an inner representation of an authoritatian conscience which hides the true conscience from sight.

(f) Two Kinds of Authority

The question as to what constitutes conscience is indissolubly linked with the further question as to the nature of authority. If the pseudo-conscience is the product of the Oedipus complex, then the genuine conscience is largely identical with Horney's concept of the 'self'. The empirical basis of Fromm's genuine conscience is not altogether convincing, however, and he is constantly obliged to have recourse to the ethics of Idealism. But his criticism of authoritarianism, which he considers need not necessarily be organized in terms of a hierarchy, as was the case in Hitler's Third Reich, but might equally well appear within the framework of an American-type economy, ultimately leads him to question Freud's interpretation of the Oedipus complex. Taking Sophocles' dramas into account (Antigone and Oedipus at Colonnos), Fromm comes to the conclusion that it is wrong to interpret the Oedipus myth in terms of sexual rivalry between the father and the son. He considers that, on the contrary, the myth represents the son's revolt against the patriarchal and authoritarian order (cf. Rank!). And the reason why Jocaste is punished in the tragedy is that she agreed to the son's murder—to his being driven out—whereby she submitted to the patriarchal order. For Fromm the Oedipus complex simply expresses the son's aggression towards his father as the representative of an authoritarian and patriarchal type of life. In the formation of the genuine conscience, which in Fromm's view is only slightly influenced by the Oedipus complex, the decision as to whether the individual will submit to the authoritarian and patriarchal order or win through to the development of a genuine conscience is normally taken in early childhood. However, this process can also take place in later years, either in adolescence or in manhood.

(g) The Unconscious and Sexuality

Although Fromm's references to the unconscious are limited to state-ments concerning the unconscious distorted attitudes which occur, for example, in socialization and assimilation, he none the less considers the unconscious to be of crucial importance. The purpose of therapy is to illumine these unconscious distorted attitudes by means of analysis and interpretation. Such attitudes are a consequence of repression, a concept to which the Neo-Freudians are obliged to have constant recourse. Fromm attributes only minor importance to sexuality. Since, unlike Freud, he does not interpret human nature in terms of hedonism, he considers sexuality to be important only if, as in the case of the 'produc-tive' character (see above), it can be said to derive from a profusion of psychic energy which is thus able to contribute to the realization of 'happiness'. And so, whereas for Freud sexual intercourse serves to release tension, for Fromm it is the physical expression of a loving attitude of give and take.

(h) Basic Conflict

For Fromm neurosis is the sign of a breakdown in the process of indivi-duation (cf. also Jung). In the light of this philosophical definition basic conflicts and individual empirical data become almost irrelevant. If *Adler's* conception of basic human conflict may be said to consist of man's attempt to reconcile his striving for superiority with the obstacles with which society opposes the realization of his striving and if *Horney's* conception may be related to man's defence against anxiety and his overcoming of anxiety, then in Fromm's case we may speak of a basic conflict between the waking self and the unbearable situation of the 'bound self'. The individual is drawn into neurosis by his fear of freedom and by the risk of freedom. It should be added, however, that this basic conflict is historically determined, for the process of self-realization is itself historically determined. The more warmth, love and security a child receives, the more harmonious and stable its environment in early childhood, the greater are its chances of being able to endure the risk of freedom 'from' and freedom 'to'.

(i) The Development of Erich Fromm's Views Between 1955 and 1965

In his book, *The Sane Society*,[1] Fromm deals with the concrete problems with which the individual has been confronted as a result of the indus-trialization of modern life. His anthropological view of man as an 'unintegrated animal' that is subject to nature but at the same time superior to nature now acquires a pessisimtic undertone. Fromm con-trasts man's birth, which he calls a 'negative event', with the instinctual

[1] *The Sane Society*, New York, 1955.

functioning of animals. In support of his view of man as 'an animal that is no longer integrated with nature' and is in dire need of a new order Fromm adduces the fearfully high rates of suicide and alcoholism in the ultra-civilized western world. But how does Fromm envisage this new order? He develops his view in terms of polarities: for example, he contrasts creative and destructive forces, brotherliness and 'psychic incest', individuality and herd identity, reason and the irrational. Man's great passions, his love, his quest for truth, his vanity or his striving for power, are not rooted in his libido but in his particular anthropological situation. Reason and love alone can save him. Man's integration is not to be conceived in terms of adaptation to the social requirements of a given milieu but rather in terms of his overcoming the incestuous or similar bonds by which he is held captive (cf. above *Fear of Freedom*).

Fromm considers that these ethical ideals can be realized by re-aligning our present political and industrial aims towards the establishment of a higher spiritual order. Politically this would take the form of a return to smaller regional and municipal groups as the cadre of healthy political life, economically it would mean that industry would be run by the workers themselves, whilst culturally it would call for an education programme designed to prepare young people for productive work and to provide adults with further education in training centres. Fromm sees socialism as a 'theoretical vision', which can only be realized step by step by means of a democratic socialism that would overcome and replace the 'market orientation' of capitalist society by the spiritual attitude described above. Modern man no longer has a choice between capitalism and communism. All that remains to him, if he fails to establish a democracy of individuals, is the choice between an automaton existence under capitalism and an automaton existence under communism.

In his book *The Art of Loving*, which was published in 1956, Fromm gives an analysis of love on the basis of his 'world view'. He defines mature love, in contrast to a purely physical procreative urge and to the many sadistic or masochistic by-products of love, as follows:

'In contrast to symbiotic union, mature *love* is *union under the conditions of preserving one's integrity*, one's individuality. *Love is an active power in man*; a power which breaks through the walls which separate man from his fellow men, which unites him with others; love makes him overcome the sense of isolation and separateness, yet it permits him to be himself, to retain his integrity. In love the paradox occurs that two beings become one and yet remain two.'[1]

And again:

[1] *The Art of Loving*, Harper, New York 1957; London, Allen & Unwin; p. 21.

'Love is an activity, not a passive affect. In the most general way, the active character of love can be described by stating that love is primarily *giving*, not receiving.'[1]

In elaborating his thesis that love is not a kind of bond but a kind of *attitude*, Fromm describes the following categories of loving: love of one's neighbour, mother love, erotic love, self-love and love of God. But for all his readiness to look upon love of God as the *non plus ultra* of loving Fromm none the less deviates from Thomist Christian philosophy in certain respects. For example, he attaches particular importance to mother love as the only adequate example of the powers of human love and he also stresses the importance of self-love (in the sense of self acceptance), which the fathers of the church had assessed in purely negative terms as the root of all evil. In fact Fromm considers that self-love is the basic factor determining the individual's capacity for love of any kind; those who are unable to accept themselves cannot accept others.

Fromm describes the dangers of 'love', i.e. pseudo loves, in terms of, for example, the psychic deformity and lack of independence induced above all in men by obsessive mother love. But pseudo-loves also include the idolatrous infatuations, which alienate the personality from the forces at its disposal and project them on to the partner, and sentimental love, which is primarily a phantasy product.

Under the heading, 'The Practice of Love', Fromm advises his readers as to how to perfect themselves in this art. He recommends, *inter alia*, that they acquire the ability to practise patience and forbearance, the ability to be a good listener and the ability to concentrate.

It has been said of Freudian psychoanalysis—and not without some justification—that, when it has laid bare the patient's problems, it then fails to provide the patient with norms for his future guidance. It is above all in respect of this deficiency that Fromm's book provides a counter-balance. The virtues, whose practice Fromm recommends to his readers in order that they may acquire a 'mature personality', are the virtues which have traditionally been encouraged above all in the religious systems of Christianity and Buddhism.

D

HARRY STACK SULLIVAN

Any attempt to present the views of H. S. Sullivan,[2] who enjoys a particularly high reputation in the United States, is beset by two distinct

---

[1] *The Art of Loving*, London, p. 22.
[2] H. S. Sullivan, *Conceptions of Modern Psychiatry*, Washington D.C., 1947.

difficulties of a practical nature: (1) Sullivan did not present his work in a final and systematic form; (2) he was largely independent of Freudian psychoanalysis and created his own terminology, which it is by no means easy to interpret.

Sullivan's work on the development of a psychiatry of 'inter-personal relations' may be regarded as an attempt to establish a genetic psychology on a Behaviourist basis. In Sullivan's view all psychic processes are tensions and energy transformations and as such are subject to empirical observation. For him energy is composed of physical forces, material entities, which are also perceived in a purely subjective form as psychic entities. Since 'confusion reigns supreme'[1] in psychiatry he endeavoured to restrict psychiatry to the description and genesis of interpersonal relationships and considered that the end purpose of psychiatric enquiries should be the development of a *social psychology*. The object of Behaviourism was to investigate tensions and energy transformations in terms of aims, tendencies and impulses without having recourse to the hypotheses which had turned Freudian psychoanalysis into a largely 'academic' structure, i.e. one which in the final analysis was unrelated to reality.

(a) *Aims and Tendencies of Human Behaviour*

For Sullivan the satisfaction of physical needs (drives) such as hunger, sleep and sexuality on the one hand and man's striving for security on the other are the chief aims of human nature, i.e. the tendencies which *primarily* determine human behaviour (Sullivan does not give a precise definition of the concept of 'tendencies' but it is presumably synonymous with strivings). In the course of childhood these tendencies are joined by the striving for power, which, however, is secondary, since it serves to promote the striving for security and to ensure satisfaction of the above-mentioned drives. Striving for security and the satisfaction of the drives are indissolubly linked with one another and are to be regarded as the *integrating forces*, which also determine the transformations which take place in the development of 'interpersonal relationships'. When the satisfaction of these primary needs has been achieved (e.g. appeasement of hunger) a maximum relaxation of the skeletal musculature may be observed. Sullivan devotes a great deal of attention to the relationships between conditions of tension and relaxation within the muscular system, for it is within these relationships that he traces the (psycho-) physical energy transformations.

(b) *Disturbances Affecting the Realization of Human Aims and Tendencies*

The chief factor opposing and hindering the striving for security and the satisfaction of the primary needs (hunger, sleep, sexuality) is anxiety,

[1] H. S. Sullivan, *Conceptions of Modern Psychiatry*, Washington D.C., 1947.

which is always accompanied by a high degree of tension of the skeletal musculature and which in its most intense form can assume panic proportions. The opposite condition to panic is euphoria, a condition of complete relaxation and ease which, however, is unlikely to be realized save in exceptional circumstances, e.g. in sleep. Anxiety, especially if it is accompanied by insecurity and difficulties relating to the satisfaction of drives, may endanger a person's development from early childhood onwards. The greatest danger is to the 'self', which Sullivan describes as consisting of 'reflective appraisals'. By this he means that the self consists of the recognition which the child receives from adults in the course of its development. Due to the workings of 'empathy', i.e. the child's direct perception, based on the transference of feelings, of environmental attitudes towards it, the infant receives vague but decisive impressions at a very early age. If, whilst suckling her child, a mother regards it critically or anxiously or if she inwardly rejects it, then her attitude will be *directly* transferred by empathy to the infant. Sullivan's view of the self—the mirror of the environment established by empathy —is far removed from the concept of the self as an individual personality. It corresponds more to Freud's early conceptions of the ego as a carrier of identifications. But Sullivan considers even this concept to be too hypothetical and academic and prefers the concept of empathy (which he took from *Bergson*).

The importance of anxiety is not restricted to the fact that it constitutes an antithesis to euphoria and inhibits the development of the self. Indeed, its chief importance lies in its relationship to the processes of 'selective inattention' and 'dissociation'. Although these concepts are linguistically distinct, in fact they are both synonymous with repression. But Sullivan is unable to give his approval to the concept of repression, for he considers that it too is overburdened with hypotheses, especially hypotheses of a 'topographical nature'. And so anxiety becomes an instrument of the self, by means of which the self is able to limit its boundaries and its attention—so as to maintain its integrity and inner security (cf. *Freud's* 'defence'). 'Selective inattention' and 'dissociation' are consequences of anxiety, whilst anxiety is the consequence of the need to guarantee security and ensure the satisfaction of drives to the greatest possible extent. Over and above this, however, 'selective in-attention' and 'dissociation'—and for that matter the whole composition of the self—are partially determined by parental praise and censure. If by being praised a child is encouraged to behave in a certain way, it will naturally tend to renounce behaviour of an opposite nature which earns it censure. In this way 'selective inattention' is established. 'Dissociation', however, refers to processes of which the personality or the child is no longer conscious—and whose existence the child might perhaps even deny to the accompaniment of a vehement display of affects. The *dissociated* ideas are removed from consciousness but in principle their development is analogous to that governing the ideas involved in 'selective inattention'. Sullivan concedes that the dissociated ideas may find expression in dreams, phantasies and unobserved actions. Moreover, they are even able to threaten the self with serious danger by producing anxiety—which might conceivably be so powerful that the person concerned would 'go to pieces'. 'Selective inattention' corresponds to Freud's pre-conscious, 'dissociation' to the unconscious.

(c) The Genesis of the Self

Apart from its capacity as a mirror of praise and censure the self also possesses an organization compounded of past, present and a possible future. It has a before and an after, a foreground and a background. The processes of selective inattention appertain to the foreground whilst the background constitutes the integration of those same processes. And so the self possess a structure, even if in the final analysis this structure is no more than a product of the environment, a mirror. The development of the self, which in its genetic capacity Sullivan calls a personality, comprises six stages. These stages are as follows:

1. From babe in arms until the child is able to speak;
2. from early childhood until the child is able to live with other children of the same age;
3. from late childhood until the child is able to participate inwardly in the life of others (Isophilia);
4. from youth until the child develops sexual feelings;
5. from early puberty until the child develops sexual patterns of behaviour;
6. from late puberty until the child achieves full maturity (adult).

Re Stage No. 1: The foundations of the moral concepts of good and evil are laid when the child is still a babe in arms by means of the child's vague perceptions of either the euphoria or the anxiety lavished on it by its mother (viz. empathy). The euphoric mother is the 'good' mother, the anxious mother is the 'bad' (evil) mother. The behaviour of children at this stage, who still inhabit the world which *Ferenczi* had described in such detail—the world of magic and 'participation mystique'—, Sullivan calls 'prototaxic'. The baby is quite unaware of temporal and causal relationships. It only learns to differentiate between 'before' and 'after' when it begins to talk. Sullivan calls this second part of the first stage 'parataxic'.

Re Stage No. 2: Early childhood, which comes to an end by the time the child has learned to talk, is of particular importance for the development of the self, because in this period praise and censure, recognition and punishment are unreservedly brought to bear on the child. The child develops its powers of *sublimation* (curiously enough Sullivan adopted this problematical Freudian concept). What Sullivan understands under sublimation is the realization of impulses—e.g. aggressions—within the framework of a socially acceptable pattern of behaviour without giving rise to anxiety. Impulses which cannot be sublimated in this way may be discharged in dreams or phantasies. If sublimation is entirely unsuccessful or succeeds only to a limited extent the following substitute mechanisms are put into operation. (*a*) The old pattern of behaviour is altered to bring it into line with the new objective, (*b*) completely new patterns of behaviour are introduced, (*c*) the old pattern of behaviour is resuscitated (regression). A child, whose need for tenderness is denied by its parents, will 'associate' tenderness with disapproval and thus with anxiety. If it adapts its behaviour to pattern (*a*) (see above), it will then try to pursue its need for tenderness by indirect methods. Alternatively, it may alter its behaviour in a pathological manner, because it feels itself surrounded by a hostile world by which it feels rejected. It could then react, for example, in a paranoid manner. And this would correspond to pattern (*b*). By following pattern (*c*) it would avoid the conflict by regressing to patterns of behaviour inappropriate to its age (e.g. smearing faeces, bed-wetting, etc.).

Re Stage No. 3: The characteristic attribute of late childhood is the need to come to terms with playmates—sometimes with brothers and sisters. Rivalry and striving for power accompanied by the development of new skills and abilities are the keynote of this period. But then there is the question of starting school with all its consequences. It is also at this age that children develop their particular form of society, which is based chiefly on the reputation of the individual or his clan. And sexuality casts its first shadow in the form of childish curiosity.

Re Stage No. 4: Youth, which extends approximately from eight to twelve years of age, is characterized by the development of the child's ability to love, which during this period takes the form of friendships entered into by pairs of children of the same sex. Over and above this the child gains its first impressions of 'humanity and human beings' and utilizes its learning, its acquisition of knowledge, for purposes of security and the satisfaction of drives.

Re Stages 5 and 6: In puberty the individual is confronted with the problem of sexuality and will regress into homosexuality if in late childhood he failed to come to terms with the opposite sex on the level appropriate to that stage. But if the individual passes through puberty successfully, then he will develop self-respect and respect for others.

Above all, however, he will develop the inner freedom which will enable him to adapt to the social order of his day.[1]

(d) 'Interpersonal relations' and Sexuality

Sullivan concentrates the whole force of his arguments on 'interpersonal relations'. What he means by this concept, to which other Neo-Freudians of similar views subscribe, is the effect exercised by the whole sphere of social and cultural activity on the individual. For Sullivan the individual *per se*—Freud's cell with stimulus protection—does not exist. He is a fiction, an abstraction, from which it follows that psychic activity must necessarily be investigated and described from the point of view of interpersonal communication. Such fundamental views, however, do not prevent Sullivan from ascribing only a minor role to sexuality in spite of the surely undeniable importance of sexuality for interpersonal relationships. The six stages of development which he described are in his view all equally important as far as sexuality is concerned. He considers it wrong to attribute priority to early childhood or to the period when the child is still being suckled, priority, that is, in the sense of definitively attributing sexuality to this particular stage (see below, p. 504 ff.). However, Sullivan's neglect of sexuality does not prevent him from occasionally referring to oral, anal and genital 'pleasure mechanisms'. But then his attempt to reorientate psychiatric knowledge was altogether unsystematic.

(e) Basic Conflict and Pathological Syndromes

For Sullivan, as also for Horney, it is the need for security and the need to avoid anxiety which give rise to basic conflict. In accordance with this conception he has sketched out ten personality syndromes based on the individual's inability to come to adequate terms with anxiety and the formation of substitute solutions as a means of controlling anxiety. Classified in terms of their particular characteristics these may be stated as follows:

1. The completely self-absorbed type, for whom wishful thinking and phantasies play an important part.

Sullivan describes the origins of this attitude: as the child learns to differentiate between the good or bad mother of its phantasies and its real mother, who is neither particularly good nor particularly bad, it will come to prefer the phantasy of the 'good mother'—who always fulfils its wishes. Since every child passes through these phases it is only when particularly unfavourable conditions obtain that a fixation to these phantasies takes place, which then stamps the child's later character (its 'career-line', cf. *Adler's* life style).

[1] H. S. Sullivan, *Conceptions of Modern Psychiatry*, Washington D.C., 1947.

2. The 'psychopathic personality', which Sullivan does not attempt to explain and which he labels as 'non-integrated'.
3. The 'negativist syndrome' which occurs with egocentric, negating types and which is due to a lack of praise and recognition during childhood.
4. The fourth syndrome is commensurate with the 'incorrigible' person who is hostile and unfriendly and considers himself beyond criticism and whose development Sullivan ascribes to the influence of parents who are never satisfied.
5. Obsessionally ambitious types.
6. A-social types who, although possessing their own fully developed scale of values, fail to see that they are also liable to be judged by others.

The eighth syndrome embraces the 'inadequate' characters, under which heading Sullivan understands all forms of masochistic dependence. Homosexuality (ninth syndrome) Sullivan does not consider to be an actual illness but rather a vice that is acquired through habit. The tenth syndrome is the 'eternal youth' who is always looking for his ideal and never finds it.

E

HARALD SCHULTZ-HENCKE

Harald Schultz-Hencke is one of the few Neo-Freudians to have succeeded in presenting his views in a systematic and comprehensive form. His principal work is *Der Gehemmte Mensch*, which first appeared in 1940[1] and reappeared in an enlarged edition in 1951 as a *Lehrbuch der analytischen Psychotherapie*.[2] H. Schultz-Hencke has also carried out detailed investigations into the psychotherapy of psychoses, psychosomatic medicine and the interpretation of dreams. Within the framework of this present book it will not be possible to make an individual assessment of these investigations, but it is none the less important that they be mentioned, since they substantiate Schultz-Hencke's claim to be considered as one of the leading protagonists of Neo-Freudianism.

(a) Basic Conflict and Types of Drive

In Schultz-Hencke's view the basic conflict of the human condition consists of the inhibition of expansive tendencies. Expansive tendencies (cf. Freud's 'id') 'consist 'principally of man's strivings'.[3] 'Strivings',

---

[1] Leipzig. [2] Stuttgart.
[3] H. Schultz-Hencke, *Der gehemmte Mensch* ('Inhibited Man').

we are told in Schultz-Hencke's *Lehrbuch der analytischen Psychotherapie*, are drives; and drives he subdivides as follows:

1. The intentional drive experience. This he considers to be one of the basic characteristics of animal cum human existence, for he equates it with the curiosity which may be observed both in animals and in babies. The process of emotionally 'turning towards' other things, which is the earliest expression of the child's participation in life, may be regarded as synonymous with curiosity.

2. The captative, oral drive experience. This experience represents the child's primitive desire ('I want it') at the oral stage, but it should be pointed out that Schultz-Hencke does *not* interpret the oral stage in terms of libido development, i.e. as a process that might conceivably be sexually determined. The infant gives expression to this desire by intentionally turning towards objects and putting them in its mouth in order to possess them. The concept of 'orality' is considerably enlarged —compared with Freud—for Schultz-Hencke correlates it in terms of psychosomatic organization with the digestive tract up to the point where it enters the intestine. Captative behaviour may also be observed in amoeba or in the active movement of the Fallopian tube towards the ejected ovum. The problems attendant on 'giving and taking' in social life are closely connected with primitive, oral-captative problems.

3. The retentive, anal drive experience. This corresponds in all essentials to the findings reached by *Abraham* and *Freud* (see p. 166 ff.) in their investigations into the connection between the phase of cleanliness training in childhood and the tendency observed in infants to retain their faeces. Schultz-Hencke also stresses the aggressive character which defecation can assume. Psychosomatic illnesses of the intestinal tracts on the one hand and faulty patterns of character such as greed on the other hand or even under certain circumstances impotence are usually connected with inhibitions of anal-retentive behaviour.

4. Aggressive drive experiences which strive for recognition. Schultz-Hencke traces aggression back to a motoric need for discharge such as may be observed in infants, a need which is intensified by resistances. When the child expresses its aggression it does not intend to be destructive, nor indeed is it destructive until such time as its aggression comes to grips with its environment. It is the environment which makes the child destructive and especially so if the child's need for motor discharge meets with resistance from its environment. The relationship between aggression and striving for recognition (cf. Adler's striving for power) is manifestly present if by virtue of its aggression the child triumphs over its environment and possibly receives recognition for having done so. In this way striving for recognition serves aggression.

5. The urethral drive experience. This also refers to an original drive experience which is first met with in childhood and which might for example find expression in a compulsive desire to urinate and the urge to yield to this desire. This drive becomes identified with the child's desire to lie in the damp warmth of the sheets after it has wet them: occasionally it also becomes identified with sexuality.

6. The loving sexual drive experience. In Schultz-Hencke's view love and sexuality (Freud's libido) are not the same thing. He argues that sexuality derives from man's need for tenderness, from Eros. He takes exception to Freud's view that tenderness is simply inhibited sexuality and instead he speaks of an original primary striving for tenderness. He comments on the desire for surrender and the desire for security and their multiple relationship to eros in this respect:

'For everyone, man or woman, feels an undeniable need to trust in his or her feelings and to surrender to the *Dasein* (human reality, being-there) and *Sosein* (being thus) of the other person or of other persons. This is a matter of the greatest importance for the psychology of neuroses (and also of the greatest practical importance). For if we analyse the phenomenon of self-surrender more closely we discover that the *desire for surrender* and the *desire for security* are intimately connected. We discover that wherever people seek security (which is always of a situational nature, a feeling of someting protective), the drive quality consists of the need to be allowed to surrender oneself *trustingly*, to be allowed to be as one is, as one originally wanted to be and then to be assured that one is positively accepted as such, that one is protected from dangers'.[1]

Both a strict upbringing and a pampered upbringing lead in their different ways to the inhibition of the various types of drive which subsequently re-emerge in the form of neurotic symptoms as *fragments of drives* (cf. Freud's description of the neurotic symptom as a compromise between the drive and the repressed material. Symptoms are also forms of drive satisfaction). But what are the consequences of 'inhibition'?

(b) The Consequences of Inhibition

In describing the consequences of inhibition Schultz-Hencke is unable to avoid equating[1] inhibition with repression, which prompts us to ask why he should choose to introduce new terminology. Schultz-Hencke divides the consequences of inhibition into those which relate directly to the inhibited material (expansive tendencies) and those which take the form of personality changes in the inhibited person. But what is it

[1] H. Schultz-Hencke, *Lehrbuch der analytischen Psychotherapie*, p. 38 ('Manual of Analytic Psychotherapy').

that inhibits expansive tendencies ? With Freud it was the environment which limited id activity—from which Freud assumed the presence of a primary drive hostility in society—and with Schultz-Hencke it is also the environment which inhibits expansive tendencies. This inhibition may be the outsome of a strict upbringing (prohibitions) or of a pampered upbringing. If the child is pampered it may desist from captative, retentive and aggressive striving because it fears a withdrawal of love. But the expansive tendencies which have thus been inhibited either by strictness or by pampering are not deprived of all their influence, for it is these same expansive tendencies which form man's *attitudes*. Schultz-Hencke regards human attitudes as specific fundamental tendencies in a man's character which function as unconscious motivations and so influence his actions. They correspond to *Freud's* symptoms in that they establish the same compromise between expansion and inhibition and also to Freud's character traits in as far as these constitute a conflict between the id and the environment. Schultz-Hencke defines these attitudes as follows:

'Right at the beginning of this study we described in a separated short chapter what was to be understood under an attitude. This was done advisedly, in order to demonstrate from the outset that from now on increasing importance would be attached to the attitudes, whilst general and coarse striving would be a factor of diminishing importance. We indicated that such attitudes are often more influential in establishing and determining the total life of a human being than are the strivings, no matter how noisily these latter may impose themselves. Meanwhile we have also attributed to these strivings the content which is relevant to our present purpose; we have established captative, retentive, aggressive and sexual strivings. And so there are also attitudes with the same attributes . . .'

'What remains of the inhibited material after the inhibition has taken place consists of such attitudes. What these attitudes lack in clarity they make up for in tenacity. They float around vaguely in the conscious mind, and yet they are directed. Their object is unknown, and yet they are avid for an object. They permeate foreign strivings which are different in kind and they direct them. They remain obscure. They belong "exclusively" to the realm of shadows in the soul, but they organize and guide to a surprising degree the actions of those in whom they are active. They have lost their old objects, but they are fixated to the qualities appropriate to those objects. They still seek them as of old.

'If infantile orality[2] sought the particular mother, then the later cap-

[1] H. Schultz-Hencke, *Der gehemmte Mensch*, p. 61.
[2] In a non-sexual sense: (footnote in *Der gehemmte Mensch*, p. 63).

tative attitude longs for motherliness. Indeed, even individual traits of contemporary persons can become a signal for the release of captative attitudes. The colour of a person's hair, their walk, some small similarity, attracts the captative attitude. These attitudes might well be called *fragments of the unconscious*, which, obscure, tenacious and intense, now produce their effect. The person who is full of such attitudes is guided by them, just as a migratory bird is guided by its instinct. The bird doesn't 'want' to fly south either, but it makes the journey as if it wanted to. Conscious intentions nearly always succumb to such attitudes; they are shattered, dissolved, dispersed by them. Care is overcome, foresight, moderation and reason are unable to take effect quietly and peaceably because they are constantly involved in new battles. Although this description may be of a conscious order, although it may be "anthropomorphic", it none the less touches upon the essential points.'[1]

But how does the 'inhibited man', i.e. the man in whom oral-captative and anal-retentive drives, strivings for recognition and quite conceivably sexual strivings are inhibited, how does such a man deal with his inhibitions? His character, which has already been deformed as a result of the inhibition of such strivings, develops further abnormal traits as a reaction to the inhibitions, namely, indolence, enormous demands and enormous expectations, over-compensation and substitute gratification. 'Inhibition, indolence and enormous demands form the structural nucleus of the inhibited person'[2] is Schultz-Hencke's own definition. Indolence, for example, is developed by children who realize that compliance and passivity meet with the approval of their environment in general or of certain adults in particular. Such children will subsequently make their 'careers' by currying favour with their fellows through their compliance and passivity. In fact, however, they are devoid of initiative and their drives are inhibited. Schultz-Hencke has the following to say on the subject of enormous demands:

'If indolence is a direct derivative of inhibition, then the psychic structure with which we are at present concerned is a descendant of the remaining attitudes.'[3]

Enormous demands derive from enormous expectations, For example, a pampered child which is suddenly exposed to a 'tough' environment by which it is rejected will submit to the environment in external matters but will unconsciously continue to make the same enormous demands

[1] H. Schultz-Hencke, *Der gehemmte Mensch*, pp. 62–3.
[2] *Ibid.*, pp. 79 ff.
[3] *Ibid.*, pp. 75 ff.

as it had always been accustomed to making, save that now those demands will appear in the form of enormous expectations *vis-à-vis* the
world. Such demands constitute a continuation of the child's oral-
captative attitude.[1] Over-compensation also occurs as a consequence of
inhibition and corresponds to what Adler understood under this concept
(see above): the child feels inferior and finds itself restricted in its natural
desire for expansion and so it engages in extraordinary (e.g. foolhardy)
undertakings in order to overcome its inhibition or at least to conceal it
both from itself and its environment.

Freud's description of substitute gratification (see p. 68 ff.) was
so thorough that it is quite unnecessary to repeat it here. In his description of substitute gratification Schultz-Hencke takes the opportunity of
dissociating himself from the libido theory:

'When researchers first noticed that sexual gratification was subject to
replacement by other forms of gratification, it was not surprising that
they should look upon these other forms as a special substitute for
sexuality in the normal course of events. The next step was to assume
that these substitute gratifications were "therefore" themselves of a
sexual nature. It is understandable that other strange phenomena, i.e.
the frequent coupling to non-sexual and sexual phenomena, should have
contributed to this view. But let it be said from the outset that these
phenomena do not support a theory of sexual libido. It is evident from the
aforegoing that these interconnections and retroactive connections
between one type of gratification and another do not indicate an
"identity of essence" between the strivings concerned. These afford
general gratification. And man is a creature who is quite happy to
abandon one form of gratification, which has been rendered loathsome
to him, and turn to another, which at that particular time contains no
menace.'[2]

(c) The Release of Neuroses. The Structure of Neuroses

Schultz-Hencke attributes particular importance to the release of
neuroses by situations in which the individual is exposed to temptation
or denial (e.g. promotion or demotion at work, rejection by women,
defeat at the hands of rivals, unexpected prosperity). In either eventuality the inhibited man (i.e. the neurotic) will find himself in a conflict,
which can lead to the development of manifest neurotic symptoms.
Schultz-Hencke's view of neurosis is easier to follow if we subdivide it
into the following sections:

[1] Cf. *Abraham's* prior comments on the oral character and on oral demands!
[2] H. Schultz-Hencke, *Der Gehemmte Mensch*, p. 82.

(*a*) Inhibition and Inhibitions. What Schultz-Hencke understands under these terms is the inhibition of oral-captative, anal-retentive aggressive drives, the inhibition of the individual's striving for recognition, of his sexuality and of his striving for tenderness. These inhibitions correspond to those listed above in respect of 'attitudes'. Those inhibited in an oral-captative sense are unable to come to grips with things, they often lack initiative, they avoid making decisions and are unable to assert themselves. Those inhibited in a retentive sense, on the other hand, 'radiate inhibition';[1] often they are the selfless individuals who are prepared to make sacrifices and are only too willing to surrender themselves up to a cause, but whose introversion, whose ability to withdraw into themselves and to engage in self-reflection, is in itself an inhibition. Aggressively inhibited individuals are those noted for—amongst other things—their extreme modesty and reserve; impotence and frigidity are common signs of aggressive inhibition. The inhibition of the urethral drives finds expression in, for example, lack of ambition and lack of spontaneity. The inhibition of the individual's sexual striving and his need for tenderness gradually deprive him of all possibility of effecting human contact and result in stunted forms of psychic existence.

(*b*) The 'inferior functions'. The neurotic is characterized both by the various forms of inhibition of the different types of drive and by the inferiority of certain of his basic functions, which Schultz-Hencke describes, by analogy with C. G. Jung, as the functions of feeling, sensation, thought and intuition. It remains an open question as to whether the inferiority (deficiency) is constitutionally determined or an acquired characteristic. Schultz-Hencke none the less tries to link the inferiority of these basic functions with the inhibition of specific types of drive. Inferiority in feeling is not far removed from a disturbance involving 'surrender' which derives from an inhibition of the individual's striving for tenderness. Inferiority of thought as revealed, for example, in compulsive brooding corresponds to an inhibition of motor aggressiveness, indeed it derives from it.

(*c*) The actual neurotic structures are then divided into four types:
1. The schizoid structure. This is commensurate with an infantile inhibition of intentional strivings (see above). We are concerned here with disrupted, ambivalent individuals who, as a result of the inhibition of their intentional strivings, show a tendency towards schizophrenia.
2. The depressive structure. In this case 'oral-aggressive' strivings were inhibited in early infancy. The aggressive strivings are projected on to the outside world, which is then felt to be demoniac and negative, with the result that the reaction to temptation or denial of the person

[1] H. Schultz-Hencke, *Lehrbuch der analytischen Psychotherapie*, p. 60.

whose oral-aggressive strivings have been thus inhibited is one of hopelessness.

3. The structure of obsessional neurosis. This is due to the inhibition of motor-aggressive strivings. The obsessional neurotic avoids decisions because these involve actions which he is obliged to avoid because of his inhibition.

4. The hysterical structure. This structure is created if the child, after passing without hindrance through every stage of its development up to the point where it is due to release its motor-aggressive strivings, then meets with unexpected severity and strictness. The only thing the child can do is to reject all hope of further maturation, i.e. to refuse to renounce the magic world in which it lives (see Ferenczi p. 172 ff.). Infantilism, inability to accept reality, are the consequence of such an attitude. Schultz-Hencke summarizes the relationship of the four different carriers of neurotic mal-development to the external world as follows:

'The *schizoid type* fears all form of contact. The *depressive type* fears to surrender himself because he thinks that this means surrendering himself up and being devoured.

'The *obsessional neurotic* fears lest tenderness be demanded from him; for his unintegrated aggressiveness, which has become latent, has deprived him of his capacity for spontaneous tenderness.

'The *hysteric*, especially the female hysteric, fears sexuality as a chronologically necessary platform for the confirmation of interpersonal relations because the hysteric is completely immature. (The hysteric has not reached the "genital stage"; *Freud*.)

'These four structures or, alternatively, these four carriers may also be characterized independently of one another in respect of their experiences from the point of view of the "nature of the demands" made by the environment:

'The *schizoid* reacts to the demands made by the environment in an instinctive manner and so quickly that in fact he defends himself against them long before they are able to acquire a subjectively oppressive character. But for this very reason there are times when he may, in certain circumstances, be "overcome" by his "actual" view of the environment.

'The *depressive* is smothered by the demands of the environment and so scarcely registers them. To him they are simply an oppressive burden.

'The *obsessional neurotic* reacts with tense interest to the nature of environmental demands. He tries to come to terms with them but senses in a vague and coarse way the presence of opposing tendencies.

'The *hysteric* comes to terms immediately and impetuously with the demands made by the environment, which he experiences perfectly clearly, but his reaction is excessive due to his naturally inadequate and highly expansive mode of activity.'[1]

Neurosis he sums up as:

'(a) Neurotic symptoms are a fragment of a complete drive experience.
(b) There is *the* neurosis.
(c) The structural "core" of neurosis is inhibition.
(d) There are primarily three drive *spheres*[2] subject to inhibition.
(e) The "testa" consists of phenomena caused by inhibition.
(f) There are four or five principal neurotic structures.
(g) In situations in which the individual is exposed to temptation and frustration drives and needs which had been latent until then "break out".'[3]

(d) The Problem of Anxiety

Whereas the Neo-Freudians, *Horney, Sullivan, Rado* and—despite his different approach—*Fromm*, consider that anxiety, which for them is diametrically opposed to security, is the chief force at work in the genesis of neurosis and have thus moved right away from Freud's basically dynamic conception (drives versus suppression), Schultz-Hencke has kept much closer to the Freudian conception. His antithesis between striving and inhibition corresponds to the Freudian antithesis between the drives (id) and repression. Although Freud never tired of pointing out that anxiety is the actual cause of neurosis he never actually treated it as a cardinal point of his theory. Neither did Schultz-Hencke make it the focal point of his theories. Indeed he tended to underestimate its importance. He concedes that feelings of anxiety and guilt must be present before any inhibition of expansive strivings can take place. But then how are the feelings of anxiety and guilt themselves inhibited? This is extremely difficult to follow, for it really does raise the question as to what inhibits what. And in order to explain this problem Schultz-Hencke is obliged to fall back on the concept of 'vital defence', which is far from being a precise definition. None the less, it is this 'vital defence' which is responsible for the inhibition of feelings of anxiety and guilt and thus for the existence of unconscious feelings of anxiety and guilt.

'For we failed to point out that feelings of anxiety and guilt may also be repressed. After they have existed for a certain time these inhibiting

---

[1] H. Schultz-Hencke, *Lehrbuch der analytischen Psychoterapie*, p. 111.
[2] *Ibid.*, p. 112: footnote: 'Spheres', however, which are not strictly delimited!
[3] *Ibid.*, p. 112.

emotional components may also be subjected to inhibition. This is due to the fact that in the long run these components constitute an intolerable experience. In fact we would expect them to persist. Apart from their being subject to a certain degree of mechanization we would expect them to be activated whenever an inhibited striving was *tempted* to emerge. Then, although it might be more mechanical, we would expect the game to start all over again: instead of emerging an expansive impulse would be stifled *in statu nascendi* by feelings of anxiety and guilt. In point of fact, however, the process is like this only at the beginning. Afterwards the constant repetitions of fear and guilt are opposed by vital and violent defence, which leads to the repression of these emotional reactions, until finally "nothing" is left.'[1]

(e) *The Unconscious*

Schultz-Hencke considers that the unconscious plays only a minor role. In this he resembles the Neo-Freudians. Wherever possible he avoids using the term and restricts his definition of it to 'the aggregate of all things difficult to remember'.[2] He attacks Freud's concept of the unconscious in the following passage:

'Those who have enquired into the thought processes of Romanticism, into the writings of *Carus* for example, will also have found that the expression, the unconscious, is used there in a sense that is largely identical to that attributed to it at a later date by *Schopenhauer* and *Hartmann*. And if we enquire a little more closely into the meaning of the unconscious in that context we will find that it has practically nothing in common with the Freudian unconscious. In the earlier usage what is meant is simply a metapsychical or metaphysical unconscious, the existent or activating substratum underlying both the physical world and the world of the soul. Consequently we are certainly justified in asking how, within half a century and within the same language, a researcher can consider himself justified in attributing a new content to a concept which had been used often enough and which had been very clearly defined. The present author is of the opinion that this dual use of the same pretentious word *should* have been avoided. At least the descendant should have indicated in an appropriate footnote that he was prepared to respect the traditional sense of the word and to recognize the limits of his own position.'[3]

Schultz-Hencke subdivides the concept of the unconscious into:

1. its metaphysical (philosophical) aspect,

[1] H. Schultz-Hencke, *Der Gehemmte Mensch*, p. 83.
[2] *Ibid.*, p. 60.
[3] *Ibid*, pp. 60-1

2. its ontogenetic aspect (i.e. subjective, personal Ucs),
3. its phylogenetic aspect (i.e. the Ucs is linked with the inheritance of certain dispositions),
4. its collective aspect (i.e. C. G. Jung's collective Ucs).

Schultz-Hencke describes the Freudian process of raising unconscious material into consciousness or alternatively the process of suspending repression as the process whereby 'inhibited material is made manifest'. The technique of making inhibited material manifest embraces all the techniques previously developed by Freud and his disciples such as day dreaming, free association and the interpretation of dreams, which Schultz-Hencke describes by analogy with Freud's findings. It should be noted in this connection that Schultz-Hencke accords only minor importance to transference, which lies at the very heart of Freudian analytic therapy.

In a work which he devoted exclusively to dreams and dream interpretation Schultz-Hencke investigates the various drive disturbances, i.e. disturbances in the captative-oral, retentive and sexual spheres, on the basis of clinical dream material. Apart from this his method of dream evaluation, like the method employed by Freudian psychoanalysis, is diagnostic.

(f) Contributions to Psychosomatic Medicine

Both in their investigations into the structure of neurosis and above all in their psychosomatic research Schultz-Hencke and his disciples (*A. Dührssen, W. Schwidder, Baumeyer* inter alia) have made extensive use of statistical material. The major part of this material is taken from the case histories or examinations of the patients at the Berlin Zentral-institut for psychogenic illnesses. According to Schultz-Hencke the number of cases evaluated between 1950 and 1952 was already in the region of 8,000 to 10,000 anamneses. Schultz-Hencke claims that on the basis of this extensive empirical evidence he is able to establish correlations between the various functional and to a lesser extent the organic illnesses and their specific drive spheres. (He speaks of 'simultaneous correlations', thus establishing a new formulation for psycho-physical parallelism). For example, diseases of the mouth and stomach (such as stomach ulcers) are correlated with disturbances of the oral-captative drive sphere, although these may overlap with disturbances of the anal-retentive sphere. The following graph,[1] in which specific organs and their illnesses are correlated with the relevant drive spheres, gives an adequate indication of the process involved.

[1] H. Schultz-Hencke, *Lehrbuch der analytischen Psychotherapie*, p. 134.

Drives, needs	Organs	Functional disturbances
Intentional	Eye	Blindness / Squinting / Tic
	Ear	Deafness
	Cortex	?
	Brain stem	
captative / oral	Hypophysis	Balimia / Anorexia
	Throat	Angina "disposition"
	Pharynx	Globus
	Oesophagus	
	Stomach	Cardiospasm / Vomiting / Gastritis / Ulcer
striving for posession		
retentive	Arteries of the skin	Acrodynia / Pruritus / Eczema
	Ureter	Ureter spasm (Pyelitis, calculi)
	Small intestine	? / Diarrhoea
anal	Liver	Hepatitis
	Gall bladder	Enteritis
	Pancreatic gland	?
striving for recognition	Large intestine	Obstipation / Colitis
aggressive	Arteries of the Head	Migraine
	Galea muscles	
	Articular muscles	"Spasms"
	Heart	Stenocardia
striving for recognition	Liver	Cholecystitis
urethral	Kidney	Polyuria
	Bladder	Enuresis
	Urethra	Ej. praec.
	Intestine	Diarrhoea
sexual	Arteries of the Head	Erythrophobia
	Heart	Tachycardia / Arrhythmia
	Genitals	Impotence / Priapism
	Germ glands	Vaginism / Frigidity
tender	Skin	Anaesthesia
sexual striving		
loving	Entire body	Restlessness
surrendering	Musculature	Astasia-Abasia
	Bladder	Incontinence
eros-sated	intestine	
anxious	Adrenal gland	Anxiety
	Diencephalon	
	Hypophysis	Tachycardia
	Heart	Stenocardia
anxious excitement	Thyroid gland	Restlessness
	Intestine	Diarrhoea
fear / frightened	Thyroid gland	Basedow
guilty	? / Frontal lobe of Brain	Depression
	Thalamus	

F

THOMAS FRENCH

(a) Behaviourism

Thomas French, who collaborated with *F. Alexander* for many years at the Chicago Psychoanalytic Institute, advocates in the *Integration of Behaviour*[1] a theory of psychoanalysis that is strongly influenced by Behaviourism. Behaviourism means behaviour research and researchers with extreme views, such as *Watson* and *Pavlov*, considered that the description of animal behaviour either in natural or artificial conditions was the only valid form of scientific enquiry. The teleological explanation of behaviour which French tries to establish is held to be only provisionally valid by the Behaviourists, who consider that the mechanism of conditioned and unconditioned reflexes will one day supplant these provisional teleological explanations.

Behaviourist research into neurosis has been promoted by J. Massermann[2] and his collaborators, who induced 'neurotic' patterns of behaviour in animals by experimental means. For example, a conditioned reflex was induced in a monkey by training it to operate the same flap mechanism every day in order to obtain its food. One day when it opened the flap, instead of finding food, it found a snake. In the course of the next few days the monkey, who was by then suffering from hunger, developed neurotic symptoms consistent with an anxiety neurosis, as it fluctuated between fear of the snake and the need to satisfy its hunger. For the time being it appeared unable to 'integrate' the trauma, and it was clear that a chain of conditioned reflexes had been disrupted and the animal had not yet been able to develop a new type of behaviour suitable to its new situation, i.e. as yet no new reflexes had been 'conditioned'. This kind of experimentally induced situation, which had previously been employed by *Pavlov*, may be taken as typical of the kind of thinking underlying Thomas French's enquiries. His fundamental question is: how can man adapt his behaviour in accordance with different situations and with the conditioned conflicts to which these may conceivably give rise; how can he 'integrate' his behaviour so that it is free from conflict and meets the needs of every situation? Starting from and constantly referring to *Freudian* psychoanalysis French advances his basic thesis in his extremely detailed and meticulous studies, namely that all human behaviour is rationally determined and that what appears to be irrational behaviour can always be traced back to rational behaviour.

[1] Chicago 1952: in this presentation of French's views we shall only be considering the first volume of his work, which comprises three volumes to date, for it is this first volume which contains his fundamental concepts.

[2] J. Massermann, *Behaviour and Neurosis*, Chicago, 1943.

(b) Behaviour and Purposiveness

French considers it a commonplace that all human behaviour (i.e. activity) is purposive. This is a prerequisite for any understanding of human behaviour. *Freud* had demonstrated that the irrational behaviour encountered in dreams or sick persons was only apparently irrational and on closer inspection turned out to be purposive: e.g. neurotic symptoms or dreams are the result of imperfect attempts to fulfil wishes. For French wish-fulfilment and purposive behaviour are identical. But what is the real ultimate purpose or ultimate wish of human and animal activity? To ensure the survival of the individual and the race by means of adaptation. In contrast to animals man is born without sound instincts and in a relatively helpless condition. On the other hand he is endowed with the ability to learn. Learning is a process of adaptation which lasts over a period of many years and which enables the child to adopt habits—long before it has acquired the use of words—on the basis of direct experience. This sort of experience is sometimes called 'intuition' but is in fact simply knowledge at a 'manipulative level'. Since all behaviour is purposive it is determined by motives. Psychoanalysis penetrates the conscious and 'unconscious' motivations underlying human behaviour and in doing so it makes use of a 'common sense' psychology, as when the analyst deduces the patient's behaviour from his knowledge of his own. If the patient appears annoyed or anxious, he is asked to name the cause of his annoyance or anxiety. If the analyst succeeds in establishing a correlation between these motives and his conception of what his own behaviour would be in a similar situation, then he will understand the annoyance or the anxiety. The ability to forecast what the patient's behaviour will be in a given situation depends on knowledge of the motives underlying his behaviour, from which knowledge—plus the knowledge of the situation in which he expects to find himself—it is possible to predict his behaviour. Psychoanalysis is motivational research and it deduces the patient's future behaviour from its knowledge of the patient's behaviour in an actual situation, e.g. one involving jealousy *vis-à-vis* a brother or sister. Psychoanalytic interpretations illuminate the patient's 'manipulative knowledge' (French's expression for the unconscious), it renders it conscious and enables it to be dealt with at the 'theoretical level', i.e. at the level of consciousness.

(c) Motives and the Realization of Motives

If we are to predict a person's behaviour in a particular situation, accurate knowledge of that situation and of the person's motives is not enough. If a person's *will* is directed towards a given purpose then, in order to predict whether he will in fact achieve his purpose, we need to know

(1) whether the person concerned knows *how* he intends to pursue his purpose and (2) whether he possesses sufficient *insight* to be able to assess his own abilities and potentials with regard to that purpose. The way in which he pursues his purpose is of course related to his external situation, whilst his insight refers to his internal situation. It is typical of the Behaviourist conception that French should have chosen an act of will as his starting-point. The confusion between actions determined by the drives and actions determined by the will which was noticeable in Freud's thinking—volition served as a model for the definition of the drives (see p. 245 ff.)—was systematically promoted in French's Behaviourism. All human activity is interpreted in terms of volition.

'Thus implicit in our common-sense understanding of behaviour is the assumption that it can be analysed into two components—motivation and 'know-how', motivation and insight. 'Patterns of motivation' arise by interaction between these two component factors. Common sense recognizes at least two kinds of interaction between them.

'First, to know how to achieve a goal means that we are able to resolve this task into a number of simpler ones. To get food to eat may mean going to a store, buying the food, preparing and cooking it, serving it on the table, and finally eating it. The dominant desire to eat will activate, each in its turn, a number of subsidiary goals; and the task of achieving any one of them, such as preparing and cooking the food, will often be resolved further into a series of still simpler acts. In brief, insight into how to achieve a goal gives rise to a hierarchy of goal-directed strivings, in which subordinate goals are related to superordinate ones as means to an end.

'A second kind of interaction between insight and motivation results from the fact that anticipating the consequences of an intended action may activate a conflicting motive. For example, when a boy knows that he will be punished if he is caught stealing, his impulse to steal an apple from a fruit stand will probably activate fear of getting caught and punished and will thus give rise a to conflict between his desire for the apple and his fear of getting punished.

'These two kinds of motivational patterns we call "functional" and "conflict" patterns, respectively. Functional patterns are those that activate and guide rational behaviour. Although psychoanalysis has dealt chiefly with the conflict patterns of neurotic behaviour, in our studies we shall be equally interested in the functional patterns of rational behaviour and in the relation between conflict patterns and functional patterns.

'A basic pattern persists while subsidiary patterns succeed one another.

Starting with this common-sense analysis, we enquire next how patterns of motivation succeed one another.[1]

'The achievement of a purpose depends on the persistence of a basic functional pattern that guides, step by step, the emergence of its subordinate goals. Similarly, when we study sequences of conflict patterns, we find that a basic conflict persists while different kinds of solution are successively attempted.'[2]

The hierarchy of aims is responsible for the over-determination of neurotic symptoms, dreams and faulty actions, in fact for all irrational behaviour. In this hierarchy the conflict or problem to which a solution is sought is first solved by means of a *substitute* action, which is subordinate to the actual solution. But a purely rational interpretation of human activity such as would proceed from considerations such as these is too insubstantial for French. If an individual wishes to attain a specific goal or perform a particular action he will not succeed in doing so if he relies exclusively on rational or intellectual planning and on his assessment of his own external situation and his insight into his personal capabilities. There is a further requirement, which is more important than anything else, namely, the 'motivating pressure'. What this means is that for a motive to be realized, i.e. for an aim to be achieved, energy must be applied, or, as French puts it, 'the intensity of a person's desire to achieve an aim is what we call the motivating pressure'. It is possible that this pressure will be maintained even if the aim is not immediately achieved, but it is also possible that it will be temporarily transferred to the substitutive aims (solutions) and return to the original aim later on. French divides the 'motivating pressure' into two aspects, the *negative* aspect (e.g. to escape from danger), and the *positive* aspect (to concentrate on an aim). He considers that the nervousness which overcomes a person who is exposed to danger and which may prompt him to undertake a whole series of purposive actions is composed of 'needs' and 'drives'.

Purposive actions (=wishes) are born of *hopes* and French speaks of a 'need' pole and a hope pole of wishes. As long as a wish is felt in the form of restlessness and dissatisfaction it is part of the 'need' pole but the moment its fulfilment is anticipated it transfers to the 'hope' pole. Hope strengthens the individual's insight into his own ability to reach the goal of a given action. It is able to give direction to what is otherwise no more than a 'motivating pressure'. The process involved in the integration of behaviour can already be defined in terms of the above concepts.

[1] Th. French, *The Integration of Behaviour*, Vol. I, pp. 43–4.
[2] *Ibid.*, pp. 43–4.

'First, the motivating pressure of a need seeks discharge in diffuse motor activity. Next, hope of satisfaction, based on present opportunity and on memories of previous success, stimulates the integrative mechanism to form a plan for realizing this hope. Finally, hope of satisfaction activates this plan so that it exerts a guiding influence, concentrating motor discharge on efforts to put the plan into execution.'[1]

(d) Disturbances in the Process of Integration

Whereas the integration of behaviour is determined by actions arising out of wishes (which consist of needs and hopes), motives and motor processes, disturbances in the integrative process are due both to external and internal obstacles and to frustration. The disturbances can affect various parts of the integrative process. In as far as this process is determined by actions a closer analysis of those actions reveals the following factors: the way in which an individual deals with a given task or with an unforseen situation will reveal the degree of integration which he has achieved. If a person is seen stealing an apple and simply runs away from his pursuers instead of trying to outwit them, then his 'integrative span' will be *small*. This 'integrative span' is determined by two factors, the individual's "integrative capacity" and the task with which he has to deal (the 'integrative task'). If the difficulties posed by the 'integrative task' increase and the individual's 'integrative capacity' remains unchanged, then clearly his 'integrative span' will have been reduced and his behaviour will begin to disintegrate. Whilst the tendency to 'integrate' tasks derives from needs (e.g. the need to find food when hungry), 'integrative capacity' is chiefly based on hope and self-confidence. If over and above this the individual has made a sufficient number of positive *experiences*, i.e. if he has already successfully dealt with similar situations (e.g. hunger and the search for food), then the forces of hope and self-confidence which promote his 'integrative capacity' will be correspondingly stronger. Thus human activity may be considered both in terms of the individual and in terms of the environment.

1. In terms of the individual we find:
(a) drives,
(b) needs,
(c) wishes with their 'need pole and hope pole',
(d) motives and motivating pressure,
(e) the plan whereby wishes are realized under the motivating pressure,
(f) the realization of the plan, which depends on self-confidence (experiences) and hope.

[1] Th. French, *The Integration of Behaviour*, Vol. I, pp. 53 ff.

2. In terms of the environment we find:

(a) external obstacles;
(b) internal obstacles in the form of *prohibitions* } frustrations.

The integration of (1) and (2) is effected by the individual's integrative capacity, which is characterized by his 'integrative span', i.e. his ability to solve an 'integrative task', where failure to do so spells disaster. The end-purpose and sole criterion of 'successful integration' is survival in the struggle for life.

(e) The consequences of frustrations

Frustrations are caused either by external or internal obstacles. Man's primitive reaction to frustrations is rage, which in the case of a kicking child assumes the proportions of total disintegration. French defines frustration as the recognition on the part of the individual that he is unable to achieve a desired aim. There are various ways in which the individual can come to terms with frustration. These include:

1. Flight (this would correspond to Freud's repression).
2. Projection, which French does not define as a distortion of reality but as 'psychological absorption'.

A child that has been beaten by its mother has a dream in which it contentedly looks on whilst its mother works at an anvil. The child's masochistic desire to be beaten by its mother has been converted into the agreeable image of the industrious mother (Freud's transformation into the opposite). The mother striking the anvil serves as a *substitute* for the child's masochistic desire for punishment by a process of 'physiological absorption', i.e. because the child is able to watch its mother working. The mother's 'physiological activity' (striking the anvil) *neutralizes* the child's masochistic desire, its 'painful motivating pressure'. French considers that anxiety, which might logically be regarded as one of the consequences of frustration, is just another motive for flight or absorption mechanisms. French's attempt to merge the concept of defence with that of 'physiological absorption' is unmistakable.

3. Further absorption mechanisms. These include:

(a) pleasurable but not necessarily purposive motor activity. For example, by charging about a child may work off tensions and recover from frustrations or its inability to gratify a desire;
(b) phantasies, which also 'absorb' the internal pressure resulting from frustrations;

(c) sleep, which neutralizes and absorbs internal pressure both physiologically and through dreams;

(d) diversions afforded by external stimuli (going to the cinema to get out of a bad mood), which also relieve the 'pressure' created by frustrations.

Purposive behaviour, as revealed in conscious planning, arises from two tendencies:

'Perception of present real situations gives rise to expectations of the probable future. This tendency to anticipate the future is supplemented by another tendency based on fantasy. Starting with fantasies based on satisfying memories, one reaches backward from the memory of past successes to recall how those successes were achieved. The integrative field of a goal-directed striving is built up by a synthesist interaction of these two processes: Looking forward from the present real situation, one forms not only a picture of the probable future but also a judgement as to how far emerging fantasies are realizable. Under pressure of this judgement, fantasies that are unattainable in reality must be replaced by others that satisfy the same needs but are more capable of realization. While fantasy is thus being modified under pressure of reality, the underlying need and the fantasies based on it are playing a large part in determining what perceptions shall be attended and reacted to; there is a continual urge to explore how the real situation and the probable future can be modified to accord better with one's wishes and fantasies.'[1]

(f) The Structure of the Personality, the Unconscious, the libido

Despite his references to Freud's organization of the structure of the personality (instances) French attaches no particular importance to them. The ego is equated with the integrative field or with integrative capacity. There is no longer any such thing as an id which transcends consciousness and the unconscious is defined as the 'manipulative level of knowledge'. The second volume of French's investigations is devoted to dream analysis. French advocates that wherever possible dreams should be considered exclusively as substitutes for actions that have gone wrong or as inferior aims in terms of the hierarchy of aims. Such advocacy renders Freud's id largely irrelevant. The libido theory, whose physiological-biological aspects Freud derived from the existence of the erotogenic zones, French would like to see replaced by a more precise 'model of physiological behaviour', in which, for example, the concepts of 'orality' and 'anality' would give way to more adequate and more comprehensive physiological functions. Although these problems obliged Freud to advance complicated and in part contradictory hypotheses, they also formed the focal point of his analysis and research

[1] Th. French, *The Integration of Behaviour*, Vol. I p. 223.

throughout the whole of his working life. The Behaviourists, however, are no longer interested in them. Their place is now taken by the conditioned and unconditioned reflexes, which constitute the sole formula for the understanding of human behaviour.

'A conditional response is an acquired adaptive reaction based on previous experience. In the classical situation of Pavlov's experiments it leads to an anticipatory secretion of saliva or to a food-seeking motor reaction in response to a stimulus that has usually been followed by food. The guiding influence of an integrative field is also an acquired adaptive reaction based in large part on past experience. Like a conditioned response an integrative field tends to activate reactions that have been successful in the past.

'In this comparison, success in achieving the goal of an integrative field corresponds to reinforcement of the conditioned reflex by the unconditioned reflex, food; hope of success corresponds to the effect of previous reinforcements in establishing a conditioned response. In other words, the integrative capacity of an integrative field parallels the strength and stability of a positive conditioned response that has resulted from previous reinforcements of this response. Similarly, failure in a goal-directed striving is equivalent to *non*-reinforcement of a conditioned response: and the impairment of integrative capacity resulting from such failure is paralleled by the internal inhibition that results from non-reinforcement of a conditioned response.'[1]

G

SANDOR RADÓ

Apart from French, Radó is doubtless the most important representative of Behaviourism within the Neo-Freudian field. His work has yet to be presented in a comprehensive form and consists at present of a large number of essays and published lectures, from which, however, it is possible to follow his development. His interpretation of human behaviour and of neuroses is centred around his theory of the 'Emergency Function', which has been described by *W. B. Cannon*[2] in his biological studies of animal reactions to fear and other stimuli. A cornered animal will react either with rage or fear, but in either case a large number of nervous and hormonal processes (the so-called sympathomimetic

[1] Th. French, *The Integration of Behaviour*, Vol. I, p. 234.
[2] W. B. Cannon, *Bodily Changes in Pain, Hunger, Fear and Rage*, New York, 1934.

processes which are controlled by the sympathetic nervous system) are released. The concept of the emergency function covers this whole combination of processes. Radó had already veered towards such ideas in his early publications (especially in his study on the fear of castration in women) which were written at a time when he was rather more closely involved with the Freudians.

(a) The Role of Anxiety, Early Phase

In his criticism of Freud's conception of the nature of anxiety Radó expresses his doubts as to whether the id really is the 'seat of anxiety', i.e. whether the id really produces the anxiety, as had been assumed by Freud in his last phase. Although he agrees with Freud that the function of anxiety, or rather the function of the fear which is the immediate cause of anxiety, is to provide a warning signal, he differs from him in his conception of what actually constitutes a state of anxiety. Radó considers that when an individual is in a state of anxiety, i.e. when he is overcome by anxiety, what actually happens is that his ego is overcome by masochism. It is due to masochism that anxiety conditions are tantamount to paralysis and prevent the patient from engaging in meaningful activity. The little girl, whose external and internal circumstances —inadequate ego maturation—render her incapable of sexual enjoyment in accordance with the pleasure principle, will develop sexual masochism instead of a 'normal' sexual drive. This then finds expression in many different patterns of behaviour: e.g. extreme passivity, rape phantasies, frigidity, etc. At the same time, however, the little girl's ego feels itself to be constantly threatened by the presence of this sexual masochism, and so out of self-defence it elects to believe in an illusory penis, a belief which may amongst other things cause the little girl to adopt markedly masculine attitudes. Over and above this the clitoris—as a penis substitute—becomes the sole source of sexual excitation. Fear of castration arises when this fictive penis is threatened and the ego is overcome by masochism in a crisis of anxiety.

(b) The Role of Anxiety, Late Phase

We have seen that Rado's attention had already been directed towards anxiety as a result of his investigations into the fear of castration in women, but following the publication of *Cannon's* investigations (i.e. as from 1934) he was to take a further important step in this direction. Whereas previously he had considered that it was the threat of masochism which constituted anxiety, he now held that anxiety was the chief criterion for the emergency function and that it was the emergency function which determined whether the individual was to survive. Neurotic distorted attitudes and neurosis were now defined as 'ego functioning altered by faulty measures of emergency control'.[1] The emergency function, which is characterized by anxiety or rage, now became the focal point of interest for the interpretation of abnormal behaviour, this latter being a remnant of the original emergency function which persists throughout the whole of life.

(c) *The Pleasure Principle and the Structure of the Personality*

In Rado's conception, which may be compared with similar conceptions entertained by *French* and *Alexander* in as far as all three espouse the cause of extreme simplification and are obliged to reduce living psychic activity to a reflex formula, the pleasure principle and, by extension, the avoidance of pain are considered to be the regulating principle of life and of consciousness. The behaviour of the amoeba, which flees from sources of pain but seeks out sources of pleasure, appears to Rado as a prototype of life itself. The emergency function which is triggered off by pain—in the case of the amoeba flight—is also the prototype within the biological sphere for the emergence of behaviour disturbances (neuroses). The spinal column in mammals still practises this very simple form of emergency function in reflex action, even though the reflex is classified as belonging to the 'non-reporting ranges' of the 'fluid section', by which Radó means the unconscious (the 'id'). It should be noted, however, that regulation by the pleasure principle is scarcely apparent in the unconscious. It is in a state of constant flux, caught up in the coming and going of unconscious tensions and sensations. If the unconscious comes into contact with the outside world in a disagreeable manner then this contact finds expression in *pain*, which is replaced by *anxiety* at the semi-conscious and *fear* at the conscious level. In the case of vertebrates the pleasure principle controls consciousness and those inherited stereotyped patterns of behaviour which need not necessarily be conscious but which are then included in that part of the unconscious designated by the 'stereotyped section of the non-reporting range' (Freud's pre-conscious) rather than the 'fluid section' (Freud's 'id'). A special 'pain barrier' (Freud's censorship) separates consciousness, which is controlled by the pleasure principle, from the 'fluid section' of the unconscious. In certain psychic disturbances, especially in depression, this 'pain barrier' is pierced, whereupon an emergency function— e.g. depression—is triggered off in the organism. The characteristic of depression is the fact that the 'action self' completely withdraws into itself, despises itself and loses in stature. Radó's 'action-self' corresponds to *Freud's* ego, save that Radó places greater emphasis on the relationship between the ego and the will, i.e. he develops this concept in terms of action and perception. Apart from depression there are also other

[1] S. Radó, *Psychoanalysis of Behaviour*, New York, 1956, pp. 134 ff.

behaviour disturbances, which may be regarded as 'unsuccessful attempts at reparation' on the part of the organism, i.e. as unsuccessful attempts to deal with the uncontrollable contents of the 'fluid section' of the 'non-reporting range' which have broken out. Attempts at reparation on the part of the organism are to be considered as remnants of the emergency function. The whole of this process as described by Radó constitutes an attempt to clothe in biological-behaviourist concepts *Freud's* views on the pleasure principle and the psychic instances, perhaps with a view to making them more accessible to the pragmatic American mentality.

(d) Sexuality

The reorganization of sexuality in terms of different behaviour patterns also constitutes a re-formulation in behaviourist language of *Freudian* concepts. It should be pointed out, however, that Radó abandons both the libido theory and the concept of the duality of the instincts (life drive and death drive). Radó assumes that the development of sexuality in vertebrates has followed a 'Push and Pull Principle', which in turn derives from the behaviour of ovum and sperm-cell. This latter type of behaviour represents copulation at the *physiological* level. Copulation at the psychological level is of course regulated by the pleasure principle, i.e. the desire to have an orgasm. Radó conceives the 'standard coital pattern', which presupposes 'average behaviour in copulation', as follows:[1]

'Internal stimulation establishes receptivity to psychodynamic stimulation.

↓

'Arousal by sensory and intellectual stimulation of each other.

↓

'In both mates, this sets up sexual motive state which mobilizes and organizes the organism's emotional and other resources for orgastic pleasure.

↓

'In both mates this state elicits automatic responses of preparedness: —sensory: selective mechanism of attention—intellectual: selective mechanisms of memory and wishful thought—motor: engorgement of erectile structures—glandular: release of sperms; secretion of vehicular and lubricative fluids.

↓

'Male woos and secures consent of the female.

↓

'Foreplay: mutual stimulation of responsive extragenital regions

[1] S. Radó, *Psychoanalysis of Behaviour*, Fig. 3, 'Standard Coital Pattern', p. 191.

sends tributary streams of pleasure into orgastic main stream in both mates.

↓

'Male: rise of impetus to penetrate—Female: rise of desire to be penetrated.

↓

'Inplay: intramural stimulation by pelvic thrust.

↓

'This reflexly evokes pleasurable orgastic peristalsis of genital structures and brings mounting emotional tensions to a climactic discharge in both male and female.

↓

'Sleep.

↓

'Pride.'

Deviations from this standard norm of the sexual act in neuroses and perversions arise as a result of infantile fears and aggressions. At this point Radó takes up the old trauma doctrine once more. The traumas take effect at that point in the standard coital pattern where normally the desire to penetrate or to be penetrated would have made itself felt. Radó supplies the following table:[1]

	→ Arousal	
	→ Motive State	
	→ Sensory	
	→ Intellectual	preparedness
	→ Motor	
	→ Glandular	
	→ Wooing	
	→ Foreplay	penetrate
	→ Impetus to	be penetrated
Damaging action of the	→ Inplay	
fears and Resentments	→ Orgasm	
of sexual degradation.	→ Sensual love	
	→ Magic love	
	→ In-love	
	→ Interest in Security	
	→ Desire for Offspring	
	→ Marriage	
	→ Pride	

The resultant disturbances to sexual behaviour, such as perversions, masturbation, homosexuality, are interpreted as patterns of behaviour

[3] S. Radó, *Psychoanalysis of Behaviour*, p. 198, Fig. 5.

which deviate from the standard norm. Radó divides them up into the following groups:[1]

'1. Organ replacement.
2. Sexual pain-dependence.
3. Contact avoidance:
   (a) the self-exposure pattern;
   (b) the *voyeur*, or peeping, pattern;
4. Patterns of solitary gratification:
   (a) the fetishistic pattern;
   (b) orgastic self-stimulation in cross-dressing;
   (c) orgastic self-stimulation in the illusory twosome of a day-dream or dream;
   (d) blank orgastic self-stimulation in the waking state;
   (e) surprise orgasm in the waking state or in sleep, in particular, the paradoxical orgasm.
5. Homogeneous pairs.
6. Adult-child pairs.
7. Human-animal pairs.
8. Patterns involving more than two mates.'

The cause of all these abnormal patterns of behaviour is the mutual fear of the partner's sexual organ (truncation, penetration). But the detailed interpretation of homosexuality, for example, follows the principles laid down by the *Freudian* school, although special emphasis is placed on the fear of the partner's genital, which is responsible for the deformation of the 'standard coital pattern' (i.e. the man's fear of the vagina, the woman's fear of the penis).

For Radó, as also for French and Alexander, the psyche is simply the subjective perception of physiological processes. He even extends the reflex schema to include the ego when (*ibid.*, p. 136) he speaks of a 'reflex organization of the ego'. This view is bought at the cost of complicated constructions on the one hand and simplifications of complex problems on the other. Constructions and simplification are particularly evident in the description of sexual relations given above. But since these are typical attributes both of the Neo-Freudian conception and also of the constructional element in Freudian psychoanalysis, their critical assessment will be reserved for the final part of this book.

[4] S. Radó, *Psychoanalysis of Behaviour*, p. 200.

H

ABRAM KARDINER

Although all Neo-Freudians tend to stress the importance of the environment rather than biological, constitutional factors for the emergence of neuroses, it was Kardiner[1] who made the most detailed investigations into the relationship between the individual and society in primitive cultures and also into the condition of minorities within a given society. Kardiner takes from Freud no more than the latter's assumption of a predominantly irrational unconscious, which is subsequently shaped and developed by cultural influences. The unconscious is made manifest in a large number of so-called 'projective systems', which give expression to the individual's most profound experiences, his ideals, his conscience and his desires and which form one basis of culture.[2] The other basis of culture is supplied by the 'basic personality'. Certain primary needs are common to all men, such as hunger, thirst, longing for security, sexuality, etc. (Kardiner gives a list of primary needs.) But the way in which these needs are gratified varies from culture to culture. Kardiner tries to interpret specific cultural institutions in the light of the type of gratification of primary needs pursued in the culture concerned. For example, the children of the Aloresians grow up without receiving any particular care from their mothers and fathers. They are either brought up by older brothers and sisters or they are left to fend for themselves. Their fathers deal only with finance, spending all their time in saving and hoarding their small fortunes. The heavy work in the gardens and the fields is done by the women. The relatively low status of this particular culture, the suspicious and hostile character of the Aloresians, their practice of hoarding objects of relatively little value (with its anal-erotic overtones) begins to make sense when we consider the loveless upbringing of the children. The behaviour of primitive cultures is comparable to the behaviour of those individuals in Western Civilisation whose primary needs have been frustrated. The upbringing of the Comanche Indians was very different. They were taught from infancy that they must not repress their aggressions (like the Aloresians) but on the contrary must direct them outwards on to their environment. The result was that

[1] *Malinowski* may be regarded as one of Kardiner's precursors, since he too did not restrict himself to ethnological descriptions of the life of primitive cultures but also attempted to interpret them in psychological terms.

[2] See A. Kardiner, *The Individual and his Society*, New York, 1939, and *The Psychological Frontiers of Society*, New York, 1945; M. Mead, *Man and Woman*, New York, 1953; R. Linton, *The Science of Man in the World Crisis*, New York, 1945.

over a long period of time the Comanche were famed as a warrior tribe, who inspired fear in their enemies, enriched themselves at the expense of their neighbours and lived off war.

Of course no answer is given to the question—which Adler had already posed—as to what comes first: the culture or the particular upbringing of which the culture is a logical correlate. Kardiner does not in fact put this question. Instead he tries to elucidate the multiplicity of possible relationships between the shaping of childhood, the gratification of primary needs and the particular type of culture concerned and to make these more intelligible to Western readers by drawing comparisons with Western civilization.

I

JANE PEARCE AND SAUL NEWTON

In their joint work *The Condition of Human Growth*,[1] these two authors, both of whom are connected with Sullivan's school, have attempted to establish a developmental psychology with a minimum of hypothetical concepts. Their investigations have been conducted at the same level as those carried out by *Schultz-Hencke* and *Karen Horney* but differ from them in that they avoid any polemical or critical confrontation with Freud. Pearce and Newton also differ from Sullivan in that they do not subscribe to his Behaviourist simplifications (reflex theories of human behaviour).

The 'self-system' is the basis of the great majority of personal experiences. Certain experiences, however, are excluded. But those which are included are arranged in a logical system which serves to maintain the individual's illusions about himself and the world in which he lives throughout the whole of his life. Quite apart from its capacity as an agent of 'repression', however, the self-system also fulfils those functions which are connected with the productive gratification of wishes and drives in as far as these are experienced by the individual concerned in a state of total awareness. Thus the self-system is seen to possess a polar structure from the outset: on the one hand it excludes anything that might question its validity, whilst on the other hand it promotes and develops productive forces. The *need for security*—cf. *Sullivan*—is regarded as the principal factor in deciding which elements would threaten the security of the self-system and must therefore be excluded from it. Parental influences are directly integrated in the self-system, which differs from the self-image, i.e. the symbolic condensation of the self-system, in as far as it cuts off disagreeable influences.

[1] Pearce & Newton, *The Condition of Human Growth*, New York, 1963.

'Central paranoia' is at the heart of all neurotic distorted attitudes and neuroses. Its foundations are laid in childhood and it constitutes the sum-total of the illusions which are maintained by the self-system and the self-image. Central paranoia develops into a cultural phenomenon of universal proportions.

Tensions between antithetical tendencies arise within the self-system if the individual's need for security imposes severe restrictions on his sense of awareness, thus stunting his original tendency towards growth and maturity, if, over and above this, ungratified wishes oppose his need for security and finally if, as a result of his need for security, all the other factors involved in his development are allowed to atrophy. By way of an example Pearce and Newton quote some—but not all—of the influences which a frustrated or anxious mother may exercise on the child's need for security, whilst scarcely making any mention at all of the father, a fact which would surely illustrate the practice whereby the father tends to be excluded more and more from his child's upbringing. Pearce and Newton consider that the important factors in the evaluation of the self-system—as opposed to the importance of the need for security —are self-respect and the respect of other people, the ability to communicate and empathy. Evaluating factors, communication and productivity are described in greater detail above all in respect of the learning process and of the dependence of this process on the mother's attitude. Any deficiency in mother love, let alone an aggressive attitude on the part of the mother towards her child, is incorporated into the self-system in the images of the 'bad' and the 'chaotic' mother (in contrast to the 'good' mother), a process which, although outlined only in very general terms by Pearce and Newton, none the less corresponds to *Melanie Klein*'s conception. It is above all the 'bad' mother who is the cause of severe integrative disturbances at a later stage, of so-called 'hostile integration' and of the emergence of central paranoia, which appears in the form of an autonomous system that grows more and more self-contained. In this connection it is perhaps apposite to consider Pearce and Newton's definition of the integrated personality, which is as follows:

'The integral personality is the dynamic organization of all conscious and unconscious experiences in the individual. This organization of the personality is directed towards the extension of experience and the gratification of wishes ... Integral personality is selective, it promotes development where development, due to blockages, is most urgently required.'[1]

When this integral system breaks down the 'central paranoia', which

1 *The Condition of Human Growth*, p. 21.

until then had maintained the condition of self-deception within the integral system, is made manifest and develops into a dominant and hence psychotic system.

Acting on these premises, which represent a developmental conception of psychology, the authors describe various illnesses with reference to clinical case histories according to the degree of disintegration of the self-system or of the self-image. They also give a detailed description of their therapy, which is directed from the outset towards the establishment of improved communication (empathy) between doctor and patient with the object of overcoming the patient's 'central paranoia' by making up for the frustration of his earlier needs for love.

Pearce and Newton's book may be summed up as a product of Neo-Freudianism as follows:

1. The main burden of human development is placed on ego psychology which reappears here, unencumbered by the hypotheses of libido development, in the form of the self-system and the self-image.

2. The defence mechanisms and repression are amalgamated under the heading of 'central paranoia'. The dualism between the repressing agent and the repressed content reappears in the contrast between the self-system and 'central paranoia', although it would seem that Pearce and Newton regard the latter as an integrated component of the personality and certainly not as identical with Freud's 'id' in its capacity as the seat of the wishes and drives.

3. Sexuality and the father problem (Oedipus complex) no longer have any part to play. The principal drive is not sexuality but the need for security. Even the drives described by *Adler* (power drive) and *Schultz-Hencke* are given only marginal consideration.

4. Inadequate mother love is looked upon as the primary factor underlying neuroses and psychoses.

K

ERNEST G. SCHACHTEL

Ernest G. Schachtel's detailed investigation in his work on *Metamorphosis*[1] has afforded American psychiatry access to (*a*) the latest findings of the research being carried out into the instincts, (*b*) neurobiological research in the field of perception and motility and (*c*) existential analysis. Schachtel's views coincide in various important respects with

[1] Ernest G. Schachtel, Metamorphosis: *On the Development of Affect, Perception, Attention, Memory.* London, 1963.

those of the present author, especially in respect of his criticism of Freud's basic principles.

Schachtel considers that the fundamental structure of human reality lies in the conflict between man's embeddedness in a particular environment and the realization of his available powers. This conflict is grounded in the developmental structure of human existence, which has already been described by *von Gebsattel* and *M. Scheler*; it was of course Max Scheler who derived the feeling of temporalness from capacity (powers). Neuroses are disturbances of man's potential self-realization and actualization. But this idea, which Schachtel holds in common with *Rank*, *Horney* and *Fromm*, is one which he succeeds in subjecting to a detailed analysis without succumbing to the dangers of vague generalization.

Schachtel criticizes the *Freudian* theory of affects, according to which affects are primarily a pathological product of conflicting sensations (feelings), in three respects: (1) Freud's interpretation of the affects was based on the processes involved in hysterical fits, (2) actions and affects were diametrically opposed to one another in respect of the influence they exercise on the environment, (3) Freud neglected to consider the positive influence exercized by the affects on the environment, which is of great importance for the establishment and integration of environmental relationships. Schachtel considers that the active movements made by the child in the so-called oral phase, when it searches for and sucks at its mother's breast, constitute an important affect—one which orthodox Freudians are prone to underestimate— since the infant is in fact making a possitive attempt to communicate. The orthodox view of the affects as the outcome of pathogenic conflicts is not borne out by those affects which are intent on active participation and are a necessary component of human existence. Their importance lies in their capacity for establishing a relationship between the individual and his environment.

Schachtel then proceeds to enumerate two different categories of affects: those which enable the infant to indulge its phantasy and to adapt its behaviour in such a way as will enable it to continue in its intra-uterine existence and those which induce the infant actively to intervene in and to reshape its environment. The first category reinforces man's tendency towards embeddedness, whilst the second promotes his self-realization.

'While the activity-affects culminate in the feeling of relatedness (openness and responsiveness) in the ongoing processes of the person's encounter with the world and with his fellow men, the embeddedness-affects result from wishes and attempts to remain, at least partly, in a state of quasi-uterine embeddedness and from rejecting and resenting the relatively separate existence in the post-natal state.'[1]

Schachtel demonstrates the limitations of the Freudian principle of pleasure and displeasure, which quite simply fails to cater for a whole range of feelings, by considering it with reference to emotions such as joy, hope and fear.

By analogy with his theory of affects Schachtel also enumerates two categories of perception, the autocentric and the allocentric, which are based on a thorough analysis of both ontogenesis and existential analysis. Autocentric perception is subjective and refers to the ego, whilst allocentric perception refers to the objective world. In autocentric perception there is little objectification, the tactile, olfactory or visual qualities of the senses tend to merge and perception is of a passive nature. By contrast, allocentric perception tends towards objectification and it proceeds more by way of knowledge than by way of sensation. If autocentric perception gains the ascendancy, a neurotic distorted attitude will develop, which forms a counterpart to the affect of 'embeddedness'. This will prevent the individual concerned from perceiving objects divorced from himself and from establishing contact with them by means of empathy and will develop into 'secondary autocentricity' if that which is perceived is regarded simply in terms of exploitation or anxiety. Allocentric perception, on the other hand, transcends the utilitarian and conventional world and is able to break through to 'reality' by virtue of its ability fully to infer the elements of the world which are potentially present in autocentric sensation. And so, like those affects which are intent on 'active participation', it too serves the cause of self-actualization.

Perception of the world may be distorted in three different ways, thus giving rise to three distorted attitudes:

1. The distorted attitude of the 'pseudo-realist' who, as an 'all-round man', is able to answer any question that is put to him but who in fact only scratches the surface of reality in his transit through the world.

2. The distorted attitude of the 'pseudo-detached' person who, if he is a scientist, will believe, for example, that he lives in a completely objective world and that he himself is quite detached, whereas in actual fact, due to excessive intellectualization, he is simply isolated and severely impaired in respect of his ability to establish contact.

3. The distorted attitude of the aesthete, who lives in a world of images, in which, by 'diluting' reality, he establishes aesthetics (semblance) in its place and avoids any real meeting.

[1] Ernest G. Schachtel, Metamorphosis: pp. 74–5.

Schachtel also argues that memory and the difficulties encountered by many people in recalling their childhood are in part determined by affective and perception factors. The great dearth of genuine childhood memories is due in no small measure to the 'conventionalization' of memory by environmental influences. The creative way in which the child first perceived its world is subjected to a conventional 'patterning' in the course of its upbringing and education with the result that the child is denied access to its earliest memories. Schachtel regards perception as as a creative process, which is analogous to the 'playful' way in which young children take in and transform their world by means of perception and phantasy, but which is accessible in this particular form only to the artist and the contemplative personality. Not regression —as postulated by *Freud* and *Kris*—but progression is the basis of artistic perception.

L

THERAPY IN THE NEO-FREUDIAN SCHOOLS (THE PROBLEM OF 'CONFORMITY')

Since the Neo-Freudians accorded greater importance to actual conflicts (with superiors, parents, husband or wife, etc.) than did the Freudians, it is not surprising that in their therapeutic method they were less interested in the past, i.e. in the possible sources of neurotic faulty actions, which was the chief sphere of Freudian therapy, than in the present. As a result of this tendency towards actualities they were labelled as 'conformists' by the Freudians (cf. Adorno's comments p. 519 ff.). In this context 'conformity' meant that in Neo-Freudian therapy the patient was not required to make the 'ultimate' confrontation with his most secret wishes or with his defence and escape mechanisms. The self-knowledge which he acquired through the (superficial) analysis of the actual conflicts and situations in which he found himself was of a limited, intellectual order, which merely enabled him to adapt his behaviour to suit particular situations which would otherwise give rise to conflict. The emphasis laid on adaptation to prevailing social conditions by the various Neo-Freudian schools in the United States (especially those those of Horney, Sullivan and F. Alexander) bears out this Freudian accusation of 'conformist tendencies' to some extent. But it should be borne in mind in this respect that Freud's therapeutic aim of rendering the patient 'capable of work and pleasure' is also conformist. (When von Weizsaecker asked what the 'capacity for work and pleasure' in the Vienna of 1900 actually meant he was making a perfectly valid criticism of these concepts). The Neo-Freudians might well argue that their conformism is far less time-consuming that Freudian conformism, since by incorporating advisory and pedagogic measures into their therapy they restore the patient's capacity for work and pleasure more speedily. In the Neo-Freudian submission it would appear unnecessary to trace back to its roots in early childhood a neurosis which has broken out in the form of an acute conflict in order to restore to the patient his lost control over the situation (i.e. marriage or profession) in which that conflict appeared. Thus in the light of their declared aim of enabling the patient to reassert his control over his neurotic symptoms as quickly as possible we find the Neo-Freudians less favourably disposed towards the lengthy procedures of free association, dream analysis and trans-ference analysis. The patient acquires his intellectual knowledge of the (possible) cause of his conflicts and neurotic distorted attitudes from the therapist in the course of their conversations. The patient is also encouraged to train and exercise his will in order to prove his ability to cope with his anxieties at the earliest possible moment, from which it naturally follows that Neo-Freudian therapy assumes a more advisory and pedagogic character. The accusation of conformist tendencies is justified in as far as the patient runs the risk of failing to come to terms with himself, of failing to probe his really basic problems and of accepting instead a ready-made social, conventional and moral 'pattern' on which to base his behaviour. In Freudian terms this means that the conscious sections of the personality, i.e. ego and super-ego, are strengthened without any attempt being made to come to terms with the 'id'. Within the Neo-Freudian schools the group led by *Schultz-Hencke* is to some extent an exception to this general rule. This group is more conservative and follows the Freudian therapeutic methods more closely, employing both free association and dream interpretation but making relatively little use of the analysis of the transference relationship. However, even this group is inclined to rouse the patient to independent activity at an early stage and the stress which it lays on acts of will and demonstrations of co-operation on the part of the patient is not inconsiderable.

PART TWO

PHILOSOPHICALLY ORIENTED
THEORIES OF DEPTH PSYCHOLOGY

A
C. G. JUNG

Next to Freud C. G. Jung must surely be considered the most important personality within the various schools of depth psychology. Fundamentally opposed to Freud's scientific-mechanistic conceptions C. G. Jung endeavours to interpret human behaviour and existence in terms of philosophy on the one hand and religious mysticism on the other, whilst at the same time attempting to place them on a scientific (empirical) basis. In support of his conceptions of the human psyche Jung draws on the mythological and alchemical teachings, to which he has devoted a great deal of attention in the course of his extensive life's work, especially over the past three decades. He is not so much concerned with sick people, with their psychopathology and cure, as with the question of self-knowledge as such, self-knowledge conceived in terms of 'Become the man you are' and directed at the very roots of human personality.

(a) The Libido Theory

Just as for Freud the Libido became a general concept for the sexual tendencies in man—irrespective of whether these tendencies displayed the characteristics of full sexual feelings such as appear after puberty or of the less specific emotions of childhood—so for Jung Libido simply meant psychic energy. The break between Jung and Freud came about as a result of their discussion of the libido concept, although it had been threatening for some time before and although—just as with Freud and Adler—personal differences also played their part. However, in their discussion of the libido economy in psychosis (schizophrenia) Freud himself, so Jung tells us, no longer insisted on the equation of the libido with the sexual drive. On that occasion Freud had equated the libido with the concept of interest, because he considered that the loss of reality in schizophrenics was due to the diversion of the libido (interest) from the outside world (see p. 114 ff.).

On the one hand Jung doubts whether this explanation does justice to the profound change which takes place in the psychotic's sense of reality, whilst on the other hand he points out that the concept of interest can be traced back to sources 'other than' purely sexual ones, that in fact in this particular instance Freud is using the libido in a wider sense. He has stated his own attitude to this question:

'Earlier in the *Psychology of Dementia Praecox* I made use of the term "psychic energy", because what is lacking in this disease is evidently more than erotic interest as such. If one tried to explain the loss of

321

relationship, the schizophrenic disassociation between man and world, purely by the recession of eroticism, the inevitable result would be to inflate the idea of sexuality in a typically Freudian manner. One would then be forced to say that every relationship in the world was in essence a sexual relationship, and the idea of sexuality would be deprived of all meaning.'[1]

In order to understand the nature of Jung's libido concept, which, in 'the form of energy', is considered to be the basis of all psychic impulses, it will be necessary to consider the following points:

1. The libido develops out of the procreative drive.
2. It is 'freed' as a result of the fructification of the egg by the sperm-cell.
3. It is an instinctive action (building of nest).
4. In the course of man's phylogenetic development it is sublimated from the level of the procreative drive for cultural purposes.
5. It is the will and actions determined by the will (in which it is presumably diametrically opposed to the instincts).
6. It is affect and emotion, productive or destructive.
7. It is both conscious and unconscious.
8. It is subject to all drive impulses but it is not itself a drive.
9. It affords its own symbolic representation.
10. It can regress, be blocked, channelled, projected or introjected, it can become inflated, is on occasions repressed, split or transformed, it will sink back into the collective unconscious, it can be tamed and even stored.

In order to describe the power of the libido to afford its own symbolic representation Jung has recourse to numerous examples of myths and authors of antiquity, which cannot really be said to furnish proof of his argument, in as far as their primary purpose is to illustrate Jung's specific method of 'amplification' (see below). For Jung symbols of light, of fire, of force, such as were attributed to the sun or the sun God in mythology, are indications that the libido is synonymous with cosmic energy. Even the cosmogonic Eros of Hesiod, the figure of 'Phanes' (Orphic), the figure of Kama, the Indian God of Love (*inter alia*) are, in Jung's view, incarnations of the libido, of energy, which is both cosmic and biological, physical and spiritual. In order to free the libido from the (unclear) burdens of a theory of drives Jung defines it in the following way, revealing in the process his conception of the origin of neuroses.

'The energetic standpoint has the effect of freeing psychic energy from

---

[1] *Symbols of Transformation*, Collected Works of C. G. Jung, London, Routledge & Kegan Paul; New York, Pantheon Books; Vol. 5, p. 135.

the bonds of a too narrow definition. Experience shows that instinctual processes of whatever kind are often intensified to an extraordinary degree by an afflux of energy, no matter where it comes from. This is true not only of sexuality but of hunger and thirst too. One instinct can temporarily be depotentiated in favour of another instinct, and this is true of psychic activities in general. To assume that it is always and only sexuality which is subject to these depotentiates would be a sort of psychic equivalent of the phlogiston theory in physics and chemistry. Freud himself was somewhat sceptical about the existing theories of instinct, and rightly so. Instinct is a very mysterious manifestation of life, partly psychic and partly physiological by nature. It is one of the most conservative functions in the psyche and is extremely difficult. if not impossible, to change. Psychological maladjustments, such as the neuroses, are therefore more easily explained by the patient's attitude to instinct than by a sudden change in the latter. But the patient's attitude is a complicated psychological problem, which it certainly would not be if his attitude depended on instinct. The motive forces at the back of neurosis come from all sorts of congenital characteristics and environmental influences, which together build up an attitude that makes it impossible for him to lead a life in which the instincts are satisfied. Thus the neurotic perversion of instinct in a young person is ultimately tied up with a similar disposition in the parents, and the disturbance in the sexual sphere is a secondary and not a primary phenomenon. Hence there can be no sexual theory of neurosis, though there may very well be a psychological one.'[1]

(b) Dynamics of the Libido and Self-regulation

With his libido theory Jung aspires to a monistic conception of the psyche, which extends from the individual via nature to the Cosmos and which no longer has anything in common with the development of the libido within specific phases (oral, anal, phallic). The dynamic processes within the libido, for which Jung also uses the terms regression, projection, split (see 10. Def. of libido), do not originate, as they do with Freud, in the antithesis between pleasure and displeasure. If a Freudian patient regresses, then he does so because his libido has been subjected to internal or external inhibitions and experiences certain denials. Freud's libido economy is determined on the one hand by pleasure and displeasure but more specifically by defence against anxiety and by the defence exercised by the defence mechanisms at the disposal of the patient (see A. Freud p. 205 ff.). The antithesis of pleasure and displeasure, which is a crucial part of Freud's theory, is given only marginal

[1] C. G. Jung, ibid., pp. 138–9.

consideration by Jung. Denial processes, which, according to Freud, influence and determine the specificity of the neuroses, are for Jung only of secondary importance. The dynamic processes at work in the libido, as seen by Jung, are comparable to a closed system of communicating tubes through which the energies are driven by means of a self-regulating 'motor'. In Freud's view the libido economy inside the communicating tubes is determined by the conditions prevailing at the open ends of the tubular system: pleasure and displeasure. Excessive pressure ('displeasure') exerted from without is transmitted through the entire system and can, if the pressure remains unadjusted, cause one of the tubes to burst, and this—*cum grano salis*—would constitute a symptom. With C. G. Jung there is no direct connection between the system and the outside world that could in any way exercise a decisive influence on the internal pressures. The system is a closed one and it is self-regulating. This principle of 'self-regulation' Jung also calls 'compensation'. He defines it as follows:

'The more one-sided his conscious attitude is, and the further it deviates from the optimum, the greater becomes the possibility that vivid dreams with a strongly contrasting but purposive content will appear as an expression of the self-regulation of the psyche.'[1]

'It is only through our knowledge of the conscious condition that we are able to decide how to characterize the unconscious contents ... The relationship between consciousness and the dream is very finely balanced ... In this sense the compensation theory may be considered to be a fundamental rule for psychic behaviour as such.'[2]

In terms of Freud's theory of the importance of pleasure and displeasure for the psychic processes the concept of the self-regulation of the psyche means that in point of fact only an inordinate degree of displeasure could ever disturb the self-regulatory process. And even this conceivable disturbance would only be of the shortest possible duration. If, for example, the individual concerned were to lapse into psychosis, having been driven to it by experiences of extreme displeasure, then even in psychosis some form of equilibrium would be restored. The power wielded by the collective images over the individual psychotic would be the characteristic of this state of equilibrium. From this it follows that with Jung the dynamics of the libido can never have an indeterminate result, one that might be understood as deriving from the intensity of the opposed forces as, for example, drive and repression. Be they regression, inflation, projection or introjection of the libido, these pro-

[1] C. G. Jung, Coll. Wks., Vol. 8, p. 253, London.
[2] C. G. Jung, 'Wirklichkeit der Seele, 'Psychol. Abhandlungen, Zürich, 1947, Vol. IV, p. 90.

cesses, although conceived by Jung as dynamic 'modes of action', are 'transformations and symbols of the libido', i.e. the automatous wheel of psychic energy drives them either backwards or forwards, transfers images to the outside world or carries images from the outside world back into the psyche. This system of dynamics may be compared to the closed circuit of an electric railway, in which the current (the libido) drives the train through self-regulating points around the Outer Circle or into the station, into the sheds or through the tunnels. For Jung dynamics means 'modes of action'. What it does not mean is that individual forces confront and test each other.

(c) The Structure of the Psyche
(i) The Collective Unconscious

If the dynamics of the libido are controlled by self-regulation and compensation, then we are entitled to ask in this respect to what extent Jung is reporting his observations and to what extent he is putting forward hypotheses. In his book, *The Relations Between the Ego and the Unconscious*[1] he describes a woman patient who, in the course of her analysis, transferred to an extreme degree her infantile wishes and longings for the all-powerful and superior father on to the analyst—Jung. It proved impossible to dissolve this transference by rational considerations and Jung asked himself:

'What was the source of this obstinacy and what was its purpose. That it must have some purposive meaning I was convinced, for there is no truly living thing that does not have a final meaning, that can in other words be explained as a mere left-over from antecedent facts. But the energy of the transference is so strong that it gives one the impression of a vital instinct. That being so, what is the purpose of such phantasies? A careful examination and analysis of the dreams, especially of the one just quoted, revealed a very marked tendency—in contrast to conscious criticism, which always seeks to reduce things to human proportions—to endow the person of the doctor with superhuman attributes. He had to be gigantic, primordial, huger than the father, like the wind that sweeps over the earth—was he then to be made into a god? Or, I said to myself, was it rather the case that the unconscious was trying to "create" a god out of the person of the doctor, as it were to free a vision of God from the veils of the personal, so that the transference to the person of the doctor was no more than a misunderstanding on the part of the conscious mind, a stupid trick played by "sound common sense"? Was the urge of the unconscious perhaps only apparently reaching out towards the person, but in a

[1] Darmstadt, 1928.

deeper sense towards a god? Could the longing for a god be a "passion" welling up from our darkest, instinctual nature, a passion unswayed by any outside influences, deeper and stronger perhaps than the love for a human person? Or was it perhaps the highest and truest meaning of that inappropriate love we call transference, a little bit of real "Gottesminne", that has been lost to consciousness ever since the fifteenth century?'[1]

After he had informed his patient of this view, although she did not accept his thesis out of hand, he was none the less able to observe in subsequent dreams that the God-father transference was being increasingly undermined; at the same time the patient withdrew from the analysis.

Jung believes that what he observed in this connection was the self-regulation of the libido within the psyche, in as far as an autonomous process, one which had developed out of itself, permitted the patient to 'outgrow' the inappropriateness of her attachment. A Freudian would have interpreted the process described by Jung as follows: (1) The patient had sacrificed her personal wishes out of consideration for the physician. (2) She had entered into another, real-life relationship, on to which she had continued to transfer her wishes and phantasies. But even if we accept that self-regulation was observable in the process described above, then we shall still want to know the answer to a further question, namely, how this self-regulation is brought about. It is guided by the archetypes, which emerge from the collective unconscious and, as it were, take control of the psyche. Jung continues his argument as follows:

'This change took place, as I showed, through the unconscious development of a transpersonal control-point; a virtual goal, as it were, that expressed itself symbolically in a form which can only be described as a vision of God. The dreams swelled the human person of the doctor to super-human proportions, making him a gigantic, primordial father who is at the same time the wind, and in whose protecting arms the dreamer rests like an infant. If we try to make the patient's conscious and traditionally Christian idea of God responsible for the divine image in the dreams, we would still have to lay stress on the distortion. In religious matters the patient had a critical and agnostic attitude, and her idea of a possible deity had long since passed into the realm of the inconceivable, i.e. had dwindled into a complete abstraction. In contrast to this, the God-image of the dreams corresponded to the archaic conception of a nature-daemon, something like Wotan. Θεὸς τὸ πνεῦμα, "God is spirit', is here translated back into its original form where πνεῦμα means "wind": God is the wind, stronger and mightier than man, an

[1] C. G. Jung, Coll. Wks., London, Vol. 7, p. 130.

invisible breath-spirit. As in the Hebrew "ruah", so in Arabic "ruh" means breath and spirit.[1] Out of the purely personal form the dreams develop an archaic god-image that is infinitely far from the conscious idea of God.'[2]

Jung's observation in respect of this patient of the manifestation of primitive, archaic symbols, a manifestation whose systematic occurrence he claims to have noted in other patients as well, led him to assume the existence of a layer in the unconscious which has stored and passed on all human experiences in symbolic form (Archetype) for as long as man can remember. This layer is common to all mankind and is therefore collective. He defines this layer as follows:

'The collective unconscious is the whole spiritual heritage of mankind's evolution born anew in the ... structure of each individual.[3]

But according to Jung the collective unconscious does not only contain those archaic images and symbols which are the decisive factor in the self-regulation of the psyche and whose origin Jung imagines to be phylogenetic. In his later works (from 1920 onwards) Jung also attributes drives, affects and emotions to the collective unconscious. Over and above this it incorporates strange foreign substances, relics of the most distant past, which the ego can never overcome or assimilate, and which can occasionally enter into consciousness in visions and ecstacies, in psychoses or neuroses.

(ii) *The Personal Unconscious and the Ego*

For Jung the libido is undifferentiated and autonomous, attributes which might equally well be applied to the collective unconscious. For the collective unconscious regulates the psyche largely autonomously, it is undifferentiated, it contains in the form of a precipitate the sum-total of human experience—including the individual's typical patterns of behaviour. Jung contrasts the collective unconscious with the personal unconscious, which has been incorrectly equated by Jungians (e.g. Jacobi) with Freud's unconscious. It can, however, at most correspond to Freud's preconscious, because for Freud the unconscious is a primary process and as such is incapable of being raised into consciousness. Jung defines this personal unconscious in the following passage and in doing so he again reveals his views on the nature of compensation and neurosis. For him neurosis is simply the need to render conscious through the torments of illness certain unconscious portions of the psyche.—Com-

[1] For a fuller elaboration of this theme see *Symbols of Transformation*, Coll. Wks. Vol. 5, Index under 'wind'.
[2] C. G. Jung, Coll. Wks., London, Vol. 7, p. 132.
[3] *Ibid.*, Vol. 8, p. 158.

pensation is implicit in this need, which in turn is a consequence of self-regulation.

'From what has been said it is clear that we have to distinguish in the unconscious a layer which we may call the "personal unconscious". The materials contained in this layer are of a personal nature in so far as they have the character partly of acquisitions derived from the individual's life and partly of psychological factors which could just as well be unconscious. It is readily understandable that incompatible psychological elements are liable to repression and therefore become unconscious; but on the other hand we also have the possibility of making and keeping the repressed contents conscious, once they have been recognized. We recognize them as personal contents because we can discover their effects, or their partial manifestation, or their specific origin in our personal past.'[1]

But where exactly does the ego stand in respect of the persona and the collective unconscious? It is extraordinarily difficult to define the position of the ego in Jung's conception, because, in his endeavours to get away from Freud's terminology, he created his own concepts and for this reason gives only marginal consideration to the ego concept. Even the question as to whether Jung considers the ego to be conscious or unconscious is capable of both a positive and a negative answer in either respect. The fact that the ego is inadequately defined does not, however, prevent it from constituting a decisive factor in Jung's 'Heilsweg' (the way of healing and the way of salvation), which is individuation. In one of his latest works Jung defines the position of the ego as follows:

'For it appears that the ego consciousness is dependent on two factors: firstly, on the conditions of the collective, alternatively social, consciousness, and secondly on the unconscious collective dominants, alternatively archetypes. These latter fall phenomenologically into two categories, on the one hand into the sphere of the drives and on the other into the archetypal sphere. The former represents the natural impulses, the latter those dominants which enter into consciousness in the form of general ideas . . . The contrast between the collective consciousness and the collective unconscious, which is the precise point where the subject finds himself placed, is almost incapable of being bridged.'[2] In the *Psychological Types* (1921) he defines the ego as follows: 'Under the ego I understand a complex of ideas, which constitutes the centre of my

---

[1] C. G. Jung, Coll. Wks., London, Vol. 7, p. 133.
[2] *Ibid.*, Vol. 8, pp. 217–18.

sphere of consciousness and which appears to me to show a high degree of continuity and identity within itself.'[1]

(iii) *The Collective Psyche and the Persona*

Jung uses the concept 'collective psyche' to summarize the immediate expression of the collective unconscious. He defines it as follows:

'The universal similarity of the brain yields the universal possibility of a similar mental functioning. This functioning is the collective psyche. In so far as differentiations exist that correspond to race, tribe or even family, there exist also a collective psyche limited to race, tribe or family over and above the "universal" collective psyche. To borrow an expression from Janet, the collective psyche comprises "les parties inférieures" of the psychic functions, that is to say, the deep-rooted, well-nigh automatic, hereditary elements that are ubiquitously present, hence the impersonal or transpersonal portions of the individual psyche. Consciousness plus the personal unconscious constitutes "les parties supérieures" of the psychic functions, those portions, therefore, that are ontogenetically acquired and developed.'[2]

According to this definition the individual develops, if he develops at all, in opposition to the community or to the 'collective psyche'. Just as the chief of a primitive tribe will on occasions put on a mask (persona), in order to set himself apart from the other members of the tribe, and to this day high-ranking officials and military men adopt special forms of dress in order to distinguish themselves from the 'collective', so the personality makes use of the persona in order to establish a line of demarcation between itself and its environment. (Jung does not necessarily understand under personality an individual who has passed through the process of individuation—although here too there is no hard-and-fast rule.) The development of the persona (mask) amongst primitive people contributes not least to the building up of prestige. Without an audience, however, prestige is not possible. Consequently the persona must always remain a compromise between the personality and its audience, which is the collective, the collective psyche. In other words the persona is a 'segment of the collective psyche'. C. G. Jung defines the persona as follows:

'This arbitrary segment of collective psyche—often fashioned with considerable pains—I have called the "persona"! The word "persona" is really a very appropriate expression for it, since it originally meant the mask worn by an actor, signifying the role he played. For, if we hazard

---

[1] C. G. Jung, *Psychological Types*, London, Routledge & Kegan Paul; New York, Pantheon Books; 1923, p. 540.
[2] C. G. Jung, Coll. Wks., Vol. 7, pp. 1444-5.

the attempt to distinguish exactly between what is to be regarded as personal, and what as impersonal, psychic material, we soon find ourselves in the greatest dilemma because, fundamentally speaking, we are bound to admit that what we said of the collective unconscious is also true of the persona's contents, that is, they are of a general character. Only by reason of the fact that the persona is a more or less accidental or arbitrary segment of collective psyche can we make the mistake of accepting it *in toto* as something "individual". But, as its name shows, it is only a mask for the collective psyche, a mask that "feigns individuality", and tries to make others and oneself believe that one is individual, whereas one is simply playing a part in which the collective psyche speaks.

'When we analyse the persona we strip off the mask, and discover that what seemed to be individual is at bottom collective; in other words, that the persona was only a mask for the collective psyche. Fundamentally the persona is nothing real: it is a compromise between individual and society as to what a man should appear to be. He takes a name, earns a title, represents an office, he is this or that. In a certain sense all this is real, yet in relation to the essential individuality of the person concerned it is only a secondary reality, a product of compromise, in making which others often have a greater share than he. The persona is a semblance, a two-dimensional reality, to give it a nick-name.'[1]

It cannot be maintained that Jung's derivation of the persona is based exclusively on empirical facts. Jung's thought processes follow even more tortuous paths than do those of Freud or his disciples (see also W. Reich, K. Abraham and A. Freud), who interpret certain characteristics as a compromise between drive and repression and call this compromise (in certain circumstances) a 'façade' of the neurotic character. The persona concept is not only supposed to define the character of the individual, it is also supposed to embrace his function in the community as well. Indeed, it is intended to be quite as comprehensive a concept as that of the libido or the collective unconscious. A doctor, for example, is said to have a typical 'persona', i.e. his particular professional manner, the same as a parson or a counter clerk. Jung's observation that this manner is determined to a considerable degree by the expectations of the community—which would, for example, expect a parson to behave with dignity and decorum—is a true one, and it is also true that Freud and his followers have paid too little attention to this particular function of the individual. The problematical nature of the 'persona', which in fact tells us no more than that high office is a mere semblance, the relationship—

[1] C. G. Jung, Coll. Wks., Vol. Vol. 7, pp. 155–6.

not entirely clarified—of the persona to the character and its development, which also incorporates much that is 'typical' and is capable of
adjusting to the collective, can only be understood in terms of the
Jungian method of 'amplification' (see above), in which a *single* observation is supplemented by further material.

Is it now possible to determine the position occupied by the ego (see
above, p. 328) in relationship to the personal unconscious, the collective
unconscious and the persona? Jung describes the persona as a 'cloak
around the ego', from which it follows that the ego is veiled by the
persona, concealed by it.—A man who has largely identified with his
rank hides his 'actual ego' behind that identification.

J. Jacobi writes of the ego:

'Beyond our ego lies not only the collective social consciousness but also
the collective unconscious, our own depths, which harbour equally
attractive figures.'[1]

From this it may be assumed that the ego is not the same as either the
persona or the collective unconscious and that it must therefore be
largely identical with the personal unconscious.

(iv) *The Freeing of the Individuality from the Collective Psyche*
The freeing of individuality from the collective psyche is the purpose of
individuation.

'Individuation means becoming a single homogeneous being, and, in as
far as "individuality" embraces our innermost, last and incomparable
uniqueness, it also implies becoming "one's own self". We could therefore translate individuation as "coming to selfhood" or "self-realization".[2] The aim of individuation is nothing less than to divest the self of
the false wrappings of the persona on the one hand and the suggestive
power of primordial images on the other.'[3]

What Jung understands under individuality cannot be clarified to an
extent that would permit of an exact definition, especially as regards the
question of whether individuality and the ego are identical. 'Become the
man you are' is the philosophical requirement underlying these concepts
and Jung sets about the task of presenting this requirement in terms of a
psychological process. Due to the self-regulation and compensation of
the psyche a person who, for example, professes a purely rational and
conscious attitude runs the risk of being swamped one day by the pent-

---

[1] Jolande Jacobi, *The Psychology of C. G. Jung*, London, Routledge & Kegan
Paul; U.S.A., Yale University Press; 1962, p. 30.
[2] C. G. Jung, Coll. Wks., Vol. 7, p. 171.   [3] *Ibid.*, p. 172.

up, unconscious contents of his libido. This inflation of the collective unconscious leads to psychosis, if the conscious mind—ego or individuality—is unable to assimilate or adapt the unconscious contents.

'A collapse of the conscious attitude is no small matter. It always feels like the end of the world, as though everything had tumbled back into original chaos. One feels delivered up, disoriented, like a rudderless ship that is abandoned to the moods of the elements. So at least it seems. In reality, however, one has fallen back upon the collective unconscious, which now takes over the leadership. We could multiply examples of cases where, at the critical moment, a "saving" thought, a vision, an "inner voice", came with an irresistible power of conviction and gave life a new direction. Probably we could mention just as many cases where the collapse meant a catastrophe that destroyed life, for at such moments morbid ideas are also liable to take root, or ideals wither away, which is no less disastrous. In the former case some psychic oddity develops, or a psychosis, i.e. a state of disorientation and demoralization. But once the unconscious contents break through into consciousness, filling it with their uncanny power of conviction, the question arises of how the individual will react. Will he be overpowered by these contents? Will he credulously accept them? Or will he reject them? (I am disregarding the ideal reaction, namely critical understanding.) The first case signifies paranoia or schizophrenia; the second may either become an eccentric with a taste for prophecy, or he may revert to an infantile attitude and be cut off from human society; the third signifies the regressive restoration of the persona.'[5]

Under the 'regressive restoration of the persona' Jung understands an inability to cope and backsliding to an 'earlier stage of development' in respect of both professional and personal matters, such as can occur if the personality is subjected to severe reverses of fortune or, alternatively, to an inflation of consciousness by unconscious contents. In this instance the freeing of the individuality from the collective psyche will have failed, the individuality will in fact regress into the collective psyche and either become psychotic or identify in a state of delusion with contents of the collective unconscious. In psychosis or in the ostentatious behaviour of prophets and eccentrics the individual concerned simply identifies with the collective psyche: he follows the call of his delusion or destiny, which means that the individual is under the direct control of the autonomous complexes of the collective unconscious. In this connection Jung also regards incest, which is the very kernel of the Freudian theory of neuroses, in a symbolic light.

[1] C. G. Jung, Coll. Wks., Vol. 7, p. 161.

'As I have shown elsewhere, there lies at the root of the regressive longing which Freud conceives as "infantile fixation" or the "incest wish" a special value and a special cogency. This is brought out in myths, where it is precisely the strongest and best man among the people, the hero, who gives way to the regressive longing and deliberately exposes himself to the danger of being devoured by the monster of the maternal abyss. He is, however, a hero only because in the final reckoning he does not allow himself to be devoured, but conquers the monster, not once but many times. The victory over the collective psyche alone yields the true value, the capture of the hoard, the invincible weapon, the magic talisman, or whatever it be that the myth deems most desirable. Therefore, whoever identifies with the collective psyche—or, in terms of the myth, lets himself be devoured by the monster—and vanishes in it, is near to the treasure that the dragon guards, but he is there by extreme constraint and to his own greatest harm.'[1]

(v) *Anima and Animus*

On the path of individuation the individuality is faced with the task of assimilating certain contents of its collective unconscious. Jung relates the whole process of individuation to the symbolic night sea journey of the hero, the descent into darkness and the capture of the hoard (Individuality). In this process human beings not only meet their shadow, which is a sort of unconscious opponent, but the man also meets his anima, the woman her animus. J. Jacobi sums up, by 'amplification', Jung's ideas on the nature of the shadow as follows:

'The first stage leads to the experience of the shadow, symbolizing our "other side", our "dark brother", who is an invisible but inseparable part of our psychic totality. For the living form needs deep shadow if it is to appear plastic. Without shadow it remains a two-dimensional phantom.'[2,3]

But what does Jung understand under the 'anima'?

'As we know, there is no human experience, nor would experience be possible at all without the intervention of a subjective aptitude. What is this subjective aptitude? Ultimately it consists of an innate psychic structure which allows man to have experiences of this kind. Thus the whole nature of man presupposes woman, both physically and spiritually. His system is tuned in to a woman from the start, just as it is prepared for a quite different world where there is water, light, air, salt, carbo-

[1] C. G. Jung, Coll. Wks., Vol. 7, pp. 167–8.   [2] *Ibid.*, pp. 236–7.
[3] J. Jacobi, *The Psychology of C. G. Jung*, p. 106.

hydrates, etc. The form of the world into which he is born is already inborn in him as a virtual image. Likewise parents, wife, children, birth and death are inborn in him as virtual images, as psychic aptitudes. These *a priori* categories have by nature a collective character; they are images of parents, wife and children in general, and are not individual predestinations. We must therefore think of these images as lacking in solid content, hence as unconscious. They only acquire solidity, influence and eventual consciousness in the encounter with empirical facts, which touch the unconscious aptitude and quicken it to life. They are in a sense the deposits of all our ancestral experiences, but they are not the experiences themselves. So at least it seems to us in the present limited state of our knowledge. (I must confess that I have never yet found infallible evidence for the inheritance of memory images, but I do not regard it as positively precluded that in addition to these collective deposits which contain nothing specifically individual, there may also be inherited memories that are individually determined.)

'An inherited collective image of woman exists in a man's unconscious, with the help of which he apprehends the nature of woman. This inherited image is the third important source for the femininity of the soul.'[1]

The anima, then, would appear to be a collective image of the woman, a collective image, however, which each man modifies in his own individual way in accordance with his personal experience and knowledge. This archetype (for def. see below), like its feminine counterpart in real life, is capable of appearing in many different forms, which are often mythological in character: elf, nix, sorceress, witch, Goddess, amazon, etc. Moreover, the archetypal images are usually of a compensatory nature: a mild effeminate man, for example, has an amazon as his anima, a strong masculine type of man might well have an elf. Jung lends to this (purely hypothetical) derivation of the anima the support of a more empirically based derivation in as far as he speaks of 'feminine qualities' of the psyche. (He avoids using Freud's term: homosexuality or homoeroticism or, alternatively, bisexuality.)

'No man is so entirely masculine that he has nothing feminine in him. The fact is, rather, that very masculine men have—carefully guarded and hidden—a very soft emotional life, often incorrectly described as "feminine". A man counts it a virtue to repress his feminine traits as much as possible, just as a woman, at least until recently, considered it unbecoming to be "mannish". The repression of feminine traits and inclinations naturally causes these contrasexual demands to accumulate in the unconscious. No less naturally, the imago of woman (the soul-

[1] C. G. Jung, Coll. Wks., Vol. 17, p. 188.

image) becomes a receptacle for these demands, which is why a man, in his love choice, is strongly tempted to win the woman who best corresponds to his own unconscious femininity—a woman, in short, who can unhesitatingly receive the projection of his soul. Although such a choice is often regarded and felt as altogether ideal, it may turn out that the man has manifestly married his own worst weakness.'[1]

The relations between a man's persona and his anima are of a similar order. For example, the man who is completely absorbed in his profession and outwardly appears to be unrelentingly stern, is often mild, submissive and sentimental in his private life. The unconscious qualities of the anima are strengthened to compensate for the conscious adjustment of his persona, which is the reason why the type of man who behaves like a tyrant at the office and gives in without as much as a whimper at home has come into being.

The purpose of individuation can only be said to have been achieved when a man is able to differentiate between himself and both his persona and his anima. (This is especially so if, as in the case of the tyrannical official, who in actual fact is henpecked, he tends to identify with his anima. One result of this might well be that a man of this type will one day turn away from the domineering woman and fall in love with some other woman, i.e. he will once again project his own anima on to a woman and then identify with it. In this case the unconscious anima image will simply have changed partners and the man will once again have become the victim of his own projections.) The task of freeing the ego from the spell of the anima follows complicated processes involving the interaction of the personal and collective unconscious, which Jung claims to have observed, not so much in his patients in a casuistic sense, as—and this above all—in investigations of mythological and alchemical parables.

Although a man has only one anima, a woman has several animi. To demonstrate the truth of this thesis, however, is an even more difficult undertaking than that concerning the existence of the anima. Jung himself admits as much:

'If it was no easy task to describe what was meant by the anima, the difficulties become almost insuperable when we set out to describe the psychology of the animus.'[2]

He derives the existence of the animus as follows:

'An inferior consciousness cannot *eo ipso* be ascribed to women; it is merely different from masculine consciousness. But, just as a woman is

[1] C. G. Jung, Coll. Wks., Vol. 17, p. 187.　　　　[2] *ibid.*, p. 204.

often clearly conscious of things which a man is still groping for in the dark, so there are naturally fields of experience in a man, which, for woman, are still wrapped in the shadows of non-differentiation, chiefly things in which she has little interest. Personal relations are as a rule more important and interesting to her than objective facts and their interconnections. The wide fields of commerce, politics, technology and science, the whole realm of the applied masculine mind, she relegates to the penumbra of consciousness; while, on the other hand, she develops a minute consciousness of personal relationships, the infinite nuances of which usually escape the man entirely.

'We must therefore expect the unconscious of woman to show aspects essentially different from those found in man. If I were to attempt to put in a nutshell the difference between man and woman in this respect, i.e. what it is that characterizes the animus as opposed to the anima, I could only say this: as the anima produces "moods", so the animus produces "opinions"; and as the moods of a man issue from a shadowy background, so the opinions of a woman rest on equally unconscious prior assumptions. Animus opinions very often have the character of solid convictions that are not lightly shaken, or of principles whose validity is seemingly unassailable. If we analyse these opinions, we immediately come upon unconscious assumptions whose existence must first be inferred: that is to say, the opinions are apparently conceived "as though" such assumptions existed. But in reality the opinions are not thought out at all; they exist ready made, and they are held so positively and with so much conviction that the woman never has the shadow of a doubt about them.'[1]

(vi) *Self-realization and the Self*

The things with which the analysand who submits to a Jungian analysis must come to terms are not only centred on the contents of the collective and the personal unconscious, of the shadow, the persona and the anima (alt. animus). The 'mana' constitutes an essential quality of the unconscious, one which can take possession of the ego in a dangerous fashion, if the ego should identify with it. For Jung 'mana' means the magic power which impinges on the images and symbols of the collective unconscious, especially of the anima. But if the analysand has succeeded in coming to terms with the anima in the sense that identification with the anima has ceased, then the mana is transferred to the ego.

'Now when the anima loses her mana, what becomes of it? Clearly the man who has mastered the anima acquires her mana, in accordance with the primitive belief that when a man kills the mana-person he assimilates his mana into his own body.

[1] C. G. Jung, Coll. Wks., Vol. 17, pp. 204-5.

'Well then: who is it that has integrated the anima? Obviously the conscious ego, and therefore the ego has taken over the mana. Thus the ego becomes a mana personality. But the mana personality is a dominant of the collective unconscious, the recognized archetype of the mighty man in the form of hero, chief, magician, medicine man, saint, the ruler of men and spirits, the friend of God. This masculine collective figure who now rises out of the dark background and takes possession of the conscious personality entails a psychic danger of a subtle nature, for by inflating the conscious mind it can destroy everything that was gained by coming to terms with the anima. It is therefore of no little practical importance to know that in the hierarchy of the unconscious the anima occupies the lowest rank, only one of many possible figures, and that her subjection constellates another collective figure which now takes over her mana. Actually it is the figure of the magician, as I will call it for short, who attracts the mana to himself, i.e. the autonomous valency of the anima. Only in so far as I unconsciously identify with his figure can I imagine that I myself possess the anima's mana. But I will infallibly do so under these circumstances.

'The figure of the magician has a no less dangerous equivalent in women: a sublime, matriarchal figure, the Great-Mother, the All-Merciful, who understands everything, forgives everything, who always acts for the best, living only for others and never seeking her own interests, the discoverer of the great love, just as the magician is the mouthpiece of the ultimate truth. And just as the great love is never appreciated, so the great wisdom is never understood. Neither, of course, can stand the sight of the other.

'Here is cause for serious misunderstanding, for without a doubt it is a question of inflation. The ego has appropriated something that does not belong to it. But how has it appropriated the mana? If it was really the ego that conquered the anima, then the mana does indeed belong to it, and it would be correct to conclude that one has become important. But why does not this importance, the mana, work upon others? That would surely be an essential criterion! It does not work because one has not in fact become important, but has merely become adulterated with an archetype, another unconscious figure. Hence we must conclude that the ego never conquered the anima at all and therefore has not acquired the mana. All that has happened is a new adulteration, this time with a figure of the same sex corresponding to the father-imago, and possessed of even greater power.'[1]

Only when the ego has ceased to be possessed by the mana, when it has resolved this condition, which is identical with self-adulation and

[1] C. G. Jung, Coll. Wks., Vol. 17, pp. 226-7.

self-delusion, can the ultimate stage of self-knowledge be approached. Jung describes this resolution almost exclusively in terms of mythological and alchemical symbols. The self, which is aroused and attained following the resolution of the mana condition, he then defines as follows:

'The self could be characterized as a kind of compensation for the conflict between inside and outside. This formulation would not be unfitting, since the self has somewhat the character of a result, of a goal attained, something that has come to pass very gradually and is experienced with much travail. So too the self is our life's goal, for it is the completest expression of that fateful combination we call individuality, the full flowering not only of the single individual, but of the group, in which each adds his portion to the whole. Sensing the self as something irrational, as an indefinable existent, to which the ego is neither opposed nor subjected but merely attached, and about which it revolves very much as the earth revolves around the sun—thus we come to the goal of individuation. I use the word "sensing" in order to indicate the apperceptive character of the relation between ego and self. In this relation nothing is knowable, because we can say nothing about the contents of the self. The ego is the only content of the self that we do know. The individuated ego senses itself as the object of an unknown and superordinate subject.'[1]

(vii) *Complex, Archetype, Symbol*

In her book *Complex, Archetype and Symbol* J. Jacobi has endeavoured to throw light on the problems posed by these concepts, which occur time and again in C. G. Jung's work. The authoress defines the manifold meanings of the complex in the following way:

'(*a*)   The complex is unconscious but not yet sufficiently charged with energy to be experienced as an "independent will", an autonomous entity; still, it more or less blocks the natural psychic process. It has preserved a relative connection with the totality of the psychic organization (e.g. it is manifested only in slips or other trifling symptoms).
'(*b*)   The complex is unconscious, but already so "swollen" and independent that it acts as a second ego in conflict with the conscious ego, thus placing the individual between two truths, two conflicting streams of will, and threatening to tear him in two (as, for example, in certain forms of compulsion neurosis).
'(*c*)   The "complex ego" can break completely out of the psychic

[1] C. G. Jung, Coll. Wks., Vol. 17, p. 237.

organization, split off and become autonomous. This leads to the well-known phenomenon of "dual personality" (Janet), or to a disintegration into several partial personalities according to the number and nature of the patient's unconscious complexes.

'(d) If the complex is so heavily charged as to draw the conscious ego into its sphere, overpower and engulf it, then the complex has to a greater or lesser degree become ruler in the house of the conscious ego; then we may speak of a partial or total "identification" between the ego and the complex. This phenomenon can be clearly observed in men having a mother complex or women having a father complex. Unbeknownst to them, the words, opinions, desires and strivings of the mother or father have taken possession of their ego, making it their instrument and mouthpiece. Such identity between complex and ego can of course vary in degree; it may cover only parts or the whole of the ego. In the former case, difficulties of adaptation, a relative loss of reality, psychic disorders of greater or lesser intensity will result; in the second case the unmistakable characteristics of a disastrous inflation will be manifested, as may occur, for example, in individuals, who identify themselves with God or the devil, with a child or a goblin, with political or historical figures, or all manner of animals, and in the various forms of psychosis involving partial or total loss of the ego.

'(e) Since unconscious contents are experienced only in projected form, the unconscious complex appears first in projection as an attribute of an outward object or person. If the unconscious complex is so markedly "split off" as to take on the character of an entity (often of a menacing nature) assailing the individual from outside, or if it appears as an attribute of an object of outward reality, such sumptoms occur as may be observed in persecution mania, paranoia, etc. This object may either belong to the actual outside world, or it may merely be thought to come from outside but actually stems from within, from the psyche. Such "objects" may take the form of spirits, animals, figures, etc.

'(f) The complex is known to the conscious mind, but known only intellectually and hence retains all its original force. Only the emotional experience coupled with the understanding and integration of its content can resolve it.'[1]

'Accordingly the ego can take four different attitudes towards the complex: total unconsciousness of its existence, identification, projection, or confrontation. But only confrontation can help the ego to come to grips with the complex and lead to its resolution.'[2]

These conceptions of Jung's on the nature of the complex, which he

[1] J. Jacobi, *Complex, Archetype and Symbol in the Psychology of C. G. Jung,* London, Routledge & Kegan Paul; Yale University Press; 1959, pp. 15–16.

[2] J. Jacobi, *ibid.,* pp. 17–18.

professed until the mid-twenties, were still identical with Freud's views in all important respects. But as a result of his growing preoccupation with the 'archetypes' he came to speak of the complex more and more in the sense of a structure of the psyche which was by no means necessarily of a morbid nature. In the course of an analysis the complex is divested of its attachment to the contents of the personal unconscious, i.e. of the chains that bind it to the conflict-laden experiences of, for example, childhood. The complex then contains as its kernel or node a collective, impersonal symbol which is identical with the archetype. The complex in the sense of morbific psychic constellations conceals an archetype; it represents archetypal modes of activity, as it were, in personal-subjective terms. Jung's formulation of the difference between the complex and the archetype is as follows:

'The contents of the personal unconscious are for the most part the so-called feeling-toned complexes, which go to make up the personal intimacy of life. By contrast the contents of the collective unconscious are the so-called archetypes.'[1]

But what are the archetypes? Jung defines them as follows (see also top of p. 327):

'The archetypes are, by definition, factors and motives which arrange psychic elements so as to form certain images (which may be called archetypal), and this they do in a way that can only ever be recognized from the effect. They are pre-consciously present and it is to be presumed that they form the structural dominants of the psyche as such... As *a priori* conditions the archetypes represent the special psychic instance of the "patterns of behaviour" which are known to the biologist and which determine the specific manner of all living creatures. Just as the manifestations of this basic biological plan can change in the course of development, so too can the archetypes. Empirically speaking, however, the archetype has not come into existence within the span of organic life. It appeared on the scene together with life.'[2]

'Whether the psychic structure and the archetypes, which are its elements, ever came into existence is a question for metaphysics and consequently not to be answered.'[3]

Since the archetype constitutes the most important content of the collective unconscious it follows that, like the collective unconscious, it

[1] C. G. Jung, Coll. Wks., Vol. 9, Part 1, p. 4.
[2] *Ibid.*, Vol. 11, p. 149 n.   [3] *Ibid.*, Vol. 9, Part 1, p. 101.

must be hereditary and, in a manner comparable to that of the instincts, must serve to regulate psychic life.

'Just as we have been compelled to postulate the concept of an instinct determining or regulating our conscious actions, so, in order to account for the uniformity and regularity of our perceptions, we must have recourse to the correlated concept of a factor determining the mode of apprehension. It is this factor which I call the archetype or primordial image. The primordial image might suitably be described as "the instinct's perception of itself", or as the self-portrait of the instinct.'[1]

Jung regards the hereditary transition of the archetype through its connection to the nerve elements of the brain as follows:

'I understand under archetype ... a structural quality or condition peculiar to the psyche, which is somehow connected with the brain'.[2]

The relationship between archetype and drive he formulates as follows:

'The archetype is not only an image in its own right but also a "dynamism which makes itself felt in the numinosity and fascinating power of the archetypal image. The realization and assimilation of instinct never take place ... by absorption into the intellectual sphere, but only through integration of the image which signifies and at the same time evokes the instinct, although in a form quite different from the one we meet on the biological level. ... It (instinct) has two aspects: ... it is experienced as physiological dynamism, while on the other hand its multitudinous forms enter into consciousness as images and groups of images, where they develop numinous effects, which offer, or appear to offer, the strictest possible contrast to instinct physiologically regarded. ... Psychologically ... the archetype as an image of instinct is a spiritual goal towards which the whole nature of man strives.'[2]

Jung endeavours to reconcile this biological aspect of the archetype with the conclusions both of the research carried out into instincts and of the Gestalt theory, an attempt which certainly opens up wide areas to speculation. Jacobi[3] quotes the Basle Zoologist *Portmann* in this connection:

[1] J. Jacobi, *Complex, Archetype and Symbol in the Psychology of C. G. Jung*, p. 36 (Quoted by Jacobi from C. G. Jung, 'Instinct and the Unconscious', par. 277).
[2] *Ibid.*, p. 37 (Quoted by Jacobi from *Psychology and Religion*, par. 165.)
[3] *Ibid.*, pp. 39–41.

'To-day this line of thinking has advanced to the point where Adolf Portmann, who has written a number of interesting works on the subject, speaks of the problem of "primordial images, preformed by heredity, in the experience of man and the animals",[1] and observes:

'". . . Biological research on the central nervous system of animals reveals structures which are ordered in the manner of Gestalten and can provoke actions typical of the species. . . ."[2] And he goes on to say: "Many people have forgotten how to experience consciously what is amazing in all living organizations—consequently they are surprised that the quality of an animal's inward experience should be predetermined, ordered and given by fixed structures." '[3]

The building of the nest is just as much a process typical of the species as are the ritual dance of the bees, the defence mechanism of the octopus, or the unfolding of the peacock's tail. Here Portmann remarks:

'. . . this ordering of the animal's inner life is controlled by the formative element, whose operation human psychology finds in the world of the archetypes. The entire ritual of the higher animals has this archetypal imprint in the highest degree. It appears to the biologist as a marked organization of the instinctual life, which secures the supraindividual living-together of the members of a species, synchronizes the mood of partners, and hinders rivals from endangering the species by destroying one another in combat. *Ritual behaviour appears as a supra-individual order valuable for the preservation of the species.*'[4]

The comparison with the child psyche calls for consideration and Jung states that the reactions of a small child are also archetypally pre-formed.

But in this connection it must be remembered that the archetypes are not inherited in the form of ideas. What is inherited is simply the ability to form and develop ideas. Jacobi writes about this as follows:

'They are channels, pre-dispositions, river-beds into which the water of life has dug deep. These "channels" form a kind of psychic mesh with "nodal points", corresponding, as we have seen, to the complex structure of the psyche, with its "nuclei of meaning". We must presume them to be the hidden organizers of representations; they are the "primordial

[1] A. Portmann, *Das Problem der Urbilder in biologischer Sicht* ('A biological view of the problem of original images'), *Eranos Jahrbuch* 1950, Special Volume, Zürich, p. 413) (footnote in Jacobi, *ibid.*, p. 40).

[2] *Ibid.*, p. 424 (footnote in Jacobi, *ibid.*, p. 40).

[3] *Ibid.*, p. 422 (footnote in Jacobi, *ibid.*, p. 41).

[4] A. Portman, *Riten der Tiere* ('Animal Rituals'); *Eranos Jahrbuch*, 1950, Zürich, p. 386 f. (footnote in Jacobi, *ibid.*, p. 41).

pattern" underlying the invisible order of the unconscious psyche; down through the millennia their irresistible power has shaped and reshaped the eternal meaning of the contents that have fallen into the unconscious, and so kept them alive. They form a "potential axial system" and—like an invisible crystal lattice in a solution—are pre-figured, as it were, in the unconscious. They possess no material existence; they are a sort of *éternals incréés* (Jung sometimes uses this Bergsonian term for them), which must first be endowed with solidity and clarity, clothed as it were by the conscious mind, before they can appear as "material reality", as an "image", and in a manner of speaking, be "born". Even when we encounter them "within us" (in dreams, for example), the archetypes, as soon as we become consciously aware of them, partake of the concrete outside world, for from it they have drawn the matter in which they are "clothed". The archetype is, so to speak, an "eternal presence", says Jung,[1] and to what extent it is perceived by the conscious mind depends only on the constellation[2] of the moment.'[3]

And Jung emphasizes the difficulty involved in clothing the meaning or content of the archetype in conceptual terms:

'No archetype can be stated as a simple formula. It is a vessel that can never be emptied and never filled. It has in fact only a potential existence, and when it takes on material form, it is no longer the same thing as it was before. It endures throughout the millennia and constantly demands to be interpreted anew.'[4]

The only difference that Jung sees between the archetype and the Platonic idea—Jung took his concept from early Christian Neo-Platonic mysticism—lies in Plato's philosophical formulation of psychological experiences. But there can be no doubt that for Jung the archetypes are structures which determine perception in an *a priori* manner. Jacobi makes the following formulation:

'There is no important idea or view that is not grounded in primordial archetypal forms. They are primordial forms that arose at a time when the conscious mind did not yet think but only perceived, when thought

---

[1] C. G. Jung, Coll. Wks., Vol. 12, p. 211.

[2] J. Jacobi, *Complex, Archetype and Symbol in the Psychology of C. G. Jung*, p. 53. Footnote: 'In this context "constellation" means the state of consciousness to which the unconscious stands in a compensatory relation; it is manifested in the distribution of psychic energy and the corresponding charge of the archetype that has been touched and "called awake" by a current problem.'

[3] *Ibid.*, pp. 52-3.

[4] C. G. Jung, Coll. Wks., Vol. 9, Part 1, p. 179.

was still essentially revelation; not invented but imposed on the mind from within, they are convincing by virtue of their immediacy.[1] Thus the archetypes are nothing other than typical forms of apprehension and perception, of experience and reaction, of active and passive behaviour, images of life itself, "which takes pleasure in creating forms, in dissolving them, and in creating them anew with the old stamp: a process that takes place in the material, the psychic and the spiritual realm as well".'[2,3]

The importance of the archetype for consciousness lies in the clarification and the breaking down of the archetypal contents, which—see above under 'inflation'—, if they are not assimilated into consciousness, endanger the individual. It is in their conception of the 'symbol' that the divergence between Jung's and Freud's views is most extreme. Freud (see pp. 87 ff. and pp. 96 ff.) explains the symbol empirically in accordance with the following considerations:

1. The difficulty experienced by a small child in differentiating between different concepts results, *inter alia*, in the fact that it will, for example, call every animal a 'bow-wow'. Because of the importance of the genitals and their erotogenic zones the child, since it has difficulty in differentiating linguistically and ideationally, will also give the same name as it gives to the genitals to every object that resembles them (pointed objects or those shaped like a hole). In addition to this there is the principle of pleasure and displeasure: the child is too lazy to learn new concepts and sticks to the old 'symbols'.

2. These names (concepts! see p. 530 ff.), which derive from early childhood, are identical with dream symbols. They are the basis of the subsequent process of repression, in which—either in sleep or in a state of hallucination—they are recharged with libido in the characteristic manner (see p. 91 ff). But they are also a compromise between the repressed 'complexes' and the repressing instance, the censor.

3. From this it follows that for Freud the symbol is a preliminary stage of conceptual thought, it is a 'sign' for something—not a sign in the mathematical sense, however, but rather, in Freud's view, a sign (symbol) is identical with both an image *and* a concept.

The problematical aspects of Freud's conception of symbols, which amongst other things prompted von Gebsattel's comment that psychoanalysis is given over to a phallus fetishism, will be investigated in

---

[1] C. G. Jung, Coll. Wks., Vol. 9, Part I, p. I (footnote in Jacobi, *ibid.*).

[2] P. Schmitt, 'Archetypisches bei Augustin und Goethe' (in *Eranos-Festschrift* for Jung's seventieth birthday; special volume), Zürich, 1945, p.99 (footnote in Jacobi, *ibid.*) (The Archetype in Augustine and Goethe.)

[3] J. Jacobi, *Complex, Archetype and Symbol in the Psychology of C. G. Jung*, pp. 50–1.

greater detail in the final section of this book. Freud considers the symbol from the reductive point of view, i.e. he relates it back to genital or to earlier stages of the libido. Jung, on the other hand, evaluates the symbol—like everything else in his system—by amplification, i.e. in contrast to the theoretically conceivable reduction of each and every symbol to the phallus (or excrement and anus, mamilla and mouth), with Jung the meaning of the symbol is extended to embrace the concrete possibilities—both in terms of objective appearance and of subjective experience—that are contained within it. For example, according to Freud tower means phallus, cellar means vagina. According to Jung the tower represents isolation, self-incarceration, defence against the outside world, pride, arrogance, etc., whilst the cellar represents darkness, unconscious, chthonian and motherly aspects, etc. Freud's symbolism does not do justice to the objective image content, because he merely abstracts this content and takes it as the preliminary stage of the concept, whereby he fails to note the fundamental difference between image and concept. When a child calls every four-legged animal a 'bow-wow', then 'bow-wow' is without question a preliminary stage of the concept, since the child has characterized it by this process of identification. 'Bow-wow' is a sign. But it is not an *image*. And in drawing his (false) conclusion Freud confuses the sign (which is abstract) with the image. If the child calls every pointed object a 'wi-wi thing' [1](Freud, Analysis of the Phobia of a Young Boy), then it can also be said to have found a concept which, just as in the case of the 'bow-wow', is based on the similarity between the real objects, the *images*. But this does not prove that all pointed objects, including church towers, street lamps, swords or candlesticks, are phallic symbols, since the identity of the concept of a 'wi-wi thing' is no more based on an identity of the images than is that of the concept of the 'bow-wow'. For images are at most similar, never identical. It is not the identity of the concept (sign) for a group of different objects which makes it possible under given conditions —in sleep—for one image to represent another, but rather the objective similarity of certain objects or, alternatively, the similarity of the images, forms and shapes. It is this similarity which constitutes the basis of the symbol. For Freud and his followers the *meaning* of the symbol (see p. 199 ff.) is only a secondary consequence of the sublimation process, although it should be pointed out that Glover has already demonstrated the highly problematical nature of this particular concept. For C. G. Jung the meaning of the symbol is immanent in the symbol and is merely unfolded, which must of course lead to a view of the world, in which all phenomena stand for something else and have a specific meaning. This meaning is the basis of the phenomena; it is not,

[1] S. Freud, St. Edn., Vol. X, *Analysis of the Phobia of a Five Year Old.*

however, transcendent, but rather immanent in the phenomena themselves. And so with Jung the whole of life, with its manifold connections, is seen symbolically, "*Alles Vergängliche ist nur ein Gleichnis*" (All that is transitory is but a likeness), i.e. sexuality, perversions, neurosis, are also symbols for something else. In his interpretation of symbols Jung refers above all to Cassirer's *Philosophie der Symbolischen Formen*[1] (Berlin 1923) and defines the symbol in contrast to the allegory and the sign as follows:

'Every view which interprets the symbolic expression as an analogous or abbreviated expression of a known thing is *semiotic*. A conception which interprets the symbolic expression as the best possible formulation of a relatively unknown thing, which cannot conceivably therefore be more clearly or characteristically represented, is *symbolic*. A view which interprets the symbolic expression as an intentional transcription or transformation of a known thing is *allegoric*.'[2]

'An expression that stands for a known thing always remains merely a sign and is never a symbol. It is, therefore, quite impossible to make a living symbol, i.e. one that is pregnant with meaning, from known associations.'[3]

The symbol becomes a *sign* if, as a result of the wear and tear of conventional usage over several centuries, it loses its meaning. C. G. Jung dissociates himself from Freud's conception of symbols in the following passage:

'Those conscious contents which give us a clue, as it were, to the unconscious background are incorrectly called symbols by Freud. They are not true symbols, however, since according to his theory they have merely the role of *signs* or *symptoms* of the subliminal processes. The true symbol differs essentially from this, and should be understood as the expression for an intuitive idea that cannot yet be formulated in any other or better way. When Plato, for instance, expresses the whole problem of the theory of knowledge in his parable of the cave, or when Christ expresses the idea of the Kingdom of Heaven in parables, these are genuine and true symbols, namely, attempts to express something for which no verbal concept yet exists.'[4]

In *Complex, Archetype and Symbol* Jacobi states that in Jung's opinion Freud

---

[1] Berlin, 1923. [2] C. G. Jung, *Psychological Types*, London, 1923, p. 601.
[3] *Ibid.*, p. 602.
[4] J. Jacobi, *Complex, Archetype and Symbol in the Psychology of C. G. Jung*, p. 89.

'from his standpoint speaks of *symptomatic*,[1] rather than *symbolical* actions; since, for him, these phenomena are not symbolic in the sense here defined, but are symptomatic signs of a definite and generally known underlying process. There are, of course, neurotics who regard their unconscious products, which are primarily morbid symptoms, as symbols of supreme importance. Generally, however, this is not the case. On the contrary, the neurotic of to-day is only too prone to regard a product that may actually be full of significance, as a "symptom".'[2] In Jung's symbolic view of the world, in which even the incest problem is seen as a symbol (see p. 331), homosexuality is also interpreted as a symbolic search on the part of the homosexual for certain (unconscious) aspects of his own personality.

Quite apart from their universal and archetypal import symbols fulfil two essential purposes for Jung: they mediate between the collective and the personal unconscious and they serve as 'energy transformers' in respect of the libido. The polar structure of the psyche, its compensatory and self-regulatory function, the dialectical process between the conscious and unconscious minds all reappear in Jung's description of symbols. The polar structure of the symbol Jung calls the bi-polarity of the symbol, by which he means that in the symbol irreconcilable opposites are reconciled. These antitheses are chiefly those between the conscious and unconscious minds, which are joined in the symbols into a 'coincidentia oppositorum'. The dissolution of the irreconcilable opposites in the symbol which takes place in a sick person has tragic consequences for the individual concerned. What happens then is that one side of the symbol gains ascendancy over the other side, e.g. the day side gains ascendancy over the night side.

The symbol's mediatory function lies in its ability to maintain the antithetical sides of the psyche (e.g. masculine and feminine aspects) in a state of constant flux, to preserve the psyche from torpor, to facilitate the rhythmical alternation of tension and relaxation and thus to make a direct contribution to psychic life. The function whereby formed symbols are created from formless libido Jung calls the 'transformation of energy'.

'With the birth of the symbol, the regression of the libido into the unconscious ceases. Regression changes into progression, blockage gives way to flowing, and the pull of the primordial abyss is broken.'[3]

---

[1] S. Freud, *On the Psychopathology of Everyday Life*, St. Edn., Vol. VI.
[2] C. G. Jung, *Psychological Types*, p. 606.
[3] J. Jacobi, *Complex, Archetype and Symbol in the Psychology of C. G. Jung*, p. 99.

Jacobi formulates the difference between this view and Freud's view of libido transformation as follows:

'Here again we find a fundamental difference between the conceptions of Freud and Jung. In Freud the "transformation of libido", sublimation, is "unipolar"; for in it unconscious, repressed material is always canalized into a "culture-creating (i.e. positive) form". In Jung the transformation of libido can be designated as "bi-polar", for it results from the continuous parting and uniting of two conflicting elements; it is a synthesis of conscious and unconscious material.'[1]

In Jung's conception the libido is constantly converted and transformed by the symbol and is thus preserved from inflations or projections. It is for this reason that Jungians place such great importance on the interpretation of dreams, because they consider that dreams constitute an autonomous activity which leads the patient to individuation. The difference between the latent and manifest dream contents which logically follows from the assumption of a primary and secondary process, does not exist for Jung. Instead he differentiates between the objective and subjective levels of dreams: the dreamer's personal connections to the dream elements, which are established by the use of association techniques, are expressed at the subjective level, whilst at the objective level the dream is correlated with the archetypal references of meaning of the collective unconscious.

'I call every interpretation which equates the dream images with real objects an interpretation on the objective level. In contrast to this is the interpretation which refers every part of the dream and all the actors in it back to the dreamer himself. This I call interpretation on the subjective level. Interpretation on the objective level is analytic, because it breaks down the dream content into complexes of memory that refer to external situations. Interpretation on the subjective level is synthetic, because it detaches the underlying complexes of memory from their external causes, regards them as tendencies or components of the subject, and reunites them with that subject.'[2]

But it would be wrong to assume that all dream symbols are capable of being collated with archetypal elements. Many dream symbols remain individual.

In Jung's conception the process of individuation—as revealed in dreams—develops into a dialectical argument

[1] J. Jacobi, *Complex, Archetype and Symbol in the Psychology of C. G. Jung,* p. 100.　　　　　　　　　　[2] C. G. Jung, Coll. Wks., Vol. 7, p. 83.

'... between the contents of the unconscious and of consciousness; symbols provide the necessary bridges, linking and reconciling the often seemingly irreconcilable contradictions between the two "sides". Just as from the outset every seed contains the mature fruit as its hidden goal, so the human psyche, whether aware of it or not, resisting or unresisting, is oriented towards its "wholeness". Hence the way of individuation—though at first it may be no more than a "trace"—becomes deeply engraved in the course of the individual's life, and to deviate from it involves the danger of psychic disturbances. Consequently Jung says:

'The symbols that rise up out of the unconscious in dreams point rather to a confrontation of opposites, and the images of the goal represent their successful reconciliation. Something empirically demonstrable comes to our aid from the depths of our unconscious nature. It is the task of the conscious mind to understand these hints. If this does not happen, the process of individuation will nevertheless continue. The only difference is that we become its victims and are dragged along by fate toward that inescapable goal which we might have reached walking upright, if only we had taken the trouble and been patient enough to understand in time the meaning of the numina that cross our path.'[1,2]

The importance of complexes, symbols and archetypes in Jungian psychology may be summarized as follows:

(a) The archetypes represent the collective unconscious in the form of primal images of human actions, strivings and desires, of spheres of feeling and recognition, of human existence as such. The archetypes reside in the collective unconscious in a potential condition, whence they may be roused in any individual due to the workings of particular external or internal situations (e.g. a threat to his livelihood) or as a result of analysis, in which case they transfer from their potential condition to an actual condition. They can emerge into consciousness either in drive form at a biological level or in the form of an image, i.e. a symbol, at the spiritual level.

(b) Symbols are archetypes made manifest, i.e. conscious, which vary according to the particular situation, the life history and the race of the individual concerned. The symbol—and thus the archetype—can either be assimilated by the ego in the course of an analysis or it can remain isolated from consciousness and from the ego, in which case it might be experienced in psychotic hallucinations, in ecstasies and visions as a dissociated element. In this latter eventuality the symbol would express a pathogenic process.

(c) When symbols are dissociated in the course of pathogenic processes

[1] C. G. Jung, 'Answer to Job', Coll. Wks., Vol. II, p. 460.
[2] Jacobi, Complex, Archetype and Symbol, p. 133.

349

they are identical with complexes. In C. G. Jung's later writings (from the early 'twenties onwards) complexes are to a large extent identical with the archetypes and with symbols, which are pictorial representations of the archetypes. But they are not entirely identical, for on the one hand complexes tend to possess a more individual character, one that reveals the influence of the personal unconscious, whilst on the other hand they tend to refer more to the pathogenic aspect of the archetypes as revealed in neuroses or psychoses. And so an archetype can become a complex in the course of a pathogenic process. What actually happens is that the archetype becomes sated with unintegrated feelings, experiences and associations, whereupon it detaches itself and becomes an autonomous, individual part of the psyche until finally it breaks out in the form of a psychosis.

(d) The Basic Functions of the Psyche

(i) Thinking, Feeling, Sensation, Intuition

For Jung thinking, feeling, sensation and intuition are the basic functions of the psyche (strangely enough the will[1] is omitted). The fact that there are four basic functions, no more and no less, is justified *inter alia* by the symbolical and mystical meaning of the figure four (cf. the four corners of the earth, the four elements, etc.). Jung defines the concept of 'the function' as a 'certain form of psychic activity that remains theoretically the same under varying circumstances and is completely independent of its momentary contents.'[2]

It is typical of certain confusions in Jung's conception that he should have derived thinking—one of his basic functions—from speech,[3] thus revealing his partial allegiance to the mechanistic and materialistic philosophy of his preceptors, which dates from the turn of the century and which was to reappear time and again in Jung's thought both in respect of constitutional factors and in respect of the connection between the collective unconscious and the cortex. Jacobi compares and contrasts the purposes served by these four psychic functions as follows:

'Thus thinking is the function which seeks to apprehend the world and adjust to it by way of thought or cognition, i.e. logical inferences. The function of feeling, on the other hand, apprehends the world through an evaluation based on the feelings of "pleasant or unpleasant acceptance or

---

[1] Jung considers that the will is identical with libido and that it is 'a freely available psychic energy, present in each of the four basic functions'. (Jacobi, *The Psychology of C. G. Jung*, p. 16 n.).

[2] C. G. Jung, *Psychological Types*, p. 547 (quoted from Jacobi, *The Psychology of C. G. Jung*, p. 11).

[3] Especially in *Symbols of Transformation*.

rejection". Both these functions are termed *rational*, because both work with evaluations and judgements: thinking evaluates through cognition from the standpoint of "true-false", feeling through the emotions from the standpoint of "pleasant-unpleasant". As determinants of behaviour these two basic attitudes are mutually exclusive at any given time; either the one or the other predominates. It is obvious, for example, that certain political figures make decisions on the basis of their feelings and not their reason.

'Jung calls the other two functions, sensation and intuition, the *irrational* functions, because they circumvent the *ratio* and operate not with judgements but with mere perceptions which are not evaluated or interpreted. Sensation perceives things as they are and not otherwise. It is the sense of reality, *par excellence*—what the French call the "*fonction du reel*". Intuition also "perceives", but less through the conscious apparatus of the senses than through its capacity for an unconscious "inner perception" of the inherent potentialities of things. The sensation type, for example, will note all the details of an historical event but disregard the general context in which it is set; the intuitive type, on the other hand, will pay little attention to the details but will have no difficulty in discerning the inner meaning of the event, its possible implications and effects. Or another example: in viewing a lovely Spring landscape the sensation type will note every detail: the flowers, the trees, the colour of the sky, etc., while the intuitive type will simply register the general atmosphere and colour. It is evident that these two functions are just as antithetical and mutually exclusive as our first pair, thinking and feeling; they cannot operate simultaneously.'[1]

In accordance with the theory of the self-regulatory and compensatory nature of the psyche these four functions also follow a compensatory pattern: one or other of the functions will always give way to the remainder although in principle all four functions are equally represented in man. The particular function which gains the ascendancy in any given case Jung calls the superior function. In the case of Europeans, indeed of the inhabitants of the Western Hemisphere in general, this is usually the thinking function. This function is encouraged at the expense of feeling or intuition or sensation and results in the extreme intellectual and rationalistic attitude of "Western man". By contrast, feeling and intuition, the inferior functions, are directed towards the nocturnal side of life. Their roots in the unconscious are considerably deeper than are the roots of the thinking function. The antitheses of thinking and feeling are then integrated into Jung's symbolic interpretation by analogy with the masculine and feminine elements, with earth and the cosmos, with

[1] J. Jacobi, *The Psychology of C. G. Jung*, p. 12.

day and night, to which end both Oriental mysticism and alchemy supply a large number of appropriate symbols. Jacobi illustrates these inter-relationships by reference to the Chinese symbol of t'ai chi t'u, which represents a circle divided by means of a curving line into a light and a dark sphere. She defines the four psychic functions with reference to this symbol, which she describes as follows:

'*T'ai chi t'u* is a product of inner vision and one of the primal symbols of mankind. It represents the duality of light and dark, of masculine and feminine as a unit, a totality. "The line at the same time posits an above and a below, a right and left, front and back—in a word, the world of opposites.'[1] The path of the arrow, the way, does not take the form of a cross, as might have been expected, but moves from top to right (the two segments of the bright part of the circle might be called symbolic representations of father and son), then leftward where more dark enters (symbol of the daughter); in the end it descends to the fourth function, situated wholly in the darkness of the womb, the unconscious—all of which is in agreement with the findings of the psychology of functions. The differentiated and the auxiliary functions are conscious and directed; they are often represented, in dreams for example, by father and son or other figures representing the dominant principle of conscious-ness and that closest to it; the two other functions are relatively or wholly unconscious and are often represented, according to the same rule, by mother and daughter. But since the opposition between the auxiliary functions is by no means as great as that between differentiated and inferior functions, the third function can be raised to consciousness and thus become "masculine".[2] But it carries along some of its con-tamination with the inferior function and so provides a kind of mediator with the unconscious. The fourth function is wholly interwoven with the unconscious; whenever circumstances raise it to consciousness, it draws with it the contents of the unconscious, it 'invades' the field of conscious-ness with its undifferentiated contents. The resulting confrontation creates the possibility of a synthesis between conscious and unconscious contents.'[3]

It goes without saying that the supremacy of one or other of the functions

[1] I Ching, translated into German from the Chinese by Richard Wilhelm with a commentary, Diederichs, Jena 1924, p. 8. Translated into English from the German by Baynes, Vol. I, p. 36 (footnote in Jacobi, *The Psychology of C. G. Jung*, p. 15).

[2] Footnote in Jacobi, *The Psychology of C. G. Jung*, p. 14, 'In the iconography of symbols, the light ordinarily stands for the masculine, the dark for the feminine'.

[3] J. Jacobi, *The Psychology of C. G. Jung*, pp. 14–15.

is harmful to the individual and may lead to neurosis. Quite apart from this, however, it is on the basis of this differentiation between the four functions that Jung constructs his typology.

(ii) *Typology*

Jung's concept of the psychological types is determined by two factors: the supremacy of one or other of the functions (the supremacy of the thinking type over the intuitive type for example) and the individual's *reaction* in any given situation to external or internal motivations. In respect of this second factor Jung speaks of the *reaction type*, which he subdivides into extroverted and introverted types. Jacobi summarizes Jung's views as follows:

'Jung distinguishes two such attitudes, *extraversion* and *introversion*, which influence the entire psychic process. One or the other of these orientations is the reaction habitus that determines the way we respond to the objects of the outer and inner world, the nature of our subjective experience, and even the compensatory action of our unconscious. Jung calls this habitus "the central switchboard from which on the one hand external behaviour is regulated and, on the other, specific experiences are formed".[1]

'Extraversion is characterized by a positive relation to the object, intraversion by a negative one. In his adjustment and reaction pattern, the extravert orients himself predominantly by the outward, collective norms, the spirits of his times, etc. The attitudes of the introvert, on the other hand, are determined mainly by subjective factors. Often he is poorly adjusted to his environment. The extravert "thinks, feels and acts in relation to the object"; he displaces his interest from subject to object and orients himself primarily by the world outside himself. For the introvert the subject is the basis of orientation, while the object plays at most a secondary, indirect role. His first move in every situation that confronts him is to recoil, "as if with an unvoiced no",[2] and only then does his real reaction set in.

'Thus while the functional types indicate the way the material of experience is apprehended and formed, the attitude type—extraversion or introversion—marks the general psychological attitude, that is, the direction of the "libido", which to Jung means the general psychic energy. The attitude type is rooted in our biological make-up and is much more clearly determined by a certain constitutional predisposi-

[1] Footnote in Jacobi, *The Psychology of C. G. Jung*, p. 18, 'A Psychological Theory of Types', *Modern Man*, p. 99.

[2] Footnote in Jacobi, *ibid.*, p. 19, 'A Psychological Theory of Types', *Modern Man*, p. 98.

tion, the constitutional tendency can be considerably modified or even repressed by conscious effort. But a change in the attitude type can be brought about only by an "inner reconstruction", a modification of the structure of the psyche, either through spontaneous transformation (which again would stem from biological factors) or by an arduous process of psychic development such as an "analysis".[1] 'Consequently, the second and third function, i.e. the two auxiliary functions, are somewhat more easily differentiated than the fourth, inferior function, which is not only far removed from, and sharply opposed to, the principal function, but also coincides with the still unlived, hidden, and hence undifferentiated attitude type. Consequently the introversion of the extraverted thinking type, for example, has an overtone not of intuition or of sensation, but primarily of feeling."[2]

The relationship between extroversion and introversion is also compensatory. The conscious extrovert is unconsciously introverted. We have seen that the dominance of any one of the basic psychic functions over the other can lead to neurosis or psychosis. And the consequences of a one-sided habitual attitude may well be equally catastrophic.

This poses important problems for educationalists, whose purpose must be to ensure a balanced and harmonious development of the child's basic functions.

Since in the course of a successful analysis (individuation) it is possible to redress the balance of the basic psychic functions, resolving discord into harmony, it should also be possible to effect a successful change in the attitude types. But in respect of artists, in whom Jung was particularly interested, new and complicated hypotheses are required if the concepts of extroversion and introversion are not to lead to absurd results. For reasons of space it will not be possible to enter into these hypotheses here.

(e) Jungian Psychotherapy

The goal and the path of Jungian psychotherapy is individuation. Individuation is fundamentally different from Freudian psychoanalysis. The difference is contained in the following factors:

1. Amplification replaces free association;
2. the dissolution of repressions gives way to collective symbols as the focal point of therapeutic concern;
3. in the interpretation of dreams the manifest and latent dream contents are superseded by interpretations at the subject and object level;

[1] Footnote in Jacobi, *The Psychology of C. G. Jung*, p. 19, 'Concerning the relation between biologically and psychologically determined disorders and the effect of hormones on the psyche, there are numerous informative works (c.f Steinach, Freud, Meng, von Wyss, etc.). [2] J. Jacobi, *ibid.*, pp. 18–19.

4. only minor, symbolic importance is attached to the transference.

Jacobi's summary of Jung's therapeutic ideas is perhaps faintly reminiscent of similar confessions from the ranks of the Theosophists, Anthroposophists, Christian Scientists, etc.:

'Jungian psychotherapy is not an analytical procedure in the usual sense of the term, although it adheres strictly to the relevant findings of science and medicine. It is a *Heilsweg* in the two-fold sense of the German word: a way of healing and a way of salvation. It has the power to cure man's psychic and psychogenic sufferings. It has all the instruments needed to relieve the trifling psychic disturbances that may be the starting-point of a neurosis, or to deal successfully with the gravest and most complicated developments of psychic disease. But in addition it knows the way and has the means to lead the individual to his "salvation", to the knowledge and fulfilment of his own personality, which have always been the aim of spiritual striving. By its very nature, this path defies abstract exposition. Jung's system of thought can be explained theoretically only up to a certain point; to understand it fully one must have experienced or, better still, "suffered" its living action in one self. And like every process that transforms man, this experience cannot be described but only adumbrated. Like all psychic experience it is very personal; its subjectivity is its most effective truth. Often as it may be repeated, this experience of the psyche is unique and only within its subjective limits is it open to rational understanding.'[1]

Whereas, in Jung's submission, Freud and Adler conducted their enquiries on the assumption of a single drive (sexuality and striving for power) and retrospectively sought the causes of actual disturbances in past events, Jung considered that with his variety of standpoints he himself was better able to do justice to the totality of psychic activity. This also includes the *spirit* and man's religious needs, factors which Freud considered to be the products of pathological repressions but which Jung held to be part of man's unconscious 'needs'. It is for this reason that he calls his psychotherapy prospective and synthetic in contrast to Freud's retrospective and analytic therapy. It is prospective because it embraces man's future and because, due to the effect of collective symbols, there is an inherent tendency in dreams which points to the future and which cannot be explained in terms of wish-fulfilment alone.

But what of the practical side of Jungian psychotherapy? Jacobi describes it as follows:

'Jung's method is "dialectical", not only because it is a dialogue between

[1] J. Jacobi, *The Psychology of C. G. Jung*, p. 59.

two persons and as such an interaction between two psychic systems. It is also intrinsically dialectical, because it is a process which, by confronting the contents of consciousness with those of the unconscious, the ego with the non-ego, provokes an interaction aimed at, and culminating in, a third term, a synthesis which combines and transcends them both. From the therapeutic standpoint it is indispensable for the psychologist to recognize and observe this dialectical principle. He does not analyse an object theoretically, from a distance; rather, he himself is just as much *in* the analysis as is the patient.

'For this reason, and also because of the autonomous action of the unconscious, the "transference", or blind projection of all the patient's ideas and feelings upon the analyst, is less indispensable in the Jungian than in other analytical methods. Under certain circumstances Jung even regards it as an obstacle to effective treatment, particularly when it takes an exaggerated form. In any case he believes that an "attachment" to a third person, a love relation for example, to be an equally satisfactory "basis" for an analytical resolution of neuroses, or for a dialogue with the unconscious that may foster psychic development. The all-important thing is not, as with Freud, to "relive" the past traumatic emotion suffered in childhood but to "live through" one's present difficulties with a concrete partner, and so reach an understanding of them. Both persons must "give" themselves, the analyst as well as the analysand, but both must also as far as possible preserve their objectivity.

'Each unconsciously influences the other and this is essential for treatment. The encounter between two personalities is like the mixing of two chemical elements; if any reaction occurs, both are transformed. "In a dialectical procedure . . . the doctor must emerge from his anonymity and give an account of himself, just as he expects his patient to do."[1] Thus the role of the analyst in the Jungian method is not largely passive as in Freudian analysis; he takes an active part, guides, encourages and participates in a personal give and take. In this form of intervention, which particularly stimulates the process of psychic transformation, because in it one living process is acting on another, the personality of the physician, its stature and scope, purity and strength, is obviously of the greatest importance, far more so than in other techniques of depth psychology. It is for this reason that Jung insists that every analyst himself undergo a thorough analysis as *conditio sine qua non* for the practice of psychotherapy. For here it is particularly true that a spiritual guide can lead his patient no farther than he himself has gone. Nor can the most expert psychotherapist get more out of his patient than what is potentially there; no treatment can stretch the constitutional limits of the

[1] Footnote in Jacobi, *The Psychology of C. G. Jung*, Coll. Wks., Vol 16, p. 67 'Principles of Practical Psychotherapy,' p. 18.

psyche. A man's psychic development is always conditioned by his individual structure, and the therapist can only do his best.'[1]

Whilst Freud used the method of free association both to lay bare the past and also for purposes of dream interpretation Jung had only occasional and temporary recourse to it. To the Jungian therapist the patient's personal existence, his symptoms, his past and future, are simply a phenomenon that will shortly recede into the background, yielding pride of place to the symbols of the collective unconscious in the modern 'initiation rites' of individuation. It is true that every Jungian will concede the importance of the 'personal unconscious', the need to deal both with drives—e.g. sexuality—and wishes. But the analysis only becomes a 'path of healing and a path of salvation' (Heilsweg) when the gates of the collective unconscious have been opened and the confrontation with the anima, the shadow (cf. the 'guardian of the threshold' of the Theosophists and Anthroposophists) and the timeless archetypes is initiated. It is at this point that the therapist becomes especially interested in his patient but it is at this point also that he ceases to be a therapist with a purely medical objective in view and becomes instead a spiritual guide in the sense of the Ancient Mysteries. And it is at this point that the method of amplification is applied, which lies at the very heart of Jung's scientific method (see above) and of his therapy.

'In Jung's amplification method the various dream motifs are enriched by analogous, related images, symbols, legends, myths, etc., which throw light on their diverse aspects and possible meanings, until their significance stands out in full clarity. Each element of meaning thus obtained is linked with the next, until the whole chain of dream motifs is revealed and the whole dream as a unit can be subjected to a final verification.'[2]

If the therapist discovers archetypal contents in his patient's dreams he will explain them by reference to analogous contents of myths, folk-tales and religion. Jungian analysis thus evolves into a conversation between therapist and analysand in which the analysand no longer lies on a couch, as with Freud, but sits facing the therapist. There are seven stages of the psychotherapeutic process in accordance with the mystical number seven. Jacobi summarizes the process as follows:

'Jung holds that before dealing with the material of the collective unconscious we must first raise the infantile contents to consciousness and integrate them. The " 'personal unconscious' ", he says, "must always

[1] J. Jacobi, *The Psychology of C. G. Jung*, pp. 66–7.
[2] J. Jacobi, *ibid.*, p. 84.

357

be dealt with first, that is, made conscious".[1] Otherwise the gateway to the collective unconscious is closed. Every conflict must first be considered in its personal aspect and examined in the light of individual experience. The accent must be placed on the most intimate life of the individual and the psychic contents acquired in connection with it, before the individual can begin to deal with the universal problems of human existence. This path, which leads to the activation of the archetypes and the unification of consciousness and the unconscious or a proper balance between them, is the path of "healing" and, from the technical point of view, it is also the way followed by dream interpretation.

'Thus, to sum up once again, the technique of analysing a dream may be divided into the following stages: description of the present situation of consciousness; description of preceding events; investigation of the subjective context and, where archaic motives appear, comparison with mythological parallels; finally, in complicated situations, comparison with objective data obtained from third persons.

'On the other hand, the course taken by the contents of the unconscious consists roughly of the following seven stages: (1) lowering of the threshold of consciousness, permitting the contents of the unconscious to emerge; (2) rising up of the contents of the unconscious in dreams, visions, phantasies; (3) perceiving the contents and holding them fast by consciousness; (4) investigation, clarification, intepretation, and understanding of the meaning of the contents; (5) integration of this meaning with the general psychic situation of the individual; (6) acquisition, incorporation, and elaboration of the meaning thus found; (7) integration of the "meaning", its organic incorporation in the psyche becoming so complete that it "enters the bloodstream" as it were, becomes a *knowledge secured by instinct*.'[2]

Jacobi reports Jung's views on the structure of dreams as follows:

'Jung found that most dreams show a certain similarity of structure. Unlike Freud, he believes that they form a self-contained whole, a dramatic action which can meaningfully be broken down into the elements of a Greek play. (1) *Place, time, dramatis personae*: this is the beginning of the dream, which often indicates the scene of action and the cast of characters; (2) *Exposition* or statement of the problem. Here is presented the central content; the unconsciou: frames the question to which it will reply in the course of the dream; (3) *Peripety*: this is the "backbone" of the dream; the plot is woven, the action moves towards a

---

[1] C. G. Jung, *Psychology and Alchemy*, Coll. Wks., Vol. 12, p. 61.
[2] J. Jacobi, *ibid.*, pp. 79–80.

climax, transformation or catastrophe; (4) Lysis, the solution, the outcome of the dream, its meaningful conclusion and the disclosure of its
compensatory message.

'This rough pattern, on which most dreams are constructed, forms a
suitable basis for interpretation. Dreams that reveal no lysis suggest a
tragic development in the dreamer's life; but these are very specific
dreams and should not be confused with those which have no lysis
because the dreamer remembers or relates them incompletely. It goes
without saying that the psychotherapist can seldom obtain a full account
of a dream all at once. A careful investigation is often needed before its
whole structure is revealed to him.'[1]

Jung contrasts his method of amplification with the (Freudian) reductive
method.

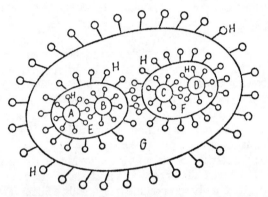

A, B, C, D. The individual dream motifs.
E, F. The elements of meaning (dream motifs) are combined into a
   whole; e.g., A = horn, B = animal, E = horned animal.
G. The whole dream as a meaningful unit, e.g. conisdered as an analogy
   to a mythologem.
H. The individual points of correspondence.'[2]

By means of this diagram Jacobi illustrates Jung's amplification method
and in the following passage she contrasts it with the method of 'reductio
in primam figuram' (cf. Diagrams 3 and 4 on p. 85 and p. 86 of Jacobi's
book):

'They start with four different elements, dream contents A, B, C, D.
Amplification combines them in all directions, taking account of all

---

[1] J. Jacobi, *Psychology and Alchemy*, pp. 80–1.
[2] J. Jacobi, *ibid.*, p. 83, Diagram 2.

possible analogies, extending their field of implication and baring their meaning as far as possible. If, for example, the figure of the real father appears as an element in a dream, amplification may enrich and broaden it into the area of the fatherly as such. The reductive method, in which it is assumed that the various dream elements are a "distortion" of contents that were originally different, carries the four points back along a chain of free association until, trapped in causal connections, they culminate in the *one* point X from which they started and which it was their function to "distort" or "conceal". Thus amplification illuminates all the possible meanings of the four points for the dreamer in his actual situation, while reduction merely carries them back to a complex point. Freud with his reduction asks "Why?" and "Whence?" Jung in his method of interpreting dreams asks primarily "To what end?" What did the unconscious intend, what did it wish to tell the dreamer by sending him just this dream and not another? An intellectual dreams, for example, that he is passing under a great rainbow bridge. Under, not over it, and this surprises him greatly. The dream aims to point out that this man has been trying to solve his problems in an unreal way, and to show him the right way—not over the bridge but under it[1] For intellectuals who suppose that they can simply exclude their instinctual nature, that they can "think away" or somehow "rationalize" their life, subjugate it with their intellect, such a hint is often very necessary. This dream, as we see, served as a warning that would open the dreamer's eyes to his real situation.

'Of course the actual meaning of the dream in all its particulars can be disclosed only by a detailed process of analysis as described above. But from the little that has been said here it is already evident that the dream had a certain "purpose", namely to disclose a fact of which the dreamer was not or did not want to be aware. Such dreams are relatively easy to interpret, for they are "parables" which can be translated directly into a warning. Such a warning is the expression of a dynamic tendency in the unconscious. This dynamic tendency, the force behind the dream and its utterances, sheds new contents into consciousness which in turn— they have been assimilated by the personality—react upon and modify the unconscious field of forces. The dynamic process that is invisible in a single dream but can easily be followed in a series prevents interruption and loss between analytic sessions, and makes it possible to carry out an analysis with meetings at fairly long intervals. And since, as we have shown, the dynamic has aim and meaning, it makes certain that when a dream is falsely interpreted other dreams will follow which will correct the error and lead the analysis back into the right path.'[2]

[1] Footnote in Jacobi, *The Psychology of C. G. Jung*, p. 84, 'Example from Kindertraumseminar 1938–9'.   [2] J. Jacobi, *ibid.*, pp. 84–6.

Jacobi also formulates the difference between dream interpretations at the subjective and objective levels:

'The subjective, individual meaning of the dream is supplied by *subjective amplifications*; i.e., the analyst asks the dreamer what each dream element means to him personally. Then the collective meaning is obtained by *objective amplification*, i.e., the dream elements are enriched with the universal, symbolic material of fairy tales, myths, etc., which illuminate the universal aspect of the problem that concerns every human being.'[1]

(f) From Jung to Personal Analysis

Jung claims to have re-discovered religious ideas and dogmas in the archetypal symbolism of the collective unconscious. The question which arises here as to whether this psychologization of religion—always assuming that the archetypes actually are psychological phenomena—serves religion has received both an affirmative and a negative answer from competent authorities.[2] Jung's detailed investigations into the Christian dogmas, especially the dogma of the Trinity, have helped many people to find new access to religion and to dogma. The work of the so-called 'personal' analysts, who regard neurosis not so much as a medical phenomenon but rather as an existential problem, whose ultimate cause is to be found in modern man's 'remoteness from God', has antecedents in both C. G. Jung and in the interpretations of human life advanced by existential analysis. But despite the undeniable influence of existential philosophy in this sphere, it was C. G. Jung who was the real founder of personal analysis, for without Jung's archetypes the 'unknown God' to whom the personal analysts refer (V. E. Frankl) would have been unthinkable. Jung's formulation of the relationship between the archetypes and Christianity is as follows:

'Although our whole world of religious ideas consists of anthropomorphic images, which could never stand up to rational criticism, we must not forget that these images are based on *numinous archetypes,* i.e. on an emotional foundation, which is immune to the attacks of critical reason. What we are concerned with here are psychic facts, which can only be disregarded but not disproved.'[3]

'A knowledge of the universal archetypal background was, in itself,

---

[1] J. Jacobi, *The Psychology of C. G. Jung,* p. 87.
[2] Cf. Affemann, R., *Psychologie und Bibel* ('Psychology and the Bible'), Stuttgart, 1957.
[3] C. G. Jung *Answer to Job,* Coll. Wks., Vol. 2.

sufficient to give me the courage to treat "that which is believed always, everywhere, by everybody" as a *psychological fact* which extends far beyond the confines of Christianity, and to approach it as an *object of scientific study*, as a *phenomenon* pure and simple, regardless of the metaphysical significance that may have been attached to it.'[1]

B

OTTO RANK

(a) *The Birth Trauma*

(i) *Rank's Influence on Psychoanalytic Theories*

Like Abraham, Ferenczi, Adler and Jung, Rank was one of Freud's first disciples. He was not a medical man but came to psychoanalysis from philosophy, art and history. Freud clearly considered Rank's background to be of particular importance, for he entrusted him with the special task of investigating comparative cultural history and mythology from the psychoanalytic point of view.

In 1924 Rank published his principal work *The Birth Trauma*, for which he expected rather more recognition and esteem from his colleagues in the psychoanalytic movement than he in fact received. Freud subjected Rank's conception to sharp criticism and in the course of the ensuing years Rank moved farther and farther away from his preceptor. He went to live in Paris and from there moved on to America, where he worked at various universities, but chiefly in Philadelphia. His influence on the Neo-Freudians, especially Horney, Sullivan and Fromm, and also at a later date on 'personal analysis' was considerable.

(ii) *The Birth Trauma as the Basis of a Theory of Neurosis*

Rank's doctrine concerning the consequences of the birth trauma for human development has been largely abandoned to-day. It is of historical interest in as far as—like many other theories advanced by Freud's disciples (e.g. Ferenczi, Reich, Adler, Klein)—it claims to solve practically every problem concerning the emergence of neuroses as well as problems of normal development from a single point of view. In his theory Rank lays relatively little stress on the anxiety trauma, which the child might conceivably experience at birth and which Freud considered to be the prototype of all anxiety conditions. Instead he places his main emphasis on the child's separation from its mother. In Rank's view the whole of man's subsequent life is governed by his (unconscious) longing to re-establish the condition of perfect bliss which he enjoyed in his intra-uterine existence. This longing constantly asserts itself as an

[1] C. G. Jung Coll. Wks., Vol. 2, p. 200.

extreme form of regression in psychoses, depressions and neuroses. However, man's longing to return to the womb is opposed by his memory of the process of birth and of the condition of anxiety which accompanied it. These opposing forces give rise to conflict and Rank considers this conflict to be the basic form from which all subsequent conflicts derive. In the fear of castration—which would involve the loss of the penis—the old fear of the birth trauma is resuscitated.[1] If perversions are considered in the light of the birth trauma it follows that the homosexual avoids the female genital because it reminds him of his birth. In normal heterosexual union the activity of the penis symbolizes the return to the womb, which also explains the pleasure derived from cohabitation. Rank considers that fear of the female genitals and thus (since the actual fear recalls the original conflict) fear of the birth trauma are factors of major importance in the genesis of neurosis. When little boys conceive incestuous wishes it is possible that they may overcome the fear to which these give rise, in which case the shock of the birth trauma is further repressed and the individual is able to normalize his development. But in the majority of cases little boys are prevented from forming an Oedipus complex by their fear of castration and must wait until puberty to master their fear of a repetition of the birth trauma.

In his subsequent development Rank retreated from many of the positions he adopted in this theory. His later arguments, as is indicated in the following section, were more concerned with the birth of individuality.

(b) The Birth of Individuality

(i) Separation and Individualtity

As Rank moved further away from Freud even his biological-evolutionist conceptions acquired a more philosophical orientation, which was destined to reappear in the theories of *E. Fromm, K. Horney, H. S. Sullivan* and even *C. G. Jung*. This theory of Rank's goes back to *Hegel* and to the philosophy of German Idealism, but above all it goes back to *Fichte* and his arguments concerning the will. Rank's first theoretical phase was governed by the contrast between the individual's longing for an inter-uterine existence and his fear of a repetition of the birth trauma. His second phase is governed by the contrast between the free and the bound individual. This contrast has been dealt with by Fromm in his work, by C. G. Jung in connection with the problems of individuation and by K. Horney, whose concept of self-realization was surely anticipated by Rank. Individuality, the self, is 'born' in the

[1] By equating castration (in which the penis is separated from the body) with birth (in which the child is separated from its mother).

course of life following the severance of those bonds, which kept the individual in a state of servitude and dependence. The initial severance of biological bonds is accomplished at birth: the child's separation from its mother is the prerequisite for the development of its (free) personality. But birth not only separates the child from its mother, it also creates in the child a feeling of complete isolation. Only when at some future time the individual has succeeded in re-establishing within his own ego the consciousness of an absolute connection and fusion with the world, with the Cosmos, and thus, at a different level, a condition corresponding to that of inter-uterine existence, only then will his individuality have been freed from all the bonds and restrictions of biological nature, only then will it have found itself. Whereas in Rank's earlier conception the birth trauma was conceived as an act taking place within the limits of man's biological condition, i.e. within the limits of physical nature, now, in view of the contrast which Rank establishes between nature and individuality, the birth of individuality is evidently conceived in terms of the individual's separation, his release, from his natural and biological bonds. In Rank's first conception fear was always the fear that the birth trauma might be repeated, whereas now it has become the fear of the loss of contact which would result from a breakdown in the process of 'Individualization', i.e. the process of self-realization, for if this process did break down then the price paid for individualization would be total isolation and loneliness.

(ii) *Will and Counterwill*

We are indebted to Rank for having dealt with the problem of volition, which has been unduly neglected by Freud's other disciples (with the exception of Adler, who dealt with it in terms of power and will). Usually the will is equated in a stereotype manner with the drives. Rank defines the will as a 'positive organization and integration of the Self, which not only utilizes the drives for productive purposes but also inhibits and controls them'.[1] Assessed in negative terms the fact that the will exists means above all that the organism is not a helpless and passive creation at the mercy of its environment. From a positive point of view the existence of the will enables the individual to guide his inner world (which he has constructed by identifying with the outside world) by projecting on to the outside world, which means that he is able to establish in the outside world conditions which accord with those obtaining in his own inner world. The will is of fundamental importance in the process of self-realization, since it is only through the will that man is able to assert himself *vis-à-vis* the anonymous biological forces of the drive world and of racial or family bonds. The will serves the

[1] O. Rank, *Will Therapy and Truth and Reality*, New York, 1945, pp. 111–12.

process of individualization. The child makes its first acquaintance with the will in the form of the 'counter-will'. Only when the child is able to say 'no', when it is able to oppose the demands and commands of grown-ups, or even to do the opposite of what they want, does it realize that it has *a will of its own*. The will is roused by defiance, or rather the first intense expression of man's self-will assumes the form of defiance. Failure to obey the demands made by parents, or worse still the act of opposing those demands, produces deep guilt feelings in the child. According to Rank these guilt feelings are of an *ethical* nature and are more deeply concealed than the moral guilt feelings which arise when the individual asserts himself *vis-à-vis* society. Ethical guilt feelings are rooted in the actual process of individualization, they are the original guilt imposed by isolation, which is incurred when the individual opposes another's will, i.e. when he exercises his 'counterwill'. Rank considers that one of the most important tasks facing psychotherapy is to teach the patient how to accept these guilt feelings.

(iii) *The Development of the Will*

The first phase in the development of the will is to be found in early childhood, when the child first starts to assert its own will in the face of counter-wills. But it is not only in parental prohibitions and environmental difficulties that the child comes up against counter-wills. For it is also 'being driven' by internal forces, i.e. the drives, and would dearly like to revolt against them. This it is able to do by exercising its will. The extent to which the child exercises its will, however, is in direct proportion to the extent of its development as an individual person. With this thesis Rank of course makes a radical departure from the Freudian view.

The second stage in the development of the child's will is brought about as a result of the comparisons which the child makes with other people: it would like to possess the same things as others possess and do the same things as others do. This engenders a spirit of rivalry and competition which is not overcome until the third stage in the development of the will has been reached, in which the mature individual no longer measures his Dasein (human reality) and his Sosein (Being thus) by comparison with others but instead pursues his own desires under the exclusive guidance of ethical principles. The close connection between desires and guilt feelings is revealed by the discrepancy between the will and the counterwill. If the child overcomes parental opposition—e.g. by disobedience—it soon realizes that it has been 'bad' and so it feels guilty. But if it strives to obey its parents' will, if it adopts their will as its own, then it is being 'good' and does not feel guilty. Rank—like Freud in his first phase—considers that repression is entirely dependent on the desire to be 'good', since 'bad' desires are repressed by feelings of guilt. Ranks claims further that the child's need for recognition and security is also dependent on adult approval of its desires and thus of its 'goodness'.

(iv) *The Position of the Ego*

In Rank's view the ego is an autonomous representative of the will. He considers the ego and the will to be largely identical (cf. Scheler's Centre of Action). Because of its close connection with the will the ego occupies a position of central importance in Rank's system. Without wishing to deny the importance, let alone the existence, of unconscious processes it is in the nature of Rank's conception that his psychology should veer strongly towards a psychology of consciousness. And indeed he considers consciousness and ego consciousness to be identical concepts, since consciousness of an object or of an inner process presupposes ego-consciousness, i.e. presupposes the possibility that a given object or condition may become capable of conscious apperception. Various stages of consciousness are involved in this process just as various stages were involved in the development of the will. At first consciousness is the organ of perception of external objects, then of internal, intrapsychic processes, after which it assumes control over external and internal activity and finally becomes the organ of self-knowledge, of self-perception in the full sense of the word. As a result of this last development consciousness is rendered largely independent of the will, for it is now in a position to support the will or, by the simple expedient of denying the objects of the will, even to repress it. (At this point we recognize Freud's defence against the drives, here translated to the will.) With this growth in self-awareness and self-knowledge, however, the individual is also made aware both of an indissoluble conflict of will, for he is unable to realize all his desires, and of an indissoluble ego conflict, for he is now aware of his separateness, of the difference which marks him off from nature, from the cosmos and from other people. The fact that he exists and is aware that he exists as a being apart from 'others' makes him feel quite as guilty as he felt in childhood when he developed his will by exercising his negative counter-will (i.e. by defiance). This conception of Rank's is not so very far removed from the conception of 'original sin'. At heart everyone longs to rid himself of consciousness and enter into a state of blissful insensibility, in which he would be reunited with the Cosmos (the intra-uterine condition of Rank's first phase). In a large number of myths and religions self-realization was held to be the root of all evil, the root of sin itself, for it was self-realization which first enabled man to oppose nature, to oppose the Cosmos. And it is this opposition which is the essential cause of man's guilt, which no psychotherapy will ever wash away. Self-realization and the development of the will are indissolubly linked with guilt, since it was through these that man first came to oppose the established order of nature.

(v) Emotions and Drives

It is in the nature of the affects and drives—especially of the drives—that they can never be fully gratified, that every gratification and every measure of control is no more than temporary. (Nietzsche: 'For desire seeks eternity . . .'.) Apart form the affects and drives Rank also differentiates between impulses and emotions. Impulses are very primitive forms of drives which find expression, for example, in a baby's uncontrolled kicking and which follow the principle of pleasure and displeasure in every instance. Emotions on the other hand—which include feelings—oppose the pleasure-displeasure principle, for they are intent on extending the pleasurable stage for as long as possible. Emotions (feelings) come about only as a result of the inhibition and blocking of impulses either by the will or by the ego. It is this which enables them to oppose the pleasure-displeasure principle. They are primarily directed towards other people, i.e. towards the partner, towards the community, for feelings, whether of hate or love, are always concerned in some fashion or form with other people. In the final analysis there are only two kinds of emotions, those which join together and those which separate, i.e. love and hate. Love embraces tenderness, gratitude, longing, submission and surrender. Hate embraces anger, fear, pride and jealousy. If the qualities of love may be said to relax the will, then the qualities of hate create hardness, tension and rigidity of the will. Rank insists that feelings are the strongest inner force at work in man, stronger than sexuality, for sexuality can always be controlled or gratified in one way or another, whereas effects and feelings are ultimately beyond the control of the will. In Rank's view sexuality has only one function, a function, however, which in no sense lessens its importance, namely, to resolve the primary conflict of the will, of consciousness (the 'original guilt' incurred by isolation) in the sexual act, the union of two individuals. The 'original sin' of consciousness, of isolation, of separateness, is resolved by sexuality.

(vi) Three Forms of Human Behaviour

In developing his theory of neuroses Rank was concerned not only with specific clinical symptoms but also with the degree of maturity which the individual had attained in the course of his 'isolation' or alternatively his self-realization. This means that in contrast to the average man both neurotics and creative individuals, i.e. artists, have broken with the unity of the collective, with anonymous conventions, moral rules and traditions. Not only does the average man continue to live his life within the deceptive unity of the collective social order, whose bankruptcy has long been apparent, he actually insists on doing so and refuses to accept himself as an individual. The inevitability of isolation, which Rank, like Hegel, considers to be historically determined, is repressed by the 'average man'. The consequence of such repression is that the average man is always playing a part although he thinks he is being himself, always 'appearing to be' but never actually 'being'. He moves in a world of deceptive and false pseudo-institutions. The neurotic on the other hand has realized the necessity for self-realization, isolation and individualization but has broken down on the way and can neither move back to the level of the average man, back into the world of pseudo-institutions, nor move forwards to creative productivity. Only neurotics and artists—in whom Rank, like Jung, sees the crowning glory of individualization—have severed their ties with the apparent unity of pseudo-institutions and so find themselves in a position from which they may proceed to engage in the productivity of the self-determining ego (cf. Fichte!). Rank claims that Freud failed utterly to grasp the nature of artistic activity. If he had understood it he would never have attempted to explain—as he did in his studies of Dostojevsky and Michelangelo—the specific and individual nature of the artistic personality in terms of the general concepts of id and super ego. For the artistic quality defies 'explanation' in terms of environmental factors (parents) or of the discrepancy between id and super ego. The artist develops his ego ideal out of himself, creating values which are new, which transcend identification and which can only emerge from an emancipated individuality, an individuality which has found itself. The guilt which the creative personality incurs stems from his disregard of the boundaries of sexuality and love, the very means by which man seeks to overcome the original guilt incurred by individuation. Both the natural and the social order set limits to sexuality and love, which may not be exceeded—and this explains why these activities can only be of brief and intermittent service to the individual in his quest for release from individuality. The artist on the other hand tries to transcend these set limits through creative work. By imposing his creative will on love and sexuality he hopes to avoid the harsh necessity of falling a victim to love, of repaying love in kind. In the processes of artistic creation the ego, intent as it is on subjecting the world to its artistic will, is diametrically opposed to the world and its laws.

There are three different ways in which the individual can escape from the harsh necessity of isolation and self-realization which history imposes. He can follow the lead of the 'average man' and either take refuge in a pseudo social order or seek release from isolation by repeatedly indulging in love and sexuality. Or else there is the way of the artist, who makes a virtue out of the vice of individualization by creating a world from within himself and subjugating the external world to his own inner world.

(vii) *The Oedipus Myth*

In his mythological, anthropological and sociological investigations Rank arrived at conclusions concerning the Oedipus complex which were diametrically opposed to Freud's. In contrast to Freud Rank bases his conceptions not only on the work of *J. J. Bachofen* but also on the current literature of anthropology and folklore, of which Freud appeared to know less than might have been expected in view of the boldness of the theses which he advanced in *Totem and Taboo*. Rank contends that Freud's primal horde has never really existed and that his theory is contradicted both by the social forms obtaining in primitive societies to-day and by modern knowledge of the life of man in early times. The most primitive form of human society involved a sort of group marriage, a practice which was closely connected with religious ideas. In the group family the children belonged to *all* the mothers and as each child began to grow up it was allocated to a particular father to be educated.[1] The group family was superseded by the matriarchy, in which the mother's brother was the male head of the family, and it was this matriarchy which was superseded by the patriarchal order and the small family groups which we know to-day. It was in the patriarchal period that the struggle between the individual and the father first began and it was in Greek mythology that this struggle found its most enduring expression. The connection between procreation and fatherhood had been unknown to the earlier forms of society, i.e. group family and matriarchy. This fact alone destroys the thesis of a primal horde descended from the apes, since this thesis presupposes at the very least that at the time when the sons killed their father they were aware of the connection between possession of the woman, intercourse and procreation. The inability of these early societies to establish the connection between fatherhood and procreation also held good for the connection between motherhood and conception. The mother simply looked after the child as a host looks

[1] Cf. Levi-Strauss, *Tristes Tropiques*, Paris, 1956, who discovered similar forms of controlled promiscuity in Brazilian Indians, whose lives were commensurate with the cultural level of the Stone Age.

after his guest. This was as far as the relationship could go—for had not the mother conceived of the spirit of her dead ancestors who had lived on in animals and plants? And so in terms of Rank's philosophy Oedipus' struggle against his father, which led to the father's death, is interpreted as the struggle of the (son's) individuality, which desires and believes in its own immortality, against the father, who is the representative of the 'group-ego', the collective and the world of sexual ideas. If it wished to make its peace with sexuality and procreation the 'individual ego' would have to renounce its immortality and the urge—one which the artist partially realizes—to perpetuate itself. It is this requirement which lies at the heart of the conflict between father and son. And so Rank considers that the Oedipus myth should be regarded from two different points of view:

1. From the point of view of pre-patriarchal societies in which the individual believed he was immortal because he was unaware of the connection between procreation and birth. When such an individual comes into contact with a patriarchal society, which is aware of the connection between procreation and birth and believes in immortality only in terms of the continuance of the race, conflict must inevitably ensue between the father, who is the representative of the patriarchal principle, and the son, who has not yet accepted that principle.
2. From the point of view of the struggle between the individual, who strives for self-realization, and the 'father principle', which stands for family ties and traditions.

Thus far the specific conflict between father and son! But there is also the question of incestuous wishes. Rank considers that these derive from myths of re-birth. He derives the Oedipus saga from primitive rites of spring and from vegetation rituals, in which the son of (mother) earth is also her husband. Rank claims that Freud's conception of the Oedipus complex as a representation of the son's desire to identify with his father is inconsistent with the genesis of this myth. On the contrary, the opposite of Freud's interpretation would appear to be correct; the son wishes at all cost to avoid identifying with his father, in order that he may overcome the father (see above). The reason why the individual seeks to establish new bonds with patriarchal society, i.e. the reason why he identifies with the father, is that the triumph of individuality since antiquity and more especially since the Renaissance and the Enlightenment, which is closely connected with the dissolution of the father principle and of family institutions, has instilled in the individual a growing fear of his own individuality. In Rank's view, therefore, the Oedipus complex is determined by sociological considerations alone and is indicative of regressive desires and tendencies on the part of the individual to reject individuality and to seek refuge in the father principle, i.e. in the patriarchal society. This conception of Rank's relates back to his earlier conception of the contrast between independence (overcoming the father principle) and dependence (identification with the father principle).

(viii) *Psychotherapy*

In order to distinguish his own therapeutic method from Freudian anlysis Rank called it 'psychotherapy'. The primary objective of Rank's psychotherapy is to enable the neurotic, vacillating between the bonds of the 'average man' and the freedom and individualization of the artist, to accept his own will and his own individuality without feeling anxiety or guilt. Rank's therapy—like Jung's—is concerned with re-education and self-education. Uncovering the past is less important than the emancipation of the individual ego from the pseudo institutions of the collective. However, in Rank's therapy the doctor-patient relationship is of greater importance than it is in Jung's. For the neurotic often feels that in accepting treatment he is being subjected to the foreign will—the counterwill—of the physician and so the success of the treatment will depend to a considerable degree on whether the patient acquires the courage to assert his own desires *vis-à-vis* the physician. It is for this reason that Rank considers resistance and aggression to be extremely positive therapeutic forces, since they are vehicles of the patient's newly aroused self-will. Rank had already made a detailed investigation into the problem of the doctor-patient relationship twenty years before this became a topic of general interest to psychotherapists (see below p. 410). Rank tried to strengthen the patient's will by encouraging resistances directed against the therapist, but at the same time he also tried to adapt the therapist's will to the patient's own will by encouraging an active, inner participation in the patient's fate on the part of the therapist. The knowledge which the patient acquires from his encounters with the therapist's will—e.g. the knowledge that patients do get better —helps him to fight his way through to his own will, to himself and to his individuality. In view of Rank's philosophical and pedagogic outlook it is scarcely surprising that in his psychotherapy particular importance is attached to the discussion of the patient's 'reality', i.e. his day to day life, and that a time limit is set for the completion of treatment. These factors, which were favoured by both Ferenczi and Adler and which were rejected out of hand by the Freudians, establish a close connection between Rank's psychotherapy and the methods of treatment employed by the Neo-Freudians.

C

PERSONAL ANALYSIS

(a) *The Concept of Personality*

In his study on *Das Personenverständnis im modernen medizinischen Denken*[1] P. Christian has revealed the confusions and contradictions which beset this concept, one which only appears meaningful if presented in dialectical terms. From the turn of the century to the present day we have been subjected to a veritable kaleidoscope of views ranging from naturalist-positivist conceptions (of which Behaviourism is the chief representative within the field of psychoanalysis at the present time) to Aristotelian-Thomist conceptions (Catholics), existential conceptions (Heidegger and his school) and the anthropological interpretations of personality advanced by thinkers such as *von Weizsäcker, Buytendijk, von Gebsattel, Kütemeyer, Kunz, Straus, Zutt, etc.* Christian outlines the difficulties involved in providing an adequate description of the concept of personality:

'The *second* fundamental difficulty encountered in attempting adequately to define the concept of personality in the field of medicine lies in the nature of the "personality" itself: we always miss the point of personality when we interpret it in scientific, universally valid and hence abstract terms. This happens *eo ipso* if I identify the personality with one of its biological functions (or with the aggregate of its biological functions), which other living creatures, e.g. animals, or life itself, share with it. What happens then is that "personality" becomes abstract, indifferent —at all events it is no longer concrete, unique "personality". But I also miss the point of "personality" if I restrict it to spiritual or mental functions: for example, to "thinking" or to the condition of "being myself" or to the general subject of feeling, willing, perceiving or doing. "Personality" underlies all of these and may therefore be defined neither in terms of any one of its particular functions nor indeed retrospectively in terms of the contents of those functions. From this it follows that personality can never be grasped in abstract terms, i.e. either as "mind" (as a logical or rational subject), or as the subject of feeling and of acting (as the general carrier of values and evaluations), but rather personality—to take this concept, which is used in an infinite variety of meanings, in its literal sense of the carrier of the "personare"—is the subject of any given act, *to whom* something appears, *who* does something, *who* acts, feels or thinks. In other words, "personality" realizes

[1] P. Christian, *Das Personenverständnis im modernen medizinischen Denken*, Tübingen, 1952. ('The Understanding of Personality in Modern Medical Thought'.)

itself in the doing of its deeds, in the experiencing of its experiences, in the thinking of its thoughts. It is of the essential nature of the personality that it lives and has its being only in the enactment of its own intentional acts. And so it is meaningless to identify it with the forms of its acts (thinking, willing, valuing, etc.). It is even less susceptible to definition in terms of the objectivizations of its own acts. Every objectifying attitude must necessarily render the Being of the personality transcendent. Consequently "personality" cannot be grasped in the objective conceptions to which im-personal objective research aspires. *Max Scheler*[1] has demonstrated this once and for all. And so it follows that *definitions of personality are necessarily casuist, unique and contingent.* 'Every patient reveals phenomena which never existed before and will never exist again in that particular condition and form and consequently in the emergence of pathological processes" (*Krehl*). Any definition of personality, therefore, can only succeed if it refers back to the *individuality* of the person concerned.'[2]

He sums up as follows:

'1. Any definition of personality in the impersonal forms of the particular science which is in the ascendancy in a given epoch is necessarily opposed by a definition of personality in terms of the personally unique nature of the individual.

'2. In connection with the above it should be said that in every generalization and every theoretical definition personality is necessarily rendered abstract. The antithesis to this is the interpretation of personality as unique and concrete Being.

'3. Every interpretation of the personality as an "individual" constitutes an antithesis to the inter-personal definition of personality as found in the relationship between doctor and patient conceived as a relationship between partners.'[3]

(b) The Concept of Personality in Psychoanalysis

The naturalist-positivist concept of personality, which reached its peak in 'l'homme machine' of the Enlightenment, formed the basis of Freud's ideas. A description of the personality, or rather of the 'psychic apparatus', in terms of the libido economy, which was itself based on the formulae of hydraulics and electro-physics, was Freud's scientific ideal.

[1] M. Scheler, *Der Formalismus in der Ethik und die materiale Wertethik*, 2nd edition, Halle, 1922 (footnote in Christian, *ibid.*) ('Formalism in Ethics and the Material Ethics of Value').
[2] P. Christian, *Das Personenverständnis im modernen medizinischen Denken*, Tübingen, 1952, pp. 5–6. ('The Understanding of Personality in Modern Medical Thought'.) [3] P. Christian, *ibid.*, p. 9.

We have already seen that this conception broke down in Freud's last phase.

Many of Freud's followers, especially the New York Group, but also *Nunberg, Glover, etc.*, reacted against Freud's positivism by developing a new concept of personality. The synthetic function of the *ego* stipulated by *Hartmann, Nunberg*, etc., and the pre-existence of an *ego* that is independent of the id are innovations which move towards *Scheler's* view of the personality and the concept of the ego as the centre of mental activity. What this means is that Hartmann, Nunberg, etc., are in fact veering away from Freud's positivist views and towards Rank's conceptions in as far as Rank equates the ego with the will and makes both independent of the drives.

Jung tried to overcome this positivist basis of Freudian psychoanalysis, but his own basis is so vastly different from Freud's in various essential respects that over large areas Freud and Jung are incommensurable and defy comparison. Jung's 'individuation', like Rank's individualization, tries to do justice to man's desire to fix the centre of personality in the spiritual self, i.e. in the 'mana personality', whereby both the purpose and the meaning of personality are ultimately rendered transcendental. It should be pointed out, however, that Jung has been accused by the existential analysts of having psychologized both the psyche and the self and of having made the ego largely dependent on the constellation of the archetypes, which would mean that in this last respect Jung was propounding the same determinist thesis as Freud, albeit in a more refined way.

To consider personality as a concept in its own right is even more alien to Adler than it is to Freud. He regards self-sensation as the nucleus of the personality and this self-sensation has to come to terms with strivings for recognition and power on the one hand and with feelings of inferiority on the other. Adler's conception of personality is not determined by the libido economy, as is Freud's, but rather by considerations of security based on a biologist type economy and governed by the requirements of a given social order. Compensation and over-compensation are, so to speak, the 'financial' regulators of self-sensation, which fluctuates between the will to power and feelings of inferiority.

With the exception of E. Fromm and K. Horney in her last phase the *Neo-Freudians* have made no noteworthy contributions to the concept of personality. Since they reject a structure of the personality in terms of instances, such as the ego and the super-ego, their definitions are necessarily restricted to the description of dynamic tendencies, which are reducible—in the case of Schultz-Hencke for example—to little more than the antithesis between expansion and inhibition. In *Behaviourism*—

Sullivan, French, Rado—the personality is reduced to the status of a conditioned reflex (see p. 524 ff.), which nobody, not even Sullivan with his emphasis on inter-personal relations, can deny.

(c) The Concept of Personality in Psychiatry: K. Jaspers and K. Schneider

In his *General Psychopathology*,[1] which opened new paths to psychiatry in Germany, K. Jaspers defined personality as 'the connection of what is meaningful in terms of the whole man'. Objective activity, i.e. chemical, physical or physiological processes, demands a causal *explanation*. But causal explanations are not an adquate means of recognizing psychic processes. Psychic activity is meaningful because it is understandable and not because it is susceptible to *causal* deduction and explanation. The essentials of Jasper's concept of personality may be summed up as follows: on the one hand personality incorporates original, elementary and irreducible existence (transcendence), whilst on the other hand it is constantly realizing itself in the world by means of intelligence, will and feeling, by means of actions and experiences. Psychological concepts can only be applied to the exploration of personality when personality is in the process of being realized, when it constitutes the connection of 'what is meaningful in terms of the whole man'. When personality is in its transcendental state, however, psychology must yield to the interpretations of 'Existential philosophy'.

   K. Schneider's concept of personality differs from Jasper's in that it reveals no transcendental bias and is restricted to the field of normal and abnormal personality conditions. He speaks of the totality of 'feeling, valuing, striving and willing', which is the exclusive province of the spiritual aspect of personality, and declares the faculties of reason, such as intelligence, conceptual and combinatory capacity, to be irrelevant to the concept of personality. K. Schneider—like *M. Scheler*—divides the personality into three spheres: the sphere of the intelligence, the vital, bodily sphere of feelings and drives and the sphere of 'feeling, willing, valuing and striving' which is the only relevant sphere for psychology.

(d) The Personality in Existential Ontology

The importance of Heidegger's existential ontology will be discussed later from the point of view of the influence it exercised on Binswanger. The concept of personality advanced by the existential ontologists constitutes a radical attempt to overcome both the positivist-scientific 'explanation' of personality in terms of causation (the scientifically oriented theories of psychoanalysis) and the interpretation of personality in 'meaningful' terms undertaken by Jaspers and his school (K.

[1] K. Jaspers, *General Psychopathology*, London, 1900.

Schneider) within the field of modern psychiatry. The existential philosopher holds that both these interpretations are doomed from the outset, since they fail to resolve the dualism between subject and object, between the individual personality and the world. Because of its 'Being in the world' the personality is traced back to its actual roots in the world. In this process the primary element is not thought, consciousness or recognition (i.e. 'cogito'). Rather it is the Being of the person-lity in the world which is primary, as in the original state of human reality (Heidegger). And so in existential analysis all expressions of the personality—e.g. clinical symptoms such as faulty actions and dreams—are interpreted in terms of their objective transcendence. The criterion for the existential ontologist is the extent to which the symptom can be said to possess human reality. The concept of personality in existential ontology is not susceptible to definitive formulation. Personality has to be distinguished both from its 'Sosein' (Being thus) and its 'Dasein' (Being there—Human reality); moreover, it constantly points beyond itself, involving the other party, i.e. the partner; and finally its *historicity* is part of its structural form. Christian gives the following summary of the development of the concept of personality from scientific positivism to existential philosophy:

'At the beginning of our investigation "personality" was concealed behind the mask of science and of the scientific view of the world. "Personality", as it were, fluctuated in accordance with these forms, but then progressively separated out from this background. In the course of a constant dialectical process the conception of personality was restricted to the image of man's own essence and proceeded to seek its objective there.

'. . . at first the concept of "personality" had possessed a content which was clearly outlined and conceived in substantial terms. Personality appeared to be subject to the limitations of space and time. It possessed a body, which was said to be a natural object, and a soul which was enclosed in that body. Biologism attributed an objective character to personality, i.e. it was one object amongst other objects. With the increasing dynamism of man's world view personality was obliged to renounce this objective character and appeared more and more as the essence of functions and acts. It became increasingly difficult to regard personality in terms of the objective forms of given objects. Within the context of an anthropological investigation of personality it is now quite impossible to interpret it in terms of objects: within this context personality appears as a pathic-personal relationship of obligation, duty, responsibility, which points beyond itself, i.e. it appears as a *"reference"*. With the radicalization of this advance personality thrusts beyond

376

itself, advancing beyond the definition of an "individual". For personality is no longer identical with the sphere of the individual subject, and from the anthropological point of view man is both an individual subject and a related factor in a meeting with the other subject. Personality is one subject amongst other subjects and reveals itself through the partner quite as much as through its own person.

'And so "personality" transcends itself in as far as it is considered in terms of the individual Being of the Self and of an individual inner essence. No sooner is "personality" considered in this individual light than it is suspended and forms the horizon for a new and different definition.'[1]

(e) *The Catholic View of Personality and Personal Analysis* (*The New Viennese School*)

V. E. Frankl, I. Caruso, P. R. Hofstätter and *W. Daim* are the leading protagonists of 'personal analysis', which has been concentrated chiefly in Vienna since its inception in 1945. For this reason its practitioners are commonly referred to as the 'new Viennese school'. After the advent of C. G. Jung both idealistic and existential philosophers began to take a growing interest in psychoanalysis, and it was doubtless this which prompted the (Catholic) theologians to take a hand in this new field of activity with the object of 'shifting the emphasis' of Freudian psychoanalysis so that it might be reconciled with Church dogma. V. E. Frankl formulates the Catholic concept of personality as derived from Aristotle and the Old Testament on the one hand and as developed by Thomas Aquinas on the other:

'But only when human Being, conceived as individuated Being, is centred around a single personality (as its spiritual-existential centre) in any given case, then and only then is human Being integrated: the spiritual personality alone establishes the unity and entity of the creature, man. It establishes this unity as a unity of body, soul and spirit. And we cannot stress often enough that it is only this threefold entity which truly constitutes man. For it is in no sense justified to speak of man as an entity of "body and soul": body and soul may form a unity—a psycho-physical unity perhaps—but this unity would never be capable of representing the entity that is man: for this entity, the entire man, also embraces the spiritual, and embraces it as its very own. And so, as long as we talk of body and soul, it follows *eo ipso* that we cannot be talking of an entity.'[2]

[1] P. Christian, *Das Personenverständnis im modernen medizinischen Denken*, Tübingen, 1952, p. 116.

[2] V. E. Frankl, *Der unbewusste Gott*, Vienna, 1949, pp. 27–8. ('The Unconscious God').

The development of the personality is now directed towards God, i.e. entelechy is its criterion, and man has a direct relationship with God. Daim writes:

'The straight and essential line of man's psychic entelechy is the line of development that leads towards God. Like all his other endowments it possesses a drive character and it is directed straight towards the Absolute. As long as the dynamics of this development is not distorted all is well. On the one hand the process of self-realization provided for in the plan for the development of man's endowments has a direct relationship to God . . ., whilst on the other hand everything that is in the world has a transparent relationship to God.

'The dynamics of this entelechy is directed on the one hand towards the establishment of an ever expanding and more differentiated relationship to God and on the other hand towards the establishment of an ever more differentiated relationship to the world. Openness *vis-à-vis* the Absolute and thus *vis-à-vis* the world opens up to human entelechy unlimited possibilities for development within the context of that entelechy.'[1]

Daim argues the inevitability of the Absolute as follows:

'For man the Absolute is unavoidable. Man must have an Absolute. Without an Absolute man is incapable of existing, even if he is unaware of the fact. But our question regarding the objective existence of an Absolute and the subjective relationship of man to that Absolute has yet to be answered.

'We are already convinced of the existence of a real and true Absolute. And for psychological reasons! If this were not the case, if there were no Absolute, then we would have to withdraw the real object of man's most central capacity, which is his power to communicate with the Absolute, and thus condemn man to despair.

'Whereas animals are organized in such a way that their organs of perception and their organs of activity allow them access to their world of perception and their world of activity, which means that—albeit intermittently in the case of animals—their subjective capacities are directed towards existentialia in the outside world, man would be the only accursed creature, whose most central capacity, one which vouchsafes him an absolute support in the world, possessed no true object.

'If this were the case, then all meaning would be an illusion. *We have to chose between the meaninglessness of psychic life and the psychological proof of God's existence*. Either the one or the other. We decide in

[1] W. Daim, *Umwertung der Psychoanalyse*, Vienna, 1951, p. 258. ('Revaluation of Psychoanalysis').

378

favour of the latter and believe in the existence of an objective Absolute which is independent of man's existence as such.

'The objective Absolute is God. Man's most central capacity is his ability to communicate with Him. *Vis-à-vis* the world God is transcendent. He is not the world and He is nothing in the world. If now the subjective Absolute and the objective Absolute come together and are as one, then man's experience of Absoluteness will meet the needs of his situation and he will be adapted to reality in the most essential aspects of his psychic life, in his experience of the Absolute and his relationship to it.'[1]

Personal analysis is now in a position to interpret neurosis as an attempt to impose absolute value on what is merely relative. Daim defines this process as 'idolatry' and he equates idolatry with the Freudian concept of fixation.

Daim follows his preceptor, Caruso, in proposing that for the most part neurosis constitutes an attempt to impose absolute values on what is merely relative. According to this thesis all men naturally tend towards the Absolute, towards God, in their innermost being. What happens in neurosis is that this existential tendency towards the Absolute is replaced by a false orientation towards relative values, such as power, sexuality, status, etc. In these faulty attitudes relative values are given preference over absolute values, e.g. sexuality is preferred to love, the driving force of man's inner entelechy, i.e. his lust for status, displaces his just desire for knowledge of his objective possibilities. The first development of these faulty attitudes takes place in early childhood, when, in the anal stage for example, because of its abnormal possessiveness the child holds on to its faeces, in fact refuses to part with them. (In this respect Daim accepts Freud's three-stage theory.) The child develops such abnormal possessiveness because it imposes absolute values on matters which are merely relative, e.g. faeces, and it is this which leads to the development of neurotic fixations. Daim also calls fixations 'idolatries' because in fixations the Absolute is displaced by relative considerations which have been made into false idols. This tendency in man to fashion false idols from relative values, a tendency which leads to neurosis, ultimately derives from original sin. The psychotherapist's task is to remove the obstacles which block man's way to the Absolute, which is his only salvation.

Whereas Daim grants psychoanalysis a subsidiary function in the task of leading sinners to God, to the Absolute, *V. E. Frankl* questions the very basis of psychoanalysis. Frankl's objections to psychoanalysis are revealing, not because they present a summary of the accusations which

[1] W. Daim, *Umwertung der Psychoanalyse*, Vienna, 1951, pp. 129-30.

have traditionally been brought against it, but because Frankl brings his thomistic philosophy to bear on weaknesses of psychoanalytic theory which have been overlooked by many psychoanalysts.

'The whole of the human soul is atomistically conceived by psycho-analysis, which considers that the soul is made up of individual parts, i.e. the various drives, and that these in their turn are made up of partial drives or drive components. As a result the life of the soul is not only atomized but an-atomized: the analysis of the soul becomes the anatomy of the soul. But this means that the soul, the human personality, has somehow been destroyed: psychoanalysis literally "depersonalizes" man; but not, it is true, without taking the individual—and often mutually antagonistic—instances within the total psychic structure, e.g. the so-called id or the association "complexes", and personifying them (namely, by transforming them into independent, arbitrary, pseudo-personal entities), if not indeed demonizing them.

'And so psychoanalysis destroys the unity and entity of the human personality—only to find itself faced with the task of having to put it together again. This is most clearly demonstrated by that particular psychoanalytic theory, according to which the ego is composed of "ego drives", which means that the instance which represses the drives, which conducts the censorship of the drives, itself possesses a drive nature. Now this is just the same as saying that the builder who makes a house out of bricks is himself made of bricks. From this example, which readily springs to mind, we already see how very materialistic (material in the sense of matter and not of essence) psychoanalytic thought really is. And of course this is the ultimate cause of its atomism.

'But we have said that psychoanalysis is not only atomistic but also energic. ... And indeed it constantly operates with concepts of drive energy and of the dynamics of affects. According to psychoanalysis the drives, or, alternatively, the drive components act in the same way as a parallelogram of forces. But what is the object on which those forces act? We are told: the ego. And so ultimately, in the psychoanalytic view, the ego is at the mercy of the drives—or, as Freud himself once said: the ego is not master in its own house.

'Thus we see that the soul is not only genetically reduced to the level of the drives but is also causally determined by the drives, and both of these processes are totalitarian. *From the very outset psychoanalysis interprets human "Being" in the sense of man's "being driven".* And this is the ultimate reason why man's ego then has to be reconstructed from the drives.'[1]

[1] V. E. Frankl, *Der unbewusste Gott*, Vienna, 1949, pp. 10–13. ('The Unconscious God'.)

Frankl turns Freud's theory of structures (id, ego and super ego) upside down. He starts from the premise that not only the drives are unconscious (as with Freud) but also the spirit. Consequently existential analysis is not so much concerned with releasing repressed drives as with rousing the unconscious spirit, a process which Daim calls the 'freeing of the unconscious'. In the following passage Frankl pours scorn on Freud's theory of structures:

'By degrading the ego to a mere epiphenomenon *Freud betrayed the ego*, as it were, *to the id*; at the same time, however, he *abused* the unconscious—namely, by regarding it only in the light of id or drive qualities and overlooking its ego or spiritual qualities.'[1]

In contrast to Freud's theory of structures Frankl advances a (thomistic) concept of personality which he proceeds to expand into a concept of depth personality. He argues that Freudian psychoanalysis concerns itself only with the animal attributes of personality and fails to deal with man's real spiritual and existential depth personality.

'But as we now know, not only the id but both this spiritual-existential personality and the ego also possess unconscious depths; indeed, by rights we ought, whenever we speak of "depth personality", to have only this spiritual-existential personality in mind, or alternatively, only *its* unconscious depths: it alone is true depth *personality*. For—let us be quite clear about it—what is traditionally understood under depth personality is not of the order of *personal* Being but rather constitutes what might be called animal Being, i.e. something which we ought to attribute to facticity and not to existence and which we ought to subsume under a psycho-physical and not under a spiritual heading.'[2]

Frankl combines his concept of spiritual depth personality with *M. Scheler's* theory of personal enactment (which goes back to *Husserl*). Spiritual enactment, whether in thought or deed, constitutes the 'pure reality of enactment' in the sense that the personality is completely absorbed in the enactment of a particular spiritual process. But such enactments are 'necessarily unconscious', from which it follows that the depth personality is the ultimate existential expression of unconscious but none the less spiritual Being. Existential analysis is not the analysis of such ultimate existentialia but rather—and in this Frankl is diametrically opposed to thinkers like Freud—an analysis leading towards such existentialia, an analysis which leads man to a meeting with himself (cf. also Rank and Jung!). Seen in this light conscience becomes an

[1] V. E. Frankl, *Der unbewusste Gott*, pp. 24.
[2] V. E. Frankl, *ibid.*, pp. 30–1.

instrument of the suprahuman Absolute, which in the case of the neurotic is either repressed or wrongly elevated to the status of the Absolute. The super ego represents only conventional morality. It does not represent the true conscience. Frankl traces the suppression of the conscience in his patients' dreams, which—as with C. G. Jung's patients—often express religious contents, i.e. often contain repressed religion.

Frankl categorically denies Freud's thesis that conscience derives from psychological factors:

But the super ego can no more be derived from the ego than the ego can be derived from the id. On the contrary, what we are faced with here is a two-fold contradiction: on the one hand the *existentiality of the ego* and on the other hand the *transcendentality of the so-called super ego.* As far as the first factor is concerned, we have already discussed the fact that man's (existential) condition of being responsible can never be traced back to his being driven, that the ego can never de derived from drive forces, that the concept of the "ego drives" is in fact self-contradictory. The drives could never repress or censor or sublimate themselves; and however true it may be from a purely biological point of view that it is drive energy which is applied in order to restrain drive forces—that which applies the energy cannot itself then be derived from drive forces.'[1]

'*What stands behind the super ego of man is not the ego of a super-man but the Thou of God; for conscience could never be a word of power in immanence if it were not the word of the Thou in transcendence.*'[2]

'In psychoanalysis not only is the super ego held to be an introjected father imago in a general sense but this is also held to apply above all to our concept of God: for psychoanalysis God is also a mere father imago.

'But we maintain the exact opposite: in reality *God is not a father imago but a father is an imago of God. For us the father is not the original image of all godliness.* On the contrary: *God is the original image of all "fatherliness".* Only ontogenetically, biologically, biographically is the father the first—for ontologically God is the first. And so, although psychologically the father-child relationship is prior to the man-God relationship, ontologically it is not illustrative but derivative. Ontologically speaking my father in the flesh, who created me in the flesh, merely happens to be, as it were, the first representative of Him, Who created everything; and so, ontologically speaking, my natural creator is

[1] V. E. Frankl, *Der unbewusste Gott*, pp. 82–3.
[2] V. E. Frankl, *ibid.*, p. 85.

only the first symbol and thus in a certain sense the imago of the super-natural creator of all nature.'[1]

Frankl regards psychoanalysis in the light of a Münchhausen escapade:

'But psychoanalysis, we now realize, is ultimately nothing but a *psychologized Münchhausen escapade*; for what it asserts is no more and no less than this: *the ego hauls itself out of the morass of the id by the hair of the super ego*.'[2]

The main tenets of existential or personal analysis may be summed up as follows:

1. Man is a unity made up of spirit, soul and body.
2. At the existential level spirit is unconscious.
3. At the existential level spirit is directed towards the Absolute, towards God.
4. The Absolute 'transcends consciousness' but speaks in man as the 'voice of conscience'.
5. The neurotic is an idolator. From early childhood onwards he has imposed absolute values on matters which are merely relative and it is this which has led to his illness. The cause of his illness is his own guilt.
6. The aim of existential psychotherapy is to free man's conscience and to re-orientate man towards God.

These theses of existential analysis have not been without their critics even in Catholic quarters. Amongst others *A. Görres*[3] has subjected them to a critical appraisal. He summarizes his views as follows:

'1. Illness may be caused by both false and correct personal decisions.
'2. Psychogenic illnesses may also emerge independently of any such personal decisions or attitudes or, alternatively, of any such distorted decisions or distorted attitudes.
'3. Consequently it is not possible to trace psychogenic illnesses back with any degree of certainty to a moral condition, i.e. to present or past guilt. Superbia cannot be diagnosed from neurosis.
'4. Illness (psychosis) may affect every act of the personality; there is no spiritual act and no species of acts which are necessarily immune to such an illness. The postulate that 'in psychosis that which has remained healthy is immune to illness" is untenable.

[1] V. E. Frankl, *Der unbewusste Gott*, p. 86–7.
[2] V. E. Frankl, *ibid.*, p. 86.
[3] A. Görres, 'Person, Psyche, Krankheit' (in the *Jahrbuch für Psychologie und Psychotherapie*, 6.Jg., H.1/3, 1958, pp. 192 ff.) ('Personality, Psyche and Illness').

'5. Illness (psychosis) can so change the individual's sense of values and his powers of moral judgement that free and responsible decisions are no longer possible or are only possible to a limited extent or within areas of experience which happen to have escaped the illness.

'6. Illness can destroy all virtue that has been made manifest in the individual's patterns of behaviour. It cannot directly affect the individual's basic moral attitude, which is concealed, for in order to do so it would at one and the same time and in one and the same respect have to give and take away the individual's freedom, since psycho-spiritual processes which are not free are not able to affect a pre-existent basic moral outlook, i.e. are unable to affect questions of good and evil. In this sense we may justly say that *moral* personality transcends health and illness.

'7. Psychic health in the sense of organization, psychic illness in the sense of disorganization, within the sphere of involuntary, pre-personal psychic processes and of the structures which carry them, i.e. in the "ordo sentiendi", must be distinguished from the organization and disorganization within the sphere of voluntary acts of will and moral attitudes emanating from the core of the personality (ordo consentiendi). Psychic illness impairs the functional efficiency, the "capabilities", which are prior to good or bad will.'[1]

D

LUDWIG BINSWANGER AND EXISTENTIAL PHILOSOPHY

(a) Binswanger's Criticism of Freud

Like M. Scheler and von Weizsäcker Ludwig Binswanger has made a probing criticism of Freudian psychoanalysis.[1] Whilst he himself remained personally loyal to Freud throughout his life and insisted time and again on the importance of Freud's work for the development of modern psychiatry he also had the courage to advance to an anthropological view of man which afforded a more adequate explanation of human personality and which provided an example for a whole generation of psychiatrists. An advance such as this and the overcoming of Freudian positivism which it involved would have been impossible, of course, but for *Husserl's* phenomenology and *Heidegger's* subsequent existential ontology. *Minkowski* in France and *Jaspers* and *Binswanger* in Germany

---

[1] A. Görres, 'Person, Psyche, Krankheit' (in the *Jahrbuch für Psychologie und Psychotherapie*, 6.Jg., H.1/3, 1958, pp. 192 ff.) ('Personality, Psyche and Illness').

were the first to apply the phenomenological method to psychiatry. They were soon followed in this undertaking by a whole host of other psychiatrists such as *von Gebsattel, E. Straus, R. Kuhn, H. Kunz, M. Boss, J. Zutt and C. Kulenkampff*. It would go beyond the scope of this present investigation, however, to afford a systematic review of the contributions made by these various authors. Traditional psychology in the form in which it was encountered first by Freud and then by Binswanger and which achieved its ultimate expression in Jaspers' *General Psychopathology* was in fact no more than a conglomeration of unrelated data based on three main theoretical factors:

1. Mental illness seen as the consequence of an organic disturbance in the brain (*Kraepelin* and *Bleuler*).
2. Mental illness seen as the consequence of pre-formed syndromes already present in the organism (*Hoche*).
3. Mental illness seen as either a chronic or a temporary reaction on the part of an abnormal personality (*Kraepelin, Jaspers*, subsequently *Bonhoeffer's* 'exogenic reaction types').

These theoretical postulates were reflected in the field of practical research in pathological anatomy, hereditary biology and characterology (*Kretschmer, Jaspers*). The sole aim of characterology was to establish a *meaningful* connection between experience and possible character change, an aim which it was inclined to pursue without any reference to biological influences whatsoever. Binswanger, on the other hand, was able to point to Freudian psychoanalysis as a single comprehensive system, whose purpose was to understand human beings and their illnesses in terms of their 'inner contradictions', i.e. in terms of conflict.

'And at this point a further fundamental characteristic of *Freudian* research is at once revealed, one which is in complete accord with the subject "matter" in which Freud as a therapist was interested, namely, the neurotic personality, and which clearly shows that he *did not in any sense* consider that the suspension of psychological conflict would be realized by existential *maturation*, by *self-realization*, as an expression of man's free capacity for Being (a process which was advocated in a certain, albeit non-existential, sense by Jung), but rather by the complete failure to effect such a realization, i.e. by repression. The difference between mental health and mental illness now consisted simply of the varying degrees of "*importance for life of the achievements*" in which the mechanisms of repression "are invested"! . . . This establishes a highly important connection, one which had been completely unknown to psychiatry until then, between the "moments of reality", by means of which the "biological nature of man as an animate being is linked with his existential capacity for Being". In other words, one of the *frontier structures*, "in which man's free capacity for Being either fulfils or fails to fulfil the possibilities inherent in the biological functions", has thereby been *freed*.'[1,2,3]

In his further criticism of Freud, however, Binswanger found himself unable to accept the naturalist-positivist concept of man advanced in psychoanalysis[4]. He demonstrates that the idea of 'homo natura', which is presented in psychoanalysis and which was the product of (1) Freud's scientific creed, (2) his method and (3) his theory, is only valid if considered as a 'scientific construction' but that it is quite unable to render an adequate account of human reality. Binswanger reveals Freud's positivist creed by quoting a passage from the 'Future of an Illusion', in which Freud clearly indicates the correlation between his conception of power and the technical exploitation of nature. 'We believe that it is possible to experience something of the reality of the world by means of scientific enquiry, which will enable us to increase our power and in accordance with which we may arrange our lives.' Binswanger calls attention to the reductive method which psychoanalysis inherited from the natural sciences by quoting the following key sentence, which makes it quite clear that there can be no real rapprochement between psychoanalysis with its genetic orientation and the phenomenological view: 'The phenomena which are perceived must in our view withdraw in favour of the strivings which are merely assumed.'[4] (Quoted from Binswanger 1/165.) Binswanger comments on this quotation as follows:

'We can now characterize the idea of homo natura more precisely by saying that it is a genuine natural-scientific construct like the bio-physiological idea of the organism, the chemist's idea of matter as the underlying basis of the elements and their combinations, and the physicist's of light, etc. The reality of the phenomenal, its uniqueness and independence, is absorbed by the hypothesized forces, drives, and the laws that govern them.'[5]

[1] See especially 'Freud's Auffassung des Menschen im Lichte der Anthropologie'; *Ausgew. Vortr. u. Aufs.*, Vol. I, Bern, 1947. ('Freud's conception of man in the light of Anthropology.')

[2] Footnote in Binswanger, *Ausgewählte Vorträge und Aufsätze*, Vol. 2, p. 11: Cf. Wilhelm Silasi, p. 84 of work quoted by Binswanger. In the original for *verbindet* read *verbinden*.

[3] L. Binswanger, *ibid.*, Vol. 2, p. 11.

[4] L. Binswanger, 'Freud's Auffassung des Menschen im Lichte der Anthropologie', *Ausgew. Vortr. u. Aufs.*, Vol. I.

[5] L. Binswanger, *Ausgewählte Vorträge und Aufsätze*, Vol. I, p. 166, (quoted from *Being in the World*, New York, 1963, p. 157).

The fact that Binswanger draws attention to the 'wish', which is the only unequivocal concept in the Freudian psychic apparatus, is also revealing:

'The entire mechanism of the psychic apparatus is set in motion from the depths, the id, by means of the psychic representation of all instinctuality, the wish. Wishing is the only context within which the Freudian homo natura is directed. But even this is merely an explanatory construct emanating from a general sundering of human being, primitive and otherwise. For in actuality man, and certainly primitive man, does not strive for pleasure as such, but for the possession or experience of a particular thing that brings him pleasure. Here, therefore, we are within the sphere of meanings and their particular specifications. Only a being that can only wish may be thought of as stretched between instinct and illusion. And, conversely, only when we posit such a being can such basic modes of human existence as the religious, the ethical, and the artistic be explained as illusion or derived from the need for illusion. Wishing is not constitutive of mankind as such, however constitutive it may in fact be for the psychic apparatus built into homo natura. What at bottom sets this apparatus and its particular mechanisms in motion is a wish. Freud developed this concept with astounding consistency, particularly with regard to the mechanisms of dream work.'[1]

But where precisely does Binswanger's criticism of Freud's conception of man reach the point of no return? He points out that in the Freudian view of man—and for that matter in every view of man based on a positivist premise—the fundamental fact of human existence, the fact that man is a creature capable of an attitude *towards himself*, is blandly overlooked, if not indeed suppressed. This fundamental fact conceals an ontological problem which any theory of human personality disregards at its peril.

'What we have called the rift or gap is thereby widened. Just as natural-scientific psychology—a "contradictio in adjecto"—systematically ignores the most basic anthropological fact that Dasein is always mine, yours or ours, and that *we ourselves* always stand in relation to the abstraction of soul as well as to the abstraction of body, so, too, it ignores the entire structure of ontological problems that surrounds the question as to the genuine *who* that so isolates itself, the question as to the human self. When this self is objectified, isolated, and theorized into an ego, or into an id, ego and super ego, it is thereby driven out of its

[1] L. Binswanger, *Ausgewählte Vorträge und Aufsätze*, Vol. I, p. 173 (quoted from *Being in the World*, New York, 1963, p. 164).

authentic sphere of being, namely existence, and ontologically and anthropologically suffocated. Instead of following HERACLITUS in *seeking himself*, and ST. AUGUSTINE in *returning to himself*, FREUD and all other scientists we have named pass by this problem of the self as though it were something too obvious to warrant attention. Precisely in regard to this issue, it becomes plain that there are two ways to practise psychology. The one leads away from ourselves toward theoretical determinations, i.e. to the perception, observation, and destruction of man in his actuality, with the aim in mind of scientifically *constructing* a scientific picture of him (an apparatus, "reflex-mechanisms", functional whole, etc.). The other leads "into our self" again, but not in the mode of *analytic-psychology* (which would again make us into objects), nor *characterologically* (which would objectify us with regard to our individual psychological "class"). The second way is that of anthropology, which concerns itself with the conditions and potentialities of the Dasein *as ours*, or—what comes to the same thing—that concerns itself with the possible kinds and modes of our existence. This path "into our self" here refers first and foremost to the self of the scientist's own particular existence. It refers to that ground upon which he stands, that which is most authentically his own. It refers to the Dasein that he assumes as his own *within the element of the worker in science*, the seeker, shaper and spokesman of scientific truth *in* and *for* the world. All this is the self-evident supposition of every scientist. In fact, however, of all things it is the least self-evident, but rather that which is sought out and questioned by any psychology that does not attempt to be just a natural science, but a genuine *psycho*-logy.'[1]

(b) *From Phenomenology to Existential Ontology (von Gebsattel, E. Straus)*

With his enquiry into man's 'Self' (which, unlike Jung, Binswanger and more especially Boss[2] interpret in an ontological and not a psychological sense) Binswanger enters the sphere of existential philosophy. Until 1927, when Heidegger's *Time and Being* was published, Binswanger's approach had been predominantly phenomenological. The phenomenology developed by *Husserl* (and in part by *Scheler*), which is in marked contrast to the genetic and positivist attitudes of psychoanalysis, has gained such momentum within the field of psychiatry that it would appear desirable to give a short account of the phenomenological

---

[1] L. Binswanger, *Ausgewählte Vorträge und Aufsätze*, Vol. I, pp. 180–1 (quoted from *Being in the World*, New York, 1963, pp. 171–2).

[2] M. Boss, *Psychoanalyse und Daseinsanalytik*, Bern, 1957 (Psychoanalysis and 'Daseinsanalysis'). See especially Boss's criticism of Jung from the existential point of view.

method, in order that Binswanger and his importance for depth psychology may be better understood. The original starting-point for Husserl's phenomenology was descriptive psychology—as opposed to genetic psychology—, whence it proceeded to establish a (temporary) position for itself in phenomenological idealism, which maintains that all Being receives its 'validity as Being from transcendental subjectivity' and is grounded in the 'absolute consciousness'. In his earlier phase (which lasted approximately up to the *Crisis of the European Economy*) phenomena interested Husserl not as intuitive perceptions but as phenomena of pure consciousness. This is elucidated by Binswanger when, in describing the phenomenon of perception, which the positivist is intent on dissecting into its individual elements, he summarizes the phenomenological method as follows:

'This is *the fundamental principle of the phenomenological method*; *the restriction of analysis to that which is really found to be present in consciousness*, or to put it in another way, *to that which is immanent in consciousness*. But what do we find present in the spiritual act or experience of perception itself? It we are agreed that what we perceive are not sensations but objects, then perhaps we shall make greater progress by visualizing the relationship of the act of perception to those objects. We then see without difficulty that the object is not contained within our perception but is outside of it. But this "outside" should not be taken in a spatial sense: for phenomenological analysis is unable to tell us where the perception takes place, where it is situated. The natural scientist says that it takes place in the brain, the psychologist in the soul. The former objectifies the act of perception and is able to say where this thing is to be found; the latter also objectifies it, only instead of turning it into a physico-physiological thing he turns it into a psychic thing and is also able to allot it its "place" within the psychic framework or organism. The phenomenologist, who takes good care not to amalgamate the phenomena of consciousness with nature, only knows one thing for certain, which is that either he himself or his ego performs the act of perception, that this act is a phenomenon of his consciousness.'[1]

The reduction (*epoché*) of the concrete contents of perception to contents of pure consciousness leads to the so-called phenomenological view of essences. Phenomenology as a 'purely descriptive doctrine of essences concerning the immanent formations of consciousness' (Husserl) becomes important for psychopathology in that it attempts to grasp the essence of specific pathogenic phenomena in terms of the phenomenologically intuited condition of Beingness. In a method such as this phenomena are not derived from so-called elementary facts, as is the

[1] L. Binswanger, *Ausgewählte Vorträge und Aufsätze*, Vol. I, pp. 25–6.

case in the natural sciences (and in psychoanalysis), nor are they traced back to underlying forces which are not directly perceptible, but instead the essence of the phenomenon—e.g. of a depression or an obsessional act—has to come up for discussion and reveal its meaning. In his analysis of a schizophrenic statement, 'No, I don't hear voices, but at night the "*Sprechsaele*" (speech halls) are open, which I would gladly dispense with', Binswanger contrasts the reductive method of the natural sciences with the phenomenological method within the sphere of psychopathology:

'Not so the *phenomenological* psychopathologist! Whereas the psychopathologist who proceeds by way of description will divide abnormal psychic activity up into natural classes, species and types, which are linked together in a hierarchical system by virtue of the properties which they possess, and will then place this system, as a total system, in contradistinction to the sphere of healthy activity, whereas, moreover, he will investigate the conditions which promote the emergence of this total system or of the individual units of which it is comprised and in doing so will always consider the individual pathological experience or the individual pathological function as a special example of the species, i.e. will always proceed by way of subsumption, thought and judgement, the phenomenological psychopathologist will constantly seek to envisage what is meant by the words and to advance from the text and its meaning to the object, the subject-matter, the experience, which is indicated by the verbal meaning. In other words, he will seek to feel his way into the verbal meanings instead of seeking to extract judgements from the verbal concepts. Here too the maxim applies: "A force de regarder l'objet se sentir y entrer!" To feel one's way, to transpose oneself into the object, instead of picking out and enumerating individual properties or characteristics! Of course the phenomenologist also requires precise descriptions of those characteristics or properties, but not for their own sake, and not in order to use them as elements of concepts, but rather in order to advance from them to the subject-matter, to the intuition of the object itself. But to this end only those properties are of value which arise out of the subject-matter, out of the phenomenon itself, and not those which reveal the conditions attendant on the emergence of the phenomenon, i.e. its relationship to other happenings of a different order. And so here too we arrive at an analysis of phenomena which reveals only those certainties which are relevant to the phenomenon itself, in our case the phenomenon of the "speech hall" (*Sprechsaal*).[1] All

[1] *Sprechsaal: Sprech* means 'speak', *Saal* means 'hall' or 'room'. *Sprechsaal* associates with *Sprechstunde* (doctor's consulting hours), with *Hörsaal* (auditorium), etc. (Tr.).

indirect fixations of this phenomenon are avoided. In this way you will try to bring the "speech hall" experience into a state of givenness as a phenomenologically unique essence—perhaps not very close and not very clear and not "pure" either, but none the less compact and to some extent condensed. Since it is an image of external perception it will sometimes be less clear (e.g. when the patient explains that the "speech hall" is also a change of title) and sometimes more clear (e.g. when the patient says: "when a lady lies in bed until eleven o'clock, in as far as she gets a connection through the Bureau with another lady au lit— 450 lit.). This disclosure puts you in mind of a telephone connection, a "telecommunication", however, which is psychologically strange and one whose phenomenological essence we have by no means clearly established, whereas schizophrenics, by virtue of their hallucinations, have evidently worked their way deeper into the essence of this condition of "being so near and yet so far", of "being there" and yet "not there" (*Dasein* and not *Dasein*).

'Now the essential thing about the phenomenological view of such psychopathological phenomena is this: you never perceive an isolated phenomenon, for the phenomenon is always enacted against the background of an "I", of a personality, or, to put it in another way, we always see the phenomenon as an expression or manifestation of a particular type of personality. In the specific phenomenon the person concerned gives information about himself and, conversely, we see through the phenomenon into the person. Thus in respect of the "speech hall" experience we see before us a person who is in contact with dark psychic powers, who moves in a psychic sphere which is quite different from our own. For this patient the "speech hall" is a constant "nemesis", a place where he "settles his account with his past life" and where indeed certain "problems are threshed out which are accompanied by a pressing need" and which are quite different from "cinema experiences", whose sole purpose is to afford entertainment. For the sick patient the "speech hall" is a "battle front", one established at great cost, "which provides him with a firm base outside the flow of events, a secure standpoint *vis-à-vis* the problems of life", and which constitutes a direct antithesis to the "relative lack of seriousness and responsibility *vis-à-vis* life" which he had shown prior to "passing through" his illness. And so we see before us a person who has undergone a change in his ethical outlook or, if you like, in his *Weltanschauung* and we see the "speech hall" as an expression of this personal *Weltanschauung*. This expression, be it noted, is always achieved largely "symbolically", always by means of "symbolic comparisons" or "by means of a largely material assimilation, which lends the necessary resonance to the sensations". Our characterology of personality in general and of the schizophrenic personality in particular is too inadequate to permit us to take a closer phenomenological look at all these matters.'[1]

Apart from Binswanger psychopathology is also indebted to thinkers such as *Minkowski, von Gebsattel* and *E. Straus* for their detailed descriptions of phenomenologically 'intuited' psychopathological disturbances, which have been supplemented only recently, thanks to the influence exercised by Heidegger's existential analysis, by other investigations into neurosis, especially those carried out by *M. Boss* (dream interpretation, psychosomatic problems, perversions). Further examples of phenomenological psychopathology have been provided chiefly by E. Straus' and von Gebsattel's investigations into depressions, phobias and obsessional neuroses. E. Straus[2] considers that endogenic depression with its hopelessness, monotony, despair and utter perplexity is caused by a 'central disruption of development' and in this connection he speaks of the 'flow of personal development' coming to a standstill. For a person suffering from depression time stands still, for such a person there is neither future nor past; and his mania for self-belittlement and self-impoverishment can only be understood in terms of a disruption of personal development, which finds expression in this reduction of time to a bare minimum. The obsessional neurotic on the other hand, whose world is described in detail by von Gebsattel, is not brought to a standstill by the disruption of his development, as is the depressive person, but rather the whole structure of his personality is subjected to a process of disintegration, reduction and decline. Seen in this light his relationship to dirt, which takes the form of exaggerated cleanliness, like his relationship to ceremony, is a senseless and stereotype repetition of an 'existential standstill'.

Von Gebsattel writes on obsessional neurotics as follows:[3]

'Normally life is cleansed by its surrender to the powers of the future and to the tasks which challenge us from the future. If man is prevented from working off the guilt of life because his movements towards self-realization have been halted, then a vague feeling of guilt will be roused in him.'

The jump from phenomenology to existential ontology was made when Heidegger introduced his postulate of man's 'Being in the World' and thus brought about the radical change in the subject-object relationship mentioned above. Where positivism is intent on fusing the subject with

[1] L. Binswanger, *Ausgewählte Vorträge und Aufsätze*, Vol. I, pp. 36–8.
[2] E. Strauss, 'Das Zeiterlebnis in der endogenen Depression; *Mschr. Psych.* p. 68, 1928. ('The Sense of Time in Endogenic Depression').
[3] V. Gebsattel, 'Die Welt des Zwangskranken'; *Mschr. Psych.* p. 99, 1938. ('The World of the Obsessional Neurotic').

the object, a form of man's Being-with-others which is clearly demonstrated by Freud's concept of 'object cathexis', phenomenology was intent on the reverse process of fusing the object, seen as an exclusively conscious phenomenon, with the subject. In the following passage Binswanger describes existential analysis in contrast to both of these processes:

'To recapitulate, with *Time and Being* the problem of subjectivity has been removed from the correlativity of the subject-object relationship and indeed from the narrow framework of *knowledge* as such and has been established on the broad basis of Being-in-the-World as a transcendant condition. Subjectivity now means the *a priori* structure not only of knowledge but of all transcendental subjectivity, which is terminologically and ontologically defined as human reality (*Dasein*) or Being-in-the-World. At the same time, however, this insight also prepared the ground for the discovery of the "forces" by means of which human reality (*Dasein*)—as Wilhelm Szilasi puts it—*preserves or loses itself within the totality of possible modes of Being*.[1] To this extent *Szilasi* is able to say that "Time and Being" constitutes the first investigation of human reality (*Dasein*) *in terms of its objective transcendence*.[2] And it is this insight which enables us to grasp the importance of "Time and Being" as a contribution towards an architectonic conception and composition of psychiatry. For now we see that the *reality* of human Being is no longer adequately described by the concepts of *consciousness* or *life*, quite apart from the fact that, by employing the concept of life, we constantly find ourselves faced with the mystery as to how it should be possible—and here too we are quoting from *Natorp*[3]—"for each given consciousness of each given subjectivity to appear as something quite new and heterogeneous at a specific point of the objective context (which has been preconceived as a totality), i.e. at a specific point of the context of the problem on which the objectivizing cognition has been brought to bear". By conceiving the reality of human Being as "human reality" (*Dasein*) *Heidegger* has for the first time "described the fullness of the objective transcendence of that which is real in terms of the real Being of man, his facticity". In doing so he has made human Being, "in a new dimension and a new intensity", into an object of scientific enquiry into the "structure of its particular mode of Being",[4] into an

---

[1] Footnote in Binswanger, *Ausgew. Vortr. u. Aufs.*, Vol. II, Bern, 1955, p. 284: W. Szilasi, *Macht und Ohnmacht des Geistes*, p. 262, Bern, 1946. ('Power and Impotence of the Mind').　　　　[2] Footnote in Bingswanger, *ibid.*, p. 261.

[3] Footnote in Binswanger, *ibid.*, p. 63.

[4] Footnote in Binswanger, *ibid.*: cf. W. Szilasi, *Wissenschaft als Philosophie*, Zürich–New York, 1945, p. 50 f. ('Science as Philosophy').

object of scientific *enquiry* into the *structure* of its particular mode of Being! And it is this which constitutes Heidegger's importance for psychiatric research.'[1]

The importance of existential analysis—in contrast to phenomenology—for the psychopathology of psychoses and neuroses lies in the fact that it enables psychopathologists to comprehend and to describe specific phenomena as existentialia, i.e. in an ultimate ontological sense, whereas phenomenology had been unable to pass beyond the limits imposed by the subjectivity of personal contexts. Existential ontologists tend to regard phenomenology in the light of a natural philosophy, as it were, one which intuits phenomena in terms of relationships of essence but then proceeds to fit them into subjective contexts, e.g. into the life history of a human being. In the formulations of existential ontology, however, definitive statements are made concerning both Beingness as such and the patterns of its realization, statements which possess a real or fundamental ontological character that transcends both subjectivity and objectivity. Clearly the claim which existential analysis is making here is a very considerable one. Whether it is a just claim only the future will tell. Psychopathology is merely concerned with the existentialia of human reality, with its patterns of qualities. But there has already been a divergence of views between Heidegger's disciples, Binswanger and Boss, as to the most suitable method of dealing with these existentialia in existential analysis. The practical importance for psychopathology of existential analysis, which considers psychopathic phenomena as existentialia, i.e. as qualities of human reality, whereby human reality is to be understood as the 'Being of that which is', is illustrated by the following passage, in which Binswanger comments on dreams of rising and falling:

'In view of the difference between the existential (*daseinsanalytisch*) and the psychopathological views those modes of the "who", which in existential analysis are expressed not in personal terms but by means of an *image*, are extremely important. To quote but *one* example, in my essay on *Dream and Existence* I have already demonstrated (and my demonstration has been fully confirmed meanwhile by *Gaston Bachelard* in his book, *L'air et les songes*, Paris, 1943) that a favourite form assumed by the "who" or the subject of "rising and falling" both in colloquial language and in poetry and dreams is that of a *bird* depicted either as rising through the air or plunging down out of the sky or shot down in flight and revealing quite specific characteristics of form and colour in each given situation, ranging from the clear-cut contours and brilliant

[1] L. Binswanger, *Ausgew. Vortr. u. Aufs.*, Vol. II, p. 284.

colours of the bird's ascent (through the reality of its Being (*Dasein*)) to the complete disruption and distortion of form and the blackest colouring which accompany its fall. These are never chance combinations but unshakable *a priori* structures of human reality (*Dasein*). If this were not so, then we could never intuit the structure of the various modes of human reality either from language or from dreams or from Rohrschach tests. I use the word *intuit* advisedly, because the opinion is often voiced that what happens here is that one thing, namely the mode of reality or the world design, is deduced from another thing, namely the image. No! What happens here is that in the image the world design reveals itself of its own accord. For the image—to quote *Szilasi*—"is the first impact of the waves of transcendence". Consequently, for existential analysis (*Daseinsanalyse*) the image is not a symbol (of something concealed behind it, as is the case in psychoanalysis) but an immediate expression. This alone explains the fact that, and the reason why, in existential analysis (*Daseinsanalyse*) all verbal expression and consequently dream language as well, i.e. the "manifest" dream content, comes into its own again, indeed, plays a decisive part.'[1]

In describing the phobia of a young girl Binswanger cites a case history from the clinical practice of existential analysis. At the age of five the young girl in question had gone skating one day and afterwards, when her skates were being removed, the heel of one of her shoes had broken away and remained wedged between the clamps of the skate. Subsequently, when walking, she often had the sensation that the heel of one of her shoes was working loose and this sensation was invariably accompanied by a condition of extreme anxiety. A Freudian would explain this anxiety condition by reference to phantasies of birth or perhaps of castration. But all such explanations would ultimately be obliged to have recourse to the concepts of disposition or constitution, if they were to establish the specificity of this particular type of anxiety condition. Binswanger rejects these biologically oriented interpretations and instead speaks of a disturbance of the specific 'world design' of *continuity*. The particular world design, in accordance with which each human being enters life, is comparable to the philosophical categories, i.e. to *a priori* structures. Binswanger quotes other case histories to demonstrate the diversity of the world designs which determine illness in the existential, ontological sense. In the case of the young girl mentioned above the world design of continuity involved an 'enormous restriction, simplification and draining away of the contents of her world' and it was this which produced in her the condition of abnormal hypersensitivity to separation or severance of any kind, as exemplified by the severed heel

[1] L. Binswanger, *Ausgew. Vortr. u. Aufs.*, Vol. II, p. 289.

of her shoe. The experience of losing the heel of her shoe when she was five years old exposed her world design of continuity to extreme danger; this gave rise to anxiety, namely, the anxiety that the continuity which she felt to be necessary might be disrupted; and this anxiety gave rise to the phobia.

M. Boss describes psychosomatic illnesses (asthma) in terms of existential analysis as follows:

'And so of all our patients it is the asthma sufferers who really leave us no choice: the very phenomenon forces us to interpret the asthmatic cramp of the bronchioli and bronchi, this organneurotic compulsion to suffocate and inhibition of the free flow of respiration, as the embodiment of an existence which came to a petrified standstill in a world pregnant with unbearable stimuli.'[1]

(c) Psychotherapy and Existential Analysis

Apart from the interpretation of certain dreams in terms of existential analysis Binswanger has also applied Heidegger's hermeneutics to numerous other spheres of psychopathology, most of which, however, are concerned with psychosis and so do not fall within the scope of this present enquiry. His arguments regarding the therapeutic application of existential analysis cast new light on the development of therapeutic method. The procedure followed by existential psychotherapists, for whom the question of basic training—whether Jungian or Freudian—is a matter of complete indifference, is described by Binswanger as follows:

'I. An existentially oriented psychotherapist (*Daseinsanalytiker*) examines the life history of the patient who is to be treated no less than any other psychotherapist, but he does so in his own very special way. For he does *not try to explain* this life history and its pathological peculiarities in accordance with the doctrines of a particular psychotherapeutic school and the categories favoured by that school but rather to *understand* them as a modification of the total structure of Being-in-the-World, as I have shown in my studies on *Ideenflucht* (Flight of Ideas), in my studies on schizophrenia and finally in the case of "Susanne Urban".

'2. Accordingly an existentially oriented psychotherapist sets out not only to show the patient but as far as possible to make him *experience* in an existential "convulsion" when and to what extent he failed to preserve the structure of human Being, when and to what extent he "*out-climbed*" himself like Ibsen's master builder, Solness, and ended

[1] Médard Boss, *Psychosomatische Medizin*, Bern, 1954, p. 190.

up in "airy heights" or in an "ethereal phantasy world". In this respect the psychotherapist might be compared to an expert mountain guide, i.e. one who knows his way about in the particular "terrain" and who attempts the journey back down into the valley with the "dilettante" tourist, who lacks the courage either to go on or to go back.

'Conversely, the existentially oriented therapist seeks to free the depressive from the world of subterranean caverns in which he has buried himself, so that he may find his feet again "on the earth", this being the only mode of human reality which permits man to realize the possibilities of Being in all their fullness.—Where the schizophrenic is concerned the existentially oriented psychotherapist will lead him back from the autistic world of contortions or distortions in which he lives and has his being into the communal world, into Heraclitus' "*koinòs Kosmos*"; or else he will try to help the sick patient who lived, as she herself put it, "at two different speeds" to—again her own word—"synchronize" those speeds. On other occasions, as in the case of anorexia mentalis reported by Roland *Kuhn*, he will realize that the therapeutic goal will be more speedily reached by examining the patient concerned not in terms of temporal structures but in terms of spatial structures. It was a surprise to us to see how many patients, who were by no means always particularly intelligent or cultured, proved to be accessible to the existential method of examination and how they felt themselves to be understood in respect of their particular individual quality as a result of the application of this method. And here, as everywhere, the establishment of natural communication is of course the prerequisite of psychotherapeutic success.

'3. No matter whether the existential analyst comes more from the psychoanalytic or more from Jungian doctrine, he will always stand on the same level with his patients, namely on the level of their common reality (*Dasein*). Consequently he will not turn the patient into an object in contrast to himself as a subject but will regard him as a partner in human reality (*Dasein*). And from this it follows that he will not denote the connection between the two partners, by analogy with the contact between two electrical batteries, as a "psychic contact" but rather as a *meeting* on what *Martin Buber* has called the "abyss of human reality", which *in terms of essence* is "in the world", and will denote it not only as self but also as "Being with" or personal intercourse and as "Being together" or love. And in an existential sense the condition which Freud has taught us to call *transference* is also a mode of the meeting. For the meeting is a condition of "Being together" in *an actual present*, i.e. in a present which certainly grows out of the *past* and which certainly contains within it a potential *future*.'[1]

[1] L. Binswanger, *Ausgew. Vortr. u. Aufs.*, Vol. II, pp. 304–6.

Binswanger describes transference:

'In every form of medical psychotherapy two people stand opposite one another, two people are in a sense "dependent on one another", two people in a sense "come to terms with one another". This inter-personal relationship, this relationship with a fellow man, is simplified or "reduced" by the expression "psychotherapy" in three different ways: firstly, because it fails to mention the one partner to the relationship, namely the sick person, and speaks instead of the "psyche", which is simply a scientific abstraction, whilst the other partner, the doctor, completely disappears behind his function towards his fellow man, i.e. behind his *"therapeia"*; secondly, because the relationship is *all one way*, namely from the subject of the therapeutic function, i.e. the doctor, to the patient's psyche, but never from the patient to the doctor; thirdly and lastly, because the process whereby doctor and patient come to terms with one another is never expressed in terms of a *relationship* between fellow-men but rather in terms of a *duty performed in the cause of therapy*. For in the medico-psychiatric sense what is meant by the psyche is not a fellow man (i.e. a person), nor even a psychological subject, but an "animated" object, an animated organism, a psychic unity of functioning, the epitome of the psychic functions of life, etc.; "therapeia" in the medical sense, however, means nursing, care, attention, treatment, activities which might equally well be bestowed on another kind of organism, an animal or plant organism; in short, therapeia means nursing duties or duties performed on an object of care. And so the literal meaning of medical psychotherapy is: medical duties performed on the psyche of a fellow man (whereby the psyche is conceived as the epitome of the functions of psychic life). If we were to restrict ourselves to this conception of psychotherapy, which is the conception implied by the word itself, i.e. by the reduction of the meaning of inter-personal Being to the level of a "one-sided" medico-psychiatric duty, we would never be in a position to understand and to communicate to one another how it is that "psychotherapy can actually function at all." '[1]

Binswanger's view of resistance is as follows:

'This communication certainly ought not to be considered—as it is considered by orthodox psychoanalysts—as a mere repetition, i.e. as transference and counter-transference in positive cases and as resistances and counter-resistances in negative cases; rather the relationship between patient and doctor always constitutes an independent communicative *"novum"*, a new providential alliance, one which is not

[1] L. Binswanger, *Ausgew. Vortr. u. Aufs.*, Vol. I, p. 133.

restricted to the doctor-patient relationship but which operates above all in terms of a purely inter-personal relationship conceived as a condition of genuine "Being together". If such a course of treatment fails, the analyst is inclined to assume that the patient has been unable to overcome his resistances towards the doctor, in whom he sees a sort of "father imago". But often the question as to whether an analysis is to achieve psychotherapeutic success is not determined by whether the patient is able to overcome resistances towards the father image which he has transferred on to the doctor but rather by whether he is able to overcome his resistances towards the father *through this particular doctor*; in other words, the operative question is whether in fact it is not the patient's rejection of this particular doctor as a human being, i.e. the impossibility of his entering into a genuinely communicative relationship with him, which prevents him from breaking through the "eternal" repetition of his resistance to his father.'[1]

(d) The Problem of Body and Soul from the Existential Point of View

Freud and his followers, as also the Neo-Freudians, solved the problem of the relationship between body and soul by assuming the psycho-physical parallelism that was in vogue at the turn of the century and whose chief advocate at that time was *Wundt*. Freud and his followers did make one reservation *vis-à-vis* Wundt, however, in that they tended to consider the psychic aspect of this relationship to be no more than a subjective expression of physiological processes, i.e. they considered that at some future date it would be possible to re-state this psychic aspect in physiological terms. The naïve fiction which this view involves, the fiction that the subject can simply be bracketed, is so patently absurd as to make it impossible for it to be taken seriously.— But it was the processes involved in the problem of hysterical conversion,[2] processes which have yet to be explained, which were the chief factor underlying Binswanger's decision to explore the question of the body and of bodiliness. In describing a case of hysterical singultus (hiccups) he deals with the concept of conversion as follows:

'In our view, therefore, the mere explanation that a psychic impulse is "converted into the physical sphere" fails to deal with the whole problem; in fact, what we must realize is that the "physical sphere", i.e. corporeality, is only one particular form of human existence; we must realize the fact that, and also the reason why, in certain circumstances it

---

[1] L. Binswanger, *Ausgew. Vortr. u. Aufs.*, Vol. I, pp. 142–3.

[2] Freud's honesty—and also his scepticism—constantly obliged him to concede that hysterical conversion was in fact 'a mystery'. It was only his disciples (especially F. Alexander) who considered that conversion, far from being a mystery, was no more than a physiological process taking place in the brain.

remains man's only "sphere of expression"; we must realize that, and why, man then uses the language of the body, i.e. instead of cursing and raging, he belches, screeches and "spews".[1]

In his principal work, *Grundformen und Erkenntnis menschlichen Daseins*, Binswanger describes the problem posed by the concept of the body, which he approached from the point of view of his enquiry into the nature of conversion, in the following light:

'What is known to common parlance and to science as the "body" can signify a tremendous number of different things in its anthropological capacity' . . . 'In love corporeality is "transparency", the transparency of the Thou, in love the physical form is part of the essential image and all partial physical forms are forms of love. In friendship corporeality is mutual support (a look in the eye, a handshake, a tone of voice). In inter-personal "taking-at" it is on the one hand tribulation as such and instrumentality, whilst on the other hand it is tribulation, impression-ability and suggestibility, in a word, tangibility. To this must be added in "taking-a-person-at-his-word" the symbolic quality such as is revealed in a handshake, in the linguistic-vocalic speech form, in ritual contact and deportment.'[2]

In an earlier work on *Lebensfunktion und Innere Lebensgeschichte* ('The Life Function and Internal Life History'), which preceded the change in his outlook brought about by Heidegger's 'Time and Being', Bins-wanger established the phenomenological cum anthropological concept of bodiliness. He summarizes his view as follows:

'What we find here is the contrast between a conception of man and a way of looking at man as a physico-psychic organism, i.e. as the epitome of organological functions which are governed by natural laws, in other words as a "*temporal process of events*", and a conception of man and a way of looking at man not only as a living person but also as a (self-) experiencing person who develops historically within the continuity of his(self-)experiencing. The context of natural laws is here replaced by a context of meaning, by the "unity of the inwardly developing motives of a meaning" or the "unity of a process of self-formation based on inner motivation". But the mere principle of the context of meaning can no more be said to constitute *research* into the life history of an actual person than the mere principle of natural causality can be said to constitute natural-scientific *research*. What is needed in the latter case is

[1] L. Binswanger, *Ausgew. Vortr. u. Aufs.*, Vol. I, p. 149.
[2] L. Binswanger, *Grundformen und Erkenntnis menschlichen Daseins*, Zürich, 1953, p. 272. ('Basic Forms and Knowledge of Human Reality (*Dasein*)').

the natural-scientific experiment and what is needed in the former case is the investigation of the actual processes of the contents of (self-)experience of the individual person, who develops historically in his own particular way and not in any other way. But here too for the phenomenologist it is not simply a question of listing actual data and contents of (self-)experience in accordance with the principle of 'motivation', which in his case would be a "psychological context of motives", for in fact both the individual contents of (self-)experience and their "contexts" must be restricted and understood in terms of their essential content, in terms of their "essence", as transparent phenomena, which, however, are then illuminated by this essence. It follows from the "fundamental phenomenological law" of the interdependence of fact and eidos, i.e. essence, that the research carried out by phenomenological anthropology can only be scientific research if it investigates the individual's *life history*. The expression "inner life history" has meanwhile become a commonplace of psychiatry.'[1]

Although Binswanger pays full tribute here to the soul and its historicity he does not yet stipulate the existential unity of body and soul propounded by Heidegger. Rather he places two different attitudes in juxtaposition, namely, the atomistic attitude of the natural sciences and the 'meaningful' interpretations of phenomenology.

Of recent years *J. Zutt* has paid special attention to the problem of the body and of bodiliness from the point of view of existential ontology. Zutt differentiates between 'living' the body and 'experiencing' the body. To live the body is a form of human reality in which man simply lives in the world and responds to the world without reflecting upon himself. Only 'by reflection, by stepping out of the immediate context of human reality is the original condition of life modified'.[2] By the act of reflecting upon himself the subject acquires his body as an object. Only then can the subject be said to 'have' a body (Zutt's 'objectified body'), which he can use, as he would use any tool, for any purpose, and with which he can above all enter into a relationship by means of reflection. 'To experience the body' means to experience the body personally, to experience it as a partner: for example, an infant experiences its body when it begins to concern itself with the erotogenic zones and in doing so receives particular sensations. But despite the fact that this differentiation between 'living' and 'experiencing' the body which Zutt advances is capable of demonstration and leads logically to the further differentiation between the human condition of 'being' a body

[1] L. Binswanger, *Ausgew. Vortr. u. Aufs.*, Vol. I, pp. 8–9.
[2] J. Zutt, *Nervenarzt*, Jg.28–7 (1957). 'Detaillierte Ausführungen über den Leib.' ('Detailed statements on the body'). See Zutt, *Über verstehende Anthropologie*, Berlin, 1961. ('On an Anthropology of Understanding').

and that of 'having' a body it has none the less been disputed by other disciples of Heidegger's (e.g. Boss) on the grounds that it introduces a new dualism.

M. Boss regards the part played by the body and thus the problem posed by the concepts of body and soul as follows:

'If man is never really an extant object, his corporeality cannot be just a body, enclosed in an epidermis and ending at its surface. Rather, the human body—including its so-called animal, vegetative and hormonal arrangements—must be understood as a specific sphere of human existence, namely that sphere which exists in that mode of being which we call the "material" one. Because the human body is a proper realm of *Dasein*, it is one of the media through which the world-disclosing life relationships which constitute existence are carried out.

'Being a partial realm of *Dasein*, the body is an inevitable, but not *the* sufficient, condition for the possibilities of human existence. It is true that man is incapable of seeing, hearing, smelling or tasting, incapable of acting or going forth in the world, unless his sense organs, his hands and his feet function properly, physiologically speaking, but it is equally true, existentially speaking, that the sense organs, hands and feet function only because man's very essence is of a primary, world-disclosing and luminating nature, and because, owing to this essential condition, he already is, and always was, in the world with its beings. In other words, man cannot see, hear and smell because he has eyes, ears and a nose; he is able to have eyes, ears and a nose because his very essence is luminating and world-disclosing.

'But since man exists in the world in this world-disclosing manner, and only in this manner, the "in" of his Being-in-the-world and his corporeal Being-in-the-world should not be confused with the "presence in the world" of an extant object which might conceivably be situated within another hollow object. Man, however, is of such a kind that he is only able to exist as the "Dasein" which he is if he is permitted by things (particular beings) to adopt a position within the context of his conceivable relationships to them; whilst on the other hand particular beings also need the illuminating nature of man if they are to "come to light". Even "natural" light that is capable of being physically recorded only appears as that which it is when it has reached particular beings and can illuminate them.'[1]

(e) *Erfahren, Verstehen, Deuten in der Psychoanalyse* (Experiencing, Understanding and Interpreting in Psychoanalysis)

As early as 1926 Binswanger published under the above title a most

[1] M. Boss, *Psychosomatische Medizin*, Bern and Stuttgart, 1954, pp. 43–44 ('Psychosomatic Medicine').

revealing investigation into the problems facing psychoanalysis in the sphere of perception. Under the concept of 'experience' Binswanger subsumed every single act of psychoanalytic perception, including not only the perception of the patient's spoken words, i.e. his reports of dreams or of day to day events but also everything deduced by means of empathy from his facial expressions, his gestures and his moods.

Binswanger regards understanding as the complete antithesis of experience, since it differs from all types of experience by virtue of two specific qualities: (1) by the emergence of a meaningful, motivational context, i.e. of a specific meaning which cannot be deduced from the world of experiences (perceptions), and (2) by the sudden appearance of a specific quality of understanding. This latter is a type of evidence which transcends experience and is thus an *a priori*. But over and above this 'the essential contents of the experiences would of themselves provide a valid or evident *a priori* indication of their link with the essential contents of other experiences'. Binswanger joins forces with *Husserl* and *Simmel* in advancing these views, which are diametrically opposed to the pragmatic and sensualist interpretations of understanding favoured by the great majority of the scientifically oriented Freudian schools. The specific motivational context of psychoanalysis is established by those factors in psychoanalytic theory which are responsible for translating a faulty action from an inadequate situational context to an adequate (meaningful) context. The fact that this motivational context remains incomplete unless certain mediatory instances of the unconscious and pre-conscious are taken into account is the essential factor underlying Freud's theory. But—according to Binswanger—this process already constitutes an attempt at interpretation. Binswanger argues that[1] 'what Freud calls interpretation involves factors deriving from acts of experiencing, from acts of rational deduction and finally from actual acts of psychological understanding'. Acts of experiencing include everything which the physician perceives in the patient and in statements made by the patient. Acts of rational deduction include all the views (judgements) formed by the physician, in which he makes deductions relevant to the patient's present behaviour or present experiences on the basis of the patient's childhood experiences. The actual acts of psychological understanding arise out of the incorporation of the acts of experiencing and of the acts of rational deduction into the higher motivational contexts, i.e. into the meaning of the whole. The most important of these higher motivational contexts within Freudian psychoanalysis is the wish (see above), but there are other essential experiences, such as revenge, anxiety or sexual desire, which also qualify as higher motivational

[1] Binswanger, *Erfahren, Verstehen, Deuten in der Psychoanalyse*, 1926 (Imago). ('Experiencing, Understanding and Interpreting in Psychoanalysis').

contexts. Binswanger argues that since these are all qualities of understanding they are all ultimately rooted in *a priori* structures of the human psyche. The accusation which has been levelled against Freud of going round in a 'hermeneutic circle', in which the individual is deduced from the whole and the whole from the individual, arose out of a misconception. For this 'whole' consists of *a priori* structures and it is in fact these *a priori* structures which, in their function as meaningful contexts, constitute the individual.

From this it follows that psychoanalytic theory is far from bieng a rational and positivist process which simply re-establishes a broken causal nexus by the assumption of an unconscious (see below p. 459 ff.). At the same time it is equally far removed from the 'common sense' psychology which the Neo-Freudians and above all the Behaviourists (French and Rado) would have us see in it. It is clear from Binswanger's arguments that the complicated nature of Freudian psychoanalytic interpretations forced psychoanalysis to exceed from the very outset the positivist limits which it had set itself.

E

PARTNERSHIP AND TRANSFERENCE
(M. Buber, M. Scheler, K. Löwith,
E. Michel, P. Christian)

(a) The 'We' as the Ontological Absolute

The influence of phenomenology and later of existential ontology on Freudian psychoanalysis was to make itself felt not only in the sphere of psychoanalytic theory but also in the sphere of therapy, where it prompted a number of therapists to rethink from first principles what actually takes place between doctor and patient in the course of an analysis. With his discovery and definition of transference Freud, it is true, had established an essential factor of psychoanalytic treatment (see p. 162 ff.). This factor was subsequently subjected to detailed investigation by members of the Freudian school in order that a faultless instrument might be fashioned for the treatment of patients in psychoanalysis (see p. 250 ff.). Freud's followers in every branch of psychoanalysis paid scrupulous attention to the whole complex range of relations between doctor and patient from the point of view of transference. Merely, the crucial problem of the meeting between doctor and patient, the problem of their inter-personal relationship, was 'repressed'. Freud himself, however, was well aware that analysis could not content itself with the purely instrumental role of manipulating transference and counter-transference as a therapeutic technique. From the letters which have only recently been published by E. Jones it is clear that Freud considers *love* to be an essential factor in therapy.

'I can unreservedly subscribe to your remarks about therapy. I have had the same experiences, and for the same reasons have taken care not to maintain in my writings more than that "the method effects more than any other". I will not even maintain that every case of hysteria is curable, let alone everything that goes under that name. Since I am not concerned with the percentage of cures I have often treated cases bordering on the psychotic, or delusional (delusions of reference, blushing phobia, etc.), and in that way at least learned that the same mechanisms apply extensively beyond the limits of hysteria and obsessional neuroses. One cannot explain things to unfriendly people. I have therefore kept to myself a good deal that I could have said about the limitations of therapy and its mechanism, or mentioned in such a way as to be intelligible only to the expert. It would not have escaped you that our cures come about through attaching the libido reigning in the subconscious (transference) which comes about with more certainty in hysteria than elsewhere. Where this fails the patient will not make the effort or else does not listen when we translate his material to him. It is in essence a cure through love. Moreover it is transference that provides the strongest proof, the only unassailable one, for the relationship of neuroses to love.'[1]

Even before Heidegger and Binswanger had undertaken their investigations the 'I-Thou' relationship, the 'meeting' and the 'partnership' had been considered from the ontological point of view above all by *M. Buber*, *M. Scheler* and *K. Löwith* (who had all been influenced by *Feuerbach* and *Dilthey*). Buber writes:

'The fundamental fact of human existence is neither the individual as such nor the aggregate as such. Each, considered by itself, is a mighty abstraction. The individual is a fact of existence in so far as he steps into a living relation with other individuals. The aggregate is a fact of existence in so far as it is built up of living units of relation. The fundamental fact of human existence is man with man. What is peculiarly characteristic of the human world is above all that something takes place between one being and another the like of which can be found nowhere in nature. Language is only a sign and a means for it, all achievement of the spirit has been incited by it. Man is made man by

[1] From Freud's letter to Jung of Dec. 6, 1906; See E. Jones, *Sigmund Freud, Life and Work*, London, Hogarth Press; New York, Basic Books; Vol. 2, p. 485.

it; but on its way it does not merely unfold, it also decays and withers away. It is rooted in one being turning to another as another, as this particular other being, in order to communicate with it in a sphere which is common to them but which reaches out beyond the special sphere of each. I call this sphere, which is established with the existence of man as man but which is conceptually still uncomprehended, the sphere of "between". Though being realized in very different degrees, it is a primal category of human reality. This is where the genuine third alternative must begin.

'The view which establishes the concept of "between" is to be acquired by no longer localizing the relation between human beings, as is customary, either within individual souls, or in a general world which embraces and determines them, but in actual fact *between* them.

' "Between" is not an auxiliary construction, but the real place and bearer of what happens between men; it has received no specific attention because, in distinction from the individual soul and its context, it does not exhibit a smooth continuity, but is ever and again re-constituted in accordance with men's meetings with one another; hence what is experience has been annexed naturally to the continuous elements, the soul and its world.

'In a real conversation (that is, not one whose individual parts have been preconcerted, but one which is completely spontaneous, in which each speaks directly to his partner and calls forth his unpredictable reply), a real lesson (that is, neither a routine repetition nor a lesson whose findings the teacher knows before he starts, but one which develops in mutual surprises), a real embrace and not one of mere habit, a real duel and not a mere game—in all these what is essential does not take place in each of the participants or in a neutral world which includes the two and all other things; but it takes place between them in the most precise sense, as it were in a dimension which is accessible only to them both. Something happens to me—that is a fact which can be exactly distributed between the world and the soul, between an "outer" event and an "inner" impression. But if I and another come up against one another, "happen" to one another (to use a forcible expression which can, however, scarcely be paraphrased), the sum does not exactly divide, there is a remainder, somewhere, where the souls end and the world has not yet begun, and this remainder is what is essential. This fact can be found even in the tiniest and most transient events which scarcely enter the consciousness. In the deadly crush of an air-raid shelter the glances of two strangers suddenly meet for a second in astonishing and unrelated mutuality; when the All Clear sounds it is forgotten; and yet it did happen, in a realm which existed only for that moment. In the darkened opera house there can be established between

406

two of the audience, who do not know one another, and who are listening in the same purity and with the same intensity to the music of Mozart, a relation which is scarcely perceptible and yet is one of elemental dialogue, and which has long vanished when the lights blaze up again. In the understanding of such fleeting and yet consistent happenings one must guard against introducing motives of feeling: what happens here cannot be reached by psychological concepts, it is something ontic. From the least of events, such as these, which disappear in the moment of their appearance, to the pathos of pure indissoluble tragedy, where two men, opposed to one another in their very nature, entangled in the same living situation, reveal to one another in mute clarity an irreconcilable opposition of being, the dialogical situation can be adequately grasped only in an ontological way. But it is not to be grasped on the basis of the ontic of personal existence, or of that of two personal existences, but of that which has its being between them, and transcends both. In the most powerful moments of dialogic, where in truth "deep calls unto deep", it becomes unmistakably clear that it is not the wand of the individual or of the social, but of a third which draws the circle round the happening. On the far side of the subjective, on this side of the objective, on the narrow ridge, where *I* and *Thou* meet, there is the realm of "between".'[1]

M. Scheler has recognized, particularly in his works on *Wesen und Formen der Sympathie*[2] ('Essence and Forms of Sympathy') and *Die Idole der Selbsterkenntnis*[3] ('The Idols of Self-Knowledge'), that the individual is always preceded by 'we-ness', that it is in fact only by virtue of 'we-ness' that the individual exists at all. This fact questions not only the validity of Freud's auto-erotic stage or his 'primary narcissism' in infants (which, it might be felt, had already been invalidated by R. Spitz's investigations (see p. 222 ff.)) but also his psychoanalytic theory of the defence against displeasure by means of projection, identification, introjection, etc., in as far as these were intended to demonstrate the thesis of libidinal cathexis of an abstract psychic neutron (see below, p. 477 ff.). These positivist conceptions are based on the Cartesian view of the world, as has been demonstrated by K. Löwith[4] and E. Straus[5] (in their criticisms of Pavlov). The misconception at the very heart of the Cartesian system lies in the concept 'cogito, ergo sum', i.e. in the primacy of 'I think' over 'I am', as a result of which the 'I' is considered

[1] M. Buber, *Between Man and Man*, London, Routledge & Kegan Paul; New York, Macmillan; 1947, pp. 202–4.
[2] Frankfurt am Main, 1948.   [3] Bern, 1955.
[4] K. Löwith, *Das Individuum in der Rolle des Mitmenschen*, Munich, 1928. ('The Individual as a Fellow-man').
[5] E. Straus, *Vom Sinn der Sinne*, Berlin, 1935. ('On the Meaning of the Senses').

from the outset as an abstract form of self-awareness which is placed in formal contradistinction to an object, e.g. the object of the psychoanalytic 'cathexis'. As a logical consequence of this conception the world and thus the partner, i.e. the 'Thou', become objects. In the final instance they become objects of scientific enquiry and instruments of technical mastery. In contrast to the Cartesian view Löwith advances his own concept of the 'contemporary world' (*Mitwelt*) which precedes the individual existentially. Von Weizsäcker (see below, p. 420 ff.) goes so far as to say that it is not the 'I' that is the metaphysical absolute but the 'We'. L. Binswanger takes a similar stand from the point of view of existential ontology in his *Grundformen und Erkenntnis menschlichen Daseins* (Fundamental Forms and Knowledge of Human Reality), in which he undertakes a critical appraisal of Heidegger's *Time and Being*. Heidegger has since dealt more exclusively with the problem of the 'We' in various publications, above all in his *Brief über den Humanismus* (Letter on Humanism). None the less, Binswanger's comments remain valid. Binswanger accuses Heidegger of having failed to recognize the human condition of Being-with-others and of having represented man either as being lost in the extremity of public life, Heidegger's 'one of many', or in the extremity of his own 'selfness'. In Heidegger's conception of human reality 'love' is 'kept out in the cold'. Binswanger argues that the individual only comes to understand himself through love, through Eros. He writes: 'Determination in respect of Being is not a blessing bestowed by Existence but a blessing bestowed by Love.' Binswanger's conception of love is Christian, it is love of one's neighbour, love of oneself, love of God, as propounded by Augustine and Pascal. In his anthropological investigations into the nature of marriage E. Michel[1] arrives at an analogous conception, although his definition of love in terms of the concrete reality of the 'meeting' and of 'living together' is less ontological (and less idealistic) than is Binswanger's definition. On the basis of von Weizsäcker's investigations into the *Gestaltkreis P. Christian* (together with *Renate Haas*) has proved by means of experiments in which two people work together on a joint task, e.g. when two people saw a block of wood with a two-handed saw, that the 'We' precedes the 'I'. These investigations, which are of fundamental importance for the theory of partnership, are best described by their author, who summarizes them as follows:

'If we investigate by physiological means a *joint task undertaken by two people* we discover the following facts:

'(*a*) The basis of their collaboration is "reciprocity": This means that partner A. does not simply pass on his activity for partner B. to take

---

[1] E. Michel, *Ehe*, Stuttgart 1948. ('Marriage').

over but rather acts on the assumption that his activity can return to him. The same applies to partner B. Neither holds back from a retro-active link with the other; on the contrary, this retro-active link is made possible by each of the partners in turn. The attitude of the two partners is such that the activity of the one may be taken over, responded to and reinforced by the other. This includes acts of anticipation and over-lapping which are so pronounced that (to take an analogy from language) one partner virtually "takes the words out of the other's mouth". What A. does for B., B. does for A. Their play (work, attitude) is *for* them both and not *between* them both.

'(*b*) The persons who participate are not "*autonomous*": strictly speak-ing, their mode of work, to which each is obliged to contribute by the other, has no bearing on the *absolute* contribution in terms of effort made by each of the partners but only on their relative behaviour. This means that in communal work one partner may well do a third or a quarter more work than the other. In the actual *performance* of the communal task *neither* of the participants *notices this*: in objective terms the extent of an individual's participation is subject to considerable variation, but any discrepancy is completely and unwittingly *compensated for* by his companion. From this the astonishing fact emerges that the question as to whether a given individual is "industrious" or "idle", "precipitate" or "tardy" cannot be determined by reference to that individual *alone* but also depends for its solution on his companion. In this context working morale, temperament and forms of reaction are not individual constants but properties which are *jointly* determined by *both* partners. It is just like a spoken dialogue: whether a person is voluble or whether he loses his tongue largely depends on his partner; and whether one of the speakers produces ideas will also depend on the other's ability to draw him out.

'(*c*) The partners' solidarity is grounded in their *self-concealment* from one another. In the performance of a joint task which involves move-ment they disappear, so to speak, from one another's sight; neither is able to separate the other from himself; each forms a part of the aggre-gate, which the task constitutes, and each plays the role assigned to him by that aggregate. Objectively one of them leads, but he is quite unaware of the fact; objectively one of them is led, but unconsciously he none the less considers his partner's activity to be his own activity. Consequently each man identifies with what is decided, what is done and what is felt.

'Even if partner A. *intentionally* and considerably modifies his contri-bution to the joint task, partner B. will automatically and quite un-wittingly compensate for this to a large extent. And so man's involve-ment in *society* is *concealed from himself*. At the precise moment when, at the successful peak of their joint task, both participants experience a feeling of maximum independence, analysis shows that, objectively speaking, both are bound together by the strict reciprocity of the work processes. From this it follows that in joint activity independence is only experienced if the *reciprocity* of that activity is objectively achieved. And so the subjective independence of the one partner is identical with the independence which he secretly gives to the other partner and which the latter positively accepts. It cannot be thrust upon him but must be accepted by him in *reciprocal* freedom.

'(*d*)   Finally the analysis of such—and similar—experiments—provides irrefutable proof that the fusion of partnership is already demonstrably present at the very *roots* of the process: although the joint task is achieved by two subjects acting in partnership, in fact it is a unified process from the very outset; segregation of the partners is neither necessary nor determinable.'[1]

(b) The 'Absolute We' and Psychotherapy (H. Trüb, F. Schottländer, A. Sborowitz, the Stuttgart School)

Together with L. Binswanger, M. Boss and the other therapists who have come under the influence of existential ontology H. Trüb[2] has been a leading protagonist in the investigation of the problem of the 'meeting' as opposed to transference. His enquiries have taken the form of conversations and collaboration with his friends *A. Sborowitz, E. Michel* and *F. Schottländer*.[3] Of the various groups engaged in psychotherapeutic practice it has been the group at the Stuttgart Institute (*F. Schottländer, W. Bitter, W. Laiblin, H. Geist*, etc.) which has dealt with this question in the greatest detail.

With the active support of F. Schottländer and the other members of the Stuttgart group H. Trüb has been the most determined apologist of a view which has subjected the central concept of Freudian psychoanalysis, namely, transference, to searching criticism. Trüb and Schottländer accuse Freud of regarding the patient as an 'it', i.e. an object, and not as a person. The concept of transference, they argue, is amongst other things a scientific fiction which the analysts invented in order to avoid a real meeting with the patient. The attempt to model the psychotherapeutic situation on the conditions prevailing in scientific experiment missed the whole point of psychotherapy, for the desire to be cured could only be engendered in the patient if the physician adopted a

[1] P. Christian, *Personenverständnis im modernen medizinischen Denken*, pp. 154 ff. ('The Understanding of Personality in Modern Medical Thought').

[2] H. Trüb, *Heilung aus der Begegnung*, Stuttgart, 1949. ('Healing through Meeting').

[3] F. Schottländer, see esp. 'Kontakt und Übertragung' in *Almanach*, 1958, E. Klett, Stuttgart. ('Contact and Transference').

genuine and personal attitude towards him. Transference meant that the patient abreacted his infantile patterns of behaviour on to the analyst in what was virtually a reflex action. For as long as the patient remained enmeshed in this process of abreaction he would remain enmeshed in his neurosis. If on the other hand he were to conceive the desire for a meeting—always provided that the therapist was himself inwardly prepared for such a meeting—then this would constitute a first and decisive indication that a cure was possible, for the neurotic, who had previously been incapable of any meeting, would then be in a position to make genuine contact. From this Trüb argues that the restrictions imposed on transference by Freud's scientific conception must be removed and the concept of transference extended to allow for the possibility of a meeting, which is a prerequisite for a successful cure. In its publications (especially in the psychological journal, Psyche E. Klett, Stuttgart) the Stuttgart group has demonstrated the efficacy of their strongly modified version of psychotherapy (as compared with Freudian therapy) by reference to clinical material and case histories.

H. Trüb studied under Jung over a period of years and the two men became personal friends. Sborowitz has told us that throughout his life Trüb was constantly coming to terms with his preceptor. His chief objection to Jung is summed up in the following passage:

'In our view Jung's achievement lies in the fact that he addressed himself in holy earnest to seek the self in the soul—and where else should he have sought it?—and that he pursued this hopeless path of inner enquiry *to its very end*, a fact which we now find very impressive. In his endless endeavours to find man's Self in the processes of introversive experience Jung in fact accurately indicated *the point of the existential breakthrough*. Although he himself did not succeed in breaking through from the *ego* to the *self*, it was through him that we, who now hold an anthropological view, were made to realize that the breakthrough to universal reality can only ever be expected to come from this point, from the Self. In his investigation of the Collective Unconscious and in its therapeutic application Jung advanced as far as an introspective psychological view could ever hope to advance, namely, to the point where the psychic sphere, pointing beyond itself, abuts on the metaphysic.'[1]

According to Trüb the breakthrough to the transcendental sphere, which he considered absolutely essential, could never be achieved by Jung's Complex Psychology. It is for this reason that Trüb speaks of Jung's 'hopeless' path and refuses 'to recognize the transcendental in any fashion or form for the realm of psychology'. But what hope of success

[1] H. Trüb, *Heilung aus der Begegnung*, p. 120.

does Trüb's anthropological psychotherapy hold out for the treatment of neurosis? *Sborowitz* comments on his therapy as follows:

'Let me try to clarify Trüb's position by means of an example, namely, that of *homosexuality*! Freudian psychoanalysis recognized that—in many cases—homosexuality was explicable in terms of an excessive attachment to the mother. Our insight into this problem is deepened when Jungian Analytical Psychology goes beyond the biographical condition of this attachment to the mother and interprets it in psychic terms: as subjection to the mother principle, to the "Great Mother". Both interpretations constitute an important aid to our understanding of homosexuality. But are they adequate in themselves? Above all, are they adequate in respect of therapy? A homo-erotic might well accept all the insights which both a Freudian and a Jungian analysis revealed to him and yet make no headway whatsoever. In such cases, Trüb argues, the patient has got stuck in the psychological sphere. He has not yet achieved the breakthrough to the Self which at some point of time, perhaps unconsciously, whilst he was under the spell of the "mother experience", opted in favour of homosexuality. And the "reason why" the sufferer did not succeed in effecting this breakthrough to the centre of his Self is that no personal relationship was established between the patient and the therapist, that the therapist did not address his partner personally, that the patient shut himself off from the call, which, if it had elicited a personal response and consummation, would have illumined the ultimate recesses. Trüb's criticism is not directed against psychology, against psychological self-illumination—for this he considers to be very necessary—but is intended rather as a reminder of the limits, beyond which psychology cannot go.'[1]

In this connection Trüb object's to Jung's therapeutic process on the grounds that the patient, i.e. the subject, is only required to come to terms with the objects of his inner world, the archetypes, whilst his relationship to his fellow men in real life is totally neglected. (In Freud's case the patient's relationship to his fellow men does at least lead a sort of shadow existence as the torso of the transference love.) If Jung's path of healing and path of salvation achieves its fulfilment in individuation, then, Trüb asks, is there a path leading back from individuation to the world? Trüb states that Jung's answer to this question was in the negative:

'He gave me to understand that it was not necessary to seek a way back to the world for the self which was attained by means of individuation, i.e.

[1] H. Trüb, *Heilung aus der Begegnung*, Poscript by A. Sborowitz, p. 123.

by means of his doctrine, because the relationship to the world was already embodied in this concept of the self.'[1]

And he goes on to say:

'So now I know definitively that my view of the doctor-patient relationship as a *meeting between partners*, which I did not conceive as a means towards the "introversive" individuation of the patient but rather as a crucial first step towards *a new meeting with the world*, can never be reconciled with Jung's therapeutic aims. For in Jung's individuation process man's essential vocation is not concerned with his capacity or readiness for meeting the world but rather with the inner-psychic meeting between the "ego" and the various strata of the unconscious, a meeting which must take place before the Self can *come into being* and into view. And so, as we have said, Jung seeks man's essential vocation in the psychological process of his relationship to himself.'[2]

Trüb considers that this crucial deficiency in C. G. Jung's Complex Psychology stems from Jung's own personality. Jung was primarily a researcher who was so fascinated by the contents of the Collective Unconscious that he cut his ties with the world and ceased to exist as a partner in relationship to the world.

'The crucial point about this achievement is not the fact that Jung plumbed the unconscious depths of the soul *as a researcher*—others have done as much and if he had done no more than this he would only be one of the great discoverers and masters. The decisive fact of the matter is that Jung clearly set out to realize himself existentially in this introversive process and then went beyond this immediate aim by raising this method, i.e. *his own* method, of self-realization both in his doctrine and in his practice to the status of a universal goal of healing and of salvation.'[3]

F

VIKTOR VON WEIZSÄCKER

(a) From 'Personal Intercourse' to the GESTALTKREIS *(Gestalt circle)*

Von Weizsäcker regards 'personal intercourse' as the foremost of human categories. He also regards it as the key to an understanding of the doctor-patient relationship. The general tendency in medical circles —a tendency which accords with the sort of attitude that has been

---

[1] H. Trüb, *Heilung aus der Begegnung*, p. 32.   [2] H. Trüb, *ibid.*, pp. 32–33.
[3] H. Trüb, *ibid.*, p. 33.

fostered by the natural sciences—is for this relationship to be considered from a single point of view only. Accordingly the patient is either evaluated as an object, i.e. as an object to be investigated in the Cartesian sense, or else he is treated by means of 'transference' and thus kept at the same distance as the object of scientific investigation. In contrast to this conception von Weizsäcker advances his own view, in which he maintains that every medical investigation is a single unified act, in which both doctor and patient are involved in a process of give and take. This single unified act von Weizsäcker has called 'personal intercourse'. The doctor gives his patient a diagnosis, enables him to acquire self-knowledge, prescribes medicine for him. In return the patient places his body at the doctor's disposal for purposes of examination, he tells him his thoughts and—last but not least—he gives him his fee. P. Christian has described this relationship as follows:

'For a genuine therapy only succeeds for as long as and in as far as the patient remains oriented towards and related to the doctor. But then the doctor's "therapeutic giving" is coincidental with the patient's "obedience" and the energy which the doctor dispenses in the act of giving he receives back again in obedience, which takes the form of increased self-confidence: the dispensation of confidence by the doctor produces an increase of confidence in the patient. This mutual give and take is the basis of the doctor-patient relationship, and it is quite evident that ontologically speaking the two are inseparable.'[1]

By introducing the concept of 'personal intercourse' von Weizsäcker has established a far deeper and far more fundamental basis for the doctor-patient relationship than did Freud or Jung. In Jung's case the reality of the transference is consumed by inner-psychic images and symbolic processes, whilst Freud's definition of transference was determined by electro-physical ideas. This does not mean to say, however, that the therapist should underestimate the importance of 'transference' and 'counter-transference'. Von Weizsäcker's purpose in formulating his concept of 'personal intercourse' was simply to establish a real basis for the doctor-patient relationship, one which would avoid the error of considering every human relationship in the light of a transference or object relationship, a practice which makes a 'meeting' and a 'personal relationship' impossible. Von Weizsäcker writes:

'Certainly Freud introduced the I (ego) into his psychology and placed the it (id) in contradistinction to it. But that this I also appears as a

[1] P. Christian, *Das Personenverständnis im modernen medizinischen Denken*, p. 142.

thou, that the thou then also has an it, its own it, that the object can be replaced by the it only within this context—this he did not see. Only when he recognized that group psychology was really unavoidable did a kind of personalism make itself felt in him; for if there are I's, thou's, i.e. if there are plurals, then the we-category is at least within hailing distance. True, he did not advance to this We. Jung hazarded an attempt; it was unsuccessful.'[1]

But how did von Weizsäcker develop the concepts of 'personal intercourse' and of the Gestaltkreis?

The importance of psychic disturbances as a factor in the genesis of internal diseases had already been recognized and described by *Ludolf von Krehl*.[2] *R. Siebeck*[3] and above all V. von Weizsäcker, both of whom had studied under von Krehl, further pursued this line of enquiry, paying special attention to the role played by the personality in the emergence and development of internal diseases. Von Weizsäcker was an experimental neurologist, a specialist for internal diseases and a psychotherapist. It was in the field of internal diseases and psychotherapy that he discovered his conception of personal intercourse, whilst his conception of the Gestaltkreis was the outcome of his biological and neurological investigations and experiments. The systematic application of psychoanalysis in the treatment of organic and functional illnesses was pioneered in Germany by von Weizsäcker and his collaborators. In adopting Freud's theories—von Weizsäcker was never deeply interested in the work of C. G. Jung—he also developed ideas[4] of his own which diverged from orthodox Freudian theory in certain essential respects. Such divergences of opinion are in fact only to be expected in view of von Weizsäcker's fundamentally different conception of human personality.

What the principle of the *Gestaltkreis* at the biological level comes down to is that seeing and moving are a single act. Von Weizsäcker gained this crucial, indeed revolutionary insight—to which unfortunately the Neo-Freudian Behaviourists and Reflexologists (e.g. Th. French, S. Rado and F. Alexander) have as yet paid no attention—from his observations of human beings walking, of butterflies in flight and from numerous experiments, chief amongst them that carried out by P. Vogel involving artificially induced vertigo. In the following passage

---

[1] V. v. Weizsäcker, *Pathosophie*, quotation taken from v. Weisäcker–D. Wyss, *Zwischen Medizin und Philosophie*, Göttingen, 1957.

[2] L. v. Krehl, *Entstehung, Erkennung und Behandlung innerer Krankheiten*, Leipzig, 1930. ('Emergence, Recognition and Treatment of Internal Diseases').

[3] R. Siebeck, *Medizin in Bewegung*, Stuttgart, 1949. ('Medicine in Movement').

[4] See especially the section dealing with v. Weizsäcker's relationship to Freud in V. v. Weizsäcker–D. Wyss, *Zwischen Medizin und Philosophie* ('Between Medicine and Philosophy').

von Weizsäcker describes his observation of the act of walking, an observation which questions the whole basis of the reflexological interpretation of this act:

'Now if we consider a common organic movement such as walking we shall find the same conditions. If a man is walking on a horizontal but undulating surface then the continuous change in the angle of inclination of his path will produce distinctly similar alternations in the forms of the innervations. True, the man's walk consists at all times of alternating flexion and extension of the major joints of the legs. But whereas on rising ground it is the tensors which effect the *extension* of the joints, when the ground falls away it is the tensors which check their *flexion* and whose stretching makes this flexion possible. On rising ground the tensors produce an *extension* but on falling ground a flexion—first they produce movement, then they check it; first by active contraction, then by active stretching, first by increasing, then by decreasing tension.

'It was a tempting speculation to interpret the act of walking, whose constitutional, physiological and morphological structure was revealed above all by Sherrington's analyses, as a combination of two co-ordinated reflexes, the flexor and the extensor. I do not believe, however, that Sherrington considered that he had explained the act of walking and failed to realize that for the composition of this act more is needed than just these two reflexes. Merely, he omitted to emphasize the fact that we can only walk on undulating ground if, for example, the co-ordination of the flexor is initiated and carried out independently of the actual outcome of the flexion—and likewise for the extensor. But this circumstance is not immaterial, since the accomplished movements can themselves become the cause of new, so-called proprioceptive reflex stimuli; thus the build-up of the movements depends not only on the innervations but also on the movements which are the outcome of the innervations.'[1]

By introducing the principle of *achievement* von Weizsäcker disposes of the reflexological interpretation of human movement once and for all.

But what is meant by this principle of achievement? Quite simply that the successful completion of any movement—the achievement which walking, standing, running, etc., constitute—depends on the operations of *various* neural pathways and reflexes. This means that the interpretation of movement as a more or less mechanical reflex function linked to specific neural affects is no longer tenable. Von Weizsäcker does in fact still attach some importance to this conception of reflex functions, but only in as far as it has greatly facilitated the task of establishing the different structures and functions of the nervous system, especially in cases where pathogenic changes have taken place. In all of man's dealings

[1] V. v. Weizsäcker, *Der Gestaltkreis*, Stuttgart, 1947, pp. 3-4.

with his environment, both when he is 'taking it in', i.e. by looking at it, and when, by means of movement, he actively intervenes, every single achievement—and this includes both simple acts of perception and simple movements such as placing one foot on top of the other—is partially determined by its outcome, i.e. by the way in which it intervenes in the environment. And so, as von Weizsäcker has stated, when a man is walking on uneven ground his walk is constantly being corrected by the unevenness of the ground, which means that *the outcome of each completed movement determines the course of the next*. This process involves various neural pathways which are connected with a great many different reflex centres. In other words: *the achievement*, the successful movement, e.g. adaptation to the uneven ground, is *supraordinate to the neural pathways and reflexes* and simply uses them as instruments. But adaptation to uneven ground also constitutes an act of *perception* of that ground, an act executed by the sense of touch and by the organs of balance, etc. And so von Weizsäcker is able to demonstrate that in every act relating to the environment perception and movement represent a *unity*. Von Weizsäcker's collaborator, P. Vogel, gave a practical demonstration of this unity when he carried out his experiment involving artificially induced vertigo. In this experiment the person submitting to the test either keeps turning round and round in circles or stands inside a cardboard cylinder which is then revolved around him. At all stages of the experiment the indissoluble connection between perception and movement was demonstrably maintained, although under certain conditions perception and movement were in fact able to replace one another: i.e. when perception moved to the fore movement withdrew and vice versa. Von Weizsäcker draws the following conclusions:

'This investigation reveals that we are linked or, as it were, bonded to the environment and its objects in quite specific relationships. There exist specific organizations which function in such a way as to ensure that the body or, alternatively, its organs remain in contact with specific pieces of the environment until such time as they are severed from one another by the intrusion of a superior force. We call this sort of connectedness *coherence*. In the visual sphere it operates in the following way: we look at a man observing a butterfly that has entered his field of vision. We may assume that in the first instance its image moves across a section of the retina. There then follows a movement of the eyes in the direction in which the butterfly is flying, which, due to the peculiar nature of this insect's flight, is soon followed by movements of the head, the body and the legs. The end object of this multiple deployment of muscular activity is always the same: to ensure that as far as possible the image of the insect shall remain imprinted on the centre of the retina. In this way, despite repeated disturbances, the observer remains in optical contact with the insect. Here too then the movement causes the object to appear in that it is by the conservation of coherence that both the observer and his movements are made apparent. Coherence then is conditional on this sequence of movements, and consequently we are entitled to call this whole process—seeing plus movement—a single act.'[1]

If one of the principal characteristics of living creatures—both of a butterfly in flight and of a man walking—is spontaneous movement then it follows that movement and perception are fused together: when I move I cause a perception to appear or alternatively when I perceive something a movement is made manifest to me. This leads to the so-called *revolving door principle* and to the *principle of mutual concealment*. What do these terms mean? The fusing of movement and perception means that the activity which prompts a perception, i.e. which prompts a look, is not itself perceived but takes place unconsciously. Such activity is a negative achievement and can only become an object of perception after it has taken place. In other words the spontaneous movement involved in the act of looking, the movement of the head in a certain direction, does not determine (or cause) the perception, rather the perception is itself a spontaneous movement. In this case the unity of movement and perception does indeed operate on the principle of a revolving door: the inside of the house is only perceived when you enter the house, once you go out again it is no longer visible. Or to put it another way: perception and movement are mutually concealed from one another. Although the act of perception is itself a spontaneous movement, the movement, as it were, 'knows' nothing about the perception and the perception knows nothing about the movement: they are concealed from one another just as the inside of the house is concealed until you have entered the house. Once the spontaneous movement of living creatures, the fusing of perception and movement, is recognized, it becomes abundantly clear that a mechanistic biology which treats living creatures as objects is quite incapable of understanding living activity. With the recognition of the spontaneous movement of living creatures subjectivity is introduced into biology as a fundamentally new principle. The importance of this discovery of von Weizsäcker's compares with that of *Einstein's* theory of relativity and *Heisenberg's* indeterminate relations. The *Gestaltkreis* is now seen to consist of the unity of the subject with his environment, which unity is constantly established by the subject by means of movement and perception.

[1] V. v. Weizsäcker, *Der Gestaltkreis*, pp. 8–9.

The same holds good for the concept of 'personal intercourse' which von Weizsäcker developed within the field of medicine:

'Personal intercourse would for example be that cyclomorphic organization which in the act of touching links the *object* of touch, the movement and the *perception* in a circular relationship; personal intercourse would also be the example described above of the pilot who intervenes in the play of forces by means of his joystick and at the same time perceives those forces in the sensations transmitted back to him by the same instrument, whereupon he again intervenes; personal intercourse is every act of walking in which the play of movement of the legs "finds a footing", whereby it sensorially perceives the next step, and is thus enabled to find a "further footing". Personal intercourse is every biological act as a fact of life. And this now *also* becomes the *general model* for the organization of that particular personal intercourse which characterizes the relationship between doctor and patient. The analogy is precise, for in the personal intercourse between doctor and patient each partner gets from the interplay of reciprocating forces what he has put into it; in other words "perception" and "treatment", provided the doctor is turned towards the patient, constitute a process of mutual illumination.'[1]

'If now we have succeeded in capturing the essence of that which is really human with all its force and all its consequence in the concept of "personal intercourse", then we shall have to make further decisions, e.g. whether, and in what sense, an animate being can only have intercourse with its own kind, or with inanimate matter as well. On this in turn will depend what meaning we actually give to the concept of "personal intercourse". This is more or less the pattern of the problems posed by the concept of the *Gestaltkreis*.'[2]

'This *Gestaltkreis* has already been described in the *biological sphere*: the essential point is that in every biological act perception and movement are mutually interchangeable conditions, that they remain concealed from one another in any given instance and that subject and object also participate in this fusion, interchangeability and concealment: "reality" appears now in one and now in the other. And so it is not a question of subjectivity alone or of objectivity alone but of the

---

[1] P. Christian, *Das Personenverständnis im modernen medizinischen Denken*, pp. 140–1.

[2] V. v. Weizsäcker, *Grundfragen medizinischer Anthropologie*, p. 14 (quotation taken from P. Christian, *Das Personenverständnis im modernen medizinischen Denken*, p. 141. 'Fundamental Questions of Medical Anthropology').

union of both in the configuration of the "Gestaltkreis". Basically this expression (in point of fact it is a precept of scientific intercourse) means a specific type of "intercourse" of subjects with objects, and the *meeting* and the *intercourse* are thus elevated to the status of a central scientific concept.

'If we transport this "precept" into the *anthropological sphere*, what follows from it is a specific *conceptual organization of the doctor-patient relationship*:

'Just as with the groping hand of the examiner the person examined is an object in a *Gestaltkreis*, so too there lies behind every therapeutic treatment, behind every diagnostic intrusion—in as far as it has been thought out in sufficiently broad terms—a cyclomorphic process, a simultaneous *give* and *take*.'[1]

(b) *From the* Gestaltkreis *to the Subject* (Personality)

But why is the *Gestaltkreis* of such crucial importance? Why is it important that the subject be introduced into physiology and biology, into the biological experiment? The *Gestaltkreis* is important because it constitutes a profound and radical revolution in the development of the natural sciences, the first—apart from Goethe's important Theory of Colour—since Newton and Descartes. The object no longer stands in contradistinction to the subject as an object of knowledge (as with Freud and Descartes), but instead enters into a relationship with the subject as a subject:

'Whereas physics presupposes that objects would continue to exist even when isolated from the subject, the object of biology is quite inconceivable unless we are prepared to come to grips with it; its independent existence cannot be presupposed. In physics perception may be affected by the object; it follows the object. By contrast the biologist feels his way into his object and experiences it through his own life. *In order to investigate living phenomena we must participate in life*. Physics is only objective, whilst the biologist is also subjective. Dead things are alien to one another, whilst living creatures, even when hostile, are gregarious.'[2]

Von Weizsäcker has furnished experimental proof of his assertion that it is not the 'I' but the 'We' which is the metaphysical absolute and in so doing he has, as it were, pulled the wool from the eyes of the Cartesian oriented natural sciences including Freudian Psycho-analysis and psycho-somatic medicine. In his work he reveals the same bent as the

[1] P. Christian, *Das Personenverständnis im modernen medizinischen Denken*, p. 141.
[2] V. v. Weizsäcker, *Der Gestaltkreis*, p. 173.

existential ontologists, *Heidegger*[1] and *Binswanger*,[2] as *M. Scheler*,[3] *K. Löwith*,[4] *M. Buber*,[5] *E. Michel*[6] and *H. Trüb*[7] in as far as these thinkers place the 'We' above the Cartesian 'I' either in an ontological sense or as a consequence of their anthropological observations. But there is none the less an essential difference between the investigations carried out by these thinkers and those carried out by von Weizsäcker, for von Weizsäcker has furnished experimental, 'scientific' proof of his enquiries by his description of the unity of the biological act of perception and movement. After subjecting the sense of touch to an investigation similar to that carried out by P. Vogel in respect of artificially induced vertigo P. Christian[8] testified to the importance of the *Gestaltkreis* as follows:

'The examples given were the act of touching and the act of preserving a state of balance: both are achievements of a subject, and these achievements evidently establish a psycho-physical relationship in terms of the *Gestaltkreis*. What the preservation of a state of balance really means, however, is *the relationship of a total organization to its environment and what the act of touching means is the rapport between a subject and its environment.* Even in the latter case the total organism (for which von Weizsäcker uses the concept "I") is interlaced and intertwined *with* this environment. The function which preserves the state of balance cannot be separated out from the condition of coherence which binds it to environmental conditions any more than the tactile process can be separated from its contact with the external object. Thus the achievement of stability *vis-à-vis* such environmental disturbances and the achievement whereby a subject is removed from its object (it only becomes an object if the attempt to free it from the subject is successful; only then is the object of touch something "outside of me") are essentially processes *in which the "I" and the environment come to terms with each other.*

'Let there be no misunderstanding: the outcome of the logical development up to this point is the precise opposite of the scientific position to date:

---

[1] M. Heidegger, *Brief über den Humanismus*, Frankfurt am Main, 1947.

[2] L. Binswanger, *Grundformen und Erkenntnis menschlichen Daseins*, Zürich, 1953.

[3] M. Scheler, *Wesen und Formen der Sympathie*, Frankfurt am Main 1948.

[4] K. Löwith, *Das Individuum in der Rolle des Mitmenschen*, Munich, 1928.

[5] M. Buber, *Das Problem des Menschen*, Heidelberg, 1948.

[6] E. Michel, *Ehe*, Stuttgart, 1948.

[7] H. Trüb, *Heilung aus der Begegnung*, Stuttgart, 1949.

[8] P. Christian, *Das Personenverständnis im modernen medizinischen Denken*, Tübingen, 1952.

' "Achievements" are processes in which the "I" and the environment, which in their original condition are intimately involved, *come to terms with each other*. What has to be explained, therefore, is not how the external object got in touch with the subject (on the basis of a duality), but rather how the subject freed and removed itself from its state of original unity with the external world. This is an extremely revolutionary mode of thought as compared with the type of thinking which stems from the natural sciences and to which we have previously been accustomed. Von Weizsäcker took this step with his *Gestaltkreis*. Likewise and independently *Arnold Gehlen*! In contrast to animals man, as a creature capable of action, is not built into an environment but has the duty to free himself, "to place himself in contradistinction". For the moment we do not propose to pursue this crucial thought any further but merely to reassert: the "I" removes itself as a subject *vis-à-vis* an environment and forms "achievements". And so "achievements" constitute, as it were, a leading concept. They are a component of living. They are either there or not there, either good or bad, either successful or unsuccessful; but they are *an a priori of every natural-scientific analysis*. They have to be presupposed, but not until they have been established am I able to analyse the conditions under which they came about. From this it follows that every natural-scientific analysis of a biological process is, so to speak, an historical act: the achievement is given, and I establish the conditions which facilitated or impeded it.'[1]

By contrast S. Freud's conception of the world remained strictly Cartesian; despite his 'discovery' of the unconscious, despite his undermining of the autonomy of consciousness, despite his endeavours to establish a dynamic conception of personality, Freud's motto remained: 'In our view the phenomena which are perceived must withdraw in favour of the strivings which are merely assumed'.[2] His attempt to express psychic relationships in terms of the libido economy, which was based on the concepts of electro-physics, quantum mechanics and hydraulics, was so typical of his nineteenth-century outlook that there is no need to go into it again here. But one of the inevitable results of such an outlook was the fact that Freud's transference concept was quite incapable of establishing the ultimate and crucial confrontation with the partner. For Freud libidinal object cathexis is the basis of human relationships and libidinal object cathexis is not able to achieve

---

[1] P. Christian, *Das Personenverständnis im modernen medizinischen Denken*, pp. 100–1.

[2] Quotation taken from L. Binswanger, Freud's 'Auffassung des Menschen im Lichte der Anthropologie'; *Ges. Vortr. u. Aufs.*, Vol. I; Bern, 1947 ('Conception of Man in the Light of Anthropology').

the personal understanding which is ultimately necessary for the success of any therapy.[1] Although the anthropologists and existential ontologists mentioned above were also engaged on the re-formulation of the concept of the personality as a subject it was von Weizsäcker who achieved this re-formulation in empirical terms. Von Weizsäcker's artificially induced vertigo had in fact produced a *crisis* under experimental conditions and it was this crisis which led von Weizsäcker from his concept of the *Gestaltkreis* to a new conception of the subject, one that was infinitely superior to the Freudian conception. It is not only in cases of inflammation of the lungs or angina pectoris that the physician is able to observe crises, for psychotherapy and even ordinary daily life produce their quota of crisis situations. What such crises have in common is that there would appear to be no way out of them. 'To be or not to be' is the question which they pose and the subject (the personality) feels that his whole existence is being questioned and weighed in the balance. If the subject fails to overcome the crisis he is destroyed, whereas if he succeeds in overcoming it he will almost certainly undergo a far-reaching transformation. The crisis interrupts the normal processes of the established order and introduces stormy and often threatening changes which cannot be 'explained' in a causal sense as the outcome of earlier stages. Often the sick person has the feeling that he is cracking up. If he overcomes the crisis he will gain a new inner form and will have become a different person. For the crisis questions the very identity of the subject *vis-à-vis* himself and those who have seen a patient sinking in a coma will have rightly asked themselves—is this a person? is this a subject? Now von Weizsäcker argues that the subject is never really noticed until such time as the crisis threatens to destroy him. But the unconscious subject, i.e. the subject in a coma who is no longer conscious of himself, is none the less a subject and becomes the very epitome of the unity of the organism which is threatened by, but also preserved in, the illness. This subject, however, is not a fixed possession; it is not an object; it must be constantly re-acquired, fought for, *suffered for* in the crisis, if it is to possess itself as a subject.

The subject, considered in terms of crisis, lies at the heart of von Weizsäcker's concept of personality. His definition of the subject was evolved from the following considerations:

1. The *Gestaltkreis*: without the subject, who creates himself in the biological act, in the unity of movement and perception, the *Gestaltkreis* would be unthinkable.
2. The crisis: this questions the unity of the subject, i.e. his identity with himself, and it questions the autonomy of the subject. It is only

[1] See p. 558 ff.

when he reacquires himself in the crisis that the subject proves himself to be the stable element in the midst of instability.

(c) The Personality (the Subject) and its Categories

Space, time, number and causation are the categories within which the natural sciences try to comprehend living nature. They are also the categories relevant to Freud's conception of man. In contradistinction to these scientific categories von Weizsäcker posits the categories of the anti-logical, the pathic and of personal intercourse as being more applicable to the subjectivity of living nature and of human personality. He arrived at these categories through the realization that man

'is not enclosed in a spatial world, nor in a temporal world, nor in a world populated by forces or energies, but rather, as it were, man lives through space, through time and through forces or energies and numbers. What is meant by "living through" is that these dimensions do not limit or constitute man's reality. Since they are newly formed in the present in each individual case, are in fact improvisations, man's view of the world here loses its classical and scientific stability and also its physical stability. Here human reality is more a process in which subject and environment are constantly coming to terms, are constantly meeting anew, are engaged in fluid intercourse. Logical definitions of this essence, which essentially is definable in terms of *intercourse*, can really only be described as a constant failure—like a house of cards that is constantly being built up and constantly falling down again. And this characteristic of logical definitions is then also designated as the anti-logic of living reality and constitutes one aspect of it.'[1]

Von Weizsäcker derives the Anti-logical, which is his most fundamental philosophical contribution, from the meeting:

'A meeting is more than a mere contact if I as a subject do not simply meet a number of objects but rather discover in those objects other subjects, who, like myself, are capable of spontaneous movement. Now the meeting is no longer a mere contact, a state of fusion in rigidity, but is instead capable of infinite development, since the other subject may move towards my own subject, or flee from it, or take evasive action by side-stepping it—I can never know which. If we wish to maintain our contact or if we wish to break it off, we, my subject and the other, must engage in personal intercourse with one another—the meeting is a present, incipient form of *personal intercourse*. And so the meeting

[1] V. v. Weizsäcker, Grundfragen medizinischer Anthropologie (in 'Forschungen und Studien'; Studiengem. d. Ev. Akad., Vol. VI, Tübingen, 1947).

between the subjects, who are mutual objects, takes the form of personal intercourse. This intercourse does not stand still, it is itself a meeting, but if the intercourse is and remains one beween two specific subjects, then it does retain as a constant property the fact that these two are the same, that this sameness delimits a special path—which is a *Gestalt*—and that despite locomotion it remains a constant property in the relationship—which is a symbol of the "circle" (*Kreissymbol*).

'But it should be said that the object which constitutes the schema of the *Gestaltkreis* is an anti-logical object, one that can be adequately apprehended in terms of anti-logic but not of logic.

'A first example is the development of organisms from fructification, division, growth, i.e. procreation. We see how in the event of fructification a new simple cell develops from sperm and egg; how this single cell is divided into two, four, eight, etc. Self-fructification and self-division, reductive and productive development contradict in a sense the unalterable character of the total number: two become one, one becomes two. This is a case of numerical anti-logic; it does not remain at the level of a contradiction, for this is overcome by real activity.—All this is repeated if, instead of the cells, we consider their nucleus, the chromosomes. Caryokinesis is just as anti-logical. This process also contains the further factor that the creature produced from two cells by fusion and then formed by division and growth is always one and the same. The newly fructified cell, the stages of the morula and the gastrula, the embryo, the child, the adult have remained one and the same creature, and for whole periods on end there exists such a marked degree of similarity in what is at the same time none the less a different organism that we are able to specify further types of anti-logic. The child looks like the youth, the youth like the man; they are the same and yet they are different. And so there is a genetic anti-logic, in which we see identity anti-logically linked with diversity by means of similarity.

'Numerical, genetic, identifying and imitative anti-logic are also examples of the great multiplicity of forms into which the anti-logical principle may be resolved.'[1]

And again:

'If we concede that there is *more* than one living creature in the world (two are quite sufficient for purposes of this demonstration), then we are also obliged to concede that these different creatures encounter different phenomena; for if everything were identical for them, then they just would not be different creatures. If on the other hand they did not both belong to the same world, then they would not encounter one another

[1] V. v. Weizsäcker, *Pathosophie*, Göttingen, 1956.

and would know nothing about one another. And so the existence of two living creatures in the world proves both the similarity and the dissimilarity of the relationship of living creatures to the world. Consequently it is inevitable that *the same* world should appear *differently*. It is likewise inevitable that to a creature that changes the same world should appear differently. And what is true of appearance (e.g. perception) is also true of activity. ("If two do the same thing, it is still not the same thing.") And so anti-logic is not an accidental property but a necessary consequence and a constitutive element of a world containing more than one living creature or of a living creature that is in the world and is capable of change. These two sub-divisions may be combined in the proposition that *a world which includes the subject must be anti-logical*. We cannot gain this perception if we deny the subject. It becomes necessary once we "introduce" the subject into the world or, more correctly, recognize the subject.'[1]

The anti-logical is not the same as a contradiction based on logic nor is it synonymous with the illogical. What von Weiszäcker understands under the anti-logical are the paradoxes which occur in life and which no amount of metaphysics can 'clear up'. But an anti-logical statement is also paradoxical in the sense that it affords both a negation and an affirmation, whereas in logic the negation of a postulate not only does not deny the logic but actually confirms it. The anti-logical contradiction inherent in living activity, the paradox, whereby affirmation and negation are simultaneously valid, becomes apparent if, for example, we consider the interrelationship between growth and decline. A man may say of himself that he is growing or that he is declining and both statements will be true. This constitutes a genuine anti-logical condition. Events such as birth and death, crises, transformations, meetings and decisions are also anti-logical occurrences. The anti-logical, as an absolute antithesis to the logical, is not to be equated with Freud's a-logic of the unconscious mind. Freud's a-logic is a construction which was established in order to denote the chaos of the irrational (the 'id'), which, in Freud's presentation, is not real but only apparent (see below, p. 511 ff.).

The recognition of the anti-logical, the recognition of concepts such as 'becoming', the 'meeting' and the 'event' signifies a movement away from the false metaphysical doctrines which have held sway in philosophy for centuries and which speak of the existence of the personality in terms of space and time, in terms of individual autonomy and identity.

[1] V. v. Weizsäcker, *Anonyma*, Bern, 1946; quotation taken from V. v. Weizsäcker and D. Wyss, *op. cit.*

The categories of the anti-logical, the meeting, the crisis and the event are further supplemented by the concept of confirmation (in place of abstract (Cartesian) identity) and the concept of responsibility (in place of freedom), concepts which are unknown to Freudian psycho-analysis. But the introduction of these concepts was to establish a a further crucial aspect of von Weizsäcker's thought, in which he places the pathic in opposition to the ontic. But what is meant by placing the pathic in opposition to the ontic? Simply that life is not determined by ontology or metaphysics but by the passions: because man is unable to escape from his situation, because he is tied to the *Gestaltkreis*, his life can only be experienced and lived in the form of a struggle, of a threat, of suffering or of guilt.

'It is possible to think of things whose only purpose is the fact that they are there. All statements about such things involve the word "is". The verb "to be" is all I need to communicate my knowledge. In respect of living beings such statements would say nothing about any of their essential properties. We are tempted to conjecture that in this respect an "is"-statement is really a non-statement. If I consider myself or another living being, my life is more essential than the fact that I am there. As one who lives I do not say "I am" but rather: I *would like to* or I *will* or I *can, must, may, should do* this; or, alternatively, I will *not*, may *not* do all this, etc. And so whereas for the first class of objects (they might be stones or raindrops) the "is"-statement says everything and is adequate, for the second class of beings, whom we call living beings, a sequence of I-statements is essential, which incidentally are also meaningful in the negative and which have no "is"-character. We shall call the mode of existence of the first class *ontic*, that of the second *pathic*. The word "ontic" is meant to indicate that naked Being decides, whilst the word "pathic" signifies that existence is not so much constituted as *suffered*.'[1]

This conception, which goes back to the pre-Socratic age, above all to Heraclitus, is pursued by von Weizsäcker to the point where he even tries to derive mind or intelligence from the pathic base of human reality:

'The intelligence can never descend far enough into the pathic base of life. If it were completely able to reach and to control it, then life would not be life. The intelligence is the balancing rod, which, however, not only regulates but must itself be regulated—such is the circle of *Gestalt* (*Gestaltkreis*). And so we cannot divide anthropology into a pathic sphere

[1] V. v. Weizsäcker, *Anonyma*, in: *Uberlieferung und Auftrag*, ed. by W. Szilasi and E. Grassi, Vol. 4, p. 11, Bern, 1946.

of passion and an ontic sphere of the intelligence. We must make up our minds to move in this circle (*Kreis*) and renounce all idea of a solution to our task. It is not possible to escape from this ambiguity. We may light a match and we must throw it away.

'But it was a great error to think the intelligence could overcome the chaos of passion. It looked as if the intelligence were withdrawing from passion, as if it were raising man above pathos. But now we see that the sounding-line of the intelligence leads towards passion. The further analysis, the further rationalism penetrates, the more it encounters passion, which behaves as if it were reacting against the intruder. This is the experience which we want to describe and which we must reproduce if we decide to investigate that part of life which relates to man and which might justly be called anthropology.'[1]

But ontic (metaphysical) reality (e.g. the reality of the various categories and of causality) and pathic reality are also related to one another in terms of the *Gestaltkreis* and in terms of mutual concealment:

'Just as, for example, when I turn round, my movement opposes itself, so too my line of vision excludes in any given case the possibility of perception in the opposite direction. That is the way the *Gestaltkreis* (circle of *Gestalt*) is constructed, and this structure of mutually exclusive antitheses illustrates quite nicely that the *Gestaltkreis* is anti-logically constructed.

'But we also learn something of the reason for restlessness, which is quite evidently an expression of the contradictory nature of our existence. The reason for both, contradiction and restlessness, is the *mutual concealment* of our existences in the *Gestaltkreis*. I call this the revolving door principle. We cannot possess the *Gestaltkreis* as an integrated whole (either by thought or by intuition) but must *pass through* it and suffer its antitheses. We must *lose it from sight* and must constantly *lose the effect* if we are to gain something new. This condition may also be expressed by saying that we must *go infinitely beyond* possession, beyond the present, and must suffer loss, in order to possess, but cannot possess entirely, since we always suffer loss. *Thus the biological act is transcendent.*'[2]

Thus in von Weizsäcker's view:
1. the personality is determined in terms of the categories of 'becoming', of the 'meeting', of the 'event', of 'confirmation' and 'responsibility';
2. the personality is rooted in 'suffering' and is related to mind and to ontology in terms of mutual concealment;
3. the personality creates the foundations and organization of human

---

[1] V. v. Weizsäcker, *Anonyma*.   [2] V. v. Weizsäcker, *ibid.*

reality in the ontic sense by taking decisions—e.g. if a man professes a philosophy of life it means that he has taken a decision. Thus decisions create organization.

'If then a basis for the perception of living nature is sought, it will not be found in ontology or metaphysics. The fundamental condition is pathic and the foundation can only be discovered in an organization in which the judgement or the antithesis of love and strife, propitiation and atonement for misdeeds, want and satiety is earlier, older and higher than the ontic categories, such as I and Not-I, Being and Nothing. This organization, then, although it does not establish a firm basis, is none the less established in the dependence of ontic on pathic existence. And so we may say that we have discovered a foundation and—in a "flash"—an organization and consequently a direction; this direction then, as may clearly be seen in the writings of the pre-Socratic thinkers, is not derivable from a firm foundation but rather is to be understood as arising out of the organization of a "tribunal". We may also say that *organization comes into being in the pathic existence as a result of a decision ("tribunal") and that thus foundations come into being.*'[1]

States of dependence are also created by decisions but where love is concerned these may be of a positive nature:

'As a result of our departure from the fundamental condition all our endeavours to establish the essence of living nature have been cloaked in a sort of mood or complexion of dependence. This involves limitation! finiteness, tension, expectation, i.e. wholesale negation. Now the last example, namely the inseparability of sex from love, means that affirmation is also possible. We might also say: *the pathic character of life rests on the pathos of love,* which affirms the fundamental condition and which gives it its name.'[2]

By tracing life back to the pathic, to wanting, to obligation (you should), permission, ability—categories which ought to be supplemented by the further categories of 'being driven', of wishing and hoping—von Weizsäcker has moved into the immediate vicinity of *Freud* and of his discovery of the extraordinary importance to man of the drives. None the less, Freud and von Weizsäcker are still separated by irreconcilable differences, which may be summarized as follows:

1. von Weizsäcker's view of personality (of the subject), which is

[1] V. v. Weizsäcker, *Arzt und Kranker*, Stuttgart, 1952 ('Doctor and Sick Person').

[2] V. v. Weizsäcker, *Pathosophie*.

determined by 'the others' (*Gestaltkreis*) and by the (anti-logical) concepts of the crisis, the meeting, becoming, confirmation, responsibility and decision, is quite alien to Freud's positivist concept of personality. Freud (in his middle phase, i.e. before the introduction of the death drive hypothesis) considered personality either in terms of a *knowing* subject in the cartesian sense (deriving from the ego and the super ego—see above) or as a subject possessed by the drives and devoid of all sense of direction (deriving in this case from the id). But, since neither the abstract personality envisaged by Descartes nor the no less abstract 'id' or instinctual personality conceived by Freud have any real existence, it follows that both views are false. In the first case the attitude towards the other person, towards the partner, is exclusively determined by an absolute ego with its motto of *cogito ergo sum*, whilst in the second case, where the ego is governed by drives and wishes, i.e. by the id, the partner is a mere *object* at the mercy of the drives, e.g. sexual drives, aggressive drives. In neither case does the *other person* exist as a subject.

2. According to Freud personality is the product of the interplay of id, ego and super ego. It might be argued that because the ego and the super ego are rooted in the id they correspond to von Weizsäcker's pathic categories. But there is an essential difference, for in the case of von Weizsäcker's categories there is a special relationship (that of the *Gestaltkreis*) between 'mind' and 'life', between pathic and ontic. In this relationship it is not a question of 'either or' but rather a question of 'both and'. In von Weizsäcker's view personality must create itself by constantly passing through the *Gestaltkreis* from the pathic to the ontic. Moreover, in Freud's conception personality is 'made up' of component parts (id, ego, super ego), which is in keeping with the positivist outlook which led him to interpret personality (the 'psychic apparatus') by analogy with a telescope or microscope. But this view destroys the concept of the subject since it renders both the subject's identity with itself and the suspension of the subject's identity in a crisis or transformation irrelevant. In other words, the concept of personality, the concept of the subject, does not exist in any real, existential sense in Freud's system.

Von Weizsäcker's concept of the personality and C. G. Jung's concept of the personality may be compared as follows:

1. In C. G. Jung's system the mature and superior 'mana' personality, which presupposes that the individual concerned is no longer identified with his mask, his persona, can only be attained by means of individuation. The concepts of transformation, crisis, confirmation and becoming all enter into Jungian individuation and have been described by Jung on

numerous occasions in connection with the symbols occurring in alchemical and other processes, which symbols are certainly 'anti-logical'. Jung's collective unconscious bears comparison with von Weizsäcker's pathic base of human reality, but Jungian compensation and self-regulation of the psyche bear no resemblance to von Weizsäcker's *Gestaltkreis* or to his revolving door principle. Jung's 'compensation' is an automatism, which, in the case of the extreme rationalist for example, inflates the contents of the unconscious, whereas the *Gestaltkreis* and the revolving door principle (mutual concealment) are not primarily concerned with the individual's relationship to himself (as is the case in the Jungian system) but rather with his relationship to the other person or to the world. The person who passes through the *Gestaltkreis* from the pathic to the ontic 'transcends' and acquires himself by the very act of passing through this circle (*Kreis*). With Jung the circle is restricted to the individual's relationship to himself and so it leaves out the other person, it leaves out the world. The largely 'automatic' nature of Jungian compensation and self-regulation of the psyche casts doubt on the categories of transformation and decision in the Jungian system, and indeed it must be said that Jung's archetyp-l determinism misses the real point of acts of decision, confirmation, responsibility, etc. Although compensation (C. G. Jung) and the revolving door principle (von Weizsäcker) appear to be analogous, they are in fact incommensurable, and that for two reasons:

(*a*) the revolving door principles incorporate the other person whilst compensation does not;
(*b*) whereas in the case of compensation the categories of decision, confirmation, responsibility, etc., are subject to archetypal determination, in the case of the revolving door principle they are of the essence of the subject.

2. As has been demonstrated by H. Trüb in his crucial criticism of Jung's doctrines, Jung's concepts of transformation, crisis, confirmation, etc., are not intended in a personal sense and so they are diametrically opposed to von Weizsäcker's concepts. The 'other person', the 'thou', the 'we', are *not* embraced by individuation, which—although doubtless of the greatest possible interest to both therapist and analysand—might well be compared to a process in a test-tube, since the psyche is only required to come to terms with itself in its quest for maturity. Jung's concept of personality, which is based on quite different assumptions than those underlying the Freudian concept, was no more successful in its attempt to grasp the 'personality' than was the Freudian concept, for if the essential meaning of the personality is to be comprehended the other person and the categories of the *Gestaltkreis* are indispensable.

431

(d) Special Contributions made by von Weizsäcker on Psychoanalysis

In conclusion von Weizsäcker's comments on Freud's theory of drives, the pleasure principle, sexuality and dreams are reproduced below:

1. The Theory of Drives

'In the natural sciences biology with its constant growth is looming up behind physics. Instead of purposes the talk is of drives, instincts, strivings towards a goal, libido. Of none of these concepts can it be said that it is either entrenched clearly on the physical side or clearly and exclusively on the psychic side. There is always something provisional about them, something unclear, and practical research treats them, although they are pure hypotheses, as if they were real things. They derive in part from everyday life, in part they enter into everyday life, and there too they behave like things which "really" exist. The concept of the drive affords the best example. Are there such things as a drive and a sexual drive? As far as I know, the Greeks, who have supplied us with nearly all of our basic concepts, had no knowledge of them. And if we have all of us yet to see an atom or an elementary quantum, we have all of us yet to see a drive. In such a case we do what the physicist does when he wants to find out about one of his basic concepts which bears a physical name but has a metaphysical nature: we experiment. Whether there are such things as forces, atoms, waves or quanta is a question which only becomes meaningful when we attempt to establish which observable facts these concepts are capable of representing. And the same procedure must be applied to the concept of the drives as well.'[1]

2. Sexuality and the Pleasure Principle

'The first error unearthed by experience is the unequivocalness of the sexual drive. We know that the drive is driving towards some goal or other, but a counterforce is also present which inhibits or drives away from the goal. Shame, chastity, loathing and other less easily defined forms of repulsion are just as natural to the sexual sphere as the forces of libidinal attraction. It is strange that Freud, who with his couple of the life drive and the death drive quite evidently grasped the polar structure of psychic life, did not attribute the forces which oppose this couple to the region of the drives but rather to the sphere of the ego or subsequently the id. I am unable to allay the suspicion that Jewish and Christian conceptions of the antithesis between nature and spirit may have exercised some influence here, although Freud's intentions would virtually exclude the independence of the spirit. It was Christianity which declared phallus worship to be of the devil; and so the isolation

[1] V. v. Weizsäcker, *Begegnungen und Entscheidungen*, Stuttgart, 1950.

of the sexual drive could be the work of Christian and ecclesiastical doctrines. The resultant conception of paganism would then be a projected idea, in fact a Christian intention. But if the repelling counter-forces—shame, chastity and loathing—also possess a drive nature and if, as I assume, the sexual drive is constructed in accordance with the principle of polarity, then we are bound to ask whether the concept of the drive still makes sense in terms of sexuality. It is not the weights which give the weighing machine its name but the function whereby they are weighed. It is not force but a balance of forces which is sought, and the characteristic of sexuality is not the libido but a rise and fall about a point of balance effected by force and counterforce. In Plato's Symposium Diotima says that Eros is a philosopher. And what Eros longs for is the Beautiful; where he is unable to take possession of the Beautiful he prefers to forgo pleasure and to suffer. And the force of desire is a non-starter when it transforms itself into its opposite, into aversion. Nature itself follows the pleasure principle only for as long as a more primal and more real instance permits pleasure to remain pleasure; where it does not displeasure arises instead. Pleasure and displeasure, attraction and repulsion are—to use an archaism—not primary but secondary qualities.'[1]

And again:

'The following brief comments are intended to give a more accurate idea of the correction or conversion of Freud's sexual theory which we are here presenting: (1) The sexual drive (libido) is not considered as an unequivocal but as a polar structure. Attraction and repulsion are seen as inherent properties of the sexual drive itself. (2) The sexual drive is not conceived as a force which simply exercises attraction or retention in respect of different objects (such as the self in the case of narcissism, such as another person, a woman or a man, such as a thing in the case of fetishism or such as rational thought in the case of science, etc.); rather I maintain that there is no such thing as a libido that is able to switch objects but that rather all those orientations towards other objects, which either seem to be or clearly are genital, become what they are by virtue of the objects, i.e. they become sexual when directed towards the genitals; social when directed towards society; political, artistic, scientific, etc., when directed towards politics, art, science, etc. The masculine or feminine aspects of these orientations do not derive from the sexual drive but from what is evidently the diametrically opposed (or complementary) nature of the objects themselves.'[2]

[1] V. v. Weizsäcker, *Begegnungen und Entscheidungen*, Stuttgart, 1950.
[2] V. v. Weizsäcker, *Pathosophie*, Göttingen, 1956.

'So now we find ourselves in a new dilemma. What they are asking now is not "what is sexuality in itself" but "how is sexuality related to non-sexuality", "where does the border lie" and so on. I am no longer entirely persuaded that the protest against sexuality stems exclusively from the repressed sexuality of those who protest. It is of course true that a "both and" situation is never very pleasant. But we are not guided by a desire for formal, rational uniformity. Of the various possible solutions I pick on one which is also of interest to non-psychoanalysts. It is what Kant called the intellectual intuition and what Schelling took as the basis for his concept of genius. As often happens, what had been reserved for the genius turned out to be the common property of most, if not of all men, and even of all living creatures. In every normal or perverse sexual action, but also in every nutritive, vegetative or animal and indeed every biological act, we may observe a tendency to assume forms (*Gestaltung*). Of course we may interpret every biological act in a sexual sense; but what is a sexual sense? If somebody holds that the differentiation between right and wrong or honour and dishonour or love and lovelessness is stronger, earlier and more essential than the difference between man and woman and adduces childhood memories and things of that sort in support of his view, then the sexual theory of neuroses and other illnesses begins to totter. The grounds for the sexual theory are then neither better nor worse than the grounds for a theory of right or a theory of honour would be; in other words, these explanatory theories stand in juxtaposition to one another at parity. In this connection psychoanalysis discovers in the pre-oedipal phase its anal-sadistic stage, whose sexual character is more than doubtful, and has even discovered in the death drive an opponent of Eros.

'And so the dilemma between what is sexual and what is non-sexual is to be understood in the following terms: anything can become sexual if I approach it with the concept of sexuality, anything can become non-sexual if I approach it with a non-sexual concept. Perceptions and experiences are formed in a corresponding manner. And so the outcome of this chapter on sexuality is this: anything is sexual, which we call sexual, which we deal with as sexual. No more, but no less. What then also becomes apparent is the insight, which would seem to be the prerogative of man, that the concealed root of sexuality is procreation; where procreation is hindered, the work, the spirit, must appear. More than this I am at present unable to say.' [1]

3. *The Relationship between Sexuality and Love*

'The separation of sexuality from the totality of man, its remoteness from his consciousness, spirituality, inwardness, is by no means exclusively

[1] V. v. Weizsäcker, *Pathosophie*, Göttingen, 1956.

due to a sort of cultural sickness. It is an observable fact that in sexual life not only do two people love one another but their sexual organs exercise a mutual attraction. The anatomical specialization of the sexual cells and of the organs which support and preserve them already constitutes a process of dissociation or even, we might feel tempted to say, of defection, as a result of which the sexual parts and the other parts of the body are also removed from one another and no longer know or understand one another very well. And so we are able to move from psychic consciousness to material consciousness and back again—the condition of concealment is always there. It is there as the primal illness.

'But the characteristic feature of the sexual act in human beings is the fact that it takes place in time, which precludes the possibility of a stable order in space. In the preparatory stage man experiences physical *attraction* and *turns towards* the partner. In the stage of enactment, i.e. of coition, a specific technique that is controlled by consciousness must be applied; in the orgastic stage any such freedom of activity is destroyed and both the attraction and the orientation towards the other person (which may be considered as love) and the controlled technique disappear. And so there are at least three quite distinct types of present desultorily organized into an historical sequence. The third of these, the orgasm, defies subsumption under a general concept and can only be defined in terms of itself; there is something unapproachable about it.

'If now a man brings his faculty of judgement to bear on sexual activity and either before or after the act adjudges it to involve both guilt and loss, then this concept of guilt and loss can never refer to the orgasm (even if it is secretly held to derive from it), but only to the preparation and to the technical phase. It is as if with the orgasm guilt and loss were obliterated, and it looks very much as if the orgasm were itself the obliteration of the guilt and loss. It is after all, at least for the man, coupled with potential procreation.

'This fact also offers some inducement to attempt a greater clarification of the problem posed by strife, an undertaking which it is proposed to pursue under a special heading. Earlier the idea was expressed, one incidentally which is by no means original, that sexuality which has been dissociated from love or which at least functions independently is perhaps already a pathological phenomenon, so that although we are justified in using it in its independent condition as an argument for the existence of such a condition, at the same time we place it—this sheer sexuality—in the group of undesirable phenomena. Now this really is to anticipate and assume something that is more than doubtful and must now be withdrawn. The dissociation of sexuality from Eros can lead to the degradation of love life but it can also lead to its sublimation. In asceticism, in ideal or romantic love and in the realism of social life both these things happen. If people were to insist on establishing the unity of sexuality and Eros, most of them would come to grief either by destroying themselves or by ruining their environment.'[1]

4. *The Interpretation of Dreams*

'It was Freud who, so to speak, re-christened dreams in a positivist epoch. During and since his lifetime there have been many new changes and developments.

'What follows are a few comments on the *Interpretation of Dreams* of 1900.

'1. At that time it was said that the "remnants of the day" were un-important for the meaning of the dream. But I have noticed that the selection from the day's activities is by no means unimportant for the meaning of the dream.

'2. The meaning of dreams and the structures of dreams change in the course of the years. Not only is there a difference between childhood dreams and adult dreams, but the dreaming of old people also differs from the dreaming of younger people. I shall return to this point.

'3. Of particular importance in this context is the ever-growing con-nection between dreams and meditation. What occurs to me here is the investigation by Ellenberger, who reminds us that the waking conscious-ness of so-called primitives is dream-like.

'4. The reason why Freudian dream interpretation strikes us as being so intellectual is that the interpretation is undertaken with the instru-ments of the waking and conscious mind. But if a dream is a letter—albeit a censored letter—from the unconscious, then dream interpreta-tion finds itself in the dilemma that this unconscious is perhaps quite differently structured from consciousness. And a contradiction arises when Freud later asserts that in the unconscious neither the proposition of contradiction nor the laws of time are relevant. For if logic is not relevant in the unconscious, then the interpretation conducted by the conscious mind must be false. For example, the assertion that there is a latent dream thought, which underlies dreams and which must be sought out, must be false if this thought is an anti-logical non-thought.

'5. It is obvious that the reality principle, which is so important in psychoanalysis, is of very little use to us. Is life a dream or is the dream life? Due to the processes of civilization we have experienced the supremacy of the social and rational principle and it is no longer to our liking. The realities of pre-revolutionary Vienna were the ability to bear arms, the ability to work and the ability to procreate, i.e. "realities"

[1] V. v. Weizsäcker, *Pathosophie*, Göttingen, 1956.

which have lost their reality. Consequently adaptation to this reality is no longer a matter of course.

'6. Thought as a logical process is like a stilt-walker with only one stilt, who, because he has only one stilt, will never make a move. To explain thought as the product of conscious feelings (logophony) may be a conviction. To assert this one-sided dependence of thought, intellect and reason on feelings will surely be an exaggeration born of a particular epoch. But the autonomy of reason is no less provisional. Kant wrote that notions without intuitions are empty, intuitions without notions are blind; if then in the dreams—and only in the dreams—of civilized man notions (concepts) achieve full intuitive representation, then these dreams have a certain advantage over matters which are purely notional (conceptual).'[1]

G

HENRI EY

Henri Ey is a leading French psychiatrist and an author whose thought reveals a close affinity to Existential philosophy. His investigation into *Consciousness*,[2] like Binswanger's *Grundformen und Erkenntnis menschlichen Daseins*, is one of the works which have opened up new paths and exercised a decisive influence on psychoanalytic research. After a period of several centuries, during which the primacy of consciousness was the dominant feature of philosophy, and after a further period, during which the Romantics and *E. von Hartmann* and finally *Freud* transferred this primacy from consciousness to the unconscious, whilst degrading both consciousness and thought to the level of an epiphenomenon (see p. 97 ff.), it would now seem that the phenomenological investigations into the essence of consciousness have established for the human mind a synthesis between metaphysics on the one hand and psychoanalysis on the other.

By thinking further along the lines developed by *Husserl*, Ey was able to reveal the completely intrinsic quality of consciousness and to demonstrate that in the final analysis the structure of the unconscious is specific for consciousness.

'To be conscious means to live the intrinsic quality of one's own experiencing by translating that experiencing into the generality of knowledge.'[3] 'Immanence and transcendence, direct givenness and

[1] V. v. Weizsäcker, *Pathosophie*, Göttingen, 1956.
[2] Henri Ey, *La Conscience*, Paris, 1963.
[3] *Ibid.*, p. 3.

reflection—these are the antinomies between which consciousness is formed. This fusion of experience and judgement is the reality of the consciously living creature.'[1]

Like *Klages*, *Palagyi* and *Scheler* Ey considers that the act of experiencing is rooted in man's vital layer and is subject to the rhythmical pulsations which obtain there. The affects, which Ey describes in the same way as *von Weizsäcker* and on whose relatedness to meaning Ey, in contrast to *Freud*, places considerable stress, are also rooted in this same vital layer. In memory, attention, perception and language, which are the basic categories of consciousness, consciousness gives itself that which has been experienced (memory), grasps that which has been experienced (perception), imagines that which has been experienced (language and reflection). Reflection is defined as the 'conjugation of pronouns (I observe myself, I feel myself, I make my decision), i.e. the relationships of a content of consciousness to the conscious subject; it (reflection) is an original property of consciousness.'[2] It is reflection which opens up the actual sphere of thought, the sphere of intentional references and significations of meaning; and these constitute the achievement of consciousness, although they do not constitute consciousness itself. Consequently, 'self-consciousness' means 'to establish oneself as a personality', to take possession of one self. In moral consciousness consciousness comes into being in the form of a value, of a sense of responsibility and of openness towards the world.

Ey's conclusions may be summed up as follows:

1. Consciousness embodies an original (and independent) organization.
2. Consciousness objectifies and reflects itself in the model of its world.
3. Consciousness possesses itself within the mode of its temporalness.
4. Consciousness is like a repetition of the ego that is structured in terms of its experience. 'To be conscious is to possess a personal model of the world.'[1] The basic structure of consciousness is concerned with the actualization of a given experience; consciousness introduces the spatial aspects of an idea into the temporal aspects of an act of experiencing. In the historicity of the ego (self) and the ego's consciousness of its own worth the quality of experiencing as such is transcended; in the relations between the ego and consciousness the ego is immanent in the act of experiencing and transcendent in the act of reflection. Ey describes

[1] Henri Ey, *La Conscience*, p. 3.
[2] *Ibid.*, p. 27.
[3] *Ibid.*, p. 39.

438

the latter as the axis of consciousness and the former as the field of consciousness—and the paradoxical structure of consciousness is grounded in both modalities.

Within the framework of this present enquiry it will not be possible to describe the detailed arguments derived both from the history of philosophy and from neurobiology on which Ey bases his thesis.

But in view of the fact that Ey describes sleep, dreams and psychosis as stages in the de-structuring of consciousness and of the ego, which in his view constitute the basic functions and categories of the personality, the question arises as to what function is fulfilled by the unconscious in Ey's conception.

If we are to understand his views we must start with his ego concept. The ontogenesis of the ego follows the principle of the dynamic integration of undifferentiated systems into differentiated systems, whereby the former, far from being eliminated, in fact partially determine the differentiated functions in terms of the *Gestaltkreis* (circle of *Gestalt*). And so the ego develops as the subject of its own perception both in respect of its own corporeality and its environment; it develops its logical capacity in its relationship to the environment and to its own body, when, after 'coming to its senses', it is able to recognize the limits of its own intelligence. Only as a result of its relationship to its environment does it develop a 'World view', in which it makes use of phantasy and ideas, and only through this 'world view' does it acquire the crucial experience of its own identity.

Ey places the ego's dynamic structure, which, by analogy with the categories of consciousness, he first describes as an ego axis that is created by the ego's *consciousness of its own value*, in juxtaposition to the ego's developmental structure. And the capacity of the ego axis for 'containing' and embracing an infinite number of potentialities, which include corporeality, speech and world view, then culminates in its historicity.

'The ego is the temporalization of a series of events or of the experiences to which those events give rise in as far as it concerns itself not only with a selection of actions but also with a selection of memories.'[1]

In the 'ego' the 'I' transcends itself in as far as it constitutes historicity or a field of experience that has been experienced by the individual. By contrast, the unconscious—whose importance Ey does not in any way deny—is regarded in the dialectical light of a negation that is inherent in consciousness. Paradoxically, it is the unconscious which establishes the unity of the ego, which insists on this unity, but which also questions it.

[1] Henri Ey, *La Conscience*, p. 361.

'... the unconscious appears in the light of unreal images in the dis-structuring of consciousness and in the speech of the other person [in negation—Author], in the dissolution of the ego, in its alienation.'[1]

In this respect, therefore, Ey is opposed to the *Freudian* conception of the primacy of the unconscious over consciousness and advances instead a fundamentally different conception, in which man appears as a bipolar creature, whose one pole points towards 'consciousness—ego—transcendence—reason' whilst the other is determined by the concepts of the 'unconscious, of automatisms, of instinct'.

With this conception Ey establishes a definition of the conscious/unconscious system, which, whilst owing much to the phenomenological view, is also dialectically related to *Hegel* and to a certain extent to *Sartre*. If we consider the fact that even Jung held that the unconscious was far more important than consciousness, if we consider Binswanger's position and the position adopted by the Catholic Existential analysts in their attempts to solve the problem posed by the relationship between consciousness and the unconscious, then it is clear that Ey's conception of the fundamental bipolarity of human nature constitutes an important advance in the discussion of this problem.

[1] Henri Ey, *La Conscience*, pp. 375 ff.

PART THREE

FUNDAMENTAL PROBLEMS OF THE VARIOUS THEORIES OF DEPTH PSYCHOLOGY WITH SUGGESTIONS AS TO HOW THESE MIGHT BE RESOLVED

A

THE CLAIM OF SIGMUND FREUD'S PSYCHOANALYTIC THEORIES TO SCIENTIFIC VALIDITY[1]

(a) The Character of Scientific Research

(i) The axiomatic (consistent) system

The nature of scientific research consists in attempting to proceed from experience to general statements about the objective origination of the objects of experience. Although of a hypothetical character, these general statements are intended to represent laws. The system of natural science aspires to become a system of statements with the status of laws. Moreover, each branch of natural science, especially physics and chemistry, endeavours to organize its statements in the context of an axiomatic system. That is, statements may not be inconsistent with one another. In this rigorous form, which dates back to Aristotle, the criterion of the axiomatic system has been met above all by physics and chemistry, including their various sub-divisions and related fields, e.g. electro-chemistry and colloidal chemistry. The branches of science dealing with living matter, however, such as biology, physiology, and pathological physiology, have not satisfied the demands of axiomatization. In the ancient world, Euclidean geometry served as the prototype of an axiomatic system. Today axiomatic systems are being developed in microphysics and chemistry, especially in connection with the problem of the conversion of atomic into molecular statements. An axiom denotes simply a valid, recognized statement about a state of fact which affords the possibility of deducing other statements from it.

(ii) Definition

An axiom, however, as a statement about a specific state of fact, presupposes definition of the latter. Every area of science consequently attempts to define its fundamental concepts before going on to the formulation of propositions. Only real definition, in contrast to nominal definition (by means of a symbol), bears on the present investigation. R. Robinson[2] has identified 12 meanings of the concept of definition. Only two of these are relevant to our discussion: definition as a determination of cause (genetic definition, which describes the origins of an

[1] This Chapter (pp. 463–468) has been translated by Mr. Jeremy Shapiro.
[2] R. Robinson, Definition, London, 1950.

object) and as analysis of a state of fact into its various aspects. Definition in the sense of a determination of essence, of what a thing is, as employed by existential ontology and phenomenology, will only be of marginal interest for the time being. A scientific system endeavours as far as possible to avail itself of a definition of an empirical state of fact in order to arrive at generally valid statements about the latter. This process, however, should not be viewed as a norm. It is, rather, an ideal case, which the mechanical side of physics has realized, within definite limits, in passing from definitions to general propositions. Other scientific disciplines, e.g. chemistry, have taken essentially more complicated paths towards the establishment of generally valid propositions (laws). The most common path leading to such universally valid propositions usually takes the following course:

1. Purely empirical data are first noted and collected (so-called 'protocol statements').
2. The protocol statements (observations) are explained through recourse to an already existing theory and to generally valid statements from which they are logically deducible.
3. These explanations are hypothetical in nature.
4. The hypotheses gain the status of laws when they are verified by further protocol statements (experiments). (Hypotheses are verified by experiments.)
5. The laws are explained with the aid of a further level of statements. These statements can be equated with a newly developed theory, which is considered to be established when it is capable of explaining a sufficiently large number of statements and laws.

It need not be specially mentioned that science takes only those statements seriously which admit of being mathematically formulated. That is, only such statements are held to be *true*. This applies to the entire range of propositions from the primary, generally valid ones with the character of definitions to those which constitute theories. Space, time, and numerical measurement are decisive for the truth or, in modern physics, the 'correctness' of a statement.

In natural science experiment and theory never come to an end. New discoveries necessitate changing the theory, which is disposed of when it no longer explains the most recent observations.

(iii) *Reduction and induction*

In contrast to mathematics, which is deductive, the natural sciences belong logically to the reductive and inductive fields of knowledge. This complicates matters considerably, for, as Aristotle demonstrated in a proof which has never been refuted, inductive syllogisms are not logically binding. (In deduction, a proposition is deduced from a conditional, 'If . . . then' statement and its premise. The reductive method works in the opposite manner: the premise is derived from a conditional, 'if . . . then' proposition and its minor term.

Example of deduction: If A, then B
but A,
therefore B
Example of reduction: If A, then B
but *B*,
therefore A.

Induction consists in the *generalization* of the minor term and is thus to be considered a special case of reduction.) The concept of reduction is here interpreted otherwise than in the Jungian characterization of the peculiarity of Freudian psychoanalysis as a method of tracing specific phenomena back, for example, to earlier experiences, i.e. of 'reducing' them. All scientific explanation consists in so-called regressive reduction. That is, one proposition is derived from another which is already known. This process becomes essentially more complicated, however, if the truth value of the explanatory proposition has not yet been confirmed (verified).

(iv) *Explanation*

What information does closer examination yield about scientific explanation? The latter has three components:

1. Demonstration of the conditions which lead to a specific phenomenon. This procedure led to the (fateful) separation of secondary from so-called primary qualities and to the accreditation of only the measurable factors of sense perception in contrast to other perceptual contents.
2. Causal explanation.
3. Teleological (final) explanation.

The conditions which are supposed to have led to the occurrence of a specific phenomenon are classified as sufficient, necessary, or sufficient and necessary. We follow Bochenski's summary:[1]

'1 *Sufficient conditions.* We say that A is a sufficient condition of B in the case where the statement "If A, then B" holds. For in this case it is sufficient for A to be given in order for B to be given also.

2. *Necessary conditions.* We say that A is a necessary condition of B in the case where the reverse statement holds: "If B, then A". For if A were not given B would not occur. Thus A is here the necessary condition of B.

[1] I. M. Bochenski, *Die Zeitgenössischen Denkmethoden*, Bern, 1954. ('Contemporary Methods of Thought'.)

'3. *Sufficient-and-necessary conditions.* We say that A is a sufficient and necessary condition of B when both of the above-mentioned statements hold, i.e. "A if and only if B" or, more briefly, "A precisely when B".[1]

In causal explanation the ontological and so-called empirical (phenomenalistic) forms must be distinguished from one another. A state of fact is explained ontologically and causally when it arises from another one or when a specific state of fact is produced by a previous one. The ontological concept of causation, which is of significance in neo-Thomism, was banished from natural science by the philosophy of the Enlightenment. This does not exclude the fact that it is still made use of in certain disciplines, for example in chemistry, medicine, and geology. (In the complicated process of chemical change, for example, a process is thought of as being caused in a direct, spatio-temporal way by a previous one.) Today the ontological concept of causation has retreated in favour of the empirical conception. The latter, however, admits in principle of being reduced to the *factors* which spatially and temporally *condition* a phenomenon. The problem of teleological explanation, which is recognized by Kant only as a regulative possibility, will be discussed below (see p. 489 ff.) in another context.

Explanation, definition, and the establishment of hypotheses, laws, and theories are by no means processes which need occur one after another in a definite temporal order. This holds particularly for the relation of explanation to definition, for these are often employed synonymously. That is, a phenomenon can be defined by being explained to be composed of this or that element. From a logical point of view, definition should be reserved for those elementary statements which, in conjunction with protocol statements (point 2, p. 444), lead to the establishment of the first hypotheses. An example here would be the setting up of the periodic table of elements in chemistry through employment of the definition of 'element'. The sciences engaged in studying living matter—not to speak of psychology—meet with the greatest difficulty in arriving at elementary statements of the order of definitions. Explanation and definition can here only seldom be separated from one another.

(v) *The Copernican system as a model*

The Copernican theory may now be taken as an example of a scientific proposition and theory, since it serves well for comparison with Freud's libido and other theories. We follow Bochenski's summary exposition:

'If we ask what is given as the epistemological foundation of this theory,

[1] I. M. Bochenski, *Die Zeitgenössischen Denkmethoden*, p. 113.

we obtain the answer: protocol statements, which report that certain luminous points are to be found at determinate locations of the apparent sky. That is all. We cannot observe either the "real" movement of the earth or the "apparent" motion of the stars. All we can see are luminous points at various places in the "sky".

'First the explanatory hypothesis is set up, that the luminous points move along a definite curve in the apparent sky. This curve can be represented by a mathematical function.

'Once such a function has been adopted, the possible deductions from it are not limited to the already ascertained statements about the position of any luminous point in question, but also include predictions of the position of the same point at other times. We observe the corresponding sector of the sky at the time obtained through deduction (calculation) and determine that the point in question actually is located where it should be according to deduction. The hypothesis is thereby verified and becomes a law.

'A class of such laws, a rather comprehensive class, is gradually obtained. These laws are now given a reductive explanation in just such a manner as to establish the Copernican theory. We assume that the luminous points are stars and planets and that the planets revolve about the sun in definite curves. This description naturally simplifies the real scientific process to a great extent. The actual situation involves a highly complicated structure of mathematical propositions, derived in part from geometry and physics and, in part, shaping the theory. By means of calculation, all those laws which have already been determined, as well as those which have not yet been established, are deduced from this complex. New, verifiable protocol statements about occurrences in the sky are then deduced from the laws. If these statements accord with observation, then the theory has been verified. It is now formalized and manifests itself as a powerful axiomatic system in which the Copernican theory together with the above-mentioned mathematical and physical theories form the axioms from which the protocol statements can be deduced.'[1]

The 'explanation' of the Copernican system was later provided by Newton's law of gravitation, from which e.g. the ellipse was deduced as the necessary form of planetary motion.

(b) *The development of some of Freud's theories in the light of natural science*

(i) *The first explanation of hysteria*

We reproduce here our discussion on page 50, for it clarifies the relation-

[1] I. M. Bochenski, *Die Zeitgenössischen Denkmethoden*, pp. 109–10.

ship prevailing between observation, hypothesis, and theory in the earliest stage of psychoanalysis.

Freud *observed* in his patient the *symptoms* of sleeplessness, loss of appetite and inability to give suck (*a*) Other hysterical patients displayed, that changed state of consciousness, in which they did things which they would never have dreamt of doing in their normal lives. (*b*) The fact that hysterics tended to do the opposite of what they wanted Freud connected with the following observation taken from normal psychology. (*c*) That in anticipating or carrying out an intended course of action a healthy person will also consider the possibility that he might come to grief. Freud extends this observation from the sphere of normal psychology:

1. to the concept of the painful antithetic idea;
2. which is repressed by the healthy person;
3. which is often unconsciously present in the hysteric, in whom it exists as a 'disassociated idea';
4. which then asserts itself as the counter-will.

Observation (*a*) was linked with observation (*b*) and both were explained by (*c*), resulting in the introduction of three hypotheses:

1. the hypothesis of the antithetic idea;
2. the hypothesis of the repression and inhibition of the antithetic idea in healthy persons;
3. the hypothesis of the (pathogenic) unconscious and disassociated idea in hysterics.

In this stage of psychoanalysis, the formation of hypotheses (explanation) did not differ considerably from analogous theories in medicine or biology, in the form in which these were generally current at the turn of the century. It was assumed that the psychic realm is just such an object of observation as other things in the world of perception. (The fundamental difference between psychoanalysis and the mechanical sciences lies in the immeasurability of the processes observed and the impossibility of giving them or the hypotheses introduced to explain them a quantitative, mathematical form.) Aside from its plausibility, the above-mentioned explanation of hysteria does not have the character of compelling necessity and does not admit of being developed to the level of a natural law or a universally valid proposition. The hypotheses cannot be experimentally verified, apart from the qualification of hypnosis as 'artificial hysteria', which was brought forward as an indirect proof of the correctness of Freud's theses. But hypnosis cannot be designated an experiment in the scientific sense, for the factors which lead to hypnosis do not possess the perspicuity which is necessary in an experiment.

This stage of hypothesis formation corresponds to points 2 and 3 on page 444. In comparison with the Copernican theory, Freud's interpretation of hysteria would correspond to the stage in which the luminous points in the sky—the symptoms of hysteria—follow a curve. Whereas the Copernican theory, however, because, it is mathematically founded, affords the possibility of predicting the appearance of points at a definite location, no similar step is possible with regard to hysteria. In order to be able to predict symptoms, it would be necessary for psychoanalysis (as for internal medicine) to have in full view all of the determinants 'conditioning' a symptom, and this requirement cannot be fulfilled (for reasons, see p. 459 ff.). The value of hypothesis formation at this stage of scientific statement is that phenomena seemingly remote from one another suddenly exhibit a definite internal connection, whether of the mathematically formulated sort of the Copernican theory or the 'intelligible' (plausible) sort of Freud's explanation of hysteria. In the latter, physical and psychic symptoms (a and b) are linked to observations drawn from normal psychology (c). The latter have above all the character of (synthetic) general propositions, which can be compared to those propositions of the Copernican theory, for example, which designate certain points of light as planets and others as fixed stars. Since a requirement of every scientific theory, however, even at this level, is that it may be used in making predictions, Freud also followed this course. In order to be able to predict hysterical symptoms, a criterion is needed in order to distinguish between health and disease. As we stated above (p. 50–51).

The fact that the antithetic idea is not pathogenic (does not produce illness) in a healthy person, although it logically follows that in the healthy person it is also unconscious and also excluded from the interchange of associations made by the normal ego, Freud explains by the introduction of two further hypotheses:

1. The antithetic ideas in hysterics are not 'exhausted', whereas in healthy persons they are, in which respect Freud understands under 'exhaustion' a reduction of the sum of excitation contained in the ideas, which excitation has been determined by the affect;

2. What has been exhausted in the hysteric, however, are 'those elements of the nervous system which form the material foundation of the ideas associated with the primary consciousness'.

Freud considered on the one hand that these elements were constitutionally determined changes within the cellular elements of the brain and on the other hand that they formed the basis of the later 'ego'.

These theses of Freud's, however, are not appropriate to rendering intelligible the difference between healthy and diseased, to say nothing of providing a basis for making predictions. In order to verify a theory through predictions, no additional theories may be adduced. Nevertheless Freud does this in practically every sentence, even to the extent of introducing entirely new and problematic conceptions ('nervous excitation', 'constitution', etc.).

In summary, this early stage of the formation of psychoanalytic hypotheses prompts the following observation: although very diverse pathological phenomena are subsumed under the concept of hysteria (a and b), normal psychology is invoked in order to arrive at general (but not necessary or binding) propositions which are supposed to explain hysteria (a and b) through recourse to further hypotheses (1, 2 and 3). The hypotheses are not verified, predictions cannot be made, and explanation follows reductively and inductively. Hypotheses 1, 2, and 3 are only to be thought of as *possible* conditions of the genesis of hysterical symptoms.

(ii) *Idea and affect*

Proceeding from the discovery that the moving points of light in the sky describe curves to the statement that the planets revolve around the sun was a significant step within the Copernican theory. With this statement (point 5, p. 444) a theory had been created which was capable of going on to explain all foregoing laws and statements. Freud accomplished this step by means of his hypothesis of the separability of affect and idea, which furnished him with the possibility of 'explaining' not only hysterical symptoms (conversion) but other disease groups as well, such as compulsion neurosis, phobia, and paranoia. In comparison with the last proposition of the Copernican theory, an analogous step seems to have been taken here, yielding a central proposition which explains all previous phenomena and provisional hypotheses. Freud conceived of the separability of an affect from its idea (association)—cf. the first part of the exposition of Freud in *From Symptom to Personality*—as a process whereby, in accordance with association theory, an affect, as a quantity of excitation, could at random attach itself to or split itself off from any association in the chain of ideas. In hysteria the quantity of excitation was discharged in the bodily sphere as a conversion symptom. In compulsion neurosis the affect was affixed to a substitute or inappropriate association, while in phobia, conversely, an inappropriate affect was joined to an association. In psychosis affect and idea were rejected, and in paranoia the affect of blame (a combination of idea and affect) was projected on to the environment. The view of affect as a quantity of excitation and its displaceability and separability from the associations in the chain of ideas, along with the pleasure-pain principle, may be held to be the most important foundation of the theses of psychoanalysis.

Individual theories such as the libido theory, the classification of the personality into various agencies, and the theories of repression and defence mechanisms are unthinkable without these two main supports of the edifice of psychoanalytic theory. The hypothesis of the random separability of affect and idea has gained the character of a universally valid proposition and is comparable to the last point (5) in a scientific system. Nevertheless it is *not* a scientific proposition, for the latter results only from the systematic, logical course of comparing and collecting verified laws already at hand. The character of Freud's hypothesis can be compared at best with other theoretical structures to be found in biology, e.g. the vitalistic assumption of an entelechy.[1] The assumption of an entelechy which can be further divided into sub- and co-entelechies apparently permits the comprehension of numerous contradictory biological phenomena. Whether processes actually take place in reality in the manner described, for example, by Conrad-Martius cannot be answered at the present time, since we do not yet possess adequate means with which to apprehend and comprehend the complexity of biological processes. But while vitalism and other, analogous scientific theories remain conscious of their markedly hypothetical character, Freud's writings do not clearly indicate to what extent he was aware of the extremely hypothetical character of his thesis of the random separability of affects from ideas. His correspondence with Fliess in particular indicates that he seems to have considered this thesis a comprehensive proposition of an axiomatic sort and a foregone conclusion. To the contrary, it should be noted that the relaton between affect and idea is at all events a problem, not a statement representing the final, axiomatic point of a scientific system. Even if we were to overlook the fact that Freud's preceding hypotheses about hysteria are not verifiable and merely indicate intelligible conditions and possibilities for a definite type of behaviour or for a disease, there would still be no doubt to the effect that Freud did not even attempt to establish the theory of the random displaceability of affects along specific series of associations as the *logical* conclusion of his total observations. As early as in the paper he published in 1892, when he did not yet clearly perceive the connection between hysteria and the other psychoneuroses, this theory was mentioned *en passant*; it goes back to Herbart's association mechanics. In Copernicus' theory, the thesis that the planets revolve around the sun may well have been a tacit assumption underlying the theory, but this had no effect on the objectivity of the laws, since the latter led to that final axiom. But if the theory of affect displaceability is a tacit assumption, and hysteria, phobia, and compulsion neurosis

---

[1] Cf. H. Conrad-Martius, *Der Selbstaufbau der Natur*, Berlin, 1944. ('The Automatous Structure of Nature').

are only used to *corroborate* it, then the Freudian theory takes on a form fundamentally different from that of the Copernican. For explanation here would have the character of arranging the phenomena to fit into a *preconceived* pattern, one which has not, however, been inferred from the phenomena themselves as in the Copernican case. It could then no longer be maintained that the assertion that affect and idea are separable and displaceable has the character of a logically inferred, final axiom. If it is assumed nevertheless that Freud's observation of pathological phenomena was guided by the phenomena rather than by a preconceived theory, an assumption which contradicts the facts, it remains to be said, not only that the relation of affect to idea poses a difficult problem, but moreover that this problem cannot be solved in as simple a fashion as that envisaged by Freud.

Only a detailed, many-faceted investigation would be able to shed light on this problem, whose 'solvability' is questionable by nature. Nevertheless, *without* anticipating such an investigation, some critical remarks are in place here. Affect determines the character of possible ideas or associations through its very nature, and associations can only be changed through the exercise of *conscious will* upon an affect. That is, affect is never that abstract quantity of excitation of which Freud was in the habit of speaking, and which does not exist. Affects, taken here primarily in the sense of passionate surges of emotion and changes of mood, are always quite *specific* affects such as hate or love. Freud's characterization of affect as 'quantity of excitation' derives from his tendency to replace quality with quantity in the manner of natural science. This process leads inevitably to a total misunderstanding of the peculiarity of the psyche, as has been repeatedly and substantially established in other quarters.[1] This definition of affect as 'quantity of excitation', which goes back to Herbart, is the basis of one of the two decisive mistakes in Freud's conception, The other, which is no less significant, lies in his association mechanics. This theory, which even strict behaviourists and reflexologists no longer take quite seriously, and whose significance for psychoanalysis has been subjected to thorough criticism by the author elsewhere,[2] states that knowledge and cognition

---

[1] Cf. P. Matussek, *Metaphysische Probleme der Medizin*, Heidelbeg, 1948 ('Metaphysical Problems of Medicine'); L. Klages, *Der Geist als Widersache der Seele*, Bonn, 1954 ('Mind versus Soul'); Kunz, *Die anthropologische Bedeutung der Phantasie*, Basel, 1946 ('The Importance of Phantasy from the Point of View of Anthropology'); Meinertz, *Psychotherapie als Wissenschaft*, Stuttgart, 1952 ('Psychotherapy as Science'); Scheler, *Wesen und Formen der Sympathie*, Frankfurt, 1948 ('The Essence and the Forms of Sympathy').

[2] See D. Wyss, 'Die Bedeutung der Assoziationstheorien fuer die Psychoanalyse', *Conf. Psychiat.*, Vol. I, 1958, pp. 1–3. ('The Imporatnce of the Association Theories for Psychoanalysis').

are composed of *accidentally* perceived (heard) scraps of e.g. a conversation, an observation, an experience, etc. As association chains, these more or less arbitrary fragments of memory and perception constitute the groundwork of thought and cognition. By means of them, for example the patient in psychotherapy is supposed to grope his way back to his recollections or complexes. On the one hand, Freud was loyal to association mechanics. On the other, he noted down a large number of observations which, in his view, could no longer be explained only by association theory. For wherever psychic material exhibits structure or is dealt with in its stratification and transformation, as in the interpretation or genesis of dreams for example, synthetic forces are at work, and these cannot be derived from association mechanics. The psychology of acts and gestalt psychology dealt association mechanics the decisive blow, and even before their appearance numerous scholars had already turned away from the latter theory. Freud adopted both the association theory and the doctrine of affect from Herbart and applied them to pathological phenomena. The results were the two above-mentioned basic principles of psychoanalysis: the depicted relationship between affect and idea and the pleasure-pain principle. Neither the *content* of affect, its experientially tangible substance, nor the content of ideas (associations) plays an essential role in the Herbartian–Freudian theory, where they are ascribed the character of 'secondary' qualities and accordingly neglected. Freud then ran into the difficulty of suddenly attributing a decisive significance to content in the form of sexuality. The random displaceability of affect and idea with respect to each other presupposes the irrevelance of their contents, which is incompatible with the theory of sexual traumas. A sexual trauma (hysteria) and behaviour which disguises sexuality (compulsion neurosis) can only function pathogenically on the basis of their content, their real relation to sexuality. Affect and idea can only be separated arbitrarily if their content is irrelevant. The Herbartian theory presupposed by Freud, based on the irrelevance of contents as 'secondary qualities', has the effect precisely of making *impossible* the Freudian claim that content (sexuality) conditions the displaceability of affect and idea. Let us take the case of a female patient who must perform a complicated compulsive ritual before being able to go to bed, where it is believed that she can be proved to be imitating the primal scene (among other things) through this ritual. In Freud's interpretation this means that the actual affect involved, the sexual excitement or fear induced by possible observations of the primal scene, has dissociated itself from its sexual associations and attached itself to the new, irrelevant associations of the ritual. The sexual notion is 'repressed', and the affect associated with it returns as (among other forms) the 'affect of blame', which can link itself to other, random associations and which conditions the compulsive ideas. The compulsive ceremonial, the going-to-bed ritual, can be further classified as a second- ary symptom of defence (see p. 59). This interpretation of compulsion presupposes that a sexual affect or an anxiety state, in any case an affect with *specific* content, was at one time present. Otherwise it would not have been repressed. The affect is now divested of its specific content, its associations, is quantified as a sum of excitation, affixes itself to blame, and then to the allegedly irrelevant associations of the compulsive ritual. This affect, which now accompanies the compulsion, is on the one hand no longer the original one, which, on the other hand, it is supposed to remain. For it has not changed, having merely been con- nected to another association in accordance with its properties as a quantity of excitation. The inconsistency of this view, which *has* to interpret the affect specifically as a sexual or anxiety affect at the same time as it considers this affect to be merely quantitative and divested of its associations, is so obvious, that it is astonishing how theories of this sort were accepted more or less uncritically for decades as founda- tions of psychoanalysis. This situation is unquestionably due in part to those disciples of Freud who, like Jung and Rank, turned away from him and advanced their own theories without engaging in a sufficiently critical analysis of the foundations of psychoanalysis or giving special attention to clinical phenomena. Accordingly, and disregarding the phenomenological investigations undertaken outside of the analytic schools, no other theory appeared attempting to explain compulsion neurosis, hysteria, phobia, and paranoia on a new basis. Investigating hysteria, with its problematic concept of conversion—which even Freud did not explain satisfactorily—or phobia and paranoia from the point of view of the random separability of affect and idea would lead to contradictions even more confusing. To exhibit them would overstep the boundary of the present work. In any case, the thesis of the separa- bility of affect and idea is not fit to be the axiomatic conclusion of a scientific system, for it is an unverified assumption of an extremely problematic nature. With this foundation of psychoanalytic theory made doubtful, the entire edifice begins to totter. For the critical observer, Freud's case histories of the wolf-man and the rat-man, which are grounded on the hypothesis discussed above, become interesting con- structions which nevertheless may be as remote from reality as the notion of the world as a flat disc is from Copernicus' findings. In conclusion, we cite Freud's interpretation of a case of (hysterical) blushing:

'Do you know why our old friend E. turns red and sweats whenever he sees a certain class of acquaintance, particularly at the play? He is ashamed, no doubt; but of what? Of a phantasy in which he figures as the "deflowerer" of every person he comes across. He sweats as he deflowers, because it is hard work. Whenever he feels ashamed in someone's presence, an echo of the meaning of his symptom finds voice in him like a growl of defeat: "Now the silly idiot thinks she has made me feel ashamed. If I had her in bed she'd soon see whether I felt embarrassed in front of her!" And the period of his life during which he turned his wishes on to this phantasy has left its traces on the psychical complex which produced the symptom. It was in his Latin class. The theatre auditorium reminds him of the classroom; he always tries to get the same regular seat in the front row. The entr'acte corresponds to the "break", and "sweating" was the slang word for operam dare ("working"). He had a dispute with the master over that phrase. Moreover, he can never got ever the fact that at the University he failed to get through in botany; so he carries on with it now as a "deflowerer". He owes his capacity for breaking into a sweat to his childhood, to the time when (at the age of three) his brother poured some soapsuds over his face in the bath—a trauma, though not a sexual one. And why was it that at Interlaken, when he was fourteen, he masturbated in such a peculiar attitude in the WC? It was so that he could get a good view of the Jungfrau (literally, "maiden"); since then he has never caught sight of another—or at all events not of her genitals. No doubt he has intentionally avoided doing so; for why else does he form liaisons only with actresses? How like a "clever work of fiction", and yet how characteristic of "man with all his contradiction"!"[1]

According to this interpretation of (hysterical) blushing by means of the theory of the separability of affect and idea, the (unconscious) idea of defloration has discharged its affect (sexual desire plus aggression) as a quantity of excitation in the bodily sphere, causing the present symptoms of blushing and perspiration. That is, the affect is conceived as specific (sexuality)—the prerequisite of its repression—as in the interpretation of compulsive behaviour. It is then taken to be unspecific (which would make repression superfluous) in order for it to be able to produce the symptom. Substitute ideas such as botany and the Jungfrau (virgin) mountain generate the hysterical symptoms. This would *not* be possible if they did not come into contact with the specific sexual affect. That is, the explanation of the symptoms, which appear as the result of specific, but repressed, sexuality, would be quite absurd without specificity of affects. What is the way out of this dilemma? Surely not the assumption that it is possible to reduce all psychopathological

[1] S. Freud, *The Origins of Psychoanalysis: Letters to Wilhelm Fliess*, pp. 278–9. London, 1954.

phenomena and illness to a common denominator and to find a pat solution, a key, which will suddenly explain the most diverse phenomena. Freud, however, was extraordinarily dominated by this idea, one might say, of finding the philosopher's stone. His desire to develop an axiomatic system and to be able scientifically to deduce one proposition from another continually comes to light, e.g. in his correspondence with Fliess. Unquestionably an axiom hovered before him, like Kekule's theory of the benzene ring, which suddenly made it possible to comprehend organic compounds quantitatively and to 'explain' them. The theory of the separability of affect and idea seemed to provide the key, even though the question remained open as to the mysterious *something* which caused the cleavage and gave rise to new connections. Psychic events, whose quantifiability in the Freudian sense is no more than a fiction, apparently do not admit of being ordered in an axiomatic system as do chemistry and physics. In other words, the positivist approach is false. This thesis, which has already been advanced by other scholars,[1] should be investigated in detail in connection with other Freudian hypotheses. In order to investigate psychic events and processes, then, it seems necessary to abandon the search for a common denominator which would explain everything in the manner of Kekule's benzene ring, and to extend the 'back to the phenomena' method of phenomenology to the realm of psychoanalysis. This would be in sharp opposition to Freud's view that not the phenomena, but the drives behind them, are important. Here, however, in contrast to those phenomenologists, such as Von Gebsattel, Straus, and Kuhn, who already have made essential contributions to the investigation of compulsion neurosis and other phenomena, we shall only refer to certain fundamental psychological relations, such as that of affect and idea, as far as the scope of the present work allows.

What is true in a comprehensive sense for the relation between instinct and idea (image) holds here as well: the affect itself contains the idea or image, and with it the range of *possible* images and thus the relation to the environment. When a person perceives rage or hatred within himself, he feels more than the impulse to expresss this emotion through an action such as stamping his feet or pounding his fist on the table. Simultaneously, either consciously or unconsciously, a larger or smaller number of ideas (images) will pass before his inner eye, images with the common feature of destructiveness. Whether he imagines striking the person who occasioned his anger, throwing an object at the wall, or even shedding blood, his interior is ruled by destructive images. The images brought forth by a surge of the feeling of love are of contrasting content: making the beloved happy, giving her presents, drawing her

[1] See above all Klages, *op. cit.*, Meinertz, *ibid.*, Kunz, *op. cit.*

near, caressing her, etc. *While the image is thus determined by the affect* and pictorially reveals, as it were, the latter's innermost essence in its manifold possibilities, the path from image to affect is the reverse. It starts with the affect in the form of having gone outside of itself, become an image, and 'lost' itself in the image, and returns to the affect itself. While the image is determined by the affect's essence—an erotic image by love—, it is not necessarily emotionally accompanied by the affect. It can, however, be affectively tinged. It is thoroughly possible to let erotic images run through one's mind without feeling love or Eros. The affect which constitutes the essential root of a particular idea is not necessarily always combined with it *in consciousness*.

The connection between affect and idea can be effected consciously by an act of the will, as well as arise involuntarily through mere submersion in the image (idea) and its objective qualities. An affect can flare up spontaneously in response to an image. One can imagine a devastated house without feeling hatred or sadness. But one can produce these feelings voluntarily, thereby establishing the link with the supporting affect. One can also perceive the corresponding feelings without conscious exertion. Or the affect can flare up spontaneously at the occurrence of the idea. The dissociation of image and affect through conscious will can proceed to the point where a person can look at a devastated house and feel, not sadness or hatred, but joy. It is even possible to link the last-mentioned emotion voluntarily (*consciously*) with the idea of destruction. The relation to the environment, which is present unambiguously in the affect and more ambiguously in the image (in the idea) as well, *can be extensively influenced, perverted, and modified by the will*. In the author's judgment, this is the *only* possible inappropriate affect or inappropriate idea.

These remarks should have adequately indicated that the relation between idea and affect certainly is not to be determined in the unilateral manner followed by Herbart and by Freud after him. Their theory was founded on the observation of the conscious, will-directed possibilities of *not* connecting affects and ideas according to their essence. They overlooked the *essential* connections between affect and image, the primary environment-relatedness of affect, *and the fact that perverted relations between affect and image (joy in destruction) are disturbances of the arbitrarily connecting agent, the will*, and are not based on a generally arbitrary 'separability' of affect and idea. Both realms, affect (feeling and emotions) and image, are essentially related to each other, yet belong nevertheless to *different psychic regions*. Their *qualitative* difference seems to be related to the difference between 'mind' (*Geist*, idea) and 'soul' (affect). But this qualitative and essential distinction between the two realms disappears in the Herbartian–Freudian conception. The scope of the present work does not permit us to pursue this distinction further.

Nevertheless, it is worth indicating the possible consequences attendant upon the seemingly all-explaining common denominator of the Herbartian–Freudian theory. It has already been shown that the Freudian explanation of compulsion neurosis and hysteria, for example, leads to unresolvable contradictions within the theory of the random separability and displaceability of affect and idea, due to the simultaneous employment of quantitative and qualitative aspects. From the foregoing depiction of the relationship obtaining between affect and idea it becomes understandable that it is thoroughly possible for an idea to exist in consciousness without the affect which in essence belongs to it. But for a particular idea and behavioural pattern, such as the above-mentioned going-to-bed-ritual, to be based upon a completely different idea in the presence of a neutralized affect ('quantity of excitation') would require a profusion of additional auxiliary and intermediate hypotheses in order to be made intelligible. (This is the course followed by Freud's psychoanalysis. Cf. e.g. the assumption of two censors in the unconscious.) In contrast to this, we assert here the thesis that—as has been indicated—the 'inappropriate' affect and inappropriate ideas (associations) of psychoanalysis do *not* exist. Rather, although the connection between affect and idea is conditioned by the relatively limited number of affects on the one hand and the profusion of possible ideas (images) on the other, *the connection still remains always objective and conditioned by the essence of both affect and idea*. Only because the connection is conditioned through essence and, in the last analysis, always appropriate are symbolic connections, such as those, in Freud's above-mentioned case, between interrupted botanical studies and defloration and between the 'Virgin' mountain and the concrete virgin, possible in the first place. A symbol already contains affect and idea *in nuce*, potentially, but avails itself of an (archaic) language, which precedes the development of possible ideas and images out of the affect and is made possible by symbolic and analogous essential features. Allowing for symbolism, the relation between affect and idea could be provisionally described as follows:

(a) The limited number of affects stands in juxtaposition to a multiplicity of possible ideas, which in their multiplicity are nevertheless rooted, *in accordance with their essence*, in affect.

(b) The conscious ego (the will) can arbitrarily connect affects with 'inappropriate' ideas, that is, associations which do not correspond to the affect in question. In like manner, the ego can bring about the reverse connection. Here lies the solution of the problem of the 'inappropriate affects' of psychoanalysis, which is to be sought in a disturbance of the combining ego (or will).

(c) For unconscious psychic life, the rooting of idea in affect is represented by the symbol. The symbol exhibits on an archaic level the unity of affect and idea. This makes possible the comprehension of archaic (symbolic) forms of reaction in normal and pathological behaviour (for example, botany—defloration). The essential root of idea in affect is objectively exhibited by the symbol in all of its possibilities of variation. Abstract concepts such as defloration and botany can be brought into an intelligible connection only when objectively grounded in the affect of aggression, seizure, and destruction. The affect and its numerous inherent ideas can be expressed through one or more symbols.

(d) Contrary to this is Freud's mechanistic view that:

(a) affects and ideas devoid of inner (essential) connection can be attached to each other arbitrarily at any time (quantities of excitation in chains of associations) and that their content is of secondary significance.

(b) Affects are grasped purely quantitatively.

(iii) *The Problem of Causality*

The problem of causality, the question of cause and effect, is not given a uniform answer today even by the exact natural sciences[1] (see above p. 443 ff.). In the beginnings of psychoanalysis trauma played the same role as did bacilli as causes of disease in the medical conceptions of that time. Causality was viewed less as condition than as ontogenesis. In the past 70 years, however, the concept of causality has changed extraordinarily within medicine, too.[2] The establishment of an unambiguous causal chain, explaining, for example, why the tubercle bacillus produces certain specific symptoms instead of others, is impossible due to the incalculability of the determining factors. This can be considered to hold for life processes as such. This is the reason why there is no exact prediction in medicine, e.g. about the course of an illness, in the sense of an axiomatic system. In so far as predictions are made, they are supported by reference to the course of similarly diagnosed diseases and experience gained from the latter. This sort of empirical prediction is quite remote from that of the exact natural sciences.

Freud soon saw through the overestimation of trauma as the genetic factor in neurosis. Nevertheless, the trauma has been retained indirectly by the Freudian and neo-analytic schools right up to the present as the

[1] See also B. Bavink, *Ergebnisse und Probleme der Naturwissenschaften*, Berlin, 1938. ('Findings and Problems of the Natural Sciences').

[2] See R. Siebeck, *Medizin in Bewegung*, Stuttgart, 1952 ('Medicine in Movement'); v. Bergmann, *Funktionelle Pathologie*, Berlin, 1933 ('Functional Pathology'); L. v. Krehl, *ibid*.

most important explanatory factor in the genesis of neuroses. The Oedipus complex replaced the trauma as the central cause of neurosis, to be followed by the castration complex, to which very many neurotic symptoms were suddenly attributed at the beginning of the 'twenties. In the following years frustrations during the pre-Oedipal, anal, and oral phases were made increasingly responsible for the formation of neuroses. This trend reached its climax in Rank's all explaining birth trauma. The drastic concept of causation which originally underlay the explanation of hysteria through one or more traumas was merely replaced by the more refined notion of frustration. But at bottom the simple causal concept, analogous to the bacillus as disease-producer, remained. For a frustration is no more than a trauma used as a *causal explanation* (in contrast to *psychological understanding* [Jaspers, Dilthey]). Although neither a precise concept of causation, in the sense of a clearly visible chain of causes, nor exact predictability are possible in medicine, e.g. in the doctrine of infectious diseases, medical hypotheses have been experimentally verified none the less. Medicine has thus approached the realm of the exact sciences. In experiments with animals tuberculosis is induced through the injection of bacilli. This form of verification of hypotheses is impossible in psychoanalysis for purely practical reasons. While a decisive element of scientific demonstration for the corroboration of the trauma hypothesis must thereby be dispensed with, it has been justifiably asserted that the frequency, bordering on regularity, of observation of the Oedipus or castration complex in neuroses makes their role as causes of neuroses appear practically a certainty. On the other hand, to be adduced against this view held by Freudians,[1] is the fact that the occurrence of the Oedipus or castration complex is always inferred through a complicated process *after* the appearance of the neurosis, *post festum*, a procedure resting on extremely shaky logical ground. Both complexes are moreover ubiquitious in nature, i.e. they also occur in so-called 'normal' individuals. The psychoanalytic conception of the causal determination and the explainability of the neuroses is thus of dubious character from the scientific viewpoint. We subscribe to Jasper's view 'that psychoanalysis is a *psychology of understanding* (*verstehende Psychologie*) which misunderstands itself.'[2,3] The reasons for this are the following:

It has not been possible to trace back a so-called neurotic symptom to a *single* frustration in the way that the specific illness tuberculosis

---

[1] Cf. O. Fenichel, *The Psychoanalytic Theory of Neurosis*, Introduction.

[2] K. Jaspers, *General Psychopathology*.

[3] See in the third part of the section on the 'Specific and Unspecific Quality of Neurosis', p. 556 ff.

can be traced back to a specific bacillus. The impossibility of such a causal reduction is due to the following points:

(a)   The absence of a universally valid distinction between neurotic and healthy. Numerous so-called frustrations such as those taking the form of the Oedipus or castration complex are also manifest in so-called normal individuals and do not always cause neurotic symptoms (cf. training analysis for example).

(b)   Overdetermination of neurotic symptoms contradicts unambiguous causality. (Cf. the factors cited by Freud as determinants of hysterical fits (see p. 96).) The neurotic symptom thereby becomes an 'as-well-as' and a 'could-be' phenomenon.

(c)   The complexity of psychic processes admits of causal explanation only within the narrow limits of action and reaction,[1] especially as such explanations always analyse that which is to be explained into an infinite regress.[2,3] Psychoanalysis has been in part a victim of *regressus ad infinitum*. This becomes clear in the theories of Rank and Melanie Klein. (The cause of neurosis is located in even earlier and scarcely accessible phases of childhood whose empirical content is extremely questionable. This is observable above all in E. Bergler's work *The Basic Neurosis*. Freud followed the same tendency.)

The need to match natural science in the establishment of one-way causal connections and in the perspicuity of determining factors led the positivist schools into a conflict of opinions rather than a dispute about knowledge. Numerous examples were adduced in this conflict of opinions (unproven hypotheses): one need only think of the discussions of the problem of transvestism, the perversions, homosexuality, sublimation, psychosomatic problems, and the question of distinguishing between the primary and the secondary. At least five or six differing explanations are provided for most neuroses and neurotic symptoms,[4] and each of them contradicts the others. In the end, the *logically* most obvious (most intelligible) explanation apparently wins out.

One theory of transvestism, for example, is that the transvestite would like to be simultaneously a man and a woman and to possess a vagina as well as a penis. This theory cited here only as one of many analogous psychoanalytic theories,[5] is seemingly supported by material

[1] See also H. Kunz, *Über den Sinn und die Grenzen Psychologischen Erkennens*, Stuttgart, 1957. ('On the Meaning and the Limitations of Psychological Perception').

[2,3] E. Bergler, *The Basic Neurosis*, New York, 1949.

[4] See especially O. Fenichel's *The Psychoanalytic Theory of Neurosis*, where this assertion is proved in every chapter.

[5] Again see O. Fenichel, cf. p. 18 n.

yielded by analysis, which is assumed to admit of being observed in the same neutral manner as does a chemical process in a test-tube. But the material itself, the patient's utterances, dreams, and reactions during analytic treatment, allow fundamentally differing interpretations. This follows from the reasons given above (p. 461) under *a, b* and *c*. That is why Sadger's and Boehm's theories of transvestism are not less convincing and intelligible than Fenichel's. None of them, however, goes beyond the realm of *possible* causes of the formation of this perversion. To be sure, the above-mentioned explanation of transvestism diverges from the trauma theory of neurosis inasmuch as it is not directed at the alleged causes supposed to be found in castration anxiety or the Oedipus complex. Instead, transvestism is thought of here as conditioned by a (chronic) conflict, and exhibits the typical compromise character of the symptom, which develops out of two opposing tendencies, the desire to be both man and woman. Nevertheless, this explanation is far removed from the causal concept of either medicine (cf. tuberculosis) or the exact sciences. For, above all, there can be no question here of causality in either the ontic sense (of actually producing an effect) or in the sense of perspicuous and calculable conditions.

How were these explanations arrived at through the psychoanalytic method? Since there are several explanations for every neurotic symptom, and since these are in part contradictory in content, due to the described overdetermination of the symptom, the question arises as to whether the numerous explanatory statements, such as those about transvestism, may not actually be selected *arbitrarily* from the 'material' obtained in analysis. Fenichel's transvestite did not only exhibit indications of a castration complex and feminine tendencies in the sense of the negative Oedipus complex and use his male identification as a defence against castration anxiety, etc. In addition, processes were apparently detected whose occurrence can be readily and analogously demonstrated in the case of other neuroses. The hypothesis that the transvestite wishes to possess simultaneously a vagina and a penis may have the following basis: out of the many explanations possible of the more or less unspecific and ubiquitous material of analysis, material with a constant internal resemblance due to its unmistakable stereotypy, one has been selected highly arbitrarily and advanced as binding *because it offers itself as the logically most comprehensible explanation*. The material of analysis certainly provides objective support for Fenichel's hypothesis. But why just this thesis is advanced when another one would apply just as well can not be derived from the empirical observations alone, since these would seem to substantiate other hypotheses (Sadger and Boehm) in the same measure. Although Freud was less audacious than his disciples in advancing specific hypotheses to explain a neurosis or symptom, it never seems to have dawned on either him or them that the problem dealt with here belongs to the essence of overdetermination. Otherwise the attempts to provide a *single* explanation for a symptom would not be so numerous. This difficulty comes to light most impressively in the hypotheses of psychosomatic medicine. Without doubting the correctness of the psychosomatic approach or questioning its necessity for the treatment of numerous functional diseases and, within limits, of organic illness, it is still impossible to overlook the unequalled audacity of psychosomatic hypotheses. Even Freud admitted that the 'final' cause of neurosis, which would explain why one individual becomes neurotic while another remains normal, is unknown. Nevertheless, theorists of psychosomatic medicine have not hesitated to use simple schemata to explain 'causally' the highly complicated functioning of both psychic *and* physiological processes. To be sure, structures similar to those of neuroses in general or even to those present in so-called normal individuals also appear during the treatment of psychosomatic disease. But in psychosomatic medicine, these analogous structures are presented as specific and generally valid by bringing in numerous auxiliary hypotheses and employing analogical inferences and symbolic thought, which is an anachronism in scientific research. A look at the psychosomatic explanations of hypertension (p. 243) and colitis (p. 243) will show the manner in which, in the former illness, the simultaneously present positive and negative Oedipus complexes are interpreted as an instinctual conflict between passive-masochistic and ('overcompensating') aggressive-masculine tendencies. The resulting, partially unconscious state of tension is supposed, by means of vegetative centres, to cause tension in the cardiovascular system as well as hypertension. Although the occurrence of the positive and negative Oedipus complexes has a ubiquitous character in Freud's work, too, it is taken here *arbitrarily* as a basis for the assumption of a state of chemical and unconscious tension, which in this case is alleged to precede hypertension temporally in the causal sense (ontonic causality) and 'produce' it. If the so-called oral and anal phases were taken into account, the 'material' of a psychoanalytically treated hypertensive patient could provide many other no less plausible hypotheses dealing with this disturbance.[1] Aside from this, the possible (physiological) tension occurring between the passive and aggressive attitudes is completely unproven. One or the other of two courses is followed to give plausibility to this explanation of the

[1] In this connection see D. Wyss, 'Psychosomatische Aspekte der juvenilen Hypertonie', *Nervenarzt*, Vol. 26, p. 5, 1955 ('Psychosomatic Aspects of Juvenile Hypertonia'); D. Wyss, 'Psychosomatische Aspekte der Paroxysmalen Tachykardie', *Z. Klin. Med.* pp. 153, 311, 1955 ('Psychosomatic Aspects of Paroxysmal Tachycardia').

influence of the alleged unconscious tension upon the cardio-vascular system. Either reciprocal action between psyche and body (through the midbrain) is assumed, or analogical inferences and symbolic thought are adopted to interpret hypertension as an expressive equivalent of the chronic unconscious tension. The attribution of hypertension and other diseases to purely instinctual conflicts of a sexual nature is already a hypothesis in itself. Here it is apparently presupposed as proven. Not least because psychosomatic hypotheses are so obviously pure hypotheses and yet are ascribed a factual character have they been received by doctors with little approbation and much scepticism, being more harmful than useful. They are even inferior to the psychoanalytic hypotheses dealing with the formation of neuroses, since the latter were at least concerned with proving the compromise character of the symptom in a consistent manner. The self-contradictory nature of psychosomatic theses can be summarized as follows:

(a) Psychoanalytic theory is presupposed along with its ballast of major hypotheses and problems.

(b) In the 'explanation' of psychomatic phenomena, psychoanalytic theory is arbitrarily pared down to the extent of

1. abandoning the compromise character of the symptom or evaluating it only symbolically (cf. 'giving' in diarrhoea in the discussion of colitis on p. 243) and,

2. while presupposing the sexual content of psychosomatic symptoms (e.g. double Oedipus complex), asserting their *asexual* character in contrast to neuroses (pure 'states of tension').

(c) General factors (double Oedipus complex, castration complex, etc.) irrelevant to the specificity of a neurosis, to say nothing of other forms of illness, are elevated arbitrarily to the status of specific theses. Unconscious and chronic states of tension in the vegetative nervous system are assumed (as in hypertension, ulcus ventriculi, colitis, hyperthyroidism, etc.). These states are deduced from the ubiquitous elements of neurosis (and of the so-called normal realm).

(d) Analogical inference, the interpretation of expression, and symbolic thought (as in 'giving' in colitis) are arbitrarily employed in supporting these hypotheses and in order to make bodily symptoms understandable (misunderstood as *causal*).

(e) Physiological theories are adapted arbitrarily by means of analogical inferences to suit the psychological need of explanation. This is exemplified by the concept of 'tension' in hypertension, which is taken in both a physiological and psychological (expressive content) sense. Furthermore, no account is taken of the significance of real and complicated processes which physiologists themselves have not fully elucidated in such phenomena as hypertension. Instead, psychosomatic medicine falls back upon general notions, such as 'tension' in the circulatory system. That is, connections which still elude explanation by pathological physiology, whether in hypertension, ulcus ventriculi, asthma, or hyperthyroidism, are simplified and squeezed into the mould of psychological theory.

(f) This hypothetical construction receives its finishing touch in the attempt to declare the subject's subjectivity a temporary weakness of method (p. 243). This leads the whole undertaking *ad absurdum*.

We can now summarize the role played by causality in psychoanalysis. Due to its character as a 'psychology of understanding (*verstehende Psychologie*) which misunderstands itself' and to the above mentioned particulars, psychoanalysis is not capable of yielding causal explanations as these are understood in the natural sciences and in medicine (cf. infectious diseases). The psychoanalytic claim to scientific validity of this sort is fictitious. Where this claim is asserted, hypothetical constructions result (cf. psychosomatic medicine). This does not exclude the fact that psychoanalysis has discovered *possible* conditions of the formation of neuroses and the development of the individual. But these conditions are not of the nature of laws or generally binding or necessary propositions and cannot be applied causally to the specificity of individual diseases. The factors revealed by psychoanalysis as affecting the development of the individual have the quality of 'could-be' and 'as-well-as' conditions, which vary greatly from person to person. Which of these factors can be considered to be ensured will emerge later in the present investigation.

(iv) *The dialectical principle of psychoanalytic theories*

With the exception of the views of existential analysis and Von Weizsäcker, all psychoanalytic theories including Jung's have the common feature of being dialectical. That is, they rest upon the assumption that psychic activity is determined by antitheses, which culminate in particular in the concept of *ambivalence* (Bleuler). In Freud's early and middle phases, these antitheses are manifested in the antithetical structure of the instincts, the distinction between ego instincts and libido, aggression and libido, conscious and unconscious, sadism and masochism, active and passive, and feminine and masculine. In his last phase, the opposition between the death and life instincts became central. The polarity of psychic processes in Freud's works can be demonstrated in detail, e.g. in the antithesis between heterosexual and homosexual tendencies. As early as his correspondence with Fliess, Freud designated the latter as the actual 'repressed': men were asserted to repress their homosexual (feminine) tendencies and women their masculine ones. Moreover, the antitheses of superego and id, pleasure and pain, tension and relaxation, and will and counterwill (in his publication of 1892) are not to be forgotten. Adler's theories are based exclusively on the opposition between inferiority feelings and overcompensating power strivings, and Horney's and Fromm's systems are constructed completely dialectically upon questions of defence against anxiety. The antithesis between expansion and inhibition forms the foundation of Schultz–Hencke's system, and Jung's psychology of complexes is likewise dialectically constituted, with its oppositions of anima and animus, conscious and unconscious, compensation and self-regulation, and extroversion and introversion. Even Klages' interpretation of psychic activity has a polar structure. The striking concurrence of psychoanalytic theories in this regard prompts the conjecture that real relationships have been apprehended here, although such observations had already been made by philosophers of classical antiquity and of the Romantic period and then, in particular, by German idealism. The antithetical nature of psychic processes becomes problematic in psychoanalytic explanations when the existence of an unconscious tendency opposing the conscious is assumed from the outset. Thus the sadist turns out to be a concealed masochist and vice versa, the heterosexual reveals himself to be a repressed homoxesual and vice versa, the exhibitionist is really a voyeur and vice versa, an aggressive personality is only a screen for a passive and feminine one and vice versa, boasting is a cover-up for self-depreciation and vice versa, the antithesis of manic and depressive follows an analogous dialectic, and so forth. The antithetical nature of psychic strivings induced Freud, especially in his last phase, to let the assumption of external frustrations (traumas) as a cause of neuroses recede increasingly into the background. Neuroses and neurotic behaviour were understood to arise from the conflict between contrary drives, instincts or forces and from the opposition between the parts of the personality. The intra-psychic realm, the conscious and unconscious, through their preformed content came to be considered the determining factors in the genesis of neuroses. It became unimportant (e.g. Melanie Klein) whether the child had a 'good' or 'bad' mother in reality, for in either case he would still project the 'bad' mother on to the real one on the basis of his inherent aggression. For Jung—analogously here to Melanie Klein—it is self-evident that all possible and antithetical father and mother imagoes are at the disposal of the individual and that the latter carries these imagoes over into reality. The assumed contradictory nature of psychic processes runs into the danger of resulting in the most banal of dialectical explanations. For if an opposite (unconscious) tendency is assumed for any (conscious) tendency, then it would seem impossible to run into empirical error. At this point the possibility of distinguishing between that which has been really observed and that which has been dialectically inferred becomes questionable, and the process reveals itself as possibly a tautology. The philosophy of idealism (Hegel) solved the problem of dialectics by having objective Spirit (*objektiver Geist*) evolve triadically and come to an end. Thesis and antithesis led to synthesis, which resolved the contradictions. As seen by psychoanalytic theories, the dialectic of psychic processes dispenses with synthesis—unless Jung's process of individuation and concept of mana are considered to unite the contradictions, as elucidated by him through symbolic representations. The positivist schools, on the contrary, do not overcome the dialectic of the contradictions.[1] This holds for Freud no less than for his disciples and, in a limited sense, for the neo-Freudians (behaviourists). It seems difficult to understand how, in the dialectical process of an analysis, in which the unconscious opposite of a conscious tendency—he loves his father consciously, but unconsciously would like to kill him—becomes conscious, simply becoming conscious of these antitheses can be surpassed and a cure arrived at, unless some form of synthesis of the contradictions is assumed. For practical psychotherapy this problem is that of how it would be possible, notwithstanding full insight into the ambivalence of emotional impulses, not to be 'dialectically' dominated by them.

It is thus necessary to differentiate:

1. The postulated antithesis of all psychic tendencies leads misguidedly to banal explanations, since the assumption of the existence of an opposing unconscious tendency for a conscious one always proves to be logically-dialectically correct.

2. To be sure, the analysis of a patient itself leads to becoming conscious of the contradictions. But the necessary theoretical foundation for the synthesis of these contradictions is lacking (apart from Jung and the philosophical schools).

The central problem which further arises is the following: Are the observed contradictions of the psychic process real contradictions, or are they antitheses based merely on the structure of man's cogn··ive faculty, which is capable of thinking only in contradictions (Kant)? This problem has been raised by philosophy since the pre-Socratics, who, like Heraclitus, made antithesis the fundamental principle of existence, and it has received very diverse solutions.—In the present

[1] See especially the New York Group, the problem of synthesis in Anna Freud, the 'self' in K. Horney. These thinkers have taken the first steps towards a synthesis of antithetical forces.

investigation it is our intention merely to refer to this problem in its capacity of conditioning or impeding psychological knowledge by enticing us into tautologies.

To summarize the discussion of the claim of Freud's psychoanalysis to scientific validity:

1. Freudian psychoanalysis and the work of its disciples are far from possessing the form of an axiomatic system based on verified hypotheses and capable of claiming scientific validity.

2. The character of scientific (causal) explanation within psychoanalysis is largely fictitious. Freud's psychoanalysis is a *verstehende* psychology which does (empirically) record observations,[1] but which inserts them into a teleological system of intelligible and possible conditions of phenomena. In most cases, moreover, causal explanation is continually abandoned in favour of teleological explanation.

3. The predominant idea of the teleological system of psychoanalysis is the principle of pleasure and pain (reality principle). Living substance lives for the sake of 'pleasure' and for this reason avoids pain (see following chapter).

4. The antithetical structure of psychic processes (ambivalence, polarity) misleads explanation into establishing tautologies. It is not always possible to tell whether the conclusions drawn from the dialectic of psychic events are based on real observations or simply on the application of dialectic.

5. Apart from (fictitious) causal explanation based on abstract energetic representations which are transferred to the psyche, and apart from teleological (pain/pleasure) explanation, psychoanalysis works with analogical inferences on the basis of symbolic interpretations, which overstep the bounds of the possibilities of scientific knowledge.

6. The psychoanalytically observed conditions of the normal and pathological development of the individual, which are inferred partly by means of complicated processes of interpretation, are exclusively 'could-be' conditions, which are inferred retroactively through analysis and which permit the prediction of specific phenomena only within certain limits of probability, even in the case of conditions which are not inferred, but observed, as in the case of infant behaviour (see p. 210 ff.).

[1] See above all Binswanger's extended concept of empirical observation in psychoanalysis, p. 403 ff.

B

FURTHER PROBLEMS OF FREUDIAN PSYCHOANALYSIS
(FREUD AND HIS FOLLOWERS)

(a) The Theory of Pleasure and Displeasure

In the preceding section the Copernican theory was taken as a 'perfect example' of an axiomatic system and this system was then compared and contrasted with psychoanalytic theory. It was pointed out that a theory such as that of the relationship between affect and idea, which appears to be universally binding, is in fact making false claims by demanding to be considered in the light of an ultimate theory, i.e. one which embraces and confirms all previous theories. The part played by causal explanation within an axiomatic system in the exact natural sciences varies from one discipline to another. The causal explanation and thus the crowning glory of the Copernican system is afforded by Newton's Law of Gravitation: the elliptical course of the planets around the sun is due to the laws of gravitation. The part played by causal explanation in psychoanalysis was discussed in the preceding section and the conclusion reached was that causal explanation cannot really be said to obtain in psychoanalytic theory in the sense in which it is applied in the natural sciences. There is of course no problem once it is agreed that the issues with which psychoanalysis is concerned have nothing to do with causality but rather with the illumination of meaningful relationships. But the disarray which besets psychoanalytic theory is due in no small measure to the fact that causal and meaningful relationships (meaningful in Jaspers' sense) have been confused. Over and above this, however, it is also questionable as to whether these meaningful interpretations—which constantly and falsely lay claim to universal validity as causal explanations—actually correspond in an objective sense to 'observable' facts of psychic life or whether they do not in fact merely project on to the psyche the biased views of the interpreter (views which ultimately derive from Herbart and the Philosophy of the Enlightenment). It is therefore proposed to investigate these interpretations further.

The theory of pleasure and displeasure is also one of the basic tenets of psychoanalysis. It is, however, no longer possible to maintain in respect of this theory—as is maintained in respect of the relationship between affects and ideas—that it is universally binding, since it is abundantly clear that its function is purely explanatory and that it therefore constitutes no more than a meaningful relationship. With the theory of pleasure and displeasure it becomes apparent that the 'mechanics' of mind and soul (idea and affect) have been abandoned, for at this point even Freud introduces teleological principles, the principles of the preservation of the species and of the conservation of energy.

The view that human behaviour is determined by the desire to obtain pleasure and to avoid displeasure, which is known to philosophy under the concept of hedonism, was one which Freud unquestioningly accepted from his preceptors, i.e. both from the physiologists and from Herbart, Fechner and above all Meynert. The theory of pleasure and displeasure, like the theory of the arbitrary dissociation of ideas and affects, is of particular importance for psychoanalysis because the whole problem of repression and of the unconscious is derived from it: displeasurable experiences are repressed, whereupon they form the basis of pathogenic complexes in the unconscious. At no time did Freud express any doubts as to the validity of his theory of pleasure and displeasure. Despite its teleological bias he considered it to be as axiomatic as the theory of the relationship between affects and ideas. The theory of pleasure and displeasure is accepted by all the positivist oriented schools of psychoanalysis. But whenever this theory tries to explain human behaviour in terms which are intended to be universally binding it always overshoots the mark, a failing which it shares with all theories which are committed to generalizations. Quite apart from the failure of this hedonistic interpretation of human behaviour to consider the problem of values,[1] which is of such crucial importance to man, quite apart from its failure to realize that there is not even such a thing as an 'abstract' animal that blindly follows its impulses (failures which must in themselves cast doubt on the validity of the interpretation), there is also the further fact that this theory eschews quality and attempts to comprehend psychic activity in quantitative terms alone, thus revealing the full measure of its problematical nature. It is not just that one type of pleasure differs from another type of pleasure, the real fact of the matter is that the concept of pleasure covers an infinite number of varying and highly differentiated experiences, which Freud here tries to reduce to an abstract common denominator. In point of fact the full diversity of possible pleasurable experiences can really only be expressed by the full range of human experiences.—'Pleasure' and 'displeasure' cannot really be said to exist as such. They are abstract concepts which Freud here presses into service as cornerstones for his whole edifice of explanations and interpretations of human behaviour. There is a difference between the pleasures of exercise and the pleasures of relaxation, between shoot-

[1] Cf. also M. Scheler's criticism of hedonism in: Der Formalismus in der Ethik, Bern, 1954 ('Formalism in Ethics').

ing a deer and committing a sexual murder, between drinking Burgundy, Rhenish and Beer, between eating game and eating baked fish, between climbing a mountain and taking a woman 'by force'. The qualitative diversity of pleasurable experiences is completely submerged in the abstract concept of pleasure. To tell a man that he is *only* seeking his own pleasure and avoiding displeasure is to falsify reality to a very considerable extent, for the objects of pleasure which he seeks and the objects of displeasure which he is supposed to repress cover an extraordinarily vast range. A child tries out its various skills and takes delight in them: it takes 'pleasure' in building a house with its bricks, but it also feels pleasure when it goes paddling or when it gains the upper hand in a fight.—The infinite diversity of human behaviour is lost and reality is distorted when psychoanalytic theory does away with these subdivisions and then proceeds further to restrict the common denominator of pleasure to sexuality alone. This sudden transition from the purely abstract concept of 'striving for pleasure' to the concrete reality of sexual strivings would appear to be both biased and unwarranted. Man's 'striving for pleasure' is then contrasted with reality (reality principle, 'the necessities of life') and with the displeasure which arises out of the clash between pleasure and reality, whereby the concept of 'reality' is even more abstract, even more alien to 'living' reality than was the concept of pleasure, which, if it was linked with nothing else, was at least linked with sexuality. And yet the totality of environmental, educational, social and cultural influences is to be subsumed under the concept of the reality principle. The interaction between pleasure and reality (displeasure) then gave rise to the theory of repression, which was to have such far-reaching consequences and which—at least in the beginning—was concerned only with displeasurable sexual experiences. And with the theory of repression the actual 'genetic' aspect of psychoanalysis was established.

In the light of these considerations the following provisional assessment can now be made of the problems attendant on the concepts of pleasure and reality (displeasure):

1. The 'pleasure principle' and the 'reality principle', with which psychoanalysis operates and whose interaction is said to produce displeasure, are both based on unreal abstract and purely quantitative concepts.
2. The 'pleasure principle' is then translated into concrete but exclusively sexual terms.

But a further question arises at this point, namely, to what extent is the hedonistic attitude adopted by psychoanalysis a true or relevant attitude? Does it correspond to the observable data of psychic life? It is a true attitude in as far as constant and productive growth is a natural attribute of man and one in which he takes pleasure. But growth is not restricted merely to those processes whereby man learns to walk, to talk, to control motor activity, to realize his abilities and to implement his will, to assert and surrender himself, to exercise pleasurable vegetative functions such as eating and drinking and sexuality. Aesthetic pleasures and the pleasure afforded by intellectual and artistic activity also play their part. It would seem that every internal or external development, whether it consists of looking at a landscape or building a house, provided it involves the controlled application of human skills and results in human achievement, will afford man 'pleasure'. And then there is the special position occupied by the orgasm in respect of pleasure, which has been described by von Weizsäcker (see p. 432 ff.), and there is also *ecstacy* which is the ultimate objective of all pleasure and on which *Klages*[1] lays great stress. The hedonistic attitude can only be justified if the view of pleasure which it advocates is *extended* to include all such aspects, aspects which psychoanalysis has not even considered. Psychoanalysis either reduces all pleasures to sexual pleasure by suppressing the diversity of quality and essence which these actually involve, or it interprets man's striving for pleasure in terms of an abstract 'pleasure principle', or it speaks of 'secondary' libidinizations.

But in point of fact, whenever man engages in a *productive* relationship with *reality*, when he masters it, records it, plays with it or transforms it into a phantasy product, he experiences 'pleasure'. In other words, *the pleasure principle and the reality principle are not the fictive antitheses which Freud imagines them to be, but rather 'pleasure' is generated when—and only when—the individual encounters and confronts reality in the widest possible sense of the word.* This applies with equal force to a baby sucking at its mother's breast and to an adult experiencing the pleasure of seeing some undertaking brought to a successful conclusion. *In either case, and indeed in every case, reality plays its part.* The concept of a pleasure principle diametrically opposed to a reality principle is a mere abstraction which has nothing to do with living reality, *for pleasure and reality are necessarily related to one another, fused together, by virtue of their common link in man.* (The child who is punished for dirtying itself will doubtless feel displeasure—but to consider such punishment as a criterion of the 'reality principle' is to equate reality with prohibitions. And if reality is understood as the totality of 'real Being' then prohibitions are not the same as reality and do not furnish an adequate criterion for the establishment of a reality principle. Moreover, this (abstract) concept of reality is quite incapable of explaining how it is that the child,

[1] L. Klages, *Vom kosomogonischen Eros*, Leipzig, 1924. ('Cosmogonic Eros')

after mastering the technique of defecation, should come to regard this as a *pleasurable* activity.)

In fact, the process whereby a man (or child) comes to terms with what we call reality is determined by the immanent relationship *between pleasure and reality. For pleasure and reality are interdependent and intertwined.* It is for this reason that the equation between reality and displeasure which is made by Freudian psychoanalysis cannot be raised to the level of an axiomatic truth. For man displeasure simply means that his natural tendency towards growth, towards self-development, which is a source of pleasure to him, is limited by external considerations both of a biological and a sociological nature, viz. death. The process of learning in children (see Piaget's analysis),[1] the process whereby pleasure is actually gained by overcoming resistances (see Rank p. 363 ff.), the acquisition of any new skill (always a source of pleasure) *all presuppose the possibility of displeasure,* e.g. having to accept defeat (displeasure), having to pocket an injury.[2] What this means is that 'pleasure' is always challenging 'reality' and thus always provoking 'displeasure', for these concepts are fused together in a multiple and living network of relations. The process whereby man is constantly coming to terms with his environment (reality), a process which may equally well follow the pattern of von Weizsäcker's *Gestaltkreis* or of Heidegger's 'Being in the World', the process of growth promoted by man's interaction with environmental resistances, the pleasure derived from overcoming obstacles and —on the negative side—the possibility that the individual may be broken by his environment, the threat (displeasure) which the environment constitutes for the invidual—*these processes become meaningful only when considered from the point of view of an innate, fundamental (ontic) relationship between man and his environment (reality).*

This innate relationship is then transcended by virtue of man's inclination to outgrow the environment and the resistances it imposes. In other words, the desire for pleasure is not to be understood in the sense of a blind natural force. On the contrary, the realization of such desires presupposes that the individual concerned is capable of acts of systematic evaluation, acts of learning, acts of applied skill, acts of will and thus capable of accepting 'reality' and *possible* displeasure. Man's constant attempts to come to terms with his environment, which may take the form of direct action *vis-à-vis* the environment or of retrospective

---

[1] Piaget, *Die Bildung des Zeitbegriffes beim Kinde,* Zürich, 1955 ('How the Child forms its Concept of Time').

[2] H. Hartmann found it neccessary to ascribe a pleasure gain to the reality principle and was thus obliged to question the Freudian practice of drawing a sharp distinction between the pleasure principle and the reality principle. See H. Hartmann in *The Ps. St. of the Child,* Vol. XI, pp. 531 ff.

action *vis-à-vis* himself, but which are always indissolubly bound up with pleasure and displeasure, *are not a genetic consequence of an antithesis between his desire for pleasure and reality, but rather, as has been stated above, they are immanent in the original relationship between man and the world, a relationship which can only be metaphysically determined.* It is this original relationship which ultimately 'regulates' the relationship between man and the world, or, as Heraclitus has it: strife is the father of all things.

But in psycho-analysis pleasure is not regarded as a symbol of human productivity and human capabilities. Instead it is pressed into service for the preservation of the species and the conservation of energy. In the form of sexual desire it is required to serve the purposes of the 'procreative drive', which means that in this capacity it serves to increase and strengthen life. But in another capacity pleasure is simply the means whereby man achieves a condition—the only desirable condition —of peace and relaxation. This way of thinking, which does justice[1] neither to the extraordinary diversity and growing differentiation of life on earth (which has been going on since primeval times) nor to man's all-embracing 'desire for pleasure', which has been described above, goes back to the unfortunate correlation which Freud established between pleasure and displeasure on the one hand and relaxation and tension on the other, a correlation which has led to irresolvable contradictions. This correlation was largely due to Wundt's influence, deriving, as it did, both from the quantifying tendency of late nineteenth-century psychology and from certain experiments carried out by Wundt. In these experiments displeasurable sensations which had been induced in a human subject gave rise to observable tensions in the body musculature. Once the effect of the stimuli had worn off these tensions gave way to relaxation accompanied by a sense of well-being. Freud soon got into difficulties with this correlation, however, when he noticed that certain pleasurable sensations of a sexual nature were accompanied by a condition of tension, which meant that pleasure and relaxation were far from being synonymous in all circumstances.[2] But due to the scotoma induced in them by sexuality and libido development Freud and his disciples revealed a marked tendency to disregard conditions in which pleasurable activity was combined with extreme tension just as they tended to disregard the innumerable moments of displeasure which were accompanied by enervation, debility, depression and relaxation of

---

[1] Cf. R. Woltereck, *Allgemeine Biologie und Ontologie des Lebendigen* (Vols. 1 and 2), Stuttgart, 1942 ('General Biology and Ontology of Animate Creatures'), where Woltereck demonstrates the immense reproduction, differentiation and specialization of life: 'Anamorphose'.

[2] For examples of pleasurable 'tension' see pp. 470–1

tension. But the false correlation between pleasure and relaxation, between displeasure and tension, which had been established as a purely abstract construction, was to have far-reaching consequences for psycho-analysis, for the primal cell which strives to preserve a condition of energic constancy, the Nirvana principle and the death drive all resulted from this thesis. The idea that life is exclusively concerned with the 'conservation of energic constancy', an idea which accompanied Freud from his early *Project for a Scientific Psychology* right through to his death drive hypothesis, was given concrete form by the assumption of a sort of primal cell, whose sole desire was for the re-establishment of a condition of absolute peace and relaxation. The only movements which this cell might be induced to make would be reflex movements undertaken as a means of flight and prompted by external stimuli, which Freud calls the 'necessities of life'. Where the need to take nourishment or the need to procreate stem from is not explained. (The concept of the primal cell and that of the reflex form the basis of the primary process in the Ucs.) *The assumption of a cell that is exclusively governed by the principle of energic constancy is one of those pseudo-scientific fictions which, like the pleasure principle, the causal explanation of neuroses or the theory of the arbitrary displacement of affects and ideas, because it is totally abstracted from living reality, shows up the dubious nature of the scientific theory on which psychoanalysis is based. Like the primal horde, which Freud also postulated on the basis of inadequate factual knowledge, the primal cell has never really existed* (cf., *inter alia*, Rank's criticism of Freud's concept of the primal horde).

What has actually been established by biologists is that all animate creatures, even amoebae and viruses, are linked by specific bonds to a particular environment (v. Uexküll).

In the light of such knowledge and in view of the fact that this abstract cell was clearly intended to solve the problem posed by the gap in human knowledge concerning the primitive stages of biological development, a problem which had proved intractable to factual analysis, Freud's concept appears to be highly questionable. (The hypotheses concerning the 'origin of life'.) Even if we bear in mind the tenor of the times in which Freud made these interpretations it is difficult to-day to conceive how a hypothesis such as this could ever have been advanced, let alone believed in, for what it in fact proposes is a gigantic anamorphosis of life, whereby all development and growth are to be traced back to a single arbitrary factor, namely, 'the necessities of life', a factor which, by the influence it brings to bear on the primal cell, produces not only all organized systems of living reality but also the infinite range of diverse individual and unrepeatable phenomena. Over and above this, however, living reality is said to be controlled by the principle of the conservation of energy, a proposition which, if we consider the multiplicity of cultural products which the species *homo sapiens* has brought forth in the course of a few thousand years, must surely seem absurd.

The following points cover the principal criticisms of the theory of pleasure and displeasure:

1. The genetic derivation of human development from the antithesis between the pleasure principle and the reality (displeasure) principle is not only a questionable hypothesis, but—since it is abstracted from reality—a completely false hypothesis. This is so because:

(a) The pleasure and reality principles are abstractions which, as has been demonstrated by individual observations, do not in fact apply in real life, where they are superseded by a relationship in which both man and environment (pleasure and reality) find themselves constantly intertwined (i.e. a relationship which is in fact a metaphysically based *Gestaltkreis*). In the process whereby man comes to terms with his environment (i.e. whereby 'pleasure' comes to terms with 'reality')—since, if man is to be capable of existing at all, he must necessarily be 'directed towards his environment'—man and reality are fused together to such an extent that it is only possible to stipulate *in abstracto* but never *in concreto* where man begins and where the environment ends.

(b) The hedonistic disposition implied by the so-called pleasure principle is only justified in as far as the concept of pleasure involves an organizing and evaluating principle, i.e. in as far as pleasure is related to both value and reality. It is also justified if man's tendency towards productive growth is recognized as a basic characteristic of human existence and if the sexuality which is undoubtedly one part of this tendency is considered *as a part* and not as the whole. The antithesis between sexuality and reality (the latter here understood in terms of prohibitions) is also an unreal abstraction. With the whole range of human development to draw on a *single* hypothesis of human development, one which claims universal validity, has here been fashioned from what are no more than mere aspects of reality.

(c) For the same reasons the equation which Freud makes between the reality principle and displeasure is also misleading. For if the relationship between the environment (reality) and man (pleasure) is immanent, so too is the constant struggle whereby they come to terms with one another. This struggle involves the risk that one side will gain the ascendancy over the other. If reality (environment) conquers man, the result will be displeasure. If the process is reversed, the result will be pleasure.

2. The equation made between pleasure and relaxation and between

displeasure and tension is by no means universally valid. There are probably quite as many tensions which produce pleasurable effects as there are relaxations which produce displeasurable effects.

3. The subjection of living and psychic processes to control by the principle of the conservation of energy, to which the pleasure principle is also subject, is incompatible with the fact of phylogenesis and is also incompatible with man's propensity for cultural achievement.

(b) Repression and Defence

A comprehensive description of the development of the crucial Freudian concept of repression from a *conscious* process to an *unconscious* process was given on p. 158. Repression is intimately connected with pleasure and displeasure, since displeasure is supposed to be the cause of repression. The process which Freud calls repression—certainly that part of it which concerns the conscious repression of unpleasant experiences—has undoubtedly been substantiated by empirical observations. When it comes to demonstrating the existence of unconscious repression, however, it is not quite so easy. When Freud realized that many of the statements made by his patients and many observations which he himself had made were virtually incompatible with the concept of conscious repression he was forced to the conclusion that there must also be a further process involving unconscious repression. But the assumption of an unconscious 'mechanism of repression' which would logically include the hypothesis of repression by unconscious instances (subsequently the unconscious sections of the ego and super-ego) goes far beyond the concept whereby 'man' is held to be governed by two principles, namely the pleasure and reality principles. This abstract creature pursues its desire for pleasure but comes to exercise repression when it encounters the reality principle. But if the possibility of unconscious repression is assumed—and with his concept of primal repression Freud has postulated it for early infancy—then, even if we disregard the inadvisability of basing any argument on the assumption of two abstract principles (see above), it is difficult to see why it should be necessary for 'secondary' repression to be implemented by means of the reality principle. In other words, if the derivation of repression from the reality principle furnishes the theoretical basis for the genetic interpretation of human behaviour, then the existence of unconscious repression and primal repression is essentially a *constitutional* factor, which would mean that *repression is fundamental to Beingness, is immanent in Beingness*. But if man—in contrast to other living creatures—inclines towards repression as he inclines towards society[1] for the simple reason

[1] See above all A. Gehlen's comparison between man and the higher primates in *Der Mensch*, Bonn, 1952 ('Man').

that repression is part of his nature, then this constitutes a further important reason why the antithesis between the pleasure and reality principles is misleading, *for if man accepts reality by exercising 'unconscious repression' then it follows that the reality principle must be immanent in man*. Now there is a crucial difference between a conception of human nature in which man—like the fictive primal cell—is 'primarily' engaged in the pursuit of pleasure and has to be 'educated' to reality and society in what is no more than a secondary process and a conception of human nature in which reality and society are immanent in man as primary factors. In the first case the conception of *homo natura* which Binswanger tried to establish for Freud would apply (save that this *homo natura* can no more be said to exist than the fictive primal cell out of which the living cosmos is said to have developed in response to the demands made by the 'necessities of life'). But if *unconscious primal repression* is assumed, then repression becomes one of the essential human attributes, which on the one hand effectively gives the lie to the concept of *homo natura* but which on the other hand is intimately tied up with the problem of so-called narrowness of consciousness. To the best of my belief this concept does not appear anywhere in Freud's writings, since Freud—at least in the beginning—considered the problem of repression only from the point of view of the pleasure and reality principles. The concept of man's narrowness of consciousness, a concept which can scarcely be denied and which has been made the subject of numerous investigations by psychologists of widely differing persuasions, involves—at least from the point of view of the conscious mind—unconscious or primal repression. The reasons why narrowness of consciousness constitutes one of the principal features of human consciousness are no doubt of a highly complex order and this in itself raises a further crucial objection to the hypothesis of displeasure as the sole cause of repression. In other words, the attempt to establish the antithesis between pleasure and displeasure (reality principle) as the sole basis of repression is questionable. This is so because:

1. The assumption of unconscious and primal repression renders repression largely independent of pleasure and displeasure. Repression becomes a 'constitutional' factor, which means that both 'reality' and society must be immanent in man.
2. So-called narrowness of consciousness, which is one of the principal attributes of human consciousness, involves 'primal repression', a fact which further undermines the hypothesis of displeasure as the sole basis of repression (and of forgetting).

Man's propensity for repression as a prerequisite for coming to terms with reality and adapting to society, his inherent condition of 'narrowness of consciousness', does not, however, preclude the possibility of repression in the Freudian sense. But deciding where to draw the line, deciding how much to apportion to narrowness of consciousness and unconscious repression and how much to the repression of (unpleasant) impressions, is likely to prove very difficult, if not impossible. Whether the solution of this problem matters from the point of view of therapy is a question which will be discussed on a later page. Meanwhile, in order to demonstrate the complex nature of this problem, it will now be considered from four different psychological points of view:

1. Hysterics—and subsequently so-called neurotics—were considered to suffer from 'repressed' complexes (i.e. pathogenic, unconscious ideational contents). It was because they repressed things that they fell ill. And by raising the repressed contents to consciousness an improvement or cure was sometimes brought about. Implicit in this process is the question as to why unconscious ideational contents should have a pathogenic effect, whilst conscious ideational contents do not. And we are justified in asking in this respect whether in fact the neurotic falls ill simply because his repression is 'incomplete'. Certainly not, would be the Freudian answer. For the fact that the complexes are unconscious is due in no small measure to the intensity of the repression. But on the other hand the ability to effect complete repression would appear to enable many people to indulge in a positive excess of cruelty and crime. The biographies of famous statesmen, many of whom have lived to a ripe old age in a state of perfect health, provide adequate testimony that such may be the case. It is above all the egoist, the man who makes his way in the world without regard for others, who possesses the happy gift of being able to repress much, indeed all, that is unpleasant. In other words, the ability to repress would appear to be a necessary condition of mental health. The psychoanalysts would no doubt retaliate at this point by pointing out that it all depends on the structure of the personality, on childhood experiences, etc., which influence the individual's capacity for adaptation and his capacity for repression quite as much as do considerations of 'ego strength' or 'ego weakness'. But even if one were prepared to venture on to the thin ice of questionable hypothesis (opinion) on which such arguments rest the basic fact of the matter would remain unchanged: mental health and personal achievement would appear to be intimately connected with a marked ability for repressing anything unpleasant. And this would seem to cast doubt on the view which Freud developed, according to which all enquiries into the nature of neurosis and of neurotics were to be conducted within the terms of reference of hysterical symptoms, of repression.

2. The second problem is tied up with the process of repression and remembering as revealed in the course of analysis. Amongst other things the following factors would appear to be of great importance for the successful outcome of any analysis: (1) remembering unpleasant experiences, (2) forgetting again, or repressing again, not only the unpleasant experiences which had been remembered but also the majority of the problems which had been worked through with the physician. (Freud considered that the most successful cures were those in which towards the end of the analysis the patients said that they had learnt nothing new because they had known it all already—in other words they had forgotten [repressed?] 'it all'.) From this is would follow that the original act of remembering, i.e. the act whereby the original repression was suspended, can scarcely be considered as the only factor of importance for the analytic process, in which repressed material is 'integrated' (also an unclear concept), i.e. is first remembered and then repressed again, because *this act of 're-repression' would appear to be quite as important for the success of the analysis as the original act of remembering*. The difficulties involved in trying to differentiate between the initial repression, which is suspended by the act of recollection, and the subsequent repression of the recollected material are doubtless of the same order as the difficulties involved in trying to differentiate between 'constitutional' repression, narrowness of consciousness, which includes the possibility of forgetting, and 'secondary' repression, which may conceivably be pathological.

3. But then what of the group of patients, a group made up in large measure of so-called 'neurotics', who suffer from a surfeit of reminiscences, not because they repress too much but because they are unable to repress at all? To contend that the reason why the experiences from which such patients suffer are traumatic is because they are linked with repressed experiences of a similar order, i.e. to contend that the reason why such patients are unable to repress is that in their childhood they did repress offences or other traumas, would appear to be self-contradictory to a degree. It seems obvious enough that these people are ill because they are unable to repress, unable to forget experiences to which they have been exposed, and not because they once repressed experiences, after the fashion of 'hysterics'. This group includes many 'neurotics', whose memories of an oppressive childhood are both numerous and detailed, who are perfectly well able to recall many incidents which led to the deterioration in their state of mental health and who, moreover, are conscious of the affects which these incidents have produced. From this it follows that to establish even a *meaningful* relationship between the concept of neurosis and 'repressed complexes' is no simple matter. (To establish a causal relationship is quite out of the question.)

4. Finally the *unconscious attitudes of defence*, e.g. an extreme tendency to adapt to the requirements made by the environment or alternatively a basic aggressive tendency towards self-assertion, will now be considered. These attitudes (or patterns of behaviour) are unconscious in the majority of people and so the question arises as to whether they too are repressed. Certainly they are not repressed in the sense in which an experience is repressed, which is of course what gave rise to the concept of repression in the first place. To define attitudes as a product of repressed experiences which are themselves then repressed would be an over-simplification of the problem, since such a process would presuppose the existence of an instance which not only represses the experience in the first place but also represses the product of that initial repression, namely the attitudes, whilst the at same time making constant use of them in its relationship to the environment.

The assumption of a general process of repression in respect of neurosis, which Freud made on the basis of his observations of hysterical symptoms, would thus appear to be problematical, for it fails to consider:

1. the further repression which takes place in the course of analysis;
2. those patients who are not suffering from the results of repression but rather from their inability to repress;
3. those patients who, because their capacity for repression is so great, enjoy vigorous health;
4. the problem posed by the repression of attitudes and patterns of behaviour.

Of the various 'mechanisms of defence' (see under Anna Freud p. 205 ff.) repression is the most important. Anna Freud—in conformity with S. Freud—treated projection, identification, introjection, undoing, negation, etc., as general mechanisms of defence by means of which the ego defends itself against displeasure and anxiety (see p. 205 ff.). The actual descriptions of these processes are based on empirical observations but both the concepts employed to denote the various individual processes (projection, identification, etc.) and the collective concept of 'defence' are such as might well give rise to misleading hypotheses. It has already been pointed out by psychoanalytic writers[1] that defence against anxiety or displeasure does not constitute pathological activity and that it is not yet possible to draw a line of demarcation between 'normal defence' and pathological defence. What was true of the concept of repression is also true of the concept of defence, i.e. defence cannot be derived from the pleasure-displeasure principle alone. We

[1] E.g. Lampl de Groot in *The Psa. St. of the Child*, Vol. XII, pp. 114 ff.

have seen that it is not possible to separate repression from narrowness of consciousness, from the as yet largely unclarified problem of forgetting and from man's innate disposition towards repression without having recourse to bold hypotheses. Similarly, the concept of defence includes processes, e.g. projection and identification, which are only very distantly related to conscious and unconscious (repressed) processes. In fact these defence processes are used to describe inter-personal activity which, in accordance with the basic Freudian view, serves the exclusive purpose of acquiring pleasure and avoiding displeasure. But we have already seen from the investigation carried out into the problem of the 'meeting' (see p. 404 ff.) that inter-personal relations cannot be reduced to a common denominator of this kind. After all that has now been said concerning the theory of pleasure and displeasure it would appear quite superfluous to go into the hypothesis that human relations are exclusively hedonistic in their aims and consequently to be construed in terms of defence against anxiety and displeasure. It is not merely that it seems impossible to restrict the highly complex and manifestly problematical nature of human relations to this sort of common denominator, but over and above this it is quite obvious that even in a general sense one man's 'pleasure' is likely to be another man's 'displeasure' and that in such cases displeasure is sought after with the same intensity as pleasure. Safety, security, love, confidence and their opposites are but four pairs of concepts which are of extreme importance in human relationships. But to try to reduce even these to pleasure and displeasure is to commit a gross abstraction which falsifies reality. And so the problematical nature of the concept of 'defence' is seen to lie in the fact that here too—in accordance with the principle of pleasure and displeasure—complicated human relations are reduced by a process of simplification to their lowest common denominator: the defence against anxiety and displeasure. The positivist conception on which Freudian psychoanalysis was based had many weaknesses, some of which have already been dealt with in this present investigation. Chief among these, however, was its inability to find adequate concepts with which to denote the subject, i.e. the individual person. It tried to grasp the nature of the individual with its 'object cathexis', a practice which, it was claimed, revealed a scientific attitude of mind, but which in fact amounted to no more than the transference to the living individual and to inter-personal relationships of electrophysical ideas, a process which had nothing to do with human reality. To the mind of the Cartesian-oriented scientist the 'subject' is nothing but a nuisance which he one day hopes to eradicate, whereafter, instead of having to record the subject, he will only have to record encephalic impulses. We are surely indebted to L. Binswanger, von Weizsäcker and the Existential analysts for having demonstrated in the psychiatric sphere that this way of dealing with the subject does not do justice to reality.

The concepts of defence—e.g. *identification, projection* and *regression* (which must serve for purposes of demonstration)—assume the cartesian position as their starting-point, from which they proceed to deny the 'subject', i.e. the *other* person, as far as is possible. It is of course true that but for this other person no defence mechanisms would be required at all. But first let us see what this other person, the person on whose account the defence mechanisms were first created, actually looks like.

It would seem that what happens in the process of identification is that the person who does the identifying completely assimilates the other person—and this despite the fact that from the observation of *imitation,* which affords the main empirical grounds for assuming the existence of identification, we are scarcely able to determine to what extent the subject has identified with the other person *or whether in fact the primary purpose of the identification is not to impress on the subject the essential difference between himself and the other person.*[1] Freud and his disciples have paid too little attention to this process whereby the subject is made aware that he is different and distinct from the other person, although this is probably the most important of the processes involved in identification. In other words, *in Freud's conception of identification the existence of the subject, i.e. of the one who identifies, is virtually denied; instead, and in conformity with the basic Cartesian view, the subject is supposed to be totally assimilated by the pseudo-object, which is the form in which the other person now appears.* The problematical nature of this concept is made manifest by the organization of the various forms of identification which Fenichel has established (see p. 186 ff.). It is evident that in Fenichel's view total identification only takes place in the formation of the super-ego (in normal personalities): this means that this so-called conscience represents the incorporation of the parental imago, from which it follows that the obedient child is not actually obeying its own commands but the commands of its *incorporated* parents, who then continue in their capacity as incorporated imagines to exercise a considerable influence on the child's future behaviour. This conception, which is already encumbered with the hypotheses relating to an analogous process in the sphere of melancholy, is also required to make good the assertion that conscience consists exclusively of the child's identification with its parents. But this assumption, which has already been criticized in numerous different quarters, in fact merely repeats the above-mentioned claim, that (total) identification consists of the total assimilation of the other person by the subject, *whereby the super-ego, in its capacity as a pseudo-object, is the other person.* But this would

[1] See also A. Gehlen in *Der Mensch.*

mean that the peculiar attribute of the conscience, whereby it is able to adopt a critical attitude to its own activities, would be rendered impossible, since the concept of total identification is incompatible with the concept of self-reflection, which latter derives from the conscience. Man 'himself' would no longer do anything. The other person would do everything for him—as him. Total identification and self-reflection are mutually exclusive. Upbringing and parental influence, i.e. identification, is certainly one of the factors involved in the formation of the child's conscience, *but this process of identification is a preliminary stage leading to self-reflection*. Although strictly speaking Freud's theory of melancholia does not fall within the scope of this present investigation, since it is a theory of psychosis, yet it is perhaps relevant to our immediate purpose to point out that the concept of introjection of, and identification with, the lost object is also basically Cartesian, since it too tries to fuse the subject with the object. The differentiation between partial and total identification was based less on observation than on the need to satisfy the requirements of the *theory* of identification. Since Freud and his followers expected the concept of identification to solve so many questions concerning the instances, it is not surprising that the question as to which part of the personality (id, ego or super ego) is the agent of identification should have arisen. The theory of instances should of course have been applied to the problem of identification in such a way as would have made it possible to avoid the (Cartesian) abolition of the subject and to establish a theory as to which of the instances—id, ego or super ego—is the actual agent of identification. In point of fact, however, no specific answer to the question as to *which* section of the personality actually identifies was ever given, although there was a veritable profusion of hypotheses and suppositions, none of which, however—since all were based on the theory of instances and thus caught up in *its difficulties*—was able to cast light on the problem. Hysterical identification (which might most readily be compared to the actor's imitation of, or identification with, his part) presupposes every bit as much as does so-called 'total' identification the possibility of exercising self-reflection. The more this possibility recedes, however, the more pathological the person concerned is likely to become, until a point is reached where the 'other person', the person with whom the hysteric has identified, takes complete possession of him. Only in pathological circumstances of such an extreme order would it be possible to speak of total identification. In other words:

1. Apart from the temporary 'total' identification which can occur in pathological cases every act of identification is 'partial'.
2. The reason why identification is partial is that it involves, indeed

gives rise to, self-reflection, which only ceases to function in pathological cases.

3. The possibility of an I-Thou relationship is immanent in identification. If this were not so the other person (the Thou) could not be comprehended at all as 'another person'.

4. The relationship posited between identification and the instances of the personality is purely hypothetical.

This last point is clearly illustrated by *Fenichel's* description of the relationship between identification and defence (see p. 186 ff.). Whereas Anna Freud's description of the child's identification with, for example, an aggressor is based on empirical observations Fenichel's statements are purely speculative. According to Fenichel it is not—as in Anna Freud's view—because the mother is aggressive, but because the child is afraid of its mother, that the child's ego—why not its super-ego?—suppresses the urge to show tenderness towards its mother, i.e. to turn libidinally towards her. It is at this point, Fenichel argues, that the child identifies with its mother, whereupon its need for tenderness is directed on to its own ego, which, as we have just seen, is identified with the mother. This hypothesis presupposes the following (unsubstantiated) facts:

1. A drive may take the ego as its object. But this thesis, on which the theory of narcissism was based and which accords to the drives volition and purpose, i.e. a purposively directed intelligence, presupposes at the very least the possibility of forming some conception of what the ego is supposed to be. Since, however, the concept of the ego in Freudian psychoanalysis (see p. 117 ff.) is both inadequate and contradictory, this possibility is not given. This same thesis, which ultimately derives from the concept of the arbitrary divisibility of affects and ideas (see above, p. 450 ff.), also presupposes that the drive—here the 'libido'—is able to exchange one object for another (mother for child) at will.

2. Although the drive is able to exchange one object for another at will, the ego—here perhaps conceived as a drive?—is able to deny the drive its 'object' and, what is more, to take over that object itself. Precisely how this process is to be understood remains shrouded in total darkness. But this darkness is not necessarily the darkness which veils the ultimate processes of living nature, the darkness of mystery. Rather it is a darkness born of the tendency, one which besets this kind of speculation, to stray into the void of abstract pettifoggery. The sagacity of Fenichel's speculation would command our admiration were it not for the fact that it is directed towards *this particular* void. The essence of this kind of thinking lies in the atomistic variability of its concepts, a

variability which is made possible by the loose and blurred definitions which it establishes. Both the drive and the ego are able to 'change' objects in accordance with the electro-physical concept of the inter-changeability of the 'energy' charge of different fields of force. The point to be noted here is that, whereas the electro-physical concept belongs to the world of the natural sciences and is thus subject to precise verification and definition, the psycho-analytic theory belongs to a world of theses which claims to be scientific but in fact is not. These theses miss the real point of psychic activity, its pre-eminent subjectivity, because with their positivist cartesian categories they are incapable of grasping the nature of the subject. Fenichel's views show with particular clarity how unimportant the 'other person', the 'Thou' (the mother) really is. Instead of being considered as a subject in her own right this mother is treated as a mere 'object' and is incorporated as such into the *child's* ego. But this denial of subjectivity is a necessary consequence of the theory. And this sort of solution of the problem posed by identification as a defence against anxiety, a solution which ultimately leads to the exclusion of the 'other person', of the 'Thou', falsifies the fundamental condition of human reality: 'We, not I, is the Absolute' (v. Weizsäcker). This process can only be described—described, that is, in meaningful terms—if the subject and its 'categories' (see v. Weizsäcker) are once more 'enthroned'. What this means is that if, for example, the frightened child identifies with its aggressor, it does not follow from this that it simply surrenders up its own identity, a process which, as has already been demonstrated, could only take place in extreme pathological conditions. The main concern of the child, i.e. of the subject, in identifying with the aggressor is to test its strength—for it realizes its strength every bit as much as it realizes any weakness which it still has—and to 'play itself in' to possible *future* strength and supremacy. This process, which it would be quite wrong to assess in *purely* pathological terms, is repeated time and again in the course of the child's development,[1] because the child's whole life is of course determined by its constant need to come to terms with its environment. Since, moreover, the child is able to incorporate its environment by means of 'identification'—*which presupposes the other person*—it is constantly testing the environment, i.e. the other person, in terms of the impact which its environment makes on it. This does not suggest that the sole purpose of identification is defence against anxiety. *Consequently identification is far from being just another defence mechanism, since it involves the perception, imitation and incorporation of the other person for purposes of coming to terms with him.*

[1] For examples see H. Zulliger, *Bausteine zur Kinderpsychotherapie*, etc., Bern, 1957 ('Material for Child Psychotherapy').

What has been said of the problems attendant on the concept of identification is equally valid for the problems which concern projection. Whereas in the Freudian view of identification the subject is eliminated by the 'object' (the other person), in projection *the other person* is eliminated by the subject—here conceived as an object. The fact that extreme instances of the apparently pure projection of subjective ideas on to the environment have been observed in cases of schizophrenia does not justify the Freudian view of this concept, which overlooks the fact that in both normal and 'neurotic' psychic life *all projections are prompted by some objective factor in the environment*.[1] Sensitive delusions of reference and the early stages of chronic (hallucinatory) paranoia have shown —in those cases where the investigation of the patient was sufficiently thorough—that the conjectures and suspicions which the patients voice are not simply arbitrary projections on to the environment of affects produced in the patient by some real or imagined reproach.[2] (Incidentally, Freud's projection theory also involves his theory concerning the divisibility and variability of affects and ideas (see above p. 450 ff.).) Detailed anamneses have shown time and again that the sensitive personality type of paranoic records the inter-personal tensions which are objectively present in a given situation by the application of normal sense perception and that it is only within the framework of his changed personality that he 'transfers' them on to the environment. If we are to understand sensitive delusions of reference, then it is not the projected reproach affect which should be our principal concern but rather the objective difficulties with which the patient is faced, in which indeed he may already have become embroiled as a result of pathogenic processes, and which are only too prone to link up with inner-psychic conflicts. What happens is that the patient, having registered these difficulties in a perfectly objective manner, proceeds to 'project' them on to the environment in an intensified and exaggerated form, one which, in the case of psychotics, is not always meaningful.[3] In other words the projection is probably a 'back-projection' on to the environment or on to certain persons of difficulties ('frustrations') which are objectively

---

[1] See E. Kretschmer, *Der sensitive Beziehungswahn*, Stuttgart, 1950 ('Delusions of Relation of the Sensitive Type').

[2] See D. Wyss, 'Psychotherapie einer halluzinatorischparanoiden Schizophrenie', *Der Nervenarzt*, Vol. 29, p. 6, 1958 ('Psychotherapy in the case of an hallucinatory paronoid Schizophrenic'); and 'Vorläufiger Bericht über die Psychotherapie einer katatonen Schizophrenie', *Schweizer Archiv f. Neurol. u. Psych.*, 1961. ('Preliminary Report on Psychotherpay in a Case of Catatonic Schizophrenia').

[3] In this connection see above all C. Kulenkampff's investigations in *Nervenarzt*, Vol. I, p. 26, 1925, into poisoning mania, which he traces back to the individual's relationship to food and to *confidence*.

recorded but then pathogenically distorted. What it is not, however, is the straightforward transference on to the environment of pure phantasmagoria. The psychology of transference offers ample evidence in support of this view, which has now been taken into account in the most recent investigations carried out both by followers of Freud[1] and by representatives of other schools.[2] When the analysand projects his father or mother on to the analyst, no matter whether it be a positive or a negative projection, the process involved has nothing in common with the process whereby a film is projected on to the cinema screen. Yet it was this cinematographic process which appealed to Freud as the ideal of the (solipsistic) view of projection which he had taken over from Meynert. Unless the analysand perceives 'paternal' or 'maternal' strains in the analyst, no matter how subtle these may be, it is unlikely that a projection will take place. This of course raises the question as to whether this concept, which derives from an abstract, solipsistic and entirely Cartesian view, should not be dropped altogether. The question is this: does the sensitive type or paranoic *project* on to the environment or is it simply that he *perceives* objective phenomena in a distorted form? Is it not possible that the so-called projection is actually caused by a disturbance in the act of perception, which produces a distorted view of the other person, in which case, of course, we could not really talk about 'back-projection' either (see above)? It will not be possible to reach a decision within the framework of this present investigation as to the plausibility of this alternative view, but it is an issue which ought to be considered before the process in question is allowed to fall a victim to abstract hypotheses.

Glover has shown us where such hypotheses can lead to in his analysis of the concept of sublimation (see p. 191 ff.). Although Anna Freud does not list sublimation as one of the defence mechanisms she does consider it to be one of the means whereby the ego is able to control the 'aim of the drives', e.g. by directing them towards a social aim. Logically this would mean that in the final analysis social institutions were also a product of defence against displeasure and anxiety. In other words, here too gross hedonism is assumed to have rocked the cradle of man's cultural achievements. Freud the man had a ready appreciation for cultural achievements but to Freud the scientist they appeared as mere by-products of defence against anxiety. However, quite apart from the untenable hypothesis that social and cultural institutions are secondary consequences of defence against anxiety, the concept of sublimation also suffers from the fatal equation of the drives with acts of volition, a problem which will be dealt with on a later page.

[1] See above p. 250 ff. (Lagache).
[2] Especially Frieda Fromm-Reichmann in *Principles of Intensive Psychotherapy*.

What is true of repression, projection, identification and sublimation is also true of regression. It is probable that the observation which has been made in respect of regression is correct, namely, that persons suffering from anxiety are able to cope with their anxiety if they allow themselves to slip back into the childish conditions appropriate to an earlier phase of their development. Observations pointing to this end have been furnished by adult, child and schizophrenic therapy and also by dream phenomena. Now if, on the basis of psychoanalytic theory, we attempt to separate regression from repression in a metapsychological sense, then new and complicated hypotheses become unavoidable. But if on the other hand repression is understood primarily in the sense in which it has been defined above as an *immanent* process deriving from narrowness of consciousness, *then regression simply represents an exaggerated form of repression*, one which results from primary repression and from secondary but extreme defence against anxiety. In regression, so to speak, narrowness of consciousness is completely restored. The anxiety-ridden subject literally withdraws into himself, and it is probably this extensive loss of communication with the environment which is the cause of unco-ordinated movements, childish mumbling and stuttering and stuporous apathy such as may be observed in the catatonic forms of schizophrenia. Here again it is not possible to define regression as a defence mechanism which functions more or less automatically and solipsistically à la Descartes. The phenomena which are here subsumed under the concept of regression are due to the subject's loss of communication with the environment and with the partner.

(c) *Problems attendant on the Theory of Drives and the Theory of Instances*
Like the other factors already mentioned in this section (ideas and affects, pleasure and displeasure, anxiety and defence) the theory of drives is one of the really fundamental components of Freudian psychoanalysis. L. Klages' claim[1] that 'nothing but a load of nonsense has so far been expounded' on the subject of the drives is no doubt exaggerated, but it would be difficult to maintain that his charge was completely unfounded. In his definition of the drives Freud tries to assess them from strictly teleological points of view. Sexuality serves the preservation of the species and the ego drives serve self-preservation, which is also to some extent the object of aggression. Moreover, Freud also speaks of the 'aim' of the drives, which consists of the suspension of somatic excitation. L. Klages writes on the teleological interpretation of the drives as follows:

'Those who are blind to the concept of life and yet investigate the drives,

[1] L. Klages, *Der Geist als Widersacher der Seele*, Vol. I, p. 566, Bonn, 1954.

irrespective of whether they proceed intentionally like Lipps, the disector of consciousness or whether on the contrary their aim is to interpret volitional impulses by analogy with drive impulses like the thinker *Schopenhauer*, will always interpret them by analogy with the will. If they lack the insight into the difference of essence which obtains between drive impulses and volitional impulses, then, since it is rare for man to experience drive impulses without experiencing volitional impulses as well, they will unfailingly transport mind into the sub-mental drives and will misconstrue the drives in the worst possible manner at the precise moment when they attempt to interpret acts of will in terms of pure drive impulses.—Because the will pursues purposes, the life impulse is also conceived as purposive and the whole of nature as if it were a system of purposes. Because volitional purposes are realized in achievements and we have grown accustomed to deducing the former from the latter, instead of the drives themselves certain consequences arising from their activation are investigated and are then imputed to the drives as intentions which are directed towards the achievement of an effect. Thus, since only an "I" is capable of willing, an "I" which asserts itself in every act of willing, the interest of the car-rier of the will in its own self-preservation is transformed into a self-preservation drive possessed by all animate creatures. Perhaps a few examples will help to clarify this. Our domestic animals eat and drink just as we do. Although they don't know, we do know, that nobody could go on living, if he were to give up eating and drinking entirely. And so we are aware of nutritive purposes and are able to take decisions such as the decision to improve our diet or the decision to desist from unneces-sary gourmandizing; and the conclusion which has been drawn from this is that eating and drinking are original and universal functions of a nutritive drive and that in this nutritive drive the self-preservation drive makes its presence forcibly felt.

'Now if someone were to say: but animals haven't the faintest idea that in order to live they have to take in calories; for even if we assume that they are capable of acquiring such knowledge, this would not dis-pose of the fact that they perform so-called purposive actions before they acquire it (to wit the chick, which, having just broken out of the egg, immediately pecks corn), not indeed are these purposive actions restricted to the intake of food but include a thousand and one other functions as well (to wit the exodus of the migratory birds in the autumn), then the faithful disciple of the self-preservationist religion, of sacro egoismo, will in all sincerity parade those phrases which, when stripped of subterfuge and obfuscation, announce that all these things are due to non-purposive purposes, unthought thoughts and unconscious con-sciousness! Just who is thinking here and who is not? The "self-preserving" creature does not think, but its inborn "nature" certainly has its preservation in mind. In every unthinking creature there is a planning, calculating "nature", one which is undoubtedly well versed in financial techniques, which prepares its operations on a long term view and about which we shall shortly be hearing some astonishing things.'[1]

Klages' deeply probing theory of the drives, which does complete justice to living reality, was adopted in a modified form[2] by H. Kunz who has also written on the confusion of the drives with acts of will:

'Verbal statements apart, the act of will is rightly considered to be the ideal case of a form of behaviour which is both "meaningful" and at the same time "understandable" in the highest possible degree. What is characteristic of its structure—as revealed in a rough and artificial analysis—is firstly the cognitive and more or less intuitive plan of the "whither" as an anticipated "goal"; then the likewise cognitive and volitional project (intention) of reaching the goal, which project then acts as a "motive" in the precise workings of the understanding and invests the understanding with an additional "purposive character"; and finally the realisation (actualization) of the intention in the teleologically and purposively controlled performance of the action, with which the whole undertaking is brought to a relative conclusion. Such acts of will are always embedded in the overlapping total behaviour of the individual within specific contemporary and environmental situations, from which they are capable of emerging with a greater or lesser degree of significance. It is for this reason that the volitional goals and purposes are usually linked with objects which are either encountered and perceived or are absent and imagined; and the motives join up with the vital impulses, which are usually the first to become active. This explains on the one hand the fact that the vital drives, which often increase and decrease in accordance with their own inner rhythms, are wrongly identified with the motives, which may in principle be introduced at any time, and on the other hand the fact that the objects and goals are wrongly identified with the volitive purposes to which they are allocated. But this uniformity of the origins and the "whither" of concrete behaviour is not the only reason for these false equations. A more decisive factor is the structural similarity between the act of will and the act of perception by which it is understood.

'What turns volitional activity into "significant" activity and what in extreme cases also renders it senseless or contradictory is evidently the

---

[1] L. Klages, ibid., Vol. I, pp. 566–8.

[2] In Die Anthropologische Bedeutung der Phantasie, 2 vols., Basle, 1946 ('The Importance of Phantasy for Anthropology').

condition of *being directed towards something*, whereby this something may be an object encountered and perceived in the individual's inner world, a product of his mind or of his phantasy, or an activity or work that has yet to be produced. The condition of being directed as such is usually understood as an "intentional" condition, i.e. in accordance with the "purposive" reference to an object actualized in "thinking", as is made manifest above all in the "meaning" of concepts and in the linguistic designations of the objects of perception, which are immanent in the acts of perception, as this or that object. But since the "ratifying", perceiving act of understanding itself possesses an intentional character, one that is directed towards the thing to be understood, both concepts— the concept involved in volitional activity and the concept involved in understanding—achieve parity as it were; and it is this which constitutes optimum intelligibility. Every act of understanding tends to establish this condition of parity. The result of this in many cases—a result which is unintended and often enough unrecognized—is that the substantive meanings which are understood, i.e. seized upon in the act of understanding, are either conceived as intentional concepts from the outset or are unquestioningly reinterpreted as such. What this means is that the intrinsic structure of the act of understanding is set up as the authoritative criterion for the more or less forcible transformation of that which is understood. The reason why this reinterpretation is usually not noticed as such within the sphere of human behaviour and why its consequences within this sphere are not all that dire is that the references to objects and the actions which are of drive origin are nearly always permeated and controlled by (predominantly automatized) acts of will, in respect of which an intentional interpretation is adequate; for the condition of being directed by the will and the condition of being directed by thought (by the understanding) are structurally congruent in the actual deed. But the inadequacy of such an interpretation is clearly revealed in respect of those phenomena, where volitive control more or less breaks down, i.e. in respect of neurotic and psychotic disturbances, faulty actions and above all organic activity which points towards the sphere of extra-human life, within which the rights of teleological explanation have long been questioned.'[1]

The Freudian explanation of such things as faulty actions or neurotic symptoms are all based on the principle of purposive acts of will. Neither Freud nor Jung attempted to distinguish between acts of will and the drives, although the fact of the matter is that, although the drives are able to make use of the will and of motives, they cannot be equated with the will. In

[1] H. Kunz, *Uber den Sinn und die Grenzen Psychologischen Erkennens*, Stuttgart, 1957, pp. 71–2.

failing to separate the drives from the will Freud was strongly influenced by Lipps. And his attempt to comprehend and explain psychic activity in terms of acts of will was the direct consequence of this failure. This process was subsequently adopted, without first being subjected to critical appraisal, above all by the Behaviourist school. It would go beyond the scope of this present investigation to attempt to establish a theory of drives that was more compatible with reality than is the Freudian theory. But no matter what the final form of such a theory of drives may be, what is quite certain is that it must not be teleological, i.e. purposive, in character, it must not impose on nature or the psyche purposes which are quite simply translations of volitional acts to the sphere of drive activity. *Ludwig Klages and H. Kunz, J. Meinertz*[1] and *V. von Weizsäcker*[2] have already published investigations which not only free the drives from the utilitarian 'stock-market' conception which had previously characterized them[3] but which also do justice to the intimate relationship between the drive image (idea, phantasy) and reality and to the infinitely diverse qualitative nature of the drive. L. Klages, taking the phenomenon of love as his theme, demonstrates in the following passage what this concept can actually look like in reality:

'In the first place everybody loves everything that he is capable of loving in a constantly changing fashion in each of the first four seven-year periods of his life, whereupon, after a long period of growing equability and with the gradual decline of sexual drive activity, a considerable change again takes place, which is finally followed in the more or less non-sexual phase by a further transformation of the love impulse. Moreover, everyone loves in a different way in every single period of his life, for he loves with a love that is appropriate to each father, mother, brother, sister, comrades, friend, superior, inferior, workmate, public men, ruler, fellow countrymen, son, daughter, grandchild, wife, lover, etc.; and with even greater differences things which are tinged with love (e.g. memories) and utterly differently animals, plants, districts (like mountains, heath, sea, etc.), home, youth and so on, not to mention completely intangible love objects like his profession, like science, art, religion, motherland, etc. But even within the sphere of the specifically sexually toned love drives one and the same person in one and the same period of life is faced with an abundance of possible modes of loving which are not easily exhausted. For apart from the fact that, due to the abundance of drive formations, this person is capable of alternately experiencing vastly divergent processes as sources of sensual pleasure

---

[1] J. Meinertz, *Psychotherapie als Wissenschaft*, Stuttgart, 1952 ('Psychotherapy as a Science'). [2] V. v. Weizsäcker, *Pathosophie*, Göttingen, 1955. [3] See p. 101 ff.

(the usual combinations: touching and feeling, facial perceptions of the most varied kind, acts such as acts of suffering or of torment which the person inflicts or submits to) the love which this person bears for *one* individual will differ in kind from the love he bears for *another* just as surely as the images of the two individuals, which inspire that love, differ from one another.'[1]

It was characteristic of Freud—in contrast to Klages—that he should try to deprive the drives of all qualitative character and to turn them into sums of excitation of libidinal energy or, alternatively, to speak of them in terms of 'work requirements for psychic life'. The reason why he did so was that he wished to assume a 'transformation' of the drives which would be in accordance with the physical ideas of the transformation of energy and comparable with the concept of the conversion of heat into electricity. Moreover, Freud's concept of the drives constantly fluctuated between a teleological view, which involved the (banal) imposition on to the drives of final purposes, and his above-mentioned attempt to isolate the concept of the drives from all qualitative attributes and to employ it as an abstract quantity, i.e. as energy. (Only in Freud's old age did this fluctuation give way to a kind of mythology of drives in terms of a conflict between Eros and Thanatos.) In its quantitative sense the concept of the drives is supposed to furnish 'causal' explanations, but it is also used—quite arbitrarily—in a teleological sense, when Freud speaks of a drive 'aim', even when this 'aim' is simply the suspension of the somatic source of stimuli.[2] This interpretation of the drives does not differ in principle from the biological view, which, for example, tries to interpret instinctive actions or ontogenetic processes in terms of human actions (entelechy, purposive character of the instincts), an undertaking which in the final analysis is alien to reality. The movement of the drives towards objects is considered by Freud (and Bibring) to be a more or less arbitrary and secondary factor, although it is precisely this factor which constitutes the crucial qualitative character of the drives. In his conception of the drives, even if we disregard the misrepresentation which its teleological and quantitative bias involves, Freud does not escape from the solipsism of the Cartesian system: in the final analysis, as he himself has stated, the drives are auto-erotic. Primal libido finds gratification in itself, and the (unconscious) formula on which Freud's theory of the drives is based is the formula of *masturbation* and not of the environment, not of the partner. In such a theory —whose validity has meanwhile been sharply questioned by the (empi-

[1] L. Klages, *Der Geist als Widersacher der Seele*, Vol. I, pp. 578 ff.
[2] See especially the arguments in the section on The Three Scotomata . . ., p. 504 ff.

rical) observations made by R. *Spitz* and A. Freud—the environment or the partner (the 'object of the drives') must necessarily be secondary, although it is perfectly obvious that the primary relationship of the drives is to the environment, to the partner, to movement.[1]

This fluctuation between quantitative, solipsistic and teleological theory is also characteristic of the libido theory. Freud's requirements in respect of the libido theory are that it should (1) reveal a somatic base in the erotogenic zones, (2) constitute a biological ontogenetic process, (3) explain transformations of drives in energic terms. This theory has already been subjected to such thorough criticism (with which the present author concurs) by so many analysts, chief amongst them *K. Horney, H. Schultz-Hencke* and *P. Federn*, that to criticize it further would be superfluous (see especially Horney's criticism, in which she demonstrates that the neurotic's striving for love cannot in any sense be said to derive from repressed libido). It should perhaps be pointed out in connection with the theory of drives, however, that not only is the concept of 'libido' unable to grasp the qualitative specificity of the impulses which the infant senses as a result of the excitation of the so-called erotogenic zones but that the infant's inability to express itself in respect of those sensations precludes from the outset all possibility of investigating them. The comparison with similar impulses in adults or pubescent children and the clear indications of pleasure which such impulses produce in infants prompted Freud to equate infantile erotic impulses with sexuality. But as a result of this equation the 'libido' was not only required to embrace the specificity of these infantile sensations of pleasure but was also required to cover the whole range of sexuality, including adult sexuality. This was unfortunate, for the concept of the libido was now being asked to cover two qualitatively quite different spheres, namely, the specific sexuality of adults and the unclarified sensations of infants, which meant that it was over-burdened. The further over-taxing of the libido concept arising out of the need to establish a biological (teleological) and energic (abstract and causal) basis for the libido (see above) led to an evaluation of this concept which was full of contradictions and which was not entirely acceptable even to the members of the Freudian school. (Cf. Jones' and Glover's attempts to declare the libido a form of defence against anxiety, see p. 191 ff.) The libido concept becomes even more questionable when Freud speaks of *desexualized* libido in connection with sublimation or when H. Hartmann speaks of 'neutralized aggression'. The need for purely quantitative energy is here made manifest, but so too is the difficulty involved in passing off as unchanged a concept which has been deprived of its

[1] See Klages', V. v. Weizsäcker's and Buytendijk's investigations into the relationships between drive, environment and movement.

actual content (i.e. libido which has been deprived of sexuality). The energic semblance of abstract quantity which was attributed to the libido in a manner that was both pseudo-scientific and unrelated to reality made it possible to speak of a 'reservoir' of libido and thus paved the way for the concepts of narcissism. And now the libido economy—Freud's aim was to express all psychic activity in terms of the libido economy—was obliged to pursue hydromechanical and electrophysical ideas (so-called 'metapsychology)'.

As far as the ontogenetic aspect of libido development is concerned the subtle schemata which Abraham established have already been exposed to doubt within the Freudian school in as far as other Freudian authors (Phyllis Greenacre, Anna Freud, M. Klein) have observed a large-scale over-lapping of the phases and indeed have even questioned the quasi-biological basis on which the importance of these phases rests. Thus the value of Abraham's schemata is purely theoretical. Whether they retain that value will depend on whether the libido theory is retained, which seems scarcely possible in the light of the evidence advanced above.

The over-emphasis of sexuality in Freud's theory of drives, the primacy of the sexual drive over all other drives, which was only subsequently counteracted—due to Adler's influence—by the promotion of the self-preservation drive and the aggressive drive, has also been so exhaustively criticized by others (see *inter alia* Th. *Reik*, E. *Homburger Erikson*, the endeavours of the *New York Group* to accord greater importance to the ego, *P. Federn*, the *Neo-Freudians* and the *philosophically oriented schools*) that there is no need for further criticism here. The suppression of sexuality for sociological reasons and the widespread hostility to the drives which marked late nineteenth-century civilization were largely responsible for the scotomization induced in Freud by sexuality.

The theory of instances is of particular importance in psychoanalysis if for no other reason than that it demonstrated the intimate interaction of vital (drive) and 'mental' capacities. When Freud first became aware of the existence of repression he started thinking along the lines of an active ego which effected repression by an act of will. And so, because the will restrained the drives, this ego, which may perhaps have been derived from analogous concepts of Brentano's, formed the basis for the antithesis between the will and the drives—which means that in this respect it is certainly possible to speak of a 'dynamics' of psychic processes. But very soon Freud initiated the development, whereby the ego and thus in due course the other instances as well (super ego, id) were declared to be drives. The theory of instances was bound to fail when it was called upon to *derive* cognitive and other intellectual functions from the drives, especially from sexuality. It was further undermined by the fundamental condition, one which was also removed from reality, whereby the concepts of the ego and the super ego were on the one hand employed substantially, i.e. in accordance with Freud's earliest conception of the ego, whilst on the other hand they were defined in abstract energic terms. Quite apart from this, however, it is somewhat more than problematical to impose on this poor hybrid concept of the ego an assortment of unrelated conscious functions (in which respect the ego is again considered as a substantial concept) whilst at the same time attempting to establish its genetic derivation as a by-product of the id, as a 'stimulus protection' that has come into being in response to the 'necessities of life'. Before concepts such as comprehension, perception, judgement, deduction, evaluation, not to mention the concept of truth, can be naturalistically 'explained' by this kind of simplifying process they need to be subjected to a more detailed examination, the kind of examination in fact which the phenomenologists have partially initiated without having elicited a critical response from Freud. We have seen from the development which Freud's ego concept has undergone that it is far more over-burdened and over-taxed than the libido concept. Thus the ego is conceived

1. as the will and the centre of activity (1892),
2. as a drive,
3. as energic,
4. as the carrier of the most diverse cognitive and sensitive functions (perception!),
5. as the basis of character attitudes, of defence attitudes,
6. as a 'stimulus protection' of genetic origin,
7. as the dream censor.

The problematical nature of the relationship between super-ego formation and conscience has already been described (see p. 377 ff.). Although the arguments which Freud puts forward in his investigations into group psychology are doubtless acceptable to those who share his theoretical outlook, it is more than doubtful whether the processes of group formation can be reduced to this relatively simple act of collective identification. To the extent to which these processes are intended to represent *a single aspect* of group formation they are feasible.—They are no less hypothetical than the concepts in accordance with which a dream in which, for example, a young girl bites off her father's penis (Fenichel, *Collected Papers*, Vol. I, pp. 39 ff.) is interpreted as meaning that the bitten off (introjected) penis will become the girl's super-ego. Although concepts of this kind, which are by no means rare in psychoanalytic literature and on which Melanie Klein and E. Jones have based their later theses, may have taken the principle of *pars pro toto* into symbolic account in respect of unconscious processes, it would surely be a bold man who would endow them with the quality of scientific truth. The jump from the bitten-off penis to the complex functions of conscience, which, even when conscience is defined as the super ego, embrace the whole of society, is too enormous to permit of its being substantiated by logical argument.

The formation of the concept of the super ego—which has elicited sharply diverging views from Freud's followers, e.g. M. Klein, E. Jones, O. Fenichel, A. Freud, H. Hartmann—was followed by the theories concerning the pre-Oedipal Oedipus phase (see p. 212 ff.) and then by the discussions of those theories, a process which bears an unmistakable resemblance to the disputations which have regularly occurred in the late and decadent periods of particular schools: Athenian sophistry, the Talmudic discussions of the mediaeval Arabs and Jews, the catholic discussions of late scholasticism. The thought of such periods is characterized by lofty abstraction and an extensive diminution of any sense of reality. As is well known, one question which was then a matter of concern referred to the number of angels able to stand on the point of a needle, a question which is justified within the system which posed it, but which in fact transcends the limits of conceivable knowledge. It is arguable that certain disciples of the Freudian school had reached an equivalent stage to this during their founder's life-time. Today, when the British Group opposes the theories advanced by M. Klein, it does so from the point of view of Freudian psychoanalysis on the assumption that this edifice will guarantee authenticity of knowledge. But this is an assumption, for—however dubious M. Klein's hypotheses may be—the method of investigation which she employed, the method of indirect inferences, of 'interpolating' observations of psychoses, of infant behaviour and of adult psychotherapy with 'her own' observations, was *the method which Freud himself used*. And the fact that she came to different conclusions—conclusions which, it is true, critical enquiry reveals as even less reliable than the boldest of Freud's hypotheses—is surely no more than a natural consequence of the uncertainty which must inevitably attend interpretations arrived at by a methodology, which, whilst occasionally assuming the mantle of a scientific discipline, is not in fact scientific.

To sum up: essential though it is to assume the existence of psychic instances, Freud's theory of instances suffers from the amalgamation of quantitative drive abstractions with substantialized ideas which it promoted. What must be said in favour of his theory is that it has revealed the drive aspect of so-called mental functions (ego, super ego), a revelation which, however, questions the whole concept of the instances, since these are only conceivable in substantial terms. An anthropologically oriented theory of depth psychology must always bear in mind that the concept of 'firm structures' within the psychic sphere is probably a misconception. Constant centres of force which fluctuate according to the flow of events and which appear to possess in their relationship to the partner, to the environment, now a 'mental' and now a 'drive' character, probably correspond much more closely to psychic reality. In his study 'Vom Kraftfeld der Seele'[1] *G. R. Heyer* has developed ideas which, although Jungian-oriented, are along these lines. The importance of the 'id' within the psychic structures will be assessed on a later page.

(d) Concerning the Problem of Dream Interpretation, the Wish and the Irrational

The importance of Freud's interpretation of dreams for the psychopathology of the turn of the century and the special position which it occupies within psycho-analysis has already been indicated. The leitmotif of pleasure and displeasure on which the Freudian system of dream interpretation is based and which serves it as a 'guiding principle' is joined by a further specific guiding principle of psychic life, namely the 'wish'. The drives, which follow the pleasure principle in pursuit of their purpose of converting tension into relaxation, can scarcely be considered as a guiding principle in respect of Freudian psychoanalysis. —What is regrettable is that the wish, which in its repressed state becomes a factor of crucial importance for the emergence of dreams, has not been clarified in greater detail either by Freud or by his followers. In Freud's middle and last phases the wish is banished, together with the drives, to the id—but without the sharp distinction being made between wishes, drives, acts of will, hopes and hallucinations which would have been desirable. Freud's failure to clarify the concept of 'wishing' did not, however, prevent him from defining thinking, for example, as a substitute for hallucinatory wishes (see p. 125 ff.) or from stating that only the wish 'is able to encourage the psychic apparatus to work'. (Thinking, which, as is well known, Freud did not rank very highly, is a detour necessitated by experience (the 'necessities of life') and whose object is the fulfilment of (unconscious) wishes. For Freud the act of recognition means establishing the identity of images of perception and memory, a sequence which is supposed to characterize the secondary process and which was *eo ipso* present in the primary process. This extreme positivist interpretation of the process of recognition misses the point both of the process and of the concept so radically that there

[1] G. R. Heyer, *Vom Kraftfeld der Seele*, Stuttgart, 1949 ('On the Field of Force in the Soul').

would appear to be little point in entering into a discussion of this hypothesis.)

In *The Interpretation of Dreams* Freud is also positively obsessed with the systematic representation of psychic activity in terms of energy displacement, as is clearly demonstrated above all by the concepts of the progressive and regressive direction of the sums of excitation (see p. 91 ff.). Although the cathexis and thus the hallucinatory animation of memory images due to the regressive movement of energy would appear to be accepted as a fact within the Freudian school, in reality it is simply an unverified hypothesis, one which does not preclude the possibility of other forms of dream interpretation. Because he was obsessed with energic ideas and with the need to establish a closed energic system in order to explain psychic processes Freud neglected the *real* character of the wish and of the image (so-called memory). He does not enquire into the remarkable fact that man is able to wish, i.e. is able to endure a condition which not only does not signify the realization either of an act of will or of a drive but which actually presupposes their renunciation. The act of will and the act of being driven are both suspended in the wish, from which it is reasonable to assume that the wish constitutes an essential property of man which certainly does not fall into the category of primary psychic impulses in infants let alone into the category of the so-called 'primary process'. Although Freud's observation of wish-fulfilment is surely valid for a large number of dreams it is characteristic of his whole attitude that in this respect also observation should have been thrust into the background by energic considerations which are as abstract as they are fictive. In view of the *frequency with which man realizes his wishes in reality* Freud's thesis that *repressed wishes are the chief source of dream energy* would appear to be dubious. In the 'ideal case' of a man who had at his disposal the material means with which to fulfil 'all his wishes' it would logically follow that such a man would no longer dream. But a view which does not subscribe to the *crass antitheses* which Freud has established between waking and dreaming will come to perceive the wish both in the dreaming and in the waking state as an absolutely essential 'anthropological' attribute of the species 'man'.

As has been stated in the discussion of the principle of pleasure and displeasure Freud's division of the 'psychic apparatus' into a primary and a secondary system is a bold and highly improbable construction even from a purely *biological* point of view. The thought behind it was less concerned with reality than with the establishment of an energic system. But even in psychogenetic terms the primary system (Freud's id of later years), which is said to be under the exclusive control of the pleasure principle and the wish and in which (apparently) irrational chaos reigns, still remains a pure construction, since, as has already been stated, aimless drives or wishes and similarly aimless striving after pleasure do not in fact exist. Wherever psychic activity is observed, it is seen to be directed towards something. The irrational character of the drives or of wishes cannot be accounted for in terms of the chaotic conglomeration in which they appear in the primary system but only in terms of their insatiability, indefatigability and unaccountability. The primary system appears to have been 'inferred', but in reality it constitutes no more than an attempt to accommodate the a-logical in a (topically) organized system by placing it in dialectical opposition to the logical. This a-logical and irrational element, to which, in Freud's view, the postulate of contradiction does not apply, forced itself on his mind as a result of his observations of irrational symptom formations and of the absurd phenomena of dreams. As has already been stated on repeated occasions Freud's achievement consists in the fact that he interpreted these irrational phenomena as *rational acts of will* which had been dislodged, contorted, condensed, distorted, etc. (see also French). But for this process of distortion to be capable of taking place an (unconscious) system had to be assumed which, as it were, first broke down rational thoughts and purposive motives, reducing them to their component elements, and then reconstructed from these elements phenomena which were distorted or contorted and therefore irrational. What is meant by the latent and manifest dream contests is simply that a logical thought—a motive or an act of will—is first reduced to its component parts and then re-formed into manifest dream contents. When the observer recognizes the latent thought in the manifest dream content he is in fact making the return journey from the irrational manifest dream phenomenon to the (apparently) original logical thought. The *apparent intelligence, the frequently admired refinement with which the dream expresses latent dream thoughts, is without question the analyst's own intelligence, which he re-discovers on this return journey, for what the analyst sees in the irrational dream products is his own purposive thinking.* This does not mean to say that at the symbolic level of the dream the patient might not have considered similar 'associations' to those expressed by the analyst in his interpretation.—*The essential value of dream interpretation, i.e. its therapeutic value, will surely lie in the rational and purposive manipulation of irrational images.* Conscious control (will, purpose) is extended to the unconscious, thus establishing a greater degree of security from the irrational. But although the assumption of latent and manifest dream contents is one which facilitates interpretation, it none the less remains a construction since it fails to incorporate the basic function of the psyche, i.e. *its ability to give symbolic and irrational expression as well as rational and purposive expression to its own contents.*

It would appear that Freud 'inferred' the primary system because he saw no other possibility of explaining irrational phenomena save by assuming the existence of a sort of chopper, which made it possible for (1) logical contexts of thought to be broken down (primary system) so that (2) they might be joined together again into new formations in the secondary system (dream work, censorship). But this whole process would appear to be divorced from reality because:

1. The irrational, whose existence is made manifest both in the apparently absurd images and actions of dreams and in the drive section of the psyche, is in principle incapable of logical explanation;

2. all explanations of the irrational attempted by the intelligence are not in fact explanations of the irrational at all but rather explanations of the intelligence itself, which in one way or another always interpolates its own purposive procedures into the non-purposive procedures of the irrational. F. Kraus describes this process in drastic terms when he says that the psychoanalysts are hunting thimbles which they themselves have hidden.

But there is a difference between the purposive explanations of Freudian psychoanalysis and the attempts made by the philosophically oriented schools to discover *a meaning* in the irrational sequences of dream images. This meaning, which C. G. Jung tries to grasp with his concepts of 'individuation', the 'mystical wedding', 'polarization' and the 'night sea journey', is no longer identical with the purposive motivation of acts of will, on which the interpretations of the positivist schools are based (cf. the dream of Irma's injection). This meaning, which the phenomenologists discover in the phenomenon itself, which Jung establishes on the basis of his gnostic-alchemistic view of the world, is absurd when considered in terms of the purposiveness of human activity: neither 'individuation' nor a 'night sea journey' can be considered to serve a purpose. In other words, *the irrational is meaningful but not purposive.* The a-logical, which corresponds to von Weizsäcker's anti-logical, constitutes to my mind the absolute antithesis to the logical. Neither is deducible from, or explicable in terms of, the other. In the positivist analytical schools the a-logical was either treated merely as a secondary, distorted form of the logical or else it was banished to the transcendental sphere as something chaotic and meaningless—and this despite the fact that it was still considered necessary for purposes of 'explaining' a-logical phenomena (dreams, symptoms, faulty actions—Freud's primary system and subsequently his id). The positivist schools failed to master the a-logical, whereas the philosophical schools did succeed in wresting a 'meaning' from it.

Freud perceived the irrational nature of the psyche in numerous different forms. He then proceeded to banish the irrational to the id (the transcendental), where it constituted a negative but indispensable antithesis to the rational and where its activity was restricted, as it were, to breaking down rational motivations (latent dream content). In the interpretation of dreams Freud presented his view of rational motivations governed by the pleasure principle (latent dream content) which proceed in accordance with the concept of human acts of will and also in accordance with the further concept—the chief concept of the psychoanalytic system—of the avoidance of displeasure. This view cannot touch the heart of the psyche, the irrational, since it fails to emerge from the confines of purposively oriented intelligence. *That the psychoanalytic interpretation of the dream—the avoidance of displeasure—and the rational motivations of the dream will be objectively the same as the patient's motivations in many cases is not disputed.* All that is here intended is to indicate (*a*) the limitations of this conception, i.e. the fact of its being divorced from reality, and (*b*) the limitations imposed on the value of dream interpretations within the positivist schools by the fact that they do not permit man to rise above the level permitted by purposive motivations. Since dream interpretation as practised by the positivist schools fails to touch the irrational heart of the psyche and since it is tied to the concept of acts of will, it can only inform man as to *the nature of dreams in their capacity as possible acts of will.* And since the positivist schools equate the drives with the will, it follows that—despite the importance which they attach to the drives—their interpretation does not in fact apply to the drives as such. And so all such interpretations are necessarily restricted to making 'as if' statements, since they fail to grasp the essential nature of the dream, which is its a-logical content (its meaning).

These are the consequences of the positivist view, which, like Freud's own view, although it recognizes the existence of the irrational, 're-presses' it and transfers it to a sphere which completely transcends consciousness. Paradoxical as it may seem, although it was Freud who discovered the irrational for science, it was also Freud who 'repressed' it. (The second paradox in the Freudian system concerns 'thinking', which Freud disparages (see especially p. 91 ff.), although reason and purpose were the sponsors of his system.) But the discrepancy between the irrational and the rational, which is the hallmark of Freud's work, is itself simply a consequence of the process of socialization and civilization, which had progressively expelled the irrational from everyday life until finally it allocated it a place in Freud's system, a place, however, which utterly transcends consciousness. It is wrong to think of Freud as the herald of the irrational in a rationalistic epoch that had lost all sense of purpose. Even in his last phase, when he turns towards the conceptions of Heraclitus, his system still constitutes an attempt to 'rationalize' irrational psychic phenomena, a process which is diametrically opposed to the emancipation of the irrational. The intercourse between the 'ego' and the 'id' which Freud describes in this last phase is certainly a most impressive attempt to recognize the absolute importance of the irrational. But what distinguishes the ego's approach to the id and the barriers, censors and sluices it has to pass through in the process—a process which finishes up with the ego still 'on the outside' —is that it constitutes an act of total repression and not the emancipation of the irrational. Von Weizsäcker has described the irrational element as anti-logic and has traced its course in the phenomena of 'chance'[1] and in the passionate involvements which are a necessary condition of life. The irrational quality of life (which Camus in a different sphere has called the 'absurd'), the irrational quality of individual and national destinies and of human activity as such—no matter how purposive it may appear to be—still remains with us in all its irrationality in spite of the rapid growth of civilization. The clearer our general view of psychic activity becomes (bird's eye view of the general course of an individual's life) the more complicated and confused does such activity appear to be when we attempt to particularize by isolating one—let alone several— of the individual threads from the general maze. The realization that what appears to be a maze is perhaps after all a carpet is likely to come only in rare moments of ecstasy or intuition.

(e) Freud's Three 'Scotomata'; System, Sexuality, Symptom. The crisis of the positivist conception

Freud's system, which he organized in accordance with dynamic (libido-) economic and topical points of view, was his supreme achievement but also his most glaring weakness. No other thinker has equalled the intensity, logic and profundity of his speculation; and the pseudo-scientific nature of his statements has strengthened him and his followers in their belief in the validity of the positivist interpretation of the psyche. But it was precisely these pseudoscientific presuppositions on which his system was based which, as has already been demonstrated, proved most susceptible to serious criticism. For the sake of the system the reality of the psyche, the reality of clinical symptoms, the reality of man were overlooked and a distorted interpretation offered in their place. The real observations which Freud established have by now merged to such a degree with his quantitative, his dynamic and his other systematic concepts that it would be wellnigh impossible to 'distill' or separate the empirical contents from the hypotheses. The incidence of the Oedipus complex, of the fear of castration or of penis

[1] V. v. Weizsäcker, *Pathosophie*.

envy, the possibilities of defence against anxiety, repression, the psychological aspects of the formation of conscience, the effect on the child of environmental influences, Freud's contributions to an understanding of infant development as such, the importance of the child's 'identification' with specific parental attitudes—these constitute only a small selection from the total number of phenomena which Freud originally recorded on the basis of empirical observation. There can in fact be no doubt but that psychoanalytic practice is broadly based on empirical foundations. But, for the reasons given above, the theory of psychoanalysis, its attempts to 'explain' or to interpret (understand) psychic activity, certainly cannot be considered to be well-founded. Observations of the Oedipus complex or of the incest wish admit of such a large number of different interpretations—some of which have been outlined in the aforegoing—that Freud's purely sexual interpretation can scarcely be granted exclusive validity.[1] Freud's system, his positivist 'scotoma', which is typified by his proposition that it is not the phenomena which must be investigated but rather the strivings which are assumed to underlie the phenomena, has led not a few of his followers into a cul-de-sac, from which, as might have been expected in view of the highly involved and highly abstract metapsychological hypotheses which have been advanced and which are not very far removed from pettifoggery, they are scarcely able to extricate themselves. The sterility to which this situation gave rise and which prompted Glover, amongst others, to write that psychoanalysis had made no noteworthy progress since Freud's death[2] had already been censured by Jaspers before the First World War. The stereotype and repetitive way in which the presence of the Oedipus or castration complex was demonstrated both in a wide range of pathological phenomena and in the phenomena of cultural history, of anthropology, of art and philosophy, affords one example of such sterility. The sterile and the stereotype are inherent in the Freudian system, which, when applied in an 'orthodox' and dogmatic manner, merely reproduces itself, repeating trains of thought which Freud had already thought out to their logical conclusion, instead of taking the decisive step forwards from the system to the reality of the psyche and to the reality of the subject with all his crises and passions, his pathic quality and his activity. Freud himself has shown in his philosophical testimony, i.e. in *The Future of an Illusion*, in *Civilization and its Discontents* and in *Moses and Monotheism*, how this system ultimately came to set itself up as the sole arbiter of life and the answer to the riddle of the universe.

[1] At a later date this was supplemented by the 'aggressive' interpretation of the Oedipus complex, which was concerned chiefly with the overpowering of the mother.   [2] Glover, *On the Early Development of Mind*, p. 352 ff.

It should not surprise us to find in this connection that many of Freud's disciples should have followed their master's example, especially in the 'twenties and the 'thirties, by devoting their attentions to the stereotype process described above, whereby, for example, a wide variety of living phenomena are reduced to sexuality and sexual deviations to the exclusion of all else. It is true that Freud has defended himself on repeated occasions against the charge of pan-sexuality and has pointed to the fact that he attaches great importance to the ego drives and the aggressive drives as well as to sexuality. The problematical concept of the 'ego drives' has already been analysed on several occasions in the course of this enquiry—but it is of course perfectly true that if the aggressive drives are taken sufficiently into account, then there can be no question of pan-sexuality where Freud is concerned. But the fact remains that (even in purely quantitative terms) sexuality figures far more than aggression in Freudian psychoanalytic theory and the degree of importance which this theory attributes to sexuality in man is surely excessive. (In this respect see also P. Matussek, K. Horney, E. Fromm, O. Rank, C. G. Jung, V. von Weizsäcker, L. Binswanger, H. Schultz-Hencke *inter alia*.) To consider infant development predominantly from the point of view of sexuality,[1] to single out this one particular drive from the great variety of possible alternatives as being of crucial importance for man's development, is a questionable procedure, but one which has been raised virtually to the status of dogma within the Freudian school. Freud and his followers have even failed to consider the fact that in countless cases so-called 'neurotics' function quite 'normally' where sexuality is concerned and experience far greater difficulty, for example, when required to establish human contact. Quite apart from this, however, Freud has also failed adequately to investigate or clarify the *essence*, the *reality* and the *problem* of sexuality (which is hardly surprising in view of the fact that he usually dealt with sexuality in terms of quantitative 'libido'). His preoccupation with quantitative ideas, with the erotogenic zones and with abstract questions of tension and relaxation was such that it prevented him from seeing the richness and diversity of sexual reality. One aspect of this reality is to be found in the fact that no norm, i.e. no set standard of sexual functioning, can ever be established, since such a norm would necessarily have to be determined by both parties to the relationship in terms of 'bi-personality'. M. Boss[2] has demonstrated that this even holds

---

[1] Cf. for example, *Piaget's* investigations into very early childhood, which reveal a great number of problems in which sexuality plays a subordinate role or is even entirely excluded.

[2] M. Boss, *Vom Sinn und Gehalt sexueller Perversionem*, Bern, 1954. ('On the Meaning and Content of Sexual Perversions'.)

good of perversions (cf. also von Weizsäcker, p. 434, and also the investigations carried out by Kinsey[1] in which this author documented the bewildering diversity of sexual behaviour which utterly transcends the concepts of normality and abnormality). A further aspect of sexual reality and of the problems attendant on it is revealed by the quite extraordinary fluctuations in the degree of importance attributed to sexuality by different cultural and social orders both in modern times and throughout the course of history. This aspect of sexual reality also embraces the connection between sexuality on the one hand and intoxication, orgies and states of ecstasy on the other, all of which played their part in the sexual epidemics which broke out in the late Hellenic period (Dionysian cult), in late Roman times and at the end of the Middle Ages. If justice is to be done to the phenomenon of sexuality, which is an important—although *by no means the most important*—property of the human species,[2] an anthropological or phenomenological interpretation is called for. Such an interpretation would have to embrace both the differences and the similarities between sexuality and love, sexuality and tenderness, sexuality and society, factors which, although clearly of the greatest importance, Freud merely noted in passing (see Freud's definition of love p. 106 ff.).

To sum up: in his enquiries into the problem of sexuality Freud took hysteria as his model, i.e. his observations were made on ladies of a highly civilized and somewhat decadent bourgeois society. The attitude towards sexuality obtaining at the turn of the century—an attitude which no doubt persists even today—caused Freud to mount what might well be called a dialectical counter-offensive which led him to overestimate the importance of sexuality. As a result of this overestimation Freud proceeded to derive all types of clinical (neurotic), social and cultural behaviour from disturbances in the sexual sphere. Sexuality itself, however, was quantified and used as abstract libido. By overestimating sexuality as a quantitative factor Freud and his followers were able to perceive the reality of sexuality, i.e. the abundance of its phenomena, only to a limited degree. Freud's 'scotoma' *vis-à-vis* sexuality derives on the one hand from his overestimation of its importance as a quantitative factor and on the other hand from his underestimation of its importance as a phenomenon.

The characteristic of the third Freudian scotoma is *the overestimation of the symptom at the expense of the sick human being*. Freud was not so much concerned with the hysterical *patient* as with the hysterical, phobic or obsessional *symptom* and with establishing the most probable method

---

[1] Kinsey, *Sexual Behaviour in the Adult Male/Female*, 2 vols.

[2] J. Zutt, 'Über Sexualität, Sinnlichkeit und Prägung', *Beiträge z. sex. Forschung*, Vol. 6, 1955.

whereby this symptom might be logically integrated into his economic, topical and dynamic system. We have already seen how Freud's concept of personality was developed from his concept of the symptom, in other words how the subject, the sick human being, was sacrificed to the concept of the symptom and the system, i.e. was not sufficiently appreciated in his capacity as an independent person with living problems. This is made particularly clear by the case histories which Freud presents, in which he explains the symptoms but does not explain the importance which attaches to any given symptom *in its interaction with other aspects of the total living personality*. In this respect also Freud was far more dependent on the patho-physiology and psychopathology of his time than he realized. The medical men of the turn of the century were just as fascinated by symptoms as was Freud himself and whilst Freud was engaged in trying to trace hysteria in terms of causation they were no less intent on establishing the symptoms of physical illness on the same causal basis. It is only over the past twenty to thirty years that a new conception, in which the symptom appears as a factor of only secondary and occasional importance within the totality of the diseased organism, has begun to emerge in the field of medicine.[1] Freud, however, failed to realize that the neurotic symptom is no more than the ultimate objectively tangible expression of previous faulty attitudes and of a fundamental psychic disturbance.—He did not see the 'neurotic person' because in his positivist and Cartesian view of the world the subject appeared as a phenomenon of mere marginal interest. In such a view any attempt to advance from the symptom to the neurosis rather than from the neurotic person to the symptom would have been to put the cart before the horse. (It was to be the prerogative of the Neo-Freudians to take the first steps in this direction.) To argue that neurotic symptoms are simply a compromise between repressing forces and repressed forces, to argue further that this compromise is responsible for the formation of faulty actions and dreams, is a procedure which, due to its dialectical nature, is calculated to produce banal explanations. For is there any human action which, if considered within the terms of reference of the Freudian system, would not be seen to consist of the interaction of repressed and repressing forces? To how many social or cultural acts might this repressive motivation not be imputed? But in that case how are symptoms to be distinguished from cultural achievements?—The Freudian system furnishes no criteria whereby such a distinction might be made, and it is quite evident that in this system everything is capable of becoming a symptom. And indeed cultural and social achievements, anthropological, historical and philosophical facts have been quite

---

[1] L. v. Krehl pioneered this new attitude and was followed at a later date by von Bergmann, R. Siebeck, V. v. Weizsäcker, Paul Christian and W. Kütemeyer.

consistently interpreted as symptoms, as the resultants of repressing and repressed forces. This would have been quite admissible, if only the interpretations had been restricted to the human acts of will, which Freud (who, it is true, failed to grasp the essence of the will) here too held up as an ideal example of his concept of the symptom. An act of will—e.g. a man takes a glass of water and raises it to his lips because he is thirsty—can certainly be interpreted as a 'compromise' between a drive (thirst) and the will, whereby it is the will which directs the drive towards the particular glass of water and which, moreover, induces the drive to undertake a purposive act. The image of the water, or of liquid as such, for which the thirsty man is longing, is immanent[1] in his thirst —but of all the various means whereby his thirst might be quenched the will (and the conscious ego) *chose* to quench it by the *particular* means afforded by the glass of water. The will also utilizes the kinetic impulse for purposes of quenching the man's thirst by purposively raising the glass of water to his lips without spilling any of its contents. *Klages* has already demonstrated that, if the will is to transform a drive into a purposive act, it must first inhibit the drive and then direct it towards a particular goal. Similar ideas have been advanced by *M. Scheler*,[2] *A. Gehlen*[3] and *Buytendijk*. The idea of an act of will, conceived as a compromise between the will and the drive, which in fact amounts to the inhibition of the drive and its subjugation to the purposes of the will, was the basis of Freud's concept of the symptom, which he presented as a compromise between the repressing forces (will or ego) and the repressed forces (drives). This is particularly evident in Freud's early publications (see p. 48 for publication of 1892) in which he writes of the basic conflict underlying hysteria as a conflict between the *will* and the *counter-will*. Here he still considers the drive to be a counter-will and although this clearly demonstrates his dependence on the concept of acts of will it is no less misleading to interpret the will (counter-will) as a drive than it is to define a drive as the will, which Freud also does at a later date. It was this latter definition, in which drive and will were mistaken for one another, indeed identified with one another, which was responsible for the grave confusions which arose in the Freudian system. For although the act of will, conceived as a 'compromise', between the directing, inhibiting (repressing) will on the one hand and the drive on the other, was held to be binding for all teleological explanations of symptoms, dreams and faulty actions, there was this one crucial

---

[1] See also H. Kunz's interpretation of the drives, which is based on Klages' views, in *Die anthropologische Bedeutung der Phantasie* (see above).

[2] M. Scheler in: *Wesen und Formen der Sympathie* and in *Die Wissensformen und die Gesellschaft*, Bern, 1960 ('Forms of Knowledge and Society').

[3] A. Gehlen in *Der Mensch*.

difference, namely, that the will was equated with the drive or alternatively the drive was defined as the will. And so the compromise character of symptoms and dreams now became a compromise between two drives—a repressing drive (defined as a will) and a repressed drive. The problems attendant on the concept of repression which arise at this juncture have already been discussed. If now we consider the fact that the Freudian system of tracing symptoms back to the compromise between repressing forces and repressed forces, is based (a) on the crucial misunderstanding of the relationship between the will and the drives and (b) on the attempt to interpret symptoms in terms of acts of will (which Freud misconstrued), then it becomes evident that if the system is to be meaningful, then the repressing force must always originate in the conscious ego and the will and never in the drives. The formula whereby the drives and the will join forces to produce activity (whereby the will restrains and inhibits the drives) is here provided by the act of will. Symptoms or dreams are also rendered meaningful by the same token, i.e. as a compromise between the repressing will and the repressed drive. *By contrast the so-called compromise character of the symptoms remains meaningless and self-contradictory when, as in Freud's case, the compromise is supposed to be between two drives (e.g. between the so-called 'self-preservation drive' and sexuality). The Freudian system*—if I may be permitted to stress the point once more—*interprets symptoms, dreams and faulty actions and subsequently all social and cultural phenomena on the basis of a misconception as to what constitutes an act of will, as a result of which the drives and the will are equated.* As has already been pointed out on an earlier page this procedure, whereby human behaviour and human phenomena are interpreted in terms of acts of will, is anyway only partially justified, since it in fact tells us nothing about the majority of such phenomena but simply reads into them purposive ideas deriving from the acts of will. This fact alone must question the very basis of every psychology of understanding constructed along Freudian lines, unless of course an attempt is made to grasp the phenomena involved in psychic activity in *meaningful* rather than *purposive* terms such as that undertaken by the philosophically oriented schools of depth psychology.

The 'dynamic' concept which, together with the economic and topical concepts, Freud and his followers have always considered to be of such great importance for the understanding of psychic processes, can scarcely be held to derive from the dynamics of drive life. It a man feels hunger and thirst at the same time and suddenly finds himself in a position to satisfy both he will certainly undergo a brief and violent conflict between two different drives. He will give in to the drive which proves more *intense*—a concept which is unknown to Freud. To speak of a dynamics of the drives in such a context would only be justified if what was meant by dynamics was a general (inner) movement ('intensity' or 'weakness') of the drives. What Freud and his followers would have us understand under dynamics, however, is a confrontation of forces and counter-forces—analogous to physical ideas—as is made quite clear by the concept of repression. What this amounts to is a dynamics between the will (conscious ego) and the drives. And here too this is misleadingly re-interpreted as a confrontation between forces and counter-forces of pure drive origin. The 'dynamic' viewpoint of the Freudian system derives from the act of will just as the economic (abstract-quantitative) viewpoint represents a compromise between purposiveness and quantity (the best way of distributing energy in a system). We have already seen that the topical viewpoint derives from anatomy.

To sum up: *Freud defines the symptom as a so-called compromise between two drives, whereas in point of fact it represents the transference of an act of will to phenomena which are not primarily governed by the will.*[1] The artifice by means of which Freud was able to interpret symptoms, dreams and faulty actions—and subsequently many, if not all, of the phenomena of social and cultural life—in accordance with the same basic principle and thus to create a psychology of understanding for human behaviour goes back ultimately to the misleading equation which was established between the drives and the will in order that these phenomena might be explained in terms of acts of will. This fundamental error in Freud's conception, which was intensified by the equation of unconscious processes with conscious acts of will, casts considerable doubt on his whole system. *It was at this point that the real crisis of positivist oriented psychoanalysis began, for human nature can only be understood to a very limited extent in the purposive terms appropriate to acts of will.*

(f) Psychic Activity and the Problem of the Irrational

To maintain that psychic activity is entirely irrational would doubtless be an over-simplification, especially in view of the fact that most people believe beyond any possible doubt that the majority of their actions are rationally motivated. Nietzsche—and subsequently Klages—have of course largely destroyed the foundations underlying this belief. Although the question as to whether or to what extent human activity is motivated is far too wide to be suitable for consideration within the framework of this present enquiry, it is a question which psychoanalysis will one day have to face. The irrational and the a-logical, the orphan children of Freudian psychoanalysis, have none the less continued to lead a sort of negative existence within this system, e.g. in the concept of *over-*

[1] Freud adopted this fallacy, together with the catastrophic consequences to which it gave rise, from Herbart.

determination (see *inter alia* the overdetermination of an hysterical fit, p. 96). What overdetermination means is that there is no shortage of rational motives underlying symptoms or dreams, indeed, that there is probably an infinite number of such motives. But then this also holds good for acts of will. Motives can be adduced *ad infinitum* for even the most trivial deed and they become more and more complex the deeper we delve into the personal life and fate of the person who performed the deed. Of course these motives, no matter whether they refer to a symptom or an act of will, do not follow the laws of logic as do the proposition of contradiction or the Aristotelian proposition of the Third Man. And so, if human activity is investigated in detail, it becomes evident that it is fed from an infinite source of conceivable conditions which lend an irrational character to even the most banal activity. In other words, the irrational, which Freud perceived only in the apparent distortions of dream images or symptoms, controls our daily lives to a far greater extent than the founder of psychoanalysis might perhaps have cared to have realized. But the more clearly we are able to discern the irrational and anti-logical in everyday life, *the more questionable the crass distinction becomes which Freud made between conscious and unconscious, between waking and dreaming, a distinction* which was designed to enable him to impose on the irrational a purely negative existence. The observation of the irrational in everyday life—whose most impressive exponent has surely been von Weizsäcker—is likely to lead to a considerable rapprochement between what is conscious, i.e. rational, and what is unconscious, i.e. irrational. Freud's system, as has already been stated, appears to constitute on the one hand an attempt to rationalize the irrational —the id—in terms of acts of will and on the other hand an attempt to cut it off from direct participation in life by banishing it to the unconscious (which transcends consciousness). In the face of such endeavours the present author advances the thesis that the great abundance of phenomena present in life and in psychic activity cannot possibly be understood simply in terms of acts of will. In other words, *irrational and hence unconscious activity is constantly present.* The crass distinction between consciousness and unconsciousness which is characteristic of Freud's system is itself a product of its times. Conscious and unconscious activity are indissolubly fused and, in my submission, any distinction between them is artificial. This does not imply the inauguration of a new psychology of consciousness but rather of a psychology which seeks to trace the unconscious in the conscious and the *conscious* in the *unconscious.* Future research in depth psychology should endeavour to apprehend irrational activity not in the abstract positivist categories (quantity and causality) used by Freud and his school but in the categories of living and hence always *anti-logical* activity whose inception we owe to von Weizsäcker. Von Weizsäcker's enquiries were not restricted to concepts such as personal intercourse, anti-logic and the *meeting*, which have been dealt with in an earlier section of this book, but also embraced, for example, the concept of the nuance. Von Weizsäcker's views on the nuance are quoted at length in the following passage as an example of the sort of psychological and anthropological approach that is needed if the artificial antitheses of Freud's conception are to be overcome:

'But what is a nuance? The word taken from a foreign language cannot really be translated into German. An anthropology of the nuance does not stem from a concept but rather from experience of life, from experience of life of the following order: if a man wishes to be truly human as a judge or as a doctor or as an educator then, after first assessing the objective evidence in accordance with legal, natural and ethical concepts, he will rely more on his feeling than on concepts, he will follow the imponderables, the impressions which reveal themselves only to the subjective mind. And now he will realize that the dehumanized condition of the concepts has been of service to him, since (in accordance with the principle of polarity) it is by virtue of the concepts that the non-conceptual quality of the nuances is made manifest. But the emphasis is still on the elaboration of the non-conceptual nuance: that is what matters, that is the more profitable undertaking.

This experience can be stated more directly. A nuance is always a means of defending a more accurate or better feeling. If I say someone is severe, then the proposition will be meaningful, or rather it will only become meaningful once it is known whether I intended to express praise or censure. For the words alone might indicate that the person was too severe to be just or pleasantly severe and thus able to suppress badness. This longing, defending, penetratively sensitive and humane character of the nuance shows that, to use an expression from mathematical analysis, it possesses a vector quantity, a directed force. Nuances can only be correctly grasped by 'nuanced' receptivity. True, there are intellectual insights, as for example that a good politician will shape great events with a minimum of interference or that subtle differences are superior to coarse distinctions, that coarseness then cannot explain and activate subtlety but that subtlety does explain and determine coarseness. But such intelligence itself rests on a feeling for the nuance.

'If we defend "nuanced" people against the "non-nuanced" we soon come to blows with the latter. Humanity is always disputed. The fact that the nuance has become the spiritual opponent of certain concepts, ideals, absolutisms, dogmas, that it has joined battle with positions of power and dominion is a spiritual reflection of this dispute. By praising the nuance we do not enter into a paradise of peace nor into a house whose occupants live in harmony. The nuance exercises a destructive effect on all absolute ideals, it dulls the cutting edge, blurs the borders, relativizes antitheses, ruins schematic organizations.'[1]

(g) Summary

It is now proposed to set out in contradistinction to Freud's three scotomata—system, sexuality and symptom—a *sketch* for an anthropological view of man which is no longer positivist in essence.

1. Empiricism and Causality. Freud's scientific conception is a fiction in as far as psychic activity cannot be causally explained in the scientific sense. This is not to deny that Freudian psychoanalysis has made a large number of observations which satisfy the requirement of the natural sciences that all observations be empirical. In as far as these observations cast light on *meaningful* relations in the development of human personality (genetic psychology) it is true to say that they reveal possible conditions within this development but *not* necessary conditions. In my submission it is impossible to 'distil' empirical contents from this system of explanations (interpretations), because the only way to reach the observations is via the theses which have subsequently been established and which by now are so interwoven with the observations that to a certain extent every observation, despite its empirical grounding, is in fact an interpretation (e.g. the sexualistic interpretation of the Oedipus complex which was based on empirical observation). Any anthropologically oriented school of depth psychology will certainly have to consider Freud's observations, but it will not be obliged to draw the same conclusions as those drawn by Freud (his system). The so-called causality of psychic activity has to be placed in firm contradistinction to its over-determination and thus to its a-logical character. Moreover, so-called unconscious motivations are really interpretations of psychic activity based on the concepts of acts of will, whereas in reality such motivations are to be found in this form only where acts of will are actually involved.

2. Affect and Idea. The concept of the arbitrary and mechanistic separability of affect and idea, which formed the basis of Freud's conception of neurosis, must be replaced by the concept that affect and idea are essentially connected. Only the will is able to place affects and ideas in arbitrary contradistinction to one another.

3. In contrast to Freud's hedonistic conception (pleasure and reality principles) the view is advanced that, due to his immanent psychic structuring, man is so involved in the process of coming to terms with his environment (reality and displeasure) that he will either accept this

[1] V. v. Weizsäcker, *Pathosophie*, pp. 147–8.

process as a pleasurable source of productivity, self-advancement and self-development or he will be destroyed by his environment. Freud's ideas on the connection between the pleasure principle and the principle of the conservation of energy and between tension and relaxation are rejected as pure fictions.

4. In respect of the dialectical principle of psycholoanalysis the reality of the antitheses which govern psychic life is conceded but with this rider: that man (and perhaps only man) is endowed with the ability to progress from such antitheses (ambivalence) to a synthesis as a result either of a sudden decision or of a continuous development.

5. Repression and defence processes are also to be considered as specifically human and immanent, i.e. not secondary, abilities which enable man to assert himself *vis-à-vis* the environment and the partner. The limitations, the Cartesian solipsism, of the Freudian concepts of repression and defence have already been pointed out.

6. The solipsistic and chaotic character of Freud's view of the drives has already been described. By contrast the anthropological view characterizes the drives as being related in terms of organization (organized *vis-à-vis* other things). The libido theory with its problematical hybridism, which requires it to embrace both sexual and pre-sexual phenomena, is rejected. Whilst recognizing the unavoidable necessity for assuming the existence of instances, Freud's theory of instances is criticized above all for having attempted to substantiate the drives in quantitative terms and for having interpreted the structures in both substantial and purely energic terms. It is suggested that Freud's theory of instances be replaced by a 'theory of structures' based on the concept of centres of force.

7. In respect of dream interpretation Freud's tendency to interpret irrational activity in terms of acts of will (cf. also his conception of the drives) has already been demonstrated. Evidence was adduced to show how Freudian psychoanalysis failed to overcome the problem posed by the irrational and how it came to establish dichotomies between logical and a-logical, conscious and unconscious, dreaming and waking, which were entirely divorced from reality. In contrast to these hypotheses the view is advanced that the nature of life and the essence of the soul are *quite simply* irrational and that categories must be developed which would comprehend the irrational, not in quantitative terms, but in terms which are appropriate to its own specific manner (cf. von Weizsäcker). The view has also been advanced that the dichotomy between conscious and unconscious, between dreaming and waking, is artificial and divorced from reality and that in actual fact the similarity between dreaming and waking, waking and dreaming, consciousness and unconsciousness is far greater than is suggested by the Freudian conception.

C

THE RELATIONSHIP BETWEEN THE VARIOUS SCHOOLS OF DEPTH PSYCHOLOGY AND S. FREUD

(a) *Characteristics common to both Freud and the various Schools of Depth Psychology*

Whilst the Neo-Freudian and the philosophically oriented schools of depth psychology hold certain basic views in common with Freud, views which constitute a common, empirical and, as it were, non-doctrinal basis, they also diverge from Freud in other fundamental respects. The views which all the other schools, including L. Binswanger, V. von Weizäcker and personal analysis, *share with* Freud are listed below:

1. The distinction between a conscious and an unconscious mind and the assumption of some form of 'repression' ('inhibition').
2. The importance of environmental influences, especially parental influences, for the development of personality.
3. The importance of inner conflicts (conflicts of drives or of instances) for the development of personality and for mental 'health' or 'illness'.
4. Freud and the Neo-Freudians hold a largely determinist view of psychic activity. The philosophically oriented schools including Jung —although his relationship to indeterminism is not entirely clear— keep to areas of the human personality which are indeterminist (see also E. Fromm).
5. With the exception of L. Binswanger and V. von Weizsäcker all schools of analysis pursue 'dialectical psychology' (see above, p. 465 ff.).
6. The importance of so-called constitutional and hereditary factors is also recognized by all schools. (Although in this respect the boundaries are particularly fluid, e.g. just what are the hereditary factors in respect of certain distorted attitudes and what is identification with parents and thus conceivable defence against anxiety?)

Despite the great differences which existed between the various analytical schools which had seceded from Freud, e.g. between the Neo-Freudians and C. G. Jung, they were at one in their desire to overcome the three Freudian scotomata, *viz.* the system, the symptom and sexuality. Although in attempting to extend the limits which Freud had here imposed they discovered much that was new and important the Neo-Freudians, C. G. Jung, O. Rank and the philosophical thinkers (with the exception of von Weizsäcker and L. Binswanger) were unable to avoid new oversimplifications. The fact that they all disassociated themselves from Freud's proclivity towards concepts which, like that of the libido, were both formally and materially overburdened, did not prevent them from expanding and belabouring their own concepts to a point where they became even less precise than his. (This is particularly true of a large number of Jung's concepts, see below p. ·535 ff.) The Neo-Freudians have simplified human nature to a very considerable degree especially in those areas where they have been at pains to overcome Freud (see below p. 525 ff.).

(b) The Neo-Freudians

The crucial importance of Neo-Freudianism as compared with orthodox Freudianism lies in the phenotypical emphasis which it lays on 'the neurotic personality'.[1] Freud was so fascinated by symptoms that the 'sick neurotic personality' appeared to him in its capacity as a total human being only as a background figure of a highly problematical nature. Even in A. Freud's book on the *Ego and the Mechanisms of Defence*, a book which was so very important for the development of the Freudian school, although the possibilities of defence against anxiety are systematically presented, the human being, who never applies these so-called mechanisms of defence in the 'abstract', is scarcely mentioned in terms of the complex totality which in fact he is. On the contrary, A. Freud's endeavours are directed towards prescribing clear-cut definitions of the mechanisms of defence, which she then proceeds to apply as if they were prescriptions. The crucial difference between the Neo-Freudian and the Freudian schools lies in the degree of importance which they attach to environmental influences for the development of neurosis. Both schools concede that constitutional—hereditary—factors exercise an influence. In the Neo-Freudian view, however, it is above all the environment which lays in infancy the seeds of subsequent neurosis. (Insecurity with K. Horney, pampering and severity with Schultz-Hencke.) The Freudians on the other hand tend to think—although in the present circumstances no firm conclusions can in fact be drawn in this respect—that the environment merely acts as a *release mechanism* for the complexes but that it is the complexes which actually produce the neurosis. For example, weaning or the existence of fathers and mothers are factors which, although subject to certain variations, have followed the same basic patterns at all times in a large number of different cultures. Accordingly the child experiences weaning or cleanliness training as a denial (castration) whilst the existence of father and mother will *eo ipso* call forth rivalry (Oedipus complex).

[1] See Sub-section (g), *The Specific and Unspecific Quality of Neurosis*, p. 556 ff.

This kind of development is considered normal. The child is only likely to become neurotic if as a result of additional burdens—insecurity, severity or pampering—it becomes fixated to the complexes, i.e. if normal maturation does not take place.

That this discrepancy between the Freudian and the Neo-Freudian view as to the origins of neurosis is really quite unnecessary seems palpably obvious. If the Neo-Freudians were to concede that certain complexes, such as the Castration or Oedipus complex, which they themselves imply, actually exist, if over and above this they were prepared to consider their investigations as an empirical complement to particular fundamental Freudian conceptions, then the gap which now separates the two schools might be bridged (see esp. below, p. 556 ff.).

(i) A. Adler

Adler's attempt to consider man as a *totality*, a totality whose chief characteristic was the antithesis between his feelings of inferiority and his ambitious striving for power, constitutes his principal achievement. In contrast to Freud, who took the symptom as his point of departure, Adler treated the sick human being as an entity and looked upon neurotic symptoms as a *secondary* product arising out of the conflict between feelings of inferiority and over-compensation. The fact that Adler then proceeded to incorporate into his conceptions very considerable simplifications regarding human nature, simplifications which were quite as astonishing as those advanced by Freud, has already been mentioned. Like the other Neo-Freudians —with the exception of E. Fromm—he reveals a tendency to establish *one* correct observation (in his case the conflict between man's feelings of inferiority and his striving for power), which he then proceeds to regard as the sole activating source of human behaviour. And so, although Adler avoided the error of attempting to trace specific phenomena back to 'primary' energic processes, i.e. to energic processes underlying those phenomena, he none the less fell a victim to the 'reductivism' (i.e. the misconstrued process of causality), of which this error was a product, as a result of the disastrous bias—disastrous because divorced from reality—which he revealed. Although Adler tried to give man priority over the symptom he still fell a prey to bias and generalization.

(ii) K. Horney

K. Horney was less prone to the weakness for further simplifications to which Adler succumbed. Her first book, *The Neurotic Personality of our Time*,[1] made a powerful plea for the 'neurotic personality' as a phenotype. Horney describes this neurotic personality with the aid

[1] *The Neurotic Personality of Our Time*, New York, 1936.

of clinical material drawn from a wide variety of cases and in terms which are understandable to the layman. Whilst specifically neurotic faulty action such as the neurotic need for love or recognition, neurotic perfectionism and hypercriticism, neurotic fears and aggressions all form part of K. Horney's central theme, neurotic symptoms such as occur in obsessional neuroses or phobias do not. From this it is evident that in Horney's view the disturbance from which the neurotic personality suffers relates primarily to the totality of his psychic strivings, drives and tendencies and that the Freudian practice of observing neurotic symptoms in isolation cannot do justice to the neurotic personality. In such a view the 'meaning' of the particular symptom —its purpose—, the possibility of resolving it by means of so-called causal reductions is only of secondary importance. For example, Horney is not interested in establishing whether a person, who is rendered incapable of realizing his full potential because of the hypercritical attitude he adopts towards his own achievements, is suffering from a pathogenically aggravated super-ego resulting from infantile penis introjection. The metapsychological questions formulated by Freud were quietly dropped by the Neo-Freudians as being insoluble and instead of engaging in speculative research they concentrated on furnishing detailed accounts of the innumerable ways which the neurotic discovers of avoiding a confrontation with himself. But the limitations which this method of procedure necessarily imposed on more fundamental enquiries into psychic life was accompanied by the danger, one which also threatened K. Horney, of simplifying the highly complex factors involved in the neurotic personality. Striving for dependence rather than independence, fear of a loss of love and adaptation to the environment, aggressive behaviour as an overcompensation for feelings of inferiority are forms of neurotic negation and human inadequacy which do not exhaust the phenomenon of illness. The particular quality of the 'neurotic personality' is dangerously emaciated as a result of new generalizations and although Horney avoids Adler's simplifications her psychology none the less becomes dialectical to a certain extent. *T. W. Adorno* writes as follows on the dangers of this kind of psychology:

'This ready-made enlightenment not only transforms spontaneous reflection but also analytic insights, whose force is equal to the energy and passion with which they were established, into mass products and the painful secrets of an individual life, which even the orthodox method is inclined to reduce to formulae, into glib conventions. The dissolution of rationalizations itself becomes a rationalization. Instead of accomplishing the task of self-reflection the enlightened acquire the ability to subsume all conflicts of drives under concepts such as "inferiority complexes", "mother fixation", "extrovert" and "introvert", concepts which in the final analysis are quite incapable of dealing with such conflicts. The terror inspired by the abyss of the ego is removed by the consciousness that what we are actually dealing with here is not so very different from arthritis or sinus troubles. As a result the conflicts lose their menace. They are accepted; but they are certainly not healed. On the contrary, they are simply built into the superstructure of normalized life as an unavoidable component. At the same time they are absorbed as a social evil by the mechanism of direct identification which fuses the individual with the social order and which has long since adopted the supposedly normal patterns of behaviour. The erstwhile catharsis, whose successful outcome was in any case problematical, is replaced by the pleasure gained from being a fellow-representative of the majority "in one's own weakness" and consequently by the prestige previously enjoyed by the inmates of sanatoria as interesting pathological cases, as also by the privilege of proving oneself, by virtue of one's very defects, a rightful member of the collective and of assuming its power and grandeur for oneself. Narcissism, which, with the disintegration of the ego, was deprived of its libidinal object, is replaced by the masochistic pleasure of no longer being an ego; and there are few properties which the rising generation guards more jealously than its egolessness, which is its one common and permanent possession. In this way the sphere of objectification and of normalization is extended into its most extreme antithesis, the sphere of alleged abnormality and chaos. The incommensurable is made commensurable as the incommensurable. And the individual is scarcely capable of any impulse which he could not, if called upon to do so, quote as an example of this or that publicly acclaimed constellation. Such identification, which is established externally and, as it were, beyond the field of force of its own dynamics, joins meanwhile with the genuine consciousness of the impulse in order ultimately to do away with that impulse. It becomes a reflex of stereotype atoms acting on stereotype stimuli which can be switched on and off at will. Moreover, the fact that psychoanalysis has been conventionalized is bringing about its own castration: the sexual motives, which are partly denied, partly approved, are not only rendered harmless but also entirely ineffectual. Together with the fear to which they give rise there also disappears the pleasure to which they might give rise. And so psychoanalysis, having itself taught the doctrine of substitution, itself falls victim to that very doctrine by its insistence on substituting an unrelated external world for the acquired super ego. This last theorem of bourgeois self-criticism on the grand scale[1] has become a means of perfecting the process of bourgeois self-estrangement

[1] This refers to Freud's Psychoanalysis.—Ed.

in its final phase and of thwarting the discovery of the age-old wound, which could give hope of improvement in the future.'[1]

An ideal environment would presumably make neurosis impossible in Horney's view. Such a view would appear to be mistaken, for it fails to take into account the individual's reactions, which are determined by the identification and instances at his disposal and which, since they are subject to variation from case to case, are incalculable. Even the best of parents with the greatest possible understanding for their children and who provide the most harmonious home conditions are no guarantee against the possible emergence of a neurosis at a later date, because a human being's reaction to his environment does *not* reflect that environment in the sense that a harmonious environment will automatically produce harmonious, un-neurotic individuals. But K. Horney's view might be taken to imply that such is in fact the case, for in her view human reactions are largely *reflex actions*. The formula according to which 'harmonious childhood environment' = 'un-neurotic individual' and 'disharmonious environment' = 'neurotic individual' would appear to be valid only to a limited and unverifiable extent. Although in actual fact no definite conditions have as yet been established for the emergence of neuroses, what does appear to be decisive is the 'manner' in which the individual concerned integrates the relevant material. This 'manner' of integrating embodies the imponderables which were established by Freud when he described the way—one largely independent of the environment—in which the individual comes to terms with *his own* drives, wishes and demands. And this 'manner' presupposes the existence of 'instances' of one kind or another. For example, whether a father is friendly or angry, i.e. whether the super ego is 'wide' or 'narrow', whether a mother is loving or cold, i.e. whether her inner-psychic representation is loving or cold, *in either case* it is possible for feelings of aggression and guilt to be roused in the child. In the first case the child would develop guilt feelings because it had not been punished for its aggressions, whilst in the second case it would develop both aggressions and guilt feelings as a defence against the 'angry' father. The occasional constellation of 'good' or 'bad' ('angry') imagines (*not* projection!), which for the most part hold no brief for environmental objectivity, must surely be considered as an empirical fact, at least in respect of the first few years of life. Certainly this fact is born out by A. Freud, D. T. Burlingham and R. Spitz when, for example, they describe how a so-called Oedipus complex can exist in a 'pre-formed' condition even in the absence of parents and may well emerge immediately parental figures appear. K. Horney wrongly tries

[1] T. W. Adorno, Minima Moralia, Berlin and Frankfurt am Main, 1951, pp. 110-13.

R*

to deny these facts which presuppose the necessity for assuming the existence of psychic instances and whose development would appear to proceed *independently* of the environment. If K. Horney (like Fromm) still occasionally employs the concepts of the ego and the super-ego she does so primarily because she wishes, for example, to contrast the 'super ego' with the genuine conscience on the one hand and to re-establish the ego as an expression of self-realization on the other. But the fact that K. Horney uses these concepts at all only goes to show that we simply cannot get on without inner-psychic instances. And so when she rejects Freud's theory of instances she finds herself on shifting ground. But Horney's limitations, her weakness in respect of the instances, are amply made up for by the detailed description of the inadequate neurotic personality which she established and which has added a new and important dimension to our conception of the sick person.

(iii) *H. Schultz-Hencke*

With certain modifications the problems dealt with in connection with K. Horney are the same as those which face us in respect of Schultz-Hencke. Although he is more scientific and considerably more systematic in his approach than K. Horney the problems attendant on his attempt to pursue a dynamic concept of depth psychology *without instances* and *without complexes* are plain to see. Certainly Schultz-Hencke's depth psychology is dynamic in the sense that it involves the inhibition of expansive forces (drives) by counter-forces. But it would be asking too much of Neo-Freudianism if we were to expect an explanation from this quarter as to what it is in man that maintains the inhibition of particular drives. The Neo-Freudians are not interested in the substratum underlying the particular inhibition, which is what actually produces the neurotic faulty attitudes. It is possible that by restricting themselves to descriptions of forces and inhibiting counter-forces they achieve a certain initial freedom. Schultz-Hencke's statements are based on just a few facts—but they are important facts—and of the various Neo-Freudian schools it is doubtless true to say that his is the most securely based on empirical observation. Once the therapist knows which drive regions are inhibited Schultz-Hencke's system enables him to apply the 'lever' correctly and effectively. But when Schultz-Hencke attempts to derive from contexts established by empirical observation statements of *universal validity* his method becomes questionable. Even if the inhibition of, for example, aggressive motor activity in respect of obsessional neurotics has been 'statistically' proved it is not permissible —in the light of what has been said about scientific methodology (see p. 443 ff.)—to draw the general conclusion that the inhibition of such drives will lead *eo ipso* to obsessional neurosis. Moreover, the explanation of, for example, motor-aggressive inhibitedness as a consequence of civilization is not specific enough to permit the specificity of such a complex structure as that of obsessional neurosis to be derived from it. This criticism also holds good for the other theses in which Schultz-Hencke deduces specific neurotic illnesses from specific drive inhibitions and inferior functions). Here too all that Schultz-Hencke and his followers have done is to note new aspects of a (conceivably) pathological development in the individual which had not previously been established to the same extent either by the Freudians or by other schools.

The problems posed by the instances, the unconscious, the 'defence mechanisms', the repression and the emergence of complexes can no longer be denied and urgently await a solution. The 'solutions' which have been furnished to date differ greatly from one another and some of them are self-contradictory. But a self-contradictory solution which does at least attempt to satisfy the complexity of psychic Being is probably preferable to one that either fails to recognize the problems at all or greatly simplifies them.

And yet a careful analysis of Schultz-Hencke's psychology reveals his dependence on Freud in all essential respects. His dream interpretations, for example, presuppose the whole mechanism of Freudian dream interpretation, which means that by implication they also presuppose Freud's views on the pre-conscious and the unconscious, on censorship, wish-fulfilment and on the instances, towards which, in their metapsychological capacity, Schultz-Hencke is extremely reserved. The concept of 'inhibition' is identical with Freud's concept of repression, save that of the two the concept of repression—despite the fundamental objections to which it gives rise (see p. 477 ff.)—probably affords a more adequate description of the process whereby the phenomena of consciousness are transferred to the unconscious. Schultz-Hencke's theory of drives is based to a considerable extent on *Abraham's* work. In his interpretation of obsessional neurosis, for example, Schultz-Hencke is obliged to have recourse to the Freudian hypothesis of the separability of affects and ideas.[1] And in his descriptions of other psychic phenomena Schultz-Hencke also employs the concepts of projection and *identification*. To some considerable extent therefore Neo-Freudianism finds itself serving two masters.

(iv) *E. Fromm*

E. Fromm occupies a special position amongst the Neo-Freudians since his point of departure is primarily philosophical. He might in fact be considered with equal justification as belonging to the group of philosophically oriented depth psychologists. But then he combines his

[1] *Der gehemmte Mensch*, pp. 285 ff. ('Inhibited Man').

philosophical conception with sociological observations and with the 'environment theory' of the Neo-Freudians. His basic idea (which closely ressembles the views advanced by *Rank* in his second phase) that neurosis occurs when man shuns freedom must surely eclipse Freud's positivist conception of man, not only because Fromm here declares war on psychological and metaphysical determinism but above all because he tries to establish a new concept of man, one which is no longer determined by purposive acts of will. Freedom is not a 'purpose'. With Fromm meaningful activity makes its entrance into the world of psychology, man is addressed as a living creature and raised above the purposive level of thought of rational and animal psychology. Fromm— like Rank—is aware of the anti-logical processes involved in acts of decision and responsibility. He evaluates clinical symptoms as being of secondary importance only and accords them their proper place within the total phenomenon of 'man'. Like the other Neo-Freudians Fromm failed to recognize the problem posed by the instances and the difficulties which prevented Neo-Freudianism from establishing its independence from Freud in this respect. But then the clinical investigation and description of neurosis was not his primary concern.

(v) *Sullivan, French, Rado*

Sullivan, French and Rado took psychoanalysis and turned it into a combination of Behaviourism and reflexology. With their conceptions, e.g. Sullivan's conception of the self, which are concerned merely with the reflex action of environmental recognition and which may well have been prompted in the first instance by the need for patent solutions capable of general dissemination, Neo-Freudianism reached new 'lowlands' (or superficies) of the human mind. However much Sullivan may emphasize 'inter-personal' relations, however much he may try to overcome Freud's solipsism, he remains a true disciple of Descartes by virtue of his reflexological ideas. The reflex swallows up both the subject and the partner. And in no sense can it be said of Sullivan that he considers the concept of partnership to be immanent in human development in the sense of the 'absolute We'. Sullivan's idea of interpersonal relationships—which is in complete accord with the principles of the (English) Enlightenment—is restricted to the concept of human interdependence for purposes of survival. It has already been pointed out that for the behaviourists survival is the whole purpose of life. Irrational forces such as drives, wishes, hopes and fears are considered only from the point of view of man's struggle for existence. In other words, apart from Fromm the Neo-Freudians—like Freud—deal with irrational forces in terms of acts of will. In his *Integration of Behaviour* French considers human behaviour to be strictly purposive. In his conception, which, by comparison with Freud's conception, is greatly simplified and bereft of both instances and censorships, irrational behaviour appears as planned activity which has failed to achieve its purpose. The reflex schema, especially the conditioned reflex, is considered to be the actual and the only 'guide line' for human activity, a view which resurrects Freud's mechanistic concepts, according to which the primary process was a reflex action (see p. 79 ff.). At this point positivism takes total possession of the psyche and does not fail to furnish simplified causal explanations of neurosis. Rado's interpretation of sexual perversions goes straight back to the simple trauma theory which Freud had already abandoned. *One* specific childhood experience, which in most cases triggers off anxiety, is assumed to be the cause of perversions in the same way as bacteria are assumed to be the cause of disease. Even if we disregard the problem of 'Explaining and Understanding' there is no denying the fact that this method of procedure is both arbitrary and pseudo-scientific, but since this matter has already been dealt with in the critical appraisal of Freud's works there is no need to go into it again here. From the behaviourist point of view it is regrettable that man should still possess drives, wishes and hopes, anxieties and passions, for if he did not the behaviourist interpretation of human reality would be true. However, like Freud, the Behaviourists are brought low by the undeniable fact that there are irrational forces which remain immune to all purposive interpretations. The naïveté with which the Behaviourists advance their theses whilst remaining totally unaware of the very existence of certain fundamental problems of human reality can only be explained in terms of a sociological phenomenon: Western civilization, fascinated as it is by the purposive processes of technical thought, can only understand itself in terms of utility. Intellectual thought is falling into decline and sterility and is acquiring the insipid flavour of tinned goods. Despite his dependence on positivism Freud still possessed a speculative power which, although it obliged him to think in positivist categories (quantity), also drove him to the unconquered borders of the a-logical and irrational. He was a 'profound' thinker in that he was loth to accept patent solutions and was prepared to abandon hypotheses which he himself had put forward. By contrast the Behaviourists are 'shallow' thinkers, for they repress a large part of the problems of human reality and psychic activity and are constantly on the lookout for solutions which are capable of general dissemination but which are not necessarily true or even accurate.

(vi) *Summary: Freud and the Neo-Freudians*

The dependence of the Neo-Freudians on Freud is not limited to the fundamental points which all the analytic schools have in common with him. The chief reason why the Neo-Freudians (with the exception of E. Fromm) depend on Freud is that they have failed to disassociate themselves both in their critical and their fundamental thought from Freud's positivist bent. This does not mean to say that, amongst other things, their anthropological and cultural investigations did not yield a rich harvest of empirical material with which they were able to demonstrate the absurdity of, for example, Freud's thesis that cultural institutions are brought about solely as a result of drive activity. But since—despite the investigations carried out by Kardiner and others—they did not succeed in establishing the independence of such cultural activity, but instead (due to their failure to introduce a new concept of repression) continued to derive cultural activity from the interaction of the drives and the repression *of the drives* by cultural institutions, they did not really overcome Freud in this respect either. As has already been stated (see p. 311 ff.), Kardiner's investigations into the culture of the Aloresians, for example, throws no light at all on the question as to what produces what, i.e. is the severity and lovelessness of the children's upbringing the product of their suspicious and hostile ('anal-erotic') character or is it the other way round?

Quite apart from such considerations, however, the Neo-Freudians also have the following points in common with Freud:

1. Psychic processes are explained in causal terms (especially by the Behaviourists) in accordance with the formula: trauma = cause of illness.
2. The principle of pleasure and displeasure is accepted in a positivist sense.
3. The theory of the separability of affects and ideas is retained (not always explicitly but certainly by implication).
4. Drive activity and irrational expressions of psychic life (dreams, symptoms) are dealt with in terms of acts of will.
5. Repression and other defence attitudes are dealt with by analogy with Freudian procedure, whilst the concomitant problems posed by the instances are avoided.

In view of the unanimity which exists between the Freudians and the Neo-Freudians in respect of these fundamental issues it is perhaps not unreasonable to ask why we should have Neo-Freudianism at all. The explanation of human behaviour which the Neo-Freudians offer is also based on a positivist theory and does not differ in any essential respect from Freudian theory. Their rejection of the theory of instances is *not* due to their having realized that Freud's theory of instances is false but rather to their recognition of the limitations to which human knowledge is necessarily subject. Although the Neo-Freudians reject

Freud's system as a metapsychological instrument designed to explain psychic activity in quantitative terms—e.g. theory of instances and libido theory—they adopt his positivism as a fundamental scientific attitude. There are two possible explanations for their rejection of the system: either they reject it because they realized that, due to its consistent positivism, it was divorced from reality and thus misleading, or they rejected it out of resignation in the face of the limits which are necessarily imposed on psychological enquiry. Only the latter explanation can possibly hold good for Neo-Freudianism, whose resignation in the face of research has stamped it as a hybrid structure, one which clearly reveals its essential affinity with its original creator (Freud). In other words, the Neo-Freudians failed to overcome Freud's first 'scotoma', his system, and simply 'suppressed' it in its quantitative, metapsychological capacity, whilst none the less constantly assuming its existence (see above), e.g. in their explanations of dreams or of symptoms. The Neo-Freudians interpret Freud's second 'scotoma', the symptom, like Freud himself, as a 'compromise' between different forces, but, unlike Freud, they attribute only secondary importance to it. In the Neo-Freudian view the neurotic personality, who, it is true, follows the pleasure principle in the approved positivist manner, must first be assessed as a phenotype within the context of his environment before his symptoms are organized into a possible meaningful relationship. The Neo-Freudians were more successful in disassociating themselves from sexuality and the libido theory (Freud's third 'scotoma') than they had been in disassociating themselves from the system and the symptom. True, they failed to solve the problem of so-called psychic energy, whose solution Freud aspired to when he postulated his libido theory. If we assume with Schultz-Hencke, for example, that there are several types of drive, which, however, are not connected to each other by means of a biologically determined process of libido development, then we open the door to an unlimited plurality of drives. The problem of having to choose between a uniform biologically determined libido development and a plurality of drives which are only vaguely related to one another was 'solved' by the Neo-Freudians when they opted in favour of the latter alternative.

Despite these fundamental objections to Neo-Freudianism this movement has undoubtedly made an important contribution towards our understanding of human and more especially neurotic behaviour.[1] This contribution was made chiefly within the greatly enlarged context of a psychology of conflicts, a fact which is hardly surprising, for a *psychology of conflicts* (*without* instances! [see above]) is what Neo-

[1] See especially the chapter on 'The Specific and Unspecific Quality of Neurosis', pp. 556–8.

Freudianism is chiefly about. By enlarging the spectrum of human conflicts in this way the Neo-Freudians have opened a new field to the therapist. It is this which constitutes their essential achievement.

(vii) *Pre-formation, Instances, Environment*

The need to assume psychic instances—although not necessarily psychic instances of a positivist Freudian kind—has been mentioned on repeated occasions. Freud and his school have tended to allot an increasingly important and exclusive role to the instances and 'pre-formed complexes', which in their view are released *eo ipso* in a child's development and in respect of which the environment is a factor of only secondary importance, functioning simply as a release mechanism. By contrast the Neo-Freudians consider that—apart from hereditary and constitutional influences—the only factor of importance for the emergence of neurosis is an unhappy childhood environment. The empirical observations which the Neo-Freudians, especially Schultz-Hencke and the Behaviourists, have collected, in support of their view do *not* in fact *contradict* the results arrived at by the Freudian school. If the Neo-Freudians were prepared to accept that the factors which they advanced as the determinants of neuroses—severity or pampering, excessive demands, withdrawal of love, insecurity, anxiety, etc.—are only their immediate cause, i.e. the release mechanisms which activate the complex from a 'latent' to an active condition, the quarrel between the two schools might be settled.

Only the intimate fusion of individual and environment, which von Weizsäcker with his *Gestaltkreis* and his revolving door principle described as simultaneous giving and taking, is capable of illuminating the basic anthropological condition of 'Being in the World' (Heidegger). *Those factors which are held to be immanent* (see p. 469 ff. regarding the pleasure principle and p. 477 ff. regarding repression) *and those factors which are brought out by the environment determine each other: the child who chooses to play the role of the 'weak' or 'strong' father, of the 'cold-hearted' or 'warm-hearted' mother, and thus enacts pre-formed, i.e. imma-nent, complexes, is in fact realizing the indissoluble unity which exists between its environment and itself.* The question as to what is primary and what is secondary is no longer of any relevance when man and the environment are indissolubly united from the outset in the pattern of the *Gestaltkreis*. Or to quote Gehlen:

'And so the character of a man always contains what he has *become*, to be precise, what he *himself* has become, whereas in the twin concepts of disposition and environment the self does not even appear. Unfortu-nately these twin concepts are all-powerful in modern psychology. But they are also quite useless, and that for two reasons: firstly, because the "dispositions" are merely inferred from the behaviour, a procedure which involves the abandonment of the critical moment of the action: for every inclination which has achieved active expression has already become more than an attitude or is at least already in principle a conceivable object of such an attitude. And secondly the expression "environment" remains completely undefined: it can scarcely be intended in terms of a biological environment, for this, as we have already seen, is a concept taken from animal psychology. In the human sphere this expression can only mean a "cultural environment", and what is this if not a highly complex and entirely historical sphere of genuine *facts*, i.e. one that is composed of the precipitates of the actions of communities which have existed over long periods of time? Now we recognize a man's character by his manner and his point of entry into this sphere of cultural action, by the way in which he behaves in active meetings and by the way in which he is actively *changing* both within the context of these facts and meetings and by virtue of the use to which he puts them, i.e. by creating an environment which suits his requirements. To put it bluntly, the environment contains only people and things: the former actively influence one another, whilst the latter are quite simply pre-formed actions, "pre-formed" deeds: this is substantiated by even the most rudimentary tools. And so what is missing in the schema of disposition and environment in its customary ill-considered sense is in fact the most important thing of all, namely, the self and the realization that the self is embodied in *action*, which also creates the environment. And so this schema is one of those negative aids to thought, which simply impede and restrict a biological conception of *man*.'[1]

(c) C. G. Jung and Freud

(i) Jung's dependence on Freud

Jung's dependence on Freud has already formed the subject of numerous investigations, the most important being those by E. Glover[2] and W. Hochheimer.[3] Jung's dependence on Freud may be summed up as follows:

1. Jung accepts the antithesis between the conscious and the unconscious minds, he accepts a topology of the psyche similar to Freud's and

---

[1] Arnold Gehlen, *Der Mensch—Seine Natur und seine Stellung in der Welt*, p. 365, Bonn, 1950. ('Man—his Nature and his Position in the World').

[2] E. Glover, *Freud or Jung*.

[3] W. Hochheimer in *Psyche*, Vol. XI, 1958.

he also differentiates between various strata and *instances* within the psyche.

2. He accepts the theory of repression and other mechanisms of defence (Jung's 'personal unconscious', which includes the problems of identification, projection and sublimation).

3. He assumes the existence of unconscious pathogenic complexes.

4. He accepts the libido theory.

5. He accepts the theory of bi-sexuality or alternatively the presence in men and women of homoerotic elements (*anima, animus.*).

6. He assumes the existence of a collective unconscious, which, however, also embraces general, albeit unconscious, patterns of behaviour such as are contained in Freud's super ego.

7. He accepts the concept of a dynamics of psychic processes.

8. He assumes that psychic activity is determined by (dialectical) antitheses.

(ii) *The differences between Jung and Freud*

But despite Jung's indebtedness to Freud in respect of the important points outlined above the differences between these two thinkers are so fundamental that any comparison of their respective theories can only be undertaken *cum grano salis*. What is far more obvious is the incommensurability of their theories in certain essential respects. The fundamental difference between Jung and Freud lies in their interpretation of symbols. We have already seen (p. 338 ff.) that the sexological interpretation which Freud placed on all symbols was due to the disastrous mistake which he made in confusing concepts with symbols. To recapitulate briefly, what prompted little Hans to describe all pointed objects as 'wi-wi things' (phallus) was the *objective similarity* which existed between those pointed objects. It would go beyond the scope of this present enquiry to enter into the complicated relationship between the objective similarity of actual objects and the process whereby a concept comes into being. This relationship has been worked out in the psychological sphere above all by *Klages* and, subsequently, by *Meinertz*. The extremely important problem which is here involved has been ably formulated by Meinertz in his summary of Klages' theories on the relationship between symbols and concepts, i.e. on the process whereby concepts come into being, as is clear from the following excerpt:

'In brief: *Klages* is the only psychologist to have made a successful attempt to discover the native soil of the conceptual faculty in the "soul" rather than in the "mind" and who has revealed the confusion which is promoted when (as has previously been the case) we equate the process of *abstraction* with that of *generalization*. For purposes of communication and heuristic expediency it is proposed to retain the differentiation between soul and mind advanced by Klages, which is immediately understandable to everyone (and no attempt will be made to place these instances "metaphysically", since such an undertaking would necessarily be speculative and unproductive). Given this premise, it is surely impossible to deny the importance of the psychological question concerning the way in which *identifications* come about in the first place; and without such identifications the formation of concepts, which are of course the principal media of scientific comprehension, would not be possible. What is equally beyond doubt is the fact that symbolic identifications within the sphere of the soul (e.g. those of psychoanalysis; cf. our statements on the living symbol) are of a different order than conceptual identifications: according to this view symbolic identity would derive its content of meaning from the elementary "similarity of images" (to use Klages' own expression) and conceptual or substantive identity would here be opposed by symbolic identity or an "identity of essence". It is precisely the verbal contents of meaning of our language which are engendered by this original identity of essence (and in this connection *Jean Paul Richter*, to whom Klages draws our attention, has called language a dictionary of faded metaphors, so that Klages derives the living foundation for the abstractness of absolutely everything that is capable of verbal representation from the essentiality of the verbal contents of meaning.)[1]

'And so according to this conception of Klages we may say that the concept stands, as it were, with one foot in the sphere of the soul, in the world of experienced images, from which it receives its general validity ('and by virtue of which the life process, which has no boundaries, participates in the concept') and with the other foot in the "mind", its allegiance to which it demonstrates by its total isolation.'[2]

Meinertz also writes on the importance of symbols:

'The idea of different degrees of reality was not unknown to the Ancient Greeks; but since their time only Klages has considered it to be of crucial importance. We may say that the symbol, filled with varying degrees of reality, extends through all stages of Being, so that the total Being of the soul would be more appropriately comprehended, the more positively and the more accurately the degree of reality contained in the specific act of comprehension were expressed. But in this connection the degree of fullness of life present in any given case should not be considered as constituting a criterion by which to assess the living symbol. For "life" may also be sick, distorted or poisoned, and very often

[1] J. Meinertz, *Psychotherapie als Wissenschaft*, pp. 37–8.
[2] J. Meinertz, *ibid.*, p. 39.

531

we are merely able to take note of the profusion of (living!) symbolism in the life of primitive peoples, whereas the "disassociating" action of the mind is indispensable for living cultural achievements: the wealth of mental configurations is far too great "to permit of its resolution into degrees of fullness of life" (Heinemann). If at this point we give prominence to Klages' achievement in having stressed the importance of the vital forces for the actions of the mind and having put the over-valued logos in its rightful place, this should not in any sense be taken to imply that we accept either the one-sided evaluations which have been set up on the basis of this achievement or the bold metaphysical constructions which it has been possible to establish (with the aid of the devalued "mind"!). The real point at issue here is this: the symbolism of the "lower" strata and of their representative figures, which Jung with his archetypes has so forcibly described as constantly active psychic reality, the symbolism of death, of motherliness, of sexuality, of light, of the hero, of the magician, is active not only in religious, mythical and artistic attitudes, not only in inter-personal relations, but also in the rational "creation" of relationships".[1]

To get back to little Hans and his 'wi-wi thing'! What little Hans has actually done is to formulate a concept of a general and an abstract nature on the basis of the objective similarity between different objects. But to conclude from this that, for example, all pointed objects appearing in dreams are penis symbols is an error of great consequence, *for the process whereby the concept has been formulated, a process based on objective similarities, has here been mistaken for the process whereby the symbol is formulated, i.e. the symbol and the concept have been confused.* Now one of the chief properties of the concept is, of course, its intrinsic identity, i.e. its identity with itself, but one of the chief properties of the symbol is its lack of an intrinsic identity, or alternatively, its susceptibility to numerous different interpretations. Thus, to equate all pointed objects with the phallus (the 'we-wi thing') is to treat them as if they were concepts, as if they were 'intrinsically identical'.

In point of fact, however, the symbol stands for many concepts, for it derives from the pre-conceptual sphere in which, due to the psyche's strange powers of symbolization, interrelating attributes of essence represent themselves. The characteristic properties of the symbol are its flexibility and its capacity for assuming many different forms, properties which constantly permit of new interpretations. If Freud's concept of the symbol were followed to its logical conclusion a patient undergoing a Freudian analysis would not really dream of symbols but of concepts, which he would reproduce, not *symbolically*, but *objectively*,

[1] J. Meinertz, *Psychotherapie als Wissenschaft*, pp. 42-3.

on the basis of the objective similarity obtaining between different (pointed or hollow) objects. But even in this view Freud's 'symbol' (i.e. the actual, real object) cannot avoid *standing for something else*, e.g. for the *concept* of the penis or the vagina. From this it follows that Freud's attempt to interpret the symbol in purely positivist and naturalist terms (e.g. 'wi-wi thing') was unsuccessful. The reasons why it was unsuccessful may be summarized as follows:

1. Freud's concept of the symbol confuses the process whereby the concept *comes into being*, i.e. as a result of the objective similarity between different objects, with the process whereby the symbol comes into being. In contrast to the symbol the concept possesses an intrinsic identity, i.e. is identical with itself.

2. Because Freud's symbols lack flexibility and the ability to assume many different forms, which is the characteristic of symbols in their preconceptual capacity, they are in fact objects (similarities!) which are related to a concept (e.g. penis–vagina), which is intrinsically identical.

This view of symbols is diametrically opposed to Jung's view for the following reasons:

1. For C. G. Jung all human reality is allegorical in the fundamental sense that it stands for another kind of reality: 'All that is transitory is but a likeness' (Goethe).

2. This applies equally to symbols, which Jung has always held to stand for some other thing.

3. This 'other thing" however, is not, as with Freud, an object that is related to a concept (penis/vagina) but a complex hierarchical system of specific ideas of a philosophical nature: the path of individuation.

4. Basically Jung has recognized both the multiple stratification and the ambiguity of symbols as opposed to concepts and also their autochthonous origin in the lower psychic strata.

Apart from the above fundamental differences between Jung and Freud, which in themselves would be quite sufficient to render their two systems largely incommensurable, there are also the following further differences:

1. Jung opposes Freud's (positivist) system (1st 'scotoma') in the following further essential respects:

(*a*) (Individuation process). Psychic activity is no longer interpreted in terms of acts of will but in accordance with meaningful (but not purposive) supraordinate viewpoints which are rooted in archetypal references of meaning or in references of meaning arising out of the individuation process.

(b) (Pleasure/Displeasure). Since in Jung's view man is not hedonistic pleasure and displeasure are no longer operative as regulators of psychic activity.

(c) (Affects/Ideas). The relationship between affects and ideas is (hypothetically) solved by the thesis that the libido guarantees the inner unity of affects and ideas or, alternatively, that it will represent this unity in the symbols of the collective unconscious.

(d) (The Irrational). The irrational, whose fate at the hands of Freud and the positivist schools has already been described, is seen more realistically by Jung both in his interpretation of symbols and in his concepts of individuation and the archetypes.

(e) (Dreams). As a consequence of his view of the irrational Jung drops the process whereby dreams are divided up into manifest and latent contents, a process which was essential to Freud's endeavours to rationalize the irrational. Jungian dream interpretation at the subject and object level does greater justice to the irrational imagery of dream symbolism, since it avoids breaking the dream down by a process of causal reduction into rational and purposive references.

(f) (Symptom). The compromise character of symptoms which Freud arrived at as a result of applying the formula of acts of will to neurotic symptoms is also dropped by Jung. In accordance with his conception of symbols Jung interprets clinical symptoms as symbols.

2. (Sexuality). Like the Neo-Freudians Jung also attaches far less importance to the part played by sexuality both in human development and in the emergence of neuroses.

3. (Conscious/unconscious). Whereas Freud derived the contrast between conscious and unconscious in developmental (genetic) terms (primal cell, primary process, etc.), Jung simply accords it provisional acceptance as a given fact. This does not prevent him from carrying out investigations into the 'meaning' of consciousness and the 'symbolism of the mind'.

4. What Jung understands under the libido is general psychic energy. This energy is the motivating force underlying the most varied psychic processes (will, drives, sensation, feeling, thinking). Jung maintains that all psychic activity is autonomously regulated by the libido, which means that regulation by the principle of pleasure and displeasure no longer applies.[1]

5. (Archetypes). Jung's assumption of a collective unconscious, which

---

[1] This does not prevent Jung from constantly equating drive and will in his libido theory.

he distinguishes from the personal unconscious, and his further assumption of archetypes which regulate and pre-form psychic reality are also factors which distinguish him from Freud.

6. Whereas Freud developed his theory of structures and instances genetically (ego drives from the stimulus protection of the primal cell), Jung's theory of structures and instances was *not* genetic. Rather it was based on a combination of empirical observations and the specific 'meaning' of the Jungian system. (The ego constitutes one of the instances throughout the various phases of individuation, i.e. in the anima (animus) phase, the shadow phase, the phase of the mana personality and the phase of the Self.)

7. A further factor which distinguishes Jung from Freud is Jung's general topology and psychology which was built up dialectically on the basis of antitheses (conscious/unconscious—thinking/feeling—extrovert/introvert).

(iii) *Fundamental problems of C. G. Jung's theory*

1. In attempting to overcome Freud's positivism, whilst still remaining dependent on it in certain crucial respects, C.G. Jung's theory (Complex Psychology) acquired the peculiarly hybrid character which is its essential weakness. Jung came to terms with Freud's basic positivist conceptions only to a minimal and quite inadequate extent, paying only scant attention to such crucial questions as whether psychic life is regulated by pleasure and displeasure, whether the drives may be considered in terms of acts of will, whether the atomism of association psychology is justified, etc. Instead he simply advanced his own Weltanschauung which he outlined in his first major work 'Transformations and Symbols of the Libido'. He tried to substantiate this view of the world with psychological evidence, i.e. he compiled evidence in support of his view by drawing on the accumulated material of his own vast scholarship ('amplification'). His Weltanschauung is by no means new—and this speaks for it rather than against it—but is in fact quintessentially the same as the majority of philosophical and religious systems, save where the former favour a purely positivist and materialist interpretation of human reality. 'Become the man you are' and 'Know thyself' are surely as much the quintessence of the Jungian view as they are of the majority of (idealistically oriented) philosophical and religious systems. By drawing on the material furnished both by individual case histories and by sagas, myths and Weltanschauungen Jung was able to establish a broader empirical basis for his conception than can be attributed to the older doctrines and systems whose basic tenets he shares. And so there arose the impressive edifice of Complex psychology, which, however, if we consider the arguments advanced above regarding

the relationship between the natural sciences and Freudian psycho-analysis, will be seen to have even less right to the title of a scientific psychology than Freud's theories. Since, moreover, in Jung's conception the patient's motivations are fed to a considerable extent by the arche-typal contents of the collective unconscious and since the unconscious is largely autonomous it is even questionable as to whether Jung's psychology may be considered as meaningful in Jasper's sense of the word and thus as scientific in the sense in which, for example, history is scientific: for in Jung's conception the motives determining human acti-vity are not *universally* meaningful but merely meaningful within the specific context of Jungian theory. Human development, human strivings and actions only become meaningful within the framework formed by the specific contents of meaning of the Jungian system—in other words, if human activity is to be understood a knowledge of Jung's conceptions is a prerequisite. From this it is quite evident that the bond which, for example, still linked Freudian psychoanalysis as a psychology of under-standing with universally meaningful and empirically observable references of meaning has become even more fragile where Jung's Complex Psychology is concerned, *unless of course we are prepared to accept Jung's basic conception of Individuation, i.e. 'Become the man you are', as a binding and conclusive concept which is supraordinate for human reality.* But to furnish proof of individuation in terms acceptable to the natural sciences or for that matter to any branch of science would surely be difficult. Before such a concept can be recognized as valid a decision has to be taken and the motives underlying such a decision, the founda-tions on which it rests, can never be entirely rational. Complex psycho-logy has entered the sphere of Weltanschauung, where truth is not established by proof but by decisions and in some cases even by decisions which are based on faith. The fact that such a decision has to be taken in respect of Jungian psychology would appear to make Freudian psychoanalysis more acceptable to modern man, for with its scientific orientation and its empirical basis it makes its appeal to 'common sense' and presents its theses as scientific facts. We have of course already seen that this is not strictly true and that Freud's positivist conception is also a Weltanschauung. From this it would follow that no matter what type of psychology a man may choose to pursue his choice must ulti-mately depend on a personal decision, since every type of (depth) psychology is ultimately rooted in the presuppositions of a particular Weltanschauung. This situation was summed up by Viktor von Weizsäcker when he said that *the problem of truth is not one of rational decisions but rather of irrational decisions.* None the less, there is still a difference between Freud's psychology of understanding and C. G. Jung's Complex Psychology. The drives or motives imputed to human development and human activity by Freudian psychology as a psychology of understanding are to a certain extent capable of empirical confirmation. Consequently Freudian psychology retains a 'universally meaningful character' to a certain extent. Jungian psychology, however, presupposes the acceptance of a specific Weltanschauung in a far more complex sense and cannot therefore be considered 'universally meaningful'.

The hybrid character of C. G. Jung's Complex Psychology derives on the one hand from its strong predilection for Weltanschauung—as we have just seen—and on the other hand from its dependence on Freudian positivism. For in many respects Jung is more positivist than his followers perhaps realize. For example, he attempts—like the positivists —to derive thought from speech (Symbols of Transformation) whilst remaining unaware of the far-reaching consequences to which this naturalist view gives rise. Nor can C. G. Jung deny his dependence on positivist doctrines when he tries to establish a biophysiological confirmation of the collective unconscious or when he deals with the question of brain structures, instincts, etc. His relationship to positivism becomes even more problematic when, for example, in elaborating on the personal unconscious and the possibilities of neurotic disturbances, he is obliged against his will to have recourse to Freud's positivist conceptions (e.g. pleasure and displeasure) whilst attempting—literally in the same breath—to replace them with concepts of his own. Moreover, he is obliged to admit that defence against anxiety does take place by means of projection, identification, regression or sublimation, an admission which is in no sense diminished by his designation of these concepts as 'automata' of the libido, for by using them at all he reveals his firm allegiance to the Cartesian oriented positivism of his preceptor, Freud. Jung's large-scale rejection of genetic factors and his subsequent realization that he could not dispense with them entirely contributed towards this dilemma which Glover, amongst others, has investigated. There is one particular sentence in Jung's writings which throws a great deal of light on this dilemma:

'The motive forces at the back of neurosis come from all sorts of congenital characteristics and environmental influences, which together build up an attitude that makes it impossible for him to lead a life in which the instincts are satisfied.'[1]

What this statement amounts to is that Jung recognizes the principle of pleasure and displeasure as being operative in respect of the emergence of neuroses—and this despite the fact that he rejects this same principle in respect of the regulation of psychic processes. In other words, Jung failed to overcome the real crux of positivism, as is evident from the

[1] C. G. Jung, *Symbols of Transformation*, Coll. Wks., Vol. 5, p. 139.

fact that in his explanations of neurotic and other phenomena he is constantly obliged to fall back on positivist concepts. 'Become the man you are' is a maxim whose validity for human development Jung clearly recognized but despite this his view of man remained encumbered with positivist errors, as a result of which it acquired a distinctly 'hybrid' character.

2. A further weakness in Jung's conception is the tendency, which is evident in all his writings, to avoid precise definitions. It may well be that the object of his enquiries—the psyche—with its amorphous, amoeboid, Proteus-like structure, its basically irrational character and its antilogical articulation and amalgamation with the environment is by its very nature incapable of precise definition. Those who come to grips with Jung's works and are confused by what are often contradictory and apparently nebulous definitions of psychic processes—of which both Jung and J. Jacobi have said that they defy conceptual formulation—will, so to speak, have grasped the iridescent nature of the soul as a result of their reading. But even if Jung is right in his assertion that the mental and verbal objectivisation of psychic activity is a difficult undertaking he should at least have tried to avoid advancing concepts which are materially and formally over-taxed. One such is the concept of the libido, which has been so over-taxed in respect of its material contents as to have been rendered almost meaningless, as a result of which it has proved impossible to establish necessary differentiations between crucial concepts such as drive and will, feeling and thinking, sexuality and love. This concept of the libido—which, incidentally, shelves the question as to the origin and nature of psychic energy (itself an heirloom of positivism) as being momentarily insoluble—exercises an unfavourable influence on Jung's conception from the outset, since it denies it all possibility of establishing further conceptual clarifications of psychic processes. Even if the 'Proteus-like' structure of the psyche is conceded, a system which throws all the basic psychic functions into the same pot as being essentially identical loses all claim to be considered universally meaningful, let alone scientifically correct. And what is true of the libido is even more true of the archetypes. If we consider the whole host of different phenomena which are supposed to be archetypal, then this concept is seen to be even more over-taxed than the concept of the libido. Even if we refrain from pursuing the question as to whether the existence of the archetypes is capable of proof we are still confronted with the fact that the archetype is both drive and mind (concept), both symbol and will, an instinct, a pattern of behaviour and a complex and is, moreover, capable of appearing autonomously in the form of an hallucination. Over and above this the archetypes are 'typical forms of comprehending and intuiting, of experiencing and reacting, of patterns of behaviour and

suffering, images of life itself'. Attempts have also been made to connect the archetypes with the instinctual behaviour of animals and with physical theories. Moreover, in Jung's view the archetypes are of an a-priori nature and control perception. If we ask whether clarity can ever be achieved by inflating concepts in this manner, the answer must surely be that it emphatically cannot. We have seen that Freud's libido concept was by no means free from heteronomous and contradictory tendencies, but it must be said that Jung's capacity for generalizing to a point where concepts become meaningless far exceeds that of his preceptor (whom he none the less criticized in this respect). Although it is true that the psyche is anti-logical and irrational, it does not follow from this that Jung's method of procedure is suited to the task of illuminating the irrational nature of the psyche, since all it does is to introduce ambiguities *into the concept*. The irrational can only be grasped if the anti-logical nature of psychic processes is demonstrated in individual *concrete* instances. It cannot be grasped by subsuming vastly different and unclarified concepts (e.g. constant equation of drive and will) under a collective concept such as the libido or the archetypes.

3. The third weakness of the Jungian system is due to the fact that its concepts are far more difficult to substantiate: e.g. the collective unconscious, the anima, the mana personality, the shadow. Psychology must remain capable of empirical substantiation in respect of its fundamental processes at least, if it is to retain even a partial right to be considered as a science. Observation in the widest sense of the word, i.e. the recording of data which have been established by observation, must remain the basis of any 'science', no matter how questionable that 'science' may appear to be as a system. It was not only in its patients' dreams and associations that Freudian psychoanalysis was able to observe the Oedipus complex, the fear of castration and penis envy, for the direct observation of infants afforded further confirmation of the empirical nature of many such observations which had been made in the sphere of analysis. The empirical nature of the majority of C. G. Jung's concepts, however, is dubious. The question as to whether the incidence of Indo-Germanic or Mexican symbols in the dreams of modern man affords a sufficient basis for assuming the existence of a collective unconscious, whether the assumption of a collective unconscious as a reservoir of all human patterns of behaviour renders such patterns of behaviour more meaningful, certainly constitutes a problem—but not a solution. Jung's collective unconscious is distinctly preferable to Freud's 'id' in that it does not rule out the irrational and, since it is held to transcend consciousness, is regarded as essentially chaotic. The collective unconscious, which is the carrier of the archetypes, is organized to this end in a meaningful but *by no means* rational and purposive manner. Jung incor-

porates the irrational as a 'meaning' (e.g. individuation) and it lives and has its being in the collective unconscious, where it affords its own irrational and symbolic representation, thereby enabling Jung to do greater justice to the anti-logical character of the psyche than Freud. However, there is no 'proof', there is not even limited empirical verification, of the existence of the collective unconscious. Those who decide in favour of its existence will ultimately do so because they are convinced of the truth of Jung's system as a whole. And the same holds good for the majority of the concepts involved in the process of individuation: the anima, the animus, the shadow, the persona, the mana-personality and the self. In order to strengthen the empirical character of the concepts of the anima and the animus Jung would have had to have gone into the problem of homosexuality; in other words, the assumption of the anima and the animus involves the assumption of homosexual 'structures'. But this would have meant falling back on Freudian psychoanalysis and this Jung wanted to avoid, since, as has already been mentioned, his endeavours were directed towards establishing a system that would do away with the positivist and genetic derivations of these concepts. The cryptic formulation of the personal unconscious as the 'shadow', which shadow the patient was required inwardly to accept in the course of treatment, is illuminating and is not without its deeper significance. In the concept of the shadow, as also in concepts such as the anima, the animus and the persona, what we are actually dealing with are *metaphors*, which are intended to free certain observations of Freud's (homosexuality, character façade (persona), pre-conscious and unconscious) from the narrow confines of their positivist definition, in order that they might be viewed from a 'higher perspective', i.e. from the perspective of individuation. *In other words, a large part of the empirical character of these concepts has been borrowed from Freud, the concepts themselves having simply been 'realigned' and 're-formulated'.* This process demonstrates with particular clarity the weakness dealt with under Para. 1 of this section, namely, the hybrid nature of Jung's conception, for when Jung found that he was unable to escape from Freud's positivist derivation and formulation of basic concepts he proceeded to adopt and rename these basic concepts (homosexuality becomes anima) and finally to adapt them to a system which presents a Weltanschauung (apparently) based on psychology.

4. The problem of 'individuation' gives rise to the following considerations:

(*a*) it might be argued that the path of man's 'healing' and of his 'salvation' (Heilsweg) lay in individuation, i.e. in a Jungian analysis. Jung implies as much and there can be no doubt but that his complex psychology claims the same 'absolute' right—i.e, the right to make definitive statements on man and the world—as has been claimed by Freud and other analysts (Rank, the Bahaviourists, the Existential analysts and the Catholic analysts). It must surely be obvious that such an attitude, which would accord priority to analysis over life itself, is a dubious one. And the net result of such an attitude is a 'fully analysed' adherent of a philosophical view, of whom it can seldom be said that he is readily distinguishable from the adherents of other philosophical views by dint of his willingness to concede the conceivable falsity of his own view. At best analysis is a 'crutch', which people use when their problems threaten to engulf them. To argue that it ought to replace the course of life, the 'passionate movement of life' (von Weizsäcker)—which is what life really is—is to reveal a not inconsiderable measure of unworldliness and doctrinal orthodoxy. Individuation, 'self-realization' in the most definitive sense of the word, cannot be restricted to the test-tube conversation between therapist and patient, however essential this may be for the light it casts on the problems facing the person seeking advice or help. 'Self-realization' demands life itself, it demands the capacity to suffer both the heights and the depths, it demands the ability to bear the burden of guilt, the ability to break down—and begin again. Last but not least—indeed most of all—it demands the partnership and the meeting, whose fundamental importance Jung failed to realize.

(b)   In their writings Jung and his disciples imply that the process of individuation is an autonomous activity which, once it is set in motion, continues of its own accord throughout the course of the analysis. This process follows its own inner laws, which are even chronologically arranged, beginning, for example, with dreams in which the archetype of the Night Sea journey appears and ending with the 'quaternity of the circle', with one or several mandalas, etc. Whether the cases which have been documented by Jung and his followers in this respect are in fact ideal cases we have not been told.—But the fact of the matter must surely be that only very few analyses follow this process in chronological order, beginning with the Night Sea journey and ending with the mandala. Would it not be possible for an analysis to begin with a few mandalas and to end with the Night Sea journey? In reality it doubtless would be possible but to the Jungian psychotherapist the suggestion must appear highly improbable because he will expect the phenomena of the collective unconscious to present themselves in accordance with the precise terms of individuation. But, to recapitulate, the chronology of individuation, the automatism of this process, is only likely to be realized in very rare cases.

5. 'Compensation' or the self-regulation of the psyche is the factor

which regulates psychic life (and one which completely transcends consciousness). Exogenic factors (pleasure and displeasure) are no longer of any great consequence for the regulation of psychic life, although, as we have seen, C. G. Jung is obliged to have constant recourse to them.

The assumption that psychic life is 'regulated'—although deriving from mechanistic thought—is justified, even though it does involve a factor which is certainly meaningful and conceivably teleological. Jung's ideas on the regulation of psychic life are preferable to Freud's in that they are not purposively oriented in terms of acts of will. On the other hand, however, the definitions which they involve are subject to the imprecision dealt with in Para. 2 of this section. Jung's views are based on a concept of psychic balance which transcends the principle of pleasure and displeasure and which the psychic processes 'automatically' strive to achieve. They do not strive to do so, however, in accordance with the principle of the conservation of energy or the Nirvana principle but rather in accordance with the principle of a *just balance*. The extrovert is threatened by inflation of the unconscious contents of his psyche, the introvert fails to fulfil the demands made by reality, and in both cases the psychic life of the individual is 'automatically' regulated so as to establish harmonious interaction between its conscious and unconscious sections. Even if an assumption of this sort does sound plausible, even if it has been confirmed in individual cases, even if it is backed up by the symbolism of myths and sagas, it must none the less remain a highly problematical and indeed unproven generalization for as long as the problem of the 'regulation' of psychic life remains shrouded in its present darkness. Anyone who has reflected on the fact that millions and indeed thousands of millions of men and women have been reduced by the processes of civilization to living lives which are both boring and exclusively extroverted without falling a prey to the pent-up forces of an inflated libido and its archetypes will feel compelled to doubt the universal validity of Jung's view. In this view Jung again reveals his characteristic ambiguity, for in attempting to demonstrate the compensation and self-regulation of the psyche, although he tried to overcome the hydro-mechanical libido concepts which Freud and Breuer had employed, he was still obliged to fall back on those same hydro-mechanical concepts, as is clear from his use of such expressions as 'blockages', 'inflation' (inundation), etc.

(iv) *Summary: Freud and Jung*

In the light of what has been said in the aforegoing, it is of course no longer possible to pose the traditional alternative of 'Freud or Jung'. We have seen that, if only as a result of their fundamentally different interpretations of symbols, their two systems cannot really be compared. Both systems have their major weaknesses. Although Jung does greater justice to the irrational character of the psyche than Freud, in other essential respects he remains dependent on Freud, in some respects indeed utterly dependent. We have seen that the Jungian system is better able to grasp the 'Reality of the Psyche' (*Wirklichkeit der Seele*) than the Freudian system, but this advantage was purchased at the cost of concepts which are lacking in precision, of assertions which are incapable of direct substantiation and of generalizations of individual observations. There can scarcely be a single concept in Jung's system which is not open to criticism. And from this it clearly follows that Complex Psychology is not so much a scientific system as a *Weltanschauung* with psychological contents. By contrast Freud's system enjoys the advantage of being able to substantiate its claim to be considered as a scientific discipline by demonstrating conceivable and meaningful conditions for an understanding of the psyche. But the price which Freud had to pay for this scientific sanction was the fundamental error of attempting to understand psychic activity in terms of acts of will (not to mention the hypotheses which were investigated in Sections A and B of Part Three of this book). To the extent to which the Freudian system is *positivist* oriented it is no less 'philosophical' than the Jungian system. The fact that both Freudian and Jungian depth psychology were ultimately obliged to enter the domain of philosophy must be regarded as a failure on the part of psychology to realise its declared aim of achieving the status of a natural science. However, this failure is rooted in the very nature of its subject-matter, the human psyche. And this failure of psychological theory can in fact lead to therapeutic success. For example, the Jungian view of the world has shown to modern man, who has 'lost his way', new ways and new possibilities of coming to terms with the depths of his personality, with the 'invisible elements' of which Paracelsus speaks (see Motto). Like every philosophical view of the world it requires that a 'decision' be taken, a fact which is likely to prove of absolutely crucial therapeutic importance for the patient who is able to find himself again within the Jungian system. The real weakness of the Freudian system on the other hand lies in the very fact that it disclaims all pretensions to being a philosophy, whilst in fact being bound by philosophical assumptions. The Freudian patient, who in his endeavours to clarify his problems begins to look for a meaning for 'self-realization', will find that in Freudian analysis, although he is certainly confronted with his problems, he will look in vain for the 'meaning' of this confrontation, since in the positivist view life is meaningless or, alternatively, the meaning of life is 'survival'.

D

FURTHER INTERPRETATIONS OF PSYCHIC ACTIVITY

(a) Otto Rank

Otto Rank's first phase, which was governed by his theory of the birth trauma, was typical of psychoanalytic modes of thought in the 'twenties and the 'thirties (Ferenczi's 'Thalassa' was another typical product). Rank offered this theory, in which he revealed a frequent lack of cogency in argument, as a master-key that would unlock the secrets underlying all the processes of life and of human reality. The absolute claims which were advanced in this theory and which were quite characteristic of many psychoanalytic theories of its day, are so obvious in respect of Rank's first phase and so utterly divorced from reality that it is not proposed to pursue them further. In his second phase, however, which ressembled Fromm's enquiries in its endeavours to establish a supra-ordinate meaning for human reality, Rank produced results which would seem to be important. The most essential outcome of his enquiries was almost certainly the distinction which he established between the will on the one hand and the drives and emotions on the other. Although his definitions of these processes are not as precise as might be desired he does at least distinguish between them. The connections between the process of self-realization and the largely volitional process whereby the individual separates out from the environment have been confirmed to a considerable extent by observations. In applying this point of view Rank always considers the human being first and the neurosis second, a method of procedure which places him in clear contradistinction to Freud and especially so in view of the fact that his concept of man is idealistic in origin. But whilst Jung's theories of individuation were at least confirmed by 'amplification', Rank's attempts to furnish an empirical foundation for his ideas remained abortive. In his theory the philosophical and metaphysical aspect of depth psychology is clearly revealed, for what we find in Rank is not even a psychological *Weltan-schauung* such as was advanced by C. G. Jung but quite simply a *Weltanschauung*, whose object is to give a meaning and a purpose to human life. Rank also failed to make the breakthrough to the reality of the 'partner'.

(b) Personal Analysis. (Transference and Meeting)

It is at this point that personal analysis or, to be more precise, that *M. Buber* comes into the picture (see p. 404 ff.). There can be little doubt but that Buber's work constitutes a further crucial advance in the field of depth psychology, one which does justice to the reality of psychic activity and to its irrational nature both in respect of the 'meeting' and of inter-personal relations. The far-reaching importance of the I-Thou relationship for man and for neurosis and the extent to which both man and neurosis are dependent on and influenced by 'partnership' has yet to be fully appreciated. Sullivan, albeit in the sphere of Behaviourism, and to a lesser extent Horney, have shown some awareness of this kind of approach. But M. Buber (and other philosophical thinkers working along similar lines) have demonstrated to psychotherapists in general that the problem of transference cannot be solved by the test-tube processes advanced by Jung and Freud (in this connection see the arguments advanced on p. 410 ff.). It is in the nature of transference analysis as practised by the Freudian and to a lesser extent by the Neo-Freudian schools to interpret the patient's behaviour in terms of 'manipulations', of defence or of appeals for love, in which the patient repeats and transfers on the to analyst infantile reaction patterns. This view—see also p. 354 ff. for comments on projection (transference) which also apply here—does not take the patient's behaviour seriously in terms of a meeting but instead reduces it to the level of a neurotic or infantile reaction. But despite the fact that such a view places a purely negative (neurotic) value on the patient's behaviour it none the less implies—*volens nolens*—that beyond 'the manipulations of the transference relationship' a genuine relationship does exist, because if it did not, then the (negative) concept of the transference *relationship* would be meaningless. Transference presupposes relationship. Freud appears to have been aware of the difference—one which, incidentally, is by no means easy to formulate—between genuine and pseudo (i.e. transference) relationships (see p. 404 ff.). In attempting to treat all relationships as transference relationships his disciples have in fact been attempting to brand man as a creature without a personal history, whose adult relationships are no more than a repetition of the relationships of early childhood. Freud took care not to make any definitive statement in this respect which might have confirmed such an interpretation.

Whilst psychoanalysis with its concept of 'transference' implies the existence of both genuine and pseudo relationships, personal analysis goes beyond this and makes the *genuine* relationship the basis of its therapy, indeed the basis of its cure. Just what form this relationship takes in reality, however, is not yet known.[1] Certainly we should not assume that the analyst is now obliged to invite his patients to tea or to maintain any relationships which go beyond the strict rules of pro-

[1] Apart from a few publications by the Stuttgart School in *Psyche* (see especially H. Geist and F. Schottländer).

cedure prescribed by Freud for the conduct of psychoanalysis. The concept of the meeting will be restricted to the *genuine* relationship between doctor and patient which, as *M. Buber* has told us (see p. 409 ff.), pulsates in every moment of 'Being together', but which defies conceptual formulation. The tendency of the positivist schools to interpret the relationship between doctor and patient in terms of the manipulations of the transference and counter-transference situation alone, makes it all but impossible for the meeting to play a *really decisive* role. But in spite of their scientific view of the doctor-patient relationship the fact remains that the Freudian school has investigated the complications which may conceivably arise in psychoanalytic treatment from the point of view of transference relationships more thoroughly than any other school and has applied its findings in its therapeutic practice. A knowledge of these findings on the part of the therapist would appear to be indispensable for the successful outcome of any course of psychotherapy, since the therapist should know what the state of 'transference' and of so-called 'counter-transference' is at any given moment of the therapy, i.e. he should know what stage has been reached in the bout of 'shadow boxing' in which the stakes are 'power and love'. The therapist must be in a position to know whether the patient is trying to seduce or outwit him and whether he himself accepts or rejects the patient. Over and above this of course the therapist ought to be prepared for the 'meeting', for otherwise any decision he might take, e.g. a decision to help the patient, would in fact amount to no more than a desire to play the part of the father. The therapist must at all times preserve a state of balance between his knowledge of the 'transference relationship', his knowledge of the patient's neurotic and infantile needs and the genuine relationship, i.e. the meeting. If we now consider transference in the light of the meeting, i.e. in the light of a genuine relationship, it is evident that in the transference relationship the patient not only repeats so-called infantile patterns of behaviour but above all persists in striving for power or love in a neurotic manner, a procedure whose general effect is to inhibit the genuine relationship, the realization of which depends on the patient's ability to relate to himself.

(c) *Catholic Oriented Depth Psychology*

As far as the enquiries of theologically (Catholic) oriented depth psychology are concerned the 'unconscious spirit' (*unbewusster Geist*) advanced by Frankl in opposition to the theses of the positivist oriented schools is justified, although it should be pointed out that Freud and his disciples had already assumed the existence of unconscious thought processes (*Geist*). But Frankl's concept of the 'spirit' (*Geist*) is not identical with the human faculties of knowledge and reason.[1] For him spirit is essentially conscience, existence, self—faculties which for Freud are predominantly secondary products resulting from the sublimation of drives, (although Binswanger has recorded the fact[2] that in answer to his question as to whether the spirit (*Geist*) also existed Freud had said that spirit (*Geist*) was everything). It has already been pointed out on a previous page that Freud over-simplified the problem posed by man's cultural and intellectual achievements. Frankl's conception links up with E. von Hartmann's 'Philosophy of the Unconscious' and with Romantic Philosophy, which latter of course had failed to discern the intimate nature of the relationship, indeed the state of fusion, which exists between the spirit (*Geist*) and the drives, which Freud, albeit within positivist limits, had certainly seen. The problem of the relationship between the spirit and the drives, with which after all mankind has been struggling since time immemorial ('nature' and 'spirit'), is not solved simply by the emphatic assumption of an 'unconscious spirit'. Frankl merely indicates the existence of an 'unconscious spirit'. He does not attempt to establish a detailed and substantiated account of the way in which it functions as did, for example, C. G. Jung. Where psychology begins and where philosophy and *Weltanschauung* end, the extent of the drives as opposed to the extent of the spirit—these are questions which do not permit of a condensed and paradigmatic solution such as Frankl offers. To agree with Frankl's views in principle—in as far as they derive from an Aristotelian and catholic view of the world—is to agree with numerous thinkers both past and present. But what Freud has done—his realization that many human manifestations which had generally been considered to exist on an elevated spiritual or ethical plane are in fact *partly* conditioned by the drives (a realization which Nietzsche had also come to in a different sphere)—cannot be undone. Frankl has not done justice to this realization. Despite Freud's fatal equation of the drives with the will his major achievement—the discovery of the relative dependence of the 'spirit' on the 'drives'—still remains. As we have already seen, von Weizsäcker went one important step further than Freud in the elucidation of the problem posed by the spirit and the drives with his conception of the *Gestaltkreis*. What is now needed is for von Weizsäcker's conception to be followed up by investigations into the close intercommunion of spirit and drives in order that both their *fundamental differences of essence* and their *antithetical interdependencies* may be established. This is a need

[1] German *Geist* means both spirit and mind. It corresponds to French *esprit*. In view of Frankl's definition of Geist as conscience, existence, etc., it has here been rendered by 'spirit'. (Tr.).

[2] L. Binswanger, *Erinnerungen an Freud*, Zürich, 1956.

547

which Catholic oriented depth psychology has so far failed to meet.

Daims' and Caruso's view that neurotic fixations are sinful is already being criticized in Catholic quarters so that no further criticism is called for here. This view involves a process of dialectical 'reversal'; the spirit is repressed, the drives gain the upper hand and this constitutes a sin. With Freud of course it is the drive which is repressed by the 'spirit' and this produces the neurosis. (The problems which Freud's view involves, especially the problem concerning the instances which exercise the repression, have been dealt with above (see p. 477 ff.). This reversal of the original order of the psychoanalytic process does not solve the problem of the relationship between the spirit and the drives. All it does is to fix the problem in a dialectical antithesis without achieving any clarification. As far as the empirical basis of these assertions is concerned *both* can be verified by observation: drives can be repressed by an act of will ('spirit') and a resolution, i.e. an act of will, can be destroyed or 'repressed' by a drive. Von Weizsäcker's revolving door principle gets more to the heart of the matter: if two psychic impulses enter into consciousness, then, whether they be decisions taken by the will or drives prompted by passion, the former may subdue the latter whilst the latter may 'overrun' the former. What is here made manifest is only *one* side of psychic activity. For a brief moment both sides may emerge simultaneously but they will immediately proceed to conceal themselves from one another. This property of psychic processes supplies further confirmation of the fact that so-called repression cannot be derived genetically from the principle of pleasure and displeasure but is in fact imminent in 'Beingness' as a primary factor in terms of the 'revolving door principle'. The fact that conscience can be suppressed and can produce reactions which are quite as neurotic as those resulting from the repression of a drive has been empirically observed on numerous occasions, above all when, as a consequence of war, men were forced to take part in actions which violated their conscience. A Freudian interpreting such a case might conceivably speak of an abnormally strong super-ego development which hindered the release of aggression, e.g. when innocent people were to be shot. In other words, the neurotic process involved in such an act would once again boil down to the repression of aggressions or alternatively to the inadequate release of aggressive drives. From this it would follow that a normal reaction would be to participate in such executions without suffering inner conflicts either before or after (a phenomenon which no doubt also exists). In the Freudian view there is no repression of conscience, i.e. of the super-ego, and so it might conceivably be argued that this profoundly inhuman conception is implied by Freudian psychoanalysis. The ultimate grounds on which such an argument would rest are two-fold, namely that Freudian psychoanalysis is based on the concept of 'homo natura', a concept that is both abstract and utterly divorced from reality, and that it is governed by the principle of pure hedonism.

And so Frankl would appear to be justified in stressing those cases in which 'conscience' or 'spirit' is repressed. His assumption of an unconscious 'spirit', however, would only really be acceptable if he were prepared to concede that the spirit is also dependent on the drives. It has already been pointed out that what is now needed is a new conception of the principle of repression, one that would lead on from von Weizsäcker's revolving door principle.

The crucial question concerning the conceivable existence of an unconscious spirit relates to its activity (thought): is the thought of the unconscious spirit similar to the thought of the conscious mind? If thought is to be considered as one of the spiritual functions, then it should be pointed out that Freud, for example, had already assumed the existence—in the pre-conscious—of an unconscious thought process, which, like the drives, is entirely purposive, but which does not differ in principle from the conscious processes of reason. This assumption will always remain an assumption and can never be proved since the unconscious thought processes—by the very fact of their being unconscious—are not susceptible to proof. They can only be inferred from symptoms or dreams—'as if' they had taken place. For Freud the pre-conscious psyche is quite as rational as the conscious psyche. We have already seen from our investigation of the drives and of the irrational that the irrational, which *transcends consciousness*, simply disrupts the rationally conceived entelechy of the pre-conscious, 'chops it up', and then proceeds to put it together again. But the question which arises here, especially in view of what has been said on the subject of concepts, objects and symbols (see p. 529 ff.), is whether these so-called unconscious thought processes are not in fact simply relationships of symbolic forms which entirely transcend concepts of power and purpose. If such were the case it would of course be more consistent to dispense with the concept of unconscious thought processes altogether. It should also be born in mind that in the process whereby the psyche affords its own symbolic self-representation that part of the process in which the symbols emerge from the innermost layers of the psyche is quite unknown to us and that what we actually see emerging from the depths of the personality is already an end-product. Consequently, the concept of unconscious thought processes must remain a largely unproved hypothesis. The assumption of an unconscious 'spirit' (which also inhabits the drives) *as the organizing principle, as the self and as the meaning* of personality appears more probable and appears moreover to be capable of empirical substantiation. The alternative is to agree with Klages that the spirit, as an a-cosmic principle, must be banished from the depth personality entirely and that only images may be held to exist there.

What is quite evident is that the problem posed by the unconscious spirit is extraordinarily difficult and at present admits of numerous interpretations, which only tends to conceal the fact that little or nothing is actually known. By considering the process of repression in terms of the revolving door principle, according to which all psychic impulses are concealed from themselves (i.e. repressed), it has been possible to assume for the present that both drives and 'spirit' are subject to repression, although this of course can in no way be said to exhaust the complexity, indeed the probable insolubility, of this question.

(d) The Interpretations of the Existential Ontologists

Of the various philosophical interpretations of psychic activity the phenomenological interpretation has succeeded in defining its concepts with the greatest degree of precision both in respect of methodology and in respect of *Weltanschauung*. The founders and representatives of phenomenology were philosophers and not psychologists who experimented with philosophy such as O. Rank or C. G. Jung. The fact that phenomenology is subject to dispute within the various philosophical schools is only to be expected since it is in the nature of philosophical theories to be disputed. A critical investigation of phenomenology will not be possible within the framework of this present enquiry.

Whilst the phenomenological method has proved extremely fruitful for psychopathology and has contributed towards the elucidation of pathogenic phenomena, *Heidegger's* existential ontology, which has been represented by *Binswanger* since 1928 and of more recent years by *Zutt, Boss* etc., has led to the complete absorption of empirical psychology into existential philosophy. This absorption is so complete that psychopathological data and phenomena and even clinical phenomena such as asthma are considered as existentialia, i.e. they are considered ontologically. Although this is no more than the logical extension of a tendency inherent in existential philosophy it also means the end of psychology as such. The chief danger which threatens here, however, is that complex and highly involved problems may be subjected to further simplification. And yet another possible consequence of this method is that the richness and multiple stratification of the phenomena of psychic life may be reduced in accordance with Husserl's principle of 'reduction', his epoché. Although such reductions are fundamentally different in respect of method from the generalizing abstractions which Freud and Jung occasionally propounded they must necessarily involve a down-grading of the empirical facts established by observation to a position of only secondary importance. The absolute right which is claimed by existential ontology to interpret all the phenomena of life and of Being in its own way does *not* differ in principle from similar claims made by other analytic schools. And this objection is in no way invalidated by the fact that existential ontology is the only system based on precise philosophical definitions.

(e) *Depth Psychology and Weltanschauung.* (*Is there such a thing as presuppositionless psychology?*)

The crucial question, which now arises and which was implied in the description and criticism of the various conceptions presented in this book, is this: is there such a thing as a presuppositionless, empirical depth psychology which may be regarded as a science or must every psychology necessarily end up as *Weltanschauung*? Must we in fact question the scientific basis of depth psychology as such? The development of the various schools of depth psychology has clearly shown that every school tends to develop its own Weltanschauung and consequently to lay claim to 'absolute' powers. This holds true for Freud's positivist-naturalist view and it holds true for the Neo-Freudians, especially the Behaviourists. It holds true for Fromm, Rank, C. G. Jung, Catholic personal analysis and existential ontology. Only Viktor v. Weizsäcker and a few of the representatives of personal analysis—M. Buber, P. Christian—have refrained from drawing such far-reaching and binding philosophical and dogmatic conclusions from their observations. It is in the nature of man to be susceptible to the charms of Weltanschauung and of course man is the 'object' which depth psychology has elected to investigate. It is also in the nature of analysts to wish to make definitive and ultimate statements on the nature of man. The analyst's personal desire to make a definitive assessment of his own personality and of his own position amid the general confusions of life, which after all is the ultimate motive underlying his statements on the nature of man, is surely an understandable phenomenon but it is one which has led to the formulation of abstract hypotheses which are utterly divorced from life. In order that statements might be made on man, on his actions and on his behaviour and even on 'motivations' of which he himself is unaware, purposes were postulated (Freud's act of will/drives) and supraordinate interpretations were established (C. G. Jung, O. Rank, E. Fromm, Existential analysis). The interpretation of psychic activity simply meant fitting individual observations into the totality of a meaningful context. In Freud's case, as we have already seen, this was done in accordance with teleological, quantitative and causal principles. In Jung's case interpretation followed the path of his alchemical and gnostic philosophy. It is of course impossible, as has also been pointed out on a previous page, to select individual facts from the sum-total of the various systems and present them as *the* universally valid basis—one that is, so to speak, immune to all theoretical speculation—of depth psychology. A psychological system which merely attempts to describe the actions and reactions of individuals already implies purposive thinking, since the reactions of living creatures can never be completely explained in the physical sense of a collision between two spheres (reflex theory). From this it follows that no interpretation of psychic activity is ever presuppositionless, although there are *different degrees* of presupposition involved in different interpretations. If a patient's fear of authority is traced back to his fear of a strict father, then his fear of authority is in fact being considered as a reaction to the action of that strict father—and also as a reaction to his initial reaction, namely his fear. The strict father (action) produces fear (reaction) and the particular fear is held to produce a general fear of authority. In this process, which Freud mistakenly adduces in support of the views which he derived from reflex action and from the concept of physical reaction, only the patient's fear of his father is universally meaningful, whereby fear is understood purely in terms of an inner condition, in which all living creatures will tend to seek refuge if exposed to similar situations. But even the process whereby fear of authority is presented as a consequence of the particular fear of the father requires complicated hypotheses if it is to appear meaningful, since the reason why a person who was once frightened by his father should continue to fear 'fathers' for the rest of his life is not immediately apparent. In other words, the precise moment when the *interpretation* of psychic activity begins is the moment when the attempt is made to render meaningful behaviour which can no longer be directly explained in terms of a simple, concrete situation—in this particular case in terms of a situation involving menace and fear. Only if such a process were interpreted in terms of the menace and fear involved in a simple situation would the interpretation be *relatively* presuppositionless (although even then it would be purposive!) But those developments which are not directly derived from a concrete situation (e.g. fear of authority) all presuppose purposive activity or activity which must be fitted into some other such reference of meaning. And by the time the fear of the father and the subsequent fear of authority have been linked with the Oedipus complex, by the time sexuality has been declared the object of the enquiry, psychoanalysis has entered its labyrinthine edifice of hypotheses and interpretations (see Section A of Part Three). And since all hypotheses and interpretations presuppose specific philosophical doctrines (positivism/gnosticism/phenomenology/idealism) it follows that *all interpretations are relative.* Consequently it is not possible to argue that, for example, the sexual interpretation which Freud places on the Oedipus complex is the only possible interpretation and thus universally valid, because it is not possible to trace the Oedipus complex back to a simple situation that is universally meaningful, such as the above-mentioned situation involving fear of a specific threat. If the purpose of scientific enquiry is to organize data without making presuppositions and in accordance with a strictly objective empirical and logical method, then the scientific character of depth psychology is rendered questionable by virtue of its dependence on philosophical doctrines and the relativity of interpretation to which this gives rise. And since existential ontology is also a *Weltanschauung*, it must necessarily be unfavourably disposed towards empirical phenomena. *Yet it would appear to be in the nature of living reality to defy systematization.* (At this point the existential ontologists will want to know what the present author's concept of reality is. For them of course reality is either a phenomenon of pure consciousness (as with Husserl) or else it is grounded in Heidegger's Being-in-the-World.) It has already been pointed out on p. 530 ff. that Freud's method of observation and enquiry was *more than a little* less inclined to presuppositions than was Jung's. His works are a constant source of fascination to the reader, who is able to sense how Freud struggled with the phenomena, with empiricism, how he tried to observe the phenomena from different viewpoints, how he questioned his own findings—only to give his ultimate preference to positivist and mechanistic solutions. The advantage enjoyed by Freud and the other positivist schools over the philosophical schools in respect of 'presuppositionlessness' derives above all from the far greater amount of empirical material which the positivist schools have amassed. The broad basis of clinical experience which is one of their distinctive features is enough to raise them above the philosophically oriented schools, *provided their explanations are meaningful* and not causal, *do not exceed the limits of universally meaningful and universally verifiable observations* and are conceived in terms of action and reaction. Both the fact and the *manner* of the constant undermining of this broad basis of clinical experience by hypotheses on the one hand and simplifications on the other have already been pointed out. However, the advantage which this broader empirical basis gives to the positivist schools, one which is by no means inconsiderable, is their only advantage. And even their empiricism is bound to the presuppositions attendant on the positivist view of the world. On the other hand this broader framework of clinical experience affords a more precise knowledge of the *therapeutic methodology of neurosis*, which has been worked out in great detail by the Freudian school.

In this author's view, however, it is not possible to espouse the cause of any one of these systems wholeheartedly—which means dogmatically —because depth psychology is far too dependent on various philosophical doctrines. The desire for the security which is accorded to all who seek refuge in a system is too obvious for this to be a feasible choice. The constant confrontation with the individual in psychotherapy elucidates time and again various fundamental aspects of human reality: the impossibility of grasping this reality in the quantitative categores of positivism, its anti-logical character, its pathic structure, its vacillations between crisis and constancy. These different aspects—for example, the contrasts (which are of course all relative) between conscious and unconscious, rational and irrational, drive and will, dream and reality, image and concept—would readily lend themselves to far-reaching philosophical conclusions, but the temptation, which is strong, must be resisted. *The reality of psychological and empirical experience would appear to lie at the point of intersection where the concept and living activity cross.* If the border is transgressed in either direction living reality withdraws, which is why it is always possible to experience it but never possible to formulate it. This is what von Weizsäcker meant when he spoke of the 'introduction of the subject' and when he expressed the view that life is experienced only by the living. *Fundamental statements on man*—which must of course be susceptible to observation and capable of verification—*should never be divorced from their relative aspects which incorporate not only the observed phenomena but also the observer.* To expand such statements into a system is fatal, for to do so is to lay hold of human reality and force it into the abstract concepts of a system of 'mind'. The principal objection to all the philosophical schools is that they necessarily involve some such process of systematization. The dilemma is insoluble because reality, which can only be experienced at its point of intersection with the concept, is necessarily 'anti-logical'. The three major methods of depth psychology, i.e. the reductive method (Freud), the amplificatory method (Jung) and the phenomenological method (Husserl and Heidegger), which are quite different from one another, are all exposed to this basic dilemma.

(*f*) *The reductive method (Freud), the amplificatory method (Jung) and the phenomenological method (Husserl and Heidegger) and their importance for psychotherapy.*

Freud's reductive method traces specific phenomena back not only to experiences of early childhood—e.g. fear of authority to fear of the father, fear of the father to the Oedipus complex—but also to the quantitative energic strivings which underlie such childhood experiences. The advantage of Freud's reductive method—an advantage which is of course lost once the method is misconstrued in terms of causality—

lies in its empiricism. This means that Freudian therapy is centred around the patient's free associations, which fact alone marks out the Freudian method as being less subject to presuppositions than either the Jungian or the phenomenological method. But this 'presuppositionlessness' applies only within certain limits which the Freudians constantly transgress either by reducing all phenomena to sexuality or aggression or by their metapsychological hypotheses. A further advantage of reduction is the therapeutic value which it has for the patient. For example, once the patient has seen the connection between his fear of authority and his father problem he will be able to trace his fear of authority back to his fear of his father. His recognition of this connection —in conjunction with other factors—will enable him to overcome his fear of authority, which in turn provides an indirect proof for the validity of the connection which was assumed in the first place. In other words, the patient will have established the validity of this connection for himself. When in the course of therapy the patient reaches the point where he reacts to particular situations with an 'Aha!', i.e. when he begins to get the hang of certain connections, he is in fact beginning to bring irrational experience under the control of reason. And this process constitutes an important part of the cure. (As Freud has put it, 'id' becomes 'ego'.) However, this process will not effect a complete cure unless it is backed up by a corresponding emotional and thus irrational change, to which, so to speak, it sets its seal. This is conceded by the positivist schools of analysis.

Jung's amplificatory method is the most dubious in terms of theory. Only if it is conceded that the symbolic self-representation afforded by the deeper sections of the psyche is based on analogy (similarity) can Jung's method receive its full due. Jungian therapy is calculated to widen the patient's horizon and to extend the conscious sections of his personality. Although Jung's amplificatory method contains within it the seeds of mere intellectualization, which finds expression in the industrious search for parallels between dreams, myths, sagas and mandalas, it also contains the possibility of a *closer* rapprochement with the irrational than can be established by Freud's reductive method. Freud's method is 'technically' oriented, for it sets out to give the patient rational power over the irrational. It is a product of that same spirit of enquiry which gave rise to the technical sciences and to the exploitation of nature. Jung's method is governed neither by technical considerations nor by concepts of supremacy, will, purpose or power and its appeal to modern man with his naïve belief in the wonders of positivism may well be weakened by this fact alone. Nonetheless, it is better calculated than is the Freudian method of reduction to touch those aspects of the psyche which are able to promote self-realization, individuation and maturation.

The phenomenological method, which is philosophically more precise than either of the other two methods, has made an important contribution to the *elucidation of the meaning* of psychopathological conditions and symptoms. Its problems—above all the danger of succumbing to new, albeit ontological, simplifications—have already been described. It may well be that in terms of perception this method represents the acme of conceivable achievement, but we should not overlook the fact that in terms of *therapy* it is as yet relatively unimportant. A depressive is hardly likely to be helped by the mere perception that he is suffering from a disruption of internal development (E. Strauss, von Gebsattel). But the fact that a perception such as this is irrelevant from a therapeutic point of view does not of course have any bearing on the question of its truthfulness, and indeed this kind of phenomenological perception—as opposed to psychological perceptions—is considered in the light of an 'ultimate' perception, one which embraces the essence of things and which no longer stands in absolute need of empirical proof. With the phenomenological method we find ourselves in the realm of pure philosophy in which empiricism is no longer required to fulfil an analogical function such as it fulfilled in C. G. Jung's method nor to withdraw behind assumed quantities as in the Freudian method, but in which empiricism is regarded in the light of a fact of pure consciousness (*Husserl*).

(g) *The Specific and Unspecific Quality of Neurosis*

Incestuous wishes *vis-à-vis* parents—as Freud was obliged to recognize —are not restricted to hysterics but on the contrary may be observed in both 'normal' and sick persons. As a result of this observation the borders between health and sickness became fluid to the extent to which all theories of neurosis advanced to a general conception of man, i.e. to a concept of personality. The pronouncements which were made in these various theories were intended to be just as binding for 'normal' behaviour as they were for sick behaviour. The 'endogenic' causes of neurosis, i.e. *conflicts between pre-formed structures*, were opposed to 'exogenic' causes (environmental influences). But neither of these views (which, as has already been pointed out, could in fact complement each other) can do more than indicate the presence in human development of meaningful motives of a general nature. *Cogent and universally valid reasons, which would necessarily clarify the genesis of any neurosis, cannot be adduced, because within variable limits the structural and environmental influences which are found to occur are always the same and these are only of relative importance in determining whether behaviour will be healthy or sick.* This also applied in respect of Schultz-Hencke's theory of drives and in respect of his attempt to explain the specific quality of neurosis. All that the genetic derivation of neurosis reveals is a limited number of conceivable situations and conditions in which neurosis might emerge. No genetic explanation will ever succeed in demonstrating that the process whereby one child reacts to a frightening situation with anxiety (and may conceivably become neurotic as a result) whilst another child does not, is a *necessary* process—no matter how many analogous situations (i.e. situations inducing fear in children) are adduced in its support. *In respect of any individual case all that the (Freudian) genetic derivation of neurosis can ever do is to reveal general tendencies which influence personality development.* The specific quality of any individual case cannot be stated in terms which are universally binding. If a patient's fear of authority is traced back to his fear of his father then in respect of this particular case a meaningful connection will have been established, but no 'natural law' (not even a general rule, e.g. strict fathers produce fear of authority) will have been pronounced. We are now in a position to establish the following formulation: those factors in human development which are (relatively speaking) universally valid are not specifically applicable to the emergence of neuroses. They simply concern personality development as such within variable limits. These factors which are (relatively speaking) universally valid are *eo ipso* (relatively speaking) universally meaningful.

It was due to these universally valid (and universally meaningful) observations of personality development that no sharp distinction could be made between sick and healthy behaviour. This fact prompted Horney and Fromm to observe the *actual* behaviour of 'neurotic personalities' in greater detail (which they did without attempting to derive from the specificity of such behaviour universally valid and thus unspecific tendencies of a genetic order) and it further prompted them to advance the concept of *phenotypically* oriented abnormal patterns of behaviour. Horney and Fromm—and this is the really important thing about them—have focused attention on the clinical image of the neurotic and thus developed *descriptive* means whereby healthy (unspecific) behaviour may be distinguished to a considerable extent from sick (specific) behaviour. In their derivations and explanations of neurotic symptoms Horney and Fromm have considered the genetic origins of neurosis only as a secondary factor and as a result they have managed by and large not to succumb to the danger of regarding universally valid tendencies, i.e. tendencies which are found in all human development, as the specific attributes of neurosis. *The specific attributes of neurosis can only be grasped in phenotypical terms as a clinical image. If they are resolved into universally meaningful lines of development then their specific quality is lost.*

The different schools consider sick, i.e. neurotic, human behaviour in the following terms:

1. in terms of a 'Beingness' that fails in its actual purpose which is conceived either in a transcendental or an immanent and ontological sense (phenomenology, existential ontology, personal analysis);

2. in terms of an existence which fails in respect of the I-Thou relationship (philosophy and the psychology of partnership, M. Buber, H. Trüb);

3. in terms of an existence which fails to fulfil its process of individuation, of self-realization (personal analysis, O. Rank, C. G. Jung, E. Fromm);

4. in terms of an existence which displays aggression, hunger for power, anxiety, etc. (Freudians and Neo-Freudians);

5. in terms of a life which is immature and mal-developed, i.e. whose development has been restricted as a result of fixations arising out of preformed complexes (which had been triggered off by environmental factors) (Freudians).

The philosophical definitions of sick and healthy behaviour (1–3) can really only be held to be specific by those who share the fundamental philosophical view in question. Once these definitions are brought to bear on individual clinical and empirical facts it soon becomes apparent that it is by no means easy to find any forms of human existence at all which have not in some way failed to fulfil their 'purpose' and which ought therefore to be declared sick. The parallel which is here implied between sickness and failure to fulfil an inherent purpose could lead to a state of affairs in which such a parallel might be established in every single clinical case, whereby other existences, which had also failed to fulfil their purpose, but which had succeeded in establishing 'healthy' achievements of one kind or another, would not be included in such an assessment.

Points 4 and 5 have been covered by the comments in the earlier part of this section.

The clinical phenotype of neurosis has been described in the greatest detail by the Neo-Freudians.

(h) Psychotherapy and the Gestaltkreis
(Perception and Love)

The extraordinary dissemination of the various psychotherapeutic schools which has taken place over the past thirty to forty years, especially in the United States, means that the reserve and scepticism which S. Freud, the founder of modern psychotherapy, entertained in respect of its popular appeal is no longer justified. Psychoanalytic Institutes, which are usually attached to Universities, are working in conjunction with psychiatrists, with specialists for internal diseases and other specialists in numerous cities in many different countries. Child guidance, social welfare, children's clinics and policlinics would be inconceivable today without the collaboration of trained and experienced therapists. Depth psychology has become a widespread movement which has influenced both medicine and the mental sciences, the political and social sciences and even literature and fine art. To attempt to deny this influence would be an anachronism. But the triumphant progress of psychotherapy would not have been possible if it had not achieved therapeutic success capable of substantiation by means of catamneses[1] and to a certain extent even by statistics (although this author is well aware of the reservations to which statistics and statistical criteria are subject). It should be pointed out, however, that the successful cures achieved by psychotherapy are not the exclusive property of just a few schools but that on the contrary successful cures (which, due to the reservations to which this concept is also subject, are here understood as *symptomatic cures*) have been effected by each and every one of the various schools and doctrines. This is due to the fact that in every course of psychotherapy, although the methodology and the emphasis may vary from one school to another, the patient is always confronted with himself. Moreover, in every course of treatment, no matter what school or doctrine the therapist may espouse, the fact remains that a trained therapist applies himself to the patient's problems for a large number of hours and often over a period of years. These two factors would appear to constitute the true principle underlying therapeutic success. On the one hand the patient is required to confront himself, to confront his weaknesses (defence, façade, persona), his potential talents, his world of drives and his world of ideas and above all, he is required to confront his own past. On the other hand there is the conversation with the therapist which, whether it be more of a monologue as with the Freudians or more of a dialogue as with the Neo-Freudians and the philosophically oriented schools, enables the patient to live through new and often shattering experiences.

The fact that the various schools of depth psychology have these two crucial factors in common has unfortunately not persuaded them to drop their traditional hostility to one another or to desist from belittling their respective achievements. But despite these two common therapeutic factors and despite the considerable fund of empirical observations which has been established the fact still remains, a fact which has been demon-

---

[1] In Germany statistical findings based on catamneses have been furnished by the Berlin Zentralinstitut für psychogene Erkrankungen (Schultz-Hencke) and by the Abteilung für Psychosomatische Medizin, Heidelberg (A. Mitscherlich).

strated in the course of this present investigation, that the theses which have been advanced by the various schools cannot in any sense be considered in the light of conclusive or established scientific knowledge. Any attempt to syncretize the different schools could only succeed in camouflaging the conflict of ideas but could never hope to illuminate the fundamental problems of psychic reality which underlie that conflict.

But where is the chief danger for psychotherapy to be found? In the first place in the tendency—one to which the posivitist schools are particularly prone—to degrade the patient by considering him as a mere object of research in the Cartesian sense. And secondly in the tendency—one to which the philosophically oriented schools are prone and which arises out of the need which they feel for the 'cure to proceed from the meeting'—to 'love' the patient at the expense of adequately perceiving him and seeing through him. Both the Freudian and the Neo-Freudian positivist schools provide ample material with which to document the patient's flight from himself and the broadly based and precise methodology which they have established ensures that the patient is made aware of any such attempted flight. On the other hand they tend—especially the Freudians—to fall a prey to positivism and to adopt a view in which the patient appears as an object but not as a subject. The philosophical schools, including C. G. Jung, do not have access to a correspondingly wide range of empirical material and also lack the (albeit relative) precision of conceptual definition with which to demonstrate to the patient the manoeuvres by which he tries to deceive himself. Their greater willingness to enter into a dialogue with the patient i.e. a conversation, a meeting, is fraught with the danger that, although the patient may be lovingly accepted, he may well be spared the confrontation with himself which is the fruit of perception. These two dangers are the Scylla and Charybdis of psychotherapy and every therapist is exposed to one or other of them according to his persuasion. The difficulty facing psychotherapy here, the need to strike a balance between perceiving and loving, the need to see through the patient whilst yet lovingly accepting him, the need to regard him not only as an object of transference but also as a human being in his own right, should not be underestimated. This point of balance, it would seem, is no sooner established than it is lost again. Indeed, if we analyse the therapist,[1] it would appear from the thoughts, impulses and feelings to which he is subject in the course of treatment that therapy constantly oscillates between these two poles. By perceiving his patient, by seeing through him, the therapist withdraws from the patient, treats him as a thing to be thought about, reduces him to the status of a mere object. By accepting him again with understanding and love he reinstates him as a

[1] Cf. esp. Th. Reik, *Listening with the Third Ear*, London–New York, 1950.

subject, as a real person. (Always provided that the therapist is aware of his own emotional relationship to the patient, his so-called 'counter-transference'!) And so the patient's importance in the eyes of his therapist is constantly changing in the course of even a single session. And the change is virtually tantamount to a complete *volte-face*. By passing through the different stages of this relationship, the stages of perception, withdrawal and objectivization on the one hand and the stages of acceptance, understanding and loving on the other, the therapist passes through the *Gestaltkreis*, which, once it has been established as a *total* act, is able to guarantee psychotherapeutic success in an existential sense. The same holds true for the patient: whether he feels himself accepted by the therapist as a human being or whether he finds himself forced by the therapist's interpretation of his behaviour—which is based on the therapist's perception of the patient as an object—into a confrontation with himself, in either case he passes through one side of the circular process which in its entirety forms the circle of *Gestalt* (*Gestaltkreis*).

And so the basic factors involved in psychotherapy, no matter what its origin, are perception and love, and they meet in the *Gestaltkreis* which therapist and patient pass through in the course of treatment.

INDEX[1]

[1] *See also* Table of Contents, pp. 15–41, where the subject matter dealt with in the individual chapters is set out in considerable detail.

INDEX OF NAMES